WebSphere Application Server

Step by Step

WebSphere Application Server

Step by Step

Rama Turaga
Owen Cline
Peter Van Sickel

MC PRESS

MC Press Online, LP
Lewisville, TX 75077

WebSphere Application Server, Step by Step
Rama Turaga, Owen Cline, and Peter Van Sickel

First Edition

First Printing—April 2006

Every attempt has been made to provide correct information. However, the pulisher and the author do not guarantee the accuracy of the book and do not assume responsibility for information included in or omitted from it.

The following terms are trademarks of International Business Machines Corporation in the United States, other countries, or both: IBM, AS/400, OS/400, iSeries, i5, and i5/OS. All other product names are trademarked or copyrighted by their respective manufacturers.

MC Press offers excellent discounts on this book when ordered in quantity for bulk purchases or special sales, which may include custom covers and content particular to your business, training goals, marketing focus, and branding interest.

For information regarding permissions or special orders, please contact:
MC Press
Corporate Offices
125 N. Woodland Trail
Lewisville, TX 75077 USA

For information regarding sales and/or customer service, please contact:
MC Press
P.O. Box 4300
Big Sandy, TX 75755-4300 USA

ISBN: 1-58347-061-1

Contents

PART II: Single Node Installation and Configuration

1

WebSphere Application Server V6: Packaging and Architecture

With complete J2EE compatibility and integrated Web services support, Version 6.0 of WebSphere Application Server delivers high performance and a highly scalable transaction engine for dynamic and mission-critical e-business applications. The product, the cornerstone of the IBM WebSphere product family, forms the foundation for IBM's other middleware offerings. Leading-edge products such as WebSphere Commerce Server, WebSphere Process Server (formerly WebSphere Business Integration Server Foundation), WebSphere Enterprise Service Bus, and WebSphere Portal Server (to name just a few) are built on top of this powerful application server.

In Version 6, WebSphere Application Server supports the full Java 2 Platform, Enterprise Edition (J2EE) 1.4 programming model, including servlets, Java Server Pages (JSPs), Enterprise JavaBeans (EJB), and Web services. WebSphere V6 also continues to support applications developed using the J2EE 1.2 and 1.3 specifications, making it easier to migrate applications deployed on WebSphere Application Server 4.x and 5.x. Figure 1-1 summarizes the standards support in WebSphere Application Server V6. (For complete documentation of the J2EE 1.4 specification, see the list of Web references in the Appendix.)

- Java 2 Platform, Enterprise Edition (J2EE) 1.4
  - › Servlet 2.4, Java Server Pages (JSP) 2.0
  - › Enterprise JavaBeans (EJB) 2.1, Java Message Service (JMS) 1.1, J2EE Connector Architecture (JCA) 1.5
  - › Java Specification Request (JSR) 109, Java API for XML-based Remote Procedure Call (JAX-RPC/JSR 101), Simple Object Access Protocol with Attachments API for Java (SAAJ) 1.2
  - › Java Database Connectivity (JDBC) 3.0, JavaMail 1.3

- Java Development Kit (JDK) 1.4.2
- WebSphere programming model extensions
  - ActivitySessions
  - Application Profiling
  - Asynchronous Beans
  - Distributed Map
  - Dynamic Query
  - Internationalization
  - Last Participant Support
  - Object Pools
  - Scheduler
  - Startup Beans
  - Work Areas

Figure 1-1: Standards support in WebSphere Application Server V6

WebSphere V6 is supported on many platforms, including Windows (Windows 2000, 2003, and XP), Unix (AIX, HP-UX, Linux, and Solaris), and IBM's i5/OS (OS/400) operating system. For a complete list of supported platforms, see the Web references list in the Appendix. In this chapter, we look at how IBM packages the product in Version 6 and examine the architectures associated with each variation. Before concluding the chapter, we'll review some of the significant new features in V6, including administrative console improvements, high-availability features, and deployment and management enhancements. Chapter 2 gives you an overview of the installation and configuration process and provides an introduction to the rest of the book.

Packaging

IBM offers WebSphere Application Server V6 in the following packages:

- *WebSphere Application Server V6 – Express* — The Express package provides a fully functional, affordable, and easy-to-use Java application server and development environment. Unlike Version 5, the V6 Express package provides full J2EE support, including an Enterprise JavaBeans container.

- *WebSphere Application Server V6* — In addition to the functionality supported by the Express runtime, the base application server product — what we call "the Base package" in this book — delivers high performance and a highly scalable transaction engine for dynamic e-business applications. The Base package provides the same functionality as the Express package, but an expanded license agreement supports the ability to federate (i.e., add) an application server node to a WebSphere Deployment Manager cell. (You'll learn more about WebSphere nodes and cells later in this chapter.)

- *WebSphere Application Server V6 – Network Deployment* — In addition to the functionality provided in the Base/Express package, the Network Deployment (ND) package delivers advanced deployment services, including clustering, edge-of-network services, Web services enhancements, and high availability for distributed configurations. Figure 1-2 illustrates the relationship among the Base, Express, and Network Deployment packages.

- *WebSphere Application Server V6 – Extended Deployment* — Installed on top of the Network Deployment package, the Extended Deployment (XD) package helps customers with multiple mission-critical and complex applications improve availability and performance by balancing and sharing the workload of multiple application server nodes and clusters to provide on-demand computing.

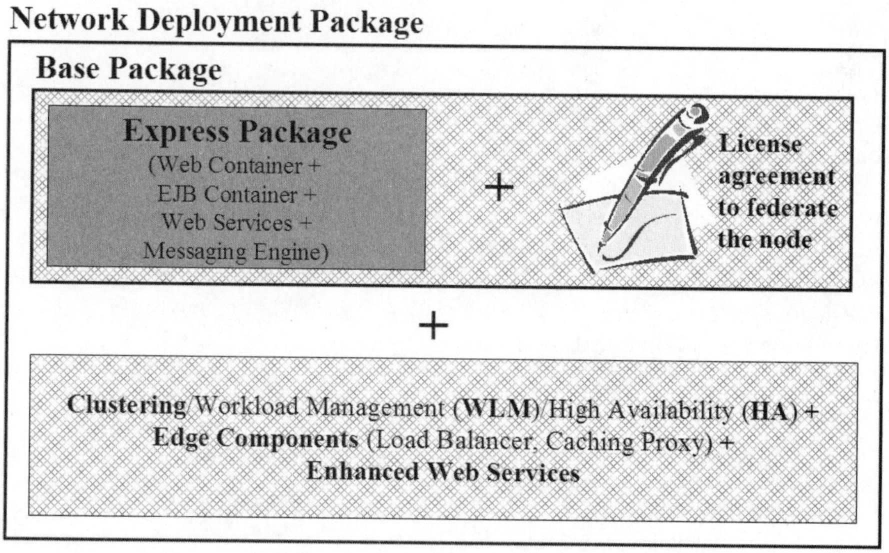

Figure 1-2: WebSphere Application Server V6 product packaging

Base/Express Package Software

Figure 1-3 depicts the software products that come with the Express and Base versions of WebSphere Application Server. These two packages include essentially the same set of software (the development tool provided is the only difference). The Base/Express package includes the following software:

- Standalone application server node with support for multiple instances

- Application client

- IBM HTTP Server V6

- Web server plug-ins

- IBM Rational Web Developer (iRWD) V6 (with the Express package) or a trial version of IBM Rational Application Developer (iRAD) V6 (with the Base package)

- Application Server Toolkit (AST)

- DB2 Universal Database (DB2 UDB) Express Edition 8.2

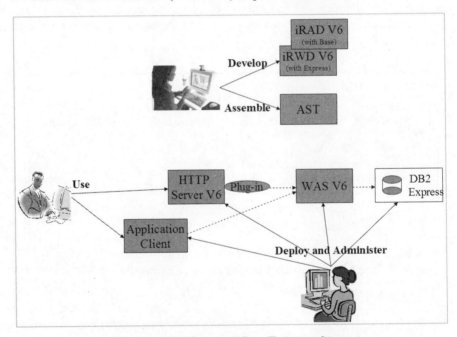

Figure 1-3: WebSphere V6 Base/Express software

It's important to understand that no functionality or feature differences exist between the Express and Base versions of WebSphere Application Server in the WebSphere V6 runtime. These packages are built of the same code base and therefore are identical in terms of features and functions. The difference between the two packages is simply a licensing issue. To be able to federate an application server node to a WebSphere cell, you must have a paper agreement; only the Base package permits use of this feature.

A license agreement also grants Base installations unlimited CPU use, while Express package users are limited to two CPUs.

Network Deployment Package Software

To the Base/Express package's support for a standalone application server environment, the WebSphere Application Server V6 – Network Deployment package adds the ability to create and manage a distributed server configuration. This product includes the following software in addition to the software provided in the Base/Express package:

- Deployment Manager

- Edge Components (Load Balancer, Caching Proxy)

- IBM Tivoli Directory Server (a Lightweight Directory Access Protocol, or LDAP, server)

- Tivoli Access Manager (TAM) server

- DB2 UDB Server Edition 8.2

- IBM Cloudscape database

Figure 1-4 depicts the software products that come with the Network Deployment package.

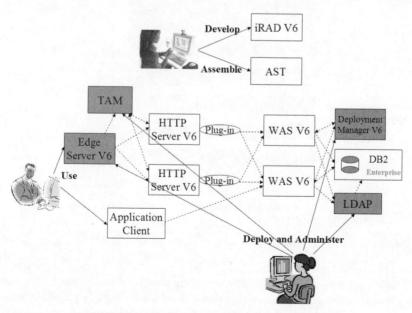

Figure 1-4: WebSphere V6 Network Deployment software

The key additional features provided in the Network Deployment package are support for workload management, high availability, and clustering and the ability to run the Web server as a managed node. (If you use IBM HTTP Server V6 as your Web server, you can manage it through IBM HTTP Admin Server V6 instead of using a node agent process from the WebSphere administrative console. This feature is not available with other supported Web servers.)

Standalone Application Server

The heart of a WebSphere Application Server installation is the application server itself. The application server provides a runtime environment in which to deploy, manage, and run J2EE applications. Both the Base and Express packages support a standalone application server structure. Figure 1-5 illustrates the components of this basic architecture, which forms the foundation of every WebSphere Application Server installation.

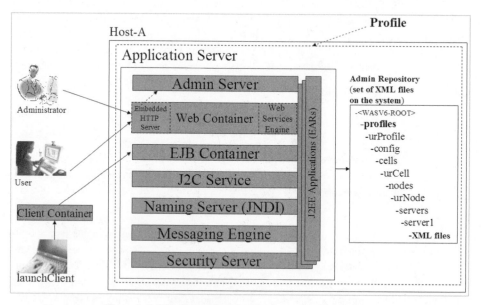

Figure 1-5: WebSphere Application Server V6 architecture

Each application server runs in its own Java Virtual Machine (JVM). As you can see in the diagram, the application server process contains the following services and containers:

- *Admin server* — The administrative server maintains and manages the administration configuration repository (which consists of Extensible Markup Language, or XML, flat files in the file system). The admin server accepts requests from the WebSphere administrative console (a browser-based graphical interface for configuring and managing WebSphere resources) and wsadmin commands and changes the configuration information accordingly. If you've enabled global security, the admin server also secures the administrative repository by authenticating and authorizing the user role.

■ *Web container* — The Web container provides a runtime environment for servlets, JSPs, JavaBeans, and static content (if you've enabled the file-serving servlet). These artifacts are typically packaged as a Web module and run inside the Web container. A Web module is packaged as a file with a .war (Web archive) extension. If necessary, the Web container works with the application server's EJB container or the Web services engine to process requests. Files with .war and .jar (Java archive) extensions run inside the Web container.

■ *Embedded HTTP Server (EHS)* — The application server's EHS component receives requests from an external HTTP server (e.g., IBM HTTP Server) using Hypertext Transfer Protocol (default TCP/IP port 9080) and passes the requests to the Web container for processing. The embedded server can serve all static content, just like an external HTTP server. EHS isn't meant to replace an external HTTP server in a production environment, but you can use it to test your WebSphere applications. By using EHS as an HTTP server to serve static content without an external HTTP server, you can save system resources in development and functional testing environments.

■ *Web services engine* — The Web services engine is the part of the application server runtime that supports Web services. Web services are self-contained, modular applications that you can describe, publish, locate, and invoke over a network.

■ *EJB container* — The application server's EJB container provides a runtime environment for deploying, managing, and running Enterprise JavaBeans. These artifacts are typically packaged as an EJB module and run inside the EJB container. An EJB module is packaged as a file with a .jar extension. Files with a .jar extension and an EJB deployment descriptor run inside this container. Java clients communicate with Enterprise JavaBeans in the EJB container. The client container depicted in the figure provides services for running standalone Java clients that use the application server. You invoke the client application container by executing the launchClient command.

■ *J2C service* — The Java 2 Connector (J2C) service provides connections between J2EE applications running inside the application server and applications running in legacy enterprise information systems. Connections and their runtime

7

environment are pooled and managed as defined in the J2EE 1.4 specification's J2C architecture.

- *JNDI naming server* — You can register resources in the application server's Java Naming and Directory Interface (JNDI) namespace. Client applications can then obtain the references to these resource objects in their programs.

- *Messaging engine* — The messaging engine provides the core messaging functionality of a Service Integration Bus (SIBus). To enable the messaging engine in the application server process (default messaging provider with WebSphere V6), you create an SIBus and attach the application server to it as a member. This messaging engine is all-Java based and runs in-process with the application server. Applications can use an external JMS provider such as WebSphere MQ, a third-party JMS provider such as TIBCO, or the WebSphere V5 embedded messaging provider instead of the default messaging engine. In this book, we cover use of the default messaging engine only.

- *Security server* — The security server provides authentication and authorization services.

Application Server Profile

Notice that Figure 1-5 depicts the application server as enclosed within a *profile*. The concept of profiles is new in WebSphere Application Server V6. A profile contains a set of files that enable the runtime environment for a WebSphere server process. You create a profile for the application server during the installation process.

Using the Base/Express package, you can create only one type of profile: an application server profile. The Network Deployment package supports two additional profile types, deployment manager and custom, both of which we describe later.

As the diagram in Figure 1-6 illustrates, when you install the WebSphere V6 package, the installation program copies to a directory on the server machine the product binaries, which include a default application server *template* and other files required to create a profile. During the installation process, you use the profile template to define the configuration settings of the new server you're going to create.

When you create an application server profile, an application server (named server1) is created by default, and necessary applications are deployed on it to help manage the configuration (adminconsole, filetransfer) and verify the installation (default application, installation verification test). You can use the same set of product binaries (and template) to create multiple profiles.

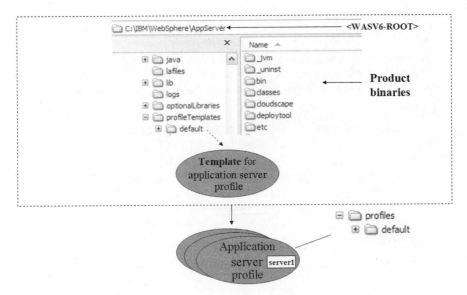

Figure 1-6: Relationship between an application server template and a profile

If you desire, you can create multiple application servers (e.g., server2, server3) within the same profile. But for easy maintenance, you may want to create a new profile (an application server process gets created with a profile) if you ever expect to have multiple application servers.

IBM HTTP Server

You can use WebSphere Application Server's Embedded HTTP Server (available inside the Web container) to serve static content, but EHS isn't meant to be used this way in a production environment, due to scalability and availability limitations. For this reason, IBM includes the "full-strength" IBM HTTP Server Web server as part of the WebSphere V6 product.

IBM HTTP Server V6, which comes with both the Base/Express and the Network Deployment packages, is based on the Apache Web Server 2.0.47. As a Web server, HTTP Server's purpose is to process and serve static content, such as Hypertext Markup Language (HTML), images, Cascading Style Sheets (CSS), and JavaScript.

Figure 1-7 shows the basic architecture of HTTP Server in V6. The server contains the following services:

- *Apache service* — This is the core Apache service that processes HTTP requests.

- *Admin service* — If you configured the Web server node as an unmanaged node, the WebSphere admin service can use the HTTP admin service to manage HTTP Server, change the configuration of the HTTP plug-in and HTTP Server, and propagate the plug-in configuration file remotely from the WebSphere administrative console.

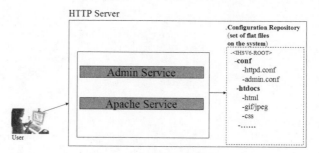

Figure 1-7: IBM HTTP Server V6 architecture

WebSphere V6 Plug-in for HTTP Server

When a Web application user sends a request, the external HTTP server processes the request first (here we are assuming that the plug-in module is not installed and configured to run with the HTTP server). If the request is for static content only, the HTTP server can serve it. (Requests for static content can be served using the file-serving enabler servlet from the application's Web module running in the application server's Web container or, if configured appropriately, from the document root of IBM HTTP Server.) However, if the request is to display dynamic content (served through a servlet and/or a JSP), an application server must fulfill it. In this case, the HTTP server needs to know where and how to divert the request. For this reason, WebSphere provides a *plug-in module* that runs with HTTP Server. The plug-in module uses an XML-based file containing a request-routing table to divert requests to the appropriate application server. Figure 1-8 illustrates the plug-in's relationship with WebSphere V6 and HTTP Server V6. Once you've installed and configured the WebSphere plug-in module on the HTTP server, the plug-in process receives the request from the client first. If the request

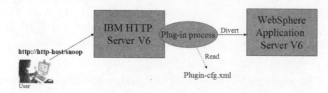

Figure 1-8: Plug-in relationship to WebSphere V6 and HTTP Server V6

is for dynamic content, the plug-in diverts the request to the WebSphere application server. If the request is for static content, the plug-in forwards it to the HTTP server.

Architectures Possible with the Base/Express Package

When it comes to architecting a WebSphere V6 Base/Express application server, you have various options with respect to IBM HTTP Server and the plug-in module. In this section, we review a few possibilities to give you a general idea of how you might build a WebSphere V6 system. You can create any of the architectural variations described here (and others) by following the steps given in Chapters 3 through 6.

Local Plug-in

In a local plug-in configuration, both WebSphere Application Server and the HTTP server (along with the plug-in module) exist on the same machine. Figure 1-9 illustrates this architecture. This simple configuration works well in training and functional/unit testing environments.

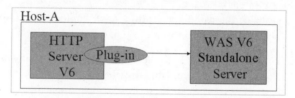

Figure 1-9: Standalone server: Local plug-in architecture

Remote Plug-in

In a remote plug-in configuration (Figure 1-10), WebSphere Application Server and the HTTP server (and plug-in module) exist on different machines. You can use this type of configuration for noncritical, small production or test environments.

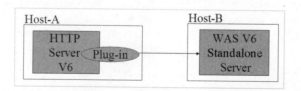

Figure 1-10: Standalone server: Remote plug-in architecture

Multiprofile Local or Remote Plug-in

In a multiple-profile configuration (Figure 1-11), multiple application server instances share one WebSphere V6 Base/Express installation (i.e., a single set of product binary files).

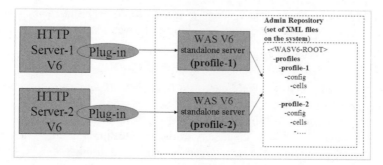

Figure 1-11: Single WebSphere V6 install: Multiple profiles with local or remote plug-in architecture

In this setup, the plug-in module can be local or remote. The important point to note is that each plug-in module can talk to only one profile built using the Base/Express package software. You can use this configuration to host different applications as follows:

- one application on each profile
- different versions of the same application, each deployed to their own profile
- one profile for each department in an organization

Of course, you can also have multiple installations of WebSphere V6 (multiple binary files) on a single machine, each with multiple profiles.

Architectures Not Supported

The plug-in file generated from Base/Express servers cannot spray, or route, requests to multiple instances. Figure 1-12 illustrates this limitation. If you need this kind of capability (i.e., workload management in the plug-in), you must use the Network Deployment package. In addition, even though you technically can federate an application server installed using the Express package to a Deployment Manager cell, it's illegal to do so without a Base package license.

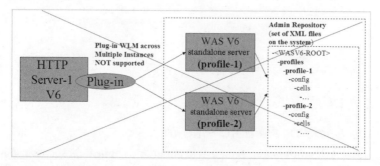

Figure 1-12: No Base/Express ability to spray requests across multiple application servers

Network Deployment Package: A Cell of Application Servers

WebSphere Application Server's Network Deployment package builds on the features of the Base/Express package by providing support for a distributed server configuration, complete with centralized administration, advanced deployment services, workload management, and high availability. Figure 1-13 depicts the basic architecture of the Network Deployment version of WebSphere Application Server.

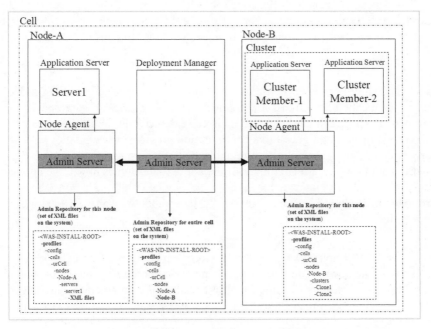

Figure 1-13: WebSphere Application Server V6 – Network Deployment architecture

The figure shows a WebSphere *cell* that consists of two nodes: node A and node B. Each node is a collection of WebSphere managed server processes (application server, Web server, generic server, and so on). Nodes in a cell can be managed or unmanaged. (You'll learn more about managed and unmanaged nodes later in this chapter and in the remainder of this book.) Many people wrongly think that a one-to-one relationship exists between a WebSphere node and a physical machine (which is sometimes also called a node). But in a WebSphere cell, a single physical machine can contain multiple WebSphere nodes.

Within each cell, the Deployment Manager process, as its name implies, is responsible for managing the administrative configuration for the entire cell. In the Network

Deployment environment, the WebSphere administrative console connects to the Deployment Manager to work with the cell configuration. You thus have a centralized, single point of administration for all the nodes in a cell. (Each node will contain one or more application servers.) The Deployment Manager runs in its own JVM.

Every WebSphere node that has been federated to the Deployment Manager contains one *node agent*. The node agent is responsible for propagating administration configuration changes from the Deployment Manager to its node. Like the Deployment Manager, each node agent process runs in its own JVM. A managed node contains a node agent on that node.

A *cluster* (shown in node B of the figure) is a collection of application server processes hosting an identical collection of J2EE applications, thus providing workload management and high availability. The architecture depicted in the figure has a limitation, though. As you might guess, this configuration provides *process* failover — if cluster member 1 fails, the application remains available through cluster member 2 — but it can't provide *system* failover. If the entire node B goes down, the applications running in the cluster are unavailable entirely. To maintain high availability during system failover, it would be wise to move a cluster to node A or create an extra cluster member there.

A new feature in WebSphere V6 is the ability to group nodes within a cell for better manageability. The node group feature (not depicted in the figure) is useful if you have nodes on different operating systems and/or platforms. In such an environment, support for node groups lets you organize nodes by operating system or platform.

Profiles Supported in the Network Deployment Package

As you learned earlier, a WebSphere profile contains a set of files that enable a runtime environment for a WebSphere server process. The WebSphere V6 Base and Express packages support one kind of profile, an application server profile. In addition to the application server profile, the WebSphere V6 Network Deployment package supports two more profile types: deployment manager and custom.

As Figure 1-14 illustrates, when you install the Network Deployment package, the installation program copies product binaries containing three kinds of templates — deployment manager, application server (default), and custom (managed) — along with the files required to create the associated profiles. You can create multiple profiles from the same set of product binaries for each profile template.

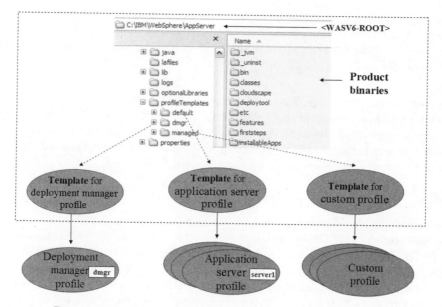

Figure 1-14: Templates and profiles in the Network Deployment package

When you create an application server profile, an application server process (server1) is created by default, along with the set of files required to run and manage that application server (server1).

When you create a deployment manager profile, a Deployment Manager process (dmgr) is created by default, along with the necessary applications to manage the configuration (adminconsole, filetransfer) and verify the installation (ivt). The Deployment Manager helps the administrator manage multiple application servers and clusters that exist on one or more nodes. To be managed from the Deployment Manager's admin console, nodes within the application server and/or custom profile must be federated (added) to the Deployment Manager.

When you create a custom profile, files are created that are necessary to

- federate a node within the custom profile to the Deployment Manager
- run and manage any application servers that will be created on the node from the Deployment Manager's admin console after federation

Unlike the application server profile, a custom profile contains no application server or applications that manage and verify the configuration immediately after its creation.

A custom profile is equivalent to the application server profile minus the application server process (server1). You use the custom profile when you know you're going to immediately federate the node and have no intention of using the profile in a standalone configuration.

If you want to manage an HTTP server remotely from the WebSphere admin console, you create a custom profile (or application server profile) on the HTTP server machine and federate it to the Deployment Manager cell. When you federate the node within the custom profile to the Deployment Manager, you'll see the creation of the node agent process on the machine where you created the custom profile.

Architectures Possible with the Network Deployment Package

You can configure WebSphere Application Server V6 – Network Deployment in various ways with respect to HTTP Server, the plug-in module, Edge Server – Load Balancer, and the DB2 database. (We should note here that WebSphere supports a variety of options in terms of caching proxy and load balancers that operate on the edge of the network. In addition, WebSphere supports a variety of JDBC-compliant databases — DB2, Informix, Oracle, SQL Server, and Sybase, to name a few — for persistent storage. The examples in this book are restricted to IBM-specific products to serve as representative samples.)

To give you a general idea how to build a WebSphere V6 ND system, let's look at a few examples. You can create any of the architectural variations described here using the Network Deployment package. This package also supports all the architectural possibilities we discussed earlier for the Base and Express packages, including those you learned weren't supported in those packages. We'll delve further into the Network Deployment architecture in Chapters 7 and beyond.

Manage Multiple Application Servers from the Deployment Manager's Admin Console

In this configuration (shown in Figure 1-15), you manage multiple application servers through the Deployment Manager's administrative console. Each profile must be federated to the Deployment Manager to permit managing the application servers on the node corresponding to the profile. Each application server can host one or more applications. Using the Deployment Manager, you can configure a Web server (or multiple Web servers) to send requests from the Web server to the application servers. This configuration works well in education, training, and noncritical small production environments.

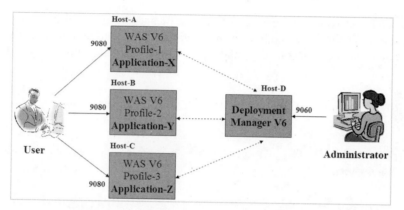

Figure 1-15: Managing multiple application servers from the Deployment Manager's admin console

Vertical Clustering with Distributed Local Plug-in

In this configuration (Figure 1-16), all the components (HTTP Server, plug-in module, WebSphere V6 cluster members, and Deployment Manager) exist on the same node. The plug-in module sprays requests to all the application servers in the cluster. This configuration is suitable for education and training environments.

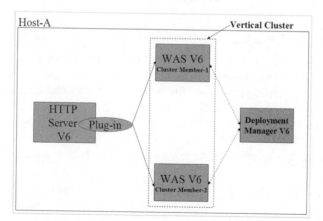

Figure 1-16: Vertical clustering with distributed local plug-in

Vertical Clustering with Distributed Remote Plug-in

In this configuration (Figure 1-17), the Deployment Manager and HTTP Server (along with the plug-in module) exist on separate nodes. Application servers (cluster members) can exist on the Deployment Manager machine or on a separate machine. The plug-in module can spray requests to both application servers. This configuration works well for education, training, stress testing, staging, and noncritical midsized production environments.

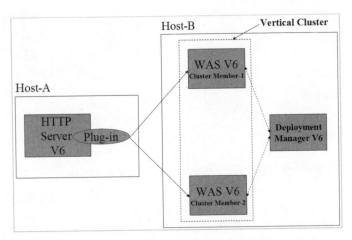

Figure 1-17: Vertical clustering with distributed remote plug-in

Highly Available/Workload-Managed Horizontal Clustering

In this configuration (Figure 1-18), WebSphere Application Server, HTTP Server (and the plug-in module), the Deployment Manager, Edge Server – Load Balancer, and the DB2 database exist on different nodes. This configuration provides high availability for each component (WebSphere Application Server, HTTP Server, and Edge Server). The only single points of failure here are the database and the LDAP server. (LDAP serves as the user registry to validate users.) You can use this configuration in production environments once you've configured the database and LDAP for high availability.

In the highly available/workload-managed scenario, when a user issues a request from a browser, the primary Edge Server – Load Balancer processes the request first. If the primary Load Balancer fails, the secondary Load Balancer starts receiving the requests from users. After receiving a request from the browser, the Load Balancer (also known as an *IP sprayer*) sprays requests to multiple HTTP servers. If one HTTP server fails, the remaining HTTP server (or servers) receives all the requests.

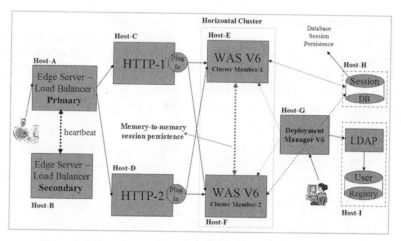

Figure 1-18: Highly available/workload-managed horizontal clustering

After receiving the request from the Load Balancer, the plug-in module on the HTTP server receives the request and sprays it to multiple application servers:

- If one application server fails, the remaining application server (or servers) serves the requests.

- If you've enabled persistent sessions, the user sessions stored in the session database of the failed application server are retrieved by the application server that is serving the request on behalf of the failed application server.

- If you've configured session persistence for memory-to-memory replication, the session data will be stored on the other cluster members.

After receiving the request from the plug-in module (in HTTP Server), the Embedded HTTP Server (part of the application server) receives the request and delegates it to the Web container (also part of the application server). In handling the request, the servlet/JSP (running inside the Web container) usually makes method calls with the help of supporting Java bean classes that may use JDBC to access a database server or method calls to Enterprise JavaBeans running in the EJB container. In handling an incoming HTTP request, a servlet/JSP may optionally invoke an EJB that thereafter accesses data in some enterprise resource, such as a JDBC-compliant database. The servlet or EJB may optionally also invoke services from utility or dependent classes that are available to the application.

WebSphere Application Server V6: New Features

We'd be remiss to conclude this introductory chapter without a brief look at some of the important new features you'll find in WebSphere Application Server V6. Among the most easily noticeable changes is a new look for the administrative console. In V6, the WebSphere admin console presents the standard look and feel that IBM has adopted across its entire WebSphere product family. You can see the console's new look in Figure 1-19.

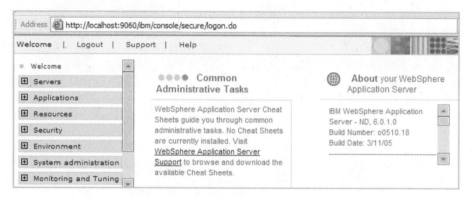

Figure 1-19: Admin console's new appearance

The new console also features simplified navigation, making it easier to find what you want than in previous versions. For example, when you click on an application, you no longer need to go through a series of screens to find all the application's properties. A single screen now provides links to all these attributes (Figure 1-20). In addition, the console's main viewing pane now displays its information in two columns, alleviating the need to scroll to locate commonly used items on the screen.

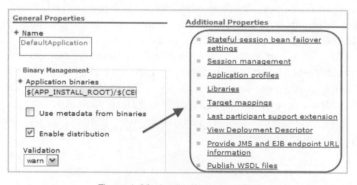

Figure 1-20: Application properties

Another console-related change in V6 involves the port number and context root you use to invoke the admin console. Instead of the URL http://washost:**9090/admin**, you now use http://was-host:**9060/ibm/console** to invoke the admin console. The WAS V5 context root, /admin, still works in V6; it is redirected to /ibm/console. For example, you can still use the URL http://was-hostname:9060/admin to invoke the admin console.

Other Changes

You'll find a host of other improvements and changes in V6, including the following highlights:

- System applications (e.g., admin console, file transfer EARs) are no longer displayed in the admin console or stored in the installedApps directory along with other enterprise applications. In V6, these applications reside in a separate repository.

- Multiple instances can now share the product binary files. As you've learned, each instance, or application server process, is called a profile in WebSphere V6.

- The default messaging provider is installed automatically when you install the application server. The messaging engine isn't enabled by default, but you can enable it by performing a few simple configuration steps.

- You can now configure and manage the Tivoli Performance Viewer (TPV) from the admin console (as shown in Figure 1-21). Chapter 22 provides a step-by-step description of how to collect data using TPV during performance monitoring.

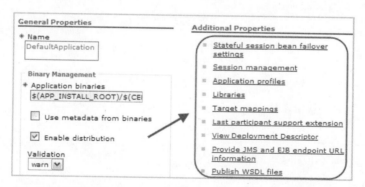

Figure 1-21: Tivoli Performance Viewer in WebSphere V6 admin console

- In V6, the Web server plug-in installation is separate from the WebSphere Application Server and IBM HTTP Server installations (Figure 1-22).

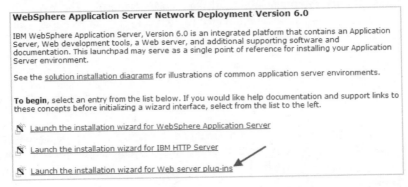

Figure 1-22: WebSphere V6 installation options

- You can manage IBM HTTP Server V6 through the WebSphere V6 admin console. You can also use the console to make plug-in file configuration changes (Figure 1-23) and propagate the plug-in to an HTTP Server V6 node (Figure 1-24).

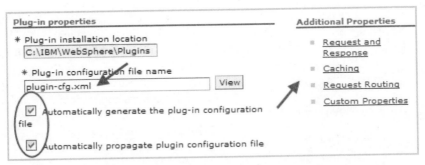

Figure 1-23: Plug-in configuration changes via WebSphere V6 admin console

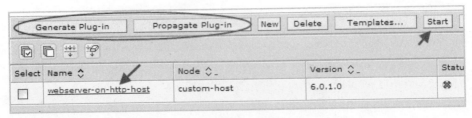

Figure 1-24: Plug-in propagation to HTTP Server via WebSphere V6 admin console

- The WebSphere Rapid Deployment (WRD) feature enables automatic installation of applications and modules onto a running application server. (This feature is intended for use only in development environments.)

- Fine-grained application-update capability lets you add, change, and/or delete parts of an installed application or selected modules of an installed application.

- Using the V6 configuration archive feature, you can export or import a full or partial configuration between different instances and applications.

- Enhanced enterprise archive (EAR) file support enables easy packaging and deployment. The new support includes the ability to include non-J2EE components (e.g., property files) inside an .ear file. In addition, J2EE resource definitions (e.g., data source definitions) can be embedded in the EAR (in the deployment.xml file) and then created when the EAR is deployed.

- You can configure resources and WebSphere variables in two new scopes (along with the existing cell, node, and server scopes):

  › *cluster scope* — The resource or variable is visible to all members of the cluster.

  › *application scope* — The resource or variable is visible to that application only.

- A new global object, AdminTask, has been introduced in the wsadmin program (along with existing objects AdminConfig, AdminApp, AdminControl, and Help). The new task enables you to run admin commands inside wsadmin.

- The default Java Message Service messaging engine available in the WebSphere V6 Base and Network Deployment packages is the Service Integration Bus technology (also known as Platform Messaging). You can configure the SIBus through the admin console or using the wsadmin command. (You can also configure applications to use any of the three other JMS provider options that WebSphere V6 supports: external WebSphere MQ, a third-party JMS provider, or the WebSphere V5-based embedded JMS provider.)

- High Availability Manager (HA Manager) is used to provide high availability for the following services:

  › the Workload Management (WLM) service —provided on all managed processes in a defined core group (in earlier WebSphere versions, this service was available only in the Deployment Manager process)

  › rapid recovery of transaction logs if a cluster member fails

  › new SIBus messaging engine components that provide JMS services on each application server

- A more optimized design of the communications layer enables improved performance, high availability, and failure recovery of Data Replication Service, or DRS (used for memory-to-memory replication between JVMs in a cluster).

- V6 supports replication and failover of stateful session EJBs.

- Service Data Objects (SDO) provide unified data access and representation across heterogeneous back-end data stores and simplify the application programming tasks required to access data.

- WebSphere V6 implements the Java Authorization Contract for Containers (JACC) specification and includes an integrated Tivoli Access Manager client for enhanced security.

2

Installation and Configuration Overview

As you learned in Chapter 1, the architectural variations you can construct using WebSphere Application Server V6 range from the very simple to the fairly complex. You can build any of the architectures we described in that chapter by following the steps outlined in the appropriate chapter or chapters of this book.

To demonstrate the steps involved in setting up a complete WebSphere Application Server installation, this book walks you through the configuration process for the most sophisticated architecture you learned about in Chapter 1: a highly available, workload-managed (HA/WLM), clustered environment built using the WebSphere V6 Network Deployment package. During the course of this book, you'll assume all the responsibilities and roles required to implement this architecture, including setup of a standalone application server (Chapters 3 and 4); IBM HTTP Server and the plug-in module (Chapters 5 and 6); the Network Deployment package (Chapter 7); node federation (Chapter 8); the HTTP Server distributed plug-in (Chapter 9); clustering (Chapter 10); HTTP session persistence (Chapter 11); the Service Integration Bus, messaging engine, and highly available persistent service (Chapter 12); and Edge Server – Load Balancer (Chapters 13 and 14). You'll learn how to build each piece of the HA/WLM architecture one at a time, step by step, adding each component in a logical way to successfully configure this system.

The steps described in Chapters 3 through 6 are performed using the Base/Express package of WebSphere Application Server. Chapters 7 and beyond require the Network Deployment package. In Chapters 15 through 26, you'll learn about some advanced topics, including security, deployment issues, and management of the WebSphere Application Server environment.

The HA/WLM Architecture

Figure 2-1 shows the sample highly available, workload-managed WebSphere architecture you're going to build. Building this system involves the following high-level tasks:

- Install and configure WebSphere in a cluster environment using the Network Deployment package.

- Configure the WebSphere cluster for memory-to-memory or database session persistence.

- Install and configure HTTP Server and the plug-in module to spray requests across application servers.

- Install and configure Edge Server – Load Balancer servers (primary and secondary) to spray requests across HTTP servers, and configure these servers for high availability.

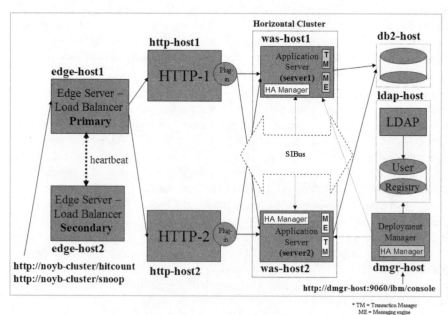

Figure 2-1: Sample HA/WLM WebSphere architecture

As you set up this system, you'll perform additional tasks to verify it, ensuring that the basic WebSphere infrastructure is foolproof and ready for application deployment. During the verification process, you'll answer the following questions about your configuration:

- Is application server failover working?
- Is HTTP session failover (memory-to-memory or database persistence) working?
- Is IBM HTTP Server (with the help of the plug-in module) spraying requests across WebSphere application servers?
- Is HTTP Server failover working?
- Is Edge Server – Load Balancer spraying requests across HTTP servers?
- Is Edge Server – Load Balancer failover working in high-availability mode?

In the rest of this chapter, we give an overview of the specific steps you'll perform to build the sample HA/WLM configuration. Figure 2-2 lists these steps. As we discuss each step in more detail, a corresponding flow chart will show you the high-level decisions and substeps required to accomplish that step.

Step 1: Verify you're ready (Chapter 2)
Step 2: Perform pre-installation tasks (Chapter 2)
Step 3: Create, configure, and verify the deployment manager profile (Chapter 7)
Step 4: Create, configure, and verify the application server profile (Chapter 7)
Step 5: Create, configure, and verify the custom profile (Chapter 7)
Step 6: Federate nodes (Chapter 8)
 Step 6a: Federate the node within the application server profile
 Step 6b: Federate the node within the custom profile
Step 7: Install, configure, and verify IBM HTTP Server (Chapter 5)
Step 8: Install the distributed remote plug-in (Chapter 9)
 Step 8a: Configure HTTP Server node as managed node
 Step 8b: Configure HTTP Server node as unmanaged node
Step 9: Create and configure the horizontal cluster (Chapter 10)
Step 10: Enable and configure highly available persistent service (Chapter 12)
Step 11: Configure HTTP session persistence (Chapter 11)
 Step 11a: Configure memory-to-memory session persistence
 Step 11b: Configure database session persistence
Step 12: Create and configure SIBus and messaging engine (Chapter 12)
Step 13: Install, configure, and verify Edge Server – Load Balancer (Chapters 13 and 14)
 Step 13a: Install, configure, and verify Edge Server – Load Balancer servers
 Step 13b: Configure Edge Server – Load Balancer servers for high availability

Figure 2-2: Installation and configuration steps

Step 1: Verify You're Ready

Figure 2-3 shows the flow chart you'll follow for Step 1.

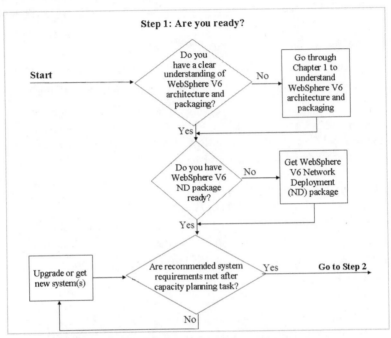

Figure 2-3: Step 1 – Verify you're ready

A successful WebSphere Application Server installation requires a clear understanding of the V6 architecture and packaging. After reading Chapter 1, you should have a good grasp of the capabilities and limitations of each package of WebSphere V6 (Express, Base, and Network Deployment). For example, you can't expect to build a WebSphere cluster environment (as for the HA/WLM example) using the Base or Express package. You can build less complex environments using the Base or Express package, as you'll see in Chapters 3 through 6. To build application server clusters, you need the Network Deployment package. Make sure you obtain the right WebSphere package for the architecture you're going to build.

After obtaining the WebSphere software, make sure the systems on which you plan to install the software will be able to run it (and your application) in the environment you require (e.g., stress test, pre-production, production). If possible, perform capacity planning to ensure you can meet any service level agreements in place. Also, be realistic:

Although a system with the minimum hardware requirements (in terms of CPU, RAM, and so on) may suffice for debugging in development, training, or functional testing environments, it's likely to prove inadequate for performance testing or production environments.

To determine the minimum operating system and hardware requirements for your platform and WebSphere package, consult one of the following Web sites:

http://www-306.ibm.com/software/webservers/appserv/doc/latest/prereq.html
http://www-306.ibm.com/software/webservers/appserv/was/requirements

Step 2: Perform Pre-Installation Tasks

Figure 2-4 shows the flow chart you'll follow for Step 2.

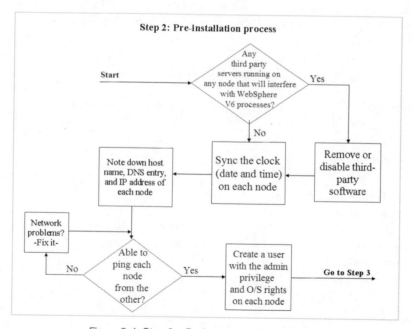

Figure 2-4: Step 2 – Perform pre-installation tasks

Before you actually install the WebSphere software, be sure to check the required configuration and administrative user privileges on each system. Doing so will save time you might otherwise end up spending on problem determination and troubleshooting.

In addition, make sure your TCP/IP network is configured properly on the machine on which you'll be installing the product. The directory structure (core directory naming) of the WebSphere administrative configuration repository uses the host name of the machine on which the WebSphere software is installed, so make sure the host name doesn't change after the installation.

If any software on your system will interfere with the TCP/IP ports used by WebSphere processes and you don't know about it, you'll spend quite a bit of time troubleshooting later. For example, you'll have trouble running HTTP Server on a machine on which a third-party Web server (e.g., Microsoft's Internet Information Server, or IIS) is already installed and running. Web servers use port 80 by default (or port 443 if you've enabled Secure Sockets Layer, or SSL). If you need to have multiple HTTP Server versions on a single physical machine, you must proactively address port-assignment issues to avoid port conflicts during the installation process. Table 2-1 lists the important port numbers used by WebSphere processes. For a complete list of WebSphere ports, consult the WebSphere Application Server V6 Information Center at http://publib.boulder.ibm.com/infocenter/ws60help/index.jsp.

Table 2-1: Default ports used by WebSphere processes

Port description	Default port number
HTTP transport port	80
HTTPS transport port	443
Embedded HTTP transport port	9080
Admin console port	9060
Embedded HTTPS transport port	9443
Admin console secure port	9043
Bootstrap port	2809
SOAP connector port	8880
SAS SSL ServerAuth port	9401
CSIV2 SSL ServerAuth listener port	9403
CSIV2 SSL MutualAuth listener port	9402
ORB listener port	9100
High Availability Manager communications port	9353
Service Integration Bus (SIB) port	7276
SIB secure port	7286
SIB MQ interoperability port	5558
SIB MQ interoperability secure port	5578

To see which ports are being used on your system, run the command **netstat –a** from the operating-system command prompt. Figure 2-5 shows sample output from the netstat command. Before proceeding with the WebSphere installation, remove or disable any third-party software that's likely to cause a conflict.

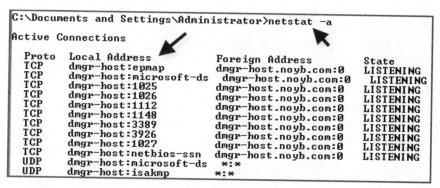

```
C:\Documents and Settings\Administrator>netstat -a

Active Connections

  Proto  Local Address             Foreign Address         State
  TCP    dmgr-host:epmap           dmgr-host.noyb.com:0    LISTENING
  TCP    dmgr-host:microsoft-ds    dmgr-host.noyb.com:0    LISTENING
  TCP    dmgr-host:1025            dmgr-host.noyb.com:0    LISTENING
  TCP    dmgr-host:1026            dmgr-host.noyb.com:0    LISTENING
  TCP    dmgr-host:1112            dmgr-host.noyb.com:0    LISTENING
  TCP    dmgr-host:1148            dmgr-host.noyb.com:0    LISTENING
  TCP    dmgr-host:3389            dmgr-host.noyb.com:0    LISTENING
  TCP    dmgr-host:3926            dmgr-host.noyb.com:0    LISTENING
  TCP    dmgr-host:1027            dmgr-host.noyb.com:0    LISTENING
  TCP    dmgr-host:netbios-ssn     dmgr-host.noyb.com:0    LISTENING
  UDP    dmgr-host:microsoft-ds    *:*
  UDP    dmgr-host:isakmp          *:*
```

Figure 2-5: Sample netstat command output

Because you'll be using the Network Deployment package to configure multiple nodes, you may encounter synchronization problems if the date and time (clock) on the application server node differ from the date and time on the Deployment Manager node to which you'll be federating the application server. To avoid such problems, synchronize the clock on each node. Also, make sure the timestamp between the Lightweight Directory Access Protocol (LDAP) server and the Deployment Manager are in sync with each other.

For each node, make a note of the host name, fully qualified name (i.e., Domain Name Server, or DNS, entry), and IP address. Be sure you can ping the nodes from each other. In some cases, you may be able to ping a WebSphere node from the HTTP server node but have trouble pinging in reverse. For help fixing this problem, consult your network administrator. It's important to solve any such issues before proceeding with the WebSphere installation.

Note: In our experience, it's best, if you can manage it, to use DNS instead of mapping host names to IP addresses through the hosts file. The latter approach can be error-prone as well as a maintenance nightmare. If you do use the hosts file, be sure to periodically validate the entries in the file and update it if a domain name, host name, or IP address changes. Otherwise, you may spend quite a bit of time troubleshooting in the wrong place. Consult your network administrator about the best way to manage the hosts file.

If a DNS entry isn't available, make sure a host name entry with the IP address exists in the etc/hosts file. If DNS entries aren't set, update the hosts file. On Windows XP systems, you'll find the hosts file in the \WINDOWS\system32\drivers\etc directory. On Unix machines, you'll find it in directory /etc.

To install and configure WebSphere software, you must have administrative privileges and certain operating system rights. For example, to install HTTP Server and WebSphere on Windows platforms, you need rights to

- act as part of the operating system
- log on as a service

On AIX, Linux, and Unix systems, you must log in as root. Before proceeding with the installation, make sure you have the appropriate rights for your operating system environment, or create the appropriate user.

Step 3: Create, Configure, and Verify the Deployment Manager Profile

Figure 2-6 shows the flow chart you'll follow for Step 3.

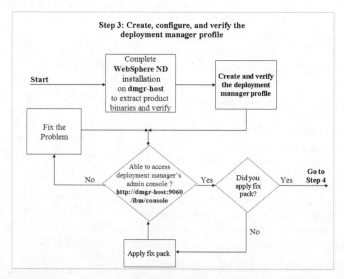

Figure 2-6: Step 3 – Create, configure, and verify the deployment manager profile

You use the Deployment Manager to manage clusters and their cluster members, Web servers and their nodes, and the entire cell configuration. To set up the Deployment

Manager, you'll need to install the WebSphere Network Deployment package on the dmgr-host system, create the deployment manager profile, and verify that you're able to connect to the Deployment Manager's administrative console. Chapter 7 explains these tasks in detail.

Figure 2-7 shows what the Deployment Manager's admin console looks like after the successful creation of the deployment manager profile on dmgr-host.

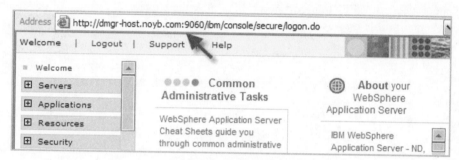

Figure 2-7: Deployment Manager's admin console

Step 4: Create, Configure, and Verify the Application Server Profile

Figure 2-8 shows the flow chart you'll follow for Step 4.

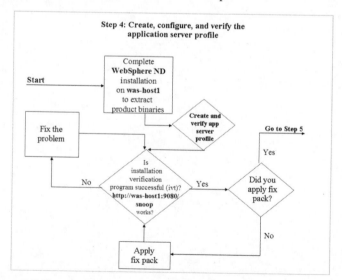

Figure 2-8: Step 4 – Create, configure, and verify the application server profile

Each application you deploy will run on an application server. When you create an application server profile on the was-host1 system, an application server (named server1) is created automatically. When you later create the horizontal cluster, you'll use this application server as a template and also as the first member of the cluster.

Chapter 7 describes how to create, configure, and verify the application server profile on was-host1. Figure 2-9 shows the output of the snoop servlet invoked through the Web container's default HTTP transport port (9080) after the successful creation of the application server profile on was-host1.

Figure 2-9: Snoop servlet output confirming creation of application server profile on was-host1

Step 5: Create, Configure, and Verify the Custom Profile

Figure 2-10 shows the flow chart you'll follow for Step 5.

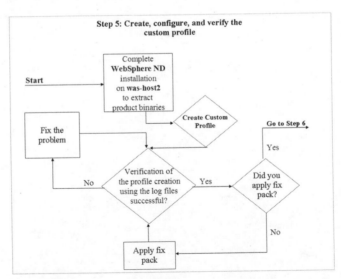

Figure 2-10: Step 5 – Create, configure, and verify the custom profile

In this step, you'll create a custom profile on was-host2 and federate the node within this profile to the Deployment Manager cell. You'll create the second cluster member (server2) when you create the horizontal cluster later.

Chapter 7 explains how to create and verify the custom profile on was-host2. Figure 2-11 shows the contents of the log file (<WASV6-ROOT>\logs\wasprofile\wasprofile_create_Custom01.log) after the successful creation of the custom profile on was-host2.

```
<level>INFO</level>
<class>com.ibm.ws.profile.cli.WSProfileCLICreateProfileInvoker</class>
<method>executeWSProfileAccordingToMode</method>
<thread>11</thread>
<message>INSTCONFSUCCESS: Success: The profile now exists.</message>
```

Figure 2-11: Log file contents after successful creation of custom profile

Step 6: Federate Nodes

When you initially create the Deployment Manager on the dmgr-host system, it's not aware of any application server profile on the was-host1 node or any custom profile on the was-host2 node. To manage the application servers and nodes from the Deployment Manager's admin console, you must first federate those nodes to the Deployment Manager cell on dmgr-host.

Chapter 8 details the steps involved in federating the node within the application server profile on was-host1 to the Deployment Manager cell on dmgr-host. Figure 2-12 shows the flow chart for this task.

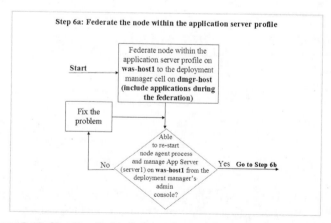

Figure 2-12: Step 6a – Federate the node within the application server profile

Chapter 8 also describes how to federate the node within the custom profile on was-host2 to the Deployment Manager cell on dmgr-host. Figure 2-13 shows the flow chart for this task.

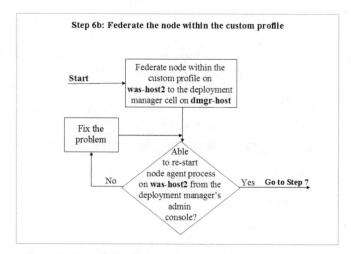

Figure 2-13: Step 6b – Federate the node within the custom profile

The screen in Figure 2-14 shows how the was-host1 and was-host2 nodes appear in the Deployment Manager's admin console after the two nodes have been successfully federated to the Deployment Manager cell on dmgr-host.

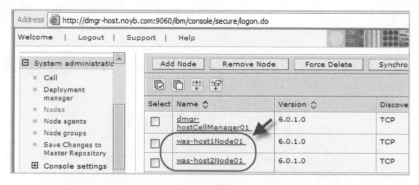

Figure 2-14: Nodes displayed in Deployment Manager admin console

Figure 2-15 shows the Deployment Manager admin console view of the node agent processes on these two nodes. Once you've successfully federated the nodes, you can use this display to manage (e.g., stop, start) the node agents and servers on each node.

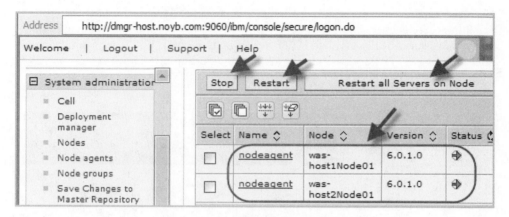

Figure 2-15: Node agent processes

Step 7: Install, Configure, and Verify IBM HTTP Server

Figure 2-16 shows the flow chart you'll follow for Step 7.

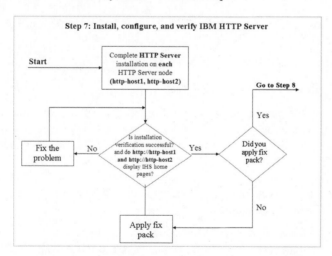

Figure 2-16: Step 7 – Install, configure, and verify IBM HTTP Server

You'll install IBM HTTP Server on two systems (http-host1 and http-host2). Later (in Step 8), you'll install the WebSphere plug-in module on each of these Web servers and configure it with the Deployment Manager to spray requests across application servers. You'll also configure both HTTP servers with Edge Server – Load Balancer to provide high availability for these servers.

Chapter 5 explains how to install, configure, and verify HTTP Server on the http-host1 and http-host2 nodes. Figure 2-17 shows the HTTP Server welcome page that appears once you've successfully installed HTTP Server on http-host1. You'll see a similar result after installing HTTP Server on http-host2 (using http://http-host2.noyb.com).

Figure 2-17: HTTP Server welcome page

Step 8: Install the Distributed Remote Plug-in

You can propagate the plug-in configuration file (plugin-cfg.xml) and manage the HTTP servers from the Deployment Manager's admin console. This feature necessitates some upfront planning and requires you to make some configuration changes in the Deployment Manager and on the HTTP server nodes after installing the plug-in. The configuration changes depend on the plug-in architecture you use. Because in this case you're dealing with a remote plug-in, you must choose which of two remote plug-in architectures you want to configure:

- *Distributed remote plug-in – Web server as managed node* — A managed node contains a node agent process that enables you to manage an HTTP server remotely from the Deployment Manager's admin console. You create a node agent process on each HTTP server/plug-in node (http-host1 and http-host2) by creating a custom profile on each node and then federating the node within the custom profile to the Deployment Manager cell on dmgr-host. (This configuration isn't recommended for production environments because the node agent runs in the demilitarized zone, or DMZ, on the Web server node, and running a full-Java process in the DMZ is not a good practice from a security perspective.)

■ *Distributed remote plug-in – Web server as unmanaged node* — In the case of IBM HTTP Server, you can use the IBM HTTP administrative server to manage the unmanaged Web server (without a node agent process). Even though it's called an unmanaged node, if you're using IBM HTTP Server, you have the same capabilities as a managed node as far as Web server management from the admin console is concerned.

> **Note:** If you're going through this process simply for educational and training purposes, consider configuring http-host1 as a managed node and http-host2 as an unmanaged node to try out both of these configurations.

Figure 2-18 shows the flow chart you follow to configure the first option, distributed remote plug-in – managed node. Figure 2-19 shows the flow chart for the second option, distributed remote plug-in – unmanaged node. Chapter 9 explains how to install the WebSphere plug-in on each HTTP Server node, how to configure each node as either a managed or an unmanaged node, and how to verify the configuration.

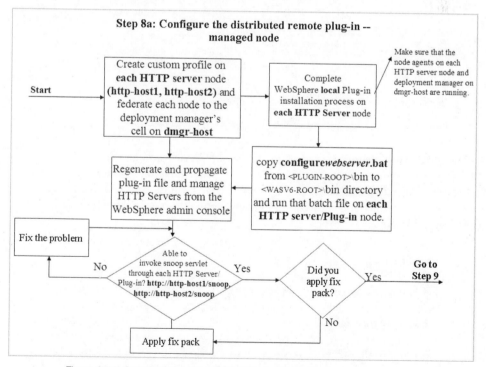

Figure 2-18: Step 8a – Configure distributed remote plug-in – managed node

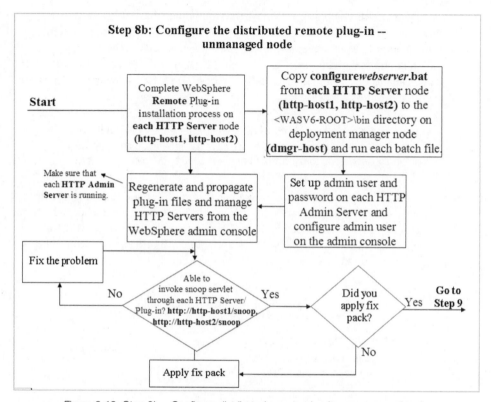

Figure 2-19: Step 8b – Configure distributed remote plug-in – unmanaged node

Figure 2-20 shows the result of invoking the snoop servlet through the HTTP Server/plug-in (http://http-host1.noyb.com/snoop) once the plug-in software has been successfully installed and configured on http-host1. You'll receive a similar result after successfully installing and configuring the plug-in on http-host2 (using http://http-host2.noyb.com/snoop).

Figure 2-20: Snoop servlet output

Once you've successfully installed and configured the plug-in software on the HTTP Server nodes, you can manage the HTTP servers remotely and change the HTTP Server configuration and plug-in properties from the Deployment Manager's admin console, as shown in Figure 2-21.

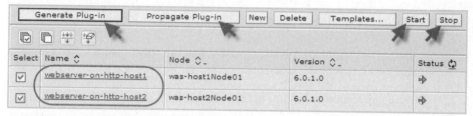

Figure 2-21: Managing HTTP servers and plug-in properties from the Deployment Manager's admin console

Step 9: Create and Configure the Horizontal Cluster

Figure 2-22 shows the flow chart you'll follow for Step 9.

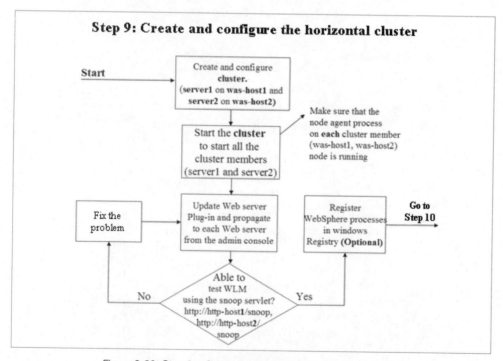

Figure 2-22: Step 9 – Create and configure the horizontal cluster

When you create the horizontal cluster, you'll use the application server named server1 on was-host1 as a template and as the first cluster member, and you'll create server2 on was-host2 as a second cluster member. Chapter 10 explains how to create, configure, and verify the horizontal cluster. If you're building this system in a Windows environment, you can optionally register and customize the service names in the Windows **Services** panel by following the instructions given in Chapter 20.

The partial screens in Figures 2-23 and 2-24 show that the client requests are being workload-managed across cluster members (server1 on was-host1 and server2 on was-host2) from the plug-in on the HTTP server node (http-host1 or http-host2). You should see the same behavior whether you use the URL http://http-host1/snoop or http://http-host2/snoop in the browser. The first figure shows that the first snoop servlet request is sent to and processed by server1 on was-host1 when a user issues either http://http-host1/snoop or http://http-host2/snoop from the browser. Figure 2-24 shows that the second snoop servlet request is sent to and processed by server2 on was-host2 when the user issues either of these requests from the browser.

Remote host	169.254.189.152
Remote port	1361
Local address	was-host1
Local host	169.254.147.4
Local port	9080
javax.servlet.context.tempdir	C:\IBM\WebSphere\App
com.ibm.websphere.servlet.application.host	server1
com.ibm.websphere.servlet.application.name	Default Web Application

Figure 2-23: First snoop servlet request

Remote host	169.254.189.152
Remote port	1359
Local address	was-host2
Local host	169.254.14.111
Local port	9080
javax.servlet.context.tempdir	C:\IBM\WebSphere\App$
com.ibm.websphere.servlet.application.host	server2
com.ibm.websphere.servlet.application.name	Default Web Application

Figure 2-24: Second snoop servlet request

Step 10: Enable and Configure Highly Available Persistent Service

Figure 2-25 shows the flow chart you follow to enable, configure, and verify highly available persistent service. If you want to recover in-flight transactions automatically should the cluster member that's processing the transactions fail, you need to enable and configure this service for the cluster. Chapter 12 explains this process.

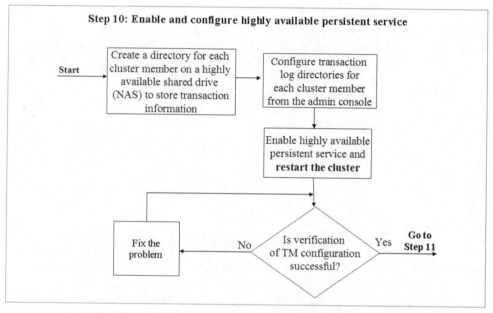

Figure 2-25: Step 10 – Enable and configure highly available persistent service

Step 11: Configure HTTP Session Persistence

You have two choices when it comes to configuring HTTP session persistence for session failover. You can choose to configure HTTP session persistence by storing the session data in another member of that cluster (known as *memory-to-memory* session persistence) or by storing the data in a database as a backup (*database* session persistence). If you like, you can configure the cluster members to use both memory-to-memory (JVM) and database session persistence, but you can enable only one of these options (or neither) at any one time.

Configure Memory-to-Memory Session Persistence

Figure 2-26 shows the flow chart you follow to configure memory-to-memory session persistence. When you configure cluster members for memory-to-memory session persistence and set the replication mode to "Both client and server," server1 (the first cluster member) on was-host1 saves the session data created on server2 (the second cluster member) on was-host2 for backup. In the same way, server2 saves the session data created on server1 as a backup to provide session failover capability.

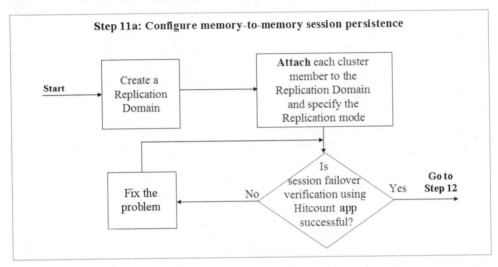

Figure 2-26: Step 11a – Configure memory-to-memory session persistence

Chapter 11 describes how to configure memory-to-memory session persistence and verify session failover. Figure 2-27 shows the session manager configuration on the first cluster member after you've successfully created the replication domain and attached each cluster member to it. You'll see similar session-manager configuration information on the second cluster member (server2) and on any other cluster members you choose to configure.

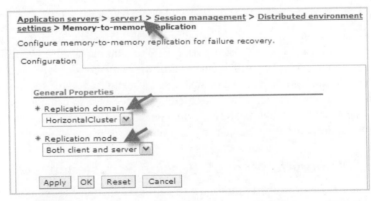

Figure 2-27: Session manager configuration on first cluster member

Configure Database Session Persistence

Figure 2-28 shows the flow chart you follow to configure database session persistence.

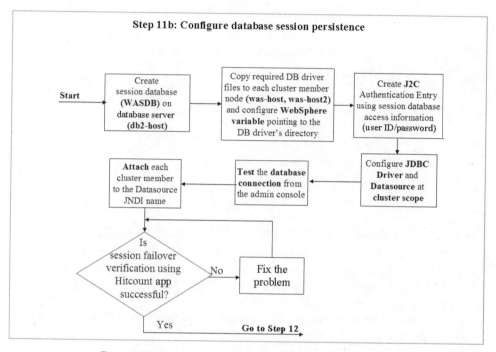

Figure 2-28: Step 11b – Configure database session persistence

When you configure a database for session persistence, all session data created on both cluster members (server1 and server2) is stored in the database as a backup for session failover capability. Chapter 11 explains how to configure database session persistence and verify the session failover. Figure 2-29 shows a successful database connection after the cluster has been configured for database session persistence from the Deployment Manager's admin console.

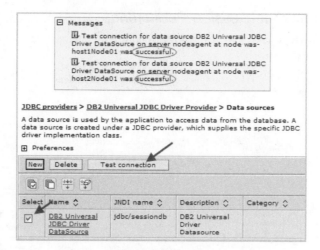

Figure 2-29: Successful database connection

Step 12: Create and Configure the SIBus and Messaging Engine

Figure 2-30 shows the flow chart you follow to create, configure, and verify the Service Integration Bus (SIBus) and messaging engine. If you plan to deploy message-based (JMS/MDB-based) applications, you need to create an SIBus and add the cluster as a member of the bus to create a highly available messaging engine on that cluster. Chapter 12 explains how to create, configure, and verify these components. If you're not deploying message-based applications, you can skip this step.

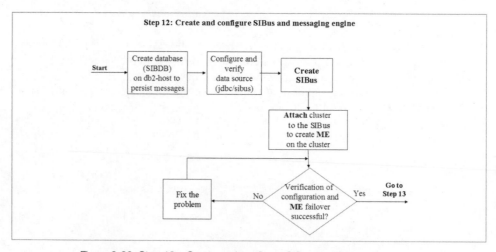

Figure 2-30: Step 12 – Create and configure SIBus and messaging engine

Step 13: Install, Configure, and Verify Edge Server – Load Balancer

The sample architecture you'll build in this book uses the Edge Server – Load Balancer's dispatcher component to spray IP requests across back-end HTTP servers (http-host1 and http-host2). You'll install edge-host1 as the primary (active) load balancer server and install edge-host2 as the secondary (standby) load balancer server.

Install, Configure, and Verify Edge Server – Load Balancer

Figure 2-31 shows the flow chart you'll follow to install, configure, and verify the primary and secondary load balancer servers to spray requests across the back-end HTTP servers. Chapter 13 describes this process.

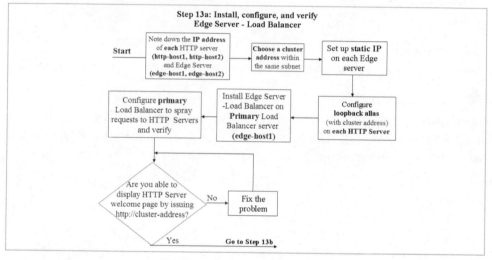

Figure 2-31: Step 13a – Install, configure, and verify Edge Server – Load Balancer

Figure 2-32 shows the output of the snoop servlet invoked through the load balancer using the cluster address or its alias (http://noyb-cluster.noyb.com/snoop). You can refresh the browser a few times and use the servlet output and Load Balancer Monitoring tool to see the distribution of load across HTTP servers and cluster members.

Figure 2-32: Output of snoop servlet invoked through the load balancer

In Figure 2-33, the Load Balancer Monitoring tool is indicating that the load balancer is spraying requests across the HTTP servers after receiving a request issued using the cluster address or its alias (http://noyb-cluster.noyb.com or http://noyb-cluster.noyb.com/snoop) to display the welcome page on each HTTP server.

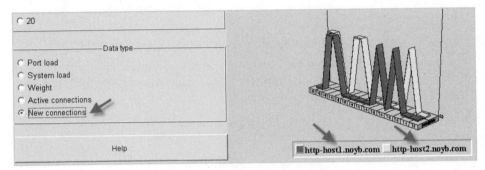

Figure 2-33: Load Balancer Monitoring tool indicating that the Load Balancer is spraying requests across HTTP servers

Configure Load Balancer Servers for High Availability

Figure 2-34 shows the flow chart you'll follow to configure the two Edge Server – Load Balancer servers for high availability. Chapter 14 explains how to perform and verify this configuration.

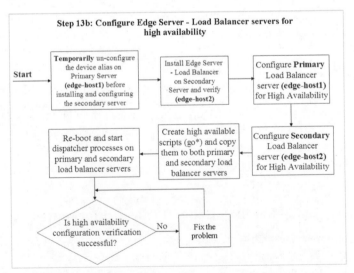

Figure 2-34: Step 13b – Configure Edge Server – Load Balancer servers for high availability

The status display in Figure 2-35 shows that the state of the secondary load balancer on edge-host2 has changed to Active (from Backup) and indicates that this load balancer is serving client requests after primary server failure.

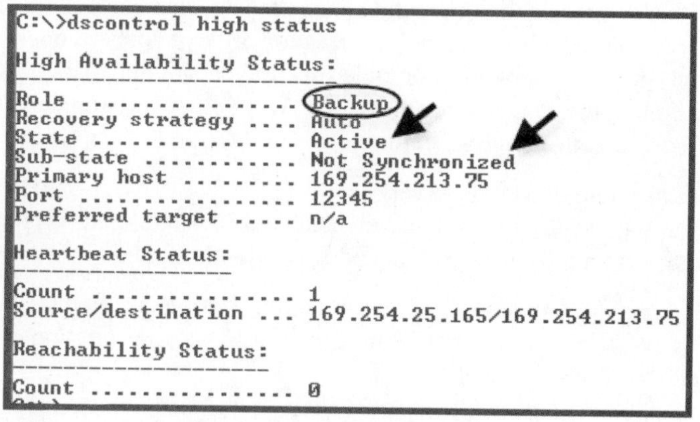

```
C:\>dscontrol high status

High Availability Status:
----------------------------
Role ................. Backup
Recovery strategy .... Auto
State ................ Active
Sub-state ............ Not Synchronized
Primary host ......... 169.254.213.75
Port ................. 12345
Preferred target ..... n/a

Heartbeat Status:
----------------------------
Count ................ 1
Source/destination ... 169.254.25.165/169.254.213.75

Reachability Status:
----------------------------
Count ................ 0
```

Figure 2-35: High availability status

Additional Tasks and Topics

Once you've installed, configured, and verified your WebSphere Application Server environment, some additional tasks and topics await you. The later chapters of this book address these issues and provide step-by-step instructions to guide your efforts.

Dynamic cache. WebSphere's dynamic caching functionality lets you cache dynamic content generated by J2EE application components (servlets and Java Server Pages) and push that content to the HTTP server/plug-in and/or a caching proxy. Use Chapter 15 to understand and configure the dynamic caching feature.

Security. To protect your WebSphere configuration from unauthenticated and unauthorized access, you should enable WebSphere security even if your applications don't use J2EE security. Chapter 16 provides step-by-step instructions for enabling security and setting up an admin group for WebSphere administrators who need to have access to the cell. There are three kinds of user registries you can use to keep a database of users and the groups to which they belong: custom, operating system, and Lightweight Directory Access Protocol (LDAP). Chapter 16 describes the use of each of these kinds of registries. Use this chapter to enable global security and create and configure admin roles.

Tivoli Directory Server. The preferred user registry is one based on the LDAP protocol. IBM Tivoli Directory Server (ITDS) is an LDAP server that you can download from *http://www-306.ibm.com/software/tivoli/products/directory-server*.

Chapter 17 provides step-by-step instructions on installing, configuring, and verifying ITDS for use as the user registry with WebSphere Application Server.

Secure Sockets Layer. Many sites need to use SSL to encrypt communications with browser clients on the Internet. Commerce sites that process financial transactions and sites that deal in personal information are examples of operations for which encryption is important. For added security, a site may use SSL for communications among the systems that make up a WebSphere environment. Chapter 18 explains how to configure SSL between

- a browser and an HTTP server
- a Web server plug-in and the Web container in WebSphere application servers
- WebSphere application servers and IBM Tivoli Directory Server

WebSphere product updates. A common administrative task is installing product updates for WebSphere. Chapter 19 gives a step-by-step description of this task for the nodes in a WebSphere cell.

Register WebSphere processes. Use Chapter 20 to register WebSphere processes in the Windows registry and run them from the Windows **Services** panel if you're using a Windows operating system.

Web services enablement. Use Chapter 21 to understand and configure the architecture necessary to invoke Web services through the SIBus.

Managing WebSphere Application Server. Consult Chapter 22 to understand WebSphere tracing, the collector tool, First Failure Data Capture, Log Analyzer, thread dumping, heap dump analysis, configuration archive backup and restore, and performance monitoring with Tivoli Performance Viewer.

Application Server Tool (AST) Kit. Use Chapter 23 to understand J2EE packaging.

Enterprise archives (EARs). Use Chapter 24 to understand EAR installation, enhanced EARs, fine-grained application updates, and mapping EAR modules to specific application servers.

WebSphere Rapid Deployment. Use Chapter 25 to understand and configure WebSphere Rapid Deployment.

J2EE system management. Use Chapter 26 to understand system management using the J2EE Management API.

3

WebSphere V6 Standalone Application Server: Install, Configure, and Verify

One of the core tasks involved in building the WebSphere architecture we described in Chapter 2 — a highly available, workload-managed (HA/WLM), clustered application server environment — is to set up a standalone application server. You can perform this task using any of the available packages of WebSphere Application Server V6: Express, Base, or Network Deployment. To use Network Deployment features such as clustering, you must upgrade the Express or Base package to the Network Deployment package.

The process of creating, verifying, configuring, and managing the standalone application server is the same whether you use the Base/Express package or the Network Deployment package. In this chapter, we step you through the install process for WebSphere V6 – Base/Express and show you how to create, configure, and verify the application server profile that's created using the binaries that are copied to disk when you install this package. (For a reminder of the relationship among product binaries, profiles, profile templates, and application servers, see Chapter 1.)

Chapter 7 covers the Network Deployment version of this process. Before using the Network Deployment package to create a standalone application server, we strongly advise you to read the present chapter from beginning to end to gain a complete under-standing of the standalone application server and how it works. Consider this chapter a prerequisite to understanding the topics covered in Chapter 7. We'll refer to parts of this chapter to perform most of the steps required in Chapter 7 to create and manage the application server profiles for the sample HA/WLM environment.

Installation Essentials

It's important to understand that the WebSphere V6 installation process has two phases:

- Phase 1 — Copying the product binaries to an installation directory you specify during the installation. Throughout the book, we represent this directory as <WASV6-ROOT>.

- Phase 2 — Creating, under the <WASV6-ROOT>\profiles directory, a default profile (called 'default') that defines the runtime environment (set of files) for an application server process (server1). Throughout the book, we represent the profiles directory as <PROFILE-ROOT>.

Table 3-1 provides a key, by operating system, to the directory locations for the symbolic directory references we use in our discussions.

Table 3-1: Directory locations for symbolic references

Symbolic reference	Windows	AIX	Linux/Unix
<WASV6-ROOT>	C:\IBM\WebSphere\AppServer	/usr/WebSphere/AppServer	/opt/WebSphere/AppServer
<PROFILE-ROOT> for default profile	<WASV6-ROOT> \profiles\default	<WASV6-ROOT> /profiles/default	<WASV6-ROOT> /profiles/default
<NEW-PROFILE-ROOT> for profile added after AppSrv01 install	<WASV6-ROOT> \profiles\AppSrv01	<WASV6-ROOT> /profiles/AppSrv01	<WASV6-ROOT> /profiles/AppSrv01

For the Base and Express packages, both phases of the install process are performed automatically for you during installation. If you use the Network Deployment package, the installation process performs only Phase 1 — copying the product binaries to the installation directory. You must then use the Profile Creation wizard or the wasprofile command-line utility to create a profile (Phase 2) yourself. For this reason, you won't see the default application server profile after installing the ND package.

Figure 3-1 shows the architecture and components that are created after you successfully install the application server using the Base/Express package.

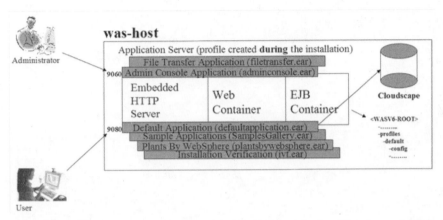

Figure 3-1: Architecture and components created after installation of the Base/Express application server

As a result of the installation process, the following elements are created:

- product binaries and a configuration repository, all stored in the file system. (WebSphere V6 doesn't require a database to store the configuration repository.)

- a default profile (default) containing an application server (server1).

- file transfer and administrative console applications on the default application server (server1). You use these applications to make changes to the configuration repository. By default, the applications are available at administrative port 9060.

- the DefaultApplication application (consisting of the snoop, hello, and hitcount servlets) and an installation verification application on the default application server (server1). You use these applications to verify installation and configuration. By default, the applications are available at HTTP transport port 9080. The Cloudscape database is also installed to support container-managed persistence (CMP) entity beans in the hitcount application.

- optionally, the SamplesGallery and PlantsByWebSphere applications, if you choose to deploy these additional sample applications during the installation.

Installing WebSphere Application Server V6 Using the Base/Express Package

The flow chart in Figure 3-2 depicts the high-level steps required to install, configure, and verify the application server profile for the standalone application server. In this section, we walk you through each step of this process.

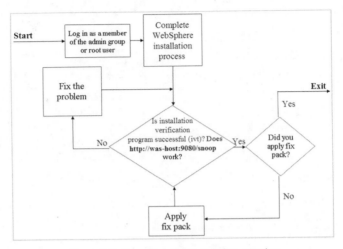

Figure 3-2: Base/Express installation overview

Our instructions assume that you're working in a Windows XP environment. If you're using a Unix operating system to perform the steps, you'll need to execute the appropriate commands for your operating system (i.e., .sh instead of .bat) and substitute the forward slash (/) for the backward slash (\) in directory and path names. We'll point out other differences for Unix in "Unix Notes" as needed. Now let's get started.

Step 1. If you plan to use the trial version of the WebSphere Base or Express package, your first step is to register for and download the software from the Web. The trial version is good for 60 days, and you can submit a problem ticket to IBM support during the trial period. For more details about the trial version and to download the software, go to either of the following URLs:

http://www-106.ibm.com/developerworks/websphere/downloads
http://www14.software.ibm.com/webapp/download/home.jsp

Figure 3-3 shows how the directory structure looks after you've downloaded the trial version of the Base package and extracted the files to a temporary directory. Note the location of the Launchpad program (launchpad.bat on Windows, launchpad.sh on Unix). This Web application is the starting point for installing all WebSphere Application Server products. If you're using the licensed Base or Express package, you'll find the Launchpad program in the root directory of the WebSphere product CD.

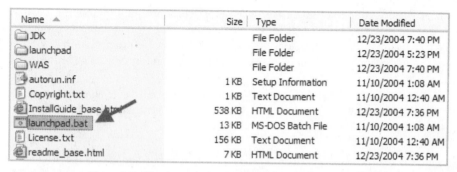

Name ▲	Size	Type	Date Modified
JDK		File Folder	12/23/2004 7:40 PM
launchpad		File Folder	12/23/2004 5:23 PM
WAS		File Folder	12/23/2004 7:40 PM
autorun.inf	1 KB	Setup Information	11/10/2004 1:08 AM
Copyright.txt	1 KB	Text Document	11/10/2004 12:40 AM
InstallGuide_base.html	538 KB	HTML Document	12/23/2004 7:36 PM
launchpad.bat	13 KB	MS-DOS Batch File	11/10/2004 1:08 AM
License.txt	156 KB	Text Document	11/10/2004 12:40 AM
readme_base.html	7 KB	HTML Document	12/23/2004 7:36 PM

Figure 3-3: Directory structure for Base package trial version

Step 2. Log in to your Windows system as a member of the Administrators group. On the Windows desktop, right-click **My Computer**, select **Properties**, and go to the **Advanced** tab. Click the **Environment Variables** button to display the user and system variables. In the "User variables for user" list, note the value set for the temporary directory, TMP. The WebSphere installation program uses this directory to store temporary files during the installation.

If you don't see TMP in the variable list, click **New** to add the variable. In the window shown in Figure 3-4, variable TMP has been edited to point to directory C:\temp.

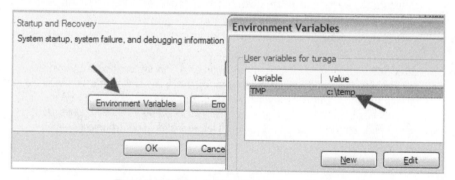

Figure 3-4: TMP variable set to directory C:\temp

Unix note: On Unix systems, log in as root. If necessary, run the command **umask 022** to set permissions for the temporary directory (usually /tmp on these systems). You can verify the current umask setting by running **umask** with no arguments.

Step 3.   The WebSphere Base/Express V6 product requires a minimum of 1,030 MB of disk space: 100 MB for the temporary directory and 930 MB for the installation root directory (<WASV6-ROOT>). Before proceeding with the installation, verify that your system meets this minimum space requirement.

Unix note: Make sure the file systems mounted on the temporary and installation directories meet the minimum disk space requirements of 100 MB and 930 MB, respectively.

Step 4.   If you're using the licensed Base or Express package, insert the product CD and navigate to the directory where the Launchpad program is located. If you're using the trial version of the software, navigate to the temporary directory containing the downloaded product files.

To start the installation wizard, double-click **launchpad.bat**. (As an alternative, you can invoke the install.exe program under the WebSphere directory where you downloaded the installation product files.)

From the moment you invoke it, the Launchpad program begins logging information about your installation activities under the TMP directory. If you have trouble starting the Launchpad (or install.exe) or encounter problems during the early part of the installation, consult this log. To learn more about WebSphere logging, see the "Logging: Problem Determination and Troubleshooting" section of this chapter.

Unix note: Before starting the Launchpad on a Unix system, make sure you can execute the **xclock** or **xeyes** command to display one of the graphical images shown in Figure 3-5. If you have a problem displaying the image, set the terminal emulation properly. If you can display these images but can't start the Launchpad, consult "Logging: Problem Determination and Troubleshooting" for more information.

Figure 3-5: Images displayed by xclock and xeyes commands

Step 5. The Launchpad program displays an initial welcome panel similar to the one shown in Figure 3-6. If you're using the licensed package, you'll see additional options (e.g., HTTP Server, Plug-in, AST) on the left side of this panel.

Read through the contents of the welcome panel, and then select the option to "Launch the installation wizard for WebSphere Application Server." (If you're using the Express package, you may need to choose the option "WebSphere Application Server – Express Installation" on the task menu to the left of the welcome text.) Click **Next**.

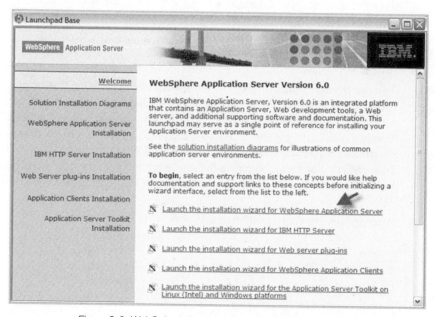

Figure 3-6: WebSphere Application Server V6 welcome panel

Step 6. On the next panel, click to accept the terms of the license agreement, and then click **Next**.

Step 7. The next panel informs you that the installation program is checking system prerequisites. If the wizard reports that the check was successful, click **Next**. If the prerequisites check fails, cancel the installation program, and open and read the log file that was generated during the check (file log.txt in the TMP directory). Correct your system to meet the requirements, and then run the installation program again. For more information about logging and troubleshooting, see "Logging: Problem Determination and Troubleshooting."

If the wizard detects an existing WebSphere installation (Version 5 or 6) when it runs the prerequisites check, an informational panel informs you that you'll need to assign unique port values for each installation. Read through the details on this panel, and then click **Next**. (If no other version of WebSphere exists on the machine, you won't see this panel.)

> **Note:** The sequence of panels hereafter depends on various conditions, such as whether there's an existing WebSphere installation on the machine you're installing (and which features were installed previously).

Step 8. You use the next panel (Figure 3-7) to specify the installation directory for the application server — that is, the <WASV6-ROOT> directory. You can accept the default directory or specify a different location. If you're using the Windows operating system, make sure the directory name you use contains no spaces (even though the install program and Windows permit spaces in path names). For the sample installation described here, we used C:\IBM\WebSphere\AppServer as the application server installation directory.

After specifying your installation directory, click **Next**.

Figure 3-7: Specifying the installation directory

Step 9. On the next panel (Figure 3-8), select **Custom installation**, and click **Next**. (This panel won't appear if you have an existing installation of WebSphere V6 on this machine.)

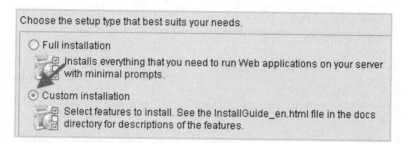

Figure 3-8: Choosing a custom installation

Step 10. When you choose the custom install option, the wizard lets you specify which WebSphere features you want to install. If you're performing this installation for educational or training purposes, select the **Application Server Samples** check box (shown in Figure 3-9) in addition to the preselected options the wizard presents. These sample applications demonstrate the functionality of the application server.

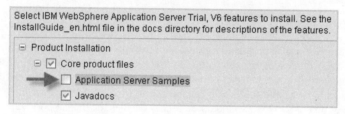

Figure 3-9: Application Server Samples option

For production and test environments, we recommend you *don't* install the Application Server Samples. You can add them later if you like by upgrading the installation (a process we cover in Chapter 4). Note that the default application (DefaultApplication), which you'll use later to verify the basic operation of the application server, will be installed even if you choose not to install the Application Server Samples.

When you've made your selection, click **Next** to proceed with the installation.

Step 11. The installation wizard next gives you a chance to change the default port numbers. Figure 3-10 shows the port number display. If the installation program detected an existing instance of WebSphere Application Server V6, each port number that appears on this panel will be incremented by 1, starting with the port number of the last instance.

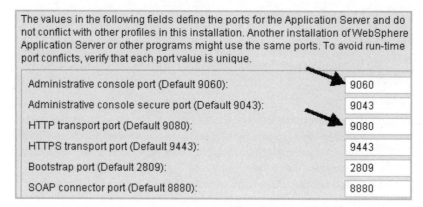

The values in the following fields define the ports for the Application Server and do not conflict with other profiles in this installation. Another installation of WebSphere Application Server or other programs might use the same ports. To avoid run-time port conflicts, verify that each port value is unique.

Administrative console port (Default 9060):	9060
Administrative console secure port (Default 9043):	9043
HTTP transport port (Default 9080):	9080
HTTPS transport port (Default 9443):	9443
Bootstrap port (Default 2809):	2809
SOAP connector port (Default 8880):	8880

Figure 3-10: Application server ports

Note: The install program keeps track of existing instances, their port numbers, and other features using the file vpd.properties. Each time you install WebSphere product binaries and/or create a new profile using the existing product binaries and the Profile Creation wizard (covered later), the program creates an entry in this file and automatically decides the default port numbers for the new profile.

The IBM support team may ask you to edit the properties file if you have problems uninstalling and/or reinstalling WebSphere. Never change this file unless IBM support asks you to do so. The file's location varies according to operating system:

> For Windows, the location is C:\Windows.
> For Windows NT, the location is C:\WINNT.
> For AIX, the location is /usr/lib/objrepos.
> For Linux, the location is root directory '/'.

At the time of this writing, HP-UX and Solaris don't use the vpd.properties file.

Here's a brief description of the ports and their use:

■ *Administrative console port – 9060* — You use this port in the browser URL when you want to connect to the application server from the admin console (e.g., http://was-host:9060/ibm/console). If you've configured the node for Secure Sockets Layer (SSL), you use the secure port (9043) instead of 9060.

- *HTTP transport port – 9080* — You use this port when you want to invoke a Web application running on the application server from a browser. For example, to invoke the snoop servlet, you'd use http://was-host:9080/snoop. If you've configured the node for SSL, you use the secure port (9443) instead of 9080.

- *Bootstrap port – 2809* — Client applications use the bootstrap port to access WebSphere's built-in Object Request Broker (ORB) to use Enterprise Java Beans (EJBs) in applications installed on the application server. The Java Naming and Directory Interface (JNDI) service provider URL used by the client application needs to reference the bootstrap port to obtain an initial context for looking up EJBs it wants to use.

- *SOAP connector port – 8880* — Client applications (e.g., wsadmin) use the Simple Object Access Protocol (SOAP) port to connect to the application server admin service. Also, when you federate a node from the Deployment Manager's admin console, you must specify the application server host name and its SOAP port (8880 in this example).

After making any port number changes required for your environment, click **Next**.

Step 12. You use the wizard's next panel (Figure 3-11) to specify the node and host names for the application server. To accept the default names, simply click **Next**.

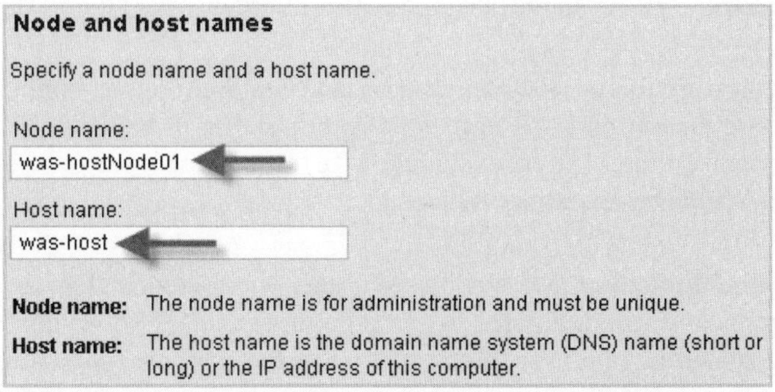

Figure 3-11: Specifying the node name and host name

If you want to change the default node name, make sure the name you choose is unique among

- multiple application server profiles on the same node per installation

- nodes in a Network Deployment domain

Also, avoid using the following reserved words: *cells*, *nodes*, *servers*, *clusters*, *applications*, and *deployments*.

The host name can be the fully qualified host name (e.g., was-host.noyb.com), the host name (e.g., was-host), or the IP address (e.g., 24.142.101.52) of the machine. Use the following criteria when deciding which option to use:

- Use the fully qualified name in production systems and/or where multiple network interface cards (NICs) exist at the time of WebSphere installation or when you may be upgrading the machine with multiple NIC cards in the future.

- Use the host name where a single NIC card exists at WebSphere installation and you're certain the machine won't have multiple cards in the future.

- We don't recommend using the IP address unless you have a valid reason to do so.

Note that the installation program doesn't validate the host name during the installation. If you specify an invalid host name or Domain Name Server (DNS) entry, you'll receive an exception (InvocationTargetException) when starting the application server after installation. For more information about this error, see "Logging: Problem Determination and Troubleshooting."

Step 13. If you want to use a Windows service to run WebSphere Application Server, choose the option to "Run the application server process as a Windows service" on the next panel (Figure 3-12). (You won't see this panel on non-Windows operating systems.)

If you don't select the Windows service option, the installation program disregards any values entered below it on this panel. If you choose the option and select the option to "Log on as a local system account," a user name and password are optional. If you choose the Windows service option and select "Log on as a specified user account," you must provide a valid user name

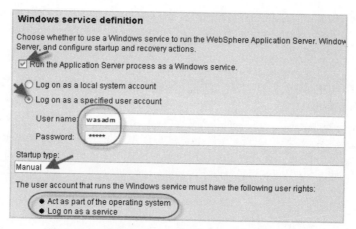

Figure 3-12: Specifying the Windows service startup type

(with no spaces) and password. This user should have "Log on as a service" authority to run the process.

If you choose the Windows service option, you must also specify a Windows service startup type (Automatic, Manual, or Disabled). When you're finished with this panel, click **Next**.

Step 14. The wizard next displays a preinstallation summary panel. Review the information on the panel, and click **Next** to proceed with the installation. You'll see a progress panel while the installation program extracts files and installs components.

You'll notice that the installation program creates the installation directory (<WASV6-ROOT>) at this stage and starts logging information under the subdirectory <WASV6-ROOT>\logs. For information about this logging, see "Logging: Problem Determination and Troubleshooting."

Step 15. When a panel reporting a successful installation appears, select the "Launch the First Steps Console" option, and click **Finish**. You'll use the First Steps tool later to verify your WebSphere Application Server installation.

Step 16. After installing any WebSphere component, you should check for and apply the latest fixes. Chapter 19 describes how to install product updates for the different WebSphere components when a refresh pack or fix pack is available to install. Consult that chapter for the steps to perform for this installation, and then return to this chapter for instructions on verification and problem determination.

Understanding the WebSphere Standalone Application Server Directory Structure

The WebSphere installation process creates several important directories under the installation root <WASV6-ROOT> (directory C:\IBM\WebSphere\AppServer in our example). Figure 3-13 depicts the directory structure of the application server profile that's created using the WebSphere Base/Express package.

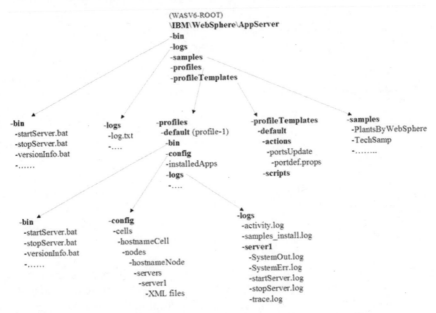

Figure 3-13: Directory structure of the application server profile

Here's a brief look at the purpose of each directory.

- *bin* — The bin directory contains all the executable commands needed to manage and configure a WebSphere application server.

- *logs* — Files under the logs directory are created during the WebSphere installation. For more information about this directory, see "Logging: Problem Determination and Troubleshooting."

- *profiles* — Each profile you create is stored under the profiles directory by default. The installation program creates a profile called default (and an application server, server1, within it) during the WebSphere V6 Base/Express installation. Each profile directory (e.g., default) contains the files (specific to that profile) that are required to run and manage the application server within that profile. When creating a profile using the Profile Creation wizard or the wasprofile command, you can choose a different destination that needn't be under the profiles directory.

- *profileTemplates* — This directory houses the profile templates used to define the configuration settings of new servers you create. The Base/Express package comes with the default profile, which the Profile Creation wizard uses when it creates a new application server profile.

- *samples* — Source and binary files for all the WebSphere samples are available under this directory.

- *_uninst* — This directory contains the uninstall execution program and related files that are used if you uninstall the WebSphere product.

Figure 3-14 provides a complete view of the structure of the default profile after the WebSphere Base/Express installation.

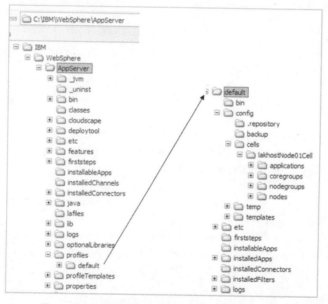

Figure 3-14: Directory structure of the default profile

Verifying the Standalone Application Server Installation

Even though the final panel of the installation wizard reported that your WebSphere installation took place successfully, it's important to verify the installation by performing a few simple checks. This way, you'll know which log files to refer to or what to verify if a problem occurs. In this section, we show you how to confirm a successful installation using the following tools:

- log files
- the First Steps console
- the administrative console
- the default application (snoop, hello, and hitcount)

We also explain how to verify that the application server process is running as a Windows service (for Windows users who choose to configure WebSphere this way).

Verify Installation by Viewing the Log Files

To confirm a successful installation of the standalone application server using the installation log files, go to the <WASV6-ROOT>\logs directory and open the file named log.txt. Scroll to the end of the file. If you see the indicator INSTCONFSUCCESS (as shown in Figure 3-15), the installation may indeed have succeeded. You need to verify a few more things (as we'll explain in a moment) before you can claim that the installation is successful.

```
com.ibm.ws.install.ni.ismp.actions.ISMPConfigManagerLaunchAction, msg1, INSTCONFSUCCESS:
successful.
com.ibm.ws.install.ni.ismp.actions.ISMPWSProfileLaunchAction, msg1, INSTCONFSUCCESS:
successful.
com.ibm.ws.install.ni.ismp.actions.ISMPLogFileAction, msg1, The Profile Creation Tool
com.ibm.ws.install.ni.ismp.actions.ISMPLogSuccessMessageAction, msg1, INSTCONFSUCCESS
```

Figure 3-15: Verifying a successful installation

If you see either INSTCONFFAIL or INSTCONFPARTIALSUCCESS, the installation program encountered problems. To determine the source of the trouble, consult this chapter's "Logging: Problem Determination and Troubleshooting" section.

As we explained at the beginning of the installation section, a default profile (and an application server, server1) is created as part of the installation process (in Phase 2). As part of verifying the installation, you should confirm the successful creation of the default profile. To do so, go to the <WASV6-ROOT>\logs\wasprofile directory, open the file wasprofile_create_default.log, and scroll to the end of the file. If you see the INSTCONFSUCCESS indicator (as shown in Figure 3-16), the installation succeeded. If you see errors in the file, consult "Logging: Problem Determination and Troubleshooting."

```
WSProfileCLICreateProfileInvoker</class>  <method>executewSProfileAccordingToMo
>INSTCONFSUCCESS: Success: The profile now exists.</message></record><record>
te>  <millis>1105284847217</millis>  <sequence>5603</sequence>
ProfileCLI</logger>  <level>INFO</level>  <class>com.ibm.ws.profile.WSProfileCLI
od>  <thread>12</thread>  <message>Returning with return code: INSTCONFSUCCESS
```

Figure 3-16: Verifying creation of the default profile

Verify Installation Using the First Steps Console

When you select the final installation panel's option to launch the First Steps console, the First Steps program is started immediately after the WebSphere installation is completed. If you perform a silent installation (a process we describe in Chapter 4), you must start this program manually. You can launch First Steps at any time by clicking the Windows **Start** button and navigating to **All programs|IBM WebSphere|Application Server v6|Profiles|default|First steps**. You can also invoke the program by opening a command window and running **firststeps.bat** from the directory <PROFILE-ROOT>\firststeps (where <PROFILE-ROOT> = <WASV6-ROOT\profiles\default).

When the First Steps program begins, it displays the First Steps wizard. This useful tool lets WebSphere administrators perform the following tasks from one screen:

- Verify the installation.
- Start or stop the application server.
- Connect to the admin console.
- Start the Profile Creation wizard.
- Invoke and work with the sample applications.
- Connect to the WebSphere Information Center.
- Invoke the migration wizard.

To confirm a successful WebSphere installation, click the panel's **Installation verification** option. (You can also run the installation verification program, ivt.bat, at the command prompt from the <PROFILE-ROOT>\bin directory.) If the installation was successful, you should see a notification screen similar to the one shown in Figure 3-17.

```
IVTL0060I: EJB Verification Status - Passed
IVTL0035I: Scanning the file C:\IBM\WebSphere\AppServer\profiles\default\logs\server1\SystemOut.log
IVTL0040I: 0 errors/warnings were detected in the file C:\IBM\WebSphere\AppServer\profiles\default\log
IVTL0070I: IVT Verification Succeeded
IVTL0080I: Installation Verification is complete
```

Figure 3-17: First Steps verification of a successful installation

If the default application server hasn't been started, the verification program starts it. Review the notification messages to ensure that the server process has been started. Also, make sure that the next-to-last line in the log indicates "IVT Verification

Succeeded." If the installation verification wasn't successful, review "Logging: Problem Determination and Troubleshooting."

Connect to the Application Server Through the Admin Console and Verify

To connect to the application server through the WebSphere Application Server administrative console, click **Administrative Console** on the First Steps main panel. For the user ID, enter any value (including blank, although we don't suggest it). WebSphere won't check against any user registry to authenticate unless security is turned on and configured; nevertheless, it's a good idea to enter a meaningful user name to enable logging and recovery of any configuration information changed using that particular user ID. WebSphere stores the activity log under the <PROFILE-ROOT>\wstemp directory.

Click **Log in** (or press Enter) to connect to the admin console and display the welcome panel (Figure 3-18). (You can also invoke the admin console from a browser using the URL http://was-host:*port*/ibm/console, where *port* is the port number of the admin console — 9060 by default.) The welcome panel offers some useful information and links (e.g., to WebSphere Support, IBM DeveloperWorks, and Documentation) and provides the WebSphere product version, build number, and build date.

Figure 3-18: WebSphere admin console welcome panel

To see the default application server that was created during the installation, expand the **Servers** item in the left pane, and click **Application Servers**. You'll see the default application server, server1, displayed on the right (Figure 3-19).

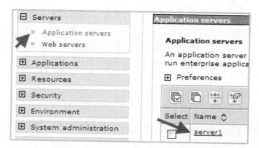

Figure 3-19: Default application server in admin console

To see the applications that have been deployed, expand **Applications** and click **Enterprise Applications**. The list of installed applications appears on the right (Figure 3-20). (If you didn't select the Application Server Samples option during installation, you won't see PlantsByWebSphere and SamplesGallery in the list.) Make sure each application is shown as running (indicted by a green arrow in the Status column). If any application is stopped, there may be a problem with the installation. For troubleshooting information, see "Logging: Problem Determination and Troubleshooting."

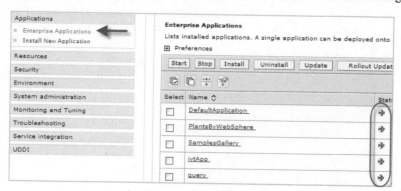

Figure 3-20: Enterprise applications

Verify Installation from the Browser Using the Default Application

Every administrator should understand how to use the three programs in WebSphere's DefaultApplication sample application — snoop, hello, and hitcount — to verify the application server configuration. Let's walk through the steps involved.

Snoop

The snoop servlet verifies the connection between the browser and the application server's Web container (through the Embedded HTTP Server). To invoke the snoop program, open the browser and enter **http://was-host:*port*/snoop** (where *port* is the HTTP transport port — 9080 by default). You should see a screen similar to the one shown in Figure 3-21. Scroll down the page, and navigate through the output to see the detailed information reported for the servlet request.

Figure 3-21: Snoop servlet

Hello

The hello servlet is designed with client type-detection support. You can invoke this servlet from a browser, a speech client, or a Wireless Access Protocol–enabled browser, for example. To invoke the servlet from a browser, enter **http://was-host:*port*/hello**. You should see a screen similar to the one shown in Figure 3-22.

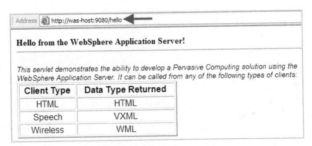

Figure 3-22: Hello servlet

Hitcount

The hitcount servlet demonstrates how to increment a counter value using several different methods. To invoke the servlet, enter **http://was-host:*port*/hitcount** after opening the browser. You should see a page similar to the one shown in Figure 3-23.

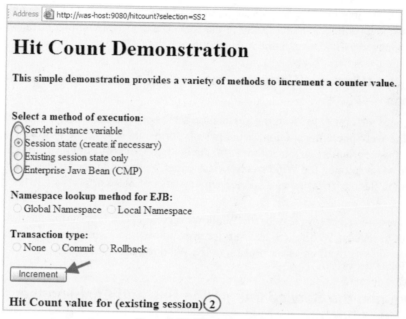

Figure 3-23: Hitcount servlet

This page offers several ways to increment a counter value:

- Select the "Servlet instance variable" option and click the **Increment** button a few times to see the hit count value for the existing session being incremented. We use this option to verify the health of the Web container.

- Select the "Session state (create if necessary)" option and click **Increment** a few times to verify that a session is created and the hit count value (attached to the session) is incremented.

- Select the "Existing session state only" option and click **Increment** a few times to see that the hit count value is incremented to the value stored in the existing session. (You'll use this option in a later chapter to verify the session persistence configuration after configuring a cluster.)

- Select the "Enterprise Java Bean (CMP)" option and click **Increment** a few times to see the hit count value incremented. This option helps you identify the connection between
  - › browser and Web container (through the Embedded HTTP Server)
  - › Web container and EJB container
  - › EJB container and the database (Cloudscape in this case)

You can use this option with the page's "Namespace lookup method for EJB" options to verify the global and local name spaces of the EJB. You can use it with the "Transaction Type" options to verify commit and rollback through the EJB.

Verify the Windows Services Panel for the Application Server Process

If you chose the option to "Run the application server process as Windows service" during the WebSphere installation (Windows platforms only), take the following steps to confirm this configuration. Click **Start** and navigate to **Control Panel|Administrative Tools|Services** to open the Windows **Services** panel. You should see IBM WebSphere Application Server V6 listed as a service with a status of Started.

If you forgot to select (or cleared) the Windows service check box during the installation and want to register WebSphere as a service now, follow the instructions in Chapter 20 to register the application server process in the Windows service registry.

Configuring the Service Integration Bus and Enabling the Messaging Engine

Unlike previous versions of WebSphere, the WebSphere V6 Java Message Service (JMS) provider runs in an application server process (JVM). When you install the standalone application server or create a new profile, the V6 messaging engine (ME) isn't enabled by default. However, the product binaries required to enable the ME are copied to the installation directory during the product installation itself.

You don't have to configure a Service Integration Bus (SIBus) or an ME if the applications installed on the application server aren't using JMS. If your application *is* using JMS and/or message-driven EJBs, you need to perform the steps outlined in this section.

To enable a messaging engine, you must complete two tasks:

- Create and configure an SIBus.
- Include the application server as a member of the SIBus to create and enable the messaging engine inside the application server (JVM).

Figure 3-24 illustrates the WebSphere V6 ME architecture. Chapter 12 provides a detailed explanation of the SIBus and the ME. When following the instructions in that chapter, add a standalone application server (instead of a cluster) as a member of the bus (as shown in Figure 3-25). When doing so, you have option to use a data source that points to a production-quality database or the default data source, which uses the built-in Cloudscape database to store persistent messages.

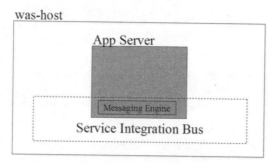

Figure 3-24: WebSphere V6 messaging engine architecture

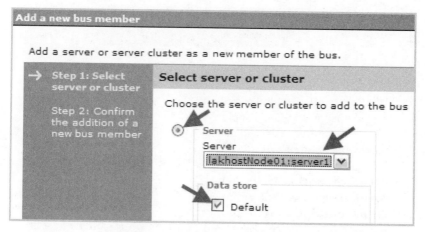

Figure 3-25: Adding a new bus member

Creating Multiple Application Server Profiles

As you learned in Chapter 1, you can use the same set of product binaries and the default application server template to create multiple application server profiles. WebSphere will deploy the administrative console and default applications (as well as the samples if you choose) on each profile you create, making it easier to manage multiple application server profiles. The diagram in Figure 3-26 depicts a system on which a second application server profile has been created. The new instance accepts requests for the admin console and installed applications at port 9061 and 9081, respectively.

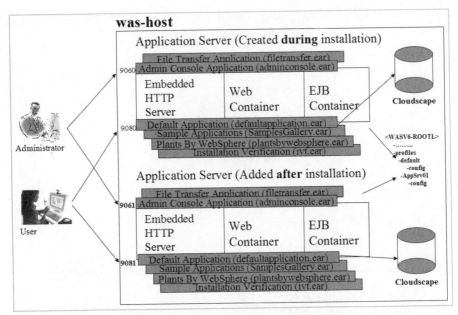

Figure 3-26: Multiprofile application server architecture

Step 1. WebSphere offers multiple methods for creating an additional application server profile. You can launch the Profile Creation wizard by clicking the **Start** button and selecting **All Programs|IBM WebSphere| Application Server v6|Profile creation wizard**. You can also invoke the Profile Creation wizard from the First Steps wizard by running **firststeps.bat** from the command prompt under the <PROFILE-ROOT>\firststeps directory. A third way to start the profile-creation tool is to run **pctWindows.exe** under the <WASV6-ROOT>\bin\ProfileCreator directory.

> **Note:** On AIX, the profile-creation executable is named pctAIX.bin. On Linux, it is pctLinux.bin. Look for the required executable in directory <WASV6-ROOT>/bin/Profile Creator.

If you want to create a new profile from the command prompt, go to the <WASV6-ROOT>\bin directory and run the command **wasprofile -create -help** first to see the arguments required to create a profile from the command line.

Step 2. The Profile Creation wizard first asks you to give the new profile a name (Figure 3-27). If you want to change the default name displayed by the wizard (AppSrv01), make sure the name you specify is unique among

- multiple application server profiles on the same node per installation
- nodes in a Network Deployment domain

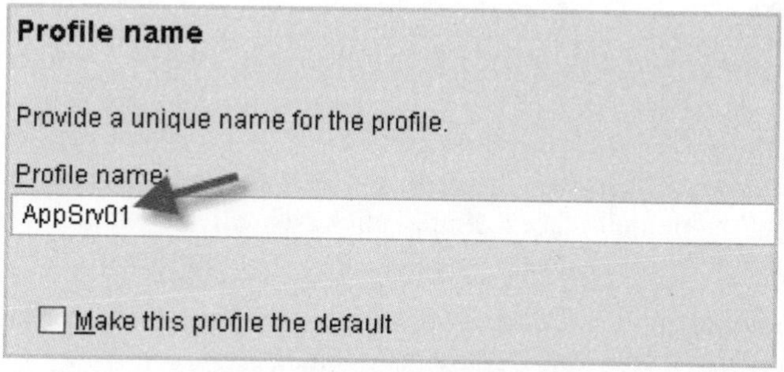

Figure 3-27: Profile name panel

The profile name panel also offers you the option to "Make this profile the default." In a multiprofile environment, you can use this option to specify one of the profiles as a default profile. You already have a profile named 'default' that was created during installation of the Base/Express package, and at this point that profile is the default profile.

It's important to understand how the default profile differs from other profiles. When you choose a profile as the default profile, you don't have to specify the –profileName argument when running any command from the <WASV6-ROOT>\bin directory. For example, to start the default profile, you can just issue

```
startServer server1
```

For all other profiles, you must specify the profile name. For example:

```
startServer server1 –profileName AppSrv01
```

In addition, during plug-in installation, the default profile configuration is updated with the Web server definition when you run the configure*webserver*.bat program. If you plan to configure the profile you're creating (AppSrv01 in our example) with HTTP Server through the plug-in, you should select the option to "Make this profile the default." You'll learn more about the plug-in installation in Chapter 6.

In summary, you should make your new profile the default profile if it will be the most frequently used profile and/or if it is the profile you want to configure with the Web server definition later. For our example, simply leave this option unchecked, and click **Next**.

Step 3. On the next panel, enter the directory where the new profile configuration should be created (or accept the default directory). (Throughout the book, we refer to this new profile root directory as <NEW-PROFILE-ROOT>.) Click **Next**.

Step 4. Next, you must specify the node and host names for the new profile. To accept the default names, simply click **Next**. If you want to change the default node name, make sure the name is unique among

- multiple application server profiles on the same node per installation
- nodes in a Network Deployment domain

Also, avoid using the reserved names *cells*, *nodes*, *servers*, *clusters*, *applications*, and *deployments*.

The host name can be the DNS entry or the host name of the machine. (You can also use the raw IP address for the host name, but we don't advise doing so.)

Step 5. Next, the Profile Creation wizard displays the assigned port numbers for the new instance (Figure 3-28). The wizard program automatically increments the port numbers by 1 from the port numbers of the last installed instance of WebSphere V6. To open the admin console for the new instance, for example, you'll use the URL http://was-host:**9061**/ibm/console. To invoke the snoop servlet, you'll use http://was-host:**9081**/snoop.

Review the assigned ports, and click **Next**.

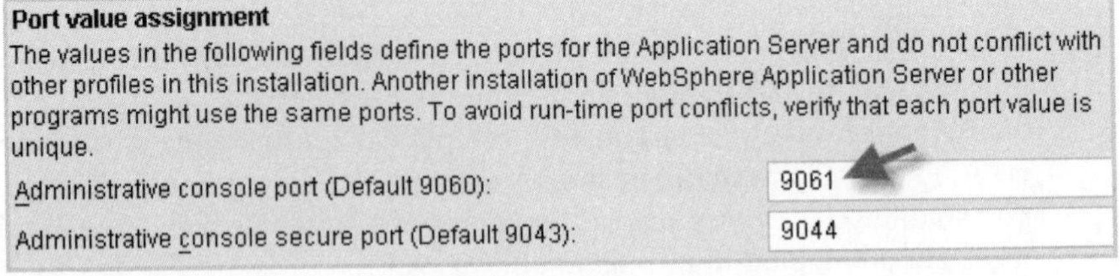

Port value assignment

The values in the following fields define the ports for the Application Server and do not conflict with other profiles in this installation. Another installation of WebSphere Application Server or other programs might use the same ports. To avoid run-time port conflicts, verify that each port value is unique.

Administrative console port (Default 9060): 9061

Administrative console secure port (Default 9043): 9044

Figure 3-28: Port value assignment

Step 6. On the next panel, select the check box option and choose a Windows service startup type if you want to run the application server process as a Windows service. Click **Next**.

Step 7. Review the summary panel, and click **Next** to create the new profile.

Step 8. On the panel indicating successful creation, select the option to "Launch the First steps Console," and then click **Finish**.

Step 9. To verify the creation of your new application server profile, follow the instructions given above for verification using the First Steps console. Substitute <NEW-PROFILE-ROOT> for <PROFILE-ROOT> when following these steps.

Step 10. If you selected to run the application server process as a Windows service, open the **Services** panel using **Start|Control Panel|Administrative Tools|Services**, and look for the new WebSphere process.

The Multiple Application Server Profile Directory Structure

Figure 3-29 shows the complete view of the WebSphere V6 multiprofile directory structure. As you can see, each application server profile uses the same binary files and has a dedicated directory (default and AppSrv01 in this case) where the items specific to that profile (its configuration, applications, log files, and so on) are stored, making it easier for the administrator to manage.

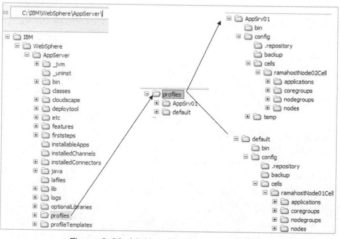

Figure 3-29: Multiprofile directory structure

Logging: Problem Determination and Troubleshooting

WebSphere Application Server V6 automatically logs all activities by default. Log files are your main source of information for diagnosing problems that occur during installation, profile creation, and server management. The location (directory) of the log files varies depending on the activity. For example, the logs generated during installation are stored in a different place than those generated when you manage (e.g., start, stop) an application server. Each activity creates logging information in one or more log files.

In this section, we describe how logging takes place, from product installation through the various stages of managing the application server. The illustration in Figure 3-30 depicts the logging architecture for the WebSphere V6 standalone application server.

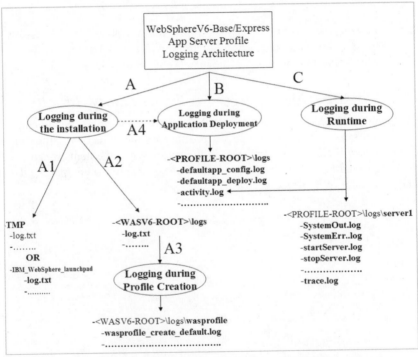

Figure 3-30: WebSphere V6 logging architecture

You can logically divide the destination of the log files into seven categories according to the activity performed on the application server. Table 3-2 provides a guide to these categories. In addition to the log files specified in the table, the log files activity.log and trace.log aid in problem determination. For more information about these two files, see Chapter 22.

Table 3-2: WebSphere logging categories

Activity	Log destination	Description	When to use these files
Installation — initial part	The TMP directory ■ File log.txt is the important log file under this destination. ■ If you used the Launchpad program to start the installation, you'll see the log files under the TMP directory's IBM_WebSphere_launchpad subdirectory. ■ If you used install.exe to perform the installation, the log files are created immediately under directory TMP. ■ On Windows, check the TMP environment variable to determine the value of the temporary directory. The examples in this chapter use C:\temp as the TMP value on the Windows machine. ■ On Unix, /tmp is usually the temporary directory.	These log files are populated immediately after invocation of the Launchpad or install.exe program. After a successful installation, the files are copied to the logs subdirectory under the installation directory (<WASV6-ROOT>).	■ Use if you have a problem starting the Launchpad or install.exe or encounter problems during the early part of the installation. ■ Use if the system prerequisites check fails and you want to see the reason.
Installation — later part Profile creation or deletion Application deployment	The <WASV6-ROOT>\logs directory specified during installation ■ File log.txt is the important log file under this destination.	These log files are populated from the moment you click **Next** after reviewing the summary report during the graphical installation.	■ Use if the installation wasn't successful and you want to know why. ■ If these log files don't provide enough information, consult the log files under the TMP directory.
Profile creation or deletion	The <WASV6-ROOT>\logs\wasprofile directory ■ File names created are as follows: wasprofile_create_profileName.log and wasprofile_delete_profileName.log. ■ If you use the Profile Creation wizard to create a profile, all the events are logged in file pctLog.txt under the <NEW-PROFILE-ROOT>\logs directory	Log files under this directory are populated when you use the Profile Creation wizard or the wasprofile command-line tool. If you're using the Base or Express package, creation of the 'default' profile is part of the installation.	■ Use if you have problems creating or deleting a profile or if installation isn't successful.

Table 3-2: WebSphere logging categories (continued)

Activity	Log destination	Description	When to use these files
Application deployment	The <PROFILE-ROOT>\logs directory ■ The log files for the applications deployed on the default profile during the sample installation were created under the C:\IBM\WebSphere\profiles\default\logs directory.	For each application installed, you'll see two log files: <appname>_deploy.txt and <appname>_config.txt.	■ Use if you have a problem invoking the default application (snoop, hello, and hitcount) or any of the sample applications after installation. ■ Use if you have a problem deploying user applications or invoking them after deployment.
Application server management (e.g., starting/stopping the server, checking the server status)	The <PROFILE-ROOT>\logs\server1 directory	You can see one log file for each initiated command. For example, if you run the command **startServer server1**, you'll see the startServer.log file under its log destination.	■ Use if execution of the command fails.
Application server JVM logging	The <PROFILE-ROOT>\logs\server1 directory ■ The log files are SystemOut.log and SystemErr.log.	Messages sent to the JVM stdout and stderr streams are directed to the SystemOut.log file and the SystemErr.log file, respectively. SystemOut.log is one of the most widely used log files for problem determination and troubleshooting.	■ Use for problems that occur during application server startup, shutdown, or run-time.
Native process logging	The <PROFILE-ROOT>\logs\server1 directory ■ The log files are native_stdout.log and native_stderr.log.	Messages sent to stdout and stderr from native code segments are directed to the native_stdout.log file and the native_stderr.log file, respectively.	■ Use for problems that occur in native code or code written using the Java Native Interface (JNI). Verbose GC (garbage collection) output goes to the native stderr log for IBM JDKs.

Accessing Log Files from the Admin Console

When you're performing WebSphere problem determination and troubleshooting, it's handy to be able to view the log files from the admin console using a browser instead of physically logging into the machine and accessing individual files. The following steps explain how to view the JVM log files SystemOut.log and SystemErr.log from the admin console. File SystemOut.log is one of the most widely used log files for problem determination and troubleshooting.

Step 1.   Connect to the admin console, and expand **Troubleshooting|Logs and Trace|server1**. You'll see a list of the different groups of logs you can view from the console (Figure 3-31).

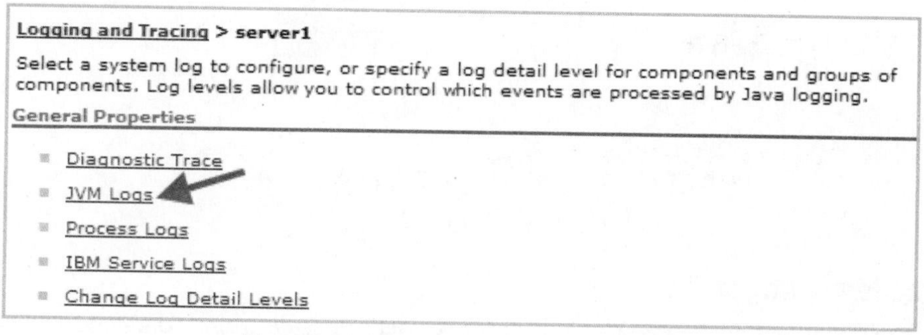

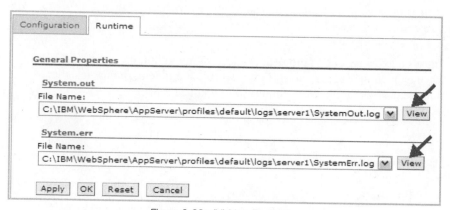

Figure 3-31: Log file groups in admin console

Step 2.   Click **JVM Logs**, and select the **Runtime** tab to see the JVM log files (Figure 3-32).

Figure 3-32: JVM log file display

Step 3.   Use the drop-down list to select the log file you want to see, and click **View**.

Step 4.   The resulting screen (Figure 3-33) reports the total number of lines in the selected file (454 in this case) and displays the first 250 of them. Enter the line number range you want to view in the **Retrieve Lines** box, and click **Refresh**. For example, to see from line 350 to the end of the sample file, you'd enter "350-454" as shown in the figure.

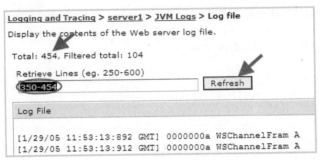

Figure 3-33: Sample log file display

Problem Scenarios

Now that you've seen how to check the log files, let's consider some common problems encountered during installation and verification of the standalone application server and explain their solutions.

Problem: *You're unable to start the installation wizard; installation fails, and no log files are created, even under the TMP directory.*

The most likely cause of this problem is a lack of minimum disk space (1,030 MB). If you have enough disk space and still experience the problem, run the installation in silent mode, using the following command to produce the log file:

```
install –options "path to response file" –silent –log # !C:\temp\log.txt
@ALL
```

(For complete instructions on performing a silent install, see Chapter 4.)

Unix note: On Unix systems, use this command:
/install –options "path to response file" -silent –log # !/tmp/log.txt @ALL

Problem: *Installation verification (IVT) shows that installation wasn't successful.*
Take the following steps to diagnose this problem.

1. Check the file ivtClient.log under the <PROFILE-ROOT>\logs directory. Because the IVT program starts the application server, also look for errors in the SystemOut.log file under the <PROFILE-ROOT\logs\server1 directory.

2. Open the file log.txt under the <WASV6-ROOT>\logs directory. If you see the INSTCONFFAIL or INSTCONFPARTIALSUCCESS indicator, a problem

occurred during product installation (copying of the product binaries). Look for the cause of the failure in this file.

3. Open the file wasprofile_create_*profileName*.log under the <WASV6-ROOT>\logs\wasprofile directory. If you see INSTCONFFAIL or INSTCONF-PARTIALSUCCESS, a problem occurred during creation of the default profile. Look for the cause of the failure in this file.

Problem: *You encounter a problem invoking the default application (snoop, hello, and hitcount) from the browser.*

Take the following steps to diagnose this problem.

1. Check the log files that were created while deploying the default application during installation: files defaultapp_deploy.log and defaultapp_config.log under the <PROFILE-ROOT>\logs directory.

2. Make sure the application server was started successfully. Open SystemOut.log, and look for the message "Server server1 open for e-business" at the end. If this message is absent, look for the errors to determine the cause of the problem.

3. Verify that the port you're using for Web applications is correct. (The default port is 9080. To invoke the snoop servlet deployed on the default application server using the default port, use http://was-host:**9080**/snoop.) Remember that in WebSphere you can have multiple application server profiles using the same product binaries. The port numbers for each profile are unique on the same node. Make sure you're connecting to the right profile.

4. If you're unsure which port you're using to invoke Web applications, open SystemOut.log, and look for a line similar to this: "Web Module Default Web Application has been bound to default_host[*:**9080**,*:80,*:9443]".
   If you see some other port number instead of 9080, invoke the application using that port.

5. If the preceding method doesn't work, look for the endpoint (port) for the WC_defaulthost in file serverindex.xml under the <PROFILE-ROOT>\config\cells*yourCell*\nodes*yourNode* directory, and use that port instead. (Figure 3-34 shows a sample endpoint entry.) *Be sure not to change any information in this file.*

6. If you're trying to connect through a Web browser from a remote machine, make sure you can ping the machines from each other using IP address, host name, and fully qualified name (DNS entry).

```
endPointName="WC_defaulthost">
        <endPoint xmi:id="EndPoint_1121184866747" host="*" port="9080"/>
```

Figure 3-34: Sample endpoint entry

Problem: *You have trouble connecting to the admin console.*

Take the following steps to diagnose this problem.

1. Make sure the application server was started successfully. Open SystemOut.log, and look for the message "Server server1 open for e-business" at the end. If this message is absent, look for the errors to determine the cause of the problem.

2. Verify that the port you're using for the admin console is correct. (The default port is 9060. To invoke the admin console that was deployed on the default application server using the default port, use http://was-host:**9060**/ibm/console.) Remember that in WebSphere you can have multiple application server profiles using the same product binaries. The port numbers for each profile are unique. Make sure you're connecting to the right profile.

3. If you're unsure which port you're using to invoke the admin application, open SystemOut.log, and look for a line similar to this: "Web Module adminconsole has been bound to admin_host[***:9060**,*:9043]." If you see some other port number instead of 9060, invoke the admin application using that port.

4. If the preceding method doesn't work, look for the endpoint (port) for the WC_adminhost in file serverindex.xml under the <DMGR-PROFILE-ROOT>\config\cells*dmgrCell*\nodes\dmgr*Node* directory, and use that port instead. *Be sure not to change any information in this file.*

5. If you're trying to connect through a Web browser from a remote machine, make sure you can ping the machines from each other using IP address, host name, and fully qualified name (DNS entry).

Problem: *Log files indicate that the installation was successful, but you receive an InvocationTargetException error while starting the server.*

To diagnose this problem, ping the host name (and DNS entry) you used during installation. If you can ping successfully, Solution 1 given here isn't likely to work for you; go to Solution 2 instead.

Unix note: On Unix systems, use the **ps –ef | grep java** command to find the java process, and then kill it using the **kill –9** command. Caution: Because the node agent process also appears in this listing (if you're in a Network Deployment environment with federated nodes), be sure to direct the kill signal to the right JVM.

```
C:\IBM\WebSphere\AppServer\profiles\AppSrv01\bin>startServer.bat server1
ADMU0116I: Tool information is being logged in file
           C:\IBM\WebSphere\AppServer\profiles\AppSrv01\logs\server1\startServer.lo
ADMU0128I: Starting tool with the AppSrv01 profile
ADMU3100I: Reading configuration for server: server1
ADMU3028I: Conflict detected on port 8880.  Likely causes: a) An instance of
           the server server1 is already running  b) some other process is
           using port 8880
ADMU3027E: An instance of the server may already be running: server1
ADMU0111E: Program exiting with error:
           com.ibm.websphere.management.exception.AdminException: ADMU3027E: An
           instance of the server may already be running: server1
ADMU1211I: To obtain a full trace of the failure, use the -trace option.
ADMU0211I: Error details may be seen in the file:
           C:\IBM\WebSphere\AppServer\profiles\AppSrv01\logs\server1\startServer.lo
```

Figure 3-38: Port 8880 conflict error message

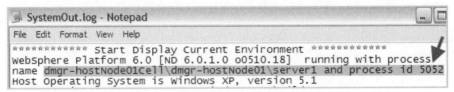

Figure 3-39: Java process ID in SystemOut.log file

4

Working with the Standalone Application Server

In Chapter 3, you learned how to install, configure, and verify the WebSphere stand-alone application server, using the Base/Express version of the product to perform the installation. With a successful installation behind you, you can begin to work with and manage the application server. In this chapter, we describe some common tasks you're likely to perform. In particular, we look at the steps required to accomplish the following operations:

- managing (e.g., starting, stopping) the application server profile environment
- upgrading an existing installation
- adding new features to an installation
- performing backup and recovery
- uninstalling the application server
- performing a silent installation

Managing the Application Server Profile Environment

There are multiple ways to manage the standalone application server, depending on the operating system used in your environment. Let's examine some frequently used operations involved in managing the application server.

Start or Stop the Application Server

To start or stop the application server that was created after the creation of the 'default' profile, you can use any of the following methods. If the name of the profile you're managing has a name other than default, substitute that profile name. If you create a default profile using the Network Deployment package, the name of the default application server profile will be AppSrv01.

- Click **Start**, navigate to **All Programs|IBM WebSphere|Application Server V6|Profiles|Default**, and click **Start the Server** or **Stop the Server**.

- Use **Start|All Programs|IBM WebSphere|Application Server V6|Profiles|Default|First Steps** to start the First Steps tool, and then click **Start the server** or **Stop the server**. (You can also invoke First Steps by running **firststeps.bat** from the <PROFILE-ROOT>\firststeps directory.)

- If you registered the application server process as a Windows service, you can start and stop the server from the Windows **Services** panel. (Use **Start|Control Panel|Administrative Tools|Services** to get there.)

- From a command-line prompt, go to the <WASV6-ROOT>\bin directory, and run either **startServer.bat server1** or **stopServer.bat server1**. Figure 4-1 shows this method of starting the server. The procedure starts the server server1 in the default profile. If the server you're dealing with isn't in the default profile, go to <PROFILE-ROOT>\bin instead of <WASV6-ROOT>\bin.

```
C:\IBM\WebSphere\AppServer\bin>startServer server1
ADMU7701I: Because server1 is registered to run as a Windows Service, the
          request to start this server will be completed by starting the
          associated Windows Service.
ADMU0116I: Tool information is being logged in file
          C:\IBM\WebSphere\AppServer\profiles\default\logs\server1\startServer.
log
ADMU0128I: Starting tool with the default profile
ADMU3100I: Reading configuration for server: server1
ADMU3200I: Server launched. Waiting for initialization status.
ADMU3000I: Server server1 open for e-business; process id is 1840
```

Figure 4-1: Starting the server from the command line

Start a Particular Profile

In a multiprofile environment, use one of the following methods to start a particular profile — in this case, AppSrv01.

- Use **Start|All Programs|IBM WebSphere|Application Server V6|Profiles|AppSrv01**, and click **Start the Server** or **Stop the Server**.

- Use **Start|All Programs|IBM WebSphere|Application Server V6|Profiles|AppSrv01|First Steps** (or run **firststeps.bat** from <NEW-PROFILE-ROOT>\firststeps), and click **Start the server** or **Stop the server**.

- Go to <WASV6-ROOT>\bin, and run one of these commands:

```
startServer.bat server1 -profileName AppSrv01
stopServer.bat server1 -profileName AppSrv01
```

Figure 4-2 shows the start command. Note that if you execute these commands from <PROFILE-ROOT>\bin, you don't have to provide the –profileName argument. For example, to start server1 in the AppSrv01 profile, you need execute only **startServer server1** from <NEW-PROFILE-ROOT>\bin.

```
C:\IBM\WebSphere\AppServer\bin>startServer server1 -profileName AppSrv01
ADMU7701I: Because server1 is registered to run as a Windows Service, the
           request to start this server will be completed by starting the
           associated Windows Service.
ADMU0116I: Tool information is being logged in file
           C:\IBM\WebSphere\AppServer\profiles\AppSrv01\logs\server1\startServer.log
ADMU0128I: Starting tool with the AppSrv01 profile
ADMU3100I: Reading configuration for server: server1
ADMU3200I: Server launched. Waiting for initialization status.
ADMU3000I: Server server1 open for e-business; process id is 3728
```

Figure 4-2: Starting the AppSrv01 profile

Verify the Status of the Application Server

The following methods let you check the status of an application server in the default profile.

- Go to <WASV6-ROOT>\bin, and run **serverStatus.bat server1** or **serverStatus.bat –all**. The sample command in Figure 4-3 checks the status of server1 in the default profile. If the server you're dealing with isn't in a default profile, go to <PROFILE-ROOT>\bin instead of <WASV6-ROOT>\bin.

- In a multiprofile environment, go to <WASV6-ROOT>\bin and run the following command from the command prompt to see the status of a particular profile (AppSrv01 in this case):

```
serverStatus.bat server1 -profileName AppSrv01
```

Figure 4-4 shows this command and its results.

If you execute this command from the <NEW-PROFILE-ROOT>\bin directory, you needn't provide the –profileName argument. For example, to check the status of server1 in the AppSrv01 profile, just execute **serverStatus server1** from <NEW-PROFILE-ROOT>\bin.

Connect to the Administrative Console

Use the following methods to connect to the default application server using the WebSphere administrative console. (If the application server isn't started, you must start it first.)

- Use **Start|All Programs|IBM WebSphere|Application Server V6|Profiles| Default|Administrative Console**.

```
C:\IBM\WebSphere\AppServer\bin>serverStatus server1
ADMU0116I: Tool information is being logged in file
           C:\IBM\WebSphere\AppServer\profiles\default\logs\server1\serverStatus
.log
ADMU0128I: Starting tool with the default profile
ADMU0500I: Retrieving server status for server1
ADMU0509I: The Application Server "server1" cannot be reached. It appears to be
           stopped.
```

Figure 4-3: Checking the status of server1 in the default profile

```
C:\IBM\WebSphere\AppServer\bin>serverStatus server1 -profileName AppSrv01
ADMU0116I: Tool information is being logged in file
           C:\IBM\WebSphere\AppServer\profiles\AppSrv01\logs\server1\serverStatus.log
ADMU0128I: Starting tool with the AppSrv01 profile
ADMU0500I: Retrieving server status for server1
ADMU0508I: The Application Server "server1" is STARTED
```

Figure 4-4: Checking the status of profile AppSrv01

- Use **Start|All Programs|IBM WebSphere|Application Server V6|Profiles|Default|First Steps,** and select **Administrative Console.**

- Open a browser, and enter **http://was-hostname:*port*/ibm/console**. For the application server created during installation (default), the default port is 9060. For the application server created after installation (AppSrv01), the default port is 9061.

Start or Stop Enterprise Applications

To start or stop one or more enterprise applications, connect to the admin console, expand **Applications**, and click **Enterprise Applications**. Select the check box next to the application (or applications) you want to start or stop, and click either **Start** or **Stop**, as Figure 4-5 demonstrates.

Figure 4-5: Starting and stopping enterprise applications

Uninstall Enterprise Applications

To uninstall one or more enterprise applications, connect to the admin console, expand **Applications**, and click **Enterprise Applications**. Stop any applications you want to uninstall. Then select each application's check box, and click the **Uninstall** button. Click **OK** to remove the applications, and then click **Save** to save your changes.

Delete a Profile

To delete a profile, open the command prompt, and go to the <WASV6-ROOT>\bin directory. You use the wasprofile.bat command to delete a profile. For information about the required command arguments, run **wasprofile.bat –delete –help**.

To list the existing profiles, run **wasprofile.bat –listProfiles**. The command results in Figure 4-6 show two profiles: default and AppSrv01.

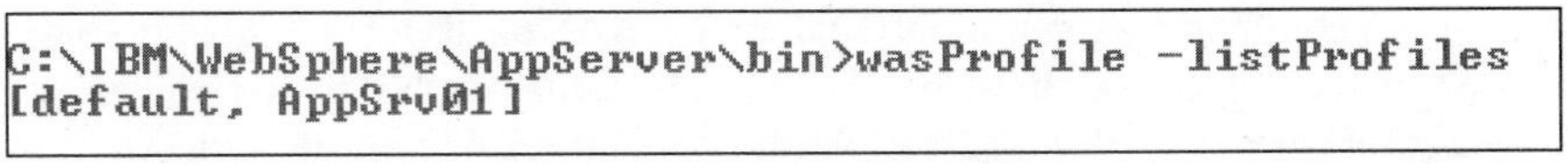

```
C:\IBM\WebSphere\AppServer\bin>wasProfile -listProfiles
[default, AppSrv01]
```

Figure 4-6: Listing existing profiles

To delete profile AppSrv01, first make sure that the server associated with the profile isn't started. To check the server's status, use the command

```
serverStatus.bat server1 -profileName AppSrv01
```

If the AppSrv01 server1 status is running, stop it using the command

```
stopServer.bat server1 -profileName AppSrv01
```

To delete profile AppSrv01, run the command

```
wasprofile.bat -delete -profileName AppSrv01
```

As a last step, delete the AppSrv01 subdirectory under <WASV6-ROOT>\profiles. The wasprofile –delete command doesn't delete the profile directory entirely, so you must perform this step manually.

A Note About bin Directories

You may be wondering about the multiple bin directories (three in our case) that exist under the WebSphere installation directory, each containing the same executable commands (e.g., startServer, stopServer). What is the significance of multiple bin directories, and which one should you use?

- The first bin directory, <WASV6-ROOT>\bin, is created after you install product binaries.

- The second, <PROFILE-ROOT>\bin, is also created when you install product binaries. It contains the 'default' application server profile that's created when you install the Base/Express package.

- The third, <NEW-PROFILE-ROOT>\bin, is created when you create a second application server profile (AppSrv01 in our example).

In a multiprofile environment, you must provide the –profileName profile argument for each command you execute from the <WASV6-ROOT>\bin directory *unless* the profile is the default profile or the command is issued from the profile's profile root. This means that if you want to start server1 in the AppSrv01 profile, you can do so using either of two methods:

- Open a command prompt, go to directory <WASV6-ROOT>\bin, and issue the command **startServer.bat server1 –profileName AppSrv01**. (If you issue **startServer.bat server1**, server1 in the default profile will be started.)

- Go to <NEW-PROFILE-ROOT>\bin, and issue **startServer.bat server1**. Here, you don't have to provide the –profileName argument because you're in the profile root.

To avoid any confusion as to which profile you're dealing with — especially when working in a multiprofile environment — it's best to run these commands from directory <PROFILE-ROOT>\bin (or <NEW-PROFILE-ROOT>\bin) rather than from <WASV6-ROOT>\bin.

Upgrading an Existing WebSphere V6 Product

At some point in your work with WebSphere Application Server, you may decide that you want to upgrade your V6 installation — from the Express to the Base package, for example, or from a trial to a licensed version. The steps to upgrade WebSphere Application Server are similar for all of the following product upgrades:

- Express trial version to Express licensed version
- Express trial version to Base licensed version
- Express licensed version to Base licensed version
- Base or Express package to Network Deployment package

To acquaint you with the upgrade procedure, let's step through upgrading the Express licensed version to the Base licensed version. You'll find parts of this process quite similar to the initial installation.

Step 1. First, log in to the WebSphere administrative console to verify which package is currently installed on your system. You'll find details about the installed package in the "About your WebSphere Application Server" section of the console's welcome panel. (You can optionally run **versionInfo.bat** from the <WASV6-ROOT>\bin directory to obtain version information.) In the sample welcome panel portion shown in Figure 4-7, the machine's current product is WebSphere V6 – Express.

After verifying the installed package, log out of the admin console.

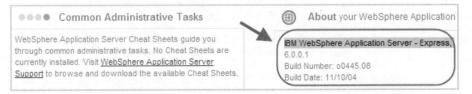

Figure 4-7: WebSphere version information in admin console welcome panel

Step 2. Stop the application server.

Step 3. Change to the directory where the Launchpad program is available for the Base package (remember, you're upgrading from Express to Base). Double-click **launchpad.bat** (or invoke **install.exe** under the directory where the installation files are available).

Unix note: Before starting the Launchpad program, make sure you can run the **xclock** or **xeyes** command to display a graphical image. If you have trouble displaying the images, set the terminal emulation properly.

Step 4. In the left pane of the Launchpad welcome panel, click **WebSphere Application Server Installation**. Then select the option to "Launch the installation wizard for WebSphere Application Server." Review the contents of the panel, and click **Next**.

Step 5. Accept the terms of the license agreement, and click **Next**.

Step 6. If the system prerequisites check is successful, click **Next**.

Step 7. When the installation wizard reports that it has detected an existing version of WebSphere (as in the panel shown in Figure 4-8), select the option to "Upgrade an existing copy of the V6 Application Server product," and verify the installation directory (C:\IBM\WebSphere\AppServer in the example) for the version of WebSphere you're updating. Then click **Next**.

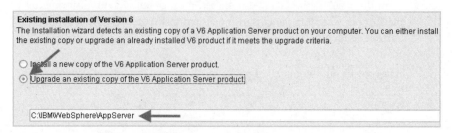

Figure 4-8: Upgrading an existing WebSphere version

Step 8. Review the summary panel, and click **Next**. The installation program will now upgrade WebSphere from Express to Base.

Step 9. When the wizard reports a successful installation, click **Finish**.

Step 10. Restart the application server.

Step 11. Log in to the admin console, and check the installed package again. You should see (under "About your WebSphere Application Server") that the WebSphere Base package has replaced the WebSphere Express package.

Adding a New Feature to an Existing Installation

Another possible task you'll face is adding new features to an existing WebSphere installation. For example, perhaps you didn't choose to install the Application Server Samples during the initial product installation but want to add them to your configuration now. The steps to add a new feature to WebSphere are similar to the steps required to upgrade.

Step 1. To verify which applications are currently installed on your system, connect to the admin console. Expand **Applications**, and click **Enterprise Applications**. If you see only the three applications listed in Figure 4-9 (DefaultApplication, ivtApp, and query), you might not have chosen to deploy the sample applications during installation.

Step 2. Stop the application server.

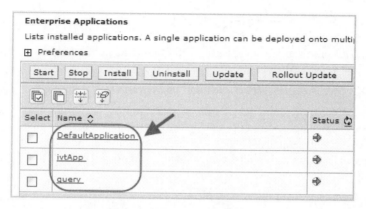

Figure 4-9: Installed applications

Step 3. To copy the sample files and deploy them, you need to upgrade the installed WebSphere product. To do so, follow Steps 3 through 6 in the "Upgrading an Existing WebSphere V6 Product" section above.

Step 4. When the installation wizard reports that it's detected an existing version of WebSphere, choose the option to "Add features to an existing copy of the V6 Application Server product" (Figure 4-10 shows this option), and click **Next**.

Figure 4-10: Adding features to an existing installation

Step 5. On the next panel, select the **Application Server Samples** check box (shown in Figure 4-11), and click **Next**.

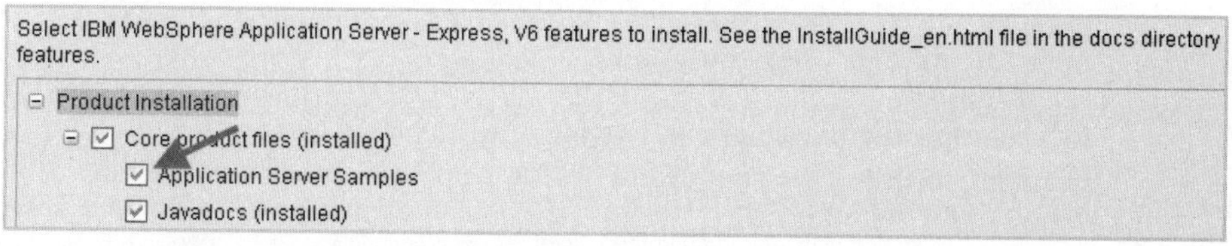

Select IBM WebSphere Application Server - Express, V6 features to install. See the InstallGuide_en.html file in the docs directory features.

⊟ Product Installation
  ⊟ ☑ Core product files (installed)
    ☑ Application Server Samples
    ☑ Javadocs (installed)

Figure 4-11: Installing the Application Server Samples

Step 6.   Review the summary panel, and click **Next**.

Step 7.   When you see the successful installation panel, click **Finish**.

Deploying the Application Server Samples

The installation program simply copies the sample applications to the
<WASV6-ROOT>\samples directory during the upgrade. You must deploy the
applications yourself manually. To view the list of available samples, navigate to the
<WASV6-ROOT>\samples\bin directory, shown in Figure 4-12.

📁 PlantsByWebSphere		File Folder	1/3/2005 4:34 PM
📁 SamplesGallery		File Folder	1/3/2005 4:34 PM
📁 Scheduler		File Folder	1/3/2005 4:35 PM
📁 TechSamp		File Folder	1/3/2005 4:34 PM
📁 WebServicesSamples		File Folder	1/3/2005 4:34 PM
📁 WebSphereBank		File Folder	1/3/2005 4:34 PM
📁 WorkArea		File Folder	1/3/2005 4:35 PM
AdminUtil.jacl	56 KB	JACL File	1/3/2005 4:34 PM
install.bat	1 KB	MS-DOS Batch File	1/3/2005 4:34 PM
samplesMaster.jacl	18 KB	JACL File	1/3/2005 4:34 PM

Figure 4-12: Sample applications

We'll use the command prompt to install one of the Application Server Samples, the
SamplesGallery application. This interesting collection of sample programs is useful for
gaining administrative experience with application installation, configuration, and
administration. To install the application, take the following steps.

Step 1.   Go to <WASV6-ROOT>\samples\bin, and issue the following command,
substituting the appropriate values for your cell and node:

```
install -cell yourCell -node yourNode -server server1 -samples
SamplesGallery
```

For example:

```
install -cell was-hostNode01Cell -node was-hostNode01 -server
srver01 -samples SamplesGallery
```

In a multiprofile environment, use the –profileName option as well. For
example, to install the samples in profile AppSrv01, use the following-
command:

```
install -cell yourCell -node yourNode -server server1 -profileName
AppSrv01 -samples SamplesGallery
```

If you specify **–samples all** on the install command (instead of **–samples SamplesGallery**), all the WebSphere samples will be deployed.

If you're not sure of the cell and node values for your system:

a. Start the server.

b. Connect to the admin console.

c. Expand Servers, and click **Application Servers**.

d. On the **Runtime** tab, note the values in the **General Properties** section, as shown in Figure 4-13.

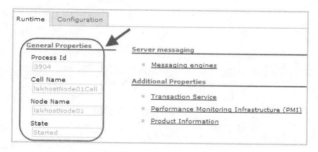

Figure 4-13: Application server general properties

Step 2.   Restart the application server, and connect to the admin console.

Step 3.   Expand **Applications**, and click **Enterprise Applications**. The SamplesGallery application should now appear in the application list, with a status of running (indicated by a green arrow), as shown in Figure 4-14.

Figure 4-14: SamplesGallery successfully installed and running

The PlantsByWebSphere Application

You can use the SamplesGallery to install, configure, and run other sample applications, including the sample online store application called PlantsByWebSphere. This user-friendly and self-explanatory application demonstrates several J2EE functions. To install PlantsByWebSphere:

1. Open a browser, and enter the URL **http://was-host:*port*/WSsamples** (case-sensitive) to see the sample applications you can install from the SamplesGallery.

2. Expand **Installable Samples|Application Server|Applications|Plants By WebSphere**.

3. Read the information about how to install the application. If you've created multiple application server profiles, click the **here** link at the end of the "Samples install help" paragraph to learn how to install the sample application(s) on a given profile.

4. To install the application, issue the following command from the <WASV6-ROOT>\samples\bin directory (substituting your own cell, node, and host values):

```
install -cell yourCell -node yourNode -server server1 -samples
PlantsByWebSphere
```

To start the PlantsByWebSphere application:

1. Open a browser, and connect to the SamplesGallery application using **http://was host:*port*/WSsamples**.

2. Expand **Installed Samples|Application Server|Applications**, and click **Plants By WebSphere**.

3. Read the instructions, and then click **Run** to invoke the application. (You can also invoke PlantsByWebSphere directly from the browser using the URL **http://was-host:*port*/PlantsByWebSphere**.) Figure 4-15 shows part of the opening page of the PlantsByWebSphere application.

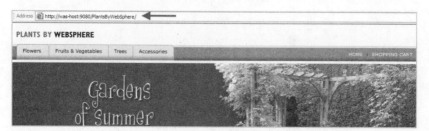

Figure 4-15: PlantsByWebSphere application

Backup and Recovery

For WebSphere Base/Express and Network Deployment installations, the configuration repository is stored in Extensible Markup Language (XML) files (flat files) in the configuration directory tree. By default, configuration information for each profile is housed in the <WASV6-ROOT\profiles*profileName*\config directory. To back up the configuration, use one (or a combination) of the methods described here.

Method 1

If you have no constraints on disk space, stop the application server process, and make a copy of the entire <WASV6-ROOT> directory (Figure 4-16). This method is the easiest way to back up the environment containing all the profiles you created (if you used the default profile directory). If you created your profiles outside <WASV6-ROOT>, you also need to copy <PROFILE-ROOT>. You can use Method 2 or 3 to perform an incremental backup as needed.

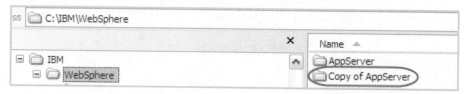

Figure 4-16: Backing up <WASV6-ROOT>

Method 2

Go to the <WASV6-ROOT>\bin or <PROFILE-ROOT>\bin directory, and run **backupConfig.bat** to make a backup of the default application server configuration. The backupConfig utility generates a ZIP archive file called WebSphereConfig_*date*.zip under the bin directory, as shown in Figure 4-17. It's recommended that you perform a backup using this command before making any major changes to the configuration, such as applying a fix pack, federating a node to the Deployment Manager, or performance tuning the application server.

To restore the configuration from the backup, run the following command:

```
restoreConfig.bat filename.zip
```

Method 3

In a multiprofile environment, go to the bin directory under each profile root and run **backupConfig.bat**. For example, to back up the AppSrv01 application server

```
C:\IBM\WebSphere\AppServer\bin>
C:\IBM\WebSphere\AppServer\bin>backupConfig
ADMU0116I: Tool information is being logged in file
           C:\IBM\WebSphere\AppServer\profiles\default\logs\backupConfig.log
ADMU0128I: Starting tool with the default profile
ADMU5001I: Backing up config directory
           C:\IBM\WebSphere\AppServer/profiles/default\config to file
           C:\IBM\WebSphere\AppServer\bin\WebSphereConfig_2004-12-30.zip
ADMU0505I: Servers found in configuration:
ADMU0506I: Server name: server1
ADMU2010I: Stopping all server processes for node ramahostNode01
ADMU7702I: Because server1 is registered to run as a Windows Service, the
           request to stop this server will be completed by stopping the
           associated Windows Service.
ADMU0116I: Tool information is being logged in file
           C:\IBM\WebSphere\AppServer\profiles\default\logs\server1\stopServer.l
og
ADMU0128I: Starting tool with the default profile
ADMU3100I: Reading configuration for server: server1
ADMU3201I: Server stop request issued. Waiting for stop status.
ADMU4000I: Server server1 stop completed.

-----------------------------------------------------------------------
-----------------------------------------------------------------------
ADMU5002I: 172 files successfully backed up
```

Figure 4-17: backupConfig utility

configuration, go to <NEW-PROFILE-ROOT>\bin and run the command. The command generates a ZIP file, WebSphereConfig_*date*.zip.

As an alternative, you can run the following command from the <WASV6-ROOT> \bin directory:

```
backupConfig.bat -profileName AppSrv01
```

You can assign your own name to the ZIP file using the syntax

```
backupConfig.bat app-server-backup.zip -profileName AppSrv01
```

If global security is enabled, you must supply a user name and password on the command:

```
backupConfig.bat app-server-backup.zip -profileName AppSrv01 -username
noyb -password noyb
```

For more information about the configuration archive utility, see Chapter 22.

Uninstalling WebSphere Application Server

WebSphere Application Server's uninstall utility removes all the profiles you've created, including their configurations and applications. If you want to delete only a particular profile, you must use the **wasProfile –delete** command instead (as described above).

If you've configured the application server to run with IBM HTTP Server V6 (through the HTTP server plug-in), you must also uninstall the WebSphere plug-in on each HTTP

Server node. Follow the instructions in Chapter 6 to uninstall the plug-in. The following steps describe how to uninstall WebSphere Application Server.

Step 1.   If you want to use the configuration and applications in the future and have no constraints on disk space, back up the <WASV6-ROOT\profiles directory before uninstalling WebSphere. If disk space is a concern, making a copy of the config, installedApps, and installableApps directories under each profile is sufficient.

Step 2.   Log in as a member of the Administrators group.

Unix note: On Unix systems, log in as root.

Step 3.   If security isn't enabled, the uninstall program will stop all the application server instances. If security is enabled, you must stop the application servers manually. To do so, go to <WASV6-ROOT>\bin, and issue the command

```
stopServer.bat server1 -profileName profile -user username -password
password
```

As an alternative, disable security before uninstalling the product.

Step 4.   Go to the <WASV6_ROOT>_uninst directory, and double-click **uninstall.exe** to start the uninstall wizard. (You can also invoke the uninstall program by clicking **Start**, navigating to **Control Panel|Add or Remove Programs**, choosing **IBM WebSphere Application Server V6** from the program list, and clicking **Change/Remove**.)

Step 5.   Click **Next** until you see a screen reporting a successful uninstallation. Then click **Finish** to exit the wizard.

Step 6.   Next, delete the <WASV6-ROOT> directory. (The uninstall program doesn't delete the installation directory entirely.)

Step 7.   Open file uninstlog.txt under <WASV6-ROOT>\logs, and scroll to the end of the file. If you see the INSTCONFSUCCESS indicator (as shown in Figure 4-18), the uninstallation was successful.

If you plan to reinstall WebSphere, it's a good practice to reboot the Windows machine before starting your installation again.

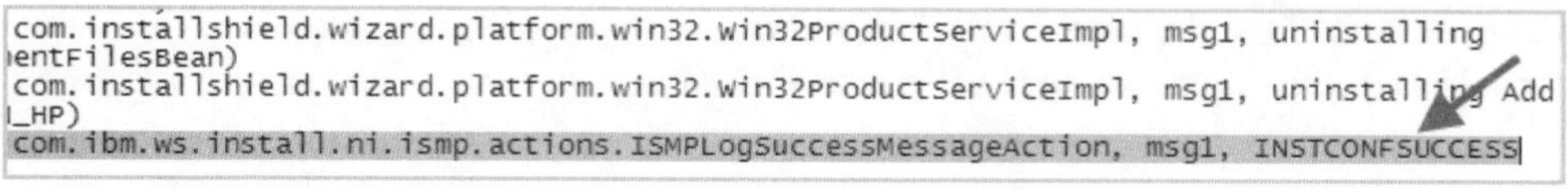

```
com.installshield.wizard.platform.win32.Win32ProductServiceImpl, msg1, uninstalling
lentFilesBean)
com.installshield.wizard.platform.win32.Win32ProductServiceImpl, msg1, uninstalling Add
l_HP)
com.ibm.ws.install.ni.ismp.actions.ISMPLogSuccessMessageAction, msg1, INSTCONFSUCCESS
```

Figure 4-18: Successful uninstallation indicator

Silent Installation

As an alternative to using the installation wizard panels described in Chapter 3 to install WebSphere Application Server, you can perform a silent installation. With this method, instead of displaying a graphical interface, the installation program determines installation options by reading responses from a text file you provide. You can use silent installation if you're not using a graphical screen, if you want to use a batch process instead of one that requires frequent user interaction, or if you need a process you can use to install WebSphere on multiple systems with minimal changes. The silent install option is typically used to build out large workstation-farm–like topologies in an automated fashion. To perform a silent install of the WebSphere product binaries and the default profile, use the following procedure.

Step 1.   Log in as a member of the Windows Administrators group that possesses the following rights:

- act as part of the operating system

- log on as a service

Silent installation will fail unless the user has these rights, even if the user is a member of the Administrators group. Restart the machine after granting these rights and before starting the silent installation.

> **Unix note:**   On Unix systems, log in as root. If necessary, run **umask 022** to set permissions for the temporary directory. To verify the present setting, run **umask.**

Step 2.   Create a temporary directory (e.g., \wasv6-silent-install), and copy into it the file responsefile.base.txt (for the Base package) or responsefile.express.txt (for the Express package) from the WebSphere installation package (usually found in the WAS directory of installation files). Give the file a meaningful name (e.g., *hostname*.responsefile.base.txt).

Step 3.   Open the file using your favorite text editor, and examine its entries. For each panel presented by the graphical installation program, you'll see a corresponding line (or lines) in the text file providing a response. For example, the following line represents the license acceptance panel, where you click to accept or not accept the terms of the license agreement.

```
-W silentInstallLicenseAcceptance.value="false"
```

For each option, the response file documents the possible values and provides other useful information. You're going to customize each line of the file to silently install WebSphere the same way you did using the graphical installation in Chapter 3.

Step 4. First, edit the file to change the license acceptance value from "false" to "true" to accept the terms of the license agreement.

```
-W silentInstallLicenseAcceptance.value="true"
```

Step 5. You use the next line to set the installation directory. The graphical installation used directory C:\IBM\WebSphere\AppServer (the default install directory). If you choose to provide a different name, be sure it contains no spaces.

```
-P wasProductBean.installLocation="C:\IBM\WebSphere\AppServer"
```

Step 6. For the setup type ID, keep the default value of "Custom". (This value is your only option for a silent installation.)

```
-W setuptypepanelInstallWizardBean.selectedSetupTypeId="Custom"
```

Step 7. To install the sample applications, you'd leave the next line's value set to "true". For now, choose not to install the samples by specifying "false". You'll see later how to add the samples using the silent install process.

```
-P samplesProductFeatureBean.active="false"
```

Step 8. If you want to install the Javadoc (Java documentation) feature during installation, leave the next entry's value set to "true"; otherwise, change it to "false".

```
-P javadocsProductFeatureBean.active="true"
```

Step 9. The next several response-file lines specify the port numbers the application server will use. Unlike the Profile Creation wizard, silent installation can't dynamically assign port numbers by looking at the vpd.properties file. If existing instances of the application server are going to run simultaneously, you must adjust the port numbers yourself (by adding 1 to the port number of the last installed instance). For the sample installation, you don't have any existing instances on your machine, so you can use the default values. Figure 4-19 shows the response file's port-number entries with default values.

```
#############################################################################
# The following entries are used to reset port numbers used in the configuration
#
# They are currently set to the defaults.
# Please check to make sure there are no Port Conflicts
#
-W defaultprofileportspanelInstallWizardBean.WC_defaulthost="9080"
-W defaultprofileportspanelInstallWizardBean.WC_adminhost="9060"
-W defaultprofileportspanelInstallWizardBean.WC_defaulthost_secure="9443"
-W defaultprofileportspanelInstallWizardBean.WC_adminhost_secure="9043"
-W defaultprofileportspanelInstallWizardBean.BOOTSTRAP_ADDRESS="2809"
-W defaultprofileportspanelInstallWizardBean.SOAP_CONNECTOR_ADDRESS="8880"
-W defaultprofileportspanelInstallWizardBean.SAS_SSL_SERVERAUTH_LISTENER_ADDRESS="9401"
-W defaultprofileportspanelInstallWizardBean.CSIV2_SSL_SERVERAUTH_LISTENER_ADDRESS="9403"
-W defaultprofileportspanelInstallWizardBean.CSIV2_SSL_MUTUALAUTH_LISTENER_ADDRESS="9402"
-W defaultprofileportspanelInstallWizardBean.ORB_LISTENER_ADDRESS="9100"
-W defaultprofileportspanelInstallWizardBean.DCS_UNICAST_ADDRESS="9353"
-W defaultprofileportspanelInstallWizardBean.SIB_ENDPOINT_ADDRESS="7276"
-W defaultprofileportspanelInstallWizardBean.SIB_ENDPOINT_SECURE_ADDRESS="7286"
-W defaultprofileportspanelInstallWizardBean.SIB_MQ_ENDPOINT_ADDRESS="5558"
-W defaultprofileportspanelInstallWizardBean.SIB_MQ_ENDPOINT_SECURE_ADDRESS="5578"
```

Figure 4-19: Setting the port value options

Step 10. When you run the graphical install, the WebSphere installation program automatically generates the default node name from the host name of the system and the number of the WebSphere instance (i.e., *hostname* + Node + *instance#*). For example, when you ran the install in Chapter 3, it generated *hostname*Node01. For the silent installation, you must provide a name for the WebSphere node you're going to install:

```
-W nodeostandcellnamepanelInstallWizardBean.nodeName="was-hostNode01"
```

Step 11. When you run the graphical install, the WebSphere installation program automatically picks up the host name from the hosts file. For the silent install, you must provide the host name, using either a Domain Name Server (DNS) entry or an IP address (not recommended). To find out the host name of your machine, go to the command prompt, and run the command **host-name**. To determine the DNS entry and IP address, run the command **ping** *your-host-name*.

```
-W nodehostandcellnamepanelInstallWizardBean.hostName="was-host"
```

Step 12. You don't have to change the next entry, which specifies the value for the Cell option. The silent installation program generates this value from the information you've provided thus far.

Step 13a. For the next option, winServiceQuery, specify "true" if you want to run the application server process as a Windows service. (This option obviously is valid only for Windows systems.) If you specify "false" for this option, the installation program ignores the remaining entries in the response file.

```
-W winservicepanelInstallWizardBean.winServiceQuery="true"
```

Step 13b. For the account type of the Windows service, you have two choices. If you specify the "localsystem" value, the Windows service will log on using the local system account. If you use the "specifieduser" value, the Windows service will log on as the user whose user name and password you specify on the next lines of the response file:

```
-W winservicepanelInstallWizardBean.userName="wasadmin"
-W winservicepanelInstallWizardBean.password="noyb"
```

(Before running the silent install, make sure the user name you provide is a member of the Administrators group and has the right to log on as a service.)

Step 13c. The next line specifies the desired startup type for the Windows service (automatic, manual, or disabled).

```
-W winservicepanelInstallWizardBean.startupType="manual"
```

Step 14. When you're finished editing the response file, scroll up to the beginning of the file to view the instructions for running the silent installation program. Figure 4-20 shows this part of the file.

```
##########################################################################
#
# InstallShield Options File
#
# Wizard name: Install
# Wizard source: setup.jar
#
# A common use of an options file is to run the wizard in silent mode. This lets
# the options file author specify wizard settings without having to run the
# wizard in graphical or console mode. To use this options file for silent mode
# execution, use the following command line arguments when running the wizard:
#
#    -options "D:\installImage\WAS\responsefile.base.txt" -silent
#
```

Figure 4-20: Silent installation execution instructions

Step 15. Save the response file, and exit your editor.

Step 16. Open a command-line prompt, and go to the WebSphere installation directory where the install.exe program is available (the same directory from which you copied the responsefile.base.txt file — usually the WAS directory). Run the following command to start the silent install, substituting the appropriate path to your response file:

```
install.exe –options "path-to-response-file" –silent
```

For example:

```
install.exe –options "c:\wasv6-silent-install\rama.responsefile.txt"
–silent
```

Step 17. If you like, go to the <WASV6-ROOT>\logs directory, and open the file log.txt to see the progress of the silent installation. For a successful installation, the last few lines of the file will look like those shown in Figure 4-21.

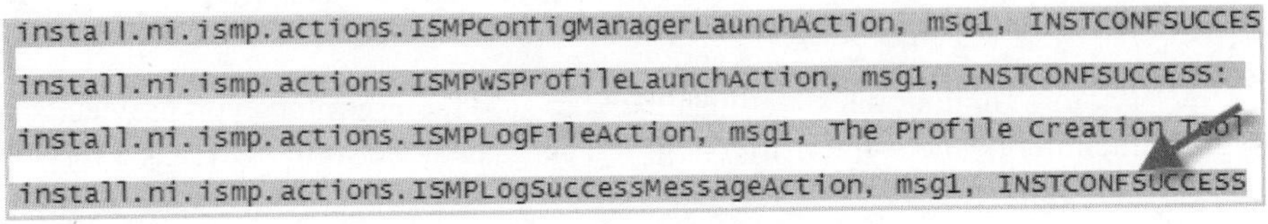

```
install.ni.ismp.actions.ISMPConfigManagerLaunchAction, msg1, INSTCONFSUCCES
install.ni.ismp.actions.ISMPWSProfileLaunchAction, msg1, INSTCONFSUCCESS:
install.ni.ismp.actions.ISMPLogFileAction, msg1, The Profile Creation Tool
install.ni.ismp.actions.ISMPLogSuccessMessageAction, msg1, INSTCONFSUCCESS
```

Figure 4-21: Silent installation log file

> **Unix note:** On Unix systems, go to the <WASV6-ROOT>/logs directory, and issue the command **tail –f log.txt** to view the installation's progress.

Step 18. Verify the silent installation using the same instructions you followed in Chapter 3 for the graphical install. In this case, you'll need to start the First Steps program manually. Open a command-line prompt, go to the <PROFILE-ROOT>\firststeps directory, and run **firststeps.bat**. If the installation verification is unsuccessful, review the "Logging: Problem Determination and Troubleshooting" section of Chapter 3 for more information.

Upgrading or Adding Features Through Silent Installation

The following steps explain how to upgrade a WebSphere installation installed without samples by adding the sample applications using the silent install process. The steps are similar for the following product upgrades:

- Express trial version to Express licensed version
- Express trial version to Base licensed version
- Express licensed version to Base licensed version
- Base trial version to Base licensed version

Step 1.   Connect to the admin console, and expand **Applications|Enterprise Applications**. If you don't see the SamplesGallery and PlantsByWebSphere applications in the application list, or if you don't see the 'samples' directory under the \<WASV6-ROOT> directory (or the samples directory is empty), you chose not to deploy the sample applications during installation.

Step 2.   Stop the application server.

Step 3.   Copy the response file you used earlier (*hostname*.responsefile.base.txt in the temporary directory) to a new file, and give the file a meaningful name (e.g., upg.*hostname*.responsefile.base.txt).

        a. Open the file using your favorite text editor.

Step 4.   To tell the silent install program that you're adding a new feature to the existing installation, uncomment (i.e., remove the # sign from) the line that reads

```
-W detectedexistingcopypanelInstallWizardBean.choice="addFeatures"
```

Step 5.   Point the installLocation option to the existing installation directory:

```
-P wasProductBean.installLocation="C:\IBM\WebSphere\AppServer"
```

If you wanted to upgrade WebSphere from a trial to a licensed version or from the Express to the Base package, you would uncomment the line at this point in the response file that reads

```
-W detectedexistingcopypanelInstallWizardBean.choice="upgrade"
```

This change would tell the silent install program that you're upgrading the existing installation. If you uncomment this line, you must also uncomment the following line and specify the existing installation directory

```
-P globalconstantsProductActionBean.
detectedExistingPanelUpgradeMatchInstallLocation="INSTALL-LOCATION"
```

In this case, you're only adding features to the existing product, so you should leave both of these lines commented.

Step 6.   For the setup type, keep the default value of "Custom".

Step 7.   Change the samples option to "true" to indicate that you want to add the samples to the existing installation.

Step 8.   Change the javadocs option to "false" (because you've installed javadoc already).

Step 9.   Because you specified the "addFeatures" choice in Step 4, the silent install program will ignore the values in the response file beyond this point. (It would do the same had you specified the "upgrade" choice.) Save the response file, and exit the editor.

Step 10.   Open a command prompt, go to the WebSphere installation directory containing install.exe, and run the command to start the silent installation:

```
install.exe -options "path-to-response-file" -silent
```

For example:

```
install.exe -options "c:\wasv6-silent-
install\upg.rama.responsefile.txt" -silent
```

> **Note:**   To upgrade the product, be sure to use the install.exe program from the package you're upgrading. For example, to upgrade from the Express trial version to the Express licensed version, use the install.exe in the Express licensed package.

Step 11.   Navigate to the <WASV6-ROOT>\samples\bin directory to see the list of samples available. To deploy the SamplesGallery and PlantsByWebSphere applications, follow the steps given earlier in this chapter.

5

IBM HTTP Server V6: Install, Configure, Verify, and Manage

The Web server included with WebSphere Application Server V6, IBM HTTP Server V6, is based on the Apache HTTP Server developed by the Apache Software Foundation. Instead of serving the static content of your Web applications (e.g., HTML, images, JavaScript) through WebSphere Application Server (using the file-serving enabler), you can choose to serve the content through HTTP Server. In this chapter, you learn how to install, configure, verify, and manage IBM HTTP Server V6 and the IBM HTTP Administration Server V6 product. We also describe how to configure and manage multiple HTTP Server processes on the same machine.

Figure 5-1 shows the architecture and items created after a successful installation of IBM HTTP Server V6. As a result of the installation process, the following items are created:

- product binaries and a configuration repository (stored in the file system)
- the Apache Web server
- the Admin (HTTP Administration) service (used to manage the Apache Web server through the WebSphere V6 administrative console)
- the Tivoli Global Security Kit

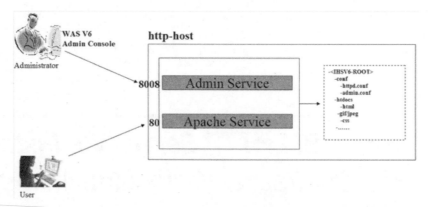

Figure 5-1: Architecture and components created after installation of IBM HTTP Server V6

Installing IBM HTTP Server V6

The flow chart in Figure 5-2 depicts the high-level steps required to install, configure, and verify HTTP Server. In this section, we walk you through each step of this process. As in the previous chapters, our instructions assume you're working in a Windows XP environment. If you're using a Unix operating system to perform the steps, you'll need to execute the appropriate commands for your operating system (i.e., .sh instead of .bat) and substitute the forward slash (/) for the backward slash (\) in directory and path names.

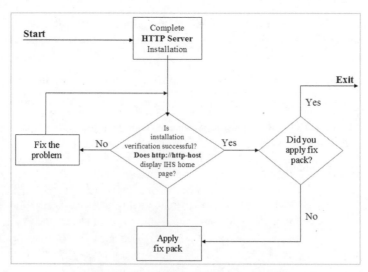

Figure 5-2: HTTP Server installation overview

Step 1. If you want to use the trial version of IBM HTTP Server V6, your first step is to download it. (You may need to register before downloading the software.) The trial version is good for 60 days, and you can submit a problem ticket to IBM support during the trial period. For more information about the trial version and to download the software, go to either of the following URLs:

http://www-106.ibm.com/developerworks/websphere/downloads
http://www14.software.ibm.com/webapp/download/home.jsp

Figure 5-3 shows the directory structure after you've downloaded the trial version and extracted the files to a temporary directory. You'll use the install.exe program in the IHS directory to install this version of the software. If you're using a licensed package of WebSphere Application Server to install HTTP Server, you'll use WebSphere's Launchpad to install the software.

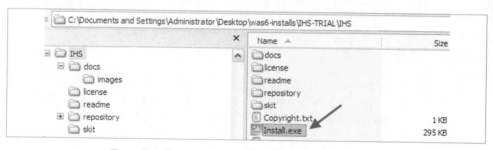

Figure 5-3: Directory structure for HTTP Server trial version

Step 2. Make sure the TMP environment variable, which specifies the working directory used during installation, is set appropriately. If you followed the instructions in Chapter 3 to install the standalone application server and you want to install HTTP Server on the same node as WebSphere, you've probably already set this variable. If you want to install HTTP Server on a different node, log in as a member of the Administrators group on that node to check the TMP variable. On the Windows desktop, right-click **My Computer**, and select **Properties|Advanced|Environment Variables**. In the "User variables for user" list, note the value set for the temporary directory (TMP). If you don't see TMP in the variable list, click **New** to add the variable. For this example, we'll assume variable TMP has been edited to point to directory C:\temp.

> **Unix note:** On Unix systems, log in as root. If necessary, run the command **umask 022** to set permissions for the temporary directory (usually /tmp). To verify the current umask setting, run **umask**.

Step 3. Your Windows system needs at least 235 MB of disk space to install the IBM HTTP Server V6 product (110 MB for the installation root directory, 25 MB for the Global Security Kit, and 100 MB for the temporary directory). Verify that your machine meets this requirement.

> **Unix note:** Make sure the file systems mounted on the HTTP Server, Global Security Kit installation, and /tmp directories meet the minimum disk space requirements of 110 MB, 35 MB, and 100 MB, respectively.

Step 4. If you're using a licensed WebSphere package to install HTTP Server, mount the CD, change to the directory where the Launchpad program is available (the root directory of the WebSphere product CD), and double-click **launchpad.bat**. If you're using the trial version, navigate to the IHS directory, and double-click **install.exe**. (The install.exe program works for the licensed packages, too.)

From the moment you invoke it, the installation program begins logging information under the TMP directory. For more information about this logging, see the "Logging: Problem Determination and Troubleshooting" section of this chapter.

> **Unix note:** Before running the installation wizard, make sure you can execute the xclock or xeyes command to display a graphical image. If you have trouble displaying the images, set the terminal emulation properly. If you can display the images but can't start the Launchpad, consult "Logging: Problem Determination and Troubleshooting" for more information.

Step 5. If you used launchpad.bat to start the installation, you'll see a welcome panel similar to the one shown in Figure 5-4. Review the panel's contents, and select the option to "Launch the installation wizard for IBM HTTP Server." You'll then see the IBM HTTP Server welcome panel.

If you used install.exe to start the installation, you'll be taken directly to the HTTP Server welcome panel. Click **Next** on the panel to proceed with the installation.

Step 6. On the next panel, select to accept the terms of the license agreement, and click Next.

Welcome	**WebSphere Application Server Version 6.0**
Solution Installation Diagrams	IBM WebSphere Application Server, Version 6.0 is an integrated platform that (Server, Web development tools, a Web server, and additional supporting softw documentation. This launchpad may serve as a single point of reference for ins Server environment.
Application Server Installation	See the <u>solution installation diagrams</u> for illustrations of common application s
IBM HTTP Server Installation	
/eb Server plug-ins Installation	**To begin**, select an entry from the list below. If you would like help documenta these concepts before initializing a wizard interface, select from the list to the
Application Clients Installation	<u>Launch the installation wizard for WebSphere Application Server</u>
ation Server Toolkit Installation	<u>Launch the installation wizard for IBM HTTP Server</u>
	<u>Launch the installation wizard for Web server plug-ins</u>

Figure 5-4: Launching the installation wizard for IBM HTTP Server

Step 7. The next panel (Figure 5-5) specifies the installation directory for HTTP Server. In this example, we've used C:\IBM\HTTPServer. For Windows, make sure whatever name you use contains no spaces. Click **Next** after specifying the directory.

:aller

Click Next to install "IBM HTTP Server 6.0" to this directory, or click Browse to install to a different directory.

Directory Name:

C:\IBM\HTTPServer

Figure 5-5: Specifying the installation directory

From now on, we refer to the HTTP Server installation directory as <IHSV6-ROOT>. Table 5-1 lists the default location of this directory for each operating system.

If you have an existing version of IBM HTTP Server 2.0.x and want to upgrade to V6, specify the installation directory of the existing HTTP Server instance on the installation directory panel. The installation program doesn't upgrade HTTP Server 1.3.x versions. You must have at least HTTP Server V2 to upgrade.

Table 5-1: HTTP Server installation directory locations

Symbolic reference	Windows	AIX	Linux/Unix
IHSV6-ROOT	C:\IBM\HTTPServer	/usr/IBMIHS	/opt/IBMIHS

If you specify the installation directory of an existing version of HTTP Server, a panel similar to the one shown in Figure 5-6 is displayed. Review the information on this panel, and then click **Next** to upgrade the existing version.

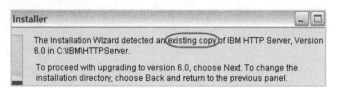

Figure 5-6: Existing HTTP Server copy notification

Step 8. You use the next panel (Figure 5-7) to specify the type of installation you want to perform: Typical, Custom, or Developer. Review the description of the Typical and Developer options to see whether they apply to your situation. For this example, select the **Custom** option, and click **Next.**

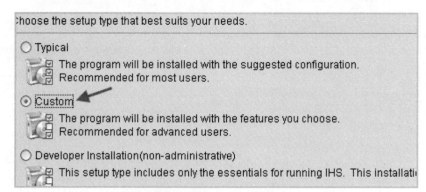

Figure 5-7: Choosing the installation type

Step 9. On the next panel (Figure 5-8), make sure the options to install the HTTPServer base and Security components are selected. Then click **Next**.

Figure 5-8: Product installation options

Step 10.   Next, review the port number assignments (Figure 5-9). The default port values for HTTP and HTTP Administration are 80 and 8008, respectively. You may need to assign different port numbers if an existing HTTP server is using the default ports and you plan to run both servers at the same time.

After verifying the port numbers, click **Next**.

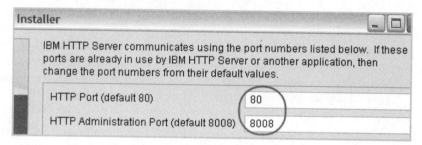

Figure 5-9: HTTP Server ports

Step 11.   The next panel (Figure 5-10) lets you specify whether you want to run the HTTP Server and HTTP Administration processes as Windows services. (You won't see this panel on non-Windows operating systems.)

If you intend to manage (e.g., start, stop) HTTP Server from the Deployment Manager's admin console and plan to configure the HTTP Server node as an unmanaged node, you must register HTTP Server as a service in a Windows environment. You'll need to specify the HTTP Server service name when you configure the Web server as an unmanaged node. (For more information about this topic, see Chapter 9.) If you want to configure the Web server as a managed node (using the node agent process instead of HTTP Admin Server), you don't need to register HTTP Server as a service.

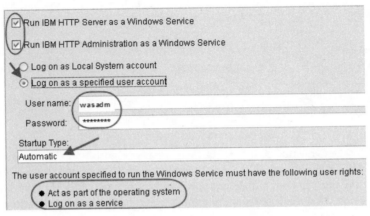

Figure 5-10: Windows service options

To run the HTTP Server and HTTP Administration processes as Windows services, select the two check-box options at the top of the wizard panel, and specify how the services will log on. If you choose "Log on as Local System account," a user name and password are optional. If you choose "Log on as a specified user account," you must provide a valid user name (containing no spaces) and password. The user should be a member of the Administrators group. Last, choose a startup type (Automatic, Manual, or Disabled) for the Windows services. When you're finished with this panel, click **Next**.

Step 12. Review the summary panel presented by the wizard, and then click **Next**. You'll notice that the install program creates the installation directory (<IHSV6-ROOT>) at this point and starts logging installation information in two files there: ihsv6_install.log and gskitInstall.log. For more information about this logging, see "Logging: Problem Determination and Troubleshooting."

Step 13. When the wizard displays a successful installation panel, click **Finish**.

Verifying the HTTP Server Installation

In Chapter 3, you used various methods to verify the successful installation of the stand-alone application server. Similar methods are available to you for confirming the success of your HTTP Server installation. In this section, we perform three types of verification:

- verify installation by viewing the log files
- verify the Windows **Services** panel for the HTTP Server processes
- verify installation from the browser

Verify Installation by Viewing the Log Files

To confirm a successful installation of HTTP Server using the installation log files, go to the <IHSV6-ROOT> directory, open log file ihsv6_install.log, and scroll to the end of the file. If you see the indicator INSTCONFSUCCESS, the installation of HTTP Server was a success. If you see INSTCONFFAIL or INSTCONFPARTIALSUCCESS, problems occurred during the installation. To determine the source of the trouble, consult "Logging: Problem Determination and Troubleshooting."

Verify the Windows Services Panel for the HTTP Server Processes

If you opted to run the HTTP Server and HTTP Administration processes as Windows services during the installation (Windows platforms only), take the following steps to confirm this configuration.

1. Click the **Start** button, and navigate to **Control Panel|Administrative Tools|Services**.

2. In the Services panel, locate the "IBM HTTP Server 6.0" process (shown in Figure 5-11), right-click it, and select **Start** to start the service. (You can also start the service from a command prompt under the <IHSV6-ROOT>\bin directory by running **Apache.exe –k start**.) If the service doesn't start, consult "Logging: Problem Determination and Troubleshooting."

3. Use the same method to start the "IBM HTTP Administration 6.0" process. (As an alternative, open a command prompt, go to <IHSV6-ROOT>\bin, and run **Apache.exe –f conf\admin.conf**.) If the service doesn't start, consult "Logging: Problem Determination and Troubleshooting."

Name	Description	Status
IBM HTTP Administration 6.0	IBM_HTTP_Server/6.0 Apache/2.0.47 (Win32)	
IBM HTTP Server 6.0	IBM_HTTP_Server/6.0 Apache/2.0.47 (Win32)	
IBM KCU Service		Start

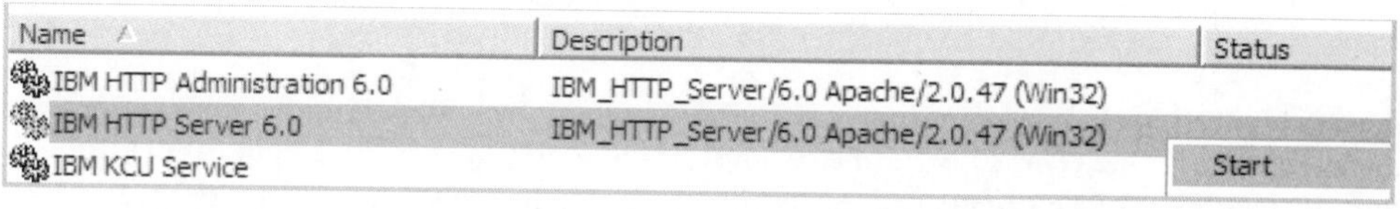

Figure 5-11: HTTP Server processes in the Windows Services panel

Unix note: On Unix, go to <IHSV6-ROOT>/bin, and run **./apachectl start** to start the HTTP Server process. To start the HTTP Administration process, run **./adminctl start**.

Some notes about the HTTP Administration process:

- You can use the IBM HTTP Admin process to administer IBM HTTP Server remotely. The Deployment Manager or a standalone application server on a remote machine uses HTTP Server's Admin Server to propagate the plug-in file to the HTTP Server machine.

- If WebSphere and HTTP Server are on two different systems, you need to run, on the WebSphere node, a configuration batch file that's generated when you install the WebSphere plug-in on the HTTP Server machine. (You'll learn about this batch file in Chapter 6.) If WebSphere and HTTP Server are on the same machine (in a standalone server environment), this step takes places automatically.

- You don't need to use the HTTP Admin Server if the WebSphere standalone server and HTTP Server are on the same machine.

If you forgot to select (or cleared) the options to register the HTTP Server and HTTP Administration processes as Windows services during installation and you want to register them now, follow the instructions at the end of this chapter to register the processes in the Windows service registry.

Verify Installation from the Browser

To verify HTTP Server installation from the browser:

1. Open a browser, and display the IBM HTTP Server V6 welcome page by providing the host name, Domain Name Server (DNS) entry, or IP address of the machine on which you installed HTTP Server. If you have trouble bringing up this page (shown in Figure 5-12), consult "Logging: Problem Determination and Troubleshooting."

2. Apply the required fix pack for HTTP Server, and verify.

At this point, if your Web server serves a production environment and you've placed it in a demilitarized zone (DMZ), you may want to remove the Java JDK (folder _jvm) from the <PLUGIN-ROOT> directory for security reasons. The JDK is used only during installation. (Additional actions may be necessary for the deployment to be DMZ-ready. A full treatment of how to ensure a DMZ-ready deployment is beyond the scope of this book.)

Understanding the IBM HTTP Server V6 Directory Structure

The HTTP Server installation process creates several important directories under the installation root, <IHSV6-ROOT> (C:\IBM\HTTPServer in this chapter's example). Figure 5-13 depicts the directory structure that's created during the installation.

Figure 5-12: IBM HTTP Server welcome page

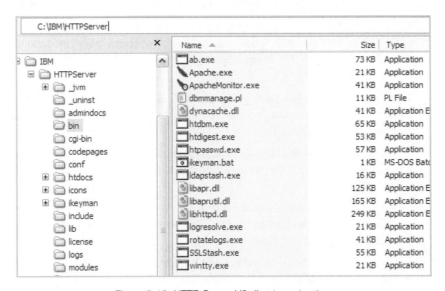

Figure 5-13: HTTP Server V6 directory structure

Here's a brief look at the purpose of the key directories:

- *bin* — The bin directory contains all the executable commands used to manage and configure IBM HTTP Server. Some important executables to note under this directory are

    › Apache.exe — used to start or stop HTTP Server
    › ApacheMonitor.exe — used to manage and monitor HTTP Server processes
    › htpasswd.exe — used to create and change the admin user ID and password
    › ikeyman.bat — used to create Secure Sockets Layer (SSL) certificates

- *conf* — HTTP Server and HTTP Admin Server read the default configuration information in certain files in this directory. Some important files to note under this directory are

    › httpd.conf — HTTP Server reads this ASCII file before startup. You can edit this configuration file manually to change the Web server configuration. If you configure HTTP Server as a managed node, you can change the configuration through the WebSphere admin console. You'll learn more about managed and unmanaged nodes in Chapter 9.

    › httpd.conf.sample — This sample configuration file contains examples of how to configure different parameters (e.g., how to configure SSL).

    › admin.conf —HTTP Admin Server reads this ASCII file before startup. You can edit the file manually to change the HTTP Admin Server configuration.

- *htdocs* — By default, this directory contains all the static content served by HTTP Server. For example, when you invoke the welcome page, by default it comes from htdocs\en_US\index.html.

- *logs* — The logging that takes place during HTTP Server runtime is stored in the files in this directory. For more information about these files, see "Logging: Problem Determination and Troubleshooting." In addition to the log files, the following files are created here:

    › httpd.pid — This file stores the process ID of the HTTP Server process. It is created when HTTP Server is started and is deleted when HTTP Server is stopped.

    › admin.pid — This file stores the process ID of the HTTP Administration process. It is created when the HTTP Admin Server is started and is deleted when the HTTP Admin Server is stopped.

- *modules* — This directory contains modules, known as Dynamic Shared Objects (DSO), that can be configured to work inside the Apache server to enhance the basic functionality of the Web server. File <IHSV6-ROOT>\conf\httpd.conf contains the configuration for these modules. Some files to note under this directory are

> mod_ibm_ssl.so — used to load the SSL module before configuring SSL on the HTTP server

> mod_afpa_cache.so — used to load the Fast Response Cache Accelerator (FRCA) to cache static content for improved performance

■ _uninst_ — This directory contains the uninstall program and related files used during product uninstallation.

Managing IBM HTTP Server V6

You can start, stop, and manage IBM HTTP Server V6 in multiple ways, depending on the operating system you're using. This section describes some frequently used methods of working with the server.

Starting or Stopping HTTP Server

To start or stop HTTP Server, you can use any of these methods:

■ Click **Start**, and navigate to **All Programs|IBM HTTP Server 6.0|Start HTTP Server** or **Stop HTTP Server**.

■ If you registered the HTTP Server processes as services in the Windows registry, right-click **My Computer** on the Windows desktop, and select **Manage|Services Applications|Services** to display the **Services** panel. In the list of services, right-click the HTTP Server service, and select **Start** or **Stop**.

■ From the command prompt, go to the <IHSV6-ROOT>\bin directory, and run **Apache.exe –k start** or **Apache.exe –k stop** to start or stop the server. (Use **Apache.exe –h** for help if needed.) You can also use the command **Apache.exe –n** *service-name* **–k start** [or **stop**], where *service-name* is "IBM HTTP Server 6.0" by default.

> **Unix note:** Go to <IHSV6-ROOT>/bin, and run ./**apachectl start** or ./**apachectl stop**. (These commands are case-sensitive.)

Starting or Stopping HTTP Administration Server

Use the following methods to start or stop HTTP Admin Server.

- Use **Start|All Programs|IBM HTTP Server 6.0|Start Administration Server** or **Stop Administration Server**.

- If you registered the HTTP Server processes as services, right-click **My Computer**, select **Manage|Services Applications|Services**, right-click the HTTP Administration service, and select **Start** or **Stop**.

- From the command prompt, go to <IHSV6-ROOT>\bin, and run **Apache.exe –f conf\admin.conf** or **Apache.exe –k conf\admin.conf**. (Use **Apache.exe –h** for help if needed.) You can also use **Apache.exe –n** *service-name* **–k start** [or **stop**], where *service-name* is "IBM HTTP Administration 6.0" by default.

> **Unix note:**   Go to <IHSV6>/bin, and run ./adminctl start or ./adminct; stop. (These commands are case-sensitive.)
>
> On Unix, you need to run the setupadm script (located under <IHSV6-ROOT>\bin) to grant read and write access to the configuration and authentication files in order to perform Web server configuration data administration. The script prompts you to enter values for User ID, Group name, Directory, File name, and Processing based on your configuration. For more information about the setupadm command, see the IBM HTTP Server V6 Information Center,
> *http://publib.boulder.ibm.com/infocenter/wasinfo/v6r0/index.jsp*.

Managing HTTP Server Through the Apache Monitor Tool

Apache Monitor is a graphical tool included in the IBM HTTP Server product that helps you manage and monitor the HTTP and Administration servers. To use the tool:

1. Open a command prompt.

2. Go to <IHSV6-ROOT>\bin.

3. Run **ApacheMonitor.exe**.

4. You should see the instantiation of an Apache Monitor tray icon, usually on the lower-right side of the screen, that looks like a Play button with a feather, as shown in Figure 5-14. Double-click the icon to bring up a window from which you can manage and monitor the HTTP Server and HTTP Administration processes (Figure 5-15).

   - Select the HTTP Server or HTTP Administration process, and click the desired button (**Start**, **Stop**, or **Restart**).

- Click the **Services** button to display the Windows **Services** panel.

- Click **OK** to minimize the monitor window.

- Click **Connect** or **Disconnect** to connect to or disconnect from the host.

- Click **Exit** to shut down the monitor process.

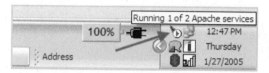

Figure 5-14: Apache Monitor icon

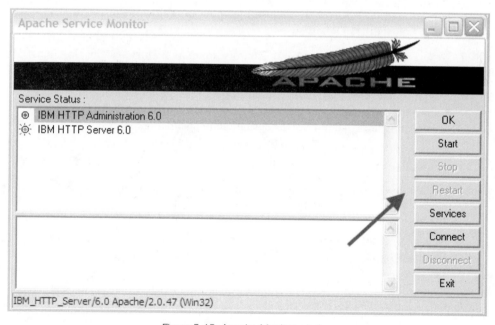

Figure 5-15: Apache Monitor window

Backup and Recovery

Configuration information for HTTP Server and HTTP Admin Server are stored in two ASCII files, httpd.conf and admin.conf, in the <IHSV6-ROOT>\conf directory. Before making any major changes to the configuration (e.g., performance tuning the parameters, configuring security), it's wise to make a copy of these files.

If you have no constraints on disk space, the easiest way to back up the HTTP Server environment is to stop the HTTP Server and HTTP Administration processes and make a copy of the entire <IHSV6-ROOT> directory.

Uninstalling IBM HTTP Server V6

The uninstall command removes HTTP Server and HTTP Admin Server, as well as their configuration information, from your system. If you want to use the configuration and any existing static content in the future, make a backup of the conf and htdocs directories under <IHSV6-ROOT> before uninstalling the product.

If you've configured WebSphere Application Server to run with HTTP Server (through the WebSphere plug-in), you may need to uninstall the plug-in on the HTTP Server node before uninstalling HTTP Server. To uninstall the plug-in, follow the instructions in Chapter 6. To uninstall HTTP Server:

1. Log in as a member of the Administrators group. (On Unix systems, log in as root.)

2. Go to the <IHSV6-INSTALL>_uninst directory, and double-click uninstall.exe to launch the uninstall wizard. The uninstall program automatically stops HTTP Server and HTTP Admin Server during the uninstallation process.

3. Click **Next** on the wizard panels until you see a panel reporting a successful uninstallation. Then click **Finish** to exit the wizard.

4. The uninstall program logs its activities in file ihsv6_uninstall.log under <IHSV6-ROOT>. If you have any problems during uninstallation, review this file.

5. Delete the <IHSV6-ROOT> directory. (The uninstall program doesn't delete the installation directory tree entirely. You must delete it manually.)

If you plan to reinstall HTTP Server, reboot the Windows machine before starting the installation again.

Logging: Problem Determination and Troubleshooting

The log files generated for HTTP Server fall logically into three categories, according to the activity being performed on the server. Logging takes place during the initial and later parts of the installation and as you manage (e.g., start, stop) the HTTP server. The diagram in Figure 5-16 depicts this logging architecture. Table 5-2 provides a guide to the logging activities.

Problem Scenarios

Review the following problem scenarios and solutions if you encounter problems while installing or verifying HTTP Server.

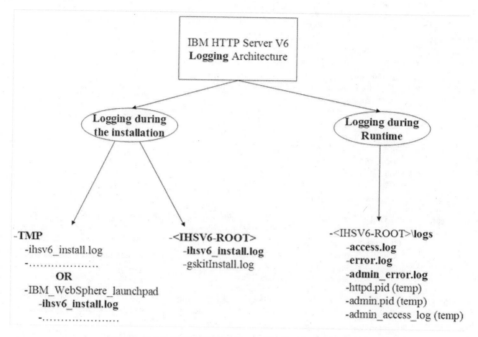

Figure 5-16: IBM HTTP Server V6 logging architecture

Table 5-2: HTTP Server logging activities

Activity	Log destination	Description	When to use these log files
Installation —initial part	The TMP directory ■ File ihsv6_install.log is the important log file under this destination. ■ If you used the Launchpad program to start the installation, you'll see the log files under the TMP directory's IBM_WebSphere_launch pad subdirectory.	These log files are populated immediately after the Launchpad or install.exe program is invoked. After a successful installation, the files are copied to the logs directory under the installation directory (<IHSV6-ROOT>).	■ Use if you have trouble starting the Launchpad or install.exe or encounter problems during the early part of the installation. ■ Use if the system prerequisites check fails and you want to see the reason.

Table 5-2: HTTP Server logging activities (continued)

Activity	Log destination	Description	When to use these log files
Installation —initial part (continued)	■ If you used install.exe to perform the installation, the log files are created immediately under directory TMP. ■ On Windows systems, check the TMP environment variable to determine the value of the temporary directory. This chapter's examples use C:\temp as the TMP value on the Windows machine. ■ On Unix, /tmp is usually the temporary directory.		
Installation — later part	The <IHSV6-ROOT> directory that was specified during the installation ■ File ihsv6_install.log is the important log file under this destination.	These log files are populated from the moment you click Next after reviewing the summary report during the graphical installation.	■ Use if the installation failed or was partially successful and you want to see the reason ■ If these log files don't provide enough information, consult the log files in the TMP directory.
Managing (e.g., starting, stopping) HTTP Server	The <IHSV6-ROOT>\logs directory ■ The important log files under this directory are access.log, errors.log, and admin_error.log.	■ File access.log is where HTTP Server records information about the content it has processed or served. The level of logging performed depends on the values set for the CustomLog and LogFormat parameters in file httpd.conf. ■ File errors.log is where HTTP Server sends diagnostic and error information. The level of logging depends on the value set for the LogLevel parameter in file httpd.conf. The default value is "warn". Set LogLevel to "debug" if the logging information is insufficient to troubleshoot the problem.	■ Use if you want a record of the static contents processed by HTTP Server. ■ Use if you have trouble starting or stopping HTTP Server or encounter problems during the HTTP server runtime. ■ Use if you have trouble starting or stopping HTTP Admin Server or encounter problems during the HTTP Admin Server runtime. ■ To record the greatest amount of information in the error log file, set LogLevel=debug in file httpd.conf.

Table 5-2: HTTP Server logging activities (continued)

Activity	Log destination	Description	When to use these log files
Managing (e.g., starting, stopping) HTTP Server (continued)		▪ File admin_error.log is where HTTP Admin Server sends diagnostic and error information. Logging in this file depends on the parameters set in file admin.conf. ▪ You must restart HTTP Server for new parameter values in these files to take effect.	

Problem: Logon fails while starting HTTP Server from the Windows Services panel.
Make sure the user you assigned to manage the HTTP Server service has the "Log on as a service" right, or assign a different user who has this right. Also, make sure you typed the password correctly when registering the service during installation.

Problem: You have trouble starting HTTP Server from the command prompt using **apache –k start** *and receive the error "... make_sock: could not bind to address 0.0.0.0:80. ..."*

HTTP Server may already be running on the node. Look for the Apache process on the machine, and try stopping it (**apache –k stop**) and then restarting it (**apache –k restart**). Also, make sure no third-party server is using port 80. (To see a list of ports in use, run the command **netstat –an**.)

Problem: You have trouble connecting to the HTTP Server welcome page.
Make sure HTTP Server was started successfully. If it wasn't, check file error.log in directory <IHSV6-ROOT>\logs for the cause. If you're trying to connect through a Web browser from a remote machine, make sure you can ping the machines from each other using IP address, host name, and fully qualified name (DNS entry).

Configuring Tracing on IBM HTTP Server

Sometimes, the information in the error.log file may be insufficient to troubleshoot a problem you're having with HTTP Server. In such cases, you can configure HTTP Server to log more information to help you debug the issue. To configure tracing, take these steps:

1. Using your favorite editor, open file httpd.conf in the <IHSV6-ROOT>\conf directory.

2. Change the LogLevel (logging level) value to "debug" as shown in Figure 5-17.

3. Restart HTTP Server.

4. Re-create the problem you encountered, and check file error.log for clues to the problem.

5. After resolving the issue, reset the LogLevel value to "warn".

6. Restart HTTP Server.

```
ErrorLog logs/error.log

#
# LogLevel: Control the number of messages logged to the error.log.
# Possible values include: debug, info, notice, warn, error, crit,
# alert, emerg.
#
#LogLevel warn
LogLevel debug
```

Figure 5-17: Setting the logging level for tracing

Silent Installation

As an alternative to the graphical installation procedure described earlier in this chapter, you can install HTTP Server silently. With this method, the installation program determines installation options by reading responses from a file you provide. You use this procedure if you're not using a graphical screen or if you want to use a batch process or one you can use to install HTTP Server on multiple systems. To perform a silent install of HTTP Server, use the following procedure.

Step 1. Log in as a member of the Administrators group with the following rights:

- act as part of the operating system
- log on as a service

Silent installation will fail unless the user has these rights. Restart the machine after granting these rights and before starting the silent installation.

Unix note: On Unix systems, log in as root. If necessary, run **umask 022** to set permissions for the temporary directory. To verify the present setting, run **umask**.

Step 2. Create a temporary directory (e.g., ihsv6-silent-install), and copy into it the file responsefile.txt from the HTTP Server installation package (usually located under the IHS directory). Give the file a meaningful name (e.g., *yourhost*.http.responsefile.txt).

Step 3. Open the file using your favorite text editor, and take a look at its entries. The options in this file correspond to the panels presented in the graphical installation. You're going to customize each line of the response file to silently install HTTP Server the same way you did using the graphical installation.

Step 4. First, to accept the terms of the license agreement, edit the file to change the license acceptance value from "false" to "true":

```
-W silentInstallLicenseAcceptance.value="true"
```

Step 5. For the setup type ID, keep the default value of "custom" (the only option for a silent installation).

```
-W setupTypes.selectedSetupTypeId="custom"
```

Step 6. Set the installation directory to C:\IBM\HTTPServer (the default Windows install location). If you choose to change the directory, make sure the directory name contains no spaces.

```
-P ihs.installLocation="C:\IBM\HTTPServer"
```

Step 7. Set the security value to "true" to install IBM HTTP Server SSL security.

```
-P security.active="true"
```

Step 8. Set the installAfpa value to "true" to install the Fast Response Cache Accelerator. This feature improves HTTP Server performance by caching previously served static content.

```
-P installAfpa.active="true"
```

Step 9a. To run HTTP Server and HTTP Administration as Windows services (on Windows systems only), specify "true" for the createIHSService and createAdminService options. If you specify "false" for these options, the installation program ignores two other response-file entries that are specific to these options (Steps 9b and 9c).

```
-W WinServicePanel.createIHSService="true"
-W WinServicePanel.createAdminService="true"
```

Step 9b. For the account type (the logOnAs option) of the Windows service, you have two choices. If you use the "localsystem" value, the Windows service will log on using the local system account.

```
-W WinServicePanel.logOnAs="localSystem"
```

If you use the "specifieduser" value, you must *comment out* the line that specifies "localsystem" and enter a user name and password in the response file. Figure 5-18 shows what these entries should look like. Make sure the user name you provide is a member of the Administrators group and has the "Log on as a service" right before you run the silent installation program.

```
#-W WinServicePanel.logOnAs="localSystem"

# *********
# Replace YOUR_USER_NAME with your username.
# *********
-W WinServicePanel.user="htadmin"

# *********
# Replace YOUR_PASSWORD with your valid password.
# *********
-W WinServicePanel.password="noyb"
```

Figure 5-18: Specifying a user name and password for the Windows services

Step 9c. Specify the start type for the HTTP and Admin services: "automatic", "manual", or "disabled".

```
-W WinServicePanel.startType="automatic"
```

Step 10. Specify the HTTP and Admin ports, or accept the default ports (80 and 8008, respectively).

```
-W portPanel.httpPort="80"
-W portPanel.adminPort="8008"
```

Step 11. Now, scroll to the beginning of the response file to see the instructions for running the silent installation program. Then save the response file, and exit the editor.

Step 12. Open a command-line prompt, and change to the directory where the install.exe program for HTTP Server is available. The program will be in the same directory from which you copied the response.txt file (usually the IHS directory). To start the silent install, run the following command, substituting the appropriate path to your response file.

```
install.exe -options "path-to-response-file" -silent
```

Step 13. Open file ihsv6_install.log in the <IHSV6-ROOT> directory, and scroll to the end of the file. If you see the INSTCONFSUCCESS indicator, the installation of HTTP Server was successful.

Step 14. Verify the silent installation using the same instructions given above for the graphical installation of HTTP Server V6.

Installing and Configuring Multiple HTTP Servers on the Same Machine

The diagram in Figure 5-19 illustrates an environment with multiple HTTP Servers on the same machine. As you can see, the second HTTP Server uses different ports (81 and 8009) to run alongside the first. The diagram also shows that a second set of items is created after the successful installation of the second HTTP Server. The following items are created after the second installation:

- product binaries and a configuration repository (stored in the file system)
- the Apache Web server
- Admin service
- the Tivoli Global Security Kit

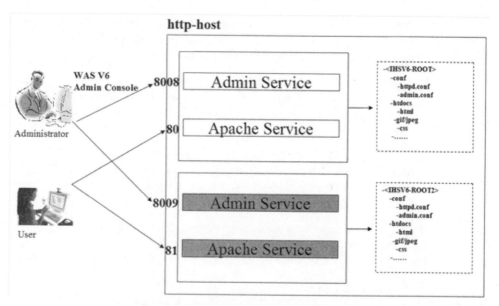

Figure 5-19: Multiple HTTP Server architecture

You can create multiple instances of HTTP Server by copying and renaming files httpd.conf and admin.conf and editing the parameter values in these files to customize the environment. In this section, however, we'll use the installation wizard to create a second HTTP Server on the machine used in this chapter's installation example.

Step 1.   If you registered the HTTP Server and HTTP Administration processes as Windows services, you must unregister them before proceeding with this installation. To do so:

   a. Go to the <IHSV6-ROOT>\bin directory.
   b. Run the following command to unregister the HTTP Server you installed earlier:

```
apache.exe -k uninstall -n "IBM HTTP Server 6.0"
```

   c. Run the following command to unregister the HTTP Admin Server you installed earlier:

```
apache.exe -k uninstall -n "IBM HTTP Administration 6.0"
```

Step 2.   Follow Steps 1–11 of the graphical HTTP Server installation process to create the second HTTP Server, making the following adjustments for the second instance:

   a. When you're prompted to specify the installation directory, use a different directory (e.g., C:\IBM\HTTPServer2) for the second HTTP Server. In the remainder of this discussion, we refer to this directory <IHSV6-ROOT2>.

   b. To avoid conflicts with the default ports of the first HTTP Server, change the port numbers to 81 and 8009 for HTTP and HTTP Administration, respectively. If you assign the defaults ports (80 and 8008), you can start only one HTTP server at any given time.

   c. For the second HTTP Server, *don't* select the options to run the HTTP Server and HTTP Administration processes as Windows services. You'll register these processes manually after completing the installation and verifying it.

Step 3.   When the wizard displays the summary panel, click **Next**. The install program creates the installation directory <IHSV6-ROOT2> and starts logging installation information in files ihsv6_install.log and gskitInstall.log there.

Step 4.   When you see the successful installation panel, click **Finish**.

Verify Installation by Viewing the Log Files

To confirm the success of your second installation, open file ihsv6_install.log in <IHSV6-ROOT2>, and scroll to the end of the file. If you see the INSTCONFSUCCESS indicator, installation of the second HTTP Server was successful. If you see INSTCONF-FAIL or INSTCONFPARTIALSUCCESS, problems occurred during installation. For troubleshooting information, see "Logging: Problem Determination and Troubleshooting."

Verify Installation from the Browser

To verify the installation from a browser, open the browser, and bring up the IBM HTTP Server V6 welcome page by providing the host name, IP address, and DNS entry of the machine with the port number you specified during the installation (81 in our example). If you have trouble displaying the welcome page, refer to "Logging: Problem Determination and Troubleshooting."

Register HTTP Server Processes as Windows Services and Verify

Now, to register the second set of HTTP Server processes in the Windows **Services** panel, take the following steps.

1. For this example, we'll register the second HTTP Server with the name "IHSV6 (2)". To do so, go to the <IHSV6-ROOT2>\bin directory, and run

   ```
   Apache.exe -k install -f "c:\ibm\httpserver2\conf\httpd.conf" -n
   "IHSV6 (2)"
   ```

   To start this HTTP Server from the command prompt, you run

   ```
   apache.exe -n "IHS V6 (2)" -k start
   ```

2. We'll register the second HTTP Admin Server with the name "IHSV6 Admin (2)". To do so, go to <IHSV6-ROOT2>\bin, and run

   ```
   apache.exe -k install -f "c:\ibm\httpserver2\conf\admin.conf" -n
   "IHSV6 Admin (2)"
   ```

   To start this HTTP Admin Server from the command prompt, you run

   ```
   apache.exe -n "IHS Admin V6 (2)" -k start
   ```

3. Next, you need to register the first HTTP Server and HTTP Admin processes installed under <IHSV6-ROOT>. To do so, repeat the preceding two steps using

the service names "IHS V6 (1)" and "IHS V6 Admin (1)" for HTTP Server and HTTP Admin, respectively. If necessary, run the command

```
Apache.exe -k uninstall -n "service-name"
```

to remove the existing service names ("IBM HTTP Server 6.0" and "IBM HTTP Administration 6.0" in this case) from the registry.

Once you've successfully registered all your HTTP processes, the list of services in the Windows **Services** panel should look similar to the one shown in Figure 5-20.

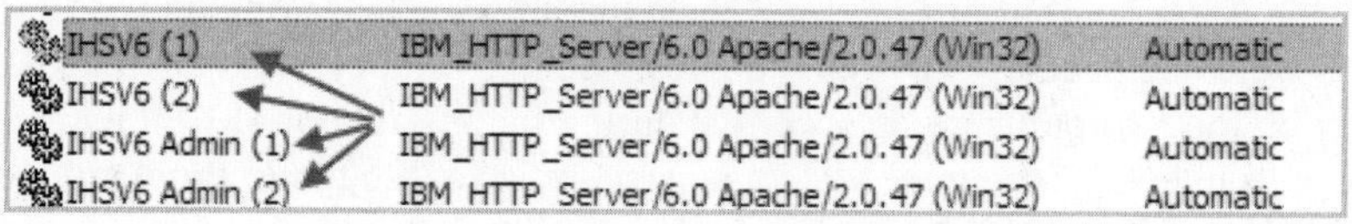

Figure 5-20: Updated list of Windows services

6

IBM HTTP Server V6 Plug-in for WebSphere V6: Install, Configure, Verify, and Manage

As you learned in Chapter 1, the plug-in module on the HTTP server is responsible for diverting requests for dynamic content (e.g., servlets) to WebSphere Application Server using information in an XML-based plug-in file. If the plug-in module (with HTTP server) resides on the same machine as the application server, you have a *local plug-in* configuration. If the plug-in module (with HTTP server) resides on a different machine from the application server node, you have a *remote plug-in* configuration.

In this chapter, we show you how to configure both a local and a remote plug-in for WebSphere Application Server V6 and IBM HTTP Server V6. We also explain how to add a Web server definition to the WebSphere administrative configuration so that you can use the WebSphere admin console to manage the HTTP Server and plug-in configurations. Near the end of the chapter, you'll find instructions for uninstalling the plug-in and for performing a silent install.

The procedures presented here cover configuring the plug-in with a standalone application server (created using the WebSphere V6 Base, Express, or Network Deployment package). If you want to install the plug-in in a *distributed* local or remote plug-in configuration (using the Network Deployment package, the Deployment Manager, and federated nodes under the profiles), you need to follow the instructions in Chapter 9.

The Local Plug-in Architecture

Figure 6-1 illustrates the architecture created when you install the IBM HTTP Server local plug-in for WebSphere. As a result of the installation, the following items are created:

- plug-in modules for the supported Web servers (e.g., IBM HTTP Server, Lotus Domino Web Server, Microsoft Internet Information Services) and a configuration repository (stored in the file system)

- batch file configure*webserver-definition-name*.bat (.sh on Unix) — When executed, this batch file will configure the Web server definition in the WebSphere repository, enabling the administrator to manage the Web server from the WebSphere admin console. In a local plug-in environment, where the Web server and the application server reside on the same machine, the batch file is executed automatically.

- default plug-in file plugin-cfg.xml — In the local plug-in scenario, the installation creates the plug-in file under the WebSphere root installation directory (<WASV6-ROOT>).

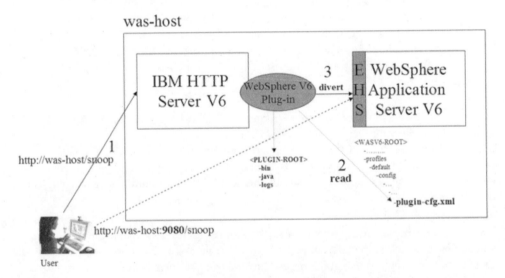

Figure 6-1: Local plug-in architecture

Figure 6-1 also illustrates how HTTP Server (with plug-in) behaves when a user issues a request — in this case, to process the snoop servlet (http://was-host/snoop):

- The plug-in receives the request from the browser. (Once installed on the Web server, the plug-in initially receives all requests on behalf of the Web server.)

- The plug-in reads the plug-in file from its cache. (In the case of a local plug-in, this file is stored in the config directory under <WASV6-ROOT>.)

- If the plug-in file contains matching Uniform Resource Identifier (URI) entries for the requested servlet, the plug-in diverts the request to the application server. In effect, what we have in the configuration file are the components of the URI, the server relative URI, the virtual hosts, and schemes associated with the Web resources hosted on the application servers. (The plug-in file also contains the application server process host name, port numbers, and protocols for opening connections between the plug-in and the application server's Embedded HTTP Server, or EHS.)

  - If the plug-in file contains no matching URI for the servlet, Java Server Page (JSP), or static file (if you've enabled file serving), the plug-in passes the request to the Web server. The Web server then either serves the request or displays an error page if it doesn't find static content that matches the URI of the request.

  - When the requested URL includes the application server host name and port, the plug-in is bypassed. For example, you can invoke the snoop servlet using WebSphere's EHS directly by issuing the URL http://was-host:9080/snoop. This technique often proves useful for troubleshooting, helping you isolate a problem in either the plug-in or the application server.

Installing IBM HTTP Server V6 Local Plug-in for WebSphere

The flow chart in Figure 6-2 depicts the high-level steps required to install, configure, and verify the local HTTP plug-in for WebSphere. In this section, we step you through each part of this process. As in earlier chapters, our instructions assume you're working in a Windows XP environment. If you're using a Unix operating system, you'll need to execute the appropriate commands (i.e., .sh instead of .bat) and substitute the forward slash (/) for the backward slash (\) in directory and path names. Table 6-1 lists, by operating system, the default directory locations for the symbolic references used in this chapter.

Step 1.   If you want to use the trial version of the WebSphere HTTP plug-in, download it from one of the following URLs. (You may need to register first.) The trial version is good for 60 days, and you can submit a problem ticket to IBM support during the trial period.

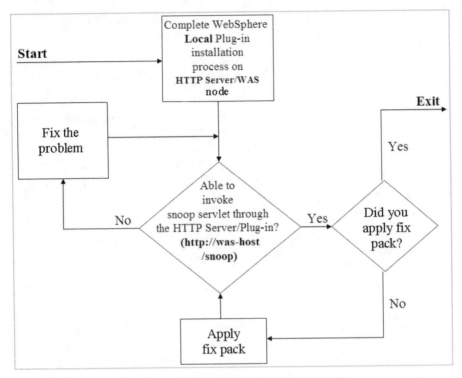

Figure 6-2: Local plug-in installation overview

Table 6-1: Directory locations for symbolic references

Symbolic reference	Windows	AIX	Linux/Unix
<IHSV6-ROOT>	C:\IBM\HTTPServer	/usr/IBMIHS	/opt/IBMIHS
<PLUGIN-ROOT>	C:\IBM\WebSphere\Plugins	/usr/WebSphere/plugins	/opt/WebSphere/plugins
<PROFILE-ROOT> for default profile	<WASV6-ROOT>\profiles\default	<WASV6-ROOT>/profiles/default	<WASV6-ROOT>/profiles/default
<WASV6-ROOT>	C:\IBM\WebSphere\App Server	/usr/WebSphere/App Server	/opt/WebSphere/AppServer

http://www-106.ibm.com/developerworks/websphere/downloads
http://www14.software.ibm.com/webapp/download/home.jsp

Figure 6-3 shows how the directory structure looks after you've downloaded the plug-in trial version and extracted the files to a temporary directory. You'll use the install.exe program in directory plugin to install the trial version of the software. If you're using a licensed package of WebSphere Application Server, you'll use WebSphere's Launchpad to install the plug-in.

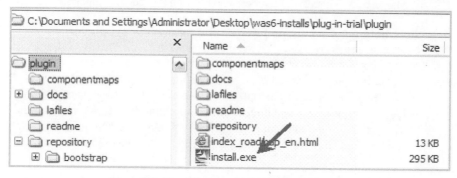

Figure 6-3: Directory structure for plug-in trial version

Step 2.   As with the other installations we've covered, you must make sure the TMP environment variable is set appropriately. If you followed the instructions in prior chapters, you've probably completed this step already. If not, log in as a member of the Administrators group, right-click **My Computer** on the desktop, and select **Properties|Advanced|Environment Variables**. In the "User variables for user" list, note the value set for the temporary directory (TMP). If you don't see variable TMP in the list, click **New** to add it. For this example, we'll assume a TMP value of C:\temp.

Unix note: On Unix systems, log in as root. If necessary, run the command **umask 022** to set permissions for the temporary directory (usually /tmp). To verify the current umask setting, run **umask.**

Step 3.   Make sure at least 325 MB of disk space is available to install the plug-in (200 MB for the <PLUGIN-ROOT> directory, 25 MB for the Global Security Kit [which provides Secure Sockets Layer, or SSL, communications], and 100 MB for the TMP directory).

Unix note: Make sure the file systems mounted on the Web server plug-in, Global Security Kit, and /tmp directories meet the minimum disk space requirements of 200 MB, 25 MB, and 100 MB, respectively.

Step 4.   If IBM HTTP Server or a third-party Web server is running on the machine on which you plan to install the plug-in, stop the Web server before starting the installation. To see whether any HTTP Server or Apache process is running on the Windows system, press Ctrl+Alt+Del to display the Windows Task Manager, and check the **Processes** tab for an Apache.exe entry.

Unix note: Run the **ps –ef | grep apache** command to see whether any Apache processes are running on the Unix system.

Step 5.   If you're using a licensed package of WebSphere Application Server to install the local plug-in, mount the CD, go to the directory containing the Launchpad program, and double-click **launchpad.bat**. If you're using the trial version of the plug-in, go to directory plugin, and double-click **install.exe**. (The install.exe program works for the licensed packages, too.)

The installation program immediately starts logging information under the TMP directory. For more information about this logging, see the "Logging: Problem Determination and Troubleshooting" section of this chapter.

Unix note: Before running the installation wizard, make sure you can execute the **xclock** or **xeyes** command to display a graphical image properly. For more information about these commands, see Chapter 3.

Step 6.   On the WebSphere welcome panel (displayed for Launchpad installations only), select the option to "Launch the installation wizard for Web server plug-ins."

Step 7.   Read through the information on the plug-in installation welcome panel. Then clear the **Installation roadmap: Overview** option, and click **Next** to start the installation.

Step 8.   On the next panel, accept the terms of the license agreement, and click **Next**.

Step 9.   The installation wizard now performs a prerequisites check. If the wizard reports a successful check, click **Next**. If the check fails, cancel the installation program, and open and read log file temporaryPluginInstallLog.txt in the TMP directory. (For more information about this log, see "Logging: Problem

Determination and Troubleshooting.") Correct the system to meet the prerequisites, and then run the installation program again.

Step 10. Next, on the panel shown in Figure 6-4, select the Web server you want to configure. For this example, you'll be using IBM HTTP Server V6, so select this option and click **Next**.

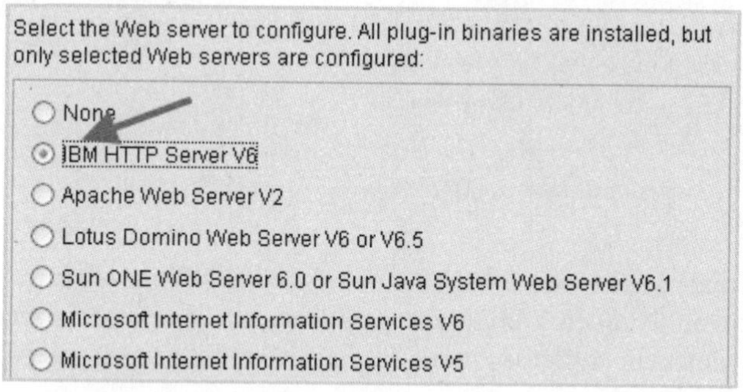

> Select the Web server to configure. All plug-in binaries are installed, but only selected Web servers are configured:
>
> ○ None
> ⊙ IBM HTTP Server V6
> ○ Apache Web Server V2
> ○ Lotus Domino Web Server V6 or V6.5
> ○ Sun ONE Web Server 6.0 or Sun Java System Web Server V6.1
> ○ Microsoft Internet Information Services V6
> ○ Microsoft Internet Information Services V5

Figure 6-4: Selecting the Web server to configure

One note about the first option on the Web server panel, **None**: A successful plug-in installation modifies the Web server configuration file (httpd.conf) to load the plug-in module during HTTP Server startup. In some situations, you may want to manually change this file after the installation. In such instances, you would select the **None** option.

Step 11. You use the next panel (Figure 6-5) to specify the plug-in installation scenario: remote or local. For this example, we're assuming HTTP Server and the application server reside on the same machine (a local plug-in), so choose the option "WebSphere Application Server machine (local)" and click **Next**.

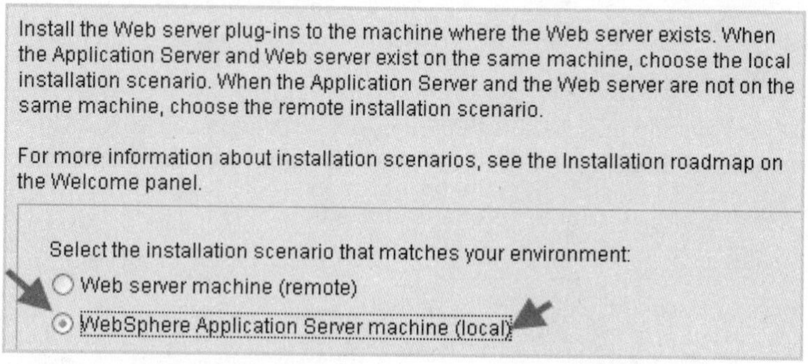

> Install the Web server plug-ins to the machine where the Web server exists. When the Application Server and Web server exist on the same machine, choose the local installation scenario. When the Application Server and the Web server are not on the same machine, choose the remote installation scenario.
>
> For more information about installation scenarios, see the Installation roadmap on the Welcome panel.
>
> Select the installation scenario that matches your environment:
> ○ Web server machine (remote)
> ⊙ WebSphere Application Server machine (local)

Figure 6-5: Selecting a local plug-in installation

Step 12. Next (Figure 6-6), set the installation directory for the plug-in. For Windows, make sure whatever directory name you use contains no spaces. For this example, simply accept the default directory, C:\IBM\WebSphere\Plugins, and click **Next**. From now on, we refer to the plug-in installation directory as <PLUGIN-ROOT>.

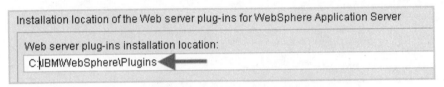

Figure 6-6: Specifying the plug-in installation directory

Step 13. The wizard next asks for the name of the installation directory you used when you installed WebSphere Application Server on this machine (Figure 6-7). Enter the directory name (C:\IBM\WebSphere\AppServer in this case), and click **Next**.

Figure 6-7: Specifying the WebSphere directory

Step 14. Next (Figure 6-8), identify the location of the Web server's configuration file (httpd.conf) and the port number at which the Web server receives requests. The plug-in installation program will use this information to add two entries to the end of the configuration file:

- the location and name of the plug-in module that must be loaded during Web server startup

- the location and name of the plug-in file (plugin-cfg.xml), which tells the plug-in module how to direct requests to the application server

When you're finished with this panel, click **Next**.

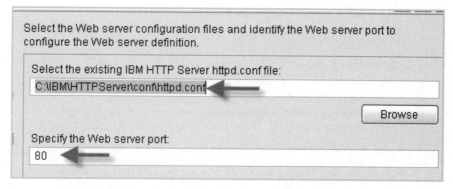

Figure 6-8: Identifying the Web server configuration file and port

Step 15. Now (Figure 6-9), you must provide a name for the Web server definition in the WebSphere application server repository. This example uses the name webserver-on-was-host. The plug-in installation will use the name you specify to create, under the <PLUGIN-ROOT>\bin directory, the batch file that will be executed during the local plug-in installation to configure the Web server definition. With that task completed, you'll be able to manage the Web server through the WebSphere admin console.

The batch file is named using the format configure*webserver-definition-name*.bat. In this example, the file will be named configurewebserver-on-was-host.bat. After specifying a meaningful name for the Web server definition, click **Next**.

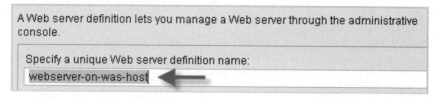

Figure 6-9: Specifying the Web server definition name

Step 16. Next, choose the default location for the plug-in file. For a local plug-in installation, the file will be generated under the directory <PROFILE-ROOT>\config\ . . . *webserver-definition-name,* as shown in Figure 6-10. The plug-in module will read this file during the Web server's startup and at an interval specified by the file's RefreshInterval parameter, which has a default value of 60 seconds. (You can tune this parameter value as needed after installation.)

After specifying the plug-in file location, click **Next**.

Select the plugin-cfg.xml file to use for the selected Web server. The Wizard uses the following location below to generate a plugin-cfg.xml file if one does not exist. If you change the location, the plugin-cfg.xml file must exist.

Web server plugin-cfg.xml file:
C:\IBM\WebSphere\AppServer\profiles\default\config\cells\lakhostNode01Ce ll\nodes\webserver-on-was-host_node\servers\webserver-on-was-host\plugi n-cfg.xml

Figure 6-10: Location of the plug-in file in a local plug-in configuration

Step 17. The wizard next displays the panel shown Figure 6-11 in preparation for creating the Web server definition. As the panel indicates, when the configuration batch file is executed, the Web server definition will be configured with the default profile. If you installed WebSphere using the Base or Express package, the name of the default profile is 'default'. If you installed WebSphere and created an application server profile (standalone server) using the Network Deployment package, the name of the default profile is 'AppSrv01'.

Review the information on this panel, and then click **Next**.

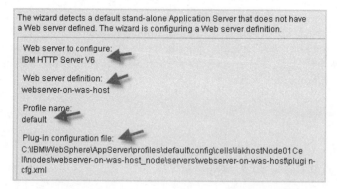

The wizard detects a default stand-alone Application Server that does not have a Web server defined. The wizard is configuring a Web server definition.

Web server to configure:
IBM HTTP Server V6

Web server definition:
webserver-on-was-host

Profile name:
default

Plug-in configuration file:
C:\IBM\WebSphere\AppServer\profiles\default\config\cells\lakhostNode01Ce ll\nodes\webserver-on-was-host_node\servers\webserver-on-was-host\plugi n-cfg.xml

Figure 6-11: Web server definition summary panel

Note: A local plug-in installation can configure only the default profile with the Web server definition. In a multiprofile environment, you must therefore make sure the profile you want to configure is in fact the default profile. To do so, open file profileRegistry.xml under the <WASV6-ROOT>\properties directory (in read-only mode). *Do not change the contents of this file.* If isDefault="true" is specified for the profile you want to configure, that profile is the default profile.

Step 18.   The next three panels of the wizard are summary screens. Review these, and click **Next** on each one. Then, to complete the plug-in installation, click **Finish**.

Understanding the Plug-in Directory Structure

The plug-in installation process creates several important directories under the installation root, <PLUGIN-ROOT> (C:\WebSphere\Plugins in this example). Here's a brief look at the purpose of the key directories.

- *bin* — The bin directory contains plug-in modules for the various Web servers supported by HTTP Server and WebSphere. It also contains batch files to create and update SSL certificates and provides information about the version and fix pack level of the product. Two important files to note under this directory are

  › mod_was_ap20_http.dll — This file is the plug-in module (defined in file httpd.conf) that is loaded during HTTP Server startup.

  › configure*webserver-definition-name*.bat (.sh for Unix) — This batch file, generated during the plug-in installation, contains the information to configure the Web server definition to enable managing the Web server from the WebSphere admin console.

- *config* — This directory is the default location for the plug-in file in a remote plug-in configuration (under subdirectory *webserver-definition-name*). In the case of a local plug-in configuration, the default plug-in file is installed in the <PROFILE-ROOT>\config\ . . . *webserver-definition-name* directory.

- *etc* — Files related to security (SSL certificate and database information) are stored under this directory.

- *logs* — The files in the logs directory contain the log information generated during the plug-in installation and runtime. For more information about this directory, see "Logging: Problem Determination and Troubleshooting."

- *_uninstPlugin* — This directory contains the uninstall execution program and related files used to uninstall the plug-in.

Verifying the Plug-in

To verify the installation of the plug-in (whether local or remote), you should examine the log and configuration files and verify operation from the browser.

Verify Installation by Viewing the Log and Configuration Files

Step 1. Go to the machine on which you installed the plug-in. Open the file log.txt under the <PLUGIN-ROOT>\logs\install directory, and scroll to the end. If you see the indicator INSTCONF_COMPLETE, as shown in Figure 6-12, the plug-in installation was successful. If you see INSTCONFFAILED or INSTCONFPARTIALSUCCESS, problems occurred during installation. For troubleshooting information, see "Logging: Problem Determination and Troubleshooting."

```
C:\IBM\webSphere\AppServer\profiles\default\config\cells\lakhostNode01Ce
11\nodes\webserver-on-was-host_node\servers\webserver-on-was-host\plugi n-cfg.xml
(Feb 6, 2005 11:23:26 PM), Plugin.Install,
com.ibm.ws.install.ni.ismp.actions.ISMPLogFileAction, msg1, INSTCONF_COMPLETE :
Installation is complete.
(Feb 6, 2005 11:23:26 PM), Plugin.Install,
com.ibm.ws.install.ni.ismp.actions.ISMPLogFileAction, msg1,
```

Figure 6-12: Indicator of successful plug-in installation

Step 2. Open the Web server configuration file — file httpd.conf under the <IHSV6-ROOT>\conf directory — and scroll to the end of the file. Make sure you see two entries similar to those shown in Figure 6-13 that represent

- the name and location of the HTTP Server plug-in module
- the name and location of the plug-in file (plugin-cfg.xml)

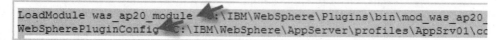
```
LoadModule was_ap20_module    C:\IBM\WebSphere\Plugins\bin\mod_was_ap20_
WebSpherePluginConfig C:\IBM\WebSphere\AppServer\profiles\AppSrv01\cc
```

Figure 6-13: Plug-in entries in Web server configuration file

Step 3. Click the Windows **Start** button, and navigate to **Control Panel|Add or Remove Programs**. Check to make sure you see a WebSphere plug-in entry in the program list, as shown in Figure 6-14. Exit the window without changing anything.

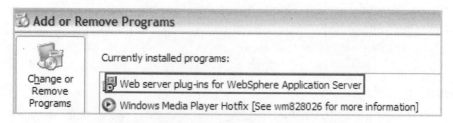

Figure 6-14: WebSphere plug-in entry in Add or Remove Programs window

Step 4. Go to the machine on which you installed and configured WebSphere with the Web server definition, navigate to the <PROFILE-ROOT>\config\cells\ *hostname*Node01Cell\nodes directory, and verify the creation of the Web server node definition here (the result of executing the batch file described above). Figure 6-15 shows the entry for our example.

> **Note:** If you're configuring a remote plug-in (standalone server or distributed), you'll need to come back and verify this entry after running the batch file on the WebSphere node. For a distributed remote plug-in – managed node, you run the batch file on the Web server node itself.

Figure 6-15: Creation of Web server node definition as a directory in the repository

Verify Installation from the Browser

Step 1. Start the default application server you configured with the Web server's definition. To do so, open a command prompt, go to the <PROFILE-ROOT> \bin directory, and run **startServer.bat server1**. (You can also start the WebSphere process from the Windows **Services** panel. For information about starting and managing WebSphere Application Server, see Chapter 4.)

Step 2. Connect to the WebSphere admin console: **http://was-host:9060/ibm/console**.

Step 3. Expand **Servers**, and click **Web servers** to see the listing of the Web server definition you configured to enable management through the admin console (Figure 6-16).

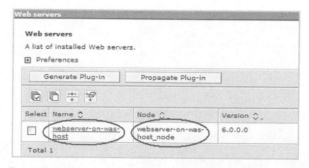

Figure 6-16: Web server definition in WebSphere admin console

Step 4.   Log out of the admin console by clicking **Logout** on the top horizontal menu bar.

Step 5.   From the browser, issue the URL to invoke the snoop servlet through the WebSphere Embedded HTTP Server (EHS): **http://was-host:9080/snoop**. If you have problems invoking snoop through EHS, refer to Chapter 3 to fix the problem, and then return here.

Step 6.   Start HTTP Server. To do so, open a command prompt, go to the <IHSV6-ROOT>\bin directory, and run **apache.exe –k start**. (You can also start the HTTP Server process from the Windows **Services** panel.) The plug-in module will be read and loaded from the Web server configuration file (<IHSV6-ROOT>\conf\httpd.conf) during HTTP Server startup.

Step 7.   Open a browser, and enter the URL **http://was-host** (for a local plug-in) or **http://http-host** (for a remote plug-in) to bring up the HTTP Server welcome page. If you have trouble starting or displaying this page, consult "Logging: Problem Determination and Troubleshooting."

Step 8.   Open a browser, and invoke the snoop servlet through the plug-in on HTTP Server: **http://was-host/snoop** (local plug-in) or **http://http-host/snoop** (remote plug-in). The plug-in module will receive this request and check file plugin-cfg.xml stored in the cache (read during startup) for an entry and routing information for the snoop servlet, as shown in Figure 6-17.

```
<ServerCluster CloneSeparatorChange="false" LoadBalance="Round Robin" Name="server1_lakhos
    <Server ConnectTimeout="0" ExtendedHandshake="false" MaxConnections="-1" Name="lakhost1
        <Transport Hostname="was-host" Port="9080" Protocol="http"/>
        <Transport Hostname="was-host" Port="9443" Protocol="https">
            <Property Name="keyring" Value="C:\IBM\WebSphere\Plugins\etc\plugin-key.kdb"/>
            <Property Name="stashfile" Value="C:\IBM\WebSphere\Plugins\etc\plugin-key.sth"/>
        </Transport>
    </Server>
</ServerCluster>
<UriGroup Name="default_host_server1_lakhostNode01_Cluster_URIs">
    <Uri AffinityCookie="JSESSIONID" AffinityURLIdentifier="jsessionid" Name="/snoop/*"/>
    <Uri AffinityCookie="JSESSIONID" AffinityURLIdentifier="jsessionid" Name="/hello"/>
    <Uri AffinityCookie="JSESSIONID" AffinityURLIdentifier="jsessionid" Name="/hitcount"/>
```

Figure 6-17: Snoop servlet entries in the plug-in file

If you have trouble invoking snoop:

1. Connect to the WebSphere admin console again.

2. Expand **Servers**, and click **Web servers**.

3. Select the Web server in the Web servers list (as shown in Figure 6-18), and click **Generate Plug-in** to regenerate the plug-in file.

4. Select the Web server again, and click **Propagate Plug-in** to move file plugin-cfg.xml to the required location.

Unix note: On Unix machines, make sure the plug-in file has permission for the WebSphere admin console user to overwrite it. To do so, open a command prompt, go to the directory where the file is available, and issue the command **chmod 666 plugin-cfg.xml.**

---

5. Restart HTTP Server, or wait 60 seconds (or the number of seconds specified for parameter RefreshInterval) for the plug-in module to load the new plug-in file.

If you still have problems invoking snoop, see "Logging: Problem Determination and Troubleshooting" for more information.

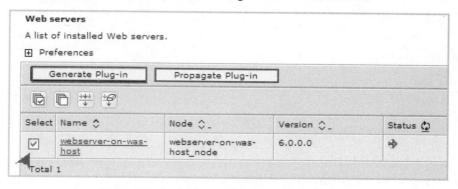

Figure 6-18: Generating and propagating the plug-in file

The Remote Plug-in Architecture

Figure 6-19 illustrates the architecture created on the HTTP Server node when you install the HTTP Server remote plug-in for WebSphere. As in the local plug-in installation, the following items are created:

- plug-in modules for the supported Web servers and a configuration repository

- batch file configure*webserver-definition-name*.bat (.sh on Unix)

- default plug-in file plugin-cfg.xml — In the remote plug-in scenario, this file is created under the <IHSV6-ROOT>\config*webserver-definition-name* directory.

As with the local plug-in, you'll use the configuration batch file to configure the Web server definition in the WebSphere repository to manage HTTP Server from the Web Sphere admin console. In the remote plug-in environment, however, WebSphere resides on a different node than HTTP Server, so you must manually copy the batch file to the WebSphere node and execute it there.

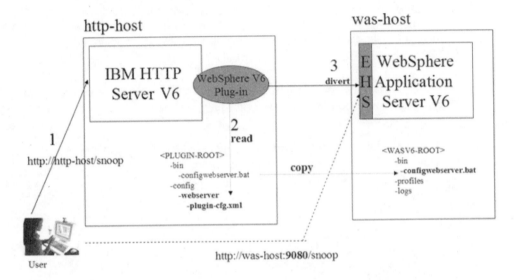

Figure 6-19: Remote plug-in architecture

Figure 6-19 also shows how HTTP Server (with plug-in) behaves when you issue a request to process the snoop servlet (http://http-host/snoop):

1. The plug-in receives the request from the browser.

2. The plug-in reads the plug-in file (plugin-cfg.xml) from its cache.

3. If the plug-in file contains entries sufficient to serve the snoop servlet, the plug-in diverts the request to the application server. If the file does not contain entries for the requested servlet (or JSP or static content if file serving is enabled), the plug-in passes the request to the Web server. The Web server then either serves the request or displays an error page if it doesn't find the static content. (Note that you can also invoke snoop using WebSphere's Embedded HTTP Server with the URL http://was-host:9080/snoop.)

Figure 6-20 illustrates how a request passes from the WebSphere admin console to HTTP Server to manage HTTP Server and its configuration when WebSphere and HTTP Server reside on different machines (remote plug-in configuration):

- After receiving a request from the console, the WebSphere admin server sends the request to HTTP Administration Server V6 on the remote HTTP Server machine (http-host in the example). Along with the request, the admin server sends the Web server's administrative user ID and password.

- HTTP Admin Server validates the user ID and password against the admin.passwd file, fulfills the request, and returns the status to the WebSphere admin server to display on the admin console.

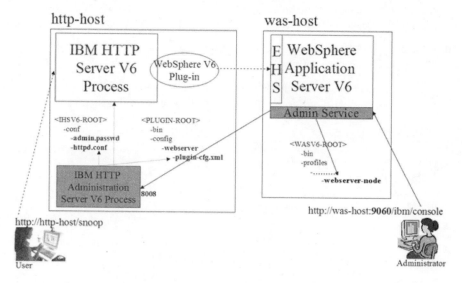

Figure 6-20: Managing HTTP Server from the WebSphere admin console

Note that the level of capability to remotely manage HTTP Server from the admin console depends on whether you connected to the standalone application server or the Deployment Manager and whether the HTTP Server node is a managed (with node agent) or an unmanaged node. (In a standalone server environment, you can only generate and propagate the plug-in file; in a Network Deployment environment, you can also start and stop HTTP Server and create a new Web server definition from the Deployment Manager's admin console.) The diagram in the figure represents the unmanaged node architecture because no node agent process exists on the HTTP Server machine.

Installing IBM HTTP Server V6 Remote Plug-in for WebSphere

The flow chart in Figure 6-21 shows the high-level steps required to install, configure, and verify the HTTP plug-in for WebSphere in a remote plug-in configuration. Because IBM HTTP Server and WebSphere reside on different machines in this scenario, you must complete a few additional steps beyond those required to install a local plug-in:

- After installing the plug-in on the HTTP Server node, you must copy the configuration batch file from the HTTP Server node to the WebSphere node and execute it there. This step creates the Web server definition in the WebSphere repository.

- To be able to manage HTTP Server remotely from the WebSphere admin console, you must define an administrative user ID and password for the HTTP Admin Server and configure the WebSphere admin console.

- You must regenerate and propagate the plug-in file to the HTTP Server node from the WebSphere admin console.

- To manage HTTP Server remotely, you must also start HTTP Admin Server. (In a local plug-in configuration, you don't need to perform this step.)

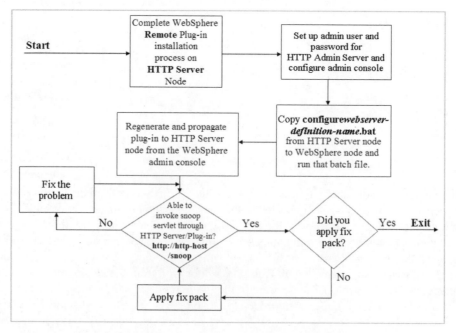

Figure 6-21: Remote plug-in installation overview

Install the Remote Plug-in

Step 1. Go to the machine on which you've successfully installed and tested HTTP Server (http-host in this example), and complete Steps 1–10 of the local plug-in installation procedure.

Step 2. When prompted to select the installation scenario, select the option "Web server machine (remote)" as shown in Figure 6-22.

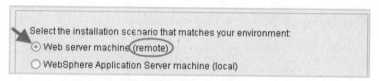

Figure 6-22: Selecting a remote plug-in installation

Step 3. Next, set the installation directory (<PLUGIN-ROOT>) for the plug-in. (For Windows, make sure the name contains no spaces.) For this example, simply accept the default directory, C:\IBM\WebSphere\Plugins, and click **Next**.

Step 4. Next, specify the location of the HTTP Server configuration file (httpd.conf) and the port number at which HTTP Server receives requests. As for the local plug-in, the installation program will add two entries to the end of this file:

- the location and name of the plug-in module to be loaded during Web server startup
- the location and name of the plug-in file (plugin-cfg.xml)

When you're finished with this panel, click **Next**.

Step 5. Next (Figure 6-23), specify a meaningful name for the Web server definition that will be created in the WebSphere application server repository. The plug-in installation uses this name to create the configure*webserver-definition-name*.bat batch file under the <PLUGIN-ROOT>\bin directory. For this example, we'll use the name webserver-on-http-host for the Web server's definition to reflect the location of the remote plug-in. The batch file name will thus be config-urewebserver-on-http-host.bat. Later, you'll copy this file to the WebSphere node and execute it to configure the Web server's definition.

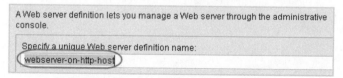

Figure 6-23: Specifying the Web server definition name

Step 6. On the next panel (Figure 6-24), specify the default location for the plug-in file. For a remote plug-in installation, the file will be under the <PLUGIN-ROOT>\config*webserver-definition-name* directory on the HTTP Server machine. Later, you'll propagate the plug-in file from the WebSphere machine to the HTTP Server (with plug-in) machine. The plug-in module will then read the plug-in file during the Web server's startup and at the interval specified by the plug-in file's RefreshInterval interval parameter (60 seconds by default).

After specifying the plug-in file location, click **Next**.

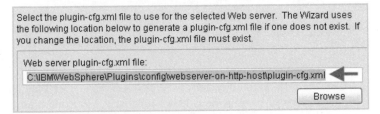

Figure 6-24: Specifying the plug-in file location

Step 7. You use the next panel (Figure 6-25) to identify the WebSphere machine. Enter the host name or Domain Name Server (DNS) entry of the system where you installed WebSphere Application Server and want to configure the Web server definition. (The plug-in installation will proceed regardless of whether the HTTP Server node can ping the WebSphere node.)

Note: If you are in a Network Deployment environment and have federated the node within the application server profile to the Deployment Manager cell, you must enter the host name or DNS entry of the Deployment Manager (dmgr-host) system instead of was-host on this panel.

Click **Next** when you're finished with this panel.

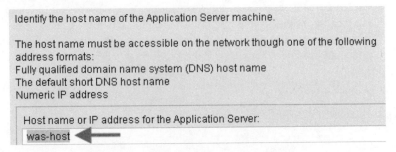

Figure 6-25: Identifying the WebSphere node

156

Step 8. Now, review the wizard's four summary panels, clicking **Next** on each one. Then click **Finish** to complete the remote plug-in installation.

Step 9. To verify installation of the remote plug-in, follow the steps given above (in the section "Verifying the Plug-in") to review the log and configuration files as described for the local plug-in.

Step 10. Apply the required fix pack for the plug-in, and verify. For information about how to install product updates, see Chapter 19.

Step 11.. If your Web server will operate in a production environment and you've placed it in a demilitarized zone (DMZ), you may want to remove the Java JDK (folder 'java') from the <PLUGIN-ROOT> directory for security reasons. The JDK is used only during installation of the plug-in.

Create an Administrative User ID and Password for HTTP Server

Once you've successfully installed the plug-in on the HTTP Server machine, you need to assign an administrative user ID and password that you'll use to manage HTTP Server through HTTP Admin Server from the WebSphere admin console. Take the following steps to create this user ID and password.

Step 12. Open a command prompt on the machine on which you installed HTTP Server (with plug-in), and go to the <IHSV6-ROOT>\bin directory. Issue the following command, and press Enter to create the user ID in file admin.passwd:

htpasswd –cm <IHSV6-ROOT>\conf\admin.passwd userid

For example:

htpasswd –cm c:\ibm\httpserver\conf\admin.passwd htadmin

Step 13. Next, specify and confirm a password.

Step 14. Restart HTTP Server and HTTP Admin Server to have your changes take effect.

Configure WebSphere to Include the Web Server Definition

Next, you need to add the Web server's definition to the WebSphere repository by copying and executing the configuration batch file that was created when you installed the plug-in.

Step 15.   Go to the <PLUGIN-ROOT>\bin directory on the HTTP Server machine (http-host), and copy the configuration batch file for the Web server definition (generated during the plug-in installation) to the <WASV6-ROOT>\bin directory on the WebSphere machine (was-host). Figure 6-26 shows the location of this file for our example.

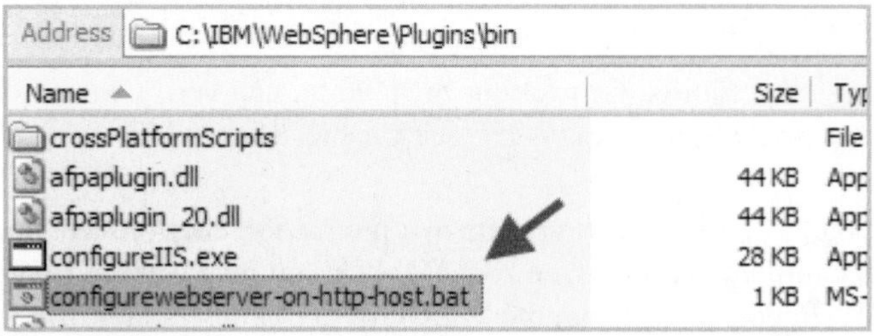

Figure 6-26: Configuration batch file on HTTP Server machine to be copied to WebSphere node

If WebSphere and HTTP Server happen to be on different operating systems — for example, if HTTP Server with the plug-in is on a Windows system and WebSphere is on a Unix machine — you'll find the configuration batch file in the <PLUGIN-ROOT>\bin\crossPlatformScripts directory on the HTTP Server machine.

Step 16.   Log on to the WebSphere node, and start the default server.

Step 17.   On the WebSphere node, go to the <WASV6-ROOT>\bin directory, and execute the Web server definition configuration batch file you copied in the earlier step. Figure 6-27 shows the batch file for our example, configurewebserver-on-http-host.bat, being executed to create the Web server definition on was-host.

Caution: Before executing the batch file, make sure you log out of the admin console; otherwise, you may see warnings about workspace conflicts, as shown in Figure 6-28. If you're curious about the batch file's operation, open it using your favorite editor to see the commands it contains (Figure 6-29) before running the script. You can also view the wsadmin JACL script (configurewebserver Definition.jacl), which the batch file uses to configure the WebSphere repository. Make sure you don't change the entries in either of these files.

```
C:\IBM\WebSphere\AppServer\bin>configurewebserver-on-http-host.bat

C:\IBM\WebSphere\AppServer\bin>wsadmin.bat -f configureWebserverDefinition.jacl webser
ver-on-http-host IHS "C:\\IBM\\HTTPServer" "C:\\IBM\\HTTPServer\\conf\\httpd.conf" 80
MAP_ALL "C:\\IBM\\WebSphere\\Plugins" unmanaged http-host http-host windows
WSUR0027I: The product will expire in 30 days.
WASX7209I: Connected to process "server1" on node lakhostNode01 using SOAP connector;
 The type of process is: UnManagedProcess
WASX7303I: The following unrecognized options are passed to the scripting environment
and are available as argv: "[webserver-on-http-host, IHS, C:\\IBM\\HTTPServer, C:\\IBM
\\HTTPServer\\conf\\httpd.conf, 80, MAP_ALL, C:\\IBM\\WebSphere\\Plugins, unmanaged, h
ttp-host, http-host, windows]"
```

Figure 6-27: Executing the configuration batch file

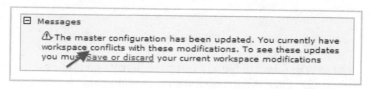

Figure 6-28: Workspace conflict messages

Figure 6-29: Sample configuration batch file

Configure WebSphere to Manage HTTP Server from the WebSphere Admin Console

Your next task is to configure WebSphere to manage HTTP Server through HTTP Admin Server from the WebSphere admin console. You'll do this by storing the administrative user ID and password you created earlier in the WebSphere admin console.

Step 18. Open a browser, and log on to the WebSphere admin console.

Step 19. Expand **Servers**, and click **Web Servers**. You should see the Web server's definition, as shown in Figure 6-30.

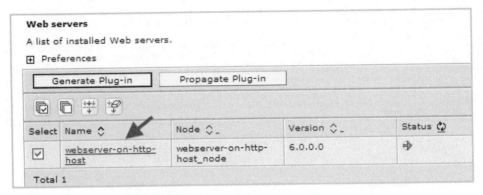

Figure 6-30: Web server definition in WebSphere admin console

Step 20. Click the Web server definition name (webserver-on-http-host in our example), and then click the **Remote Web server management** link in the **Additional Properties** section.

Step 21. On the resulting page (Figure 6-31), enter the administrative user ID and password you created earlier for HTTP Admin Server. Then click **OK**, and save the configuration.

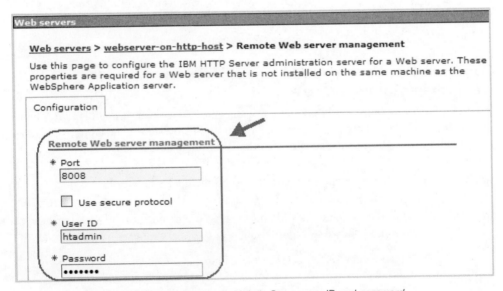

Figure 6-31: Configuring the Admin Server user ID and password

Generate and Propagate the Plug-in File

Only a few more steps to go before you're finished setting up the remote plug-in environment! Your next task is to generate the plug-in file (plugin-cfg.xml) and propagate it to the remote Web server machine.

Step 22. In the WebSphere admin console, expand **Servers**, and click **Web Servers**.

Step 23. Select the check box in front of the Web server definition, and then click the **Generate Plug-in** button. (You can see this button in Figure 6-30 above.) You should receive a message saying that the plug-in configuration was updated successfully, as shown in Figure 6-32.

Figure 6-32: Successful plug-in generation message

Step 24. Again, select the check box in front of the Web server definition. Then click the **Propagate Plug-in** button. You should see a message saying that the plug-in configuration was propagated successfully, as shown in Figure 6-33.

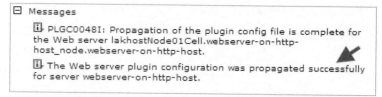

Figure 6-33: Successful plug-in propagation message

Troubleshooting Problems Propagating the Plug-in File

If you receive error "PLGC0049E — A problem was encountered transferring the designated file" (Figure 6-34) after clicking the **Propagate Plug-in** button, check the following:

- Make sure you created the HTTP Server administrative user ID and password using the method described above (Steps 12–14 for the remote plug-in). IBM HTTP Server uses file admin.passwd in the <IHSV6-ROOT>\conf directory (by default) to store this user ID and password. Even though HTTP Server is based on the Apache Web server, you need to follow the specific instructions given for IBM HTTP Server because the instructions for creating an administrative user for the Apache Web server are different.

■ Make sure you entered the same administrative user ID and password when configuring WebSphere to manage HTTP Server (Steps 18–21 for the remote plug-in).

Unix note: On Unix machines, make sure file plugin-cfg.xml has permission for the WebSphere admin console user to overwrite the file. To do so, open a command prompt, go to the directory where the file is available, and issue the command **chmod 666 plugin-cfg.xml.**

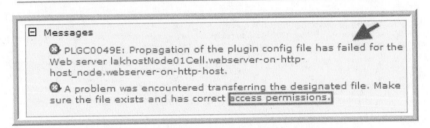

Figure 6-34: Problem transferring the plug-in file

If you receive error "PLGC0049E — Could not make a connection to the node agent or IBM HTTP Server administration server" (Figure 6-35) after clicking the **Propagate Plug-in** button, check the following:

■ Make sure you can successfully ping the Web server node from the WebSphere node.

■ Make sure HTTP Admin Server is started on the remote Web server node.

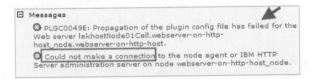

Figure 6-35: Problem connecting to HTTP Admin Server

If the Web server status on the admin console is always shown as "stopped" even though both HTTP Server and HTTP Admin Server are started on the Web server machine, check the following:

- Click the Web server definition, and make sure the host name and port specified for the Web server node (Figure 6-36) are correct. Also make sure you can ping the Web server using the **Host name** entry.

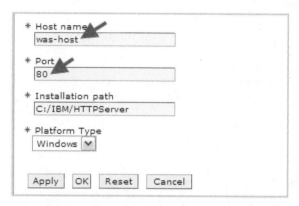

Figure 6-36: Verifying Web server host name and port

Logging During Plug-in Propagation

The following log files provide more information about problems related to propagating the plug-in file to the Web server from the WebSphere admin console.

- On the WebSphere node:
    - › \<PROFILE-ROOT>\logs\server1\SystemOut.log
    - › \<PROFILE-ROOT>\logs\server1\trace.log

- On the HTTP Server (with plug-in) node:
    - › \<IHSV6-ROOT>\logs\admin_error.log
    - › \<IHSV6-ROOT>\logs\admin_access.log

Follow the instructions in the "Verify Installation from the Browser" section above to verify the plug-in configuration after propagating the plug-in file. If you have problems verifying the configuration using the browser, refer to "Logging: Problem Determination and Troubleshooting."

Logging: Problem Determination and Troubleshooting

The destination of the log files created for the plug-in fall logically into three categories based on the activity performed on the plug-in. The diagram in Figure 6-37 illustrates the plug-in logging architecture, and Table 6-2 explains the three categories.

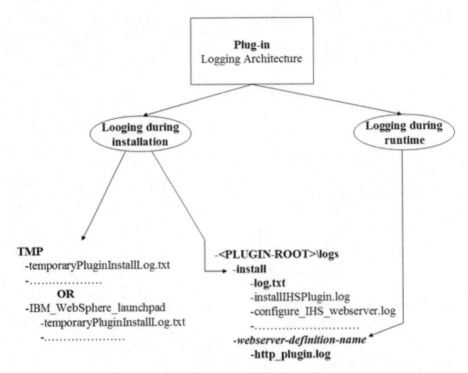

Figure 6-37: HTTP plug-in for WebSphere V6 logging architecture

Table 6-2: Plug-in logging activities

Activity	Log destination	Description	When to use these log files
Installation – initial part	The TMP directory ▪ File temporaryPluginInstallLog.txt is the important log file under this destination. ▪ If you started the installation using the Launchpad program, you'll find the log files under the TMP directory's IBM_WebSphere_launchpad subdirectory.	These log files are populated immediately after you invoke the Launchpad or install.exe program. After a successful installation, the files are copied to the logs\install subdirectory of the installation directory (<PLUGIN-ROOT>).	▪ Use if you have a problem starting the Launchpad or install.exe or encounter problems during the early part of the installation. ▪ Use if the system prerequisites check fails and you want to see the reason.

Table 6-2: Plug-in logging activities (continued)

Activity	Log destination	Description	When to use these log files
Installation – initial part (continued)	■ If you used install.exe, the log files are created immediately under the TMP directory. ■ On Windows systems, check the TMP environment variable for the TMP value (C:\temp in the examples). ■ On Unix, the temporary directory is usually /tmp.		
Installation – later part	The <PLUGIN-ROOT>\logs\install directory ■ File log.txt is the important log file under this destination. ■ Other log files here are masterConfiguration Log.txt, installIHSPlugin.log, configure_IHS_web server.log, and installGSKit.log.	■ These logs files are populated from the moment you click Next after reviewing the summary report during the graphical installation. ■ File log.txt records all installation events and indicates whether installation was successful. ■ File masterConfigurationLog.txt records all configuration events. ■ File installIHSPlugin.log records the events during installation of the IBM HTTP Server plug-in. If you're installing the plug-in for a different Web server, this file name will be different. ■ File configure_IHS_web-server.log records the events during configuration of the IBM HTTP Server plug-in. If you're installing the plug-in for a different Web server, this file name will be different. ■ File installGSKit.log records the events during installation of the Global Security Kit.	Use if the installation fails or was partially successful. If these log files don't provide enough information, see the log files under the TMP directory.

Table 6-2: Plug-in logging activities (continued)

Activity	Log destination	Description	When to use these log files
Runtime (invoking dynamic content that goes through the plug-in module — servlets, Java Server Pages, and so on)	The <PLUGIN-ROOT>\logs\web-server-definition-name directory ▪ The log file under this directory is http_plugin.log.	File http_plugin.log is the place where the plug-in module records information about the content it has processed, as well as diagnostic and error information. The level of logging depends on the value set for the LogLevel parameter in the plug-in file (plugin-cfg.xml). The default value is "error". Set LogLevel to "trace" if the default logging information isn't sufficient to troubleshoot the problem. After resolving the issue, make sure you reset LogLevel to "error". Other valid LogLevel values are ▪ "stats" — to record load balancing information and information about the server that processed the request ▪ "warn" — to record all warning and error messages during request processing You must restart the HTTP server or wait for the amount of time (in seconds) specified by the plug-in file's RefreshInterval parameter for a new LogLevel value to take effect.	▪ Use if you have trouble starting or stopping HTTP Server or encounter problems during the HTTP Server runtime after plug-in installation. ▪ Use if you want to record the dynamic content that is processed through the plug-in module. ▪ To record the most detailed level of information in the http_plugin.log file, set LogLevel="trace" in the plug-in file (plugin-cfg.xml).

Problem Scenarios

Before we look at some problem scenarios and their solutions, examine the diagram in Figure 6-38 to understand the logging that takes place for the components involved in serving dynamic content (HTTP server, the plug-in, and WebSphere Application Server). If you encounter problems after installing the plug-in module on the HTTP Server node, consult the appropriate log file or files based on the problem's symptoms.

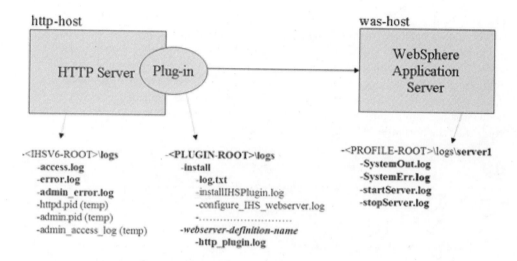

Figure 6-38: Logging of components involved in serving dynamic content

Problem: *You have a problem starting HTTP Server after successfully installing and configuring the plug-in module. (The installation log file, log.txt, indicates that the plug-in installation was successful.)*

Using your favorite editor, open the Web server configuration file (httpd.conf) under the <IHSV6-ROOT>\conf directory, and scroll to the end of the file. Comment out (using #) the lines that were added during the plug-in installation (refer back to Figure 6-13 to see these lines), save the file, and restart HTTP Server.

If you have problems starting HTTP Server after commenting out the plug-in information in file httpd.conf, the problem isn't with the plug-in configuration. Consult Chapter 5 for information about troubleshooting HTTP Server.

If HTTP Server starts successfully, there's something wrong with the plug-in configuration. Take the following steps to determine the problem's cause:

1. Open file httpd.conf again and uncomment the lines you just commented. Save the file, and restart HTTP Server. Unless the problem is an intermittent one, you should again have a problem starting HTTP Server.

2. Open file http_plugin.log in the <PLUGIN-ROOT>\logs*webserver-definition-name* directory, and look for errors related to the plug-in module during its startup.

Figure 6-39 shows a sample http_plugin.log file. The errors shown indicate that the HTTP Server node is having a problem pinging the WebSphere node. In this case, we either forgot to add a DNS entry on the HTTP Server machine for the WebSphere node or didn't update the hosts file with the WebSphere machine's fully qualified host name. In our environment, after updating the hosts file under the WINDOWS\system32\drivers\etc directory on the HTTP Server machine with the fully qualified name of the WebSphere node (was-host.noyb.com), we could successfully restart HTTP Server. (On Windows NT, you'll find the hosts file under the WINNT directory. On Unix, it is under directory /etc.)

```
http_plugin.log - Notepad

File  Edit  Format  View  Help

[Mon Feb 14 14:56:16 2005] 00000b00 00002d40 - ERROR: ws_transport:
transportSetServerAddress: Failed to resolve address [was-host@noyb.com] and port
[9080], error 11001
[Mon Feb 14 14:56:16 2005] 00000b00 00002d40 - ERROR: ws_server: serverAddTransport:
Failed to initialize server address
[Mon Feb 14 14:56:16 2005] 00000b00 00002d40 - ERROR: lib_sxp: sxpParse: End element
returned FALSE for Transport. line 14 of |
C:\IBM\webSphere\AppServer\profiles\default\config\cells\lakhostNode01cell\nodes\webserv
er-on-was-host_node\servers\webserver-on-was-host\plugin-cfg.xml
[Mon Feb 14 14:56:16 2005] 00000b00 00002d40 - ERROR: ws_config_parser:
configParserParse: Failed to parse the config file
C:\IBM\webSphere\AppServer\profiles\default\config\cells\lakhostNode01cell\nodes\webserv
er-on-was-host_node\servers\webserver-on-was-host\plugin-cfg.xml
[Mon Feb 14 14:56:16 2005] 00000b00 00002d40 - ERROR: ws_common: websphereUpdateConfig:
Failed parsing the plugin config file
[Mon Feb 14 14:56:16 2005] 00000b00 00002d40 - ERROR: ws_common: websphereInit: Failed
to load the config file
[Mon Feb 14 14:56:16 2005] 00000b00 00002d40 - ERROR: mod_was_ap20_http: as_init: unable
to initialize websphere
```

Figure 6-39: Plug-in log indicating problem pinging was-host from http-host

Problem: *You have trouble invoking the snoop servlet (http://http-host/snoop in a remote plug-in configuration or http://was-host/snoop in a local plug-in configuration) through HTTP Server after successfully installing the plug-in.*

Follow the instructions in this chapter to verify the installation from the browser. In a remote plug-in configuration, make sure you can ping the HTTP Server node and the WebSphere node from each other using the IP address, host name, and fully qualified name (DNS entry).

If you're trying to connect through the Web browser from a remote machine other than the HTTP Server or WebSphere node, make sure you can ping the HTTP Server machine from the system on which the browser was instantiated using the IP address, host name, and fully qualified name (DNS entry).

Problem: *You have trouble invoking the snoop servlet through HTTP Server after successfully generating and propagating the plug-in file. Figure 6-40 shows this error.*

Figure 6-40: Snoop servlet error

Make sure you applied the plug-in fix pack that matches the fix pack level of the application server (or Deployment Manager). If the plug-in is at a lower fix pack, the generated and propagated plug-in file may not contain entries for the enterprise applications.

If you need to apply a new fix pack to the plug-in:

1. Delete the Web server definition and node using the instructions (given later) in the uninstallation section this chapter.

2. Apply the fix pack on the plug-in.

3. Rerun the Web server definition batch file.

4. Generate and propagate the plug-in file.

5. Restart the Web server.

6. Test the snoop servlet again.

Also, make sure the directory path where the plug-in file is generated/propagated is the same as the path indicated in the <IHSV6-ROOT>\conf\httpd.conffile. Make the appropriate changes in file httpd.conf if required. The message shown in Figure 6-41 indicates that the plug-in (a local plug-in) was generated under the <DMGR-PROFILE-ROOT> \ . . . \ directory, whereas httpd.conf (on HTTP Server) is reading the plug-in file from the <PLUGIN-ROOT>\ . . . \ directory, as shown in Figure 6-42.

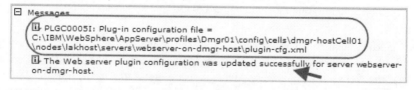

Figure 6-41: Location of the plug-in file generated from the WebSphere admin console

Figure 6-42: Location of the plug-in file configured in HTTP Server's httpd.conf file

Configuring Multiple Web Servers with Multiple Application Server Profiles

With the installation experience you've gained in this and the preceding chapters, you have all the knowledge you need to set up a WebSphere environment consisting of multiple Web servers and multiple application servers. Here's a rundown of the steps involved in this configuration.

Step 1.   Install and create an application server profile by following the instructions given in Chapter 3. If you install WebSphere using the Base or Express package, the name of the default profile is 'default'. If you install WebSphere and create an application server profile (standalone server) using the Network Deployment package, the name of the default profile is 'AppSrv01'. Verify installation of the application server as described in Chapter 3.

Step 2.   Install HTTP Server by following the instructions in Chapter 5. Verify installation of HTTP Server as described in that chapter.

Step 3.   If your Web server is local to the WebSphere node, follow the instructions in this chapter to install the HTTP Server local plug-in for WebSphere. If your Web server is remote to the WebSphere node, follow the instructions to install the HTTP Server remote plug-in for WebSphere. Verify the plug-in installation by following the appropriate sections of this chapter.

        After successfully completing the preceding steps, your architecture will look like the illustration in Figure 6-43.

Step 4.   Now, create a second profile, 'AppSrv01', by following the instructions from the appropriate section of Chapter 3. (If you create the second profile using the Network Deployment package, its default name is 'AppSrv02'.) *Important note:* Don't forget to make this profile the default profile when

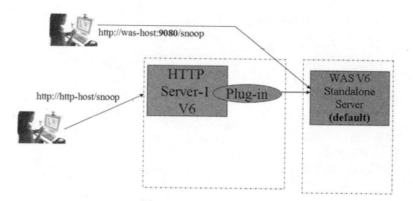

Figure 6-43: WebSphere environment with a single HTTP Server (with plug-in) and application server

you create it (as shown on the panel in Figure 6-44). Only the default profile can be configured with HTTP Server during the plug-in installation (through the configure*webserver-definition-name*.bat, or .sh, script). If the profile isn't the default profile, you'll need to configure the Web server definition manually from the administrative console.

Verify creation of the second application server profile as described in Chapter 3.

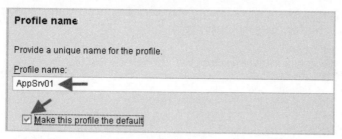

Figure 6-44: Creating the second profile as the default profile

Step 5. Log in to the WebSphere admin console. Expand **Environment,** and select **Virtual hosts|default host|Host Aliases**. As you can see from the window shown in Figure 6-45, the new profile is configured to receive requests from port 80 (along with ports 9081 and 9444). However, we want to configure this profile to receive requests from a second HTTP Server (through plug-in) whose HTTP port is 81 (not 80). To make this change:

a. Click * in the Host Name column for port 80 to display the host's properties.
b. Under General Properties (Figure 6-46), change the **Port** value to 81.

c. Click **OK,** and save the configuration.

d. Restart the application server profile (AppSrv01).

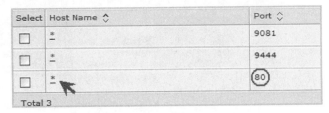

Select	Host Name ◇	Port ◇
☐	* —	9081
☐	* —	9444
☐	* —	80
Total 3		

Figure 6-45: Host configured to receive requests from port 80

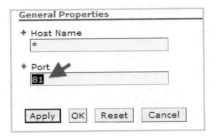

Figure 6-46: Changing the port value

After successfully completing the preceding steps, your architecture will look like the illustration in Figure 6-47.

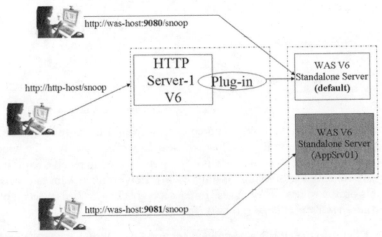

Figure 6-47: WebSphere environment with a single HTTP Server (with plug-in) and multiple application servers

Step 6.   Install a second HTTP Server by following Chapter 5's instructions for installing and configuring multiple HTTP Servers on the same machine. Verify installation of the second HTTP Server as described in that chapter.

After successfully completing the preceding steps, your architecture will look like the illustration in Figure 6-48.

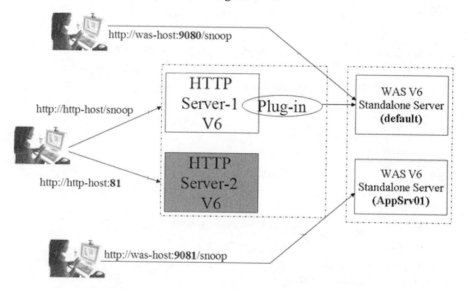

Figure 6-48: WebSphere environment with multiple HTTP Servers and application servers

Step 7.   If your Web server is *local* to the WebSphere node, create a second plug-in by following this chapter's instructions for installing a local plug-in. Take note of the following important changes:

- Substitute <IHSV6-ROOT2> for <IHSV6-ROOT> when you install the second plug-in to install the plug-in on the second HTTP Server.

- You're going to use the same plug-in binary files for both HTTP Servers, so specify the same plug-in installation directory (<PLUGIN-ROOT>) you used before. Figure 6-49 shows the panel where you specify this directory.

- When specifying the Web server configuration file, make sure you select httpd.conf from the second HTTP Server (under <IHSV6-ROOT2>\conf), and change the Web server port to 81 (Figure 6-50).

- Assign a meaningful and distinct name for the second Web server definition (Figure 6-51).

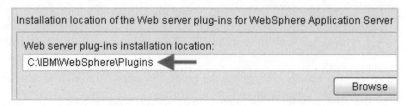

Figure 6-49: Specifying the second plug-in installation directory

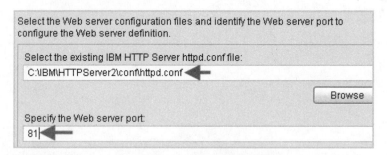

Figure 6-50: Specifying the second Web server configuration file

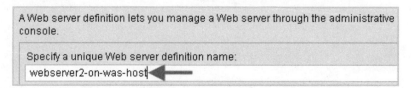

Figure 6-51: Naming the second Web server definition

If your Web server is *remote* to the WebSphere node, create a second plug-in by following this chapter's instructions for installing a local plug-in. Take note of the following important changes:

- Substitute <IHSV6-ROOT2> for <IHSV6-ROOT> to install the second plug-in on the second HTTP Server.

- Create an administrative user ID and password for the second HTTP Server.

- Configure the second WebSphere application server profile (AppSrv01) to include the second HTTP Server definition.

- Configure the second WebSphere application server profile to manage the second HTTP Server through HTTP Admin Server from the WebSphere admin console.

- Generate the plug-in file, and propagate it to the remote Web server from the admin console.

- Consult the sections "Troubleshooting Problems Propagating the Plug-in File" and "Logging During Plug-in Propagation" above if you have problems propagating the plug-in file.

- Verify installation of the plug-in by following the appropriate sections of this chapter.

After successfully completing the preceding steps, your architecture will look like the illustration in Figure 6-52.

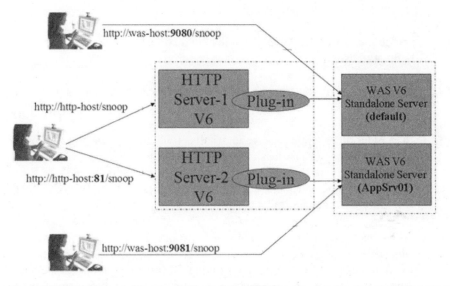

Figure 6-52: WebSphere environment with multiple HTTP Servers, plug-ins, and application servers

Backup and Recovery

No special commands exist for backing up the configuration of the WebSphere HTTP plug-in. If you have no constraints on disk space, the easiest way to back up the plug-in environment is to stop the HTTP Server and HTTP Admin Server processes and a make copy of the entire <PLUGIN-ROOT> directory.

If you've created SSL key files using the IBM Key Management utility and stored them in the <PLUGIN-ROOT>\etc directory or any subdirectory of <PLUGIN-ROOT>, make a backup of that directory.

Uninstalling the Plug-in

The uninstall command removes the plug-in, as well as its configuration information, from the system. To uninstall a local or remote plug-in, take the following steps.

Step 1.   Log in as a member of the Administrators group.

Unix note: On Unix systems, log in as root.

Step 2.   Before invoking the uninstallation process, make sure the Web server (HTTP Server in our case) is stopped. If WebSphere and/or any other Java process is running on this machine, stop it.

Step 3.   Go to the <PLUGIN-ROOT>_uninstPlugin directory, and double-click **uninstall.exe**.

Step 4.   Click **Next** until you see a panel reporting a successful uninstallation. Then click **Finish** to exit the uninstall wizard.

Step 5.   The uninstall program logs the uninstall activities in various log files under the <PLUGIN-ROOT>\logs\uninstall directory. File log.txt is the key file here. To verify the uninstallation, open this file, scroll to the end, and make sure the last line indicates, by the presence of the INSTCONFSUCCESS indicator, that the uninstallation was successful.

If you have problems during the uninstallation, review the log files in the uninstall directory, and examine file temporaryPluginUninstallLog.txt in the TMP directory. Also, verify that the uninstall script has commented out (as shown in Figure 6-53) the two lines representing the location and name of the plug-in module and plug-in file (plugin-cfg.xml) in the HTTP Server configuration file (httpd.conf). (Once the plug-in is successfully uninstalled, HTTP Server won't start if you uncomment these lines.)

```
#</VirtualHost>

#LoadModule was_ap20_module "C:\IBM\WebSphere\Plugins\bin\mod_was_ap20_http.dll"
#WebSpherePluginConfig "C:\IBM\WebSphere\AppServer\profiles\default\config\cells
```

Figure 6-53: Lines commented out by uninstall script

Step 6.   Delete directory <PLUGIN-ROOT>. (The uninstall program doesn't delete the installation directory entirely. You must delete it manually.)

Unconfiguring the Web Server Definition from the Application Server

If you've configured WebSphere to run with the Web server's definition in order to manage the Web server through the WebSphere admin console, you need to "unconfigure" the Web server's definition from the application server after uninstalling the plug-in. To do so, take this next group of steps.

Step 7.   Start WebSphere Application Server.

Step 8.   Make a note of the Web server definition name you provided when you installed the plug-in (webserver-on-was-host in our example). To see this name, log in to the WebSphere admin console, expand **Servers**, click **Web Servers**, and look for the Web server definition name in the list of Web servers.

             You'll also need the node name for the Web server in the WebSphere repository. You can derive this name by adding **_node** to the end of the Web server definition name (e.g., webserver_on_was_ host_node). You can also see the node name in the admin console by viewing the list of Web servers.

Step 9.   Open a command prompt, navigate to the <WASV6-ROOT>\bin directory, and issue the command **wsadmin** to connect to the default application server you configured with the HTTP Server plug-in for WebSphere.

Step 10.   To remove the Web server's definition from the WebSphere repository, issue the following command:

```
$AdminTask deleteServer { -serverName webserver-name -nodeName
webserver-name_node }
```

Step 11.   To remove the Web server's node from the WebSphere repository, issue this command:

```
$AdminTask removeUnmanagedNode { -nodeName webserver-name_node }
```

Note: In a WebSphere Network Deployment environment, you can perform the preceding two steps (removing the Web server definition and node) from the Deployment Manager's admin console. Navigate to **Servers|Web servers** to delete the Web server. Navigate to **System Administration|Nodes** to delete the Web server node.

Step 12.   Save the configuration you modified, and exit the wsadmin prompt:

```
$AdminConfig save
exit
```

Figure 6-54 shows the commands to perform the preceding three steps for the plug-in in our example.

```
Command Prompt - wsadmin

C:\IBM\WebSphere\AppServer\bin>wsadmin
WASX7209I: Connected to process "server1" on node lakhostNode01 using SOAP connector;
 The type of process is: UnManagedProcess
WASX7029I: For help, enter: "$Help help"
wsadmin>$AdminTask deleteServer { -serverName webserver-on-was-host -nodeName webserver-on-was-host_node

wsadmin>$AdminTask removeUnmanagedNode { -nodeName webserver-on-was-host_node }

wsadmin>$AdminConfig save
```

Figure 6-54: Removing the Web server definition and node

Step 13.   Now, log in to the WebSphere admin console again, expand **Servers**, and click **Web Servers**. Verify that the Web server definition no longer appears in the list of Web servers. If you plan to reinstall the plug-in, reboot the Windows machine before starting your installation again.

Silent Installation of the WebSphere HTTP Plug-in

You'll find that the process of silently installing the HTTP plug-in for WebSphere is similar to the other silent installation procedures we've covered. Let's step through the process for a sample local plug-in installation.

Step 1.   Log in as a member of the Administrators group with rights to act as part of the operating system and log on as a service. Silent installation will fail unless the user has these rights, even if the user is a member of the Administrators group. Restart the machine after granting these rights and before starting the silent installation.

Unix note: On Unix systems, log in as root. If necessary, run **umask 022** to set permissions for the temporary directory. To verify the present setting, run **umask.**

Step 2.   Create a temporary directory (e.g., plugin-silent-install), and copy into it the file responsefile.txt from the plug-in installation package (usually located under the plugin directory). Give the file a meaningful name (e.g., httphost-plugin.responsefile.txt).

Step 3. Using your favorite editor, open the response file and take a look at its entries. You're going to customize each line of this file to silently install the plug-in the same way you did in the wizard-based installation.

Step 4. First, edit the file to accept the terms of the license agreement:

```
-W silentInstallLicenseAcceptance.value="true"
```

Step 5. Next, set the install type to "local" to indicate you want to install a local plug-in:

```
-P pluginSettings.installType="local"
```

Step 6. Set the plug-in installation directory to C:\IBM\WebSphere\Plugins (the default Windows install location):

```
-P pluginProductBean.installLocation="C:\IBM\WebSphere\Plugins"
```

Step 7. For the wasExistingLocation parameter, specify the WebSphere installation directory (WASV6-ROOT). (The installation program ignores this parameter if the silent installation is for a remote plug-in.)

```
-W websphereLocationWizardBean.wasExistingLocation="C:\IBM\WebSphere\
AppServer"
```

Step 8. Next, specify the Web server you want to configure with the plug-in. For IBM HTTP Server, use the value "ihs" as shown in Figure 6-55. As you can see in the figure, the comments section for the Web server option provides the values to use for other Web servers.

```
# Web server to configure
#
# valid options
# : none        Install binaries only.  No web server configuration.
# : ihs         IBM HTTP Server V6
# : apache      Apache web Server v2
# : domino5     Lotus Domino web Server V5 (supported on HP-UX)
# : domino6     Lotus Domino Web Server V6 or V6.5 (not supported on HP-UX)
# : sunone      Sun ONE web Server 6.0 or Sun Java System web Server V6.1
# : iis5        Microsoft Internet Information Services V5 (supported on Windows)
# : iis6        Microsoft Internet Information Services V6 (supported on Windows)
#
# Note  : Specify only one web server to configure.
#
-P pluginSettings.webServerSelected="ihs"
```

Figure 6-55: Specifying the Web server to configure with the plug-in

Step 9.   Next (Figure 6-56), specify the location and name of the Web server configuration file. For HTTP Server, this file (httpd.conf) is located under the <IHSV6-ROOT>\conf directory. You'll find the configuration file names for other Web servers in the comments section for this option.

```
##########################################################################
#
# web server Configuration File 1
#
# valid options for web server configuration file 1
#
#                ihs              : httpd.conf
#                apache           : httpd.conf
#                domino5          : Notes.jar
#                domino6          : Notes.jar
#                sunone           : obj.conf
#
#  Note : File must exist
#
-P pluginSettings.webServerConfigFile1="C:\IBM\HTTPServer\conf\httpd.conf"
```

Figure 6-56: Specifying the configuration file

Step 10.   The next option, Web server Configuration File 2, doesn't apply for HTTP Server, so simply leave the default value ("").

```
-P pluginSettings.webServerConfigFile2=""
```

Step 11.   Next, specify the port number of the HTTP server. The default is port 80.

```
-P pluginSettings.portNumber="80"
```

Step 12.   Comment out (using the # character) the next parameter, Domino 6 User ID. This option is specific to the Domino 6 server; IBM HTTP Server V6 doesn't use this parameter.

```
#-W domino6UserIDPanel.userID="notes"
```

Step 13.   Specify a name for the Web server definition that will be created in the plug-in and WebSphere configuration repositories. (No spaces are permitted in the Web server definition name.)

```
-P pluginSettings.webServerDefinition="webserver-on-was-host"
```

Step 14.   Next (Figure 6-57), specify the location of the plug-in file (plugin-cfg.xml). As noted in the comments section, it's recommended to leave the default value ("") and let the installation program decide the location at install time.

```
# plugin-cfg.xml File Location
#
# This file will be generated by the plugin installer.
#
# Valid options:
#  ""  : leaving the string empty will result in installer generating the plugin-cfg.xml
#         file location at install time and configuring web server to use this location.
#         This is the recommended option.
#
#  "<file_location>" : User may enter an existing file location.  web server will be
#         configured to use this existing plugin-cfg.xml file location.
#         If file is specified, it must exist, otherwise install will not proceed.
#
-P pluginSettings.pluginCfgXmlLocation=""
```

Figure 6-57: Specifying the plug-in file location

Step 15.   Specify the host name of the application server:

   -P pluginSettings.wasMachineHostName="was-host"

Step 16.   Set the next option (Figure 6-58) to "true" to map all existing applications to the Web server.

```
# Advanced User Options available in silent installs only
#
# Map all the existing deployed applications to the web server.
#
# Valid options
# true :  Web server Definition is mapped as a target to the existing deployed
#          applications such as snoop and hitcount (Recommended)
# false : No applications are mapped to the web server definition.
#
# Note : If not set to a valid option of true or false, the installer will
#         set to true and continue install.
-P pluginSettings.mapWebserverToApplications="true"
```

Figure 6-58: Mapping existing applications to the Web server

Step 17.   For the next (and final) option, the host name of the Web server, keep the default value (""):

   -P pluginSettings.webServerHostName=""

Step 18.   Now, scroll to the beginning of the response file, and view the instructions for running the silent install program. Then save the file, and exit the editor.

Step 19.   Open a command-line prompt, and go to the directory where the install.exe program for HTTP Server is available (the same directory from which you copied the responsefile.txt file, usually the IHS directory).

Step 20.   Run the silent install command, substituting the path to your response file:

```
install.exe -options "path-to-response-file" -silent
```

Step 21.   Open file ihsv6_install.log under <IHSV6-ROOT>, and scroll to the end of the file. If you see the INSTCONFSUCCESS indicator, the plug-in installation was successful.

Step 22.   Verify the silent install of the plug-in using the same steps you followed to verify the graphical installation.

7

WebSphere V6 Network Deployment Package: Install, Create, Verify, and Manage

In this chapter, we install the Network Deployment package of WebSphere Application Server V6 and then create, verify, and manage a deployment manager, application server, and custom profile. You should consider this chapter an extension to Chapter 3, where you learned to install, configure, and verify a standalone application server. We'll be referencing that chapter to perform many of the steps described here. (To install an application server using the WebSphere V6 Base/Express package, follow Chapter 3's instructions.)

Figure 7-1 illustrates the components created when you install the Network Deployment package. As a result of the installation, the product binaries and profile templates necessary to create any of three profile types are created:

- application server profile
- deployment manager profile
- custom profile

For the Network Deployment package, the installation process only copies the product binaries to the installation directory, <WASV6-ROOT> (installation Phase 1). No profiles are created during the installation. You must use the Profile Creation wizard or the wasprofile command-line utility to create any of the three profiles (Phase 2). As you learned in Chapter 3, Phase 1 and Phase 2 are performed automatically for you during installation when you use the WebSphere Base or Express package. These two packages support only an application server profile, which is created during the installation itself.

For more information about the architecture of profiles and the relationship between a profile template and a profile, see Chapter 1.

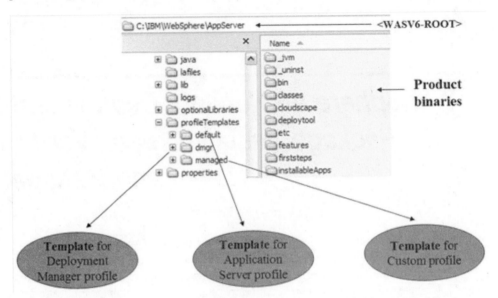

Figure 7-1: Components created after installation of the Network Deployment package

Install WebSphere V6 Network Deployment Package: Product Binaries

The flow chart in Figure 7-2 depicts the high-level steps required to install and verify the Network Deployment software. In this section, we step you through each part of this process. As in previous chapters, the instructions assume you're working in a Windows XP environment. If you're using a Unix operating system, you'll need to execute the appropriate commands for your operating system (i.e., .sh instead of .bat) and substitute the forward slash (/) for the backward slash (\) in directory and path names.

Table 7-1 lists, by operating system, the default directory locations for the symbolic references used in this chapter.

In this chapter and the one that follows, we assume you're using multiple machines (dmgr-host, was-host1, washost-2, custom-host, and http-host) to perform the steps to create a WebSphere V6 cluster environment. If you're going through the exercises for educational purposes only and want to simulate all the steps on the same machine

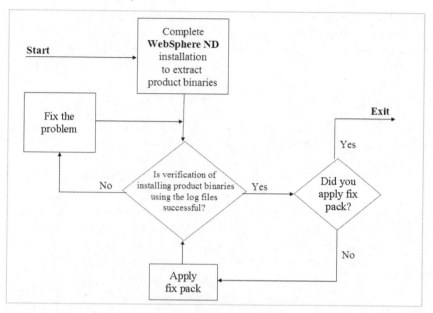

Figure 7-2: Network Deployment installation overview

Table 7-1: Directory locations for symbolic references

Symbolic reference	Windows	AIX	Linux/Unix
<WASV6-ROOT>	C:\IBM\WebSphere\AppServer	/usr/WebSphere/AppServer	/opt/WebSphere/AppServer
<DMGR-PROFILE-ROOT>	<WASV6-ROOT>\profiles\Dmgr01	<WASV6-ROOT>/profiles/Dmgr01	<WASV6-ROOT>/profiles/Dmgr01
<PROFILE-ROOT>	<WASV6-ROOT>\profiles\AppSrv01	<WASV6-ROOT>/profiles/AppSrv01	<WASV6-ROOT>/profiles/AppSrv01
<CUSTOM-PROFILE-ROOT>	<WASV6-ROOT>\profiles\Custom01	<WASV6-ROOT>/profiles/Custom01	<WASV6-ROOT>/profiles/Custom01

(assuming your system has enough resources to handle multiple JVM processes), you can do so by providing host name aliases of logical machines in your system's etc\hosts file. To do so, open the file in an editor, and enter the host names we use next to your machine's IP address, as Figure 7-3 shows. You may need to manually adjust port numbers during the installation process because you can't use the default port numbers for all the profiles. In preparing the instructions for this book, we didn't test running the whole environment on a single machine, so consider this note a hint only, and proceed at your own risk.

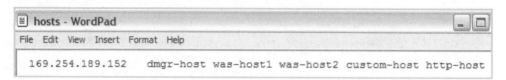

Figure 7-3: Editing the etc\hosts file to provide host name aliases

Step 1.   Figure 7-4 shows how the directory structure looks after downloading the Network Deployment package and extracting the files to a temporary directory. If you have this software on CD (i.e., a licensed version), mount the CD and change to the directory where the Launchpad program is available.

Name ▲	Size	Type	Date Modified
AppClient		File Folder	12/9/2004 3:56 PM
DataDirect		File Folder	12/9/2004 3:55 PM
GSKit		File Folder	3/12/2005 10:05 A
IHS		File Folder	12/9/2004 3:56 PM
JDK		File Folder	12/9/2004 3:55 PM
launchpad		File Folder	3/21/2005 11:09 A
migration		File Folder	12/9/2004 3:55 PM
plugin		File Folder	12/9/2004 3:56 PM
WAS		File Folder	12/9/2004 3:55 PM
autorun.inf	1 KB	Setup Information	11/9/2004 7:08 PM
Copyright.txt	1 KB	Text Document	11/9/2004 6:40 PM
launchpad.bat	13 KB	MS-DOS Batch File	11/9/2004 7:08 PM

Address: C:\Documents and Settings\Administrator\Desktop\was6-installs\nd

Figure 7-4: Directory structure for Network Deployment installation

Step 2.   Make sure the TMP environment variable is set appropriately. To do so, log in as a member of the Administrators group, right-click **My Computer** on the desktop, and select **Properties|Advanced|Environment Variables**. In the "User variables for user" list, note the value set for the temporary directory (TMP). If you don't see variable TMP in the list, click **New** to add it. For this example, we'll assume a TMP value of C:\temp.

> **Unix note:** On Unix systems, log in as root. If necessary, run the command **umask 022** to set permissions for the temporary directory (usually /tmp). To verify the current umask setting, run **umask.**

Step 3.   Make sure at least 830 MB of disk space is available to install the Network Deployment product (730 MB for the <WASV6-ROOT> directory and 100 MB for the TMP directory). You also need space for the profiles you'll create after the installation:

- a minimum of 200 MB (with sample applications) for the application server profile (<PROFILE-ROOT>) and 40 MB for the TMP directory

- a minimum of 30 MB for the deployment manager profile (<DMGR-PROFILE-ROOT>) and 40 MB for the TMP directory

- a minimum of 10 MB for the custom profile (<CUSTOM-PROFILE-ROOT>) and 40 MB for the TMP directory

> **Unix note:** Make sure the file systems mounted on the installation and temporary directories meet the minimum disk space requirements of 730 MB and 100 MB, respectively.

Step 4.   In the directory where the Launchpad program is available, double-click **launchpad.bat** to begin the installation. (As an alternative, you can invoke **install.exe** under the WAS directory.) The install program immediately begins logging information about installation activities under the TMP directory. For more information about this logging, see the "Logging During Installation of Product Binaries" section of this chapter.

> **Unix note:** Before running the installation wizard on Unix systems, make sure you can execute the **xclock** or **xeyes** command to display a graphical image properly. For more information about these commands, see Chapter 3.

Step 5.   Read through the information on the WebSphere welcome panel, and select the option to "Launch the installation wizard for WebSphere Application Server." On the resulting welcome panel, click **Next**.

Step 6.   Accept the terms of the license agreement, and click **Next**.

Step 7.   The installation wizard now performs a system prerequisites check. If the wizard reports a successful check, click **Next**. If the check fails, cancel the installation program, and open and read log file log.txt in the TMP directory. For more information about this log, see "Logging During Installation of Product Binaries." Correct the system to meet the prerequisites, and run the installation program again.

If the wizard detects an existing WebSphere V6 installation, you'll see the panel shown in Figure 7-5. Read the information on the panel, select the option to "Install a new copy of the V6 Application Server product," and click **Next**.

Note: If you previously installed WebSphere using the Base or Express package and want to upgrade to the Network Deployment package or add features to the existing product, select this panel's option to "Add features to an existing copy of the V6 Application Server product" and specify the installation directory (<WASV6-ROOT>) of the existing product.

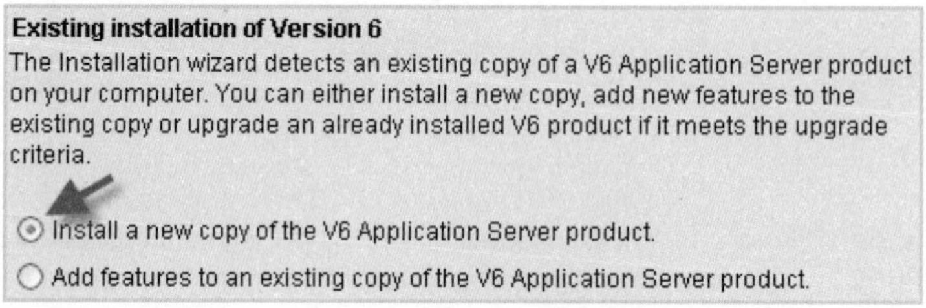

Existing installation of Version 6
The Installation wizard detects an existing copy of a V6 Application Server product on your computer. You can either install a new copy, add new features to the existing copy or upgrade an already installed V6 product if it meets the upgrade criteria.

⊙ Install a new copy of the V6 Application Server product.

◯ Add features to an existing copy of the V6 Application Server product.

Figure 7-5: Existing WebSphere V6 installation detected

Step 8.   Next (Figure 7-6), specify the installation directory for the application server. For Windows, make sure whatever directory name you use contains no spaces. For this example, we'll use C:\IBM\WebSphere\AppServer as the installation directory. (Hereafter, we refer to this directory as <WASV6-ROOT>.) Click **Next**.

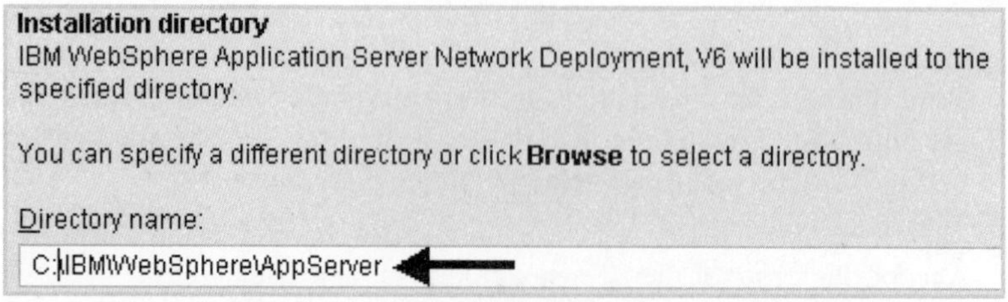

Installation directory
IBM WebSphere Application Server Network Deployment, V6 will be installed to the specified directory.

You can specify a different directory or click **Browse** to select a directory.

Directory name:

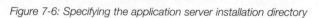

C:\IBM\WebSphere\AppServer

Figure 7-6: Specifying the application server installation directory

Step 9.   If you're performing this installation for educational or training purposes, leave the **Application Server Samples** check box, shown in Figure 7-7, selected. These sample WebSphere applications demonstrate the functionality of the application server. For production and test environments, we recommend you *don't* install the samples. You can install them later if you like by adding features to the existing installation (a process we cover later in this chapter). Note that the default application (DefaultApplication), which you'll use later to verify the basic operation of the application server, will be installed even if you choose not to install the Application Server Samples.

When you're finished with this panel, click **Next**.

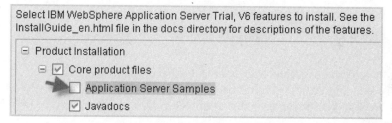

Figure 7-7: Application Server Samples option

Step 10.   The wizard next displays a preinstallation summary panel. Review the information on the panel, and click **Next** to proceed. You'll see a progress panel while the installation program extracts files and installs components.

You'll notice that the installation program creates the installation directory (<WASV6-ROOT>) at this point and begins logging information under the directory <WASV6-ROOT>\logs. For more information about this logging, see "Logging During Installation of Product Binaries."

Step 11.   When a panel reporting a successful installation appears, select the option to "Launch the Profile creation wizard," and click **Finish**.

Step 12.   Before you start creating profiles, you should verify that the product binaries were installed properly. To do so, open file log.txt under the <WASV6-ROOT>\logs directory (C:\IBM\WebSphere\AppServer\logs in this example), and scroll to the end of the file. If you see the indicator INSTCONFSUC-CESS (as shown in Figure 7-8), the product binaries were installed successfully. If you see INSTCONFFAIL or INSTCONFPARTIALSUCCESS, problems occurred during the installation. For troubleshooting information, see "Logging During Installation of Product Binaries."

```
com.ibm.ws.install.ni.ismp.actions.ISMPComponentizedFileRepositoryDeployAction, msg1,
Processing component: security.xml
(Mar 21, 2005 11:24:03 AM), Install,
com.ibm.ws.install.ni.ismp.actions.ISMPConfigManagerLaunchAction, msg1,
INSTCONFSUCCESS: Post-installation configuration is successful.
```

Figure 7-8: Successful installation of product binaries confirmed

Step 13.   Apply the latest refresh pack and/or fix pack for WebSphere. For step-by-step instructions on how to install updates, see Chapter 19. Return to this chapter for instructions on verification, problem determination, and maintenance.

WebSphere Directory Structure After Installation of Product Binaries

The installation process for the Network Deployment product binaries results in the creation of several important directories under the installation root <WASV6-ROOT> (C:\IBM\WebSphere\AppServer in this example). Here's a brief look at the purpose of these directories.

- *bin* — The bin directory contains all the executable commands needed to manage and configure WebSphere application servers.

- *logs* — Files under the logs directory are created during the installation. You'll learn more about this directory in "Logging During Installation of Product Binaries."

- *profileTemplates* — This directory houses the profile templates used to define the configuration settings of new servers you create. The Network Deployment package comes with three profile templates:

    › *default* template — When you create a new application server profile using the Profile Creation wizard, the wizard creates the profile using this template.

    › *dmgr* template — When you create a new deployment manager profile using the Profile Creation wizard, the wizard creates the profile using this template.

    › *managed* template — When you create a new custom profile using the Profile Creation wizard, the wizard creates the profile using this template.

When you use the wasprofile command-line utility, you must provide the location of the profile template using the –templatePath argument.

- *samples* — Source and binary files for the WebSphere samples are available under this directory (which appears only if you select "Application Server Samples" during installation).

- *_uninst* — This directory contains the uninstall execution program and related files that are used if you uninstall the product.

Figure 7-9 depicts the WebSphere directory structure following the installation of the Network Deployment package. Notice that no profiles directory is created when you install this package (in contrast to the directory structure created by the Base/Express package installation) — only the product binaries are copied at this time. Figure 7-10 shows the file-system view of the directory structure as it appears immediately after installation.

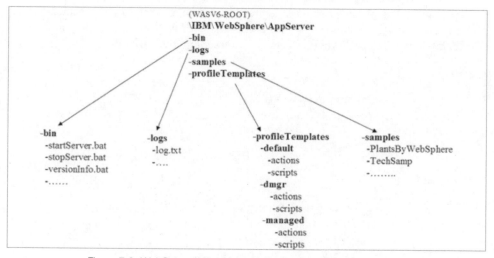

Figure 7-9: WebSphere V6 – Network Deployment directory structure

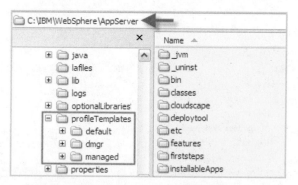

Figure 7-10: File system view of the directory structure

Logging During Installation of Product Binaries

WebSphere logs all Network Deployment installation and profile-creation activities. The log files are your main source of information for diagnosing problems you encounter while installing the package, creating profiles, and managing servers. The destination directory of the log files varies based on the activity. For example, the log files generated during installation are stored in a different place from those generated when you install, create, or manage (e.g., start, stop) the profiles. Each activity generates logging information in one or more log files.

This section describes the logging that takes place during product installation. Because the Network Deployment installation doesn't create any profiles, the logging architecture is simple during this phase. We cover the profile-creation logs later in the chapter. Figure 7-11 depicts the logging that occurs during installation of the Network Deployment product binaries. Table 7-2 provides details for these logging activities.

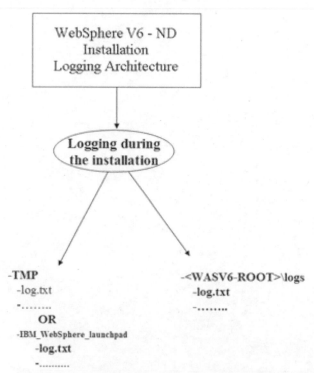

Figure 7-11: WebSphere V6 Network Deployment installation logging architecture

Table 7-2: Product binaries installation logging activities

Activity	Log destination	Description	When to use these log files
Installation — initial part	The TMP directory ■ File log.txt is one important log file under this destination. ■ If you started the installation using the Launchpad, you'll see the log files under the IBM_WebSphere_launch-pad subdirectory of the TMP directory. ■ If you used install.exe, the log files are created immediately under the TMP directory. ■ On Windows systems, check the TMP environment variable to determine the TMP value (C:\temp in the examples). ■ On Unix, the temporary directory is usually /tmp.	These log files are populated immediately after you invoke the Launchpad or install.exe program. After a successful installation, the files are copied to the logs directory under the installation directory (<WASV6-ROOT>).	■ Use if you have a problem starting the Launchpad or install.exe program or encounter problems during the early part of the installation. ■ Use if the system prerequisites check fails and you want to see the reason.
Installation — later part	The <WASV6-ROOT>\logs directory that was specified during the installation ■ File log.txt is the important log file under this destination.	These log files are populated from the moment you click **Next** after reviewing the summary report during the graphical installation.	■ Use if the installation was unsuccessful and you want to see the reason. ■ If these log files don't provide enough information, see the log files under the TMP directory.

Create a Deployment Manager Profile

Once you've installed the Network Deployment product binaries and verified that the installation was successful, you can proceed to the next phase of setting up this version of WebSphere: creating the necessary profiles. WebSphere provides a tool, the Profile Creation wizard, to help you with this part of the configuration process. You used this wizard in Chapter 3 to create a second application server profile. In this chapter, you'll use the wizard to create a deployment manager profile, an application server profile, and a custom profile.

The flow chart in Figure 7-12 depicts the high-level steps required to create, configure, and verify a deployment manager profile. The purpose of the Deployment Manager is to manage multiple application servers and their configurations from its administrative console (or the wsadmin command). You've already completed the first task in the chart, installing and verifying the product binaries. In this section, we step you through the profile-creation process.

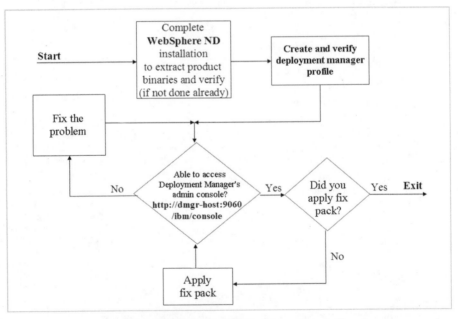

Figure 7-12: Creating a deployment manager profile

Step 1.   If you selected the option near the end of the product binaries installation process to launch the Profile Creation wizard (Step 11), the wizard is started automatically after installation is complete. You can launch the wizard at any time by clicking the Windows **Start** button, navigating to **All Programs|IBM WebSphere|Application Server Network Deployment v6|Profile creation wizard**. Another option is to run **pctWindows.exe** from the <WAS6-ROOT>\bin\ProfileCreator directory.

Note: On AIX, the profile-creation executable is named pctAIX.bin. On Linux, it is pctLinux.bin. Look for the required executable in directory <WASV6-ROOT>/bin/ProfileCreator.

When the wizard displays its welcome panel, read through the information on the screen, and click **Next** to proceed.

Step 2.   On the next panel, select the option to "Create a deployment manager profile" as shown in Figure 7-13, and click **Next**.

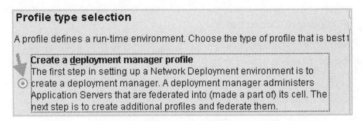

Figure 7-13: Create a deployment manager profile option

Step 3.   Next (Figure 7-14), provide a unique name for the deployment manager profile. We'll use the default name, Dmgr01.

Figure 7-14: Providing a profile name

Step 4.   Next (Figure 7-15), specify the installation directory for the profile. For Windows, make sure whatever directory name you use contains no spaces. For this example, accept the default value, C:\IBM\WebSphere\AppServer\ profiles\Dmgr01. Hereafter, we refer to this installation directory as <DMGR-PROFILE-ROOT>. Click **Next** when you're finished with this panel.

> **Note:** If necessary, the profile installation directory can be outside the <WASV6-ROOT> directory.

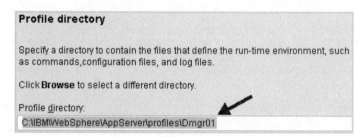

Figure 7-15: Specifying a profile directory

Step 5. Next (Figure 7-16), specify a node name, host name, and cell name for the profile. If you want to change the default node name, make sure the name you choose is unique among

- multiple instances/profiles on the same node per installation
- nodes in a Network Deployment domain

Avoid using the following reserved names: *cells*, *nodes*, *servers*, *clusters*, *applications*, and *deployments*.

The host name can be the fully qualified host name (e.g., dmgr-host.noyb.com), which is what we recommend, the host name (e.g., was-host), or the IP address (e.g., 24.142.101.52) of the machine. We strongly advise against using an IP address for the host name attribute. Use the following criteria when deciding which host name option to use:

- Use the fully qualified name in production systems and/or where multiple network interface cards (NICs) exist at the time of WebSphere installation or when you may be upgrading the machine with multiple NIC cards in future.

- Use the host name where a single NIC card exists and you're certain the machine won't have multiple cards in the future.

Note that the profile-creation program doesn't validate the host name. If you enter an invalid host name or DNS entry, you'll receive an exception (InvocationTargetException) when you start the Deployment Manager. For more information about this error, see "Logging During Creation and Management of the Deployment Manager Profile."

The cell name is common for all nodes federated to this Deployment Manager. For this example, accept the default node, host, and cell names, and click **Next**.

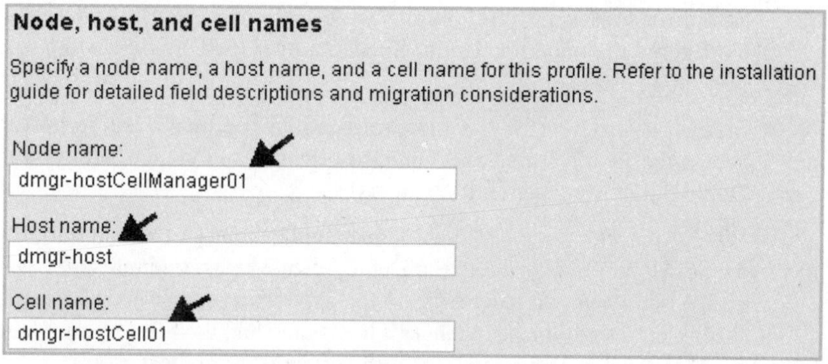

Node, host, and cell names

Specify a node name, a host name, and a cell name for this profile. Refer to the installation guide for detailed field descriptions and migration considerations.

Node name:

dmgr-hostCellManager01

Host name:

dmgr-host

Cell name:

dmgr-hostCell01

Figure 7-16: Specifying a node, host, and cell name for the deployment manager profile

Step 6. The next panel (Figure 7-17) gives you a chance to change the default port numbers if an existing WebSphere installation is already using them. If the installation program detected an existing instance of WebSphere Application Server V6, the port numbers you see on this panel will be incremented by 1 (starting with the last instance port number). If the program detected an existing instance of a previous version of WebSphere Application Server (e.g., 5.1, 5.0.x), the default ports will be displayed. In other words, the WebSphere installation program doesn't help you by automatically incrementing the port numbers for coexistence with previous versions. You must correct port number conflicts manually in this circumstance if you want to run both instances at the same time.

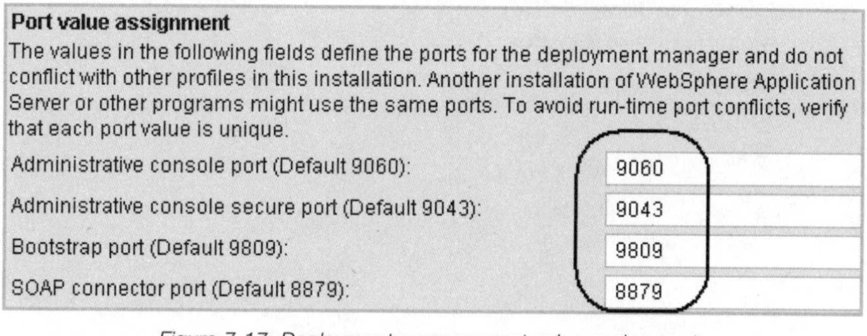

Port value assignment

The values in the following fields define the ports for the deployment manager and do not conflict with other profiles in this installation. Another installation of WebSphere Application Server or other programs might use the same ports. To avoid run-time port conflicts, verify that each port value is unique.

Administrative console port (Default 9060):   9060

Administrative console secure port (Default 9043):   9043

Bootstrap port (Default 9809):   9809

SOAP connector port (Default 8879):   8879

Figure 7-17: Deployment manager port value assignments

Here's a brief description of the ports and their use:

■ *Administrative console port – 9060* — You specify this port in the browser URL when you want to connect to the Deployment Manager from the admin console (e.g., http://dmgr-host:9060/ibm/console). If you've configured the node for Secure Sockets Layer (SSL), you use the secure port (9043) instead of 9060.

■ *Bootstrap port – 9809* — Client applications use the bootstrap port to access the Java Naming and Directory Interface (JNDI) running on the Deployment Manager (InitialContext).

■ *SOAP connector port – 8879* — Client applications (e.g., wsadmin) that use the SOAP port to connect to the Deployment Manager admin service use this port. Also, when you federate from the application server node, you must specify the Deployment Manager's host name and the SOAP port when using the addNode.bat command (e.g., **addNode.bat dmgr-host 8879**).

After making any port number changes required for your environment, click **Next**.

Step 7. The next panel (Figure 7-18) is displayed on Windows systems only. Select the check box if you want to run the deployment manager process as a Windows service. The installation program disregards the options beneath the check box unless you make this selection.

If you choose the Windows service option and select "Log on as a local system account," a user name and password are optional. If you select "Log on as a specified user account," you must provide a valid user name (containing no spaces) and a password. The user should have "Act as part of the operating system" and "Log on as a service" authority to run the process.

Figure 7-18: Windows service definition panel

If you choose the Windows service option, you must also choose a Windows service startup type (Figure 7-19): Automatic, Manual, or Disabled. When you're finished with the Windows service definition, click **Next**.

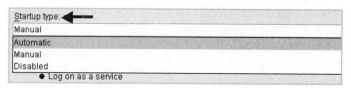

Figure 7-19: Specifying the Windows service startup type

Step 8. Review the profile summary panel, and click **Next** to create the deployment manager profile. At this point, the installation program creates the installation directory (<DMGR-PROFILE-ROOT>) and begins logging information under the <WASV6-ROOT>\logs\wasprofile directory. For more information about this logging, see "Logging During Creation and Management of the Deployment Manager Profile."

Step 9. You'll briefly see a screen informing you that the profile-creation program is installing the components. When you see the "Profile creation is complete" panel, select the option to "Launch the First Steps Console" and click **Finish**.

Step 10. Before you start verification using First Steps, check the log files to verify a successful profile creation. To do so, open file wasprofile_create_Dmgr01.log under the <DMGR-PROFILE-ROOT>\logs\wasprofile directory (you can see this file in Figure 7-20), and scroll to the end of the file. If you see the INSTCONFSUCCESS indicator, the creation of the deployment manager profile was successful. If you see INSTCONFFAIL or INSTCONFPARTIAL-SUCCESS, problems occurred during the creation. For troubleshooting information, see "Logging During Creation and Management of the Deployment Manager Profile."

Figure 7-20: Profile creation log file

WebSphere Directory Structure After Creation of the Deployment Manager Profile

By default, WebSphere stores all information pertaining to profiles in the <WASV6-ROOT>\profiles directory (C:\IBM\WebSphere\AppServer\profiles in this example). If necessary, you can choose a destination other than under <WASV6-ROOT> when creating a profile using the Profile Creation wizard or the wasprofile command. For the example, the Profile Creation wizard creates a deployment manager profile called Dmgr01 and creates a subdirectory of the same name under the profiles directory (as shown in Figure 7-21) to contain information about this profile.

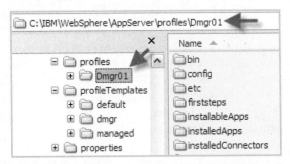

Figure 7-21: Dmgr01 subdirectory of <WASV6-ROOT>\profiles

Figure 7-22 depicts the WebSphere directory structure after creation of the deployment manager profile. Observe that there is now a profiles directory (and a Dmgr01 subdirectory under it).

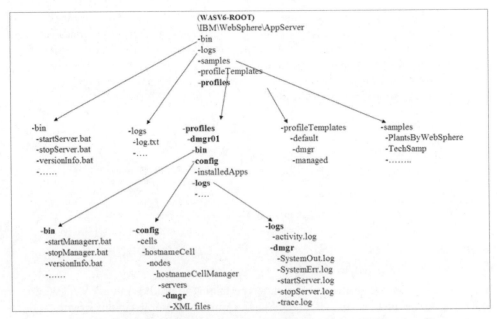

Figure 7-22: Directory structure after creation of the deployment manager profile

Verify Creation of the Profile Using the First Steps Console

Step 11.   Now, we'll use the First Steps tool to verify the creation of the deployment manager profile. If you chose the option to launch the First Steps console on the
final panel of the Profile Creation wizard, First Steps is launched automatically
once the deployment manager profile is created. You can launch First Steps at
any time by clicking **Start** and navigating to **All programs|IBM WebSphere
Application Server v6|Network Deployment|profiles|Dmgr01|First steps**.
You can also invoke First Steps by running **firststeps.bat** from the <DMGR-
PROFILE-ROOT>\firststeps directory, where <DMGR-PROFILE-ROOT> is
<WASV6-ROOT>\profiles\Dmgr01.

As you learned in Chapter 3, the First Steps wizard is a useful tool that lets
you perform a variety of administrative tasks, including profile-creation verification, from one screen. To use First Steps to confirm that the deployment
manager profile was created successfully, click the **Installation verification**
option on the console screen (you can see this option in Figure 7-23). (You
can also run the installation verification program, ivt.bat, from the command
prompt in the <DMGR-PROFILE-ROOT>\bin directory.)

Figure 7-23: Verifying profile creation using the First Steps console

If the installation was successful, you should see a notification screen similar
to the one shown in Figure 7-24. If the Deployment Manager isn't started
already, the verification program will start it. If the installation verification
was not successful, consult "Logging During Creation and Management of
the Deployment Manager Profile."

WebSphere Application Server lakhost is running on port 9060 for profile Dmgr01
Scanning the file C:\IBM\WebSphere\AppServer\profiles\Dmgr01\logs\dmgr\SystemOut.log for errors and warnings
0 errors/warnings were detected in the file C:\IBM\WebSphere\AppServer\profiles\Dmgr01\logs\dmgr\SystemOut.log
IVT Verification Succeeded
Installation Verification is complete

Figure 7-24: First Steps verification of a successful profile creation

Connect to the Deployment Manager Through the Admin Console and Verify

Step 12. Next, verify creation of the profile by connecting to the Deployment Manager through the WebSphere admin console. To do so, click **Administrative Console** on the First Steps screen.

Step 13. For the user ID, enter any value (including blank, although we don't recommend it). Unless security is turned on and configured, WebSphere won't check against any user registry to authenticate; nevertheless, it's a good idea to enter a meaningful user name to enable logging and recovery of any configuration information changed using that particular user ID. WebSphere stores the configuration work space under the <DMGR-PROFILE-ROOT>\wstemp directory.

Step 14. Click **Log in** to connect to the admin console and display the WebSphere welcome panel (described in Chapter 3). (You can also invoke the admin console from the browser using the URL **http://dmgr-host:*port*/ibm/console**, where *port* is the port number of the admin console — 9060 by default.)

Step 15. Expand **Servers**, and click **Application Server**. You'll see no application servers listed because not a single server has been federated to this Deployment Manager so far.

Step 16. Expand **Applications**, and click **Enterprise Applications**. You'll see no enterprise applications listed because there are no application servers (enterprise applications run on application servers).

Verify the Windows Services Panel for the Deployment Manager Process

Step 17. If you chose the option to run the deployment manager process as a Windows service when you created the profile, open the Windows **Services** panel using **Start|Control Panel|Administrative Tools|Services** to verify the service. You should see the Deployment Manager listed as a service with a status of Started, as shown in Figure 7-25.

If you forgot to select, or cleared, the option and want to register the service now, follow the instructions in Chapter 20 to register the deployment manager process in the Windows service registry.

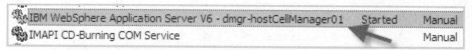

Figure 7-25: Deployment Manager process in the Windows Services panel

Managing the Deployment Manager

There are multiple ways to start, stop, and manage the Deployment Manager, depending on the operating system you're using. The following paragraphs describe some frequently used methods.

Starting or Stopping the Deployment Manager

Use one of these methods to start or stop the deployment manager instance:

- Click **Start**, and navigate to **All Programs|IBM WebSphere|Application Server V6 Network Deployment|Profiles|Dmgr01|Start the Deployment Manager** or **Stop the Deployment Manager.**

- Start the First Steps tool by using **Start|All Programs|IBM WebSphere| Application Server V6 Network Deployment|Profiles|Dmgr01 |First Steps**, and click the option to **Start the deployment manager** or **Stop the deployment manager**. (You can also invoke First Steps by running **firststeps.bat** from the <DMGR-PROFILE-ROOT>\firststeps directory.)

- If you registered the deployment manager process as a service in the Windows registry, you can start and stop the service from the Windows **Services** panel. (Use **Start|Control Panel|Administrative Tools|Services** to get there.)

- From a command-line prompt, go to <DMGR-PROFILE-ROOT>\bin and run **startManager.bat** or **stopManager.bat**. Figure 7-26 shows this method of starting the Deployment Manager. You can also start and stop the deployment manager instance by going to <WASV6-ROOT>\bin and running the following commands:

```
startManager.bat dmgr -profileName Dmgr01
stopManager.bat dmgr -profileName Dmgr01
```

```
C:\IBM\WebSphere\AppServer\profiles\Dmgr01\bin>startManager.bat
ADMU7701I: Because dmgr is registered to run as a Windows Service, the request
           to start this server will be completed by starting the associated
           Windows Service.
ADMU0116I: Tool information is being logged in file
           C:\IBM\WebSphere\AppServer\profiles\Dmgr01\logs\dmgr\startServer.log
ADMU0128I: Starting tool with the Dmgr01 profile
ADMU3100I: Reading configuration for server: dmgr
ADMU3200I: Server launched. Waiting for initialization status.
ADMU3000I: Server dmgr open for e-business; process id is 5360
```

Figure 7-26: Starting the Deployment Manager from the command line

Checking the Status of the Deployment Manager

To check the status of the deployment manager instance, go to the <WASV6-ROOT>\bin
or <DMGR-PROFILE-ROOT>\bin directory, and run **serverStatus.bat dmgr** or
serverStatus.bat –all. Figure 7-27 shows this method of checking the status of the dmgr
process.

```
C:\IBM\WebSphere\AppServer\bin>serverStatus dmgr
ADMU0116I: Tool information is being logged in file
           C:\IBM\WebSphere\AppServer\profiles\Dmgr01\logs\dmgr\serverStatus.lo
ADMU0128I: Starting tool with the Dmgr01 profile
ADMU0500I: Retrieving server status for dmgr
ADMU0509I: The Deployment Manager "dmgr" cannot be reached. It appears to be
           stopped.
```

Figure 7-27: Checking the Deployment Manager status

Connecting to the Administrative Console

The following methods let you connect to the deployment manager instance using
WebSphere's admin console. (If the Deployment Manager isn't started, you need to start
it first.)

- Use **Start|All Programs|IBM WebSphere|Application Server V6 Network
  Deployment|Profiles|Dmgr01|Administrative Console**.

- Use **Start|All Programs|IBM WebSphere|Application Server V6 Network
  Deployment|Profiles|Dmgr01|First Steps** to display the First Steps console,
  and select the **Administrative Console** option.

- Open a browser, and type **http://dmgr-host:*port*/ibm/console** to connect to the
  application server through the admin console. For the deployment manager
  instance you created during installation, the port value is 9060 (the default).

Performing Backup and Recovery for the Deployment Manager

For WebSphere Network Deployment profiles, the configuration repository consists of
XML files (flat files) stored in the configuration directory tree. The configuration
information for the deployment manager profile you created in this chapter's example is
stored under the directory <WASV6-ROOT\profiles\Dmgr01\config.

If you have no constraints on disk space, the easiest way to back up your environment, including all the profiles you created (if you used the default directory), is to stop the deployment manager process and make a copy of the entire <WASV6-ROOT> directory. If you created the deployment manager profile outside <WASV6-ROOT>, you also need to make a backup of <DMGR-PROFILE-ROOT>.

To back up the deployment manager configuration in situations where disk space constraints exist, go to <DMGR-PROFILE-ROOT>\bin, and run **backupConfig.bat** to make a copy of the deployment manager configuration. The backupConfig utility generates a ZIP archive file (named WebSphereConfig_*date*.zip) under the bin directory. You should run this command before making any major changes to your configuration (e.g., applying a fix pack).

You can assign your own name to the ZIP file using this command syntax:

```
backupConfig.bat dmgr-backup.zip
```

If you've enabled global security, you must supply a user name and password on the command — for example:

```
backupConfig.bat dmgr01-backup.zip -username noyb -password noyb
```

To restore the configuration from the backup, run

```
restoreConfig.bat filename.zip
```

In addition to backing up the deployment manager configuration, you need to make a copy of all the profiles whose nodes have been federated to this Deployment Manager in the Network Deployment environment. To perform this task, follow the instructions given later in this chapter for backing up the application server profile.

Logging During Creation and Management of the Deployment Manager Profile

Figure 7-28 depicts the logging that takes place during creation and management of the deployment manager profile. You can logically divide the destination of the log files into five categories based on the activity performed on the Deployment Manager. Table 7-3 summarizes these activities.

In addition to the log files described in the table, files activity.log and trace.log also assist in problem determination. For more information about these log files, see Chapter 22.

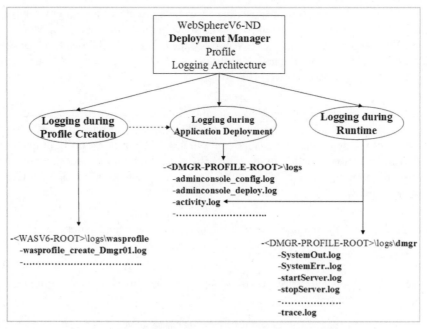

Figure 7-28: Deployment manager logging architecture

Table 7-3: Deployment manager logging activities

Activity	Log destination	Description	When to use these log files
Profile creation or deletion	The <WASV6-ROOT>\logs\wasprofile directory	The log files in this directory are populated when you use the Profile Creation wizard or the wasprofile command-line tool.	▪ Use if you have problems creating or deleting a profile.
	▪ Files wasprofile_create_profileName.log and wasprofile_delete_profileName.log are created.		
	▪ If you use the Profile Creation wizard to create a profile, the events are logged in file pctLog.txt in the <DMGR-PROFILE-ROOT>\logs directory.		

Table 7-3: Deployment manager logging activities (continued)

Activity	Log destination	Description	When to use these log files
Application deployment	The <DMGR-PROFILE-ROOT>\logs directory ■ File log.txt is the important log file under this destination.	For each admin application deployed, two log files are created: <appname>_deploy.txt and <appname>_config.txt.	■ Use if you have a problem invoking the admin application (http://dmgr-host:9060/ibm/console).
Deployment Manager management (e.g., invoking startManager, stopManager, serverStatus)	The <DMGR-PROFILE-ROOT>\logs\server1 directory	One log file exists for each initiated command. For example, if you run **startManager**, you'll see the startServer.log file under its log destination.	■ Use if the execution of the command fails.
JVM logging	The <DMGR-PROFILE-ROOT>\logs\server1 directory ■ The log files are SystemOut.log and SystemErr.log.	Messages sent to the JVM stdout and stderr streams are directed to file SystemOut.log and SystemErr.log, respectively. SystemOut.log is one of the most widely used log files for problem determination and troubleshooting.	■ Use if you have problems during JVM startup, shutdown, and runtime or at any other time.
Native process logging	The <DMGR-PROFILE-ROOT>\logs\server1 directory ■ The log files are native_stdout.log and native_stderr.log.	Messages sent to stdout and stderr from native code segments are directed to file native_stdout.log and native_stderr.log, respectively.	■ Use if problems occur in native code or code written using the Java Native Interface (JNI).

Create an Application Server Profile

The flow chart in Figure 7-29 shows the high-level steps required to create, configure, and verify the application server profile. In this section, we describe each step of this process. Chapter 3 provides a complete discussion of the standalone application server architecture. We urge you to read that chapter before creating an application server profile using the Network Deployment package. You manage the standalone application server in exactly the same way whether you create it using the Base/Express package or the Network Deployment package.

For this example, we'll assume you want to create the application server profile on a different machine from the one on which you created the deployment manager profile. Let's step through the process.

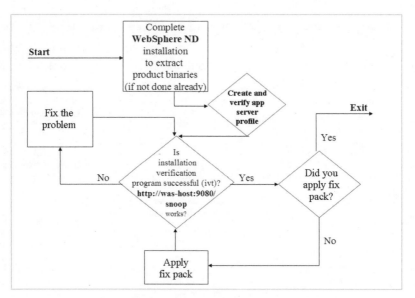

Figure 7-29: Creating an application server profile

Step 1. If you plan to create the application server profile on a machine other than the one on which you created the deployment manager profile (as in this example), your first step is to install the product binaries on the application server machine by following the instructions given earlier in this chapter (in the section titled "Install WebSphere V6 Network Deployment Package: Product Binaries"). If a deployment manager (or application server) profile already exists on the machine where you plan to create the application server profile, you don't need to install the product binaries again, so you can skip this step.

Step 2. Start the Profile Creation wizard as described in Step 1 of the "Create a Deployment Manager Profile" section above. Review the wizard's welcome panel, and click **Next**.

Step 3. On the "Profile type selection" panel, select the option to "Create an Application Server profile," and click **Next**.

Step 4. Provide a unique name for the profile. For this example, we'll use the default name, AppSrv01.

Step 5. Next, specify the installation directory for the application server profile. For Windows, make sure whatever name you choose contains no spaces. For this example, we'll use the default directory, C:\IBM\WebSphere\AppServer\profiles \AppSrv01. From now on, we refer to this installation directory as <PROFILE-ROOT>. (Logically, this profile directory can be outside the <WASV6-ROOT> directory if necessary. For example, on Unix systems it can be on a different file system.) After specifying the installation directory, click **Next**.

Step 6.   Next, specify a node name and a host name for the profile. For a description of the considerations to keep in mind when choosing these values, see Step 5 of the "Create a Deployment Manager Profile" section above. For this example, we'll use the default values shown in Figure 7-30: was-host1Node01 for the node name and was-host1 for the host name.

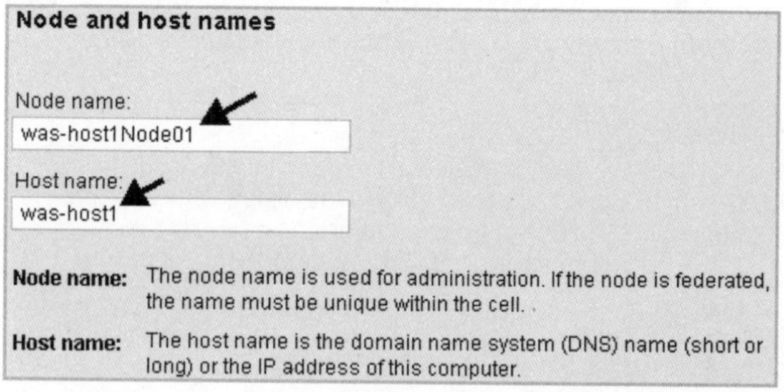

Figure 7-30: Specifying a node name and host name for the application server profile

Step 7.   The next panel (Figure 7-31) gives you a chance to change the default port numbers if the ports are already in use by any third-party software. For a description of the ports used by the application server, see Chapter 3.

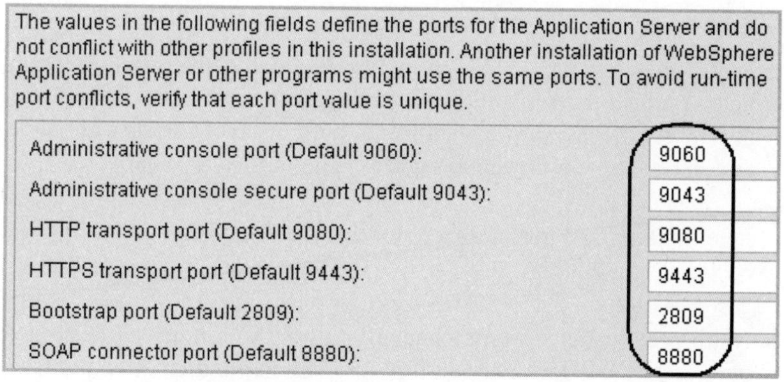

Figure 7-31: Application server default port values

If the installation program detected an existing instance of WebSphere Application Server V6 (i.e., an application server profile), each port number is incremented by 1 (from the port number of the last instance). If a deployment manager profile rather than an application server profile already exists, the installation program increments only the necessary port numbers. For example, in the application server port assignments shown in Figure 7-32, the two HTTP transport ports use the default port numbers (9080 and 9443). That's because the deployment manager doesn't host Web applications at these ports. Also note that, according to this panel, you'll need to use port 9061 when connecting to the application server through the admin console (e.g., http://was-host1:9061/ibm/console). If you've configured for SSL, you'll use the secure port, 9044. (The install program uses the vpd.properties file to keep track of information about existing instances, including their port numbers.)

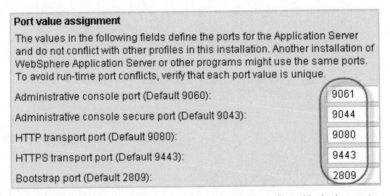

Figure 7-32: Application server port values adjusted to avoid conflict with deployment manager

If the installation program detected an existing instance of a previous version of WebSphere Application Server (e.g., 5.1, 5.0.x), the port assignment panel will show the default ports. In other words, the install program doesn't help you by automatically incrementing port numbers to coexist with previous versions. If you want to run both instances at the same time in this circumstance, you'll need to correct port conflicts manually.

After making any port number changes required for your environment, click **Next**.

Step 8.   On the next panel, specify whether you want to run the application server process as a Windows service. The installation program disregards the remaining options on the panel unless you select this option.

If you choose the Windows service option and select the option to "Log on as a local system account," a user name and password are optional. If you choose the Windows service option and select "Log on as a specified user account," you must provide a valid user name (with no spaces) and password. To run this process, the user should have "Act as part of the operating system" and "Log on as a service" authority. If you choose the Windows service option, you must also specify a Windows service startup type: Automatic, Manual, or Disabled.

Step 9. Review the profile summary panel, and click **Next** to create the profile. You'll notice that the installation program creates the installation directory <PROFILE-ROOT> at this stage and starts logging information under <WASV6-ROOT>\logs\wasprofile. For more information about this logging, see "Logging During Creation of the Application Server Profile."

Step 10. You'll see a panel informing you that the profile-creation program is installing the components. When the successful "Profile creation is complete" panel is displayed, select the option to "Launch the First Steps Console" and click **Finish**.

Step 11. Before verifying the profile creation using First Steps, check the log files to make sure the application server profile was created successfully. To do so, open file wasprofile_create_AppSrv01.log in the <PROFILE-ROOT>\logs\ wasprofile directory, and scroll to the end of the file. If you see the INST-CONFSUCCESS indicator, the application server profile was created successfully. If you see INSTCONFFAIL or INSTCONFPARTIALSUCCESS, problems occurred during the creation. For troubleshooting information, see "Logging During Creation of the Application Server Profile."

WebSphere Directory Structure After Creation of the Application Server Profile

Following the creation of the application server profile, a new directory, called profiles, is added under <WASV6-ROOT> on the application server node. Each profile you create is by default stored under this directory, in a subdirectory of the same name as the profile. For our example, the subdirectory AppSrv01 is created to contain the files required to run and manage the application server within profile AppSrv01. Figure 7-33 shows this subdirectory. (If you desire, you can choose a different destination when creating a profile using the Profile Creation wizard or the wasprofile command.)

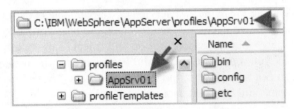

Figure 7-33: AppSrv01 subdirectory of <WASV6-ROOT>\profiles

Figure 7-34 depicts the directory structure after creation of the application server profile. Observe that there is a profiles directory (and directory AppSrv01 under it), which is created after you create the application server profile.

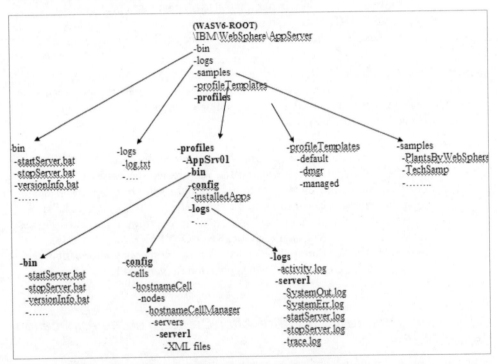

Figure 7-34: Directory structure after creation of the application server profile

Verify Creation Using the First Steps Console

Now, use the First Steps tool to verify the creation of the application server profile. If you chose the option to launch the First Steps console on the final panel of the Profile Creation wizard, First Steps is started automatically once the application server profile is created. You can launch First Steps at any time using **Start|All Programs|IBM WebSphere|Application Server v6 Network Deployment|profiles|AppSrv01|First steps** (or by running **firststeps.bat** from a command prompt under the <PROFILE-ROOT>\firststeps directory).

Step 12.   On the First Steps console screen, select **Installation verification** to confirm that the application server profile was created successfully. (You can also run the installation verification program, ivt.bat, from the command prompt in the <PROFILE-ROOT>\bin directory.)

If the installation was successful, you should see a notification screen similar to the one shown in Figure 7-35. The verification program will start the application server if it isn't already started. If the installation verification wasn't successful, consult "Logging During Creation of the Application Server Profile."

```
IVTL0035I: Scanning the file C:\IBM\WebSphere\AppServer\profiles\AppSrv01\logs\server1\SystemOut.log for errors
IVTL0040I: 0 errors/warnings were detected in the file C:\IBM\WebSphere\AppServer\profiles\AppSrv01\logs\server1
IVTL0070I: IVT Verification Succeeded   ◄━━━━━
IVTL0080I: Installation Verification is complete
```

Figure 7-35: First Steps verification of a successful profile creation

Other Verification Steps

Steps 13–15. The remaining steps to verify the creation of application server profile AppSrv01 are the same as those described in Chapter 3 to verify the creation of the standalone application server. Consult the appropriate sections of that chapter to

- connect to the application server through the admin console and verify
- verify installation from the browser using the default application
- verify the Windows **Services** panel for the application server process

In following Chapter 3's instructions, use <WASV6-ROOT>\profiles\AppSrv01 instead of <WASV6-ROOT\profiles\default for all references to the <PROFILE-ROOT> directory.

Logging During Creation of the Application Server Profile

Figure 7-36 depicts the logging that takes place for the application server profile. You can logically divide the destination of the log files into five categories, depending on the activity performed on the profile. Table 7-4 summarizes these categories. To learn about some frequently occurring problems and their solutions, refer to the "Problem Scenarios" section of Chapter 3.

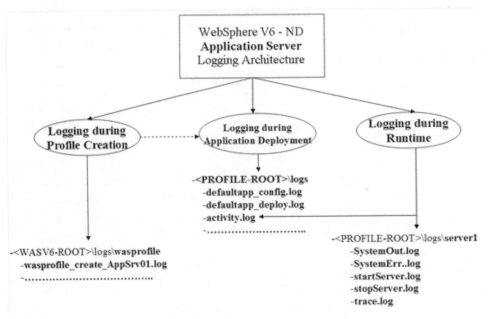

Figure 7-36: Application server logging architecture

Table 7-4: Application server logging activities

Activity	Log destination	Description	When to use these log files
Profile creation or deletion	The <WASV6-ROOT>\logs\wasprofile directory	Log files in this directory are populated when you use the Profile Creation wizard or the wasprofile command-line tool.	■ Use if you have problems creating or deleting a profile.
	■ Files wasprofile_create_profile-Name.log and wasprofile_delete_profileNa me.log are created.		
	■ If you use the Profile Creation wizard to create a profile, the events are logged in file pctLog.txt in the <PROFILE-ROOT>\logs directory.		

Table 7-4: Application server logging activities (continued)

Activity	Log destination	Description	When to use these log files
Application deployment	The <PROFILE-ROOT>\logs directory ■ In this chapter's example, <PROFILE-ROOT> is C:\IBM\WebSphere\profiles\AppSrv01.	You'll see two log files for each deployed application: <appname>_deploy.txt and <appname>_config.txt.	■ Use if you have a problem invoking the default application (e.g., snoop, hitcount) or sample applications after creating the profile. ■ Use if you have trouble deploying user applications or invoking them after deployment.
Application server management (e.g., invoking startServer, stopServer, serverStatus)	The <PROFILE-ROOT>\logs\server1 directory	One log file is created for each initiated command. For example, if you run **startServer server1**, you'll see file startServer.log under its log destination.	■ Use if the execution of the command fails.
JVM logging	The <PROFILE-ROOT>\logs\server1 directory ■ The log files are SystemOut.log and SystemErr.log.	Messages sent to the JVM stdout and stderr streams are directed to file SystemOut.log and SystemErr.log, respectively. File SystemOut.log is one of the most widely used log files for problem determination and troubleshooting.	■ Use for problems that occur during JVM startup, shutdown, or runtime or at any other time.
Native process logging	The <PROFILE-ROOT>\logs\server1 directory ■ The log files are native_stdout.log and native_stdrrr.log.	Messages sent to stdout and stderr from native code segments are directed to file native_stdout.log and native_stdrrr.log, respectively.	■ Use for problems that occur in native code or code written using JNI.

Additional Tasks and Options

Many of the activities related to the application server profile are covered in detail elsewhere in this book — primarily in Chapters 3 and 4. Review the following information about these activities, and refer to the relevant chapters for detailed instructions on performing these tasks.

Applying Fix Packs

For instructions on how to apply fix packs and eFixes, see Chapter 19. Return to this chapter for verification instructions and problem determination tips.

Configuring a Service Integration Bus and Enabling the Messaging Engine

Follow the instructions in Chapter 12 configure the Service Integration Bus and enable the messaging engine. Consult Chapter 21 for detailed instructions on installing and configuring Service Integration Bus Web Services Enablement (SIBWS).

Creating Multiple Application Server Profiles

To create additional application server profiles on the node where you created application server profile AppSrv01, follow the instructions given for this task in Chapter 3. The default name of the second profile you create in the Network Deployment package is AppSrv02, so you'll need to substitute "AppSrv02" for "AppSrv01" when following those instructions. If you use the default values, your <NEW-PROFILE-ROOT> will be <WASV6-ROOT>\profiles\AppSrv**02** instead of <WASV6-ROOT>\profiles\AppSrv**01**, and the directory names you see under the profiles directory will be AppSrv01 and AppSrv02 instead of Default and AppSrv01. For more information about the directory structure created for multiple application server profiles, see Chapter 3.

Manage WebSphere Single or Multiple Application Server Profile Environment

Chapter 4 describes the methods available to manage (e.g., start, stop, check the status of) WebSphere in a single or multiple application server profile environment.

Adding New Features

To add new features, such as the sample applications, to the existing WebSphere installation, follow the instructions in Chapter 4.

Performing Backup and Recovery for the Application Server Profile

Use Chapter 4's instructions to perform this task, making the following adjustments:

- For <PROFILE-ROOT>, use <WASV6-ROOT>\profiles**AppSrv01** instead of <WASV6-ROOT\profiles**default**.

- The default name for the second profile you created with the Network Deployment package is AppSrv02, so substitute AppSrv02 for AppSrv01 while following the instructions.

- If you're using the default values, your <NEW-PROFILE-ROOT> directory will be <WASV6-ROOT>\profiles\AppSrv**02** instead of <WASV6-ROOT>\profiles\ AppSrv**01**.

Create a Custom Profile

The flow chart in Figure 7-37 depicts the high-level tasks required to create, configure, and verify a custom profile. In this section, we step through each part of this process.

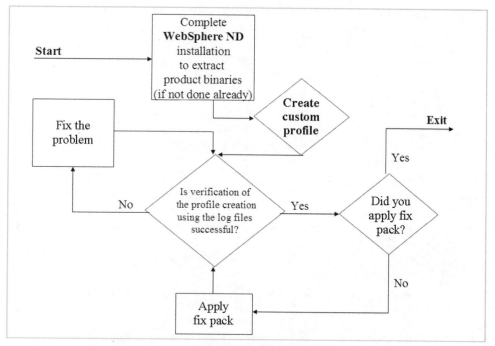

Figure 7-37: Creating a custom profile

Step 1.   For this example, we'll assume you're creating the custom profile on a different machine from the machine on which you created the deployment manager and application server profiles. In that case, you must install the product binaries (as described earlier in this chapter) before you can create the profile. When a deployment manager or application server profile already exists on the machine where the custom profile will be created, you don't need to install product binaries again.

Step 2.   Start the Profile Creation wizard as described in Step 1 of the "Create a Deployment Manager Profile" section above. Read through the wizard's welcome panel, and click **Next**.

Step 3.   On the "Profile type selection" panel, select the option to "Create a custom profile," and click **Next**.

Step 4.   A custom profile has no meaning without being federated to Deployment Manager, and the next panel (Figure 7-38) requests some information about the Deployment Manager. To federate the node within the custom profile to the Deployment Manager at the time the custom profile is created, you simply provide the host name (or DNS entry) and SOAP port for the Deployment Manager and click **Next** on this panel.

If you prefer (for example, if the Deployment Manager isn't available right now), you can opt to federate the node later by selecting the option to "Federate this node later using the addNode command." When you choose this option, the installation program ignores the host name and SOAP port values on this panel.

For this example, select the option to federate the node later so that we can examine the directory structure and logging activities before federating the node. You'll learn how to federate the node as a follow-up step in Chapter 8.

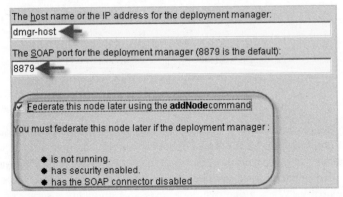

The host name or the IP address for the deployment manager:

dmgr-host

The SOAP port for the deployment manager (8879 is the default):

8879

☑ Federate this node later using the **addNode** command

You must federate this node later if the deployment manager :

- is not running.
- has security enabled.
- has the SOAP connector disabled

Figure 7-38: Choosing to federate the node within the custom profile later

Step 5.   Next, provide a unique name for the custom profile. For this example, we'll use the default name, Custom01.

Step 6.   On the next panel, specify the installation directory for the profile, and click **Next**. For Windows, make sure whatever directory name you use contains no spaces. For this example, we'll use the default directory, C:\IBM\WebSphere\AppServer\profiles\Custom01. From now on, we refer to the custom profile installation directory as <CUSTOM-PROFILE-ROOT>. (Logically, the profile directory can be outside <WASV6-ROOT> if necessary. For example, on Unix systems it can be on a different file system.)

Step 7. Next, provide a node name and host name for the custom profile. You'll usually want to change the default node name. For a description of the considerations to keep in mind when choosing these values, see Step 5 of the "Create a Deployment Manager Profile" section above. For this example, we'll use the values shown in Figure 7-39: custom-hostNode01 for the node name and custom-host for the host name.

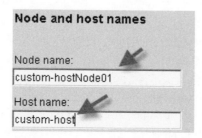

Figure 7-39: Specifying a node name and host name for the custom profile

Step 8. If you chose to federate the node during the creation of the custom profile, the next panel you see presents the port value assignments. Here, as on the port assignment panels for the deployment manager and application server profiles, you either accept the default port numbers or make changes to avoid port conflicts. Once the node within the custom profile is federated, a node agent process is created on this machine. You'll learn more about the node agent in Chapter 8 when we talk about federating nodes.

Because you chose to federate the node later, you'll see a profile summary panel at this point rather than the port value assignments. Review this panel, and click **Next** to create the profile.

The installation program creates the installation directory <CUSTOM-PROFILE-ROOT> at this stage and starts logging information under <WASV6-ROOT>\logs\wasprofile. For more information about this logging, see "Logging During Creation of the Custom Profile."

Step 9. Next, a panel informs you that the profile-creation program is installing the components. When you see the successful "Profile creation is complete" panel, *clear* the option to "Launch the First Steps Console," and click **Finish**. In the case of a custom profile, no installation verification program is available because no application server exists immediately after the installation. You therefore don't need to start the First Steps console.

Step 10. To verify the successful creation of the custom profile, open file wasprofile_create_Custom01.log in the <CUSTOM-PROFILE-ROOT>\logs\ wasprofile directory, and scroll to the end of the file. If you see the INST-CONFSUCCESS indicator, the profile was created successfully. If you see INSTCONFFAIL or INSTCONFPARTIALSUCCESS, problems occurred. For troubleshooting information, see "Logging During Creation of the Custom Profile."

WebSphere Directory Structure After Creation of the Custom Profile

Following the creation of the custom profile, a new directory, called profiles, is added under <WASV6-ROOT>. All profiles created on this node are stored in this directory by default, each in a directory of the same name as the profile. (If you prefer, you can choose a different destination when creating a profile using the Profile Creation wizard or the wasprofile command.) The profile directories contain the files required to federate the node within the custom profile to the Deployment Manager and to manage the application server (e.g., server1) that you'll create from the Deployment Manager's admin console after federation.

For our example, the subdirectory Custom01 is created to contain the files required to federate the node within custom profile Custom01 to the Deployment Manager. Figure 7-40 shows this subdirectory.

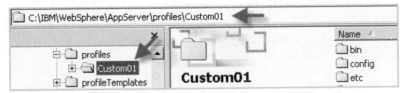

Figure 7-40: Custom01 subdirectory of <WASV6-ROOT>\profiles

Figure 7-41 illustrates the directory structure after creation of the custom profile (assuming you didn't federate the node during the creation). Observe the presence of the profiles directory (and the Custom01 subdirectory under it). Also notice that you don't see server1 (under <CUSTOM-PROFILE-ROOT>\config\cells\ . . .). That's because no application server is created during the creation of the custom profile.

If you federated the node during the profile-creation process, you'd also see directories representing the node agent process. We'll talk more about that topic in the next chapter.

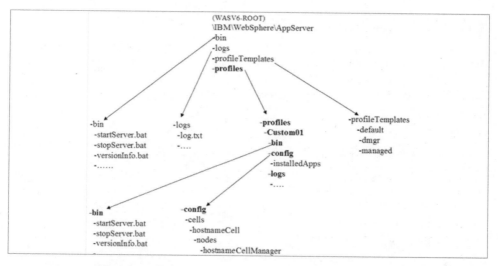

Figure 7-41: Directory structure after creation of the custom profile

Logging During Creation of the Custom Profile

The logging architecture during the creation of the custom profile is simple compared with the logging that occurs for the other profiles because the custom profile has no application server at the time of creation. Figure 7-42 depicts the logging architecture for the custom profile. Table 7-5 explains when to use the custom profile log files.

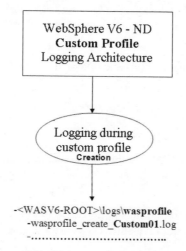

Figure 7-42: Custom profile logging architecture

Table 7-5: Custom profile logging activity

Activity	Log destination	Description	When to use these log files
Profile creation or deletion	The <WASV6-ROOT>\logs\wasprofile directory	The log files in this directory are populated when you use the Profile Creation wizard or the wasprofile command-line tool.	Use if you have problems creating or deleting a profile.
	▪ The following files are created: wasprofile_create_profileName.log and wasprofile_delete_profileName.log. ▪ If you use the Profile Creation wizard to create a profile, the events are logged in file pctLog.txt in the <PROFILE-ROOT>\logs directory.		

Silent Installation

As an alternative to using the wizard panels to install the Network Deployment package and create the necessary profiles, you can perform a silent installation. With this method, instead of displaying a graphical interface, the installation and profile-creation programs read responses you provide in text files to determine the installation and creation options. As the diagram in Figure 7-43 illustrates, the Network Deployment package contains four response files:

- one to install the product binaries and optionally call one of the other response files

- one to create the deployment manager profile

- one to create the application server profile

- one to create the custom profile and optionally federate to the Deployment Manager (if the Deployment Manager exists and is running when you create the profile)

In this section, we step you through the silent installation process for the Network Deployment product binaries and give an overview of the silent profile-creation process.

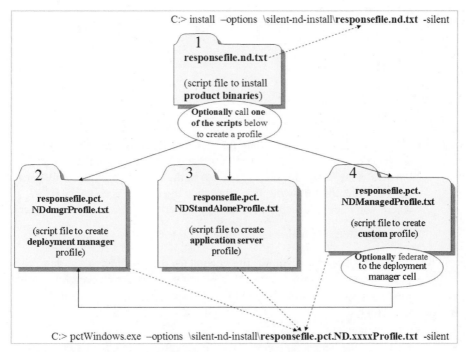

C:> install –options \silent-nd-install**responsefile.nd.txt** -silent

1

responsefile.nd.txt

(script file to install
product binaries)

Optionally call **one**
of the scripts below
to create a profile

2

**responsefile.pct.
NDdmgrProfile.txt**

(script file to create
deployment manager
profile)

3

**responsefile.pct.
NDStandAloneProfile.txt**

(script file to create
application server
profile)

4

**responsefile.pct.
NDManagedProfile.txt**

(script file to create
custom profile)

Optionally federate
to the deployment
manager cell

C:> pctWindows.exe –options \silent-nd-install**responsefile.pct.ND.xxxxProfile.txt** -silent

Figure 7-43: Network Deployment package response files

Install Product Binaries

Step 1.   Log in as a member of the Administrators group with rights to act as part of the
operating system and log on as a service. Silent installation will fail unless the
user has these rights, even if the user is a member of the Administrators group.
Restart the machine after granting these rights and before starting the silent
installation.

> **Unix note:** On Unix systems, log in as root. If necessary, run **umask 022** to set
> permissions for the temporary directory. To verify the present setting, run
> **umask.**

Step 2.   Create a temporary directory (e.g., silent-nd-install), and copy file response-
file.nd.txt from the WebSphere installation package (usually under the WAS
directory) into it. You can see this file in Figure 7-44.

Figure 7-44: WAS directory containing Network Deployment response files

Step 3. Using your favorite editor, open the response file and take a look at its entries. For each panel presented in the graphical installation of the product binaries, a corresponding line (or lines) in the text file provides a response. For example, the following line represents the license acceptance panel, where you click to accept or not accept the terms of the license agreement.

```
-W silentInstallLicenseAcceptance.value="false"
```

For each option, the response file documents the possible values and provides other useful information. You're going to customize each line of this file to silently install the Network Deployment product binaries the same way you did using the graphical installation.

Step 4. First, edit the license-agreement line to accept the agreement's terms by changing the value from "false" to "true":

```
-W silentInstallLicenseAcceptance.value="true"
```

Step 5. Next, set the installation directory to C:\IBM\WebSphere\AppServer as you did in the graphical installation:

```
-P wasProductBean.installLocation="C:\IBM\WebSphere\AppServer"
```

(If you choose to provide a different name for the installation directory, make sure the name you use contains no spaces.)

Step 6. To install the sample applications, leave the next line's value set to "true"; otherwise, change it to "false".

```
-P samplesProductFeatureBean.active="false"
```

Step 7. To install the Javadoc (Java documentation) feature during the installation, leave the next line's value set to "true"; otherwise, change it to "false".

```
-P javadocsProductFeatureBean.active="true"
```

Step 8. If, after installing the product binaries using this script, you want to invoke the profile-creation program to create one of the supported profiles (using a separate response file), set the next line's value, launchPCT, to "true"; otherwise, set it to "false". Note that if you set this value to "true", you need to be ready with the silent script for the profile you plan to create before invoking the product binaries installation script. In this case, we'll choose not to launch the profile-creation tool:

```
-W ndsummarypanelInstallWizardBean.launchPCT="false"
```

Step 9. If you set the launchPCT value to "true", you must specify, on the next line of the response file, the location of the response file that creates the profile. If you set launchPCT to "false", as in this example, comment out this line.

```
##-W pctresponsefilelocationqueryactionInstallWizardBean.fileLocation=""
```

Figure 7-45 shows the edited response-file lines you'll use for the sample installation.

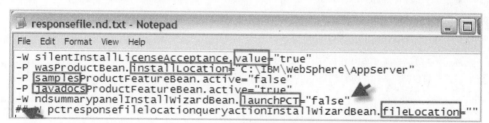

Figure 7-45: Response file to install Network Deployment product binaries

Step 10. Now, scroll to the beginning of the file to view the instructions for running the silent installation program. Figure 7-46 shows this part of the file.

```
# A common use of an options file is to run the wizard in silent mode. This lets
# the options file author specify wizard settings without having to run the
# wizard in graphical or console mode. To use this options file for silent mode
# execution, use the following command line arguments when running the wizard:
#
#    -options "D:\installImage\WAS\responsefile.nd.txt" -silent
####################################################################################
```

Figure 7-46: Silent installation instructions

Step 11. Save the response file, and exit the editor.

Step 12. Open a command-line prompt, and go to the WebSphere software directory where the install.exe program is available (the same directory from which you copied the response.base.txt file, usually the WAS directory). Run the following command, passing the location of the response file as an argument:

```
install.exe -options "path-to-response-file" -silent
```

Step 13. Verify the silent installation of the product binaries using the same instructions given for the graphical installation (Step 12 in the section "Install WebSphere V6 Network Deployment Package: Product Binaries"). If the installation verification is unsuccessful, review the section "Logging During Installation of Product Binaries" in the early part of this chapter.

Create Profiles

Before trying to create any of the profiles supported by the Network Deployment package, be sure you've installed the product binaries and verified their installation. Then open the appropriate response file for the type of the profile you want to create:

- To create a deployment manager profile, use responsefile.pct.NDdmgrProfile.txt.

- To create an application server profile, use responsefile.pct.NDStandAloneProfile.txt.

- To create a custom profile (and optionally federate the node), use responsefile.pct.NDmanagedProfile.txt.

The entries in these files correspond to the panel options you specified during the graphical creation process for each respective profile.

For more information about the profile-creation options in a silent install, consult the silent installation section of Chapter 4. One important difference to note is that, in contrast to installations performed using the Profile Creation wizard, a silent install can't assign port numbers for a profile automatically during the installation runtime. If you're creating multiple profiles on the same machine, you must resolve the port conflicts manually.

After editing the response file as required to create the desired profile, scroll to the beginning of the file to view the instructions for running the silent installation program, save the response file, and exit the editor. Then, open a command prompt, go to the <WASV6-ROOT>\bin\ProfileCreator directory, and run the profile-creation program, passing the location of the response file as an argument.

The name of the profile-creation program varies depending on the operating system. On Windows, you use pctWindows.exe to invoke the program:

```
pctWindows.exe -options "path-to-response-file" -silent
```

On AIX, you use pctAIX.bin; on Linux, pctLinux.bin; and on HP Unix, pctHPUX.bin. You'll find the required executable under the <WASV6-ROOT>\bin\ProfileCreator directory for your operating system.

As a last step, verify the silent profile creation using the instructions you followed to verify creation of the appropriate profile by the Profile Creation wizard. If the installation verification is unsuccessful, review the logging discussion in the section of this chapter pertaining to that profile.

8

WebSphere V6 Network Deployment:
Federation of Nodes

n a WebSphere environment with multiple profiles (multiple application servers), the administrator must log on to each application server's administrative console to manage the application server — a time-consuming and error-prone process. By federating the WebSphere nodes to a Deployment Manager, you can administer all the application servers from the admin console of the Deployment Manager, gaining the ability to manage multiple application servers from a single place.

Figure 8-1 depicts a sample WebSphere environment as it exists before federation of the nodes. As you can see, no relationship exists between the Deployment Manager and the application server or custom profiles, and the administrator must manage each server directly.

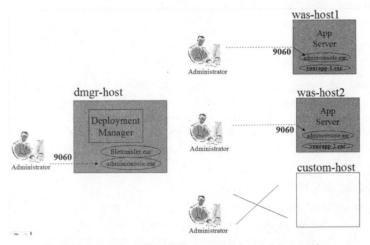

Figure 8-1: Deployment Manager and three standalone nodes

Figure 8-2 depicts the same environment after the nodes have been federated to the Deployment Manager. Now, the administrator has a single, central point from which to administer the two application servers and the custom profile.

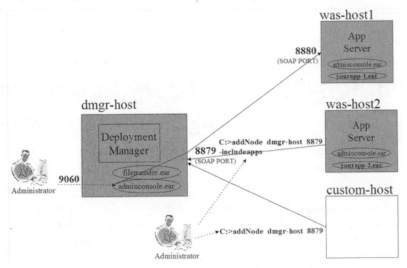

Figure 8-2: Deployment Manager and federated nodes

To federate a node to the Deployment Manager, you can use either of two methods:

- From the Deployment Manager's admin console, you can add a node using the console's graphical interface. In Figure 8-2, the was-host1 node is being federated using this method.

- From the application server's command prompt, you can use the addNode command to federate the node. In the figure, the was-host2 and custom-host nodes are being federated using this method.

In this chapter, we explain how to federate nodes within application server and custom profiles into the Deployment Manager's cell. We cover both the graphical method and the command-based procedure, providing step-by-step instructions. As in previous chapters, the instructions assume a Windows XP environment. Refer to Chapter 3 for a reminder of the symbolic directory references we use.

Pre-Federation Tasks

Before beginning the federation process, you have a few preliminary tasks to take care of. This work consists primarily of navigating the application servers and the Deployment Manager to verify connections and obtain port numbers.

Navigate the Application Servers Before Federation

Complete the following steps for the application servers in preparation for federation:

1. Open a command window on was-host1, and make sure you can ping the Deployment Manager node, using both host name and DNS entry. For example, issue both **ping dmgr-host** and **ping dmgr-host.noyb.com**.

2. Start the application server on was-host1 (if it isn't already started). (If you plan to federate a node from the Deployment Manager's admin console, the application server must be running on that node.)

3. Log on to the application server's admin console from the browser: **http://was-host1:9060/ibm/console**.

4. Expand **Servers**, and select **Server1**. Then, under the **Communications** section, expand **Ports** to display the list of ports used by the application server (Figure 8-3). Make a note of the port number assigned to the SOAP_CONNECTOR_ADDRESS port. Communications between the Deployment Manager and the application server will take place through this port. In the figure, the port number is 8880. If you changed port numbers during installation, your port number may differ.

5. Log out of the admin console.

6. Repeat Steps 1–5 for each application server you plan to federate to determine its SOAP address port. Don't forget to log out of the admin console after noting down each port number. If you're federating from the Deployment Manager's admin console, be sure to keep the application server running.

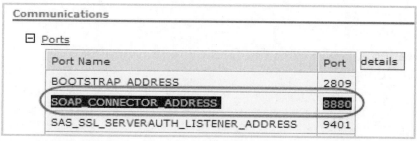

Figure 8-3: Application server's SOAP_CONNECTOR_ADDRESS port

Navigate the Deployment Manager Before Federation

Take the following steps on the Deployment Manager in preparation for federation:

1. Open a command prompt, and make sure you can ping each node you plan to federate, using both host name and DNS entry. For example:

```
ping was-host1
ping was-host1.noyb.com

ping was-host2
ping was-host2.noyb.com
```

2. Start the Deployment Manager on dmgr-host (if it isn't already started), and log on to the Deployment Manager's admin console from the browser: **http://dmgr-host:9060/ibm/console.**

3. Expand **System administration**, click **Cell**, and select the **Local Topology** tab (shown in Figure 8-4). Note that only the Deployment Manager (dmgr) is part of the cell at this point.

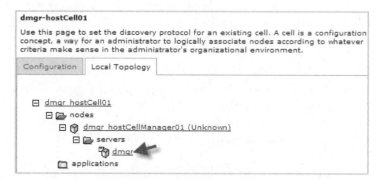

Figure 8-4: Deployment Manager's Local Topology tab

Federating a Node from the Deployment Manager's Admin Console

The diagram in Figure 8-5 illustrates the architecture you're going to build in this chapter. In the figure, the application servers have been federated and can thus be managed from a single place — the Deployment Manager's admin console. Once you federate each application server or custom profile node, a node agent process is created on that node. Notice that by default the custom profile contains no application server (server1) immediately after its federation. You can create an application server on the custom profile from the Deployment Manager's admin console at any time after federating the node.

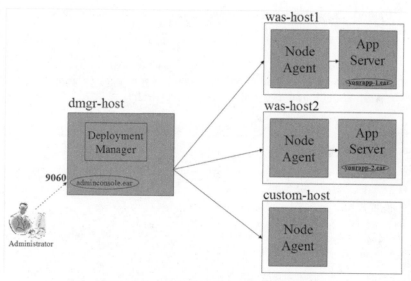

Figure 8-5: Architecture after node federation

The flow chart in Figure 8-6 depicts the high-level steps required to federate nodes within an application server profile to the Deployment Manager's cell. We cover the process to federate a node within a custom profile later.

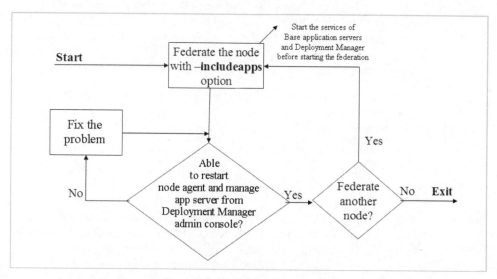

Figure 8-6: Node federation overview

To federate a node using the graphical method (i.e., using the Deployment Manager's admin console), take the following steps.

Step 1. On the Deployment Manager's admin console, expand **System administration** and click **Nodes**. On the **Nodes** page (Figure 8-7), click the **Add Node** button to add the node on was-host1.

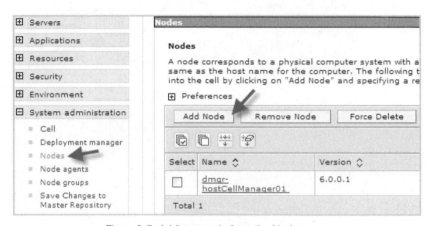

Figure 8-7: Adding a node from the Nodes page

Step 2. On the resulting page, select the **Managed node** option (shown in Figure 8-8), and click **Next**. A managed node is a node on which a node agent process will run. The Deployment Manager will communicate with this node agent process to manage the application server. The node agent process communicates with the application server.

Figure 8-8: Selecting to add a managed node

Step 3. On the next page (Figure 8-9), specify the host name and SOAP address port of the application server you're federating. To move the application server's applications (e.g., the default and ivt applications and any others you've installed) to the Deployment Manager's repository, select the **Include applications** option.

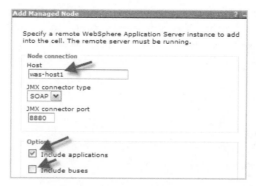

Figure 8-9: Managed node options

If you choose the option to include applications, and an application with the same name and context root as one of the application server's applications already exists in the Deployment Manager's repository, the federation process ignores that particular application and moves only the unique applications. For example, if you select to include applications when federating the second node (was-host2), you'll be notified (during federation) that the federation process isn't moving the default and ivt applications because they already exist in the repository as a result of federating the was-host1 node.

If you created a Service Integration Bus (SIBus) and enabled a messaging engine, and you want to propagate the bus, select the **Include buses** option on this page. Click **Next** when you're finished with these options. (You'll learn more about the SIBus and messaging engine in Chapter 12.)

Step 4.   If your application server is on a Windows system and you want to register the node agent process as a Windows service, select the option on the next page (Figure 8-10) to "Run node agent as Windows service." Click **OK**.

Figure 8-10: Specifying a node agent as a managed Windows service

Step 5.   Now, a series of messages informs you that the federation process is adding the node, is launching the node agent process, and finally has successfully federated the node. You're then prompted (as shown in Figure 8-11) to log out of the admin console to see the new node on the console. Click the logout link.

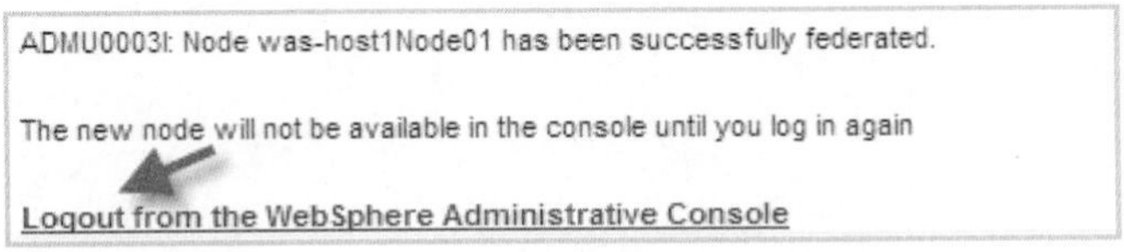

> ADMU0003I: Node was-host1Node01 has been successfully federated.
>
> The new node will not be available in the console until you log in again
>
> <u>Logout from the WebSphere Administrative Console</u>

Figure 8-11: Link to log out of the WebSphere admin console

If you see any errors during the federation, consult the "Logging During Federation of Nodes" section of this chapter for troubleshooting tips.

Verify Federation by Viewing the Log Files

As with the other procedures described in this book, your next step is verification. You'll confirm the federation of the washost1 node in several ways, first by using the log files.

Step 6.   To verify the federation by viewing the log files, first log on to the Deployment Manager node (dmgr-host in this example). Open file SystemOut.log under the <DMGR-PROFILE-ROOT>\logs\dmgr\logs directory, and look for the node you federated (was-host1 in this example). You should see messages similar to those shown in Figure 8-12, starting with "Beginning attempt to federate a node . . . " and reporting the successful update of the appropriate XML files in the master repository.

```
[5/9/05 21:27:50:096 CDT] 00000031 AdminOperatio A   ADMN1101I: Beginning attempt to
federate a node with WebSphere version 6.0.0.1 to a cell controlled by dmgr at version
6.0.1.0.
[5/9/05 21:28:00:751 CDT] 00000044 ServletWrappe A   SRVE0242I: [transfer]:
DefaultCoreGroup at Member dmgr-hostCell101\dmgr-hostCellManager01\dmgr: View change in
process.
[4/11/05 10:54:44:398 CDT] 00000034 FileRepositor A   ADMR0009I: Document
cells/dmgr-hostCell101/nodes/was-host1Node01/servers/server1/resources-pme.xml is created.
[4/11/05 10:54:44:438 CDT] 00000034 FileRepositor A   ADMR0009I: Document
cells/dmgr-hostCell101/applications/DefaultApplication.ear/deployments/DefaultApplication/
DefaultWebApplication.war/WEB-INF/ibm-web-bnd.xmi is created.
[4/11/05 10:54:44:448 CDT] 00000013 VSync        I   DCSV2004I: DCS Stack
DefaultCoreGroup at Member dmgr-hostCell101\dmgr-hostCellManager01\dmgr: The
synchronization procedure completed successfully. The View Identifier is
```

Figure 8-12: Sample SystemOut.log file

Step 7.   Next, log on to the federated node (was-host1 in this case), open file addNode.log under the <PROFILE-ROOT>\logs directory, and scroll to the end of the file. If you see a message indicating that the node has been successfully federated (as shown in Figure 8-13), the node was federated without any problem.

```
[4/11/05 10:55:31:268 CDT] 0000000a AdminTool      A    ADMU9990I:
[4/11/05 10:55:32:059 CDT] 0000000a AdminTool      A    ADMU0003I: Node was-host1Node01 has
been successfully federated.
[4/11/05 10:55:32:059 CDT] 0000000a AdminTool      3    Returning from auxiliary method
runTool with return: 0
```

Figure 8-13: Sample addNode.log file with successful federation message

Step 8.   Next, open file SystemOut.log under the <PROFILE-ROOT>\ logs\Nodeagent\logs directory, and look for the node you federated (was-host1). You should see messages indicating that the node agent was started successfully after the federation and that the configuration was synchronized successfully. If you see any error messages, consult "Logging During Federation of Nodes" for more information.

Verify Federation from the Admin Console

To verify the node's federation from the Deployment Manager's admin console, take the following steps.

Step 9.   Log in to the Deployment Manager's admin console. Expand **System administration**, and click **Nodes**. On the resulting page (Figure 8-14), you should see that the node on was-host1 has been federated and synchronized (indicated by the arrow-within-a-circle symbol in the Status column). The synchronized symbol indicates that the node's configuration information is in sync with the Deployment Manager's cell configuration. If you don't see the node you federated, refer to "Logging During Federation of Nodes" for more details.

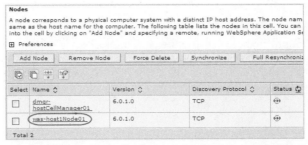

Figure 8-14: Federated and synchronized node in Deployment Manager's admin console

Step 10.   Expand **Servers**, and click **Application Servers**. You should see the application server (server1) on the federated was-host1 node, as shown in

Figure 8-15. Select the check box for server1, and click the **Start** button to start the server1 application server on was-host1 from the Deployment Manager's admin console. If you have a problem starting the application server, refer to "Logging During Federation of Nodes."

If you federated the node within the custom profile (using the command-prompt procedure, which we describe later), you won't see any entry for the custom profile here.

Figure 8-15: Starting application server server1 on the federated was-host1 node

Step 11. Expand **Applications**, click **Enterprise Applications**, and check the resulting application list to make sure all the applications are in a "running" state (indicated by a green arrow in the Status column as shown in Figure 8-16). (The applications will appear only if you chose the **Include applications** option during the federation.) If the status of any application is "stopped," consult "Logging During Federation of Nodes."

If you federated the node within the custom profile, you won't see any entry for that profile here because the custom profile has no application server by default.

Figure 8-16: Checking the status of the enterprise applications

Step 12. Expand **System administration**, select **Node agents**, and verify that a node agent process has been created on the node you federated (was-host1 in this case). Make sure the node agent's status is running, as shown in Figure 8-17.

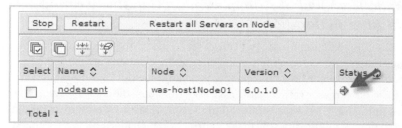

Figure 8-17: Checking the status of the node agent process

Step 13. Open a browser, and issue the URL to invoke the snoop servlet on was-host1 through WebSphere's Embedded HTTP Server (EHS): **http://was-host1: 9080/snoop**. Figure 8-18 shows the resulting page. Notice that the way you invoke snoop before and after federation is the same when you use the EHS. After the federation, you must manage the application server on was-host1 by connecting to the Deployment Manager's admin console.

If you federated the node within the custom profile, you can skip this step because no application server or enterprise applications are available on the custom profile by default.

Figure 8-18: Snoop servlet invoked on was-host1 through the Embedded HTTP Server

Verify the Windows Services Panel for the Node Agent Process

Step 14. If you selected the option to "Run node agent as Windows service" during the federation (Windows platforms only), open the Windows **Services** panel (using **Start|Control Panel|Administrative Tools|Services**), and look for the new WebSphere process that was created.

Automatic Removal of Administration Capability on Application Servers After Federation

After successful federation of an application server node, the federation process removes the administrative applications (adminconsole.ear and filetransfer.ear) from the application server. To confirm this change, you can issue the URL to invoke the admin console from the browser (http://was-host1:9060/ibm/console). Your attempt should fail (as shown in Figure 8-19) because the admin applications no longer exist on the node. If you need to deploy applications or make configuration changes on the federated node, you must do so through the Deployment Manager's admin console.

Figure 8-19: Failed attempt to invoke the admin console on the application server

Understanding the Directory Structure After Federating the Node

After federating a node to the cell, you'll see changes in the directory structure on both the Deployment Manager and the application server (or custom profile) node. Figure 8-20 shows the configuration directory structure of the Deployment Manager (under <DMGR-PROFILE-ROOT>\config\cells\dmgr-hostCell01 on dmgr-host) before and after federating was-host1. Notice that entries for was-host1 are added to the master repository as a result of federation. A nodeagent directory is also created on was-host1.

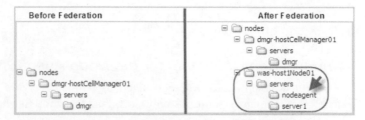

Figure 8-20: Configuration changes on the Deployment Manager (dmgr-host)

Figure 8-21 shows the configuration directory structure of the application server profile (under <PROFILE-ROOT>\config\cells\was-host1Cell01 on was-host1) before and after federating was-host1. Notice that entries for the Deployment Manager have been added to the nodes repository as a result of federation. A nodeagent directory is also created on was-host1.

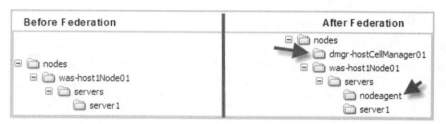

Figure 8-21: Configuration changes on federated node (was-host1)

Federating Other Nodes from the Deployment Manager's Admin Console

For each application server profile you want to federate, repeat the steps in the preceding sections to federate a node from the Deployment Manager's admin console (Steps 1–5), verify the federation by viewing the log files (Steps 6–8), verify the federation from the admin console (Steps 9–13), and (if necessary) verify the Windows **Services** panel for the node agent process (Step 14). If you're federating was-host2 (for example), substitute was-host2 for was-host1 while using those instructions.

After federating was-host2 successfully, you should see an entry for it in the Deployment Manager's admin console as shown in Figure 8-22. Figure 8-23 shows that the node agent has been created and started on was-host2 following federation of the node.

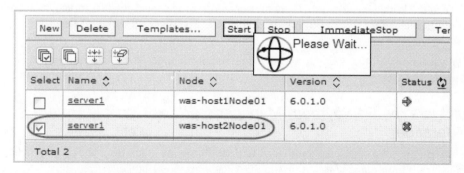

Figure 8-22: Federated was-host2 in Deployment Manager's admin console

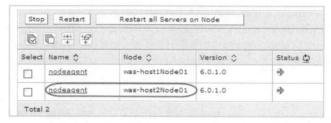

Figure 8-23: Node agent process on federated was-host2 node

Figure 8-24 shows the configuration directory structure of the Deployment Manager (under <DMGR-PROFILE-ROOT>\config\cells\dmgr-hostCell01) after federation of the second node. Notice that entries for was-host2 have been added to the master repository.

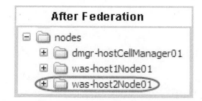

Figure 8-24: Nodes directory after federating the second node (was-host2)

Federating a Node from the Application Server's Command Prompt

In this section, we step through the command-prompt method of federating a node. You use the addNode command to perform this task.

Unless you chose to federate the node within the custom profile when creating the profile, you must use the command-based method to federate a custom profile node. That's because to make initial contact, the Deployment Manager requires an application server to be started on the node. With a custom profile, there is no application server process immediately after the profile's creation, so you can't federate the node from the Deployment Manager.

If you federated all the nodes from the Deployment Manager's admin console, you can skip this discussion.

Navigate the Deployment Manager's Admin Console Before Federation

Before running the addNode command, take the following steps from the Deployment Manager's admin console to obtain the SOAP address port number.

1. Log on to the Deployment Manager's admin console. Expand **System administration**, and select **Deployment manager**. Then, under the **Additional Properties** section, expand **Ports** to display the list of ports used by the Deployment Manager (Figure 8-25). Make a note of the port number for the SOAP_CONNECTOR_ADDRESS port. Communications between the node agent and the Deployment Manager take place through this port (if you're using the default SOAP connType). The figure lists the default port, 8879. If you changed port numbers during the installation, your port number may differ.

2. Log out of the Deployment Manager's admin console. *Warning:* If you don't log out of the console and you try to federate the node using the addNode command prompt, you'll receive synchronization warnings, so be sure to perform this step before federating a node using this method.

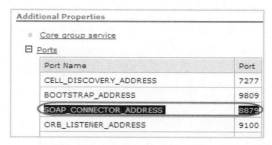

Figure 8-25: Deployment Manager's SOAP_CONNECTOR_ADDRESS port

Federate a Node from the Application Server's Command Prompt

Step 1.　On the node you're going to federate, open a command prompt, and change to the <PROFILE-ROOT>\bin directory. If you're federating a node within a custom profile, change to directory <CUSTOM-PROFILE-ROOT>\bin.

Step 2.　Start the Deployment Manager on dmgr-host (if it isn't already started). You don't need to start the application server process in this case.

Step 3.　Issue the addNode command, specifying the host name and SOAP address port of the Deployment Manager as arguments:

```
addNode.bat dmgr-host 8879
```

If you're working in a Windows environment and want to register the node agent process as a Windows service, include the **–registerservice** argument on the command:

```
addNode.bat dmgr-host 8879 -registerservice
```

Figure 8-26 shows the messages you'll see leading to a report of a successful federation.

```
C:\IBM\WebSphere\AppServer\profiles\AppSrv01\bin>addNode dmgr-host 8879
-registerservice
ADMU0116I: Tool information is being logged in file
           C:\IBM\WebSphere\AppServer\profiles\AppSrv01\logs\addNode.log

ADMU0128I: Starting tool with the AppSrv01 profile
ADMU0001I: Begin federation of node was-host2Node01 with Deployment Mana
ger at
           dmgr-host:8879.
ADMU0009I: Successfully connected to Deployment Manager Server: dmgr-hos
t:8879

           configuration have not been migrated to the new cell.
IDMU0307I: You might want to:
IDMU0303I: Update the configuration on the dmgr-hostCell01 Deployment Ma
lager
           with values from the old cell-level documents.
IDMU9990I:
IDMU0003I: Node was-host2Node01 has been successfully federated.
```

Figure 8-26: Federating a node from the application server's command prompt

Step 4. Verify the federation using the verification instructions given in the earlier sections of this chapter (Steps 9–13 of the "Federating a Node from the Deployment Manager's Admin Console" section).

Federate Other Nodes from the Command Prompt

To federate additional nodes from the command prompt, repeat Steps 1–4 of the preceding section for each application server profile you want to federate. If you're federating was-host2 (for example), substitute was-host2 for was-host1 when following these instructions.

Federate the Node Within the Custom Profile

You use the same procedure (Steps 1–4) to federate the node within the custom profile. When performing the steps for a custom profile, substitute the <CUSTOM-PROFILE-ROOT> directory for the <PROFILE-ROOT> directory and use custom-host instead of was-host1.

Figure 8-27 shows the configuration directory structure of the Deployment Manager (under <DMGR-PROFILE-ROOT>\config\cells\dmgr-hostCell01) after you've federated the custom-host node in our example. Notice that in this case there's no entry for the application server (server1). That's because the custom profile has no application server immediately after its creation. We'll create the application server (server1) on custom-host from the Deployment Manager's admin console later in this chapter. You would see similar configuration changes on the custom-host node (under <CUSTOM-PROFILE-ROOT>\config\cells\custom-hostCell01).

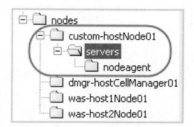

Figure 8-27: Nodes directory after federating the third node (custom-host)

Figure 8-28 shows that the node agent has been created and started on custom-host following federation of that node.

Select	Name ◇	Node ◇	Version ◇	Status ⟳
☐	nodeagent	was-host1Node01	6.0.1.0	✖
☐	nodeagent	custom-hostNode01	6.0.0.1	➡
☐	nodeagent	was-host2Node01	6.0.1.0	✖

Stop | Restart | Restart all Servers on Node

Total 3

Figure 8-28: Node agent process on federated custom-host node

Create the Application Server on the Custom Profile Node After Federation

Next, we look at the steps required to create an application server (server1) on the custom-host node. The diagram in Figure 8-29 illustrates the architecture of the cell of application servers once you've accomplished this task. Before performing these steps, make sure you've federated the node within the custom profile.

You can create an application server on any node that has been federated. Our task here is to create one on custom-host. If you like, you can create multiple applications servers on any node using the same procedure.

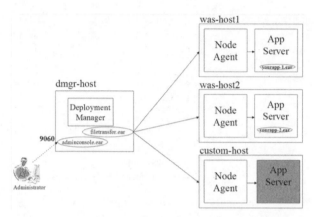

Figure 8-29: Cell of application servers

Step 1. Open a browser, and log in to the Deployment Manager's admin console: **http://dmgr-host:9060/ibm/console**.

Step 2. Expand **Servers**, select **Application Servers**, and click the **New** button to create a new application server on custom-host. At this point in our example, there are application servers on was-host1 and was-host2, as Figure 8-30 shows.

Figure 8-30: List of application servers

Step 3. In the drop-down box on the next page displayed (Figure 8-31), select the node on which you want to create the application server. For this example, select **custom-hostNode01**. Then, assign a name to the application server on custom-host. For consistency, we'll use **server1** for this example.

Step 4. Next (Figure 8-32), select the server template on which you want to base the new application server. Unless you created new templates, you should see only one option, the WebSphere Default Server Template. Select the default template, and click **Next**.

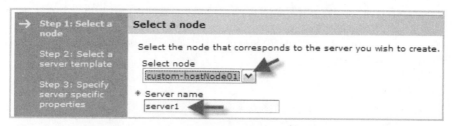

Figure 8-31: Selecting a node

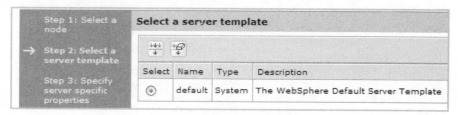

Figure 8-32: Selecting a server template

Step 5. Select the option to "Generate Unique Http Ports," and click **Next**.

Step 6. After reading the confirmation page, click **Finish**.

Step 7. *Don't forget* to save the configuration.

Step 8. Again, expand **Servers** and select **Application Servers**. You should see the application server (server1) that has been created on custom-host, as shown in Figure 8-33. You can deploy applications on this server now.

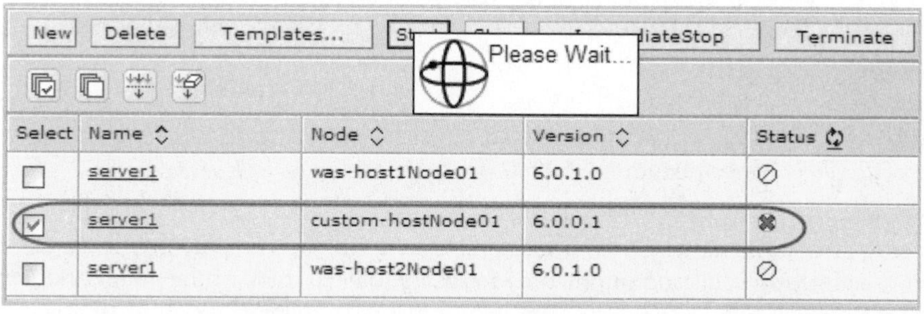

New	Delete	Templates...	St~~~~ ~~~~ ~~~~diateStop	Terminate

Select	Name ◇	Node ◇	Version ◇	Status ⟳
☐	server1	was-host1Node01	6.0.1.0	⊘
☑	server1	custom-hostNode01	6.0.0.1	✖
☐	server1	was-host2Node01	6.0.1.0	⊘

Figure 8-33: List of application servers after adding server1 on the custom-host node

Step 9. Log on to custom-host, and examine the configuration changes (the creation of a server1 directory containing XML configuration files) under the

<CUSTOM-PROFILE-ROOT>\config\cells\dmgr-hostCell01) directory. Figure 8-34 shows the nodes directory as it appears before and after the creation of server1. You'll see similar changes in the Deployment Manager configuration.

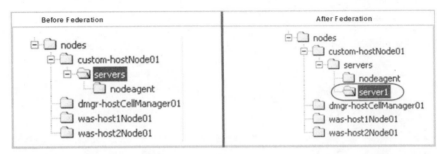

Figure 8-34: Nodes directory before and after creation of server1 on custom-host

Step 10. Navigate to the <CUSTOM-PROFILE-ROOT>\logs directory, and observe that directory server1 has been created to maintain the log files (e.g., SystemOut.log, SystemErr.log) that will be updated during the application server's runtime and while operations (e.g., start, stop) are conducted on the server.

Application Invocation in a Network Deployment Environment

The diagram in Figure 8-35 depicts an enterprise application (inventory.ear) that has been deployed on the custom-host node by an administrator from the Deployment Manager's admin console (http://dmgr-host:9060/ibm/console). The diagram also shows how a user issues requests to invoke applications on the different nodes:

Application	URL
Defaultapp	http://was-host1:9080/snoop
Payroll	http://was-host2:9080/pay
Inventory	http://custom-host:9080/inv

In an enterprise environment, enterprise applications will be available on plenty of systems, and it's difficult and impractical for users to keep track of the nodes and port numbers on which applications are available. In the next chapter, you'll learn how you can simplify the execution of applications by introducing HTTP Server and the plug-in into the architecture.

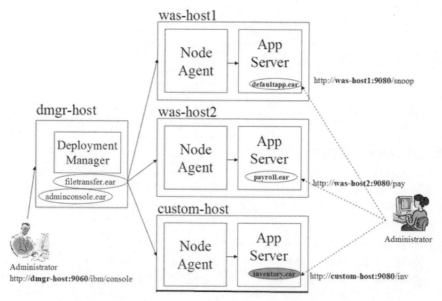

Figure 8-35: Application invocation in a Network Deployment environment

Managing a Cell of Application Servers

There are multiple ways to manage the cell of application servers environment. In this section, we look at some of the frequently used methods. To manage application servers from the Deployment Manager's admin console, make sure the following conditions are satisfied:

- The node within the application server profile must be federated.

- The deployment manager process should be running.

- The node agent process should be running (it provides services required by the application servers during startup).

Start the Deployment Manager Process

Follow the instructions in Chapter 7 to start the deployment manager process.

Verify the Status of the Node Agent

To check the status of the node agent, go to the <PROFILE-ROOT>\bin directory, and run either **serverStatus.bat nodeagent** or **serverStatus.bat –all**. Figure 8-36 shows the latter command being executed.

```
C:\IBM\WebSphere\AppServer\profiles\Custom01\bin>serverStatus -all
ADMU0116I: Tool information is being logged in file
           C:\IBM\WebSphere\AppServer\profiles\Custom01\logs\serverStatus.log
ADMU0128I: Starting tool with the Custom01 profile
ADMU0503I: Retrieving server status for all servers
ADMU0505I: Servers found in configuration:
ADMU0506I: Server name: nodeagent
ADMU0506I: Server name: server1
ADMU0508I: The Node Agent "nodeagent" is STARTED
```

Figure 8-36: Checking the status of the node agent

Start the Node Agent Process

The node agent process runs on the node that has been federated or on the node where the application server you're planning to manage is located. Use one of the following methods to start the node agent process. As a first step, log on to the node where the node agent is running.

- If you registered the node agent process as a service in the Windows registry during federation (Windows systems only), you can start it from the Windows **Services** panel. Right-click the service (shown in Figure 8-37), and click **Start**. (To stop the service, click **Stop**.)

- From a command-line prompt (on any operating system), go to the <PROFILE-ROOT>\bin directory and run **startNode.bat**. (To stop the node agent process, use **stopNode.bat**.) Figure 8-28 shows the startNode.bat command being executed to start the node agent process.

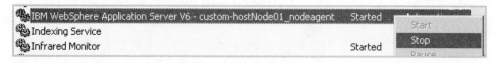

Figure 8-37: Node agent process in the Windows Services panel

```
C:\IBM\WebSphere\AppServer\profiles\Custom01\bin>startNode.bat
ADMU7701I: Because nodeagent is registered to run as a Windows Service, the
           request to start this server will be completed by starting the
           associated Windows Service.
ADMU0116I: Tool information is being logged in file
           C:\IBM\WebSphere\AppServer\profiles\Custom01\logs\nodeagent\startServ
er.log
ADMU0128I: Starting tool with the Custom01 profile
ADMU3100I: Reading configuration for server: nodeagent
ADMU3200I: Server launched. Waiting for initialization status.
ADMU3000I: Server nodeagent open for e-business; process id is 1584
```

Figure 8-38: Executing the startNode.bat command

Start the Application Server

To start the application server, use one of these methods:

- Connect to the Deployment Manager's admin console, expand **Servers**, and click **Application Servers**. Select the check box next to the application server (server1) on the node on which you started the node agent, and click **Start**. (To stop the application server, click **Stop**.)

- From the command prompt, go to the <PROFILE-ROOT>\bin directory and run the command **startServer.bat server1**. (To stop the application server, use **stopServer.bat**.)

Perform Backup and Recovery for the Cell

In the cell of application servers environment (where multiple application servers are being managed by a Deployment Manager), you need to back up both the Deployment Manager and all the nodes you've federated. If you omit any of these components, your backup doesn't represent the whole system.

To make a complete backup of the environment we've built in this chapter, you must back up the following:

- the Deployment Manager on dmgr-host — This represents the entire cell. The configuration information is stored under the <DMGR-PROFILE-ROOT>\ config directory.

- the application servers on was-host1, was-host2, and custom-host — The configuration information for these servers is stored under the <PROFILE-ROOT>\config directory on each node.

If you have no constraints on disk space, stop all the processes in the cell (at a time when it's practical to do so), and make a copy of the entire <WASV6-ROOT> directory on each node, including the Deployment Manager (assuming you used the default directory for the profiles). This method is the easiest way to back up the entire environment. If you created profiles outside <WASV6-ROOT>, also make a copy of <DMGR-PROFILE-ROOT> and <PROFILE-ROOT> on each node.

You can also back up your configuration by running the backupConfig command for the Deployment Manager and each federated node. For instructions on using this command, see Chapter 7.

Logging During Federation of Nodes

The illustration in Figure 8-39 depicts the logging that takes place when you federate a node to the Deployment Manager cell. The log file destinations fall logically into two categories based on the activities performed during federation. Table 8-1 summarizes these activities.

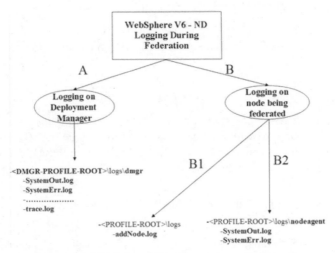

Figure 8-39: WebSphere V6 logging during node federation

Problem Scenarios

Below are descriptions and solutions for two problems commonly encountered during or after federation of a node.

Problem: *You encounter errors when trying to federate a node to the Deployment Manager.*

If you're federating from the Deployment Manager's admin console, make sure the application server of the node you're trying to federate is running to make initial contact. If you're federating from the application server node's command prompt using the addNode command, make sure the Deployment Manager is running. Also make sure you can ping the nodes from each other using both the host name and DNS entry.

Table 8-1: Node federation logging activities

Activity	Log destination	Description	When to use these log files
Logging on the Deployment Manager	The <DMGR-PROFILE-ROOT>\logs\dmgr directory ■ The log files here are SystemOut.log and SystemErr.log.	When you federate a node using the Deployment Manager's admin console, the logging initially takes place in file SystemOut.log on the Deployment Manager side.Logging during the federation also goes into SystemOut.log.	■ Use if the Deployment Manager fails to contact the node being federated. ■ Use if you see any errors during the federation or while conducting operations on the admin console.
Logging on the node being federated and	The <PROFILE-ROOT>\logs directory ■ The log file here is addNode.log.	When you federate a node using the addNode.bat (.sh) command from the node you're federating, the logging initially takes place in file addNode.log. Logging during the federation and creation of the node agent also goes into addNode.log.	■ Use if the node being federated fails to contact the Deployment Manager or you see any errors during federation ■ Use if you have problems starting or stopping the node agent during or after federation.
Logging on the node agent	The <PROFILE-ROOT>\logs\nodeagent directory ■ The log files here are SystemOut.log and SystemErr.log.	After the node agent has been created during the federation, the process tries to start the node agent. All logging that occurs during the start, stop, and runtime of the node agent goes into these files.	

Problem: You're unable to start an application server whose node was successfully federated previously. You receive an error when trying to start the server from the command prompt (Figure 8-40), and exceptions are recorded in file SystemOut.log (Figure 8-41).

```
C:\IBM\WebSphere\AppServer\profiles\Custom01\bin>startServer server1
ADMU0116I: Tool information is being logged in file
           C:\IBM\WebSphere\AppServer\profiles\Custom01\logs\server1\startServer
.log
ADMU0128I: Starting tool with the Custom01 profile
ADMU3100I: Reading configuration for server: server1
ADMU3200I: Server launched. Waiting for initialization status.
ADMU3011E: Server launched but failed initialization. Server log files should
           contain failure information.
```

Figure 8-40: Error received when running startServer.bat

After federating a node, you need to start the node agent before starting the application server because the Location Service Daemon required by the application server during startup is available on the node agent.

```
[5/15/05 21:20:14:091 CDT] 0000000a WsServerImpl  E    WSVR0009E: Error
occurred during startup
com.ibm.ws.exception.RuntimeError: com.ibm.ws.exception.RuntimeError:
com.ibm.ejs.EJSException: Could not register with Location Service Daemon,
which could only reside in the NodeAgent. Make sure the NodeAgent for this
node is up an running.; nested exception is:
      org.omg.CORBA.ORBPackage.InvalidName:
LocationService:org.omg.CORBA.TRANSIENT: java.net.ConnectException:
```

Figure 8-41: SystemOut.log exceptions

9

IBM HTTP Server V6 Distributed Plug-in for WebSphere V6: Install, Configure, Verify, and Manage

In Chapter 6, you learned how to configure the WebSphere plug-in for IBM HTTP Server in a standalone server environment. Recall that the plug-in is the element responsible for diverting requests for dynamic content (e.g., servlets) from the HTTP server to WebSphere Application Server. In this chapter, we explain how to configure the plug-in in a distributed (i.e., Network Deployment) environment. You'll also learn how to set up your WebSphere environment so you can manage IBM HTTP Server from the WebSphere administrative console.

Distributed Plug-in Configurations

To understand the configuration choices for a distributed plug-in, you first need to know about managed and unmanaged nodes. A *managed node* is one on which a node agent process is running. With a node agent present on the node, the Deployment Manager can manage the application servers and Web servers on that node through the node agent. When you install a custom profile on a machine and federate the node within the custom profile (thereby creating a node agent process on the node), you have a managed node. (If you want an application server on the node, you can install an application server profile instead of a custom profile.)

An *unmanaged node* is a node that the Deployment Manager doesn't manage or a node on which no node agent process is running. The Deployment Manager can't manage application servers or Web servers (other than IBM HTTP Server V6) on an unmanaged node. (You can manage IBM HTTP Server V6 by using IBM HTTP Administration

Server V6 in place of a node agent. For all other Web servers, this capability requires a node agent.)

Distributed Plug-in Configuration Categories

We can distinguish distributed plug-in configurations into four categories based on the presence or absence of a node agent process on the Deployment Manager box and on the location of the plug-in (and HTTP Server) with respect to the Deployment Manager:

- *Distributed local plug-in – managed node* — In this configuration, the Deployment Manager and plug-in (with Web server) reside on the same machine. The node agent process is present on the Web server (with plug-in) node. All IBM-supported Web servers can be managed from the Deployment Manager's admin console through the node agent. This configuration is suitable for nonproduction environments.

- *Distributed local plug-in – unmanaged node* — In this configuration, the Deployment Manager and plug-in (with Web server) again reside on the same machine, but the node agent process is absent. The only Web server you can manage through the Deployment Manager's admin console in this configuration is IBM HTTP Server V6. For HTTP Server, IBM HTTP Admin Server V6 plays the role of the node agent. This configuration is suitable for nonproduction environments.

- *Distributed remote plug-in – managed node* — In this configuration, the Deployment Manager and plug-in (with Web server) reside on different machines. The node agent process is present on the Web server node. All IBM-supported Web servers can be managed from the Deployment Manager's admin console through the node agent. This configuration is suitable for nonproduction environments.

- *Distributed remote plug-in – unmanaged node* — In this configuration, the Deployment Manager and plug-in (with Web server) reside on different machines. The node agent process is absent on the Web server node. The only Web server you can manage through the Deployment Manager's admin console in this configuration is IBM HTTP Server V6, using HTTP Admin Server in place of the node agent. This configuration is suitable for production environments.

Figure 9-1 illustrates the four distributed plug-in categories. (For clarity and to focus on the current subject, we've omitted some components from these diagrams.) Notice that on the managed nodes, the Deployment Manager works with the node agent process to manage HTTP Server. On the unmanaged nodes, the Deployment Manager works with HTTP Admin Server to manage HTTP Server.

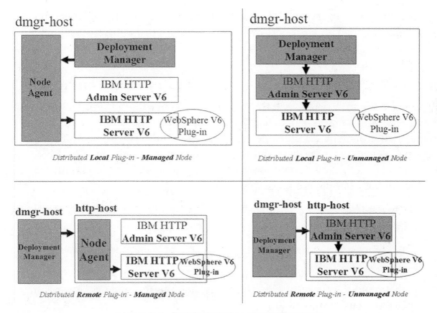

Figure 9-1: Distributed plug-in configurations

Prerequisites to Understanding and Performing Distributed Plug-in Tasks

The procedure for installing a plug-in in a distributed environment differs slightly from that for a standalone server environment. Before creating a distributed plug-in, make sure you've read Chapter 6 and understand the behavior of the plug-in in the standalone server scenario. Consider this chapter an extension of Chapter 6, which we'll be referencing to perform many of the steps here.

You should also have completed all the tasks in Chapters 7 and 8 to install the WebSphere Network Deployment package, create profiles (deployment manager, application server, and custom), and federate nodes to the Deployment Manager's cell. Use the following instructions to set up the prerequisite environment:

1. Use Chapter 7 to install, create, and verify the Deployment Manager on dmgr-host. Be sure to clear the "Application Server Samples" option when installing the product binaries. Apply the required fix pack, and verify.

2. Use Chapter 7 to install, create, and verify the application server and custom profiles on was-host1, was-host2, and custom-host. Apply fix packs, and verify.

3. Use Chapter 8 to federate the nodes within the profiles to the Deployment Manager cell. You *must* perform this step before installing a plug-in in a distributed environment.

Request Processing in a Distributed Plug-in Environment

The diagram in Figure 9-2 shows how the HTTP server (with plug-in) behaves when it receives a request from a user in a distributed plug-in configuration. In the Network Deployment environment, all the nodes are federated to the Deployment Manager, and the plug-in is generated from the Deployment Manager's admin console. The Deployment Manager knows about the applications deployed on the various nodes, and the requests in the example are processed as follows:

- If the request is for http://dmgr-host/snoop, the plug-in module forwards the request to was-host1.

- If the request is for http://dmgr-host/pay, the plug-in module forwards the request to was-host2.

- If the request is for http://dmgr-host/inv, the plug-in module forwards the request to custom-host.

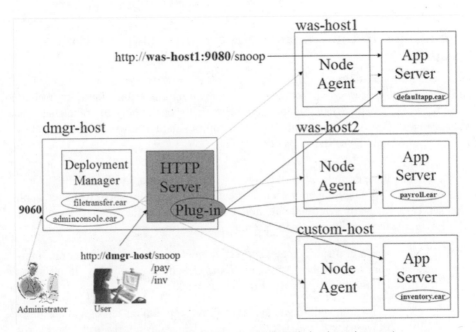

Figure 9-2: Request processing in a distributed plug-in environment

Note that you can also invoke the snoop servlet through WebSphere's Embedded HTTP Server (EHS) using the URL http://was-host1:9080/snoop. (In this scenario, HTTP Server and the plug-in don't participate in the request processing.) This method also works with other application servers that have been federated. You can use this procedure to debug and resolve problems.

In the remainder of this chapter, we step through the process of configuring and verifying the four types of distributed plug-ins. As in earlier chapters, we assume you're working in a Windows XP environment. If you're using a Unix operating system, you'll need to execute the appropriate commands for your operating system (i.e., .sh instead of .bat) and substitute the forward slash (/) for the backward slash (\) in directory and path names. Table 9-1 lists, by operating system, the default directory locations for the symbolic references we use in this chapter.

Table 9-1: Directory locations for symbolic references

Symbolic reference	Windows	AIX	Linux/Unix
<CUSTOM-PROFILE-ROOT>	<WASV6-ROOT>\profiles\Custom01	<WASV6-ROOT>/profiles/Custom01	<WASV6-ROOT>/profiles/Custom01
<IHSV6-ROOT>	C:\IBM\HTTPServer	/usr/IBMIHS	/opt/IBMIHS
<PLUGIN-ROOT>	C:\IBM\WebSphere\Plugins	/usr/WebSphere/plugins	/opt/WebSphere/plugins
<PROFILE-ROOT> for default profile	<WASV6-ROOT>\profiles\default	<WASV6-ROOT>/profiles/default	<WASV6-ROOT>/profiles/default
<WASV6-ROOT>	C:\IBM\WebSphere\AppServer	/usr/WebSphere/AppServer	/opt/WebSphere/AppServer

Distributed Local Plug-in – Managed Node

The diagram in Figure 9-3 illustrates the architecture of the distributed local plug-in – managed node configuration, including the node agent that's needed (on the Deployment Manager/Web server node) to manage HTTP Server from the WebSphere admin console. Notice that even though IBM HTTP Admin Server is installed in this configuration, it isn't started or involved in managing the Web server.

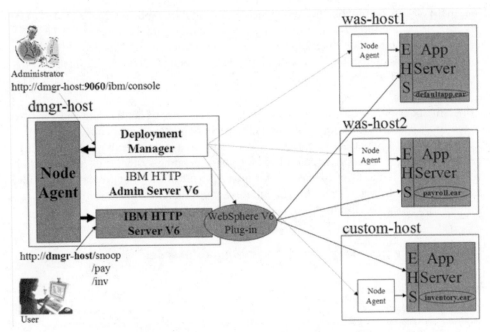

Figure 9-3: Distributed local plug-in – managed node architecture

The flow chart in Figure 9-4 shows the high-level steps to install, configure, and verify a distributed local plug-in – managed node configuration.

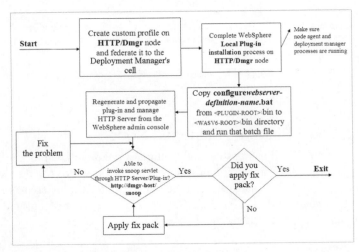

Figure 9-4: Installation overview: Distributed local plug-in – managed node

Install and Configure the Local Plug-in – Managed Node

Before proceeding, make sure you've completed the prerequisite tasks described above. Then take the following steps to set up the local plug-in – managed node environment.

Step 1.   Using the instructions in Chapter 5, install IBM HTTP Server on the same machine as the Deployment Manager (dmgr-host). Apply the required fix pack, and verify.

Step 2.   Using the instructions in Chapter 7, create and verify a custom profile on the Deployment Manager machine. Apply the fix pack, and verify.

In a local plug-in configuration, you can propagate the plug-in file (plugin-cfg.xml) from the Deployment Manager's admin console without the node agent process (because the Deployment Manager resides on the same machine as the plug-in). However, to start and stop the Web server from the admin console, you need a node agent — thus the need to create a custom profile.

> **Note:** If an application server profile already exists on the Deployment Manager machine and is federated to the Deployment Manager cell (creating a node agent), you don't need to install a custom profile. Also, if you want to deploy applications to an application server on this machine, you can install an application server profile instead of a custom profile.

Step 3.   Use Chapter 8 to federate the node within the custom profile on the Deployment Manager machine to create a node agent process on dmgr-host. Issue the following command from the <CUSTOM-PROFILE-ROOT>\bin directory to federate the node:

```
addNode dmgr-host 8879
```

Step 4.   Install a local plug-in on the Deployment Manager node (dmgr-host) by completing Steps 1–16 in Chapter 6's "Installing IBM HTTP Server V6 Local Plug-in for WebSphere" section. Take note of the following particulars for the distributed installation.

In Step 15, specify a meaningful name for the Web server definition that will be created in the Deployment Manager's repository. Figure 9-5 shows the name we'll use for this example, webserver-on-dmgr-host. The plug-in installation process uses this name to create a batch file (configure*webserver-definition-name*.bat) under the <PLUGIN-ROOT>\bin directory. In our example, the file name will be configurewebserver-on-dmgr-host.bat.

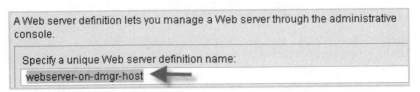

A Web server definition lets you manage a Web server through the administrative
console.

Specify a unique Web server definition name:
webserver-on-dmgr-host

Figure 9-5: Specifying the Web server definition

Unlike in the standalone server environment, the configuration batch file
won't be executed automatically during the distributed local plug-in installation. You'll run this process manually from the command prompt later. Once
you've successfully configured the Web server's definition, you'll be able to
manage HTTP Server through the Deployment Manager's admin console.

For the plug-in file location (Step 16), accept the default location and click
Next. For a local plug-in installation, the default plug-in file will be generated under the <PROFILE-ROOT>*config*\ . . . *webserver-definition-name*
directory. In this example, HTTP Server (with plug-in) and WebSphere are
on the same machine (a local plug-in), so you don't need to propagate the
plug-in file. After you generate the file, the plug-in module will read it
during the Web server's startup and at an interval specified by parameter
RefreshInterval in the plug-in file (60 seconds by default).

Step 5. Review the summary panel that's presented next (Figure 9-6). Notice that the
panel informs you that some manual configuration (i.e., executing the
configuration batch file) is required. Click **Next**.

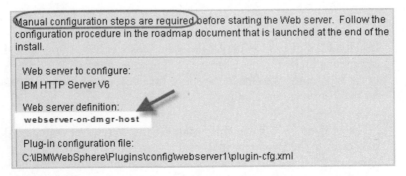

Manual configuration steps are required before starting the Web server. Follow the
configuration procedure in the roadmap document that is launched at the end of the
install.

Web server to configure:
IBM HTTP Server V6

Web server definition:
webserver-on-dmgr-host

Plug-in configuration file:
C:\IBM\WebSphere\Plugins\config\webserver1\plugin-cfg.xml

Figure 9-6: Summary panel noting manual configuration required

Step 6.   At this time, the installation program copies the required files to the <PLU-GIN-ROOT> directory. Once the binary and configuration files are copied, another summary panel provides the name of the batch file you need to run to configure the Web server definition in the WebSphere repository. Click **Next** on this panel. Then close the browser that displays the installation roadmap, and click **Finish** on the final summary panel.

Verify Installation by Viewing the Log and Configuration Files

Step 7.   To verify the installation of the plug-in, follow the instructions in the section of Chapter 6 titled "Verify Installation by Viewing the Log and Configuration Files." Then apply the fix pack for the plug-in, and verify.

Configure WebSphere to Include the HTTP Server Definition

Your next task is to configure the Web server definition in the Deployment Manager repository. To do so, take the following steps.

Step 8.   Start the Deployment Manager and node agent processes (if they're not already running) on dmgr-host. (If you're configuring for an unmanaged node, you won't have a node agent process on the Web server machine.)

Step 9.   Open a command prompt, go to the <PLUGIN-ROOT>\bin directory, and copy the Web server definition configuration batch file (configurewebserver-on-dmgr-host in our example) to the <WASV6-ROOT>\bin directory.

Step 10.   Now, go to the <WASV6-ROOT>\bin directory, and execute the batch file you just copied. Make sure you log out of the admin console before executing the batch file; otherwise, you may see warnings about workspace conflicts.

Note: When you configure the Web server definition by running the batch file, the Web server is configured with the default profile. You must therefore make sure the profile that has been federated to the Deployment Manager is the default profile on that node. (If you're running the batch file on dmgr-host, the deployment manager profile should be the default profile.)

If the federated profile isn't the default profile and you have a profile that isn't federated (i.e., it's being used as a standalone server), you must configure the Web server definition manually instead of through the batch file. (In this situation, the Web server definition is configured with the default profile that was on the standalone server as a result of running the batch file.) We describe how to configure the Web server definition manually near the end of this chapter.

Generate the Plug-in File and Propagate to the Web Server from the Admin Console

Next, you must regenerate the plug-in file and propagate it to the Web server.

Step 11.   Connect to the Deployment Manager's admin console: **http://dmgr-host:9060/ibm/console**.

Step 12.   Expand **Servers**, and click **Web servers** to see the listing of the Web server definition you configured to enable administration through the admin console (Figure 9-7). Select the Web server's check box, and click **Generate Plug-in** to regenerate the plug-in file.

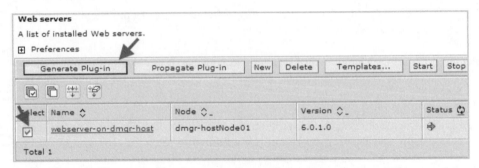

Figure 9-7: Web server definition in Deployment Manager's admin console

Step 13.   Next, select the Web server's check box again, and click **Propagate Plug-in** to move the plug-in file to the required location. (This step is optional in the case of a local plug-in.)

Step 14.   Restart HTTP Server, or wait 60 seconds (or the interval specified by the RefreshInterval parameter) for the plug-in module to load the new plug-in file.

Step 15.   Select the Web server's check box once more, and click **Stop** and then **Start** to restart the Web server. (If you configured the Web server definition with a standalone server, the start and stop capabilities won't be available; you'll be able to use this panel only to generate and propagate the plug-in file.)

Note: As a general rule to minimize troubleshooting time, try to start HTTP Server from the machine on which you installed it before trying to start it from the admin console. Doing so will help you make sure there are no log-on problems, such as an incorrect user ID or password.

Step 16. Log out of the admin console by clicking **Logout** on the top horizontal menu bar.

Verify Installation and Configuration from the Browser

To verify the plug-in installation from the browser, take these steps.

Step 17. Open a browser, and issue the URL **http://dmgr-host** to bring up the HTTP Server welcome page.

Step 18. Issue the URL to invoke the snoop servlet through the WebSphere EHS: **http://was-host1:9080/snoop**. (We're assuming you included applications when federating was-host1 to keep the default application in a cell environment.) If you have trouble invoking snoop, see the "Logging: Problem Determination and Troubleshooting" section of Chapter 6.

Step 19. Next, open a browser, and invoke the snoop servlet through the HTTP Server plug-in on WebSphere: **http://dmgr-host/snoop**. You should see the page shown in Figure 9-8. If you have trouble invoking snoop, see "Logging: Problem Determination and Troubleshooting" in Chapter 6.

Figure 9-8: Snoop servlet invoked on dmgr-host

Distributed Local Plug-in – Unmanaged Node

Figure 9-9 illustrates the architecture of a distributed local plug-in – unmanaged node configuration, which contains no node agent. Notice that IBM HTTP Admin Server is acting in place of a node agent on the dmgr-host node to manage IBM HTTP Server V6 from the Deployment Manager's admin console.

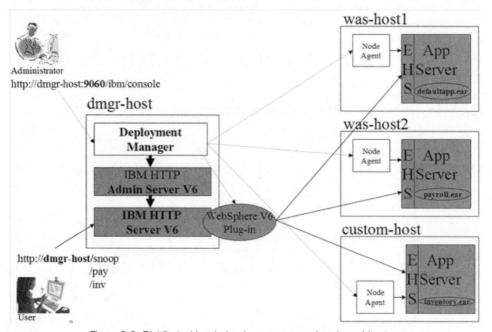

Figure 9-9: Distributed local plug-in – unmanaged node architecture

The flow chart in Figure 9-10 shows the high-level steps to install, configure, and verify a distributed local plug-in with Web server as an unmanaged node. This process has many steps in common with the local plug-in – managed node configuration, and we'll be referencing parts of that procedure in the following discussion. The main difference between a managed and an unmanaged node in a distributed local plug-in environment is the absence of a custom profile/node agent process on the Deployment Manager/Web server node.

Install and Configure the Local Plug-in – Unmanaged Node

Before proceeding, make sure you've accomplished the prerequisite tasks described near the beginning of the chapter. Then, to install and configure the local plug-in, complete the following steps from the installation procedure described above for the local plug-in – managed node:

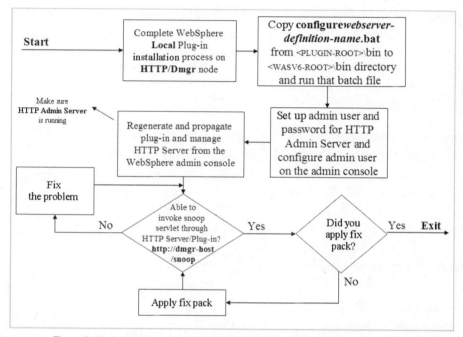

Figure 9-10: Installation overview: Distributed local plug-in – unmanaged node

1. Complete Step 1 to install and verify IBM HTTP Server V6.

2. *Skip* Steps 2 and 3. An unmanaged node won't have a node agent process, so you don't need to install a custom profile and federate.

3. Complete Steps 4–6 to install and configure the distributed local plug-in.

Verify Installation by Viewing the Log and Configuration Files

To verify the plug-in installation, follow the instructions given under this task heading for the local plug-in – managed node (Step 7 above).

Create an Administrative User ID and Password for HTTP Server

Once you've successfully installed the plug-in, you need to assign an administrative user ID and password for HTTP Server on the Deployment Manager/Web server machine (dmgr-host). You'll use this ID and password to manage HTTP Server through HTTP Admin Server from the Deployment Manager console. To create the ID and password, follow the instructions under this task heading in Chapter 6.

Configure WebSphere to Include the HTTP Server Definition

To configure WebSphere with the Web server's definition, complete the steps under this task heading as for the local plug-in – managed node (Steps 8–10). Ignore the instructions for the node agent process because you won't have a node agent on an unmanaged node. To configure the Web server definition manually instead of through the batch file (configure*webserver-definition*.bat), refer to the instructions at the end of this chapter.

Configure WebSphere to Manage HTTP Server Through HTTP Admin Server from the WebSphere Admin Console

Next, you need to configure WebSphere to manage HTTP Server through HTTP Admin Server from the WebSphere admin console. To do so, take the following steps.

Step 1. Open a browser, and log on to the Deployment Manager's admin console.

Step 2. Expand **Servers**, and click **Web servers**. You should see the Web server's definition as shown in Figure 9-11.

Figure 9-11: Web server definition in Deployment Manager's admin console

Step 3. Click the Web server definition name (webserver-on-dmgr-host in our example), and then click the **Remote Web server management** link in the **Additional Properties** section.

Step 4. On the resulting page (Figure 9-12), enter the administrative user ID and password you created for HTTP Admin Server, click **OK**, and save the configuration.

Figure 9-12: Remote Web server management page

Verify Installation and Configuration from the Browser

To verify the installation from the browser, complete the steps under this task heading as for the distributed local plug-in – managed node (Steps 17–19).

Distributed Remote Plug-in – Managed Node

Figure 9-13 depicts the architecture of a distributed remote plug-in – managed node configuration. In this scenario, you need a node agent (on the remote Web server node) to manage HTTP Server from the WebSphere admin console. Note that although HTTP Admin Server has been installed on this machine, it isn't started or involved in managing the Web server in this configuration.

The remote plug-in – managed node configuration is tricky and raises some questions initially if the concept isn't understood clearly. Even though the Deployment Manager and the Web server (with plug-in) are on different machines in this scenario, the node agent process (which is created when you federate the custom profile to the Deployment Manager cell) is local to the Web server. Imagine that there's a hard-wired connection between the node agent and the Deployment Manager (or that the Deployment Manager is virtually on the same machine as the Web server). When you install the plug-in, you install it as a local plug-in, but when you run the Web server definition batch file on the Web server machine, the process is configured with the Deployment Manager through the node agent automatically. This is the reason you federate the custom profile before installing the plug-in.

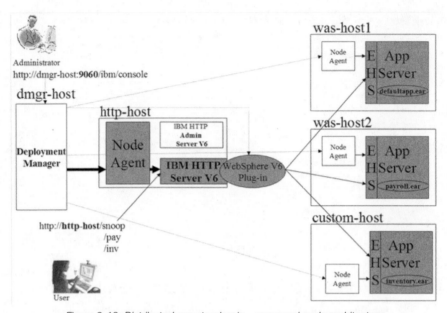

Figure 9-13: Distributed remote plug-in – managed node architecture

The flow chart in Figure 9-14 shows the high-level steps to install, configure, and verify a distributed remote plug-in with the Web server as a managed node.

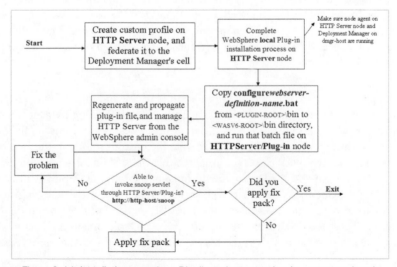

Figure 9-14: Installation overview: Distributed remote plug-in – managed node

Install and Configure Remote Plug-in – Managed Node

Before proceeding, make sure you've accomplished the prerequisite tasks. Then complete the following steps to set up the remote plug-in – managed node environment.

Step 1. Install IBM HTTP Server on the Web server machine (http-host) using the instructions in Chapter 5. Apply the required fix pack, and verify.

Step 2. Install and verify the custom profile on the Web server node (http-host) using the instructions in Chapter 7. Apply the fix pack, and verify.

Step 3. Federate the node within the custom profile on the Web server machine (http-host) to the Deployment Manager (on dmgr-host) using the instructions in Chapter 8. This step creates a node agent process on the Web server machine. Issue the following command from the <CUSTOM-PROFILE-ROOT>\bin directory to federate the node:

```
addNode dmgr-host 8879
```

Step 4. Go to the machine on which you installed and tested HTTP Server (http-host). To install the plug-in, complete Steps 1–16 of Chapter 6's "Installing IBM HTTP Server V6 Local Plug-in" section. As we noted, even though you're configuring for a remote plug-in here, you follow the local plug-in instructions because you have a node agent process locally on the Web server node. Take note of the following particulars for the distributed installation.

In Step 15, specify a meaningful name for the Web server's definition in the Deployment Manager's repository. Figure 9-15 shows the name we'll use for this example, webserver-on-http-host. The plug-in installation process uses this name to create a batch file (configure*webserver-definition-name*.bat) under the <PLUGIN-ROOT>\bin directory. In our example, the name of the batch file will be configurewebserver-on-http-host.bat. You'll run this process manually from the command line later.

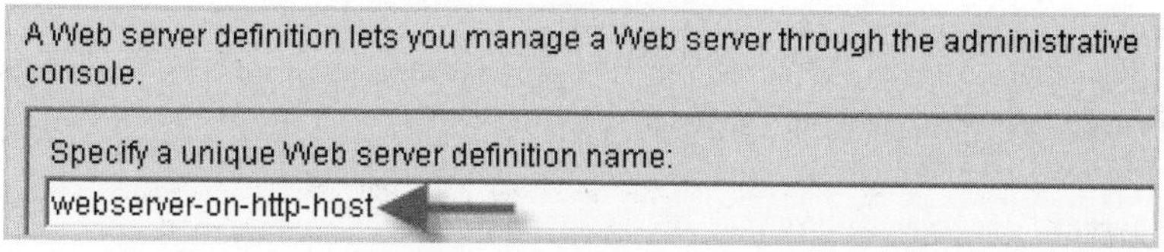

A Web server definition lets you manage a Web server through the administrative console.

Specify a unique Web server definition name:

webserver-on-http-host

Figure 9-15: Specifying the Web server definition

For the plug-in file location (Step 16), accept the default location and click **Next**. For a local plug-in installation, the default plug-in file will be generated under the <PROFILE-ROOT>\config\ . . . \webserver-definition-name directory.

Step 5. Review the summary panel that's presented next. Notice that some manual configuration (i.e., executing the configuration batch file) is required. Click **Next**.

Step 6. At this time, the installation program copies the required files to the <PLUGIN-ROOT> directory. Once the binary and configuration files are copied, another summary panel provides the name of the batch file you need to run to configure the Web server definition in the WebSphere repository. Click **Next** on this panel. Then close the browser that displays the installation roadmap, and click **Finish** on the final summary panel.

Verify Installation by Viewing the Log and Configuration Files

Step 7. To verify the installation of the plug-in, follow the instructions given under this task heading for the local plug-in – managed node (Step 7).

Configure WebSphere to Include the HTTP Server Definition

Step 8. Start the Deployment Manager (on dmgr-host) and the node agent process (on http-host) if they're not already running.

Step 9. Open a command prompt on the Web server node (http-host), go to the <PLUGIN-ROOT>\bin directory, and copy the Web server definition configuration batch file (configurewebserver-on-http-host) to the <WASV6-ROOT>\bin directory.

Step 10. Go to <WASV6-ROOT>\bin on http-host, and execute the batch file you just copied. (Be sure to log out of the admin console before executing the batch file; otherwise, you may see warnings about workspace conflicts.) When you run the batch file, you'll see (as shown in Figure 9-16) that the wsadmin JACL script (which the batch file uses to configure the WebSphere

```
C:\IBM\WebSphere\Plugins\bin>"C:\IBM\WebSphere\AppServer\profiles\Custom01/bin/w
sadmin.bat" -f "C:\IBM\WebSphere\AppServer\bin\configureWebserverDefinition.jacl
" webserver-on-http-host IHS "C:\\IBM\\HTTPServer" "C:\\IBM\\HTTPServer\\conf\\h
ttpd.conf" 80 MAP_ALL "C:\\IBM\\WebSphere\\Plugins" managed http-hostNode01 saih
ost windows
WASX7209I: Connected to process "dmgr" on node dmgr-hostCellManager01 using SOAP
connector;  The type of process is: DeploymentManager
```

Figure 9-16: Executing the configuration batch file

repository) connects to the Deployment Manager and performs the configuration remotely from the Web server node through the node agent.

When you configure the Web server definition by running the batch file, the Web server is configured with the default profile, so you must make sure the profile federated to the Deployment Manager is the default profile on that node. For more information about this requirement, see the note in Step 10 of the configuration procedure for the distributed local plug-in – managed node.

Generate the Plug-in File and Propagate to the Remote Web Server from the Admin Console

Step 11. Connect to the Deployment Manager's admin console: **http://dmgr-host:9060/ibm/console**.

Step 12. Expand **Servers,** and click **Web servers** to see the Web server definition that was configured to enable administration through the admin console (Figure 9-17).

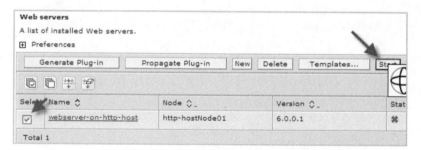

Figure 9-17: Web server definition in Deployment Manager's admin console

Step 13. Select the Web server's check box, and click **Generate Plug-in** to regenerate the plug-in file.

Step 14. Select the Web server's check box again, and click **Propagate Plug-in** to move the plugin-cfg.xml file to the required location. If you have problems propagating the plug-in file, refer to Chapter 6.

Step 15. Start HTTP Server, or wait 60 seconds (or the interval specified by the plug-in file's RefreshInterval parameter) for the plug-in module to load the new plug-in file.

Step 16.   Select the Web server's check box, and click **Start** to start the Web server.

Step 17.   Log out of the admin console by clicking **Logout** on the top horizontal menu bar.

Verify Installation and Configuration from the Browser

Step 18.   Open a browser, and issue the URL **http://http-host** to display the HTTP Server welcome page.

Step 19.   Issue the URL to invoke the snoop servlet through the WebSphere EHS from the browser: **http://was-host1:9080/snoop**. (We're assuming you included applications when federating was-host1 to keep the default application in the cell environment.) If you have problems invoking snoop, see "Logging: Problem Determination and Troubleshooting" in Chapter 6.

Step 20.   Open a browser, and invoke snoop through the plug-in on HTTP Server: **http://http-host/snoop**. You should see the page shown in Figure 9-18. If you have problems invoking snoop, see "Logging: Problem Determination and Troubleshooting" in Chapter 6.

Figure 9-18: Snoop servlet invoked on http-host

Distributed Remote Plug-in – Unmanaged Node

Figure 9-19 shows the architecture of the distributed remote plug-in – unmanaged node configuration, which contains no node agent. In this configuration, IBM HTTP Admin Server acts as a node agent to manage IBM HTTP Server V6 from the Deployment Manager's admin console. This configuration is useful when you plan to deploy the Web server in a DMZ in a production environment. For security reasons, you may not want a node agent deployed on the Web server in this situation. Using IBM HTTP Server and IBM HTTP Admin Server is a good alternative if you still want to be able to manage the HTTP server remotely from the admin console.

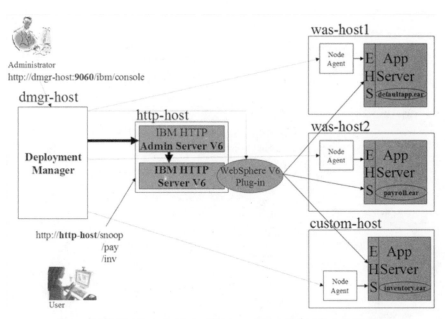

Figure 9-19: Distributed remote plug-in – unmanaged node architecture

The flow chart in Figure 9-20 depicts the high-level steps to install, configure, and verify a distributed remote plug-in with Web server as an unmanaged node. The configuration process for this environment is similar to the remote plug-in configuration you performed in Chapter 6 for a standalone server environment. If you follow the steps in that chapter to configure a remote plug-in, substitute dmgr-host (the Deployment Manager node) for was-host (the application server node). The main difference between a managed and an unmanaged node in a distributed remote plug-in environment is the absence of the custom profile/node agent process on the Web server node.

Install and Configure Distributed Remote Plug-in – Unmanaged Node

Before proceeding, make sure you've completed the prerequisite tasks described above. Then take the following steps to set up the remote plug-in – unmanaged node environment.

Step 1. Install IBM HTTP Server V6 on the Web server machine (http-host) using the instructions in Chapter 5. Apply the fix pack, and verify.

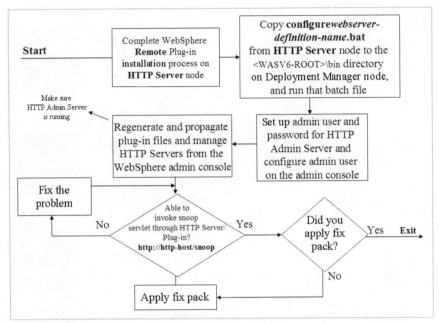

Figure 9-20: Installation overview: Distributed remote plug-in – unmanaged node

Step 2. Install the plug-in on the Web server machine by completing Steps 1–7 of the section "Installing IBM HTTP Server V6 Remote Plug-in for WebSphere" in Chapter 6. You use the remote plug-in instructions in this case because, unlike with a managed node, you don't have a node agent process locally on the Web server node. Take note of the following particulars for a distributed installation.

In Step 5, specify a meaningful name for the Web server's definition in the Deployment Manager's repository. Figure 9-21 shows the name we'll use for this example, webserver-on-http-host. The plug-in installation process uses this name to create a batch file (configure*webserver-definition-name*.bat) under the <PLUGIN-ROOT>\bin directory. In our example, the name of the

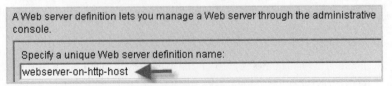

Figure 9-21: Specifying the Web server definition

batch file will be configurewebserver-on-http-host.bat. You'll run this batch
file manually from the command line later.

For the plug-in file location (Step 6), accept the default location and click
Next. For a remote plug-in installation, the default plug-in file will be
generated under the <PROFILE-ROOT>*config*\ . . . *webserver-definition-
name* directory.

Specify dmgr-host as the remote WebSphere node (Step 7).

Step 3.   Review the summary panel that's presented next. Notice that some manual
configuration (i.e., executing the configuration batch file) is required. Click
Next.

Step 4.   At this time, the installation program copies the required files to the <PLU-
GIN-ROOT> directory. Once the binary and configuration files are copied,
another summary panel provides the name of the batch file you need to run
to configure the Web server definition in the Deployment Manager repository. Click **Next** on this panel. Then close the browser that displays the
installation roadmap, and click **Finish** on the final summary panel.

Verify Installation by Viewing the Log and Configuration Files

To verify the installation of the plug-in, follow the instructions given under this task
heading for the local plug-in – managed node (Step 7).

Create an Administrative User ID and Password for HTTP Server

Next, create an administrative user ID and password for HTTP Server. To do so, follow
the instructions under this task heading in the "Installing IBM HTTP Server V6 Remote
Plug-in for WebSphere" section of Chapter 6.

Configure WebSphere to Include HTTP Server Definition

Step 1.   Open a command prompt on the Web server machine (http-host). Go to the
<PLUGIN-ROOT>\bin directory, and copy the Web server definition
configuration batch file (that was generated during the plug-in install) to the
<WASV6-ROOT>\bin directory on the Deployment Manager node
(dmgr-host). Figure 9-22 shows the location of this file for our example. You
can use any means suitable on your operating system (e.g., File Transfer
Protocol, Remote Copy Protocol, mapping a network drive) to copy the
batch file.

Figure 9-22: Configuration batch file in <PLUGIN-ROOT>\bin on http-host

---

Note: If HTTP Server and WebSphere happen to be on different operating systems in your environment (for example, if HTTP Server with the plug-in is on Windows and WebSphere is on a Unix system), go to the <PLUGIN-ROOT>\bin\crossPlatformScripts directory on the Web server machine, and copy the Web server definition configuration batch file from there to <WASV6-ROOT>/bin on the WebSphere machine.

Step 2.   Log on to the Deployment Manager node (dmgr-host), and start the default server.

Step 3.   Go to the <WASV6-ROOT>\bin directory on the Deployment Manager node, and execute the batch file you just copied. (Be sure to log out of the admin console before executing the file; otherwise, you may receive workspace conflict warnings.) To configure the Web server definition manually instead of through the batch file, see the instructions given later in this chapter.

Configure WebSphere to Manage HTTP Server Through HTTP Admin Server from the WebSphere Admin Console

Step 1.   Open a browser, and log on to the Deployment Manager's admin console.

Step 2.   Expand **Servers**, and click **Web servers**. You should see the Web server's definition as shown in Figure 9-23.

Figure 9-23: Web server definition in Deployment Manager's admin console

Step 3.   Click the Web server definition name (webserver-on-http-host in our example), and then click the **Remote Web server management** link in the **Additional Properties** section.

Step 4.   On the resulting page (Figure 9-24), enter the administrative user ID and password you created earlier for HTTP Admin Server, click **OK**, and save the configuration.

Figure 9-24: Remote Web server management page

Verify Installation and Configuration from the Browser

Complete the steps under this task heading for the distributed remote plug-in – managed node (Steps 18–20).

Configuring the Web Server Definition Manually from the Deployment Manager's Admin Console

As we discussed earlier, during certain circumstances you may want to configure the Web server definition manually from the admin console instead of running the configuration batch file. In this section, we review the steps involved in that process.

Add the Web Server Node to the WebSphere Configuration

Step 1.   If you're configuring a distributed local or remote plug-in – managed node environment, skip the steps for this task (Steps 1–4 here). Otherwise, start the Deployment Manager (if it isn't running already), and log in to the admin console.

Step 2. Expand **System administration**, and click **Nodes**. On the Nodes page (Figure 9-25), click the **Add Node** button to add a node to the WebSphere configuration.

Add Node		Remove Node		Force Delete		Synchronize		Full Resynchr

Select	Name ◇	Version ◇	Discovery Protocol ◇	Status
☐	dmgr-hostCellManager01	6.0.1.0	TCP	⊕
☐	was-host1Node01	6.0.1.0	TCP	⑦
☐	was-host2Node01	6.0.1.0	TCP	⑦

Figure 9-25: Adding the Web server node

Step 3. On the resulting page, select the **Unmanaged node** option (shown in Figure 9-26), and click **Next**.

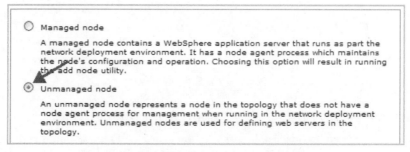

○ Managed node

A managed node contains a WebSphere application server that runs as part the network deployment environment. It has a node agent process which maintains the node's configuration and operation. Choosing this option will result in running the add node utility.

◉ Unmanaged node

An unmanaged node represents a node in the topology that does not have a node agent process for management when running in the network deployment environment. Unmanaged nodes are used for defining web servers in the topology.

Figure 9-26: Specifying an unmanaged node

Step 4. Next (Figure 9-27), enter a name for the unmanaged node, and provide the host name and operating system of the machine on which the Web server is installed. Then click **OK**, and save the configuration.

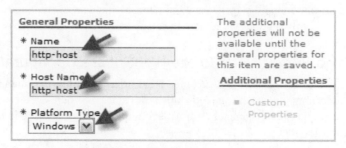

General Properties

* Name
http-host

* Host Name
http-host

* Platform Type
Windows ▾

The additional properties will not be available until the general properties for this item are saved.

Additional Properties

▪ Custom Properties

Figure 9-27: Unmanaged node properties

Add the Web Server Definition to the WebSphere Configuration

Now, take the following steps to add the Web server's definition to the WebSphere repository.

Step 5. On the Deployment Manager's admin console, expand **Servers**, click **Web servers**, and then click **New** (Figure 9-28) to create a new Web server definition.

Figure 9-28: Creating the Web server definition

Step 6. On the next page (Figure 9-29), select the Web server node from the drop-down list, and enter the Web server definition name you provided when you installed the plug-in. For this example, you'd enter the name webserver-on-dmgr-host for the distributed *local* plug-in configuration or webserver-on-http-host for the distributed *remote* plug-in configuration. Click **Next** after finishing with this page.

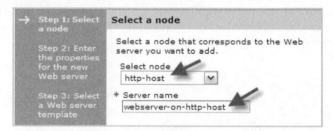

Figure 9-29: Specifying the Web server node and server name

Step 7. Next, on the page shown in Figure 9-30, enter the following values as properties for the new Web server. Then click **Next**.

- **IHS** for the Web server type

- **80** for the port

- **C:\IBM\HTTPServer** (i.e., <IHSV6-ROOT>) for the IBM HTTP Server V6 installation path

■ the HTTP Server service name (if the Web server is on a Windows system and you registered it as a Windows service)

■ **C:\IBM\WebSphere\Plugins** (i.e., <PLUGIN-ROOT>) for the plug-in installation location

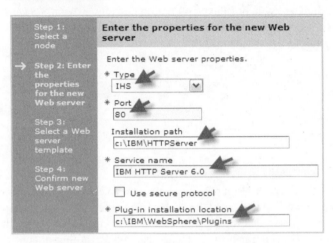

Figure 9-30: Specifying the Web server properties

Step 8. On the next properties page displayed (Figure 9-31), enter **8008** for the port, **htadmin** for the administrative user ID, and **htadmin** for the HTTP Admin Server password. (If you used different values for these fields, enter the appropriate values.) Click **Next**.

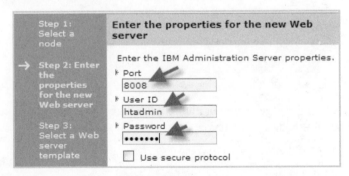

Figure 9-31: Specifying the IBM Admin Server properties

Step 9.   Next (Figure 9-32), select IHS as the Web server template, and click **Next**.

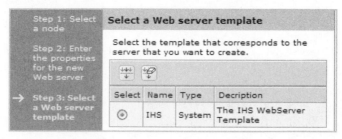

Figure 9-32: Selecting the Web server template

Step 10.   Review the summary page, click **Finish**, and save the configuration.

Step 11.   To verify the configuration, make sure HTTP Admin Server is running on the Web server machine. Then, from the Deployment Manager's admin console, expand **Servers**, click **Web servers**, and click **Start** to start HTTP Server (as shown in Figure 9-33).

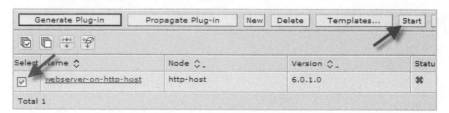

Figure 9-33: Verifying the configuration

Step 12.   To verify that HTTP Server is started, issue the URL **http://http-host** (or **http://dmgr-host**) from the browser to display the HTTP Server welcome page.

10

WebSphere Application Server V6 Network Deployment: Vertical and Horizontal Clustering

Most production applications support critical needs of an organization or its customers. These applications usually need to provide service qualities such as rapid response time and high availability. Important applications also typically serve relatively large numbers of users, so they must provide high throughput. To enable a run-time environment that can meet the requirements of such critical applications, WebSphere provides the ability to create a collection of application servers called a *cluster*. Instead of installing an application on an individual application server, you can install it on a cluster. When you do so, the application is automatically deployed on each application server that's a member of the cluster.

We use the term *vertical clustering* when the cluster members are defined on the same physical machine. We use the term *horizontal clustering* when the cluster members are defined on different physical machines. You can also use a combination of vertical and horizontal clustering within the same WebSphere cluster. WebSphere treats all clusters and cluster members the same, regardless of the allocation of cluster members to physical machines.

Request Processing in a Clustered Environment

Figure 10-1 shows the architecture of a sample cluster — in this case, a vertical cluster (where the cluster's members reside on the same physical machine). This cluster has two cluster members, server1 and server2.

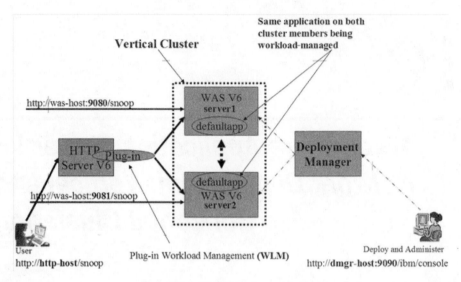

Figure 10-1: Vertical cluster architecture

The Deployment Manager and HTTP server (with plug-in) can be on the same machine as the cluster members or on separate machines, whether the cluster is a vertical or a horizontal one. For production, it's recommended that both the Deployment Manager and HTTP server/plug-in be located on different machines.

In the diagram, an application, defaultapp, has been installed on the cluster. This application was installed on both application servers (cluster members) automatically for us when we deployed the default application on the cluster through the Deployment Manager's admin console.

When you generate a plug-in configuration file (plugin-cfg.xml) for a cluster environment, the file contains information necessary to help the plug-in module on the HTTP server "workload manage" requests across cluster members. For example, if you issue the URL http://http-host/snoop, one of the cluster members (say server1) serves the request. If you issue the same URL again, the plug-in routes the second request to the second cluster member (server2 in this case). This plug-in routing behavior changes depending on various factors (e.g., HTTP session creation, LoadBalanceWeight value in plug-in file).

The flow chart in Figure 10-2 shows the high-level steps required to create and configure a WebSphere cluster. In the first part of this chapter, we show you how to set up a vertical cluster. The second part is dedicated to creating and configuring a horizontal cluster. Refer to Chapter 20 for instructions on completing the last step of the flow chart, registering the WebSphere processes in the Windows registry.

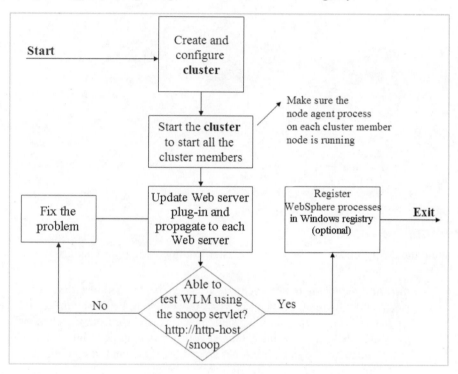

Figure 10-2: Cluster creation overview

Create and Configure a Vertical Cluster

To illustrate the steps involved in creating a vertical cluster (one where the cluster's members all reside on the same physical machine), we'll step through the process for the vertical cluster we looked at in Figure 10-1. Before creating the cluster, you must complete some prerequisite tasks to set up the WebSphere environment. After successful completion of these tasks, your system architecture should look similar to the one shown in Figure 10-3.

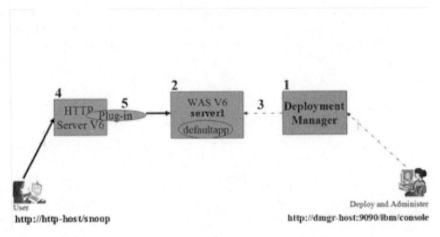

Figure 10-3: Prerequisite architecture to configure a vertical cluster

Prerequisite Tasks

To set up the environment for the vertical cluster, complete the following tasks.

Task 1: **Install a deployment manager profile.** Use Chapter 7 to install, create, and verify a deployment manager profile. As we noted, the Deployment Manager and HTTP server can be on the same machine as the cluster members or on separate machines. For this example, you'll install and configure all the components on the same machine, dmgr-host. This kind of configuration is suitable for education and training environments.

We'll assume no application server profile exists on the machine at this time, so accept the default port numbers for the deployment manager profile if possible. In the event of an existing application server profile, accept the incremented port numbers assigned by the Profile Creation wizard, and be sure to select the option to "Make this profile the default" when naming the profile. Figure 10-4 shows part of the wizard panel where this option appears.

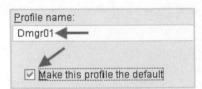

Figure 10-4: Default profile option on profile name panel

For this example, we assume you're setting up this system for a production environment, so don't select to install the Application Server Samples when installing the product binaries. After completing the installation, apply the required fix pack and verify.

Task 2:   *Create an application server profile.* Use Chapter 7 to create and verify an application server profile on the node where you created the deployment manager profile (dmgr-host). Accept the incremented port numbers the wizard suggests for the application server profile. (The deployment manager profile will use the default ports.) Figure 10-5 shows the port assignments for the application server profile.

Port value assignment

The values in the following fields define the ports for the Application Server and do not conflict with other profiles in this installation. Another installation of WebSphere Application Server or other programs might use the same ports. To avoid run-time port conflicts, verify that each port value is unique.

A̲dministrative console port (Default 9060):	9061
Administrative c̲onsole secure port (Default 9043):	9044
H̲TTP transport port (Default 9080):	9080

Figure 10-5: Port assignments for application server profile

When naming the application server profile, *don't* select the option to "Make this profile the default." The deployment manager profile will be the default profile.
Apply the fix pack, and verify.

Task 3:   *Federate the node.* Follow Chapter 8 to federate the node within the application server profile to the Deployment Manager cell. When you federate the node, be sure to select the option (shown in Figure 10-6) to "Include applications." You'll use the default application's snoop servlet to verify the cluster configuration. (If you forget to include the applications now, you'll need to deploy and configure resources for defaultapp.ear manually later from the Deployment Manager's admin console on the cluster.)

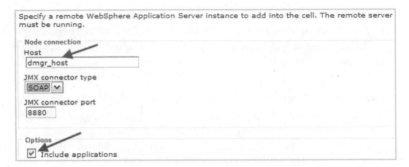

Figure 10-6: Selecting to include applications

Task 4:   ***Install HTTP Server.*** Use Chapter 5 to install IBM HTTP Server on the same node where the application server profile is located (dmgr-host). Apply the fix pack, and verify.

Task 5:   ***Install the plug-in.*** Based on your architecture, follow the appropriate instructions in Chapter 9 to install and configure one of the four distributed plug-in configurations:

- distributed local plug-in – managed node
- distributed local plug-in – unmanaged node
- distributed remote plug-in – managed node
- distributed remote plug-in – unmanaged node

In this example, you've installed the Deployment Manager and HTTP Server on the same machine, so you can configure the distributed local plug-in as either a managed or an unmanaged node.

After configuring the plug-in, make sure you can access the snoop servlet through HTTP Server. In this case, HTTP Server is on dmgr-host, so issue **http://dmgr-host/snoop**.

Steps to Create and Configure a Vertical Cluster

Next, take the following steps to set up the vertical cluster.

Step 1.   Connect to the Deployment Manager's admin console: **http://dmgr-host:9060/ibm/console**.

Step 2.   Expand **Servers**, and click **Application servers** to see the application server (server1) that you federated to the Deployment Manager (Figure 10-7). You'll use this existing application server as a template to create your cluster. At the time you create them, all the cluster members will be identical to this application server. (Cluster members have only applications in common. Other attributes of the application servers in a cluster may differ.)

Figure 10-7: Application server server1 in Deployment Manager's admin console

Step 3.   On the admin console, expand **Applications**, and click **Enterprise Applications** to see the applications that are deployed. Figure 10-8 shows these applications for our example. These applications will be deployed automatically on each cluster member you create because the applications' target mappings have been set to server1 and you'll use server1 as the template for the cluster when you create it. (To see each application's target mapping, click the application and then select **Target mappings**.)

Figure 10-8: Enterprise applications deployed

Step 4.   Now, create a cluster using the existing the application server (server1) as a template. To do so, expand **Servers**, select **Clusters**, and then click the **New** button, as shown in Figure 10-9.

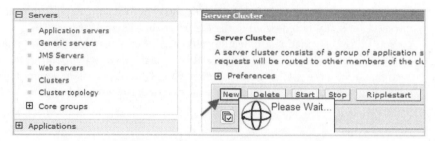

Figure 10-9: Selecting to create a new cluster

Step 5. On the next panel (Figure 10-10), assign a name to the cluster. We'll use the name VerticalCluster for this example. Set the other options as follows:

1. Select the "Prefer local" check box. This option improves performance in the clustered environment by causing Enterprise JavaBean (EJB) calls (from components in the application server's Web container) to be routed to the EJBs deployed (in the EJB container) in the same Java Virtual Machine (JVM).

2. Select the "Create a replication domain for this cluster" check box. Choosing this option during cluster creation lets you configure memory-to-memory HTTP session replication with minimum effort later. You can always disable this replication if you don't need it. (If you don't choose this option, you can create a replication domain from the admin console later.)

3. For the **Existing server** option, choose "Select an existing server to add to this cluster" to use the existing application server as the first cluster member. Then choose server1 on dmgr-host in the drop-down list.

4. You're going to create two cluster members, so keep the **Weight** value default of 2. On each cluster member, this number will be decremented by 1 after each request is processed until the value reaches 0. (Under certain conditions, the value will be less than 0.) The value will then be reset to 2 again (2, 1, 0, 2, 1, 0, 2, and so on). The cluster member with the highest weight value will usually handle a request (although this behavior changes depending on various factors, such as session affinity and the failure of one or more cluster members). For more information about this topic, see the WebSphere Application Server V6 Information Center at *http://publib.boulder.ibm.com/infocenter/ws60help/index.jsp*.

When you're finished with this panel, click **Next**.

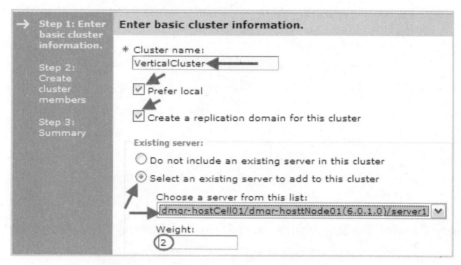

Figure 10-10: Specifying basic cluster information

Step 6. On the next panel (Figure 10-11), specify a name for the second cluster member (server2 or any name you prefer). Select the node on which your first cluster member is located — dmgr-hostNode01 in this case because you're configuring a vertical cluster. Then select the "Generate Unique Http Ports" option to avoid port conflicts, and click **Apply**.

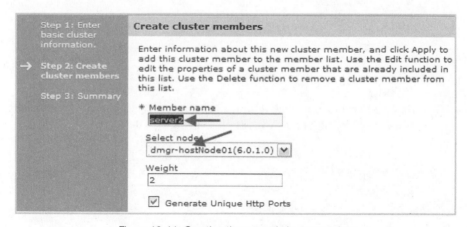

Figure 10-11: Creating the second cluster member

Step 7. On the next panel (Figure 10-12), scroll down and review the cluster member information. Then click **Next**.

Select	Application servers	Nodes	Version	Weight
☐	server1	dmgr-hostNode01	6.0.1.0	2
☐	server2	dmgr-hostNode01	6.0.1.0	2

Figure 10-12: Cluster members in application server list

Step 8. Click **Finish** on the summary panel, save the configuration when prompted, and click **OK**.

Verify Cluster Configuration and Plug-in Workload Management

To verify the cluster configuration and workload management by the plug-in, complete the following steps.

Step 9. From the Deployment Manager's admin console, expand **Servers** and click **Clusters** to see the cluster you created. Figure 10-13 shows the listing for our sample cluster, VerticalCluster.

Figure 10-13: Cluster VerticalCluster in Deployment Manager's admin console

Step 10. Expand **Servers**, and click **Application Servers** to see the cluster members you created in the VerticalCluster cluster (Figure 10-14).

Figure 10-14: Cluster members server1 and server2

Step 11. Expand **Servers**, and click **Clusters**. On the resulting panel (Figure 10-15), select the check box for your cluster (VerticalCluster), and click the **Start** button to start all the cluster members (server1 and server2) associated with the cluster.

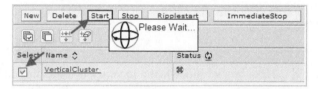

Figure 10-15: Starting the cluster members

Step 12. Next, verify that all the cluster members have been started. To do so, expand **Servers** and click **Application Servers**. You should see server1 and server2 listed with a status of "running" (green arrow), as shown in Figure 10-16.

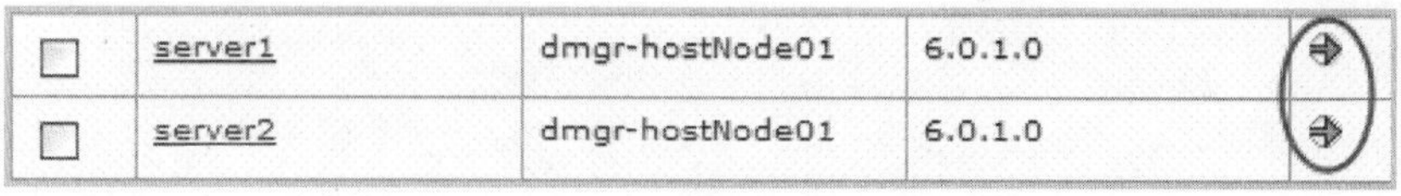

| | server1 | dmgr-hostNode01 | 6.0.1.0 | ➡ |
| | server2 | dmgr-hostNode01 | 6.0.1.0 | ➡ |

Figure 10-16: Cluster members started

Step 13. Now expand **Servers**, and choose **Web servers**. Select the check box for the Web server definition, and click **Generate Plug-in** to generate the plug-in representing the cluster environment. (If your HTTP server is on a different node from the Deployment Manager node, select the check box for the Web server definition and click **Propagate Plug-in** to copy the plug-in file according to the configuration.)

Step 14. Restart HTTP Server to make sure the plug-in module reads the new plug-in file you generated. To do so, expand **Servers**, click **Web servers**, select the Web server definition's check box, and click **Stop** and then **Start**.

Step 15. Next, open a browser, and issue the URL to invoke the snoop servlet through the HTTP Server plug-in: **http://dmgr-host/snoop**. To see which cluster member served the request, scroll down the snoop servlet page until you see the **ServletContext Attributes** section (shown in Figure 10-17). The value listed beside "com.ibm.websphere.servlet.application.host" is the cluster member that served the request (server1 in this case).

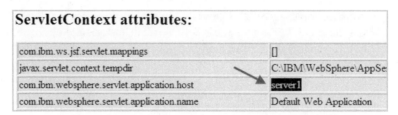

Figure 10-17: Indication that server1 served the snoop servlet request

Step 16. Issue the URL to invoke snoop again to verify that the plug-in workload manages the request. If you've configured everything properly, the second request should go through the second cluster member (server2 in this case), as you can verify in Figure 10-18.

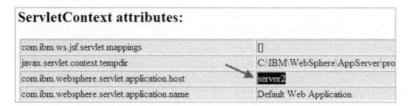

Figure 10-18: Confirmation that server2 served the second snoop request

Configure Virtual Host and Host Alias

While verifying the vertical cluster environment, you may want to invoke the snoop servlet through the Embedded HTTP Server (EHS) of each cluster member by issuing http://was-host:**9080**/snoop for server1 and http://was-host:**9081**/snoop for server2. If you try to invoke snoop through the EHS of the second cluster member after configuring the vertical cluster with the default settings (http://was-host:9081/snoop), the request will fail, reporting that the virtual host wasn't defined. You can see this error in Figure 10-19.

Figure 10-19: Virtual host not defined error

When you created the vertical cluster, you created the cluster members on the Deployment Manager machine, so you need to specify dmgr-host instead of was-host when issuing the URL for server2. To avoid the error and be able to invoke snoop using the HTTP transport port defined for server2 (port 9081), you need to define port 9081 as a *host alias* under the default_host virtual host. To do so, take these steps:

1. On the Deployment Manager's admin console, navigate to **Environment|Virtual Hosts|default_host|Host Aliases**.

2. Click **New** on the resulting panel (Figure 10-20) to create a new alias.

3. On the next panel (Figure 10-21), keep the default host name value of *****, change the port number to 9081, click **OK**, and save the configuration.

4. Navigate once again to the list of host aliases (Figure 10-22), and make sure the new host alias appears in the list.

5. Restart the Deployment Manager and VerticalCluster. Then invoke snoop again, specifying dmgr-host and port 9081: **http://dmgr-host:9081/snoop**. The request should work now.

> **Note:**   If you need to deploy different versions of the same application (with the same context root) on the same application server, you can create a new virtual host and deploy the second version of the application on that virtual host. To the end user, the application appears to be running on two different application servers. WebSphere manages each application and its resources independently even though both versions of the application are running on the same application server.

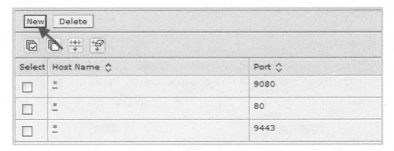

Figure 10-20: Creating a host alias

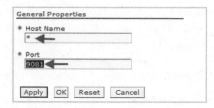

Figure 10-21: Host alias general properties

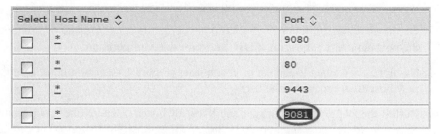

Figure 10-22: Updated host alias list

For this discussion, we've assumed that you used the default HTTP transport values (9080 and 9081) when configuring the vertical cluster. If you're unsure of the HTTP transport port of the cluster members, expand **Servers** and select **Application servers**. Click each server (server1 and server2) one at a time, scroll down, expand **Ports** under the **Communications** section, and look for the port value of WC_defaulthost (as shown in Figure 10-23).

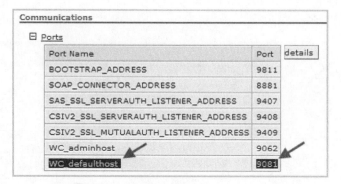

Figure 10-23: Confirming HTTP transport port values

Directory Structure After Creating the Vertical Cluster

After creating the vertical cluster, you'll see changes in the directory structure under both the <DMGR-PROFILE-ROOT> directory and the < PROFILE-ROOT> directory on dmgr-host. Figure 10-24 illustrates the configuration directory structure of the Deployment Manager (under <DMGR-PROFILE-ROOT>\config\cells\dmgr-hostCell01) after creation of the vertical cluster. Notice that entries for server2 (the second cluster member of VerticalCluster) and the Web server (webserver-on-dmgr-host) have been added to the master repository. You can observe similar changes under directory <PROFILE-ROOT>.

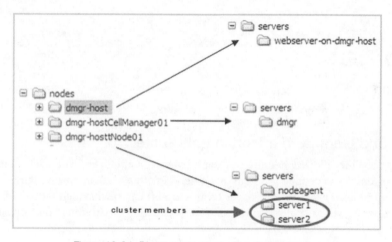

Figure 10-24: Directory structure after cluster creation

Logging in a Vertical Cluster Environment

Figure 10-25 depicts the logging architecture for a vertical cluster environment. After creating the vertical cluster, you'll see a new directory for the second cluster member (server2) under the <PROFILE-ROOT>\logs directory.

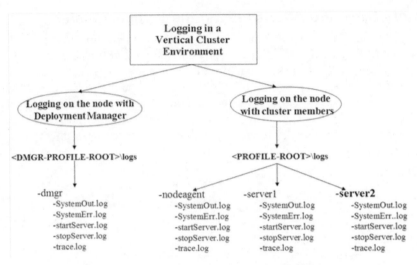

Figure 10-25: Logging in a vertical cluster environment

Create and Configure a Horizontal Cluster

Figure 10-26 shows the architecture of a sample horizontal cluster, where each cluster member resides on a separate physical machine. As with a vertical cluster, the Deployment Manager and HTTP Server (with plug-in) can be installed on one of the cluster member systems (not recommended for production environments) or on separate machines.

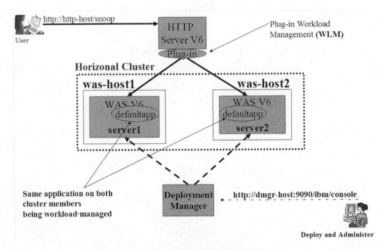

Figure 10-26: Horizontal cluster architecture

Figure 10-27 shows the high-level steps specific to creating and configuring a WebSphere horizontal cluster. Before creating the cluster, you must complete some prerequisite tasks to set up the WebSphere environment. After doing so, your system architecture should look similar to the one shown in Figure 10-28.

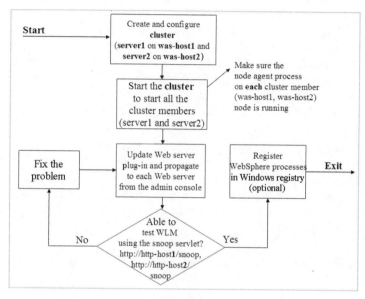

Figure 10-27: Horizontal cluster configuration overview

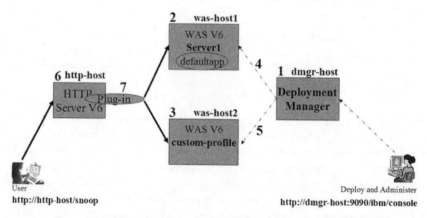

Figure 10-28: Prerequisite architecture to configure a horizontal cluster

Prerequisite Tasks

Complete these tasks to set up the required environment for the horizontal WebSphere cluster.

Task 1:   *Install a deployment manager profile.* Use Chapter 7 to install, create, and verify a deployment manager profile on the dmgr-host machine. In this exercise, you're installing and configuring the components on separate physical machines. We'll assume you don't have an existing application server profile on dmgr-host. In that case, accept the default port numbers for the deployment manager profile if possible. When installing the product binaries, don't select to install the Application Server Samples. After completing the installation, apply the required fix pack, and verify.

Task 2:   *Install an application server profile.* Use Chapter 7 to install, create, and verify an application server profile on was-host1. (You use an application server profile so you'll have a server with the default application to use as a template when creating the cluster later. In cases where you don't want the default application, you can create a custom profile instead and proceed as described in the next task.)

Do not install the Application Server Samples. Apply the fix pack, and verify.

Task 3:   *Install a custom profile.* Use Chapter 7 to install, create, and verify a custom profile on was-host2. Don't install the Application Server Samples. Apply the fix pack, and verify.

Instead of a custom profile, you can install an application server profile on was-host2. But in a horizontal cluster environment, you delete (or ignore) the application server (server1) on was-host2 in most cases. When that is the situation, it's a good idea to create a custom profile on was-host2.

Task 4:   *Federate the node within the application server profile.* Use Chapter 8 to federate the node within the application server profile on was-host1 to the Deployment Manager cell on dmgr-host. When you federate the node, be sure to include applications. You'll use the default application's snoop servlet to verify the cluster configuration. (If you forget to include the applications now, you'll need to deploy and configure resources for defaultapp.ear manually later from the Deployment Manager's admin console on the cluster.)

Task 5: **Federate the node within the custom profile.** Use Chapter 8 to federate the node within the custom profile on was-host2 to the Deployment Manager cell on dmgr-host.

Task 6: **Install HTTP Server.** Use Chapter 5 to install IBM HTTP Server on http-host. Apply the fix pack, and verify.

Task 7: **Install the plug-in.** Follow the appropriate instructions in Chapter 9 to install and configure one of the two distributed remote plug-in configurations:

- distributed remote plug-in – managed node
- distributedremote plug-in – unmanaged node

After configuring the plug-in, make sure you can access the snoop servlet through HTTP Server. In this case, issue **http://http-host/snoop**.

Steps to Create and Configure a Horizontal Cluster

Now, to create and configure the horizontal cluster, complete the following steps.

Step 1. Connect to the Deployment Manager's admin console: **http://dmgr-host:9060/ibm/console**.

Step 2. Expand **Servers**, and click **Application servers** to see the existing application server (server1) on was-host1 that you federated to the Deployment Manager cell (Figure 10-29). You'll use this server with an existing application (the default application) as a template to create a cluster. All the cluster members you create will be identical to this application server.

Select	Name ◇	Node ◇	Version ◇	Stat
☐	server1	was-host1Node01	6.0.1.0	✖

Figure 10-29: Application server server1 on was-host1

Step 3. Expand **Applications**, and click **Enterprise Applications** to see the applications deployed on the existing application server (Figure 10-30). These applications will be deployed automatically on each cluster member you create.

Figure 10-30: Enterprise applications deployed on application server server1

Step 4.   Expand **Servers**, select **Clusters**, and click **New** to create a cluster using application server server1 as a template.

Step 5.   On the next panel (Figure 10-31), assign a name to the cluster (we'll use HorizontalCluster), and set the other values as follows:

1. Select the "Prefer Local" option to improve the performance of EJB calls.

2. Optionally select the option to "Create a replication domain for this cluster."

3. Choose "Select an existing server to add to this cluster," and select server1 from the drop-down list to add the existing server as the first cluster member.

4. Keep the default **Weight** value of 2.

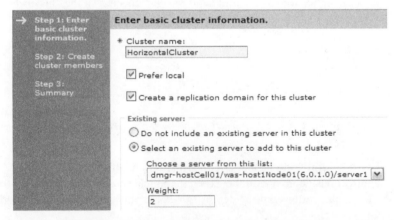

Figure 10-31: Specifying basic cluster information

For more information about these options, see the vertical cluster section of this chapter. When you're finished with this panel, click **Next**.

Step 6.   Next (Figure 10-32), enter a name for the second cluster member (server2 or any name you prefer), select the node on which you want to create the member (was-host2 in this case), clear the option to "Generate Unique Http Ports" (because you're configuring a horizontal cluster across machines where port conflicts aren't involved), and click **Apply**.

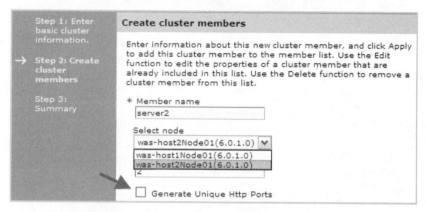

Figure 10-32: Creating the second cluster member

Step 7.   On the next panel (Figure 10-33), scroll down and review the cluster member information. You should see server1 and server2 in the application server list. Click **Next**.

Select	Application servers	Nodes	Version	Wei
☐	server1	was-host1Node01	6.0.1.0	2
☐	server2	was-host2Node01	6.0.1.0	2

Figure 10-33: Cluster members in application server list

Step 8.   Click **Finish** on the summary panel, save the configuration, and click **OK**.

Verify Cluster Configuration and Plug-in Workload Management

To verify the cluster configuration and workload management by the plug-in, complete the following steps.

Step 9. From the Deployment Manager's admin console, expand **Servers** and click **Clusters** to see the cluster (HorizontalCluster) you created. Figure 10-34 shows the cluster listing for our example.

	New	Delete	Start	Stop	Ripplestart	ImmediateStop

Select	Name ◇	Status ◌
☐	HorizontalCluster	✖

Figure 10-34: Cluster HorizontalCluster in Deployment Manager's admin console

Step 10. Expand **Servers**, and click **Application Servers** to see the cluster members you created in the HorizontalCluster cluster (Figure 10-35).

	New	Delete	Templates...	Start	Stop	ImmediateStop	Term

Select	Name ◇	Node ◇	Version ◇	Status ◌
☐	server1	was-host1Node01	6.0.1.0	✖
☐	server2	was-host2Node01	6.0.1.0	✖

Figure 10-35: Cluster members server1 and server2

Step 11. Expand **Servers**, and click **Clusters**. Select the check box for your cluster, and click **Start** to start the cluster members (server1 and server2) associated with the cluster.

Step 12. To verify that the cluster members have been started, expand **Servers** and click **Application Servers**. You should see server1 and server2 listed with a status of "running" (green arrow).

Step 13. Expand **Servers**, and choose **Web servers**. Select the check box for the Web server definition, and click **Generate Plug-in** to generate the plug-in file.

Step 14. Select the Web server definition's check box again, and click **Propagate Plug-in** to copy the plug-in file to the HTTP Server host.

Step 15. Restart HTTP Server to make sure the plug-in module reads the new plug-in file.

Step 16. Open a browser, and issue the URL to invoke the snoop servlet through the HTTP Server plug-in: **http://http-host/snoop**. To see the host name that served the request, scroll down the snoop servlet page until you see the **Request Information** section. The "Local address" line here gives the host name that served the request — was-host1 in this case, as Figure 10-36 shows.

Remote host	169.254.189.152
Remote port	1361
Local address	was-host1
Local host	169.254.147.4
Local port	9080

Figure 10-36: Indication that host was-host1 served the snoop servlet request

To see the cluster member that served the request, scroll down again until you see the **ServletContext Attributes** section (Figure 10-37). The value listed beside "com.ibm.websphere.servlet.application.host" is the cluster member that server the request (server1 in this case).

ServletContext attributes:

com.ibm.ws.jsf.servlet.mappings	[]
javax.servlet.context.tempdir	C:\IBM\WebSphere\App
com.ibm.websphere.servlet.application.host	server1
com.ibm.websphere.servlet.application.name	Default Web Application

Figure 10-37: Indication that cluster member server1 on was-host1 served the snoop servlet request

Step 17. Issue the URL to invoke snoop again to verify that the plug-in workload manages the request. If you've configured everything properly, the second request should go through the second host name and the second cluster member (was-host2 and server2 in our example). Check the lines described in the preceding step to verify this operation.

Directory Structure After Creating the Horizontal Cluster

The directory structure changes that take place for horizontal clustering are similar to those you saw for a vertical cluster except that the changes are made on multiple nodes for their respective components instead of a single node.

Logging in a Horizontal Cluster Environment

Figure 10-38 depicts the logging architecture for a horizontal cluster environment. After creating the horizontal cluster, you'll see two new directories (nodeagent and server2) on the second cluster member (server2) host under the <PROFILE-ROOT>\logs directory.

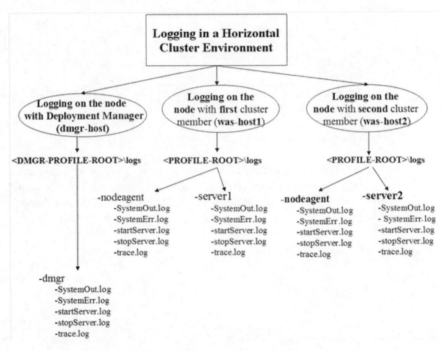

Figure 10-38: Logging in a horizontal cluster environment

Note: If you have problems during the testing of plug-in WLM across cluster members, then plug-in ESI may be caching the output. This will happen if you have configured ESI caching on a server and later used that server as a template during the cluster creation. In this case, temporarily disable ESI caching on the plug-in. To do this, open the plugin cfg.xml file in a text editor and modify the Property value of ESIEnable from true to false (<Property Name="ESIEnable" Value="false"/>). Restart the HTTP server and test the plug-in WLM again. Make sure that you set this property value back to true after plug-in WLM verification.

11

WebSphere V6 Network Deployment: HTTP Session Persistence

By configuring your WebSphere cluster for HTTP session persistence, you can protect the cluster against an HTTP session single point of failure. Depending on how critical your application is, it's usually wise to persist HTTP sessions in a clustered environment. If you've done so and a member of the cluster fails, the plug-in module redirects future HTTP requests made to that server to a different cluster member.

Depending on your architecture, you can persist HTTP user session data in memory (cluster member/JVM) or in a database. In this chapter, we show you how to configure both of these session persistence types. The steps are similar whether your cluster is a vertical or a horizontal one.

Memory-to-Memory Replication

The diagram in Figure 11-1 illustrates the architecture of memory-to-memory session persistence. In this type of replication, HTTP sessions on server1 are stored on server2 for backup, and vice versa. The diagram also shows the relationship between the cluster members and the *replication domain*, a logical place common to all members.

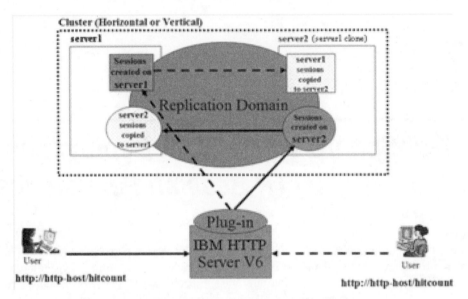

Figure 11-1: Memory-to-memory replication architecture

Figure 11-2's flow chart shows the high-level steps required to configure and verify memory-to-memory replication.

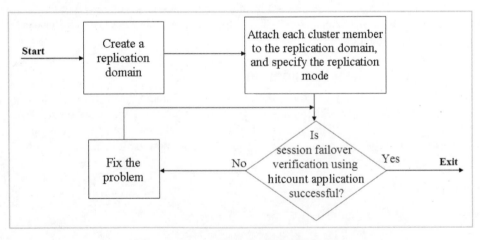

Figure 11-2: Configuration overview: memory-to-memory replication

The process to set up a cluster environment for this type of session persistence is straightforward:

1. Create a replication domain.
2. Attach the cluster members to the replication domain.
3. Specify one of three replication modes:

> *Both client and server:* In this mode, server1 (the client) sends HTTP sessions to server2 (the server) for backup, and server2 (client) sends HTTP sessions to server1 (server) for backup. This chapter's sample configuration uses this replication mode.

> *Client only:* In this mode, server1 (client) sends HTTP sessions to server2 for backup, but server2 doesn't send sessions to server1 for backup.

> *Server only:* In this mode, server2 (server) stores the HTTP sessions of server1 for backup, but server1 doesn't store the sessions of server2.

Before configuring memory-to-memory session persistence, make sure you've configured a cluster (vertical or horizontal) and verified that the plug-in workload management is working. (Refer to Chapter 10 for instructions on setting up and verifying a cluster.) We'll use the two-member vertical cluster you created in Chapter 10 (VerticalCluster) to illustrate the configuration process, pointing out any differences you'd encounter with a horizontal cluster as needed.

Configure Memory-to-Memory Replication

Step 1. First, determine whether a replication domain already exists for your cluster. If, when creating the cluster, you selected the option to "Create a replication domain for this cluster" (as in Chapter 10's example), this will be the case. Figure 11-3 shows this check box option.

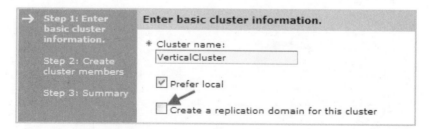

Figure 11-3: Option to create a replication domain during cluster creation

To verify that a replication domain was created, connect to the Deployment Manager's admin console, expand **Environment**, and click **Replication**

domains. Figure 11-4 shows the listing of the replication domain that was created for the VerticalCluster cluster.

Figure 11-4: VerticalCluster replication domain

Step 2. If you did not select the option to create a replication domain when you created the cluster, you need to create one manually now. To do so, take these steps:

a. From the admin console, expand **Environment**, select **Replication domains**, and click **New** to display the panel shown in Figure 11-5.

b. Enter a name for the new replication domain. For this example, we'll use the name VerticalCluster.

c. Keep the default values for the other parameters: a request timeout value of 5, no encryption, and a single replica. In a cluster environment with only two cluster members (as in this example), it in fact doesn't matter whether you select "Single replica" (the default memory-to-memory topology) or "Entire Domain" for the "Number of replicas" option. If you have more than two cluster members, you can use this option to limit the number of servers that will participate in the replication.

d. Click **OK**, and save the configuration.

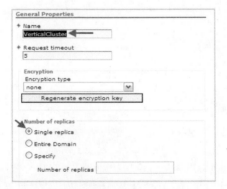

Figure 11-5: Manually creating a replication domain

Step 3. Next, set up the type of replication to be performed for server1. To do so, expand **Servers**, and navigate to **Application Servers|server1|Web container|Session management|Distributed environment settings**. In the **General Properties** section (shown in Figure 11-6), select the "Memory-to-memory replication" radio button, and then click the corresponding link.

Figure 11-6: Specifying memory-to-memory replication

Step 4. Use the drop-down lists shown in Figure 11-7 to specify the replication domain and the desired replication mode. For this example, select VerticalCluster and choose "Both client and server" as the replication mode. Click **OK**, and save the configuration.

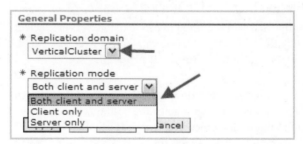

Figure 11-7: Specifying the replication domain and mode

Step 5. Repeat Steps 3 and 4 for server2 (and for any other cluster members if you have more than two).

Step 6. From the admin console, expand **Servers**, click **Clusters**, and restart (stop and then start) the cluster (as shown in Figure 11-8).

Figure 11-8: Restarting the vertical cluster

Step 7.   Next, expand **Servers**, and click **Application Servers** to make sure all the cluster members have been started. They should appear with a status of "running" (green arrow) in the server list.

Verify HTTP Session Failover

With that, you've configured memory-to-memory session persistence! Now, take time to verify that the HTTP session failover is working. To do so, you'll configure the plug-in log file for tracing and then use the hitcount application to verify failover.

Configure the Plug-in Log File for Tracing

Step 8.   To configure tracing on the plug-in, expand **Servers**, select **Web servers**, and click the Web server definition. On the resulting panel, click the **Plug-in properties** link in the **Additional properties** section.

Step 9.   On the next panel, scroll down to the **Log level** list (shown in Figure 11-9), and select **Trace**. Make a note of the path this panel shows to the plug-in log file, http_plugin.log. Once you restart HTTP Server, the plug-in tracing information will be written to this file. When you're finished with this panel, click **OK** and save the configuration.

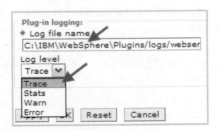

Figure 11-9: Configuring the plug-in log file for tracing

> **Note:** If necessary, you can configure plug-in tracing in the plug-in file itself instead of from the admin console. To do so, open file plugin-cfg.xml on the HTTP Server/plug-in node, and change the file's LogLevel value from "error" to "trace". It's also interesting to note that a less verbose option for LogLevel (called "stats") was recently introduced for use with session failover and connection count troubleshooting.

Step 10.   Next, stop HTTP Server if it's running, and delete the plug-in log file (http_plugin.log). (To stop HTTP Server, navigate to **Servers|Web servers**, select the Web server's check box, and click **Stop**.)

Step 11.   Start HTTP Server (navigate to **Servers|Web servers**, select the Web server's check box, and click **Start**). Now you're ready to verify HTTP session failover.

Verify Session Failover Using Hitcount

You learned about the hitcount application in Chapter 3. This servlet, part of the WebSphere default application, lets you increment a counter value using several execution methods. In this section, we'll first use hitcount to observe how HTTP requests are normally handled. Then we'll stop one of the cluster members to observe what happens when a cluster member fails.

Step 12.   Open a browser, and invoke the hitcount application through the HTTP server. (This request goes through the following components in the following order before the servlet is executed: HTTP Server, plug-in, Embedded HTTP Server, and Web container.) For a vertical cluster, issue **http://dmgr-host/hitcount**. For a horizontal cluster, issue **http://http-host/hitcount**.

Step 13.   On the page that results, select the "Session state (create if necessary)" execution method, and then click the **Increment** button. You should see the message "Hit Count value for (new session): 1" appear at the bottom of the page, as shown in Figure 11-10. The message reports a hit count value of 1 and indicates that a new session has been created for you.

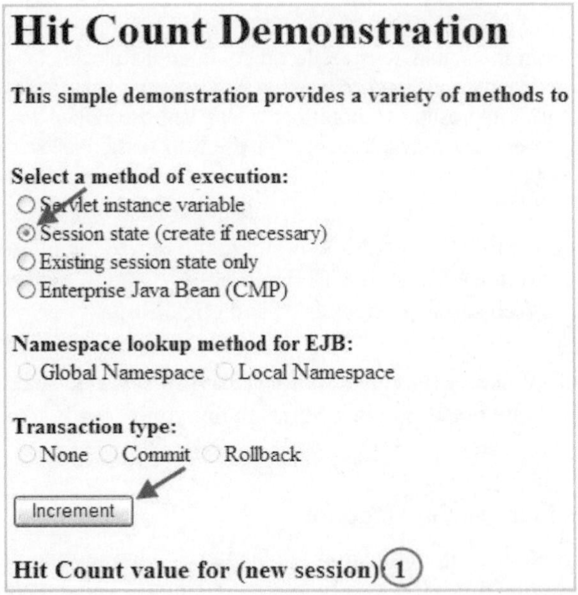

Hit Count Demonstration

This simple demonstration provides a variety of methods to

Select a method of execution:
○ Servlet instance variable
⦿ Session state (create if necessary)
○ Existing session state only
○ Enterprise Java Bean (CMP)

Namespace lookup method for EJB:
○ Global Namespace ○ Local Namespace

Transaction type:
○ None ○ Commit ○ Rollback

[Increment]

Hit Count value for (new session) (1)

Figure 11-10: Hitcount results for "Session state (create if necessary)" option

Step 14. Return to the main hitcount page by clicking the browser's Back button. Select the "Existing session state only" option, and click **Increment** to see the hit count incremented by 1. You should see the message "Hit Count value for (existing session): 2" at the bottom of the page (Figure 11-11). This message indicates that an existing session has been used. Make a note of the hit count value (2 in this case).

Do not close the browser while performing the remaining verification steps. (An open browser represents a single user and hence maps to a single HTTP session object maintained on the server. If you closed the browser and re-invoked the previous request from a new browser instance, the browser would map to a different HTTP session object on the server.)

Step 15. Now, connect to the machine on which you installed HTTP Server and the plug-in. For a vertical cluster, connect to dmgr-host; for a horizontal cluster, connect to http-host.

Step 16. Using your favorite editor, open the plug-in log file (http_plugin.log). For a vertical cluster, the file will be in the <PLUGIN-ROOT>\logs\

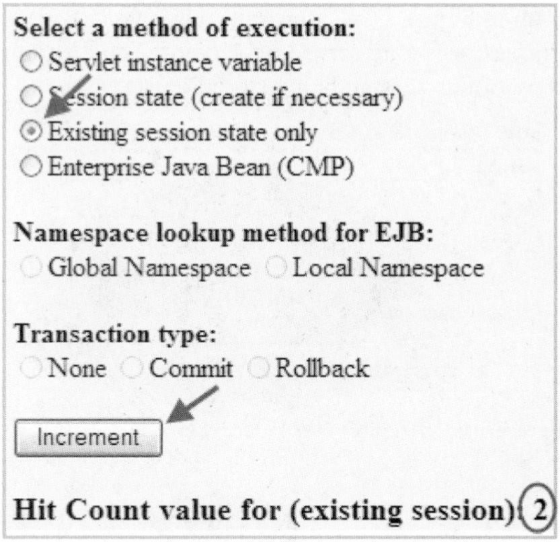

Select a method of execution:
- ○ Servlet instance variable
- ○ Session state (create if necessary)
- ⦿ Existing session state only
- ○ Enterprise Java Bean (CMP)

Namespace lookup method for EJB:
- ○ Global Namespace ○ Local Namespace

Transaction type:
- ○ None ○ Commit ○ Rollback

[Increment]

Hit Count value for (existing session) 2

Figure 11-11: Hitcount results for "Existing session state only" option

webserver-on-dmgr-host directory. For a horizontal cluster, it will be in <PLU-GIN-ROOT>\logs\webserver-on-http-host. Search for the word "picked" until you see the "Cannot find 'picked'" message, looking for the last match.

In the sample plug-in log shown in Figure 11-12, you can see that our hit-count application session was created and the request served by server2. According to the log file, **s**erver2 is on dmgr-host. For a horizontal cluster, you'd see was-host1 (and server1) or was-host2 (and server2) instead of dmgr-host (and server1 or server2) in the log file. (Depending on various factors, your request might be served by server1.)

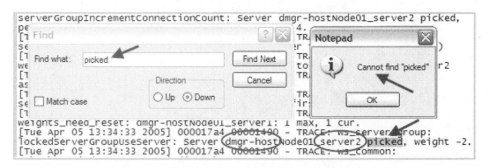

Figure 11-12: Plug-in log file for hitcount application session

The diagram in Figure 11-13 illustrates what you've observed: a hitcount request from a user being served by server2. The diagram also shows a backup copy of this session being stored on server1.

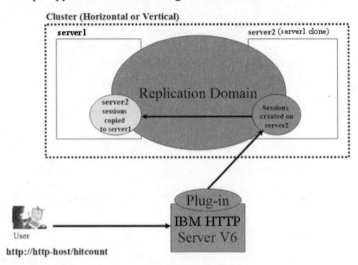

Figure 11-13: Normal handling of a hitcount application request

Step 17. Now, to test session failover, expand **Servers**, click **Application Servers**, and stop server2 (as shown in Figure 11-14). (For a horizontal cluster, stop server2 on was-host2.) If your http_plugin.log file indicated that server1 served the hitcount request, stop server1 instead. (For a horizontal cluster, stop server1 on was-host1 in this case.)

Figure 11-14: Stopping server2 to test session failover

Step 18. Select the "Existing session state only" option on the existing page in the previously opened browser, and click **Increment**. At this time, the request tries to go to server2 because of session affinity (a WebSphere behavior that returns session requests to the same application server that served them previously, using the cluster member ID saved in a cookie). But the plug-in quickly realizes that server2 is down and so sends the request to server1, which has the backup copy of this session. If you configured HTTP session persistence properly, you should see a hit count value of 3, as shown in Figure 11-15.

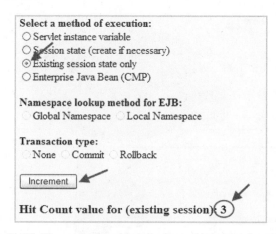

Figure 11-15: Hit count value of 3, indicating a third request was served

Step 19. To verify whether server1 indeed served the request, open the plug-in log file and search for the word "picked" again, looking for the last match. According to the portion of the log shown in Figure 11-16, server1 served the last request. (For a horizontal cluster, you'd see was-host1 instead of dmgr-host in the log file.) This information tells you that you've configured HTTP session persistence properly and tested it successfully.

```
serverGroupGetNextServer: getting the next server
[Tue Apr 05 13:38:17 2005] 000017a4 00001490 - TRACE: ws_server_group:
serve
[Tue  Find                                          ? X   Notepad        X
assur
[Tue  Find what:  picked              Find Next
serve                                                    i   Cannot find "picked"
[Tue                     Direction
serve                                   Cancel
[Tue  Match case        O Up ⊙ Down                          OK
assur
[Tue
serve  GroupGetNextServer: getting the next server
[Tue Apr 05 13:38:17 2005] 000017a4 00001490 - TRACE: ws_server_group:
lockedServerGroupUseServer: Server (dmgr-hostNode01(server1) picked, weight 0.
```

Figure 11-16: Log file confirmation that server1 handled the failover request

Figure 11-17 illustrates the failover of the HTTP session. Because server2 was down, the plug-in directed the hitcount request to server1. To serve the request, server1 picked up the session data from the backup copy in its memory.

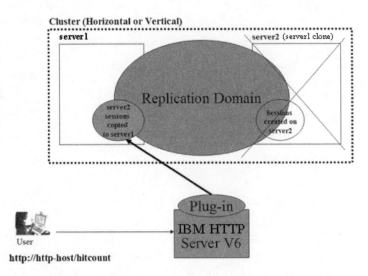

Figure 11-17: Failover handling of a hitcount application request

Remove Tracing on the Plug-in

Step 20. Tracing reduces the performance of the plug-in, so you should reset the plug-in logging level to "Error" once you've verified HTTP session failover. To do so, navigate to **Servers|Web servers**, and click the Web server definition again. Select the **Plug-in properties** link under the **Additional properties** section, scroll down, and select **Error** in the **Log level** drop-down list. Then click **OK**, save the configuration, and restart HTTP Server.

Database Session Persistence

Figure 11-18 depicts the architecture of the database form of HTTP session persistence. In this configuration, HTTP sessions on server1 and server2 are stored in a database for backup. For this example, we'll use the DB2 database on a remote machine, db2-host, to persist HTTP sessions. We'll use a Type 4 database driver to access the database. The version of the database used for this exercise is DB2 8.2.

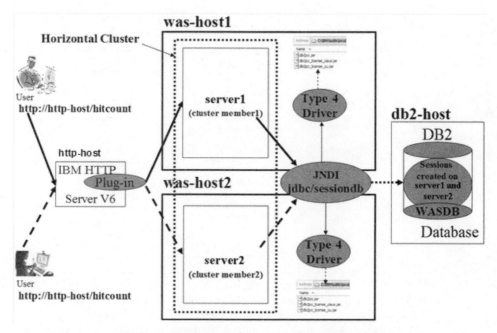

Figure 11-18: Database session persistence architecture

The flow chart in Figure 11-19 shows the high-level steps to configure and verify database session persistence. The process entails the following tasks:

1. Prepare the system for database session persistence.

2. Prepare the cluster members to access the session database through the DB2 Type 4 driver.

3. Create a WebSphere variable pointing to the location of the Type 4 driver files.

4. Create a Java 2 Connector (J2C) authentication entry to access the session database.

5. Create a Java Database Connectivity (JDBC) provider and a data source to access the session database.

6. Test the database connection from the admin console.

7. Attach each cluster member to the data source's Java Naming and Directory Interface (JNDI) name to persist sessions.

8. Verify session failover using the hitcount application.

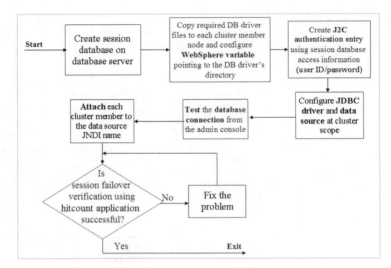

Figure 11-19: Configuration overview: Database session persistence

Before configuring for database session persistence, make sure you've configured a cluster (vertical or horizontal) and verified that the plug-in workload management is working. (Refer to Chapter 10 for instructions on setting up and verifying a cluster.)

Prepare the System for Database Session Persistence

Step 1.   Verify that the database you'll use to persist HTTP sessions has been created. For this example, we created a DB2 database named WASDB on host db2-host. We installed DB2 under the \ibm\sqllib directory, hereafter referred to as <DB2-HOME>. If you're setting up session persistence for educational purposes only and don't have a database in which to store sessions, you can use the trial version of DB2 8.2. To learn how to obtain and install the trial version, see the instructions at the end of this chapter.

Step 2.   Obtain a user name and password you can use to access the database and persist sessions. For this example, we'll use "db2admin" for both the user name and password.

Step 3.   Verify that you can access the node where the WASDB database resides from each node that has a cluster member, and vice versa. On each node, open a command prompt and issue **ping db2-host** (ping the DNS entry also).

For a vertical cluster, only one node will have cluster members (dmgr-host in this case). To verify access, open a command prompt on the dmgr-host machine, and issue **ping db2-host**. Then, from db2-host's command prompt, issue **ping dmgr-host**.

For a horizontal cluster, open a command prompt on the was-host1 (first cluster member) machine, and issue **ping db2-host**. Then, from db2-host's command prompt, issue **ping was-host1**. Repeat these steps on was-host2 (and on any other cluster member node you have).

Prepare the Cluster Members to Access the Session Database Through the DB2 Type 4 Driver

Step 4. Because you're using a DB2 Type 4 driver, you don't need to install DB2 client software on each cluster member (unlike a Type 2 driver). Simply copy the Type 4 driver JAR files to each cluster member from which you'll access the WASDB database. Figure 11-20 shows the three JAR files required on each cluster member:

- db2jcc.jar
- db2jcc_license_cisuz.jar
- db2jcc_license_cu.jar

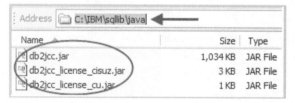

Figure 11-20: DB2 Type 4 driver JAR files

We copied these files from the DB2 server machine's (db2-host's) <DB2-HOME>\java directory (\ibm\sqllib\java in our example) to each cluster member. For uniformity, we created the same directory, <DB2-HOME>\java, on each cluster member to store the three files.

For a vertical cluster, copy the three files to the machine where you created the cluster members (dmgr-host in our configuration) because this is the machine on which all cluster members are located. For a horizontal cluster, copy the files to both was-host1 (the first cluster member) and was-host2 (the second cluster member). If you have more cluster members (was-host3 and so on), copy the files there as well.

Create a WebSphere Variable Pointing to the Location of the Type 4 Drivers

Next, you need to set up a variable in WebSphere that tells the cluster members where the Type 4 driver files are. You'll create this path variable at *cluster scope* to make it available to all members of the cluster, even if they're on separate nodes.

Step 5.   Connect to the Deployment Manager's admin console, expand **Environment**, and select **WebSphere variables**. On the resulting panel (Figure 11-21), click the **Browse Clusters** button, select the cluster you created, and click **OK**. (For a vertical cluster, select VerticalCluster. For a horizontal cluster, select HorizontalCluster.) Then click **Apply**.

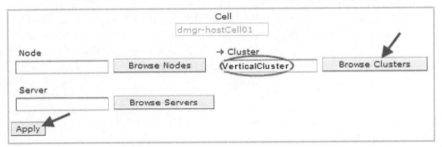

Figure 11-21: Selecting the vertical cluster

Step 6.   You may not see a list of WebSphere variables at the cluster scope by default on the next panel that appears (Figure 11-22). To create a new variable at this scope, scroll down on this panel and click **New**.

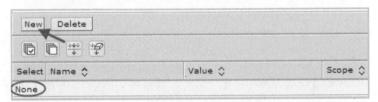

Figure 11-22: Creation of WebSphere variable at cluster scope

Step 7.   Figure 11-23 shows the resulting panel, which you use to name the variable and define the path it represents. Be sure to specify a variable that doesn't exist at a node or server scope because such values will override any value you specify at the cluster scope.

a. For the **Name** field, enter **DB2-TYPE4-DRIVER-PATH** (or any name you prefer). Make sure the variable name contains no underscore characters (_).

b. For the **Value** field, enter **c:\ibm\sqllib\java** (i.e., <DB2-HOME>\java). Make sure you copied the Type 4 driver files to this directory on all nodes of the cluster.

c. Optionally enter a description.

d. Click **OK**, and save the configuration.

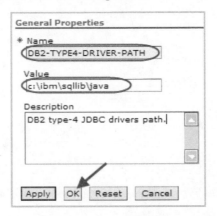

Figure 11-23: Specifying the WebSphere variable

After successfully creating the WebSphere variable, you should see its entry in the variables list under cluster scope, as shown in Figure 11-24.

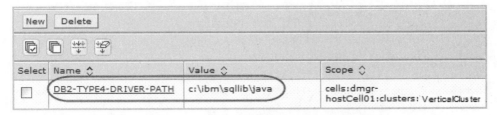

Figure 11-24: New WebSphere cluster scope variable in variables list

Create a J2C Authentication Entry to Access the Session Database

Step 8.   To create an authentication entry with a user ID (and password) that has permission to access the session database (WASDB), navigate to

Security|Global security|JAAS Configuration (under the **Authentication** section), and click **New**. Complete the resulting panel (shown in Figure 11-25) as follows:

a. For the **Alias** field, enter **db2admin**.
b. For the user ID and password, enter **db2admin** in each field.
c. Optionally enter a description.
d. Click **OK**, and save the configuration.

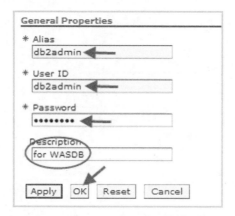

Figure 11-25: Specifying the J2C authentication entry

Create a JDBC Provider and a Data Source to Access the Session Database

Step 9.   Next, create a JDBC provider at node scope for each cluster member. To do so, expand **Resources** and select **JDBC Providers**. Click **Browse Clusters**, select the cluster, click **OK**, and click **Apply**. (For a vertical cluster, select VerticalCluster. For a horizontal cluster, select HorizontalCluster.) Then click **New** to create the JDBC provider.

Step 10.   On the resulting panel (Figure 11-26), specify the type of JDBC provider for DB2:

a. For the database type, select **DB2**.

b. For the provider type, select **DB2 Universal JDBC Driver Provider**.

c. For the implementation type, select **Connection pool data source**. (This implementation type is suitable for one-phase commit transactions, especially if performance is your main concern and your operations don't require two-phase commit. For two-phase commit transactions, you'd choose **XA data source**.)

d. Click **Next**.

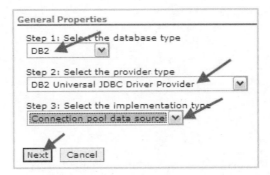

Figure 11-26: Specifying the JDBC provider type

Step 11. On the next panel (Figure 11-27), go to the **Class path** text box, and change "DB2UNIVERSAL_JDBC_DRIVER_PATH" to "DB2-TYPE4-DRIVER-PATH" as shown the figure. This is the variable you created to point to the directory where you copied the DB2 Type 4 driver files. (Notice that the variable name contains no underscore characters.) Make this change in the text area for all three instances of the variable (one for each JAR file). Then scroll down, and click **Apply**.

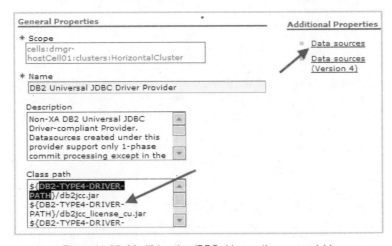

Figure 11-27: Modifying the JDBC driver path name variable

Step 12. Now, click the **Data sources** link in the panel's upper-right corner (under **Additional Properties**), and click **New** on the resulting panel (Figure 11-28) to create a DB2 data source.

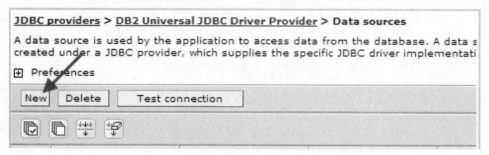

Figure 11-28: Creating a DB2 data source

Step 13. Enter a JNDI name for the data source that points to the session database (WASDB) on the DB2 server (db2-host). For this example, we'll use the name jdbc/sessiondb, as shown in Figure 11-29.

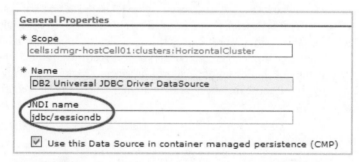

Figure 11-29: Specifying a JNDI name for the data source

Step 14. Scroll down until you see the "Component-managed authentication alias" section (shown in Figure 11-30). From the drop-down list here, select the J2C authentication alias you created earlier.

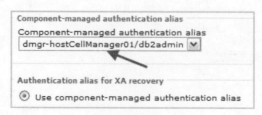

Figure 11-30: Specifying the J2C authentication alias

Step 15.   Scroll down again to the "DB2 Universal data source properties" section (Figure 11-31).

     a. For the database name, enter the name of the session database, **WASDB**.

     b. For the driver type, enter **4**.

     c. For the server name, enter **db2-host** (or the DNS entry of the DB2 database server).

     d. For the port number of the DB2 server, we've used default port **50000**.

     e. Click **OK**, and save the configuration.

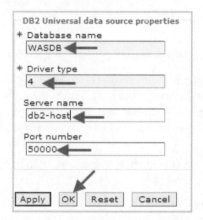

Figure 11-31: DB2 universal data source properties

Test the Database Connection from the Admin Console

With the setup steps completed, you're ready to test your database connection. Take the following steps from the Deployment Manager's admin console.

Step 16.   In the data sources list (shown in Figure 11-32), select the check box for the data source you just created, and click the **Test connection** button. If you configured the data source according to the instructions, you should see messages indicating that the test was successful. You can see these messages at the top of the figure.

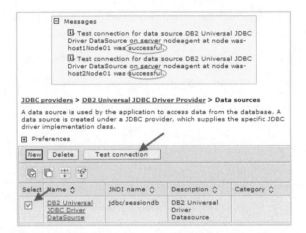

Figure 11-32: Successful test of the new data source connection

If the connection test is unsuccessful, restart the cluster and node agent on each cluster member node. For a vertical cluster, you'll have one node agent process because all the cluster members are on the same physical machine. For a horizontal cluster, every cluster member node will have a node agent.

If you see an exception such as "Undefined variable" or "No jar or zip files found," check the following:

- Make sure you created the WebSphere variable at the cluster scope as described (pay attention to the name of the variable you created).

- Verify that you copied the Type 4 jar files to the directory you defined for this variable (refer back to Figure 11-23).

- Check that there is no variable with the same name defined at the node or server scope in the cell that points to a different driver directory.

- Double-check each cluster member's session-management data source configuration to be sure you provided the WebSphere variable you created (refer back to Figure 11-27).

Attach Each Cluster Member to the Data Source JNDI Name to Persist Sessions

After confirming the database connection, perform the following tasks on each member of the cluster (server1 and server2 in this case) one at a time.

Step 17. Expand **Servers**, and click **Application Servers**. In the application server list, click **server1**. Select **Session management** (under **Web Container Settings**) and then **Distributed environment settings** (under **Additional Properties**). In the resulting display (Figure 11-33), select the **Database** radio button (because you're configuring for database session persistence), and click the corresponding link.

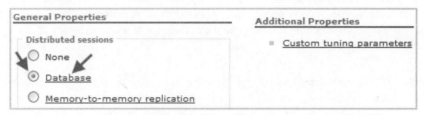

Figure 11-33: Selecting the option for database session persistence

Step 18. On the panel that results (Figure 11-34), enter **jdbc/sessiondb** in the **Datasource JNDI name** field. When overwriting the existing data source JNDI name ("jdbc/Sessions"), be sure to use the exact case and spelling of the name you created before. If you want to override the user ID and password you created for the J2C authentication alias (db2admin), enter the new values here; otherwise, leave these fields blank.

Figure 11-34: Specifying the data source JNDI name

Step 19. Repeat Steps 17 and 18 for each cluster member (in this case, for server2).

Step 20. Now, expand **Servers**, select **Clusters**, and restart (stop and start) the cluster in preparation for testing session failover using database persistence.

Verify Session Failover Using the Hitcount Application

If your cluster contains only two cluster members (as in this example), you can use a shortcut, without enabling plug-in trace, to verify session persistence after configuring the cluster for database session persistence. This shortcut won't work if you have more than two cluster members, nor can you use it to verify memory-to-memory session replication.

Step 21. If you meet the requirements, take the following steps to verify database session persistence using the shortcut. Otherwise, verify database session persistence using the procedure you performed earlier to verify session persistence after configuring memory-to-memory replication.

  a. After restarting the cluster, stop one of the cluster members (navigate to **Servers|Application Servers**). For this example, we'll stop server1. By stopping server1, you can be certain all requests will be served through server2 (because you have only two cluster members).

  b. Open a browser, and invoke the hitcount application through the HTTP server/plug-in by issuing the URL **http://http-host/hitcount**.

  c. Select the "Session state (create if necessary)" option, and click **Increment**. At the bottom of the page, you'll see the message "Hit Count value (for new session): 1" — indicating that a new session has been created for you.

  d. Next, select the "Existing session state only" option, and click **Increment**. The message "Hit Count value for (existing session): 2" indicates that the hit count has been incremented and that an existing session has been used. Make a note of the hit count value (2 in this case). If you configured database session persistence correctly, the hitcount application session data created on server2 will have been stored in the session database, WASDB.

  The diagram in Figure 11-35 illustrates what you've observed: a hitcount request being served by server2. The diagram also shows that a backup copy of this session has been stored in the session database.

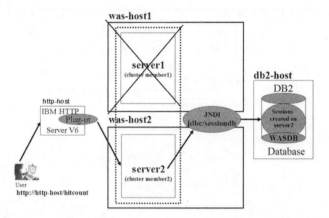

Figure 11-35: Normal hitcount application request handling

Do not close the browser while performing the remaining steps:

e. Navigate to **Servers|Application Servers**, *start* the cluster member you stopped before (server1 in this case), and *stop* the other cluster member (server2).

f. Click the browser's Back button. Select the "Existing session state only" option again, and click **Increment**. At this time, the request tries to go to server2 because of session affinity, but the plug-in quickly realizes that server2 is down, so it sends the request to server1. Server1 retrieves the session ID from the URL, pulls the session data for the requesting user from the session database (WASDB), and serves the request. If you configured HTTP session persistence properly, you should see a hit count value of 3, as shown in Figure 11-36.

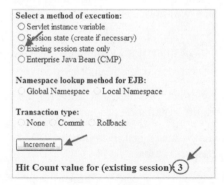

Figure 11-36: Hit count value of 3, indicating a third request was served

As the diagram in Figure 11-37 shows, the plug-in has directed the hitcount request to server1 because server2 is down. To serve the request, server1 picks up the session data from the session database.

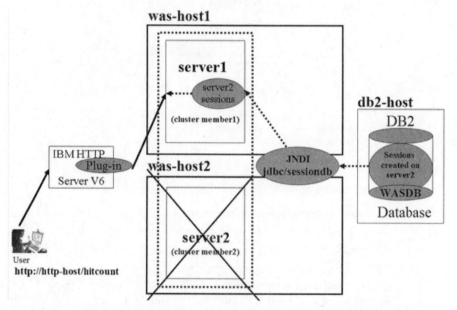

Figure 11-37: Failover handling of a hitcount application request

Installing DB2 and Creating the Session Database

If you want to use the trial version of DB2 8.2 for this chapter's exercise, complete the steps in this section before setting up database session persistence. First, obtain and install the DB2 software on a Windows system:

1. Go to *http://www-128.ibm.com/developerworks/downloads/im/udbexp* to obtain the software. Download file DB2ExEWindows.zip from the Web site, and extract the database software into a temporary directory.

2. Go to the temporary directory where you extracted the software, and click **setup.exe** to invoke the installation program.

3. Accept all the default values when installing the DB2 software. For the installation type, choose **Typical**.

4. For the installation directory, specify **c:\ibm\sqllib** (<DB2-HOME>).

5. Use **db2admin** for both the user name and password.

6. Select to create a default DB2 instance.

7. Apply the fix pack if it's available at the time of your installation.

Next, create the HTTP session database:

1. Start the DB2 and DB2 admin server (at a minimum). Figure 11-38 shows these two Windows services. (On Unix, you'd use the **db2start** command.)

DB2 - DB2-0	Started	Manual	.\db2admin
DB2 Governor		Manual	Local System
DB2 JDBC Applet Server		Manual	Local System
DB2 License Server		Manual	Local System
DB2 Remote Command Server		Manual	.\db2admin
DB2 Security Server		Manual	Local System
DB2DAS - DB2DAS00	Started	Manual	.\db2admin

Figure 11-38: DB2 and DB2 admin server started

2. Start the DB2 Control Center. To do so, click the Windows **Start** button, and navigate to **IBM DB2|General Administration Tools|Control Center**. (On Unix, run **./db2cc** from the <DB2-HOME\bin directory.)

3. To create the session database, navigate to **All Cataloged Systems|*DB2-host*|Instances|DB2**. Right-click **Databases**, and select **Create|Database Using Wizard**.

4. On the panel shown in Figure 11-39, specify the name of the database, the drive where you want to create the database, an alias (**WASDB** in this case), and an optional description. Then click **Finish**.

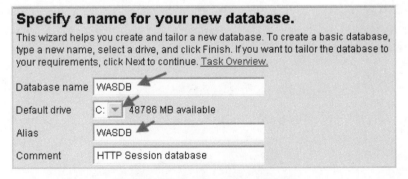

Specify a name for your new database.

This wizard helps you create and tailor a new database. To create a basic database, type a new name, select a drive, and click Finish. If you want to tailor the database to your requirements, click Next to continue. Task Overview.

Database name	WASDB
Default drive	C: ▾ 48786 MB available
Alias	WASDB
Comment	HTTP Session database

Figure 11-39: Creating a new database

5. Wait until you see a DB2 message indicating that the database has been created successfully (Figure 11-40). Click **No** to skip the Configuration Advisor. The WASDB session database is now ready to be configured from the Deployment Manager's admin console.

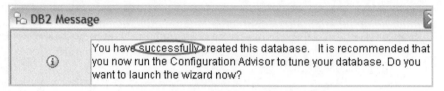

Figure 11-40: Successful database creation message

12

Service Integration Bus and High Availability Manager

WebSphere's Service Integration Bus (SIBus) is a form of managed communications that supports the integration of services through synchronous and asynchronous messaging. SIBus supports applications using message-based and service-oriented architectures. A bus must be contained within a single cell; however, a cell can contain more than one bus. When you add a cluster or an application server as a member to an SIBus, a messaging engine (ME) is created on that member to provide core SIBus messaging functionality. The messaging engine manages SIBus resources and provides a connection point for applications.

If you add multiple clusters and application servers to a bus, the messaging engines created within those members are interconnected seamlessly. Applications connected to any of the messaging engines associated with a given SIBus can exchange messages with each other without regard for which messaging engine they're connected to.

In this chapter, you'll extend the highly available cluster architecture you configured in Chapter 11 by adding messaging engines with high-availability capability. Figure 12-1 shows the architecture you'll achieve. You'll build this environment by creating an SIBus and then adding the cluster as a member to the SIBus. This configuration consists of a single messaging engine that can fail over to the messaging engine on the other cluster member if required, making the messaging engine highly available.

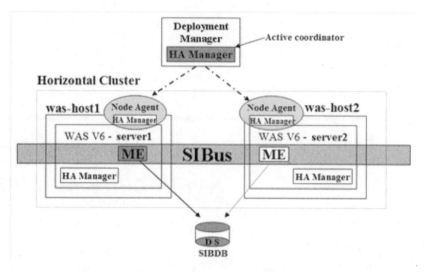

Figure 12-1: Highly available messaging engine architecture

Configure a Highly Available Messaging Engine

The flow chart in Figure 12-2 shows the high-level steps required to configure an SIBus and create a messaging engine on the cluster.

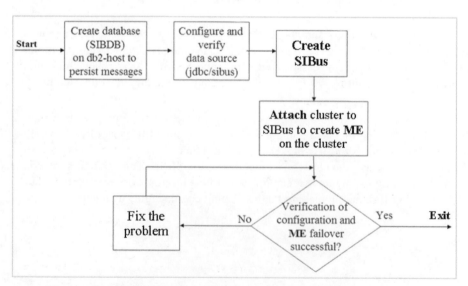

Figure 12-2: SIBus and highly available messaging engine configuration overview

To prepare the cluster environment, verify that the following processes are started:

- Deployment Manager on dmgr-host
- node agents on each cluster member node (was-host1 and was-host2)

Create a Data Store to Store Messages

Step 1. To persist messages, a messaging engine uses a Java Database Connectivity (JDBC) data source to interact with the database that contains the data store for the messaging engine. You need to specify this data source when you create an SIBus. For this example, follow the instructions in Chapter 11 to configure a data source named jdbc/sibus:

    a. Create a database to persist the messages on a production-quality database. In our example, we created the database SIBDB on DB2.

    b. Create a Java 2 Connector (J2C) authentication alias to access the database.

    c. Create a driver at cluster scope, and name the data source jdbc/sibus.

    d. Verify the data-source database connection as described in Chapter 11. A messaging engine won't start unless its data source has been successfully configured and verified. Figure 12-3 shows the successful test message you should receive.

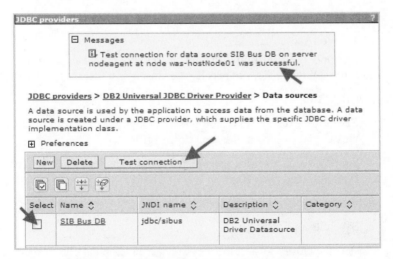

Figure 12-3: Successful test of database connection

Create the SIBus

Step 2.   Log on to the Deployment Managers admin console. Expand **Service integration**, select **Buses**, and click **New** to create a new SIBus. On the resulting panel (Figure 12-4), specify a name for the bus (NOYBBus in this example) and a description. Then click **Apply**.

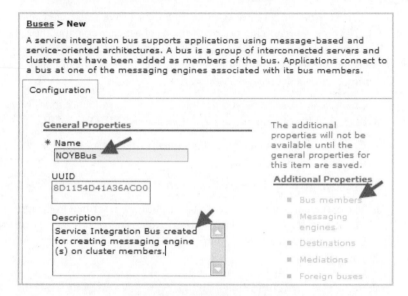

Figure 12-4: Creating the SIBus

Step 3.   Next, under the **Additional Properties** section, click **Bus members**. Then take the following steps to specify the cluster as a member to the bus:

    a. Click **Add**.

    b. Select the **Cluster** radio button (shown in Figure 12-5), and select the cluster you created in the drop-down list.

    c. Specify the data source you created and verified earlier (jdbc/sibus in this example), and click **Next**.

    d. On the confirmation page, click **Finish**.

    e. Save the configuration.

Step 4.   Restart the cluster to start the messaging engine on the cluster member. At this point, a messaging engine will be created with the default configuration. The messaging engine you created now is highly available.

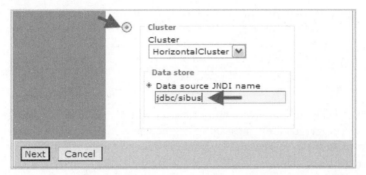

Figure 12-5: Specifying the cluster and data source

Step 5.   Navigate to **Service integration|Buses|*yourbus*|Messaging engines**, and
verify (on the panel shown in Figure 12-6) that the messaging engine's status
is "started" (green arrow). You can start or stop the messaging engine from
this panel if required.

Figure 12-6: Messaging engine verified as started

Verify Messaging Engine Configuration and Failover

Step 6.   In the default configuration, only one messaging engine will be active at any
one point. The messaging engine instance on the other cluster member(s)
will be in standby mode, ready to be started by the High Availability (HA)
Manager should the primary messaging engine fail. (You'll learn more about
the HA Manager in the next section.) To determine which cluster member the
messaging engine is started on, review the SystemOut.log file (located under
the <PROFILE-ROOT>\logs*server* directory) on both nodes. In our environment, the log file shown in Figure 12-7 indicates that the messaging engine
was started on server1 on the was-host1 node.

```
[10/21/05 17:54:12:436 CDT] 00000042 DiscoveryMBea I    ADMD0023I: The system discovered process
(name: nodeagent, type: NodeAgent, pid: 4468)
[10/21/05 17:54:13:637 CDT] 0000000a WsServerImpl  A    WSVR0001I: Server server1 open for
e-business
[10/21/05 17:54:16:722 CDT] 0000002b WorkSpaceMana A    WKSP0023I: Workspace configuration
consistency check is enabled.
[10/21/05 17:54:19:306 CDT] 00000023 SibMessage    I    [NOYBBus:HorizontalCluster.000-NOYBBus]
CWSID0016I: Messaging engine HorizontalCluster.000-NOYBBus is in state Started. ◄──
```

Figure 12-7: SystemOut.log file for server1 on was-host1

Step 7.   To check the high-availability function of the messaging engine, stop the server on which the messaging engine was initially started (server1 on was-host1 in this case). Navigate to **Servers|Application Servers** to stop a cluster member.

Step 8.   Review the SystemOut.log file on was-host2 to see that the messaging engine has been failed over and started on server2 on was-host2. The log file shown in Figure 12-8 verifies the failover of the messaging engine.

```
[10/21/05 18:13:08:319 CDT] 00000068 SibMessage    I
[NOYBBus:HorizontalCluster.000-NOYBBus] CWSIP0212I: messaging engine
HorizontalCluster.000-NOYBBus on bus NOYBBus is starting to reconcile the WCCM destination
and link configuration.
[10/21/05 18:13:08:399 CDT] 00000068 SibMessage    I
[NOYBBus:HorizontalCluster.000-NOYBBus] CWSIP0213I: messaging engine
HorizontalCluster.000-NOYBBus on bus NOYBBus has finished reconciling the WCCM destination
and link configuration.
[10/21/05 18:13:08:539 CDT] 00000068 SibMessage    I
[NOYBBus:HorizontalCluster.000-NOYBBus] CWSID0016I: Messaging engine
HorizontalCluster.000-NOYBBus is in state Started. ◄──
```

Figure 12-8: SystemOut.log file for server2 on was-host2

Step 9.   Navigate to **Service integration|Buses|*yourbus*|Messaging engines**, and verify that the status of the messaging engine still appears as started. If it does, you're ready to deploy and configure Java Message Service/Message-Driven Bean (JMS/MDB)–based applications.

Configure Highly Available Messaging Engine with Workload Sharing (Optional)

As you saw in an earlier task, the default SIBus member configuration doesn't support workload sharing because only one messaging engine is active to handle the traffic for that member. For many applications, one message engine will be enough to handle the messaging load. One reason to use a single messaging engine is to more easily maintain message sequence. For scenarios requiring high-volume message processing, you can change the default configuration by adding additional messaging engines to the cluster to support workload sharing. Figure 12-9 shows this architecture.

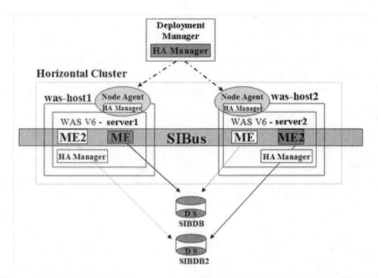

Figure 12-9: Highly available messaging engine with workload-sharing architecture

To set up this environment, complete the following steps to create a data store to store the messages of a messaging engine on the second cluster.

1. Create a second database to persist the messages. In the example, we created a second database (SIBDB2) on DB2.

2. Create the data source jdbc/sibus2, and verify the data-source database connection.

3. Navigate to **Service integration|Buses|***yourbus***|Bus members|***yourmember***, and click the **Add messaging engine** button. Figure 12-10 shows this panel for the HorizontalCluster member.

Figure 12-10: Adding a messaging engine

4. On the resulting panel (Figure 12-11), enter the name of the second data source and the J2C authentication alias you created. Leave all other values at the

defaults. Make sure the **Create tables** check box is selected. Click **OK**, and save the configuration.

5. Restart the cluster if it's practical to do so. Otherwise, start the new messaging engine on the cluster by navigating to **Service integration|Buses|*yourbus*| Messaging engines,** selecting the new message engine's check box, and clicking **Start**.

6. Use the instructions you followed earlier to verify the configuration and failover.

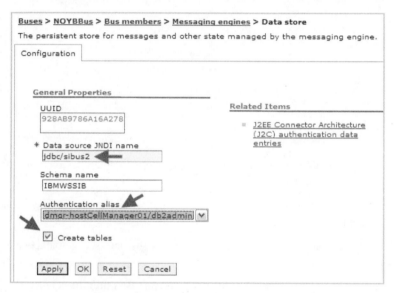

Figure 12-11: Creating the second data store

High Availability Manager

As the architecture diagrams you saw in Figures 12-1 and 12-9 depict, a High Availability Manager service runs in every application server, every node agent, and the Deployment Manager in a WebSphere clustered environment. The HA Manager is responsible for running key services (also called *singleton* services) on any available application servers in a cluster rather than on a dedicated server. Transaction managers, messaging engines, and workload-management routing are examples of singleton services. If the cluster member on which a service is running fails (or if the service appears to have failed), the HA Managers on the running cluster members detect the failure and negotiate which of the remaining servers will take over running the failed service. The goal of the HA Manager is to eliminate single points of failure.

Core Groups and the Active Coordinator

In the sample configuration, an HA Manager monitors and manages the state of a messaging engine to make the messaging service highly available. A cell can be divided into multiple highly available domains known as *core groups*. When you create a cell, a default core group called DefaultCoreGroup is created for the cell.

To see the default core group, expand **Servers**, and navigate to **Core groups|Core group settings.** Click **DefaultCoreGroup** and then **Core group servers** to view the list of servers that belong to this core group in your configuration. (The list includes the cluster members on which messaging engines are running.) Figure 12-12 shows this display for the cluster in this chapter's example.

Select	Name ◇	Node ◇	Version ◇	Type ◇	Cluster Name ◇
☐	dmgr	dmgr-hostCellManager01	6.0.1.0	Deployment manager	
☐	nodeagent	was-host2Node01	6.0.1.0	Node agent	
☐	nodeagent	was-host1Node01	6.0.1.0	Node agent	
☐	server1	was-host1Node01	6.0.1.0	Application Server	HorizontalCluster
☐	server2	was-host2Node01	6.0.1.0	Application Server	HorizontalCluster

Figure 12-12: Core group servers

Each HA Manager instance establishes connectivity with all other HA Manager instances in the same core group using a dedicated transport channel. This behavior provides a mechanism for an HA Manager instance to monitor the state of the other core group members. Within the core group, the HA Managers negotiate to "elect" one HA Manager to coordinate highly available services.

To determine the active coordinator in your configuration, review the SystemOut.log file on each server process. In the sample configuration, the SystemOut.log file under the <DMGR-ROOT>\logs\dmgr directory (shown in Figure 12-13) indicates that the HA Manager instance on the Deployment Manager is the active coordinator in our case. (In your configuration, you might find the active coordinator in a different process, such as one of the cluster members or node agent processes.) Logging related to the HA

Manager function will be written to this log file as long as this instance acts as the active coordinator. If the process that is holding the active coordinator (the Deployment Manager process in our case) goes down for any reason, an HA Manager instance on another process (one of the node agents or cluster members, for example) will be elected as an active coordinator, making the HA Manager coordinator function highly available.

```
[10/22/05 10:50:04:060 CDT] 00000016 vSync          I   DCSV2004I: DCS Stack
DefaultCoreGroup at Member dmgr-hostCell101\dmgr-hostCellManager01\dmgr: The
synchronization procedure completed successfully. The View Identifier is
(2:0.dmgr-hostCell101\dmgr-hostCellManager01\dmgr). The internal details are [0].
[10/22/05 10:50:04:150 CDT] 00000014 CoordinatorIm I   HMGR0206I: The Coordinator is an
Active Coordinator for core group DefaultCoreGroup.
[10/22/05 10:50:04:230 CDT] 00000014 CoordinatorIm I   HMGR0218I: A new core group view
has been installed. The view identifier is
(3:0.dmgr-hostCell101\dmgr-hostCellManager01\dmgr). The number of members in the new view
is 2.
```

Figure 12-13: SystemOut.log file on dmgr-host

If you want to verify the HA Manager's high-availability function, stop the process in which the HA Manager instance is the active coordinator (the Deployment Manager in our case). Review the SystemOut.log file for the remaining processes (node agents and cluster members) to see which server's HA Manager instance is the active coordinator. In the sample configuration, the SystemOut.log file under the <PROFILE-ROOT>\logs\ nodeagent directory on was-host1 indicates that the HA Manager instance on the node agent is the active coordinator.

High-Availability Policies

Every core group has an associated collection of high-availability policies. Each policy contains sets of directives governing the management of highly available components. To examine the policies associated with the default core group, navigate to **Servers|Core groups|Core group settings|DefaultCoreGroup|Policies**. You'll see a policy called "Default SIBus Policy" (shown in Figure 12-14) that is used by all the messaging engines (the match criteria of "type=WSAF_SIB" signifies all messaging engines) with a "One of N policy" policy type, which means to keep a singleton running on one server at any time. If a failure occurs, the HA Manager will start the singleton on another server.

Select	Name ◇	Description ◇	Policy type ◇	Match criteria ◇
☐	Clustered TM Policy	TM One-Of-N Policy	One of N policy	type=WAS_TRANSACTIONS
☐	Default SIBus Policy	SIBus One-Of-N Policy	One of N policy	type=WSAF_SIB

Figure 12-14: Default core group policy listing

The default policy is sufficient for many purposes, and we recommend you don't change it. If necessary, you can create and configure a specific policy by clicking **New** in the policies window.

If you do want to change the default behavior of the SIBus policy, click **Default SIBus Policy** in the policies list, and use the options under the **Additional Properties** section and/or the **General Properties** section to change the default configuration. Options here (shown in Figure 12-15) let you control which cluster servers the messaging engine can run on (use the **Preferred servers** link to specify a list of servers in order of preference) and configure the policy to control whether the messaging engine has a preference for a particular server or set of server. You also have options to **Fail back** to the preferred server whenever it resumes operation and to indicate that you want a service to run on the **Preferred servers only.** (You should avoid being restrictive about which servers can be chosen to run a service unless you have specific reasons for specifying preferred servers. It's better to give the HA Managers the freedom to choose where a service can run.)

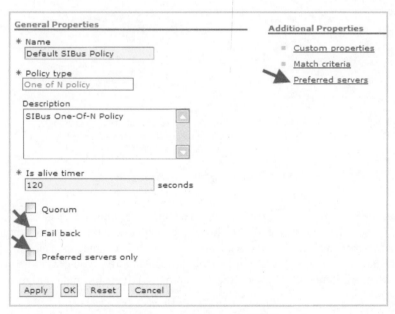

Figure 12-15: Customizing the default SIBus policy

For more information about the SIBus (and other SIBus topologies), the messaging engine, and HA Manager topics, consult the WebSphere V6 Information Center documentation *(http://publib.boulder.ibm.com/infocenter/ws60help/index.jsp)*.

Configure Highly Available Persistent Service

As the diagram in Figure 12-16 illustrates, the transaction manager (TM), which is a singleton service, is responsible for storing transaction information in a log file and recovering the transaction from that file if the server that's executing the transaction fails. The HA Manager instance makes sure the TM is highly available. By default, the transaction manager uses the "Clustered TM Policy" (the other policy listed in Figure 12-14). In this section, you'll see how to configure the cluster environment to recover "in-flight" transactions on a failed cluster member.

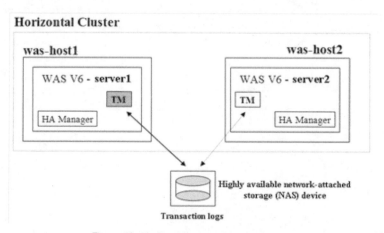

Figure 12-16: Persistent service architecture

For cluster members to perform recovery for each other, you must create the transaction logs on a device that all the cluster members can access — for example, a network-attached storage (NAS) device. You also need to enable persistent service for the cluster because this service isn't enabled by default after you create the cluster. The flow chart in Figure 12-17 shows the steps required to enable and configure persistent service.

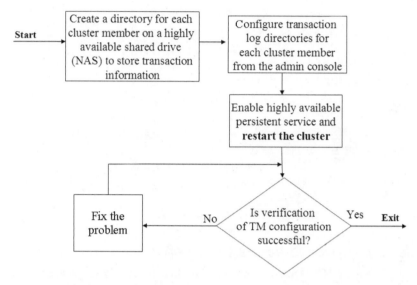

Figure 12-17: Highly available persistent service configuration overview

Create Transaction Log Directories

Step 1. Create a directory for each cluster member on a highly available shared drive to store the transaction information created by the cluster members. For the sample configuration, we created two directories on the shared drive:

- z:\wasv6\server1 to store the transaction information of the first cluster member (server1)

- z:\wasv6\server2 to store the transaction information of the second cluster member (server2)

On Unix machines, make sure you give read and write permissions to these directories so that each cluster member node can read and write transaction information.

Configure Transaction Service

Step 2. Connect to the Deployment Manager's admin console, expand **Servers**, and navigate to **Application Servers|server1|Container services|Transaction service**. Specify the transaction log directory you created for server1 as shown in Figure 12-18. Repeat this step for each cluster member (in our sample configuration, for server2).

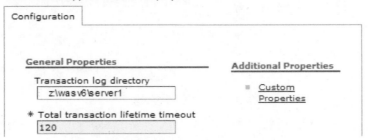

Application servers > server1 > Transaction Service

The transaction service is a server runtime component that can coordinate updates to multiple resource managers to ensure atomic updates of data.Transactions are started and ended by applications or the container in which the applications are deployed.

Configuration

General Properties

Transaction log directory

z:\wasv6\server1

* Total transaction lifetime timeout

120

Additional Properties

▪ Custom Properties

Figure 12-18: Specifying the transaction log directory

Enable Highly Available Persistent Service

Step 3.   From the Deployment Manager's admin console, expand **Servers,** and navigate to **Clusters|yourcluster.** Select the option to "Enable high availability for persistent services" as shown in Figure 12-19. Repeat this step for each cluster member (server2 in this case).

Server Cluster > HorizontalCluster

A server cluster consists of a group of application servers. If one of the member servers fails, requests will be routed to other members of the cluster.

| Runtime | Configuration | Local Topology |

General Properties

* Cluster name:

HorizontalCluster

Bounding node group name

DefaultNodeGroup ▾

☑ Prefer local

☑ Enable high availability for persistent services

Additional Properties

▪ Cluster members

▪ Backup cluster

▪ Endpoint Listeners

Figure 12-19: Enabling highly available persistent service

Step 4.   After enabling the persistence service, restart the cluster. If you have trouble starting a cluster member, review the SystemOut.log file of that member.

Verify Persistent Service Configuration

Step 5.   After successfully restarting the cluster, go to the shared device on which
you created transaction log directories, and make sure the transaction log
files have been created under the directories configured by WebSphere (as
shown in Figure 12-20). If you face any problem during or after configuring
the persistent service, review the SystemOut.log file of the relevant cluster
member to troubleshoot the problem.

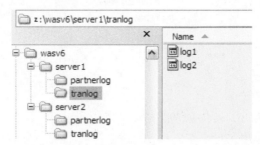

Figure 12-20: Verifying transaction log files creation

13

WebSphere V6 Load Balancer Edge Component: Install, Configure, Verify, and Manage

The Network Deployment package of WebSphere Application Server supports the ability to distribute the workloads of servers in your network to improve response time and ensure the availability of back-end servers. In this chapter, you'll learn how to set up a Load Balancer server to distribute requests across multiple back-end HTTP servers in a sample configuration. In Chapter 14, we'll extend this chapter's architecture to create a highly available workload-management environment.

The Load Balancer is part of the Edge Components for WebSphere, a set of "edge-of-network" functions that come with the WebSphere Network Deployment offering. (We cover another Edge Component for WebSphere, the Caching Proxy, in Chapter 15.) You use a Load Balancer server (also known as an *IP sprayer*) to spray, or route, client requests across multiple back-end servers. By distributing the workload, the Load Balancer can increase throughput, improve response time, and provide high availability for the servers on the back end. You can configure the Load Balancer to spray requests to a variety of server types, including e-mail, database, Lightweight Directory Access Protocol (LDAP), and Web servers.

The Load Balancer contains the following subcomponents:

- Dispatcher
- Content Based Routing
- Site Selector
- Cisco CSS Control

- Nortel Alteon Controller
- Metric Server

In this chapter, we explain how to configure the Load Balancer to spray HTTP requests across HTTP servers using the Dispatcher component of the Load Balancer. (For the remainder of the chapter, you can assume we're referring to the Dispatcher component whenever we use the term "Load Balancer.") The Dispatcher component supports three methods of forwarding requests:

- Media Access Control (MAC) address (the default)
- Network Address Translation/Network Address Port Translation (NAT/NAPT)
- Content-Based Routing (CBR)

In the first part of the chapter, we'll configure the Dispatcher using the default MAC address forwarding method. Later, we'll discuss the advantages and configuration details of the other two methods. (For more information about the other components of the Load Balancer, see IBM's Edge Components for WebSphere Information Center:

http://www-306.ibm.com/software/webservers/appserv/doc/v602/ec/infocenter/index.html).

The MAC address, which uniquely identifies each node of a network, is also known as the physical address associated with the network adapter. In the MAC forwarding method, the Dispatcher sprays incoming requests to the back-end servers (HTTP servers in our example), and those servers return the response directly to the requesting client, without Load Balancer (Dispatcher) involvement. The result is improved network performance.

Four functions of the Dispatcher interact to balance and dispatch the incoming requests to the back-end servers: *dsserver*, *executor*, *manager*, and *advisors*.

- The dsserver function relays command-line requests line to the executor, manager, and advisor functions.

- The executor distributes incoming connections and packets to the back-end servers that are part of the cluster.

- The manager gives the executor weightings to balance the new connections after collecting information from the executor, the advisors, and the Metric Server (if it's installed and configured).

- The advisors furnish the manager function with information about the response time and availability of each server on the assigned port.

Figure 13-1 illustrates how request processing proceeds in a Load Balancer environment. A key part of the configuration is the *cluster IP address*. In this example, the HTTP request that specifies the cluster IP address (169.254.213.100) in the URL is being workload-managed across two HTTP servers by the Load Balancer's Dispatcher component. When a user issues such a URL, the Load Balancer dispatches the IP packets associated with the request to one of the HTTP servers (let's assume http-host2 for this example) by swapping the MAC address of the Load Balancer with that of the HTTP server. That HTTP server, having been configured with its loopback adapter aliased to the cluster IP address (like each other load-balanced server in the cluster), accepts the request. If the Load Balancer receives another request from a different user, it will route that request to a different HTTP server (http-host1 in this case) to distribute the load.

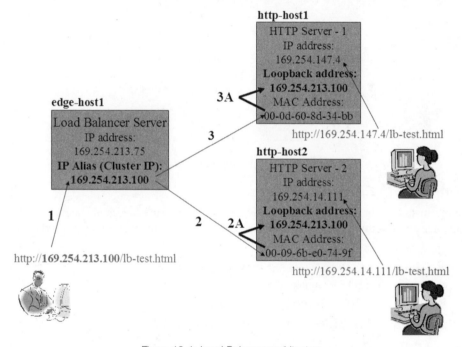

Figure 13-1: Load Balancer architecture

Installing the Load Balancer

The flow chart in Figure 13-2 shows the high-level steps required to install, configure, and verify the Load Balancer Edge Component. We'll go through all these steps in the following sections to set up a sample environment. In the example, you'll configure the Dispatcher component on a Load Balancer server (edge-host1) to load balance HTTP requests to two back-end HTTP Server machines (http-host1 and http-host2) using the MAC forwarding method.

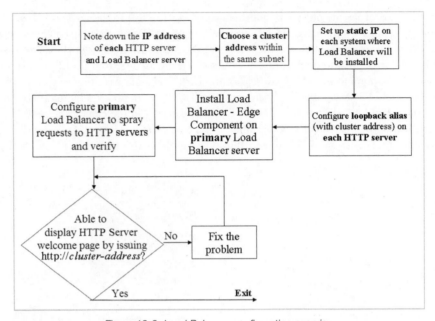

Figure 13-2: Load Balancer configuration overview

Configure the Network

Before installing the Load Balancer software and configuring the Load Balancer server, you have some setup and verification steps to perform on the network. You need to

- verify the network environment
- set up a static IP address on the Load Balancer system
- verify your HTTP connections
- obtain a cluster IP address

Let's step through the details for the sample environment.

Step 1.   The MAC forwarding method requires the Load Balancer server and the HTTP servers to be set up on the same LAN segment, with no routers or bridges in between these machines. Verify that this arrangement is the case in your environment. In our exercise, we set up the machines under the same LAN segment, with all three systems under the same subnet mask (169.254.0.0).

Step 2.   To participate in workload balancing, the machine on which you plan to install the Load Balancer (edge-host1 in this case) needs a static IP address.

In a corporate environment, ask your network administrator for a static address for this machine. The procedure to set up static IP depends on your operating system. Contact your system administrator to set up static IP on edge-host1 in your environment. On the system we used for this exercise (a Windows 2000 machine), we took the following steps to set up static IP.

a. Click the Windows **Start** button, and navigate to **Control Panel|Network Connections**.

b. Right-click **Local Area Connection**, and select **Properties**.

c. On the resulting panel (shown in Figure 13-3), select **Internet Protocol (TCP/IP)** in the list of connection items, and then click the **Properties** button.

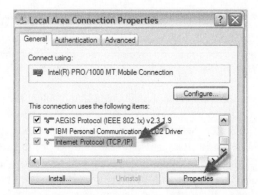

Figure 13-3: Local Area Connection Properties panel

d. Check the resulting properties panel (Figure 13-4) to see whether the option to "Obtain an IP address automatically" is selected. If it is, your

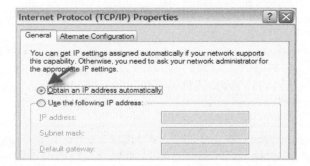

Figure 13-4: Internet Protocol (TCP/IP) Properties panel

system is not configured to use a static IP address. (For the machine in this example, we'll assume this is the case.)

e. Open a command prompt, and run the command **ipconfig** (**ifconfig** on Unix systems) to determine the IP address that's being assigned dynamically to this machine right now. The sample ipconfig results in Figure 13-5 show that the machine in this case has been assigned the IP address 169.254.213.75. We'll use this value as the static IP address for this example.

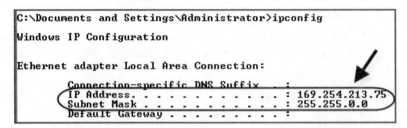

```
C:\Documents and Settings\Administrator>ipconfig

Windows IP Configuration

Ethernet adapter Local Area Connection:

        Connection-specific DNS Suffix  . :
        IP Address. . . . . . . . . . . . : 169.254.213.75
        Subnet Mask . . . . . . . . . . . : 255.255.0.0
        Default Gateway . . . . . . . . . :
```

Figure 13-5: Running the ipconfig command to determine the current IP address

f. Return to the TCP/IP properties panel, and select the option to "Use the following IP address." Figure 13-6 shows this option. Then, as shown in the figure, enter the IP address you just discovered (169.254.213.75) to be used as the static IP address from now on. For the subnet mask, accept the default value (255.255.0.0 in our case). If the ipconfig command reported a default gateway (or if your network administrator provided one), enter that value on this panel, too. In our case, we'll leave this field blank because we're going to test from systems within the same LAN segment using a switch, and our LAN isn't configured with a router to expose it to outside networks. Consult your network administrator if you need to enter any values for Domain Name Server (DNS) servers; otherwise, leave these fields blank. When you're finished with this panel, click **OK** to save the new properties, and close the main properties window.

Step 3.   Next, make sure you can ping both HTTP servers from the Load Balancer machine. To do so, open a command prompt on edge-host1, and issue the commands **ping http-host1** and **ping http-host2**. To find out the IP address of each HTTP server, run the **ipconfig** (**ifconfig** on Unix) command.

Step 4.   Make sure you can ping the Load Balancer server from each HTTP server. To do so, open a command prompt on each HTTP Server machine, and issue

ping edge-host1. To find out the IP address of each HTTP server, run the **ipconfig** (**ifconfig** on Unix) command.

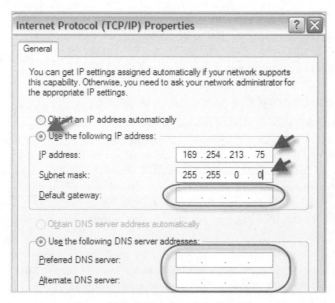

Figure 13-6: Setting the static IP address

Step 5.   Make a note of the MAC address of each HTTP server. To determine these values, open a command prompt on the Load Balancer machine, and run the command **arp –a**. (You need to ping the HTTP servers to obtain output for this command.) Figure 13-7 shows the command output for our example.

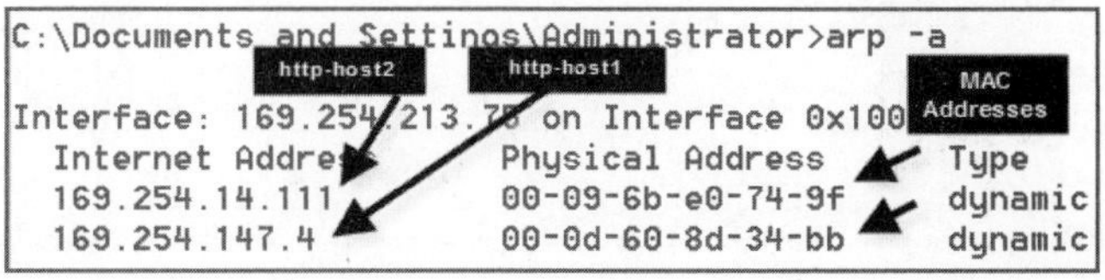

Figure 13-7: IP and MAC addresses reported for the sample configuration

Step 6.   Make sure you've set up the same content on both HTTP servers so that requests can be load balanced across these systems through the Load Balancer component.

Step 7. Obtain a valid IP address that's not being used by any other machine for the LAN segment you're setting up. You'll configure this address as the cluster address on the Load Balancer machine and as a loopback address on each HTTP server to enable workload-managing the requests across the HTTP servers from the Load Balancer server. For this example, we'll use 169.254.213.100 as the cluster IP. Notice that the cluster IP address falls under the same subnet as the other servers (169.254.0.0).

Configure and Verify the Loopback Adapter

Next on your task list is to configure the loopback adapter. You need to add the adapter and assign the cluster address to it. Once you've done so, any HTTP request received by the HTTP server machine that specifies the cluster address will be looped back to the machine's own IP address and handled by that HTTP server. Before configuring the loopback adapter, make sure you've obtained a cluster IP address as described in the preceding section; for this example, we'll use the address 169.254.213.100. Then take the following steps on each HTTP server you plan to use with the Load Balancer component.

Step 8. Verify that you can successfully ping the machine on which you plan to install the Load Balancer component (edge-host1 in this example) from the HTTP Server machine. To do so, open a command prompt, and run **ping edge-host1**.

Step 9. Execute the **route print** command to display the HTTP server machine's IP routing table (on Unix machines, use **netstat –nr**). You'll need this command's output as a reference when configuring the loopback adapter on this system. Figure 13-8 shows the command results for the http-host2 system in our example.

```
C:\Documents and Settings\Administrator>route print
===========================================================================
Interface List
0x1 ........................... MS TCP Loopback interface
0x2 ...00 00 00 00 00 01 ...... AT&T
0x1000004 ...00 09 6b e0 74 9f ...... Intel 8255x-based Integrated Fa
===========================================================================
===========================================================================
Active Routes:
Network Destination        Netmask          Gateway       Interface
        127.0.0.0        255.0.0.0        127.0.0.1       127.0.0.1
     169.254.0.0      255.255.0.0   169.254.14.111   169.254.14.111
  169.254.14.111  255.255.255.255        127.0.0.1       127.0.0.1
 169.254.255.255  255.255.255.255   169.254.14.111   169.254.14.111
       224.0.0.0        224.0.0.0   169.254.14.111   169.254.14.111
 255.255.255.255  255.255.255.255   169.254.14.111               2
===========================================================================
```

Figure 13-8: Sample route print command output for http-host2

Step 10. Verify that the HTTP Server system is functioning properly by starting it and invoking the HTTP Server welcome page. Issue the URLs pointing to the machine's host name (http://http-host2), DNS entry (http://http-host2.noyb.com), and IP address (http://169.254.14.111) from a browser.

Step 11. Next, use the appropriate procedure for your operating system to define a loopback adapter on the HTTP Server machine. For this example, we'll describe the detailed steps for a Windows 2000/2003 system. Then we'll point you to the procedures to follow on Windows NT, Linux, and AIX.

Take the following steps to configure the loopback adapter on a Windows 2000/2003 machine:

a. Click **Start**, and navigate to **Settings|Control Panel**.

b. Select **Add/Remove Hardware** to launch the Add/Remove Hardware wizard, and click **Next** on the wizard's opening panel.

c. On the next panel, select the **Add/Troubleshoot a device** option, and click **Next**.

d. Select to **Add a new device**, and click **Next**.

e. When asked whether you want Windows to search for the new hardware, select "No, I want to select the hardware from a list." Click **Next**.

f. Scroll through the **Hardware types** list, select **Network Adapters**, and click **Next**.

g. The next panel presents you with a list of manufacturer names and a corresponding list of network adapters. Select **Microsoft** in the **Manufacturers** list, and choose the **Microsoft Loopback Adapter**. Figure 13-9 shows these selections. Click **Next** when you're finished with this panel.

h. Click **Next** again, and click **Finish** to exit the wizard.

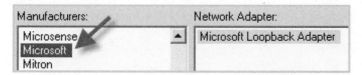

Figure 13-9: Specifying the network adapter to add

i. Now click **Start**, and navigate to **Settings|Network and Dial-up Connections**.

j. In the list of connections displayed (Figure 13-10), right-click the loop-back adapter (Local Area Connection 3 in our case), and select **Properties** from the context menu.

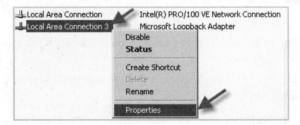

Figure 13-10: Selecting to display the loopback adapter properties

k. In the components list for the selected adapter (Figure 13-11), choose **Internet Protocol (TCP/IP)**. Then click the **Properties** button.

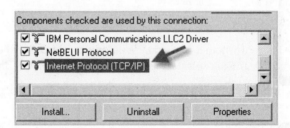

Figure 13-11: List of components used by the loopback adapter

l. On the resulting panel (Figure 13-12), select the option to "Use the following IP address," and enter the cluster IP address (169.254.213.100 in our example) and default subnet mask (255.255.0.0 in our example). Leave the gateway address field blank to use localhost as the default DNS server. Click **OK** twice when you're finished with this panel.

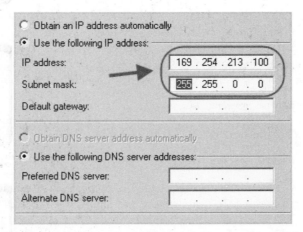

Figure 13-12: Specifying the cluster IP address and subnet mask

m. Open a command prompt, and run the **route print** command again (on Unix, use **netstat –nr**). Figure 13-13 shows the updated command output for our example. Look through this output for an entry whose Gateway column value is the cluster address (169.254.213.100) and whose Network Destination value starts with the first one to three octets of the cluster address (169.254 in this example — two octets) and ends exactly with the number of zeros reported in the Netmask column (0.0). According to this formula, we need to look for the cluster address 169.254.213.100 in the Gateway column and the network address 169.254.0.0 in the Network Destination column. In the sample output, the matching entry appears as the third route in the list.

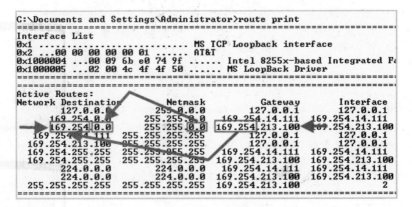

Figure 13-13: Updated route print command output

n. On some operating systems, a default route may have been created after you configured the loopback adapter. You need to delete this default route for the Dispatcher to be able to spray requests across HTTP servers. Contact your system administrator if you need to perform this step. You can delete the extra route by issuing the following command from the command prompt:

```
route delete network_destination cluster_address
```

For the example, issue

```
route delete 169.254.0.0 169.254.213.100
```

When you reboot the machine later, the duplicate entry might reappear in the route print results. To deal with that possibility, you can create a batch file containing your route delete command and place the batch file in your Startup programs folder. Figure 13-14 shows the batch file contents for our example. With the batch file in place, the extra route will be deleted automatically at startup if necessary.

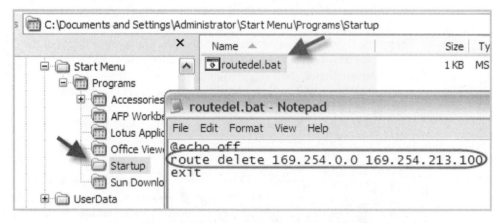

Figure 13-14: Storing the route delete command in a batch file

Configuring the Loopback Adapter on Other Operating Systems

The procedure to configure the loopback adapter on a Windows NT machine is similar to the one we've just gone through for Windows 2000/2003. For an HTTP server on Windows NT, follow the instructions shown in Figure 13-15. For a Linux machine, follow Figure 13-16. For an AIX machine, follow Figure 13-17.

Aliasing the Loopback Adapter for Windows NT

- Alias the loopback device
  1. Click **Start**, then click **Settings**.
  2. Click **Control Panel**, then double-click **Network**.
  3. Add the MS Loopback Adapter Driver if necessary (see Administration Guide for details).
  4. Set the loopback address to your cluster address.

- Check for an extra route by issuing the command **route print**
- Delete any extra route by issuing the command
  route delete *network_address cluster_address*

Figure 13-15: Configuring the loopback adapter on Windows NT

Aliasing the Loopback Adapter for Linux

Issue the following command:

ifconfig lo:1 *cluster_address* **netmask 255.255.255.255 up**

Figure 13-16: Configuring the loopback adapter on Linux

Aliasing the Loopback Adapter for AIX

- Alias the adapter by issuing the command:
  ifconfig lo0 alias *cluster_address* **netmask** *netmask*
- Check for an extra route by issuing the command:
  netstat -nr
- Delete any extra route by issuing the command:
  route delete -net *network_address cluster_address*

Figure 13-17: Configuring the loopback adapter on AIX

Step 12. To verify the successful configuration of the loopback adapter, start the HTTP server (if it isn't already started). Open a browser on the HTTP server machine, and bring up the HTTP Server welcome page by issuing the system's IP address — http://169.254.14.111 in this case. Figure 13-18 shows the result for this example.

Figure 13-18: IBM HTTP Server invoked using the IP address of the HTTP Server machine

Step 13.   Now, issue a URL specifying the cluster IP address (169.254.213.100) to bring up the HTTP Server welcome page again. Figure 13-19 shows the result for our example. This successful test demonstrates how HTTP Server behaves when a request arrives with the cluster address in the URL and how the system responds to the request.

Figure 13-19: IBM HTTP Server invoked using the cluster IP address

Step 14.   With the loopback adapter successfully configured on the first HTTP Server machine, repeat the preceding steps (7–12) for each HTTP server in your configuration (for http-host1 in the example).

Install the WebSphere V6 Load Balancer Edge Component

You'll find the installation process for the Load Balancer similar to the other WebSphere installations you've performed in this book, with the Launchpad program and an installation wizard there to guide you through the steps. For this example, you'll install the Load Balancer software on the edge-host1 system.

Step 15.   Figure 13-20 shows how the directory structure looks after you've downloaded the WebSphere Edge Components and extracted the files to a temporary directory. If you have this software on CD, mount the CD and change to the directory where the Launchpad program is available.

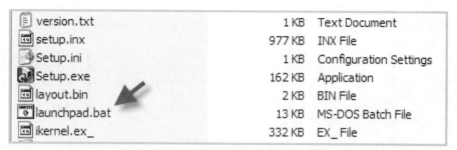

version.txt	1 KB	Text Document
setup.inx	977 KB	INX File
Setup.ini	1 KB	Configuration Settings
Setup.exe	162 KB	Application
layout.bin	2 KB	BIN File
launchpad.bat	13 KB	MS-DOS Batch File
ikernel.ex_	332 KB	EX_ File

Figure 13-20: Directory structure for WebSphere Load Balancer installation

Step 16. Make sure the TMP environment variable is set appropriately. To do so, log in as a member of the Windows Administrators group, right-click **My Computer** on the desktop, and select **Properties|Advanced|Environment Variables**. In the "User variables for user" list, note the value set for the temporary directory (TMP). If you don't see variable TMP in the list, click **New** to add it. For this example, we'll assume a TMP value of C:\temp.

Verify that at least 50 MB of disk space is available to install the Load Balancer product.

Unix note: On Unix systems, log in as root. If necessary, run the command **umask 022** to set permissions for the temporary directory (usually /tmp on these systems). To verify the current umask setting, run **umask**.
Make sure the file system mounted to the temporary directory has at least 100 MB of disk space. Before running the installation wizard on Unix systems, make sure you can execute the **xclock** or **xeyes** command to display a graphical image properly. For more information about these commands, see Chapter 3.

Step 17. In the directory where the Launchpad program is available, double-click **launchpad.bat**. (As an alternative, you can invoke **install.exe** under the WAS directory.) From the moment you invoke it, the program logs information about the installation activities in file WSES.log in the TMP directory.

Step 18. A WebSphere panel similar to the one shown in Figure 13-21 will be displayed. Review the information on this panel, and then choose the option to "Launch the installation wizard for WebSphere Application Server – Edge Components."

WebSphere Application Server - Edge Components Version 6.0

IBM WebSphere Application Server - Edge Components, Version 6.0 is an integrated platform that contains Edge Components, a Web server, and additional supporting software and documentation. This launchpad can serve as a single point of reference for installing your Application Server - Edge Components environment.

Select items from the menu on the left to access more detailed information about each installable component including links to release information, help documentation and ibm.com support pages.

To begin installing, select one of the following options:

Launch the installation wizard for WebSphere Application Server - Edge Components

Launch the installation wizard for IBM HTTP Server

Figure 13-21: Edge Components installation option

Step 19.   Read through the installation welcome panel, click **Next**.

Step 20.   Click **Yes** to accept the terms of the license agreement.

Step 21.   On the next panel, shown in Figure 13-22, select to install the Load Balancer component and the documentation. In the lower part of the panel, click the **Change Folder** button, and specify the installation directory. For Windows, make sure whatever directory name you use contains no spaces. For this example, we'll use **c:\IBM\edge\lb** as the Load Balancer installation directory. From now on, we refer to this installation directory as <EDGE-ROOT>. Click **Next** after specifying the installation directory.

Step 22.   Review the installation summary panel, and then click **Finish**. The installation program creates the <EDGE-ROOT> installation directory at this point and starts logging information in the file <EDGE-ROOT>\lbinst.log.

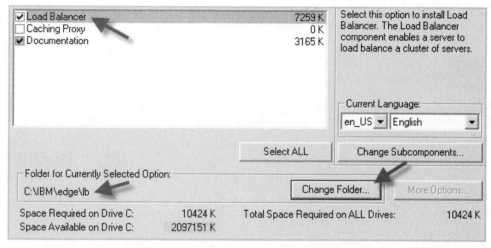

Figure 13-22: Selecting to install the Load Balancer

Step 23. You'll see a panel informing you that the installation program is extracting files and installing the components. When the **Setup Complete** panel (Figure 13-23) appears, click **Finish**. If the ReadMe file is open, close it to initiate the reboot process.

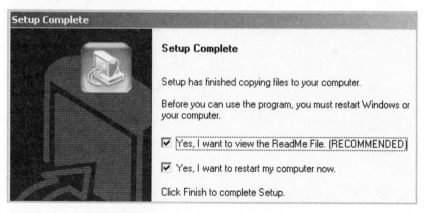

Figure 13-23: Load Balancer setup complete notification

Verify the Installation

To confirm the success of the installation steps, take time now to verify the installation. You'll do so by viewing the installation log file, starting the dispatcher process, connecting to the dispatcher process through the Load Balancer's graphical admin console, and starting the Load Balancer configuration wizard.

Step 24. Open file lbinst.log in the <EDGE-ROOT> directory, and make sure you see no errors or exceptions in the log file. Figure 13-24 shows a sample log.

```
6-19-2005 14:48:48  Set value for registry key: \SYSTEM\CurrentControlSet\Control
\Session Manager\Environment, Value name: Path, Value: C:\PROGRAM FILES\THINKPAD
\UTILITIES;%SystemRoot%\system32;%SystemRoot%;%SystemRoot%\System32\Wbem;C:\Program
Files\IBM\Infoprint Select;C:\Utilities;C:\Notes;C:\Program Files\XLView\;C:\lotus
\compnent\;C:\Program Files\IBM\Personal Communications\;C:\Program Files\IBM\Trace
Facility\;C:\WINDOWS\Downloaded Program Files;\ibm\websphere6\appserver\bin;c:\ibm
\edge\java\bin;C:\IBM\edge\lb\servers\lib;
6-19-2005 14:48:48  Exit: SetupRegistry
6-19-2005 14:48:48  Entry: SetupFolders
6-19-2005 14:48:48  Exit: SetupFolders
6-19-2005 14:48:48  Entry: CleanUpInstall
6-19-2005 14:48:48  Entry: ShowFinish
6-19-2005 14:48:48  Exit: ShowFinish
6-19-2005 14:48:48  Exit: CleanUpInstall
```

Figure 13-24: Sample lbinst.log file

Step 25. On Windows systems, you need to start the Load Balancer server from the Windows **Services** panel. To do so, click **Start**, and navigate to **Control Panel|Administrative Tools|Services**. You'll see the Load Balancer service listed in the **Services** panel with the name "IBM Dispatcher." Right-click this item, and click **Start** to start the service (Figure 13-25).

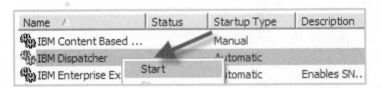

Figure 13-25: Starting the Load Balancer server from the Windows Services panel

---

Unix note: On Unix systems, issue the command **dsserver start** from the command prompt to start the Load Balancer. Use **dsserver stop** to stop the service.

Step 26. The Load Balancer comes with a graphical console you can use to perform the configuration and administrative tasks associated the Load Balancer. You'll use this console, shown in Figure 13-26, to connect to the dispatcher process to verify the installation. To start the Load Balancer console, click

Start, and navigate to **Programs|IBM WebSphere|Edge Components|Load Balancer|Load Balancer**. (You can also start the console from a command prompt using the lbadmin command.) The dscontrol command provides a command-line alternative to the graphical console for configuring the Dispatcher component; you'll learn more about this command later in the chapter.

Unix note: Open a command prompt, and run the **lbadmin** command to invoke the Load Balancer console.

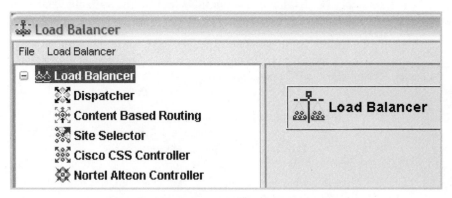

Figure 13-26: Load Balancer administrative console

If you receive a "cannot find 'javaw'" error (as shown in Figure 13-27) when starting the Load Balancer console, either JDK 1.4.2 isn't installed on this machine or the path to the JDK hasn't been set. The Load Balancer doesn't need the JDK during the installation or runtime of the dispatcher process, but you'll need later to use the Load Balancer's graphical configuration wizard.

Figure 13-27: "Cannot find 'javaw'" error

If you encounter this error, take the following steps to install the correct JDK version and set the required environment variables.

a. Go to the directory into which you extracted the Edge Components software, and locate the subdirectory JDK\repository\prereq.jdk. Copy the **java** directory from here to the Load Balancer install directory (C:\IBM\edge in this example) so that the Load Balancer graphical program can access it.

b. Right-click **My Computer** on the Windows desktop, select **Properties|Advanced|Environment Variables**, and click **New** to add a new system variable. In the resulting dialog (Figure 13-28), enter **JAVA_HOME** as the variable name, and type the path to the java directory (C:\IBM\edge\java in this case) for the variable value. Then click **OK**.

c. In the list of system variables displayed next, select the **Path** variable, and then click the **Edit** tab. In the resulting dialog, add the path for the javaw executable (C:\IBM\edge\java\bin in this case) at the end of the line, as shown in Figure 13-29. Click **OK**, and save the configuration.

d. Open a command prompt, and run **java –version** to verify the java version you installed. The command results should indicate that the 1.4.2 version of the JDK has been installed (Figure 13-30).

Step 27. Next, verify that you can start the Load Balancer's configuration wizard. You'll use this tool later to configure the Load Balancer system to spray requests to the HTTP servers. In the Load Balancer console's left navigation pane, right-click **Dispatcher**, and select **Start Configuration Wizard** from the context menu to display the welcome panel for the configuration wizard.

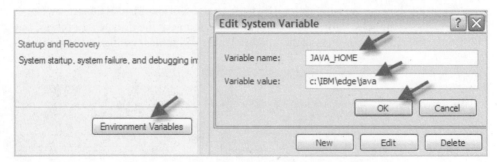

Figure 13-28: Defining the Java system variable

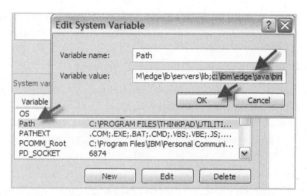

Figure 13-29: Adding the path to the javaw executable

```
C:\Documents and Settings\Administrator>java -version
java version "1.4.2"
Java(TM) 2 Runtime Environment, Standard Edition (build 1.4.2)
Classic VM (build 1.4.2, J2RE 1.4.2 IBM Windows 32 build cn142sr1w-20041028
```

Figure 13-30: Verifying the installed Java version

If you receive a "wizard already started" error, you may not have the right JDK version on this machine; the Load Balancer requires JDK 1.4.2 or later. To determine your JDK version, open a command prompt, and type **java –version** to display the installed version. If you find you have an earlier JDK, uninstall it. (To do so on Windows machines, click **Start**, navigate to **Control Panel|Add Remove Programs**, select the Java runtime, and click **Change/Remove**.) Then install JDK 1.4.2 using the instructions in the preceding step.

Step 28.   After confirming that you're able to successfully launch the configuration wizard, click **File|Exit** to exit the Load Balancer console.

Apply the Fix Pack

Step 29.   If you're applying a fix pack in preparation for configuring the Load Balancer to spray requests to multiple HTTP Servers, make sure you first make a backup copy of the configuration file default.cfg (under the <EDGE-ROOT>\ servers\configurations\dispatcher directory) and the license file lb60Full.LIC (under the <EDGE-ROOT>\servers\conf directory). Refer to Chapter 19 for instructions on applying fix packs and efixes. Then return to this chapter for instructions on verification, problem determination, and maintenance.

Set Up a DNS Entry for the Cluster Address

Step 30.   You need to create a DNS entry for the cluster IP address to provide it to users who try to access Web pages through the Load Balancer. Configure this entry on all the servers (Load Balancer and HTTP servers), as well as on the client machine from which you'll test the configuration.

In Figure 13-31, we've used the /etc/hosts file instead of DNS, assigning cluster address 169.254.213.100 the host name noyb-cluster@noyb.com and the alias noyb-cluster. If you've set up a DNS entry for the cluster address, you don't need to make any entries in the /etc/hosts file.

Make sure you can ping the cluster IP address and DNS entry from each machine in the configuration. Figure 13-34 shows the successful ping results for our example.

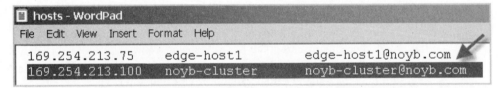

Figure 13-31: Hosts file entry for the cluster IP address

```
C:\Documents and Settings\Administrator>ping noyb-cluster

Pinging noyb-cluster [169.254.213.100] with 32 bytes of data:

Reply from 169.254.213.100: bytes=32 time=10ms TTL=128
Reply from 169.254.213.100: bytes=32 time<10ms TTL=128
Reply from 169.254.213.100: bytes=32 time<10ms TTL=128
Reply from 169.254.213.100: bytes=32 time<10ms TTL=128
```

Figure 13-32: Pinging the cluster IP address

Configure the Load Balancer to Spray Requests to Multiple HTTP Servers

With the preceding steps under your belt, you're ready to configure the Load Balancer to spray requests to the two HTTP servers in the sample configuration. You'll use the Load Balancer's configuration wizard to accomplish this task.

Step 31.   Start the dispatcher process if it's not already started. To do so, open the Windows **Services** panel (**Start|Control Panel|Administrative Tools|Services**), right-click **IBM Dispatcher**, and click **Start**.

Step 32.   Connect to the Load Balancer admin console (**Start|Programs|IBM WebSphere|Edge Components|Load Balancer|Load Balancer**).

Step 33.   Right-click **Dispatcher**, and select **Start Configuration Wizard** to display the configuration wizard's welcome panel. Review the panel's contents, and click **Next**.

Step 34.   Review the contents of the "What to Expect" panel, and click **Next**.

Step 35.   Review the configuration requirements on the "What Must I Do Before I Begin?" panel (Figure 13-33). Then click the **Create Configuration** button.

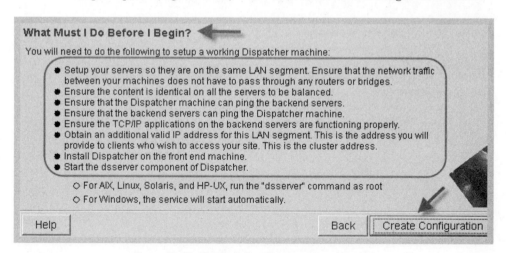

Figure 13-33: Dispatcher configuration requirements

If you receive the "No Host Keys" error (shown in Figure 13-34), you may not have rebooted the machine (Windows operating systems) after installing the Load Balancer. It's also possible you didn't start the dispatcher process after the reboot, because the system was trying to connect to the dispatcher process on an external node using host keys. Exit the Load Balancer console, reboot the machine, and repeat the preceding steps.

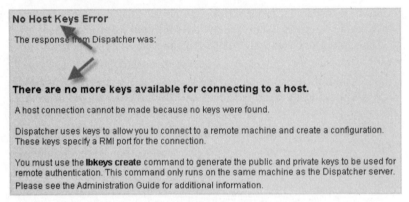

Figure 13-34: No host keys error

Step 36. When prompted to choose a host to configure (Figure 13-35), accept the default host (the host name of the machine), and click **Next**.

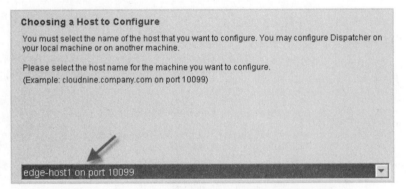

Figure 13-35: Specifying the host to configure

If you receive a "Host Connection Error" (Figure 13-36), investigate the following possible conditions, and take the appropriate action. (If you use the

Dispatcher dscontrol command from the command prompt to specify the host, this error is reported as "Server not responding.")

- You may not have started the dispatcher process. To correct the error, start the process. Then repeat the preceding steps.

- The network may not be functioning properly. To check the network status, open a command prompt, and run the **ipconfig** (**ifconfig** on Unix) and **ping edge-host1** commands to make sure the Load Balancer server (edge-host1) is configured properly in the network.

- You may have a port conflict. The Load Balancer console uses port 10199 to communicate with the dsserver function to handle command-line requests. Open a command prompt, and run **netstat –an** to see whether any third-party software is using this port or whether any processes are hanging from the previous step and holding this port. On Windows systems, check the Windows Task Manager for the javaw process. (On Unix, use **ps –ef | grep javaw**.)

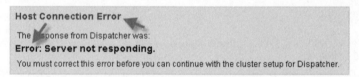

Figure 13-36: Host connection error panel

Step 37. On the next panel (Figure 13-37), enter the cluster address (or DNS entry or alias) that you previously selected. Then click the **Update Configuration & Continue** button.

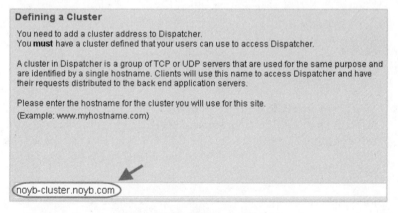

Figure 13-37: Defining the cluster

If you receive a "cluster is not valid" error, make sure a DNS entry is available for the cluster or an alias for the cluster address is configured in the /etc/hosts file.

If you receive the error "Executor is not running," the most likely cause is that you haven't set up a static IP address on this machine. (If you try to start the executor from the command line using **dscontrol executor start**, you'll receive the error "Kernel was not loaded.") When the wizard informs you that the cluster was added successfully, click **Next**.

Step 38. On the next panel (Figure 13-38), specify the port number that will handle client requests. For HTTP non-SSL traffic, the requests come to port 80 by default. If you're using SSL, select port 443. Then click **Update Configuration & Continue**. When notified that the port was added successfully, click **Next**.

Adding a Port

Every cluster needs a port that will handle client requests for a specific application. Web servers use Port 80 by default.

Enter the Port for the Service that you would like to have load-balanced, or enter a port number between 1 and 65535:

Port 80 (HTTP)

Figure 13-38: Specifying the port for client requests

Step 39. You're now ready to configure the two servers that the Dispatcher will load balance. On the **Adding Servers** panel (Figure 13-39), click the **Add a server** button to configure the first HTTP Server. Enter its name (DNS entry, host name, or alias) on the resulting panel (Figure 13-40), and then click **Next**.

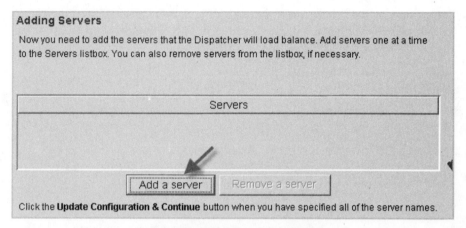

Figure 13-39: Adding Servers panel

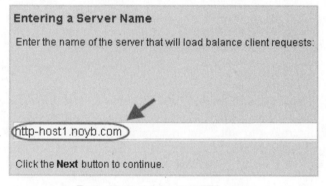

Figure 13-40: Adding the HTTP server

If you receive the error "Router address not specified or not valid for port method" when you click the **Add a server** button, you may not have set up static IP on this machine (Network Dispatcher/Load Balancer). Make sure you've also disabled the Dynamic Host Configuration Protocol (DHCP) client on this node.

Step 40.   To add the second HTTP server, click the **Add a server** button again on the **Adding Servers** panel, enter the name of the second HTTP server, and click **Next**.

Step 41. Figure 13-41 shows the updated **Adding Servers** panel with the two newly added HTTP servers listed. Click the **Update Configuration & Continue** button here to have your additions take effect.

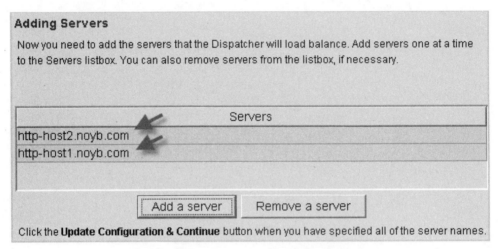

Figure 13-41: HTTP servers in Adding Servers panel

Step 42. On the next panel (Figure 13-42), select **Yes** to start the advisor for HTTP port 80, and click **Update Configuration & Continue**. The Dispatcher will use this advisor to collect information about the HTTP server's activities and relay it to the manager function. When informed that the advisor has been started successfully, click **Next**.

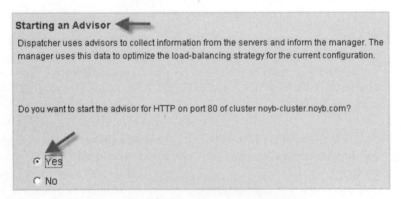

Figure 13-42: Starting an advisor for the HTTP server

Step 43.   On the next panel (Figure 13-43), select the operating system on which your HTTP servers are running (Windows 2000/2003 in this example), and then click the **View Loopback Instructions** button.

Setting Up the Server Machine

The final step required is to configure the application servers to accept traffic for noyb-cluster.noyb.com. In order to do this, you must issue a loopback command at each of the application servers.

Please select the appropriate operating system for each server:

- ⦿ Windows 2000 or 2003
- ○ Linux
- ○ OS/2
- ○ Windows NT

- ○ AIX
- ○ Solaris
- ○ OS/390
- ○ HP-UX

Click the **View Loopback Instructions** button to see the directions for the selected operating system.

Figure 13-43: Specifying the HTTP Server operating system

Step 44.   Review the instructions displayed for aliasing the loopback adapter. You completed these steps in the earlier part of this chapter. Remember that you need to perform these steps on each HTTP Server machine (not on the Load Balancer machine). Click **Next**.

Step 45.   When the Congratulations panel appears, click **Exit**, and then confirm with a **Yes** (as shown in Figure 13-44) to exit the dispatcher configuration wizard. *Do not* exit out of the Load Balancer console unless you save the configuration. Otherwise, you'll lose your changes.

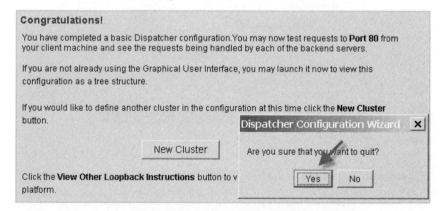

Congratulations!

You have completed a basic Dispatcher configuration. You may now test requests to **Port 80** from your client machine and see the requests being handled by each of the backend servers.

If you are not already using the Graphical User Interface, you may launch it now to view this configuration as a tree structure.

If you would like to define another cluster in the configuration at this time click the **New Cluster** button.

New Cluster

Click the **View Other Loopback Instructions** button to v platform.

Dispatcher Configuration Wizard ✕

Are you sure that you want to quit?

Yes   No

Figure 13-44: Exiting the dispatcher configuration wizard

Connect to the Host and Save the Configuration

Step 46.   Back in the Load Balancer admin console, right-click **Dispatcher**, and select **Connect to Host** from the context menu. If you receive the error "Unable to access RMI server," review the possible conditions described in Step 36, and take the appropriate action. (If you run the dscontrol command from the command prompt to make the connection, this error is reported as "Server not responding.")

Step 47.   At the Dispatcher login prompt (Figure 13-45), select the default host name displayed (edge-host1 on port 10099 in this example), and click **OK**.

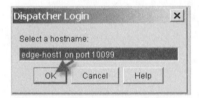

Figure 13-45: Dispatcher login prompt

Step 48.   In the left pane of the Load Balancer console, navigate to **Load Balancer|Dispatcher|Host:** *hostname* (edge-host1 in this case). Right-click the host name, and select **Save Configuration File As**, as shown in Figure 13-46.

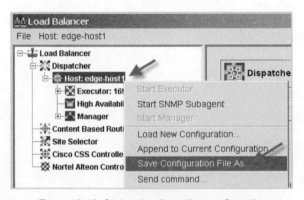

Figure 13-46: Saving the dispatcher configuration

Step 49.   When prompted to save the configuration (Figure 13-47), accept the default configuration file name (default.cfg), and click **OK**. Click **Yes** when asked whether you want to overwrite the existing file. (When you start the dispatcher process, the Load Balancer server reads the configuration information from file default.cfg by default.)

Figure 13-47: Specifying the configuration file name

Step 50. Navigate to the default.cfg file in the <EDGE-ROOT>\servers\configurations\dispatcher directory. Open the file, and review the commands it contains. Figure 13-48 shows the default.cfg file for our example. You could have used these dscontrol commands to configure the Load Balancer from the command prompt instead of using the graphical console. (Be sure to back up this configuration file before making any changes to the configuration.)

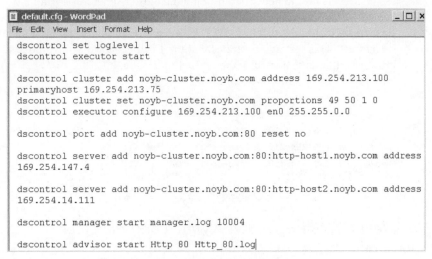

```
dscontrol set loglevel 1
dscontrol executor start

dscontrol cluster add noyb-cluster.noyb.com address 169.254.213.100
primaryhost 169.254.213.75
dscontrol cluster set noyb-cluster.noyb.com proportions 49 50 1 0
dscontrol executor configure 169.254.213.100 en0 255.255.0.0

dscontrol port add noyb-cluster.noyb.com:80 reset no

dscontrol server add noyb-cluster.noyb.com:80:http-host1.noyb.com address
169.254.147.4

dscontrol server add noyb-cluster.noyb.com:80:http-host2.noyb.com address
169.254.14.111

dscontrol manager start manager.log 10004

dscontrol advisor start Http 80 Http_80.log
```

Figure 13-48: Sample Dispatcher configuration file

Verify the Configuration from the Command Prompt

Step 51. Open a command prompt on the Load Balancer system, and issue **ipconfig** (**ifconfig** on Unix systems) to see that the cluster address has been aliased to the device. Figure 13-49 shows the command results for our example. With this configuration, the Load Balancer machine will respond to both the cluster address (169.254.213.100) and its own IP address (169.254.213.75). When a request arrives with the cluster address (169.254.213.100), the Load Balancer will forward it to one of the HTTP servers.

```
C:\Documents and Settings\Administrator>ipconfig

Windows 2000 IP Configuration

Ethernet adapter Local Area Connection 2:

        Connection-specific DNS Suffix  . :
        IP Address. . . . . . . . . . . : 169.254.213.100
        Subnet Mask . . . . . . . . . . : 255.255.0.0
        IP Address. . . . . . . . . . . : 169.254.213.75
        Subnet Mask . . . . . . . . . . : 255.255.0.0
        Default Gateway . . . . . . . . :
```

Figure 13-49: IP configuration for the Load Balancer system

Step 52. Open a command prompt on a machine other than the Load Balancer or HTTP servers on the network, and ping the cluster IP address: **ping 169.254.213.100**. You should see that the reply comes from the Load Balancer's IP address (169.254.213.75) even though you're pinging the cluster address. This test demonstrates that the Load Balancer will respond to browser requests that specify the cluster address (e.g., http://169.254.213.100/lb-test.html).

```
C:\Documents and Settings\Administrator>ping 169.254.213.100

Pinging 169.254.213.100 with 32 bytes of data:

Reply from 169.254.213.75: bytes=32 time<1ms TTL=255
Reply from 169.254.213.75: bytes=32 time<1ms TTL=255
Reply from 169.254.213.75: bytes=32 time<1ms TTL=255
Reply from 169.254.213.75: bytes=32 time<1ms TTL=255
```

Figure 13-50: Pinging the cluster IP address

Set Up a Test HTML Page to Verify the Load Balancer Configuration

Step 53. Create a simple HTML page (we'll use the name lb-test.html for this example), and save it on each HTTP server under DocumentRoot (e.g., <IHSV6-ROOT>\ htdocs\en_us, where <IHSV6-ROOT> is the directory where you installed IBM HTTP Server). (If you use a locale other than en_us, copy the file to that locale.) Use the same name for the test HTML page on each HTTP server.

Step 54. In the lb-test.html file on the first HTTP Server system (http-host1), enter the HTML script shown in Figure 13-51 so you'll know when the page has been served from http-host1.

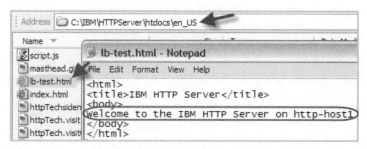

Figure 13-51: HTML script for http-host1

Step 55. In the lb-test.html file on the second HTTP Server system (http-host2), enter the HTML script shown in Figure 13-52 to know when the page has been served from http-host2.

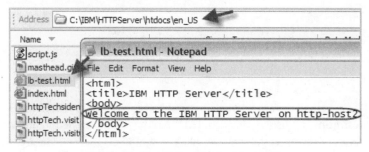

Figure 13-52: HTML script for http-host2

Verify That the Load Balancer Is Spraying Requests to the HTTP Servers

Step 56. Make sure the dispatcher process and both HTTP servers are running. Also make sure you deleted the extra route on each HTTP server if your operating system requires this step.

Step 57. Open a browser on a machine in the network other than the Load Balancer or HTTP server machines, and invoke the HTTP Server welcome page by issuing a URL specifying the cluster alias (http://noyb-cluster), the cluster's DNS entry (http://http-host2.noyb.com), or the cluster's IP address (http://169.254.213.100). Click the browser's reload button few times to distribute the load among the HTTP servers.

Step 58. Open a command prompt on the Load Balancer server, and run the command

```
dscontrol server report noyb-cluster.noyb.com:80:
```

Figure 13-53 shows sample results for our example. The numbers in the Total column show the distribution of load across the HTTP servers.

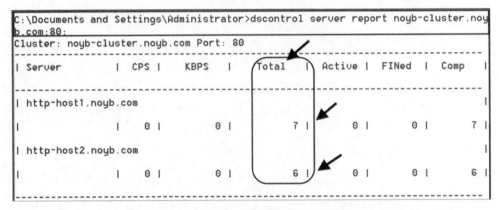

Figure 13-53: Load distribution results

Step 59. Issue **http://*cluster-address*/lb-test.html** (e.g., **http://169.254.213.100/lb-test.html**) to display the sample HTML page you created in an earlier step. Observe the request being served by one of the HTTP servers. In Figure 13-54, the request is being served by http-host1, as confirmed by the welcome message in the HTML page. Click the reload button a few times.

You may find that the same HTTP server serves subsequent requests issued from the same browser. This behavior is due to the default *sticky time* configuration. Sticky time is the interval during which subsequent requests on an existing connection are sent to the same server. If you want to observe the workload management before the sticky time expires, open a second browser and issue http://*cluster-address*/lb-test.html again to see the request served by the second HTTP server (http-host2 in this case, as shown in Figure 13-55).

Figure 13-54: HTTP request being served by http-host1

Figure 13-55: HTTP request being served by http-host2

Step 60. In the left pane of the Load Balancer console, navigate to **Load Balancer|Dispatcher|Host:** *hostname***|Executor:** *IP address***|Cluster:** *cluster address***|Port:** *port number*. Figure 13-56 shows this navigation path for our example. Right-click the port number (80 in this case), and select **Monitor** from the context menu.

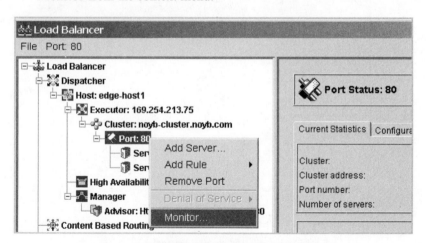

Figure 13-56: Starting the Load Balancer monitor

Step 61. On the resulting panel (Figure 13-57), click the **New Connections** radio button, and observe the activity of the new connections and the distribution of the load across HTTP servers as suggested by the advisor and the sticky time.

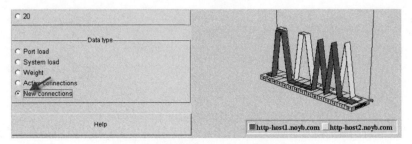

Figure 13-57: Load Balancer monitor

Step 62. Open a command prompt, go to the <EDGE-ROOT>\servers\bin directory, and run the command **dscontrol manager report** to obtain statistics from the manager. Figure 13-58 shows the results of this command for the sample configuration. As you can see, the Load Balancer manager tracks a variety of information about the activity on the cluster, including HTTP server status, active and new connections, current and new weightings.

```
C:\IBM\edge\lb\servers\bin>dscontrol manager report
----------------------------------------------------------------
|      SERVER              |   IP ADDRESS   |   STATUS   |
----------------------------------------------------------------
|           http-host1.noyb.com |  169.254.147.4 |   ACTIVE  |
|           http-host2.noyb.com |  169.254.14.111 |   ACTIVE  |
----------------------------------------------------------------

-----------------------------------
|   MANAGER REPORT LEGEND   |
-----------------------------------
| ACTV | Active Connections |
| NEWC | New Connections    |
| SYS  | System Metric      |
| NOW  | Current Weight     |
| NEW  | New Weight         |
| WT   | Weight             |
| CONN | Connections        |
-----------------------------------

------------------------------------------------------------------
| noyb-cluster.noyb.com                                          |
|   169.254.213.100 | WEIGHT | ACTV |  NEWC  | PORT  |  SYS  |
|     PORT:    80   |NOW NEW|  49% |  50%  |  1%  |  0%  |
------------------------------------------------------------------
| http-host1.noyb.com                                            |
|                   | 10  10 |   1 |    0 |   -1 |     0 |
| http-host2.noyb.com                                            |
|                   | 10  10 |   3 |    0 |   -1 |     0 |

------------------------------------------------------------------
|   ADVISOR    |   CLUSTER:PORT   | TIMEOUT  |
------------------------------------------------------------------
|        http | noyb-cluster.noyb.c | unlimited |
------------------------------------------------------------------
```

Figure 13-58: Load Balancer manager statistics

Logging

By default, the Load Balancer's Dispatcher component logs events and diagnostic information under the <EDGE-ROOT>\servers\logs\dispatcher directory. Figure 13-59 gives you an idea of the different log files available for the Dispatcher. On Unix systems, you'll also see the log file dsserver.log in the <EDGE-ROOT>\servers\bin directory. This file logs information during Dispatcher startup (when you run the **dsserver start** command).

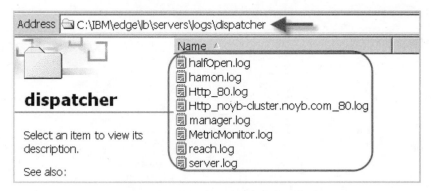

Figure 13-59: Dispatcher component log files

By default, the logging level for the dsserver function is set to Minimal. If necessary for debugging purposes, you can change this log level to verbose from the Load Balancer console. To do so, select **Dispatcher|Host:** *hostname* (e.g., **Dispatcher|Host: edge-host1**), go to the **Configuration Settings** tab, and choose **Verbose** from the list of dsserver logging level options displayed (Figure 13-60). Click the **Update Configuration** button to have the new log level take effect. (You can also run **dscontrol set loglevel 5** from the command prompt to change the logging level to verbose.) Be sure to reset the log level value to Minimal once you've resolved whatever problem you're having.

You can set the log levels for the other functions of the dispatcher process either by running a dscontrol command from the command prompt or by including the log level values in the default.cfg file and restarting the dsserver function. Use the following commands to set the logging level to verbose for the manager and advisor functions.

- Run **dscontrol manager set loglevel 5** to change the log level to verbose to record more information about problems with the manager function in the manager.log file.

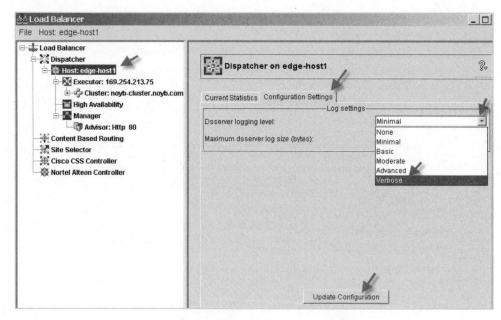

Figure 13-60: Changing the dsserver log level

- Run **dscontrol advisor loglevel http 80 5** to change the log level to verbose to record more information about problems with the advisor function in the http_80.log and http_*cluster-address*.log files.

Configure Rule-Based Load Balancing

When you configure the Load Balancer's Dispatcher component as described in the earlier part of this chapter, factors such as server availability, sticky time, and affinity address mask (*stickymask*) govern how the Dispatcher workload-manages client requests across the back-end HTTP servers. (The stickymask defines a group of clients having common subnet addresses. Using this parameter, you can configure the Dispatcher to spray requests to the selected back-end server(s) for clients having common subnet addresses.)

In some environments, you may require more control over the way client requests are routed. For example, perhaps you need to have only certain HTTP servers in a cluster handle requests during a particular time of day (e.g., to perform maintenance on the other servers). Or maybe you want to block requests that come from certain client IP addresses or route them to a specific HTTP server (or servers). You can achieve this kind of fine-tuned control by setting up a *rule-based* load balancing configuration.

With rule-based load balancing, you define how client requests are to be handled based on information contained in the HTTP request header, as well as on network conditions. The panel in Figure 13-61 lists the different rules you can apply.

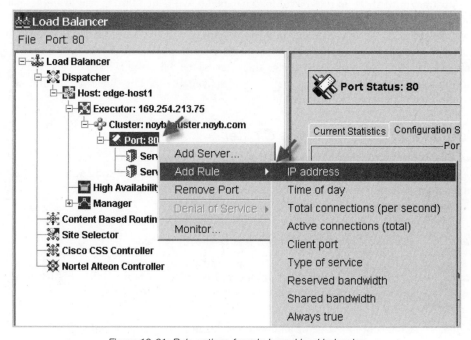

Figure 13-61: Rule options for rule-based load balancing

As you can see, the Load Balancer supports the ability to control request routing based on the following factors:

- IP address
- time of day
- total number of connections
- number of active connections
- client port
- service type
- reserved bandwidth
- shared bandwidth

An additional option, **Always true**, lets you set up a rule that is always selected if none of the rules defined at a higher priority are resolved (unless all the servers associated with the rule are down). The Dispatcher evaluates rules based on the priority you assign them, evaluating the highest-priority (lowest-value) rule first. The first rule that is satisfied is used, and no further rules are evaluated.

To illustrate how to set up rule-based load balancing, we'll step through an example that uses an **IP address** rule to block users with IP addresses between 169.254.189.0 and 169.254.189.255. We'll also set up an **Always true** rule to configure the Dispatcher to accept requests originating from clients with IP addresses between 169.254.0.0 and 169.254.255.255 and workload-manage them across the back-end HTTP servers. For more information about these and the other rules available for Dispatcher configuration, see the Edge Components Information Center.

Add an HTTP Server in the Cluster

For this example, we'll add a new HTTP server to the cluster to receive requests from the restricted IP addresses and return a message informing the requesting users that they lack authorization to invoke applications on this cluster. Adding an HTTP server for this purpose is optional.

Step 1. Start the dispatcher process if it isn't already started.

Step 2. Verify that the Dispatcher component is properly configured and is workload-managing requests across the back-end HTTP servers.

Step 3. Connect to the Load Balancer console, and navigate to **Load Balancer|Dispatcher|Host:** *hostname***|Executor:** *IP address***|Cluster:**

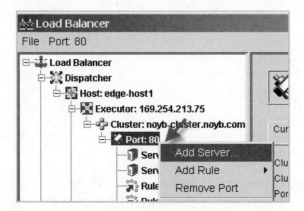

Figure 13-62: Adding an HTTP server to the cluster

cluster address. Right-click on port 80 (or port 443 if you've configured for SSL traffic), and select **Add Server** from the context menu. Figure 13-62 shows the navigation path for our example.

In the resulting dialog (Figure 13-63), provide a name for the server that will display the message to the restricted users, and specify its DNS entry or IP address. For this example, we'll name the server **NoAccess** and use the address **http-host3.noyb.com**. Click **OK**.

Figure 13-63: Specifying the server name and address

Add an IP Address Rule for Restricted Users

Step 4.   Navigate to **Dispatcher|Host:** *hostname***|Executor:** *IP address***|Cluster:** *cluster address*, and right-click on port 80 (or 443) again. Select **Add Rule** and then **IP address** to define the rule for the restricted users.

Step 5.   In the IP address rule panel (shown in Figure 13-64), enter the following values.

a. For **Rule name**, enter **Restricted-Users**.

b. For **Priority**, enter **10**.

c. Enter a **Begin range** value of **169.254.189.0** and an **End range** value of **169.254.189.255** to apply this rule to all clients that have IP addresses in this range.

d. In the server list, select the server you want to serve the requests specified by this rule — in this case, **NoAccess**. (If you didn't add a server to the cluster for this purpose, you would select no server in this list. In that case, requests from the specified users wouldn't be forwarded to any server in the cluster. They would simply receive no response, and the requests would time out.)

e. Click **OK**.

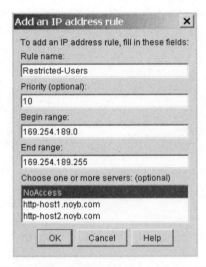

Figure 13-64: Adding the IP address rule for restricted users

Step 5.   Define the message that the NoAccess server will return to restricted users. For this example, we'll use the following text:

"Sorry you are NOT Authorized to access this application. Contact system administrator."

Add an IP Address Rule for Unrestricted Users

Step 6.   Right-click port 80 (or 443), and select **Add Rule|IP address** again to specify the rule for the unrestricted users.

Step 7.   Enter the following values in the IP address rule panel (as shown in Figure 13-65).

a. For **Rule name**, enter **Un-Restricted-Users**.

b. For **Priority**, enter **20**.

c. Enter a **Begin range** value of **169.254.0.0** and an **End range** value of **169.254.255.255** to apply this rule to all clients with IP addresses in this range.

d. From the server list, select http-host1 and http-host2 to have these two servers respond to requests from the unrestricted users.

e. Click **OK**.

Figure 13-65: Adding the IP address rule for unrestricted users

Add an Always True Rule

Next, we'll add an **Always true** rule to ignore requests from clients if their IP address is outside the range 169.254.0.0 to 169.254.255.255 (i.e., users coming from outside this subnet). We won't associate this rule with any of the back-end servers. The Dispatcher will simply ignore the requests and drop the packets.

Step 8. Right-click port 80 (or 443) in the navigation pane, and select **Add Rule|Always true** to specify the rule to ignore the users.

Step 9. Enter the following values in the always true rule panel (Figure 13-66) to define the rule.

    f. For **Rule name**, enter **Ignore-Users**.

    g. For **Priority**, enter **30**.

    h. To ignore the requests and drop the packets from the users, don't choose any servers from the list.

    i. Click **OK**.

Step 10.   When prompted, save the configuration to file default.cfg.

Figure 13-66: Adding an always true rule

Review and Test the Rule-Based Configuration

Step 11.   To review the configuration, go to the <EDGE-ROOT>\servers\configurations\dispatcher directory, and open file default.cfg. Take a look at the commands that were generated when you added the rules using the Load Balancer console. Figure 13-67 shows the contents created for our example. You could have used these dscontrol commands to configure the Load Balancer from the command prompt instead of using the graphical console.

Step 12.   Open a browser on a client that has an IP address in the range specified in the **Restricted-Users** rule (we used the client with IP address 169.254.189.152), and issue the URL **http://noyb-cluster.noyb.com**. According to our configuration, the Dispatcher will forward the request from

```
dscontrol rule add noyb-cluster.noyb.com:80:Restricted-Users type ip
priority 10 beginrange 169.254.189.0 endrange 169.254.189.255
dscontrol rule useserver noyb-cluster.noyb.com:80:Restricted-Users
NoAccess
```

```
dscontrol rule add noyb-cluster.noyb.com:80:Un-Restricted-Users type ip
priority 20 beginrange 169.254.0.0 endrange 169.254.255.255
dscontrol rule useserver noyb-cluster.noyb.com:80:Un-Restricted-Users
http-host1.noyb.com
dscontrol rule useserver noyb-cluster.noyb.com:80:Un-Restricted-Users
http-host2.noyb.com
```

```
dscontrol rule add noyb-cluster.noyb.com:80:Ignore-Users type true
priority 30
```

Figure 13-67: Dispatcher configuration file after rule definition

this user to the NoAccess server, and NoAccess will return a response informing the client that it has no authorization to access. For our test, we modified file index.html in the <IHSV6-ROOT>\htdocs directory to give the response shown in Figure 13-68.

Figure 13-68: Response to an HTTP request from a restricted user

Step 13. Open a browser on a client that has an IP address in the range specified in the **Un-Restricted-Users** rule (we used the client with IP address 169.254.25.165), and issue **http://noyb-cluster.noyb.com** or **http://noyb-cluster.noyb.cm/lb-test.html**. Use the instructions given earlier in this chapter (Steps 58–63) to verify that the Dispatcher workload-manages the request across the back-end HTTP servers.

Step 14. Open a browser on a client that has an IP address in the range specified in the **Ignore-Users** rule. Issue **http://noyb-cluster.noyb.com** or **http://noyb-cluster.noyb.com/lb-test.html** to observe that no response occurs from any server. According to the configuration, the Dispatcher will ignore this request.

Content-Based Load Balancing

As we noted at the beginning of this chapter, the Load Balancer supports two request-forwarding methods in addition to the default MAC address forwarding method:

Network Address Translation/Network Address Port Translation, or NAT/NAPT, and content-based routing, or CBR. As you worked through the sample configurations, you may have realized two limitations of the MAC method:

- The Load Balancer server and the back-end HTTP servers must be in the same subnet, with no routers or bridges between them. This arrangement may not be suitable or practical for some customers.

- The Dispatcher component can look only at the HTTP header to route requests based on rules to the back-end HTTP servers. (The NAT/NAPT method shares this limitation.)

Both NAT/NAPT and CBR forwarding overcome the first of these limitations, letting you configure the Load Balancer's Dispatcher component to work with remote back-end HTTP servers. If you need to route requests based on the content or pattern in the URL request (instead of or in addition to rule-based request routing using HTTP header information), you can use the CBR method to achieve this kind of control. (You can configure CBR forwarding on the Load Balancer server whether the back-end HTTP servers are local or remote to the Dispatcher.)

Another feature the CBR and NAT/NAPT forwarding methods offer over MAC forwarding is that the back-end HTTP servers can listen on a port other than the one on which the Dispatcher component is configured to receive requests. The HTTP servers could listen on port 81, for example, while the Dispatcher listens on port 80.

Figure 13-69 illustrates how content-based load balancing works. In the diagram, requests are routed to the appropriate back-end HTTP server depending on URL content (using the CBR forwarding method), and responses are returned to the client through the Load Balancer's Dispatcher component. The NAT/NAPT forwarding method uses a similar architecture to connect the Dispatcher to remote back-end servers.

> **Note:** There are two ways to effect content-based routing using the Edge Components for WebSphere. The Kernel CBR that is tied to the Load Balancer kernel (using the Load Balancer's Dispatcher component) can't effectively do content-based routing for HTTPS traffic (but it performs better than the other choice and is ideal if you're configuring for HTTP traffic). The CBR that is tied to the Caching Proxy Edge Component (using the CBR component of the Load Balancer) can load balance HTTPS traffic. Administration and monitoring is similar for these two modes of content-based load balancers. In this chapter, we're discussing the Kernel CBR that comes with the Dispatcher component.

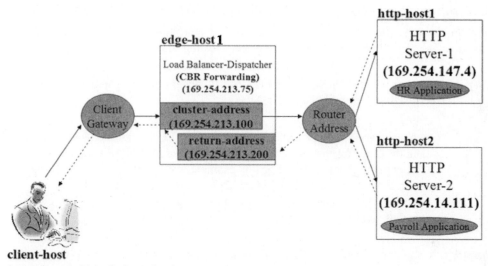

edge-host**1**

Load Balancer-Dispatcher
(CBR Forwarding)
(169.254.213.75)

cluster-address
(169.254.213.100

return-address
(169.254.213.200

Client
Gateway

Router
Address

http-host1

HTTP
Server-1
(169.254.147.4)

HR Application

http-host2

HTTP
Server-2
(169.254.14.111)

Payroll Application

client-host

http://cluster-address/hr/home.html
http://cluster-address/pay/home.html

Figure 13-69: Content-based load balancing architecture

Both CBR and NAT/NAPT forwarding rely on a second cluster IP address, called a *return address*, in addition to the primary cluster IP address. You configure the return address as an alias to the network device on the Load Balancer machine (edge-host1 in the example). When the Dispatcher receives a request from a client, it replaces the source IP address in the header information with its return address and sets the cluster IP address to the IP address of the HTTP server to which it is going to route the request. The back-end HTTP server returns its response to the Dispatcher, which restores the request to its original state and then forwards it on to the client.

The configuration steps for CBR and NAT/NAPT forwarding are similar except that with NAT/NAPT, you can configure only rule-based routing; content-based routing is available only with the CBR forwarding method. To demonstrate how to configure content-based load balancing, we'll use a content-based rule with the CBR forwarding method to configure the Dispatcher to forward requests to http-host1 if the directory portion of the URL contains the string "/hr/" (HR application) and to http-host2 if the URL contains the string "/pay/" (payroll application). First, we'll configure the Dispatcher for CBR forwarding. Then we'll set up the content-based routing.

Configure the Dispatcher for CBR (or NAT/NAPT) Forwarding

For details on how to perform the following steps to configure forwarding, refer to the instructions in the "Installing the Load Balancer" section of this chapter.

Step 1.   Set up a static IP address on the Load Balancer machine (Step 2 in "Installing the Load Balancer").

Step 2.   Choose two unused IP addresses: one for the cluster address (used by clients) and the other for the return address (the back-end HTTP servers will send responses to this address). For this example, we'll use 169.254.213.100 as the cluster address and 169.254.213.200 as the return address. If you're configuring for a production environment, you may want to set up DNS entries for these addresses.

Step 3.   You don't need to configure a loopback adapter on the HTTP servers for CBR or NAT/NAPT forwarding, so you can skip the instructions given earlier for that task.

Step 4.   Install and verify the Load Balancer on the edge-host1 machine (Steps 15–25).

Step 5.   Connect to the Load Balancer console (Step 26).

Step 6.   In the navigation pane, right-click **Dispatcher**, and select **Connect to Host**.

Step 7.   At the Dispatcher login prompt, select the default host name displayed (edge-host1 on port 10099 in this example), and click **OK**.

Step 8.   Right-click **Host:** *hostname* (**Host: edge-host1** in this case), and select **Start Executor** from the context menu to start the executor.

Specify the Client Gateway Address

Step 9.   Open a command prompt on the Dispatcher machine, and run the **tracert client-host** command (On Unix systems, use **traceroute**). Figure 13-70 shows sample output from this command. Locate the address of the client gateway (router address or default gateway) that the Load Balancer uses to respond to the client machine. The first entry in the output is usually the address (router address) you'll use as the client gateway address.

```
C:\>tracert client-host

Tracing route to client-host [169.254.189.152]
over a maximum of 30 hops:

  1   <10 ms   <10 ms   <10 ms   client-host [169.254.189.152]

Trace complete.
```

Figure 13-70: Sample Load Balancer route tracing output

If you don't have a router in your subnet, configure a machine in the subnet to perform IP forwarding, and use it as the client gateway. In our test environment, we used the client-host IP address (169.254.189.152) as the client gateway. The client-host machine is in the same LAN segment as the Load Balancer and HTTP server machines. The systems are connected using a switch, and our LAN isn't configured with a router to expose it to outside network.

Step 10. Click **Executor*: ip-address***, go to the **Configuration Settings** tab (shown in Figure 13-71), and enter the client gateway address you determined the preceding step. Then click the **Update Configuration** button at the bottom of the panel. (The client gateway address won't be recorded unless you click this button.)

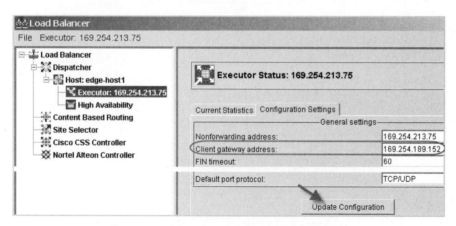

Figure 13-71: Specifying the client gateway address

Add the Cluster Address

Step 11. In the navigation pane, right-click **Executor: *ip-address***, and select **Add Cluster** to add the cluster address and other required information. Enter the appropriate values for your environment. Figure 13-72 shows the values for our example. We've used 169.254.213.100 for the cluster address and 169.254.213.75 (the IP address of edge-host1) as the primary host for the cluster. To configure the network device with the cluster address as an alias, select **Configure this cluster?** check box option. Click **OK** when you're finished with this panel.

Figure 13-72: Adding the cluster

Step 12. This step is optional in most cases. If your cluster address doesn't match any subnet for an existing address, you can use the values shown in Figure 13-73 for the interface name and netmask; otherwise, leave the fields blank and click **OK**. If you're on a Windows operating system and you have only one Ethernet card, the default interface name will be **en0**. If you have one Token-Ring card, the name will be **tr0**. If you have multiple cards (e.g., en0 and en1 or tr0 and tr1), contact your system administer to determine which value to use.

Figure 13-73: Configuring the interface address

Add the Port and Choose the Forwarding Method

Step 13. Right-click **Cluster:** *cluster-address* in the navigation pane, and select **Add Port** to specify the port and forwarding method. On the resulting panel (Figure 13-74), specify **80** (or whatever port you want to use) for the port number. Choose the **Content-based Routing** forwarding method, and click **OK**. (You won't see this option unless you've set the client gateway address and clicked the **Update Configuration** button as explained earlier.)

If your requirement is not to use content-based routing but to configure the back-end HTTP servers in a different subnet or using different ports from the Load Balancer server, select **NAT / NAPT** as the forwarding method.

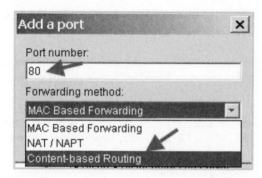

Figure 13-74: Specifying the port and forwarding method

Step 14. Next (Figure 13-75), select **HTTP** as the protocol that will be forwarded. (If you choose **SSL** here, the Dispatcher component will support content-based routing for HTTPS requests using SSL session ID affinity.)

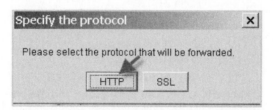

Figure 13-75: Selecting to forward the HTTP protocol

> **Note:** The Dispatcher component can serve only HTTP requests when configured for a content rule. If you also need to serve HTTPS requests while using content-based routing, you must use the Load Balancer's CBR component, which can decrypt and re-encrypt messages, instead of the Dispatcher. The content-rule configuration steps are similar for both the Dispatcher and CBR components.

Configure the Return Address

Step 15. Open a command prompt on the edge-host1 machine, and run the following command to configure the network device with the return address as an alias (Figure 13-76).

```
dscontrol executor configure 169.254.213.200
```

With this setting, the HTTP servers will respond to this return address (not directly to the client as in the MAC forwarding method) after processing an

```
C:\>dscontrol executor configure 169.254.213.200
Address 169.254.213.200 has been configured.
```

Figure 13-76: Configuring the return address

HTTP request. After you perform this step, the network device on edge-host1 will have three IP addresses to respond to:

- machine IP address: 169.254.213.75
- cluster IP address: 169.254.213.100
- return address: 169.254.213.200

Add the HTTP Servers

Next, add the two HTTP servers to the configuration.

Step 16. Right-click **Port: 80**, select **Add server**, and add the configuration information requested in Figure 13-77 for the first HTTP server (http-host1 in this example):

a. For **Server**, enter the host name: **http-host1**.

b. For **Server address**, enter the IP address of http-host1 (169.254.147.4).

c. For **Map port**, enter **80** (or whatever port number your HTTP server is listening on). The Load Balancer will map the port you add here after receiving the request at port 80 (or the port number you added earlier).

d. For **Return address**, enter **169.254.213.200**.

e. To determine the **Network router address** value to use, open a command prompt on the Dispatcher machine, and run the **tracert http-host1** command (on Unix machines, use **traceroute**) to find out the router address or default gateway the HTTP server uses to send responses to the Dispatcher machine. The first entry in the output is usually the address you need. For this example, the sample tracert output in Figure 13-78 reports the address 169.254.147.4. Enter this value as the network router address, and click **OK**. (If you don't have a router in the subnet, as in our test environment, enter the IP address of http-host1 as the network router address.)

Figure 13-77: Adding HTTP server http-host1

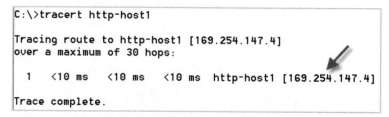

Figure 13-78: Sample http-host1 route tracing output

Step 17.   Right-click **Port: 80** again, select **Add server**, and enter the configuration information for the second HTTP server using the same procedure you did for the first. Figure 13-79 shows the values to use for http-host2 in the sample configuration. Repeat this procedure for every HTTP server you want to add to the port.

Figure 13-79: Adding HTTP server http-host2

Start the Manager and Advisor

Step 18.   Right-click **Host: *hostname***, and select **Start Manager** to start the manager and advisor functions. When the **Start the manager** panel (Figure 13-80) is displayed, you can accept the default field values and simply click **OK**. Likewise, you can accept the defaults on the **Start an advisor** panel (Figure 13-81) and click **OK** to start the advisor.

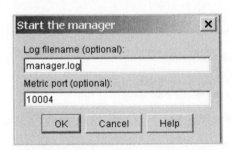

Figure 13-80: Start the manager panel

Figure 13-81: Start an advisor panel

Step 19. Save the configuration to the default.cfg file using the instructions given earlier in this chapter (Step 49 of the Load Balancer configuration discussion).

Step 20. Open file default.cfg, and review the commands (Figure 13-82). You could have used these dscontrol commands to configure the Load Balancer from the command prompt instead of using the graphical admin console.

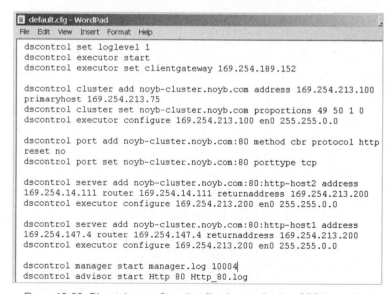

Figure 13-82: Dispatcher configuration file after configuring CBR forwarding

Verify CBR (or NAT/NAPT) Forwarding from the Command Prompt

Step 21. Open a command prompt on edge-host1, and issue **ipconfig** (**ifconfig** on Unix) to verify that the cluster and return addresses have been aliased to the device. The sample results shown in Figure 13-83 confirm that the Load Balancer machine will respond to the cluster address (169.254.213.100), the return address (169.254.213.200), and its own IP address (169.254.213.75). When a client request arrives that specifies the cluster address, the Load Balancer server will forward the request to one of the HTTP servers. When a response arrives from the back-end HTTP servers with the return address, the Load Balancer will receive that request to return to the clients.

```
C:\>ipconfig

Windows 2000 IP Configuration

Ethernet adapter Local Area Connection 2:

        Connection-specific DNS Suffix  . :
        IP Address. . . . . . . . . . . . : 169.254.213.200
        Subnet Mask . . . . . . . . . . . : 255.255.0.0
        IP Address. . . . . . . . . . . . : 169.254.213.100
        Subnet Mask . . . . . . . . . . . : 255.255.0.0
        IP Address. . . . . . . . . . . . : 169.254.213.75
        Subnet Mask . . . . . . . . . . . : 255.255.0.0
        Default Gateway . . . . . . . . . :
```

Figure 13-83: Results for ipconfig command for sample CBR configuration

Step 22. Open a command prompt on a machine other than the Load Balancer or HTTP servers in the network (we used client-host), and issue **ping 169.254.213.100** (the cluster address) and **ping 169.254.213.200** (the return address). The replies should come from the Load Balancer's IP address (169.254.213.75) even though you're pinging the cluster and return addresses. Figure 13-84 shows this result.

```
C:\>ping 169.254.213.100

Pinging 169.254.213.100 with 32 bytes of data:

Reply from 169.254.213.75: bytes=32 time<1ms TTL=255
Reply from 169.254.213.75: bytes=32 time<1ms TTL=255

C:\>ping 169.254.213.200

Pinging 169.254.213.200 with 32 bytes of data:

Reply from 169.254.213.75: bytes=32 time<1ms TTL=255
Reply from 169.254.213.75: bytes=32 time<1ms TTL=255
```

Figure 13-84: Results of ping test for sample CBR configuration

Verify That the Load Balancer Is Spraying Requests Correctly

Before you configure content-based routing with the CBR forwarding method, make sure the Dispatcher component is load-balancing requests across the back-end HTTP servers regardless of URL content. To do so, take the following steps.

Step 23. Create and set up a test HTML page on each HTTP server (Steps 53–55 of the Load Balancer configuration discussion).

Step 24. To test the basic configuration of the CBR (or NAT/NAPT) forwarding method, open a browser on the client-host system, and invoke the test page using the cluster address (http://169.254.213.100/lb-test.html) or its alias (http://noyb-cluster.noyb.com/lb-test.html). Click the browser's reload button a few times to see that the request is being workload-managed across the HTTP servers. For more information about this topic, see the verification section of the Load Balancer configuration discussion.

Configure Content-Based Routing

You're now ready to configure content-based routing. *Reminder:* You must have configured your network to use CBR forwarding before performing this configuration. You're going to set up two content rules for the Dispatcher: one to forward requests to http-host1 if the directory portion of the URL contains the string "/hr/" and the other to forward requests to http-host2 if the URL contains the string "/pay/".

Step 25. Right-click **Port: 80**, and select **Add Rule** and then **Content**, as shown in Figure 13-85. (You won't see this option if you're using the MAC or NAT/NAPT forwarding method.)

Step 26. On the content rule panel (shown in Figure 13-86), configure a rule named **hr** to send requests to HTTP server **http-host1** if the uri pattern matches /hr/* (**uri=/hr/***). Specify the desired priority, and click **OK**.

Step 27. Right-click **Port: 80**, select **Add Rule|Content** again, and configure a second rule named **pay** to send requests to HTTP server **http-host2** if the uri pattern matches /pay/* (**uri=/pay/***). Figure 13-87 shows the values to enter. Click **OK**.

Step 28. Save the configuration to file default.cfg again.

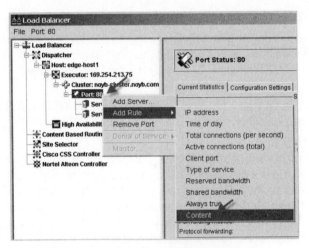

Figure 13-85: Selecting to add a content rule

Figure 13-86: Specifying the first content rule details

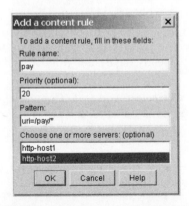

Figure 13-87: Specifying the second content rule details

Step 29. Open default.cfg, scroll down, and review the commands related to the configuration of content-based routing (Figure 13-88). You could have used these dscontrol commands to configure the content rules from the command prompt instead of using the graphical console.

```
default.cfg - WordPad
File  Edit  View  Insert  Format  Help

dscontrol rule add noyb-cluster.noyb.com:80:hr type content pattern
URI=/hr/* priority 10
dscontrol rule useserver noyb-cluster.noyb.com:80:hr http-host1

dscontrol rule add noyb-cluster.noyb.com:80:pay type content pattern
URI=/pay/* priority 20
dscontrol rule useserver noyb-cluster.noyb.com:80:pay http-host2
```

Figure 13-88: Dispatcher configuration file after configuring content-based routing

Verify the Content-Based Routing Configuration

Step 30. On the http-host1 system, create a directory called hr under DocumentRoot (<IHSV6- ROOT>\htdocs\en_us). (If your locale differs, create this directory under your locale instead of en_us.) Create a simple HTML page called home.html in this directory, entering the HTML script shown in Figure 13-89 to demonstrate when the page is served from http-host1.

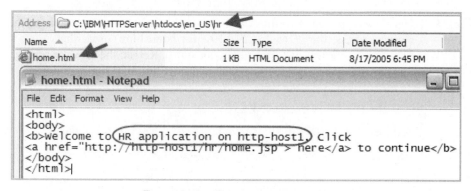

Figure 13-89: HTML script for http-host1

Step 31. On the http-host2 system, create a directory called **pay** under DocumentRoot. Create a simple HTML page called home.html in this directory, entering the HTML script shown in Figure 13-90 to demonstrate when the page is served from http-host2.

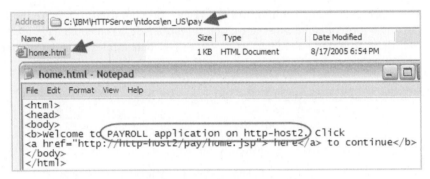

Figure 13-90: HTML script for http-host2

Step 32. Open a browser on client-host, and invoke the HR application using the cluster address (http://169.254.213.100/**hr**/home.html) or its alias (http://noyb-cluster.noyb.com/**hr**/home.html). Click the browser's reload button a few times to see the request being served from http-host1 (Figure 13-91).

Figure 13-91: Content-based routing to the HR application on http-host1

Step 33. Open a browser on client-host, and invoke the payroll application using the cluster address (http://169.254.213.100/**pay**/home.html) or its alias (http://noyb-cluster.noyb.com/**pay**/home.html). Reload the browser page a few times to see the request being served from http-host2 (Figure 13-92).

Figure 13-92: Content-based routing to the payroll application on http-host2

14

Load Balancer High Availability: Configure, Verify, and Manage

The Load Balancer's Dispatcher component supports the ability to eliminate a single point of failure (SPOF) by configuring a secondary Dispatcher machine that can take over the load-balancing work if the primary server fails. When you set up two Load Balancer servers for high availability, you configure a *heartbeat* between the primary and secondary servers. If the secondary Load Balancer server loses the heartbeat from the primary, it assumes the primary server is down and takes over the job of receiving client requests and routing packets to the back-end servers. This kind of configuration (primary and standby Load Balancer servers) is known as a *simple high availability* configuration. In this chapter, you'll learn how to configure and verify the simple high availability feature.

You can optionally configure both Load Balancer servers with one or more *reach target* servers. A reach target server can be a router or any type of server that has an IP address (other than the back-end and Load Balancer servers). In this situation, even if the heartbeat between the primary and secondary servers is okay, if the secondary server can ping more reach target servers than the primary server can, the failover occurs anyway. We describe the optional step of configuring a reach target server at the end of the chapter.

The high-availability function supported by the Load Balancer's Dispatcher component is not available for the Content Based Routing (CBR) or Site Selector component of the Load Balancer. When we use the term "Load Balancer" in this chapter, you can assume we're referring to the Dispatcher component.

Configure Load Balancer High Availability

The flow chart in Figure 14-1 depicts the high-level steps required to configure and verify two Load Balancer servers in highly available mode. (These steps assume that the primary Load Balancer system has already been installed, configured, and verified.)

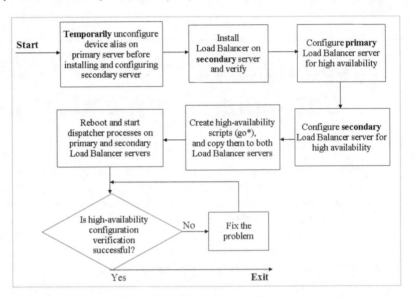

Figure 14-1: Configuration overview: Load Balancer high availability

Figure 14-2 shows the high-availability configuration you'll set up in this chapter's example. In the diagram, the edge-host1 system is acting as an active (primary) server that accepts HTTP requests from clients and balances the workload across two back-end HTTP Server systems (http-host1 and http-host2). The edge-host2 system is functioning as a standby (secondary) server that is there to take over the request-handling if the primary server fails.

For a successful configuration, the primary and secondary Load Balancer servers must be running on the same operating system and preferably on a similar hardware configuration. Both servers should also be at the same version and fix pack level. Before proceeding with the sample configuration, make sure your environment meets these requirements.

To establish Dispatcher high availability, you'll configure the same cluster IP address on both systems. This chapter's instructions assume you're setting up high availability for a

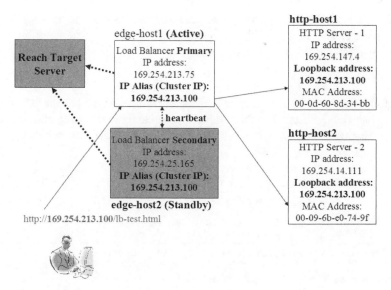

Figure 14-2: Load Balancer Dispatcher high-availability architecture

Dispatcher component that has been configured using the Media Access Control (MAC) address forwarding method (as described in Chapter 13). If you're using the Network Address Translation/Network Address Port Translation (NAT/NAPT) or content-based routing (CBR) forwarding method, you'll need to perform an extra step to configure the return address along with the cluster address. When executing this extra step, use the return address in place of the cluster address.

Set Up the Primary Load Balancer Server

Step 1. If you haven't already installed the Load Balancer on the primary server (edge-host1 in the example), do it now, and verify the configuration using the instructions in Chapter 13.

Prepare the Primary Load Balancer Server for High Availability

Before setting up the primary Load Balancer server for high-availability mode, you need to install, configure, and verify the Load Balancer on the secondary server. As we noted, both Load Balancer servers must be configured with the same cluster address to enable the secondary server to receive the client requests if a failure occurs. However, if you alias the same cluster address to two different network devices in the same LAN segment (on the primary and secondary servers), you'll receive errors reporting an IP address conflict, and the Load Balancer servers won't function normally. To avoid the IP conflict problem, you will temporarily unconfigure the cluster address on the primary server (to disassociate the cluster alias from the network interface device). After configuring and verifying the secondary Load Balancer server, you'll set up the cluster address again on the primary server.

Take the following steps to unconfigure the cluster address on the primary Load Balancer server (edge-host1). For this example, we'll assume the same cluster address we used in Chapter 13: 169.254.213.100 (DNS entry noyb-cluster.noyb.com).

Step 2.   Open a command prompt on edge-host1, and run the command **ipconfig** (**ifconfig** on Unix systems). Observe that the cluster address has been aliased to the network interface device. Figure 14-3 shows the ipconfig results for our example.

```
C:\Documents and Settings\Administrator>ipconfig

Windows 2000 IP Configuration

Ethernet adapter Local Area Connection 2:

        Connection-specific DNS Suffix  . :
        IP Address. . . . . . . . . . . . : 169.254.213.100
        Subnet Mask . . . . . . . . . . . : 255.255.0.0
        IP Address. . . . . . . . . . . . : 169.254.213.75
        Subnet Mask . . . . . . . . . . . : 255.255.0.0
        Default Gateway . . . . . . . . . :
```

Figure 14-3: Verifying the cluster address on edge-host1

Step 3.   Open a command prompt on a machine in the network other than the Load Balancer system or the HTTP servers, and ping the cluster address: **ping 169.254.213.100**. You should see the reply come from the primary Load Balancer server's IP address (169.254.213.75 in this example), as shown in Figure 14-4.

```
C:\Documents and Settings\Administrator>ping 169.254.213.100

Pinging 169.254.213.100 with 32 bytes of data:

Reply from 169.254.213.75: bytes=32 time<1ms TTL=255
Reply from 169.254.213.75: bytes=32 time<1ms TTL=255
Reply from 169.254.213.75: bytes=32 time<1ms TTL=255
Reply from 169.254.213.75: bytes=32 time<1ms TTL=255
```

Figure 14-4: Results of pinging the cluster IP address on edge-host1

Step 4.   Open a command prompt on the primary Load Balancer server, and issue the following dscontrol command to remove the cluster address as the device alias.

```
dscontrol e unconfig 169.254.213.100
```

You'll receive a confirmation that the specified address has been unconfigured (Figure 14-5).

```
C:\Documents and Settings\Administrator>dscontrol e unconfig 169.254.213.100
Address 169.254.213.100 has been unconfigured.
```

Figure 14-5: Unconfiguring the cluster IP address

Step 5.   From a command prompt on the primary Load Balancer server, run **ipconfig** again (**ifconfig** on Unix) to verify the removal of the device alias. Figure 14-6 shows the updated ipconfig results for our example.

```
C:\Documents and Settings\Administrator>ipconfig

Windows 2000 IP Configuration

Ethernet adapter Local Area Connection 2:

        Connection-specific DNS Suffix  . :
        IP Address. . . . . . . . . . . . : 169.254.213.75
        Subnet Mask . . . . . . . . . . . : 255.255.0.0
        Default Gateway . . . . . . . . . :
```

Figure 14-6: Results of ipconfig command confirming removal of cluster address

Step 6.   Once you unconfigure the cluster address from the device, the primary server shouldn't respond if you try to ping the cluster address. Nor will you receive any response if you issue a URL containing the cluster address or its DNS entry (i.e., http://169.254.213.100 or http://noyb-cluster.noyb.com) from a browser. To test this behavior, issue **ping 169.254.213.100**. The request should time out.

Set Up the Secondary Load Balancer Server

With the aforementioned tasks out of the way, you're ready to set up the Load Balancer on the secondary (standby) server. Take the following steps to do so.

Step 7.   Follow the instructions in Chapter 13 to install, configure, and verify the Load Balancer on the secondary server (edge-host2). Be sure to use the same cluster IP address (169.254.213.100 in this example) and the same back-end servers (http-host1 and http-host2) as you did in setting up the primary server.

Step 8. Open a command prompt on the secondary Load Balancer server, run **ipconfig** (**ifconfig** on Unix), and verify that the cluster address has been aliased to the device. The sample results in Figure 14-7 confirm this configuration for our example. In these results, you can also see the IP address of the edge-host2 server as 169.254.25.165, which is under the same LAN segment (169.254.0.0) as the primary server.

```
C:\>ipconfig

Windows IP Configuration

Ethernet adapter Local Area Connection 3:

        Connection-specific DNS Suffix  . :
        IP Address. . . . . . . . . . . . : 169.254.213.100
        Subnet Mask . . . . . . . . . . . : 255.255.0.0
        IP Address. . . . . . . . . . . . : 169.254.25.165
        Subnet Mask . . . . . . . . . . . : 255.255.0.0
        Default Gateway . . . . . . . . . :
```

Figure 14-7: Verifying the cluster address on edge-host2

Step 9. Open a command prompt on a network machine other than the Load Balancer or HTTP servers, and issue **ping 169.254.213.100** (cluster address). This time, the reply should come from the secondary Load Balancer server's IP address (169.254.25.165), confirming that when a URL containing the cluster address (e.g., http://169.254.213.100/lb-test.html) arrives, the secondary Load Balancer server will receive the request and route the packets to the back-end HTTP servers.

Verify the Version and Fix Pack Level

Step 10. To check the systems' current version and fix pack level, make sure the executor and manager are running on both the primary and secondary Load Balancer servers. (If necessary, issue the command **dscontrol executor start** to start the executor; use **dscontrol manager start** to start the manager.) Then open a command prompt on each system, and issue **dscontrol manager version**. Figure 14-8 shows sample results for this command.

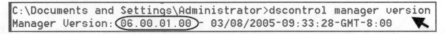
```
C:\Documents and Settings\Administrator>dscontrol manager version
Manager Version: 06.00.01.00 - 03/08/2005-09:33:28-GMT-8:00
```

Figure 14-8: Determining the Load Balancer version

Prepare the Secondary Load Balancer Server for High Availability

Step 11.   Now that you've set up the secondary Load Balancer server, you need to unconfigure the cluster IP address as the device alias on this system in preparation for configuring the primary Load Balancer server for high availability. To remove the cluster address, open a command prompt on the secondary server, and issue the following command:

```
dscontrol e unconfig 169.254.213.100
```

You'll receive a confirmation that the specified address has been unconfigured.

Set Up the Primary Load Balancer Server for High Availability

Step 12.   Restart the dispatcher process on the primary Load Balancer server to restore the cluster address association on edge-host1. (On Unix systems, run **dsserver stop** and **dsserver start** from the command prompt to restart the dispatcher.) During startup, the Dispatcher reads the configuration file default.cfg and reconfigures the cluster IP address alias with the network interface device.

Step 13.   To verify that the cluster address has been aliased to the network interface device, open a command prompt on the primary server, and run **ipconfig** (**ifconfig** on Unix).

Step 14.   Open a command prompt on a network machine other than the Load Balancer or HTTP servers, and issue **ping 169.254.213.100** (cluster address). The reply should come from the primary Load Balancer server's IP address (169.254.213.75).

Step 15.   Open a browser, and issue **http://169.254.213.100** (cluster address) or **http://noyb-cluster.noyb.com** (DNS entry). Make sure you see the HTTP Server welcome page, shown in Figure 14-9.

Figure 14-9: HTTP Server welcome page

Step 16. Connect to the primary Load Balancer server's admin console (using **Start|Programs|IBM WebSphere|Edge Components|Load Balancer|Load Balancer**). Right-click **Dispatcher** in the navigation pane, and select **Connect to Host** from the context menu. Accept the default host name displayed in the login window (Figure 14-10), and click **OK**. In this case, the default host is edge-host1 on port 10099.

Figure 14-10: Dispatcher login on the primary Load Balancer server

Step 17. Next, you need to set up the heartbeat between the primary and secondary Load Balancer servers. Once you've configured the heartbeat, the two servers will communicate with each other at a regular interval. If the secondary server doesn't hear a heartbeat from the primary, it will assume the primary server is down and begin accepting requests on behalf of the primary server.

To set up the heartbeat on the primary server, right-click **High Availability** in the console navigation pane, and select **Add Heartbeat**, as shown in Figure 14-11.

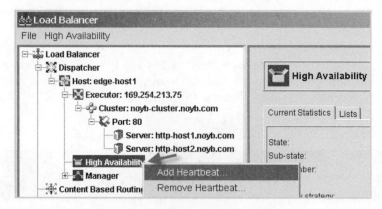

Figure 14-11: Selecting to add a heartbeat

On the resulting panel (Figure 14-12), enter the IP address (or host name) of the primary Load Balancer machine as the host name of the current machine, and enter the IP address (or host name) of the secondary Load Balancer machine as the destination address for the heartbeat.

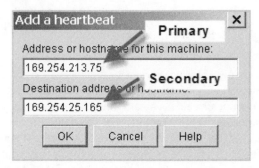

Figure 14-12: Specifying the heartbeat between the two servers

Step 18. Right-click **High Availability** again in the navigation pane, and select **Add High Availability Backup** (Figure 14-13). You'll use this option to configure the port number, role, and recovery strategy of the primary Load Balancer server.

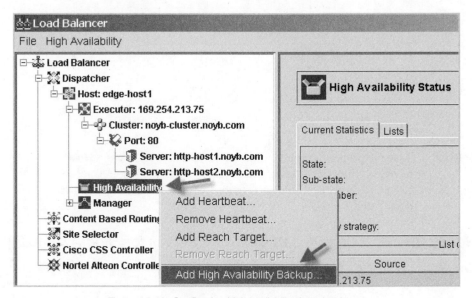

Figure 14-13: Configuring high availability for edge-host1

On the resulting panel (Figure 14-14), enter the following values as the high-availability parameters for the primary server.

a. For **Port number**, specify a port that's not being used by any of the software on the primary and secondary servers (e.g., 12345). The two servers will use this common port to exchange information.

b. For **Role**, select **Primary** to have this system serve requests from users initially.

c. The **Recovery strategy** parameter dictates whether the primary system will automatically resume routing requests once it becomes operational again (parameter value **Auto**) or must be returned to an active state manually (parameter value **Manual**). For this example, choose **Auto**. (Remember that failover to the secondary server is automatic when the primary server fails, regardless of which recovery strategy value you use.)

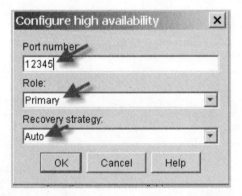

Figure 14-14: High-availability parameters for edge-host1

Step 19. Save the primary server configuration. To do so, right-click **Host:** *host-address* (**Host: edge-host1** in this case) in the navigation pane, and select **Save Configuration File As** (Figure 14-15). Save the configuration to file default.cfg.

Set Up the Secondary Load Balancer Server for High Availability

The steps to set up high availability on the secondary Load Balancer server are the same as those you just completed for the primary server.

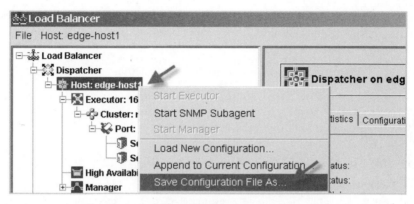

Figure 14-15: Saving the primary server configuration

Step 20.   Connect to the secondary Load Balancer server's admin console, right-click **Dispatcher**, and select **Connect to Host**. Accept the default host name displayed in the login window, and click **OK**.

Step 21.   Right-click **High Availability**, and select **Add Heartbeat** to set up the heartbeat. This time, specify the IP address (or host name) of the *secondary* Load Balancer machine (169.254.25.165) as the host name of this machine, and enter the IP address (or host name) of the *primary* Load Balancer machine (169.254.213.75) as the destination address for the heartbeat.

Step 22.   Right-click **High Availability** again, and select **Add High Availability Backup** to configure the port number, role, and recovery strategy of the secondary Load Balancer server. On the resulting panel (Figure 14-16), enter the high-availability parameters for the secondary server:

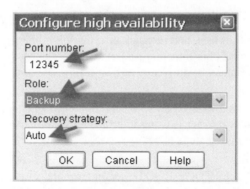

Figure 14-16: High-availability parameters for edge-host2

        a. For the **Port number** and **Recovery strategy** fields, use the same values you specified for the primary Load Balancer server (12345 and Auto in the example).

        b. For **Role**, select **Backup** to set up this system as a standby machine.

Step 23. In the navigation pane, right-click **Host:** *host-name* (**Host: edge-host2** in this example), select **Save Configuration File As**, and save the secondary server's configuration to file default.cfg.

Create and Configure High-Availability Scripts

Once you've configured the Load Balancer with the cluster address from the console, the cluster address will be aliased to the network interface device, enabling the Load Balancer (Dispatcher) server to receive requests and route the packets to the back-end HTTP servers. In a high-availability configuration, only one Load Balancer server will be active and serving requests at any time (in primary/backup mode). If the primary server fails, the secondary Load Balancer (acting as a standby) should take over serving the requests.

For the secondary Load Balancer server to serve the requests, the network interface device on that system must be aliased with the cluster address automatically as soon as the primary server fails. To achieve this functionality, you need to develop high-availability scripts that will be executed automatically to configure (or unconfigure) the cluster address with the network interface device on-the-fly. (If you're setting up high availability for the NAT/NAPT forwarding method, you'll need to add the return address along with the cluster address to the script files.)

The Load Balancer installation directory contains sample scripts you can use as a reference and customize to your environment. You'll find the scripts in the <EDGE-ROOT>\servers\samples directory (where <EDGE-ROOT> is the directory where you installed the Load Balancer). We're going to customize these scripts by updating the cluster address, interface, and netmask information in them and moving them to the <EDGE-ROOT>\servers\bin directory on both Load Balancer systems. Before changing a script, be sure to make a backup copy so you'll have the original file for reference.

The scripts will usually be the same on both servers, although exceptions are possible — for example, if the primary server is using interface en0 and the secondary server is using en1. Take the following steps to set up the high-availability scripts.

Step 24. Navigate to the <EDGE-ROOT>\servers\samples directory on one of the Load Balancer servers, and locate the sample high-availability scripts. Figure 14-17 highlights the three scripts we'll modify for this example. (If you don't see the .sample extension for the sample scripts in the directory display on a Windows system, select **Folder Options** from the **Tools** menu, go to the **View** tab, clear the "Hide extensions for known file types" check box, and click **OK**.)

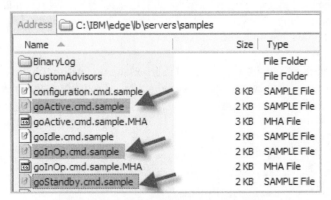

Figure 14-17: Sample high-availability scripts

Step 25. Using your favorite editor, open the goActive.cmd.sample script, and update the script with the cluster address (or DNS entry), interface, and netmask values specific to your system. Figure 14-18 shows the modified script reflecting the values for our example. (The values for your environment may differ.) Save the file with the name goActive.cmd (i.e., remove the .sample extension). Be sure you've made a backup copy of the original sample script.

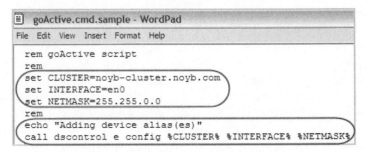

Figure 14-18: Modified goActive.cmd.sample script

As you can see in the figure, the goActive script adds the cluster address as an alias to the network interface device. Remember that only after the cluster address has been aliased to the network interface device can the server accept requests at the cluster address and route the packets to the back-end servers. This script will be run when the Load Balancer server (Dispatcher) goes into active state. In a highly available environment, the script will be invoked automatically on the primary (active) Load Balancer server. If the primary server fails to function for some reason (i.e., if the secondary server loses the heartbeat from the primary), this script on the secondary (standby) Load Balancer server will be executed. In short, this script deletes the loop-back alias and adds the device alias.

Step 26. Open the goStandby.cmd.sample script, and update it with the cluster address, interface, and netmask values specific to your system. Figure 14-19 shows the modified script for our example. After editing the file, save it with the name goStandby.cmd.

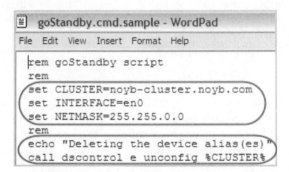

Figure 14-19: Modified goStandby.cmd.sample script

As you can see in the figure, the goStandby script deletes the device alias. Remember that once the device alias has been deleted (removing the associa-tion between the cluster address and the network interface device), the server *cannot* accept the requests and route the packets. This script will be run when the Load Balancer server (Dispatcher) goes into standby state. In a highly available environment, the script will be invoked automatically on the secondary (standby) Load Balancer server (this way, the secondary server won't respond to the client requests). If for some reason the primary server fails to function, this script on the primary Load Balancer server will be exe-cuted (this way, the client's requests won't reach this server). In short, this script deletes the device alias and adds the loopback alias.

Step 27. Open the goInOp.cmd.sample script, and update the script with the cluster address and interface specific to your system. Save the file as goInOp.cmd. Figure 14-20 shows the modified script for our example.

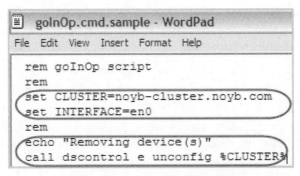

Figure 14-20: Modified goInOp.cmd.sample script

As you can see in the figure, the goInOp script deletes the device alias. Remember that once the device alias has been deleted (removing the association between the cluster address and the network interface device), the server can't accept the requests and route the packets. This script will be run when the executor on the Load Balancer server (Dispatcher) is stopped or before the executor is started. In short, this script deletes both the device and the loopback aliases.

Step 28. Move the three "go" scripts to the <EDGE-ROOT>\servers\bin directory on both the primary (active) and secondary (standby) Load Balancer servers (Figure 14-21). (On Unix machines, make sure the scripts contain executable permissions.)

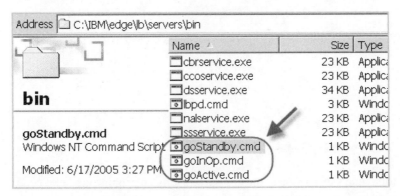

Figure 14-21: High-availability scripts in the <EDGE-ROOT>\servers\bin directory

Step 29. Take the following steps to activate the high-availability configuration and scripts (using the **Services** panel on Windows systems to stop and start the required processes):

a. *Stop* the dispatcher process on the *secondary* Load Balancer server. (On Unix systems, run **dsserver stop** from the command prompt to stop the dispatcher process.)

b. *Restart* (stop and then start) the dispatcher process on the *primary* Load Balancer server. (On Unix systems, run **dsserver stop** and **dsserver start** to restart the dispatcher process.)

c. *Start* the dispatcher process on the *secondary* Load Balancer server. (On Unix, run **dsserver start** to start the dispatcher process.)

d. Make sure the HTTP servers are running.

Verify the High-Availability Configuration

Figure 14-22 illustrates how the high-availability environment functions when the primary Load Balancer server goes down for any reason. After losing the heartbeat from the failed primary Load Balancer server, the secondary server begins responding to and serving the requests that arrive from clients.

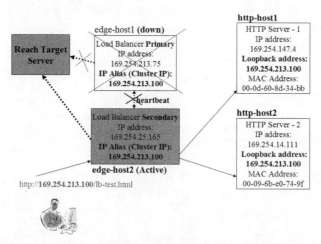

Figure 14-22: High-availability environment operating in failover mode

Use the following steps to verify the high-availability environment you've configured.

Step 30. Open a command prompt on a network machine other than the Load Balancer or HTTP servers, and issue **ping 169.254.213.100** (cluster address). The reply should come from the primary Load Balancer server's IP address (169.254.213.75).

Open a browser on the same machine, and issue **http://169.254.213.100** (cluster address or DNS). Make sure you see the HTTP Server welcome page.

Step 31. Open a command prompt on the primary Load Balancer server (edge-host1), and run the command **dscontrol high status** to verify the configuration. Make sure the command results list the state of the primary server as Active and its sub-state as Synchronized (as shown in Figure 14-23). You should also see the secondary server's IP address specified as the preferred target in the event that the primary server fails.

```
C:\Documents and Settings\Administrator>dscontrol high status

High Availability Status:
-------------------------
Role ................. Primary
Recovery strategy .... Auto
State ................ Active
Sub-state ............ Synchronized
Primary host ......... 169.254.213.75
Port ................. 12345
Preferred target ..... 169.254.25.165

Heartbeat Status:
-----------------
Count ................ 1
Source/destination ... 169.254.213.75/169.254.25.165

Reachability Status:
--------------------
Count ................ 0
```

Figure 14-23: Verifying the edge-host1 configuration

Step 32. Open a command prompt on the secondary Load Balancer server (edge-host2), and run **dscontrol high status**. The configuration should indicate the secondary server's role as Backup and its sub-state as Synchronized (Figure 14-24).

```
C:\>dscontrol high status

High Availability Status:
-------------------------
Role ................. Backup
Recovery strategy .... Auto
State ................ Standby
Sub-state ............ Synchronized
Primary host ......... 169.254.213.75
Port ................. 12345
Preferred target ..... 169.254.213.75

Heartbeat Status:
-----------------
Count ................ 1
Source/destination ... 169.254.25.165/169.254.213.75

Reachability Status:
--------------------
Count ................ 0
```

Figure 14-24: Verifying the edge-host2 configuration

Step 33. Simulate failure on the primary Load Balancer server using one of the following methods:

- Stop the executor on the primary server while the Dispatcher service is running by issuing **dscontrol executor stop** from the command prompt. (Figure 14-25 shows the results of running this command.)

- Turn off the primary server.

- Remove the network cable from the primary server.

```
C:\Documents and Settings\Administrator>dscontrol executor stop
Advisor 'Http' stopped on port 80.
The manager has been stopped.
Executor stopped at your request.
```

Figure 14-25: Stopping the executor from the command line

Step 34. Open a command prompt on a network machine other than the Load Balancer or HTTP servers, and issue **ping 169.254.213.100** (cluster address). Because the primary server has failed, the reply should now come from the secondary server's IP address (169.254.25.165).

Step 35. When the secondary server loses the heartbeat from the primary server, the dispatcher process on the secondary server executes the goActive.cmd high-availability script to configure the cluster address as the device alias to receive requests from the clients. To confirm the failover, open a browser on the same machine, and issue **http://169.254.213.100** (cluster address or DNS). Make sure you see the HTTP Server welcome page again, this time served through the secondary Load Balancer server.

Step 36. Open a command prompt on the secondary server (edge-host2), and run **dscontrol high status**. The configuration should now indicate the secondary server's state as Active and its sub-state as Not Synchronized (because the secondary server can't hear the heartbeat from the primary server). Figure 14-26 shows the command results for the example.

Step 37. If you specified the recovery strategy as **Auto** when you set up the high-availability configuration on the primary and secondary servers, reboot the primary Load Balancer server, start its dispatcher process, and make sure that system begins responding to client requests by taking over the load from the secondary server. When the secondary server hears the heartbeat from the

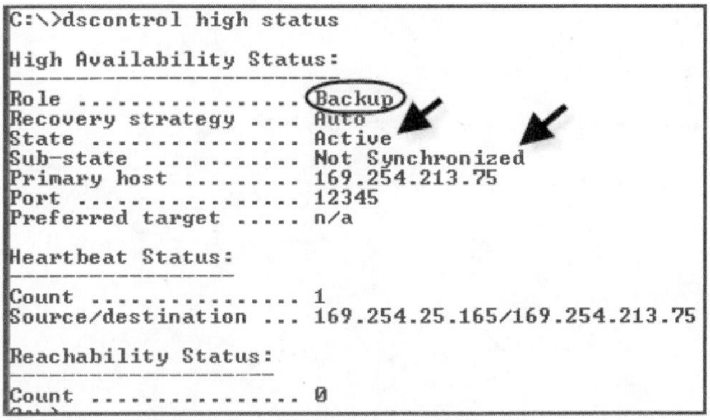

```
C:\>dscontrol high status

High Availability Status:
_____
Role ................. Backup
Recovery strategy .... Auto
State ................ Active
Sub-state ............ Not Synchronized
Primary host ......... 169.254.213.75
Port ................. 12345
Preferred target ..... n/a

Heartbeat Status:
_____
Count ................ 1
Source/destination ... 169.254.25.165/169.254.213.75

Reachability Status:
_____
Count ................ 0
```

Figure 14-26: Secondary Load Balancer server status after failover

primary server again, the dispatcher process on the secondary server executes the goStandby.cmd high-availability script to unconfigure the cluster address as the device alias on that system. At the same time, the dispatcher process on the primary server should execute the goActive.cmd script to configure the device alias there to respond to requests from the clients.

Step 38. Open a command prompt on a network machine other than the Load Balancer server or HTTP servers, and make sure the network connections have been restored on the primary server. You should be able to ping edge-host1 (169.254.213.75) again. Also ping the cluster address (169.254.213.100). The reply should come from the primary Load Balancer server's IP address (169.254.213.75).

If you still receive a response from the secondary Load Balancer server's IP address (169.254.25.165) or the request times out, open a command prompt on the primary Load Balancer server, and issue **ipconfig** to see whether the cluster IP address has been configured as the device alias. If you see 0.0.0.0 instead of the cluster IP address (as shown in Figure 14-27), the cluster IP address for some reason wasn't unconfigured when the failure occurred on the primary server (or you may not have rebooted your machine after the failure).

As a workaround (instead of rebooting the machine), you can unconfigure the device alias by running **dscontrol e unconfig *cluster-address*** from the command prompt. Or simply execute the goStandby.cmd script from <EDGE-ROOT>\servers\bin directory. Restart the dispatcher again, and verify that the primary server is responding to the requests.

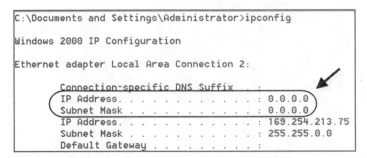

```
C:\Documents and Settings\Administrator>ipconfig

Windows 2000 IP Configuration

Ethernet adapter Local Area Connection 2:

        Connection-specific DNS Suffix  . :
        IP Address. . . . . . . . . . . . : 0.0.0.0
        Subnet Mask . . . . . . . . . . . : 0.0.0.0
        IP Address. . . . . . . . . . . . : 169.254.213.75
        Subnet Mask . . . . . . . . . . . : 255.255.0.0
        Default Gateway . . . . . . . . . :
```

Figure 14-27: Cluster address not configured as device alias

Step 39. Open a browser on the same machine, and issue **http://169.254.213.100** (cluster address or DNS). Make sure you see the HTTP Server welcome page again, served through the primary Load Balancer server.

Step 40. If you encounter problems with the high-availability function, run **dscontrol set loglevel 5** from the command prompt to change the loglevel to verbose and record more information in the hamon.log file.

Configure Reach Target Server(s) (Optional)

As we noted at the beginning of the chapter, once you've completed the high-availability configuration for the primary and secondary Load Balancer servers, you can optionally configure one or more reach target servers. In this environment, if the standby server can reach more target servers than the primary server can, failover occurs, and the secondary Load Balancer server takes over the job of responding to client requests.

Step 41. To configure a reach target server, perform the following steps on both the primary and secondary Load Balancer servers. For better failover capability, you can configure multiple reach target servers (one server address for each subnet) by repeating this procedure for each server.

    a. Start the Load Balancer server's console, and connect to the host.

    b. Right-click **High Availability**, and select **Add Reach Target**.

    c. On the resulting panel (Figure 14-28), enter the IP address of the reach target server on the network.

    d. Click **OK**.

    e. Save the configuration to file default.cfg.

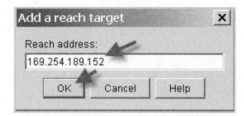

Figure 14-28: Adding a reach target server

If you encounter problems with the reach target function, run the following command from the command prompt to change the logging level to verbose and record additional information in the reach.log file.

```
dscontrol manager reach set loglevel 5
```

15

Configure WebSphere Dynamic Caching

WebSphere Application Server's caching functionality lets you cache the dynamic content generated by J2EE application components — servlets and Java Server Pages (JSPs) — and push that content to an HTTP server/plug-in and/or Caching Proxy system. (The Caching Proxy is a feature of the Edge Components for WebSphere, part of the WebSphere Application Server – Network Deployment offering.) You can also configure the application server to cache the static content (e.g., HTML, image files) served through the file-serving enabler servlet. This chapter's discussion will help you understand WebSphere caching and show you how to configure and verify dynamic caching on the application server and optionally move the cached content to the edge (HTTP server and/or Caching Proxy).

The diagram in Figure 15-1 illustrates a multitiered caching solution. This configuration relies on the Caching Proxy, the Edge Side Include (ESI) processor (a built-in processor contained in the plug-in), and the application server's dynamic caching service.

The Caching Proxy can fetch and serve public content from any Web server or application server in the deployment and can participate in caching dynamic content by being able to process invalidations. The choice of the Caching Proxy in this deployment is made based on deployment requirements, such as the need to efficiently cache large amounts of content through disk cache and the ability to support cache clustering. The ESI processor provides a fast, in-memory, public cache and can assemble fragments dynamically, caching whole pages and fragments in memory on the HTTP server/plug-in node. The application server's dynamic caching service provides an efficient dynamic cache that can be used to declare sophisticated caching policies, including declaring dependencies and invalidation policies per application. You can also configure the dynamic caching service configured for replication and offload to disk.

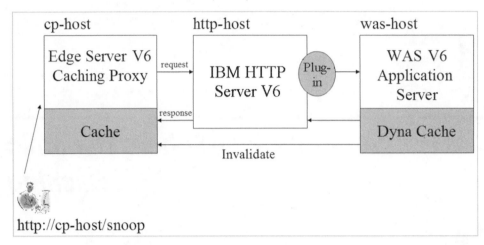

Figure 15-1: WebSphere dynamic caching architecture

When a user submits a request for the first time (http://cp-host/snoop, for example), the Caching Proxy intercepts the request from the client and sends it to the HTTP server/plug-in to process. Upon receiving the response from the HTTP server/plug-in, the Caching Proxy caches the output locally on the Caching Proxy server and then returns the response to the client. If the HTTP server/plug-in is processing the request for the first time, it sends the request to the application server to process and caches the returned output (after performing any ESI processing) before returning it to the Caching Proxy. If the application server is processing the request for the first time, it executes the servlet (or JSP) and caches the output in its JVM (after optionally including any ESI markup) before sending the response to the plug-in. Subsequent requests for the same servlet will be served from the cache instead of reprocessing the servlet, thereby reducing traffic at the back-end servers and improving performance and throughput. Timeout values or invalidation policies specified in the configuration govern when the cache's content is invalidated.

To use the caching feature on an application server and optionally push the cached content to the HTTP server/plug-in node's ESI processor or a Caching Proxy server using the external caching feature, you need to

- configure WebSphere to use the caching functionality and push data to the external cache device

- create and deploy on the server a cache specification file (cachespec.xml) to provide details about the objects (e.g., URIs, servlet classes) that you want to cache

- configure the edge device (HTTP server/plug-in or Caching Proxy) to accept cached data from the application server and serve subsequent requests

In the first part of this chapter, we explain how to configure the application server to cache dynamic content on the application server node (was-host). Next, you learn how to push static and dynamic content to the ESI processor (on http-host). Then, we show how to push dynamic content to the Caching Proxy server (cp-host).

Snoop Servlet Behavior Without Dynamic Cache

Before deploying customer applications that use the dynamic caching feature, you'd be wise to test your dynamic caching infrastructure to be sure all the elements perform as expected. You can use the default application provided in WebSphere Application Server to test your configuration.

Use the following procedure to verify the behavior of the snoop servlet before configuring the application server(s) and default application to use the dynamic cache service. Before performing this test, make sure the application server and default application are running. (If you're in a clustered environment, make sure the cluster has been started.)

1. Open a browser on a machine in the network, and issue **http://was-host:9080/snoop**, using the Web container's HTTP transport directly. Scroll through and review the snoop servlet output. The contents of the output, shown in Figure 15-2, are unique to this request. Pay attention to the values given for the remote address, host, and port.

2. Now, open a browser on another machine in the network (say was-host1), and issue **http://was-host:9080/snoop**. Again, the output (shown in Figure 15-3) is unique to the request, as you can see from the remote address, host, and port values reported for this request.

Address   http://was-host:9080/snoop

Remote user	\<none>
Remote address	169.254.189.152
Remote host	was-host
Remote port	4528

Figure 15-2: Remote address, host, and port values for initial invocation of snoop servlet

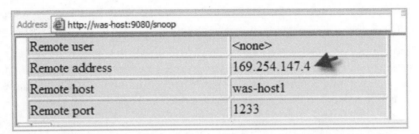

Figure 15-3: *Remote address, host, and port values for second invocation of snoop servlet*

From this test, it's evident that the snoop servlet (which is running on the application server) is invoked each time you submit a request. In the next section, you'll see how snoop's behavior changes after you configure the servlet to use the dynamic cache service.

> **Note:**   If you're in a clustered environment, you must test each cluster member separately. For example, use **http://was-host1:9080/snoop** and **http://was-host2:9080/snoop**, substituting "was-host1" and "was-host2" for "was-host" in the preceding instructions.

Task 1: Configure the Application Server and Enterprise Application to Use Dynamic Cache

In this section, you configure the application server (or each cluster member if you're in a clustered environment) and the default sample application to cache data at the application server JVM. The following steps accomplish this task:

1. Enable the dynamic cache service.
2. Enable servlet caching.
3. Deploy the CacheMonitor application.
4. Prepare the application to use dynamic cache.
5. Verify the dynamic cache configuration on the application server.

Enable the Dynamic Cache Service

Step 1.   Dynamic content caching requires the dynamic cache service to be enabled. This service is enabled by default. If you need to enable the feature, expand **Servers**, navigate to **Application Servers|server1|Container Services|Dynamic Cache Service**, and select the option to "Enable service at server startup," as shown in Figure 15-4. (In a clustered environment, navigate to **Application Servers|*cluster-member*|Container Services|Dynamic Cache Service**, and perform this step for each cluster member.)

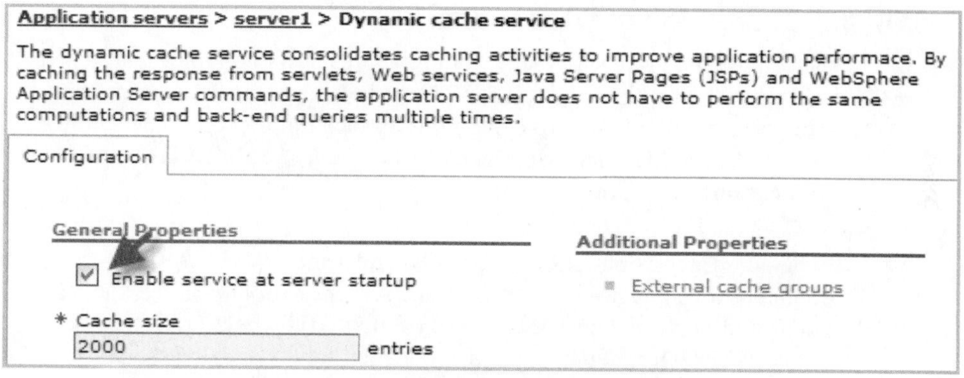

Application servers > server1 > Dynamic cache service

The dynamic cache service consolidates caching activities to improve application performace. By caching the response from servlets, Web services, Java Server Pages (JSPs) and WebSphere Application Server commands, the application server does not have to perform the same computations and back-end queries multiple times.

Configuration

General Properties

☑ Enable service at server startup

* Cache size

```
2000
```
entries

Additional Properties

▪ External cache groups

Figure 15-4: Enabling the dynamic cache service

Enable Servlet Caching

Step 2.   Next, you must enable the servlet caching feature on each Web container to cache the output from servlets and JSPs. To do so, expand **Servers**, navigate to **Application Servers|server1|Web Container Settings|Web Container**, and select the option to "Enable servlet caching," as shown in Figure 15-5. (In a clustered environment, navigate to **Application Servers|*cluster-member*|Web Container Settings|Web Container**, and perform this step for each cluster member.) Save the configuration after performing this step.

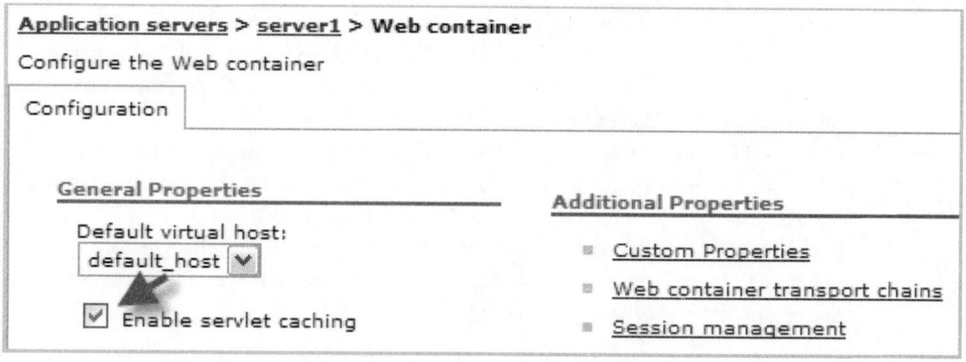

Application servers > server1 > Web container

Configure the Web container

Configuration

General Properties

Default virtual host:

default_host ▾

☑ Enable servlet caching

Additional Properties

▪ Custom Properties

▪ Web container transport chains

▪ Session management

Figure 15-5: Enabling servlet caching

Deploy the CacheMonitor Application

Step 3.   You can use the graphical CacheMonitor application to monitor the cached contents in the application server JVM and invalidate the data during the testing and tuning phases. To deploy this application, log on to the admin console, deploy file CacheMonitor.ear (navigate to **Applications|Install New Application**), and save the configuration.

By default, CacheMonitor.ear is installed under the <WASV6-ROOT>\ installableApps directory. In a standalone server environment, the application is deployed on virtual host admin-host (port 9060) by default. (Accept the default values when deploying this application for a standalone server.) To invoke the application, open a browser and issue **http://was-host:9060/cachemonitor**.

In a clustered environment, you can install the CacheMonitor application on the cluster and use default_host as a virtual host. To invoke the application, open a browser and issue **http://was-host1:9080/cachemonitor** to see the activity of the application server on the was-host1 JVM. Issue **http://was-host2:9080/cachemonitor** to see the activity of the application server on was-host2.

You can install the application on admin-host instead of default_host in a clustered environment, but to do so you must activate the Web container's transport chain (port 9060 by default) for each cluster member. Transport chains represent network protocol stacks operating within a client or server. To enable the transport chain, expand **Servers**, navigate to **Application Servers|server1|Web Container Settings|Web container transport chains|WCInboundAdmin**, and select the **Enabled** check box option (shown in Figure 15-6). Restart the cluster after making this change. Then, to invoke the application, open a browser and issue **http://was-host1:9060/cachemonitor** to see the activity of the application server on washost1. Issue **http://was-host2:9060/cachemonitor** to see the activity of the application server on washost2.

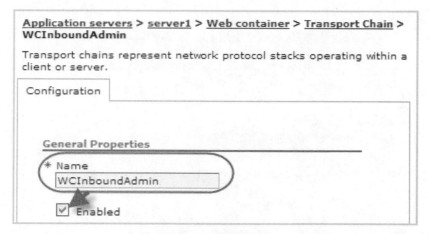

Figure 15-6: Enabling the transport chain

Prepare Enterprise Application to Use Dynamic Cache Service

Step 4.   When you install WebSphere, the sample cachespec configuration file is copied into the <WASV6-ROOT>\properties directory as file cachespec.sample.xml. To enable the default application to use the dynamic cache service, copy file cachespec.sample.xml to the application's WEB-INF directory (<WASV6ROOT>\profiles*profileName*\installedApps*yourCell*\Default Application.ear\DefaultApplication.war\WEB-INF), and rename it to cachespec.xml. (In a clustered environment, perform this step on each cluster member.)

> **Note:**   You can optionally drop the cachespec.xml file into the <WASV6-ROOT>\properties directory instead of packing it in the WAR module. In this case, you must restart the application server to have the new property values take effect.

Step 5.   The cachespec file contains entries that define the caching that will take place for different cacheable objects. Open the file, and review its contents. The first cache entry, shown in Figure 15-7, is designed to cache the snoop servlet with a cache timeout value of 180 seconds.

```
<cache>
  <!-- Sample cache entry for SnoopServlet
       cache entry is based on:
           1) request parameters if present
           2) pathinfo if present
           3) the host header if present
  -->
  <cache-entry>
      <class>servle  /class>
      <name>/snoop</name>
      <cache-id>
          <component id="*" type="parameter">
              <required>false</required>
          </component>
          <component id="" type="pathinfo">
              <required>false</required>
          </component>
          <component id="host" type="header">
              <required>false</required>
          </component>
          <timeout>180</timeout>
      </cache-id>
  </cache-entry>
```

Figure 15-7: Cache timeout cache entry

The second entry, shown in Figure 15-8, is designed to cache, on the application server JVM, all static content served through the file-serving servlet.

```
<!-- Cache Entry for the File Serving Servlet
     Will cache all static content in the web application -->
<cache-entry>
    <class>servlet</class>
    <name>com.ibm.ws.webcontainer.servlet.SimpleFileServlet.class</name>
    <cache-id>
        <component id="" type="pathinfo">
            <required>true</required>
        </component>
        <component id="If-Modified-Since" type="header">
            <required>false</required>
        </component>
        <timeout>300</timeout>
    </cache-id>
</cache-entry>
```

Figure 15-8: Cache entry for the file-serving servlet

The third cache entry, shown in Figure 15-9, demonstrates how to create multiple cache instances. We aren't using this feature in this chapter's example, so you can delete this cache instance block. Be sure you *don't* delete the end tag </cache>, which appears on the last line of the file. After removing the instance entry, save the file and exit your editor.

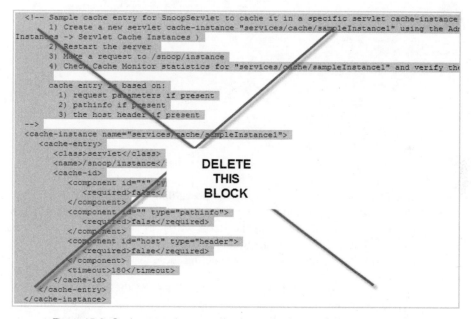

Figure 15-9: Cache entry demonstrating how to create multiple cache instances

Verify Dynamic Cache Configuration on the Application Server

With the preceding steps completed, you're ready to verify whether you've configured dynamic cache correctly. To do so, take the following steps on the application server.

> **Note:** In a clustered environment, you can test each cluster member separately by starting only one cluster member at a time. For example, to invoke snoop, use **http://was-host1:9080/snoop** and **http://was-host2:9080/snoop**. To invoke the cache monitor, use **http://was-host1:9060/cachemonitor** and **http://was-host2:9060/cachemonitor.** If you installed the CacheMonitor application using the default_host virtual host, specify port 9080 instead of 9060.

Step 6. Restart the application server. (In a clustered environment, restart the cluster.)

Step 7. Expand **Applications**, click **Enterprise Applications**, and make sure the DefaultApplication and Dynamic Cache Monitor applications are listed as running (green arrow), as shown in Figure 15-10.

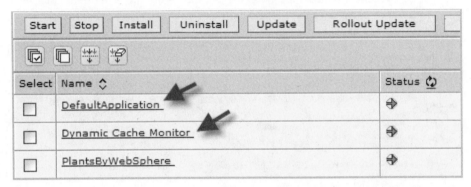

Figure 15-10: Enterprise applications panel

Step 8. Open a browser, and enter **http://was-host:9060/cachemonitor** to launch the CacheMonitor application. Perform the following tests from the panel shown in Figure 15-11. You can click the **Reset Statistics** and **Clear Cache** buttons as needed during this testing and tuning exercise. Do *not* close the CacheMonitor application after completing these tests.

a. Click the **Cache Statistics** link on the left side of the panel, and make sure the value that's displayed for the Servlet Caching Enabled statistic is Yes. (If it's not, go back and enable servlet caching as described in Step 2.) Cache Hits and Cache Misses will appear with a value of 0 (unless you invoked the snoop servlet already).

b. Click **Cache Contents**. At this time, you won't see any cached contents in the list that appears unless you invoked snoop already.

c. Click **Cache Policies**, and verify that you see entries for snoop and the SimpleFile Servlet class, as shown in Figure 15-12. (If you don't see these entries, make sure you configured file cachespec.xml as described in Step 5.)

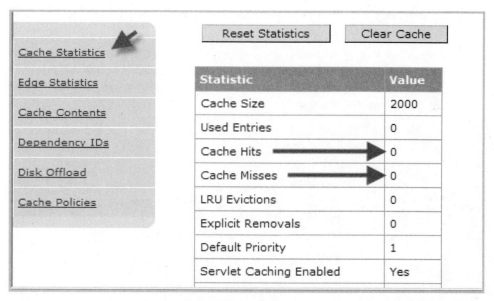

Figure 15-11: CacheMonitor application statistics

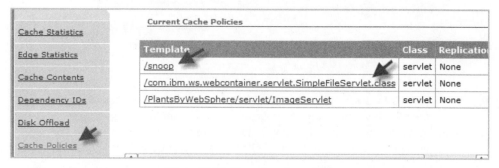

Figure 15-12: Current cache policies

Step 9. Again, open a browser on a machine in the network, and issue **http://was-host:9080/snoop** to run the snoop servlet. You'll see snoop output unique to this request, providing the remote address, host, and port values you saw in Figure 15-2.

Step 10. Go to the browser you used to invoke the CacheMonitor application, and perform these tests:

a. Click **Cache Contents**. You should now see an entry for snoop, as shown in Figure 15-13.

b. Click **Cache Statistics**, and you should see a Cache Hits value of 0 and a Cache Misses value of 1 (the first request will always be a miss), as shown in Figure 15-14. These values tell you that the snoop servlet output has been cached in the JVM.

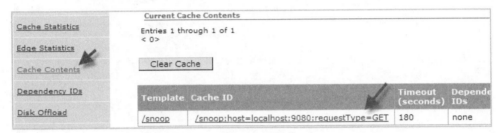

Figure 15-13: Current cache contents showing snoop entry

Dependency IDs	Used Entries	1
Disk Offload	Cache Hits ➡	0
	Cache Misses ➡	1
Cache Policies		

Figure 15-14: Cache statistics for first snoop request

Step 11. Open a browser on another machine in the network, and issue **http://was-host:9080/snoop** again. As you can observe from the snoop output, the remote address, host, and port values are the same as for the earlier request made on a different machine, indicating that this time the response was served from the cache.

Step 12. Go to the browser where you invoked the CacheMonitor application, and click **Cache Statistics**. You should see a Cache Hits value of 1 (Figure 15-15). Compare the values here with those you saw earlier. These results likewise indicate that the second snoop servlet request was served from the cache, confirming that you've configured dynamic cache on the application server successfully.

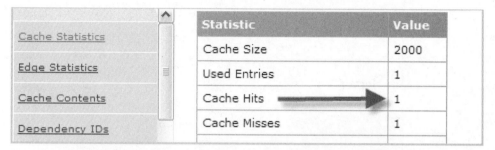

Figure 15-15: Cache statistics for snoop servlet served from the cache

---

Note: An important new feature of dynamic caching in WebSphere V6 is the ability to cache individual static content (instead of caching all the static content by caching the file-serving enabling servlet). For example, to cache index.html static content, you'd specify the following in the cachespec.xml file:

```
<class>static</class>

<name>WSsamples/en/index.html</name>
```

Task 2: Configure the Plug-in File and Application Server to Push Cached Content to the ESI Processor

WebSphere's dynamic cache can control caches outside the application server. In this section, you'll set up the external caching environment shown in Figure 15-16 to enable the application server to push static and dynamic cached content to the ESI processor on the HTTP server/plug-in node. The following steps accomplish this task.

On the HTTP server/plug-in:

1. Enable the Invalidation Monitor in the plug-in file to permit the ESI processor to receive invalidation notifications from the application server.

On each application server configured to work with the HTTP server/plug-in:

1. Deploy the DynacacheEsi.ear file to communicate with the ESI processor.
2. Configure an external cache group.

Before performing the steps for this task, make sure you've completed all the Task 1 steps and verified a successful configuration. Also, make sure you've installed the plug-in module and configured the HTTP server/plug-in system to send requests to the application server. (Use the snoop servlet to test this configuration.) If you have multiple

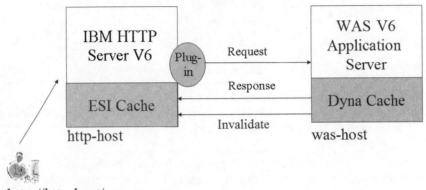

Figure 15-16: External caching architecture using ESI processor on HTTP server/plug-in node

HTTP servers/plug-ins in your configuration, you must perform the steps on each HTTP server/plug-in node.

Configure the Plug-in File

Step 1.   Open the plug-in file (plugin-cfg.xml) on the HTTP server node, and set the **ESIInvalidationMonitor** property to "true" as shown in Figure 15-17. With this setting, the ESI processor can accept cache invalidation requests from the cache monitor application running on the application server according to the timeout values set in the cachespec.xml file.

```
<Property Name="ESIEnable" Value="true"/>
<Property Name="ESIMaxCacheSize" Value="1024"/>
<Property Name="ESIInvalidationMonitor" Value="true"/>
```

Figure 15-17: Enabling the Invalidation Monitor in the plug-in file

If you've set up HTTP Server to be managed through the WebSphere admin console, you can configure this setting from the admin console instead of editing the plug-in file manually. Figure 15-18 shows the console options to select.

Step 2.   Regenerate the plug-in, and propagate it to the HTTP server node.

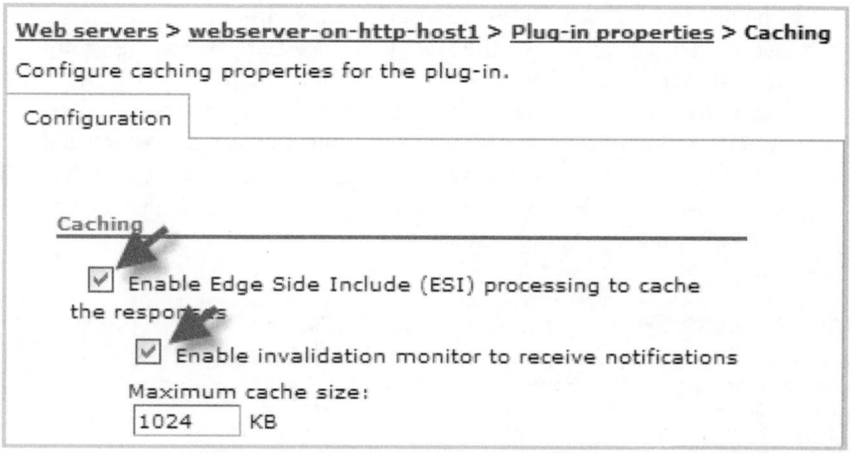

Figure 15-18: Enabling the Invalidation Monitor from the admin console

Step 3.   Restart HTTP Server.

Configure the Application Server

Complete the following steps on the application server to push cached content to the ESI processor.

Deploy the DynacacheEsi.ear Application

Step 4.   Log on to the admin console on the WebSphere node, and deploy file DynacacheEsi.ear on server1 (navigate to **Applications|Install New Application**). (If you're in a clustered environment, install the application into the cluster.) By default, the file is installed in the <WASV6-ROOT>\installableApps directory. Accept the default values when deploying the application, and save the configuration.

Configure External Cache Group and Member

When you define external cache groups, the dynamic cache matches externally cacheable cache entries with the groups and pushes cache entries and invalidations out to the groups. The content can then be served from the external cache (ESI processor in this case) instead of from the application server, thereby improving performance. To configure an external cache group for the ESI processor, take the following steps.

Step 5. Navigate to **Application Servers|server1|Dynamic cache service| Container services|Dynamic Cache Service|External cache groups**, and look for the external cache group EsiInvalidator (shown in Figure 15-19). (In a clustered environment, navigate to **Application Servers|*cluster-member*|Dynamic cache service|Container services|Dynamic Cache Service|External cache groups**.) If the group doesn't appear in the cache group list, click **New** to create it, and supply the address and adapter bean information given in the next step.

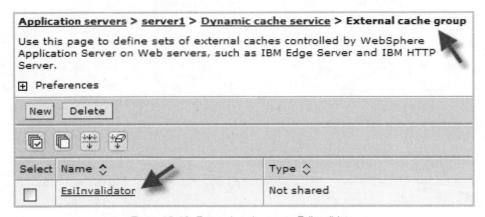

Figure 15-19: External cache group EsiInvalidator

Step 6. Verify whether the host address and adapter bean have been set. To do so, click **EsiInvalidator** in the cache group list, select **External cache group members**, and check to see that the values have been set as shown in Figure 15-20. If they have not, supply the address and adapter bean information as shown. By default, EsiInvalidator is created with localhost and the ESI adapter bean (EsiInvalidatorServlet) as parameters.

Select	Address ◇	Adapter bean name ◇
☐	localhost	com.ibm.websphere.servlet.cache.ESIInvalidatorServlet

Figure 15-20: Address and adapter bean for external cache group EsiInvalidator

Prepare the Enterprise Application

Step 7.   Open the cachespec.xml file you configured earlier for the snoop servlet. Add the **EdgeCacheable** property, and set its value to "true" as shown in Figure 15-21 to enable the default application to push cached contents to the ESI processor on the HTTP server/plug-in node. Then save the file. The application server will pick up these changes automatically. (In a clustered environment, perform this step on each cluster member.)

```
<cache-entry>
    <class>servlet</class>
    <name>/snoop</name>
    <cache-id>
        <component id="*" type="parameter">
            <required>false</required>
        </component>
        <component id="" type="pathinfo">
            <required>false</required>
        </component>
        <component id="host" type="header">
            <required>false</required>
        </component>
        <property name="EdgeCacheable">true</property>
        <timeout>180</timeout>
    </cache-id>
</cache-entry>
```

Figure 15-21: Setting the EdgeCacheable property in file cachespec.xml

Verify the External Cache Configuration

To verify the external cache (ESI) configuration, make sure the default application, Dynamic Cache Monitor, and Dynacache ESI applications are running (navigate to **Applications|Enterprise Applications** to check the status of these applications). Then perform the following steps.

Step 8.   Open a browser, and enter **http://http-host/snoop** to invoke the snoop servlet through the HTTP server/plug-in.

Step 9.   Open a browser, invoke the CacheMonitor application as described earlier, and perform the following tests. You can click the **Reset Statistics** and

Clear Cache buttons as needed during this exercise. Do not close the application after completing these steps.

a. Click **Edge Statistics** and then **Refresh Statistics**. You should see the entries shown in Figure 15-22: a value of 1 for the ESI Processes, Number of Edge Cached Entries, and Cache Misses By URL statistics and a Cache Hits value of 0 (unless you invoked snoop multiple times).

b. At the bottom of the panel, click **Contents**. You should see a cache contents entry for snoop similar to the one shown in Figure 15-23, proving that the snoop servlet output has been cached by the ESI processor.

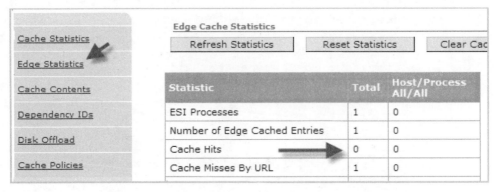

Figure 15-22: Cache monitor statistics for initial snoop request

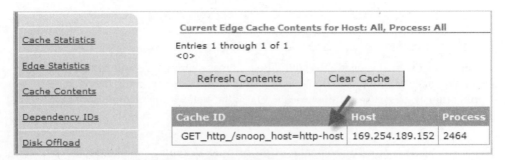

Figure 15-23: Cache contents after initial snoop request

Step 10. Open a browser on another machine in the network, and reissue the snoop servlet request through the HTTP server/plug-in.

Step 11.   Go to the browser where you invoked the cache monitor, and click **Edge Statistics**. You should now see a Cache Hits value of 1, as shown in Figure 15-24. Compare the values here with those you saw earlier to observe that an entry has been served from the ESI cache.

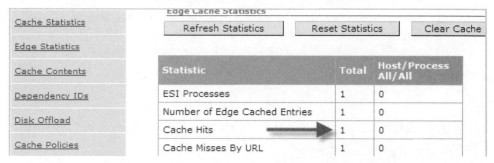

Figure 15-24: Edge statistics for second snoop servlet request

Step 12.   To verify that the static content served by the application server (using the file-serving enabler) is being cached at the ESI processor, invoke one of the sample applications you installed in an earlier chapter — for example, the SamplesGallery (**http://http-host/WSsamples**) or the PlantsByWebSphere application (**http://http-host/PlantsByWebSphere**). Then click **Edge Statistics|Contents** to see the static content cached at the ESI processor. Figure 15-25 shows the cached content for the SamplesGallery application.

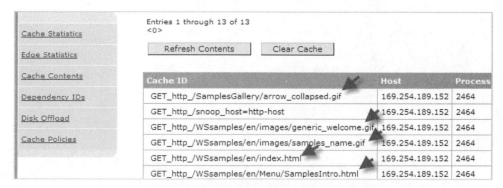

Figure 15-25: Cached SamplesGallery application contents

Configure Cache Timeout of Static Content on ESI Processor (Optional)

Step 13. When you use WebSphere to serve static data (e.g., images, HTML) on the application server, the URLs are also cached in the ESI processor as we've described. This data has a default timeout period of 300 seconds. You can change the timeout value by adding the property **com.ibm.servlet.file.esi. timeOut** to your JVM's command-line parameters. The following line, for example, sets a one-hour timeout on the static data cached in the ESI processor.

```
-Dcom.ibm.servlet.file.esi.timeOut=3600
```

Task 3: Pushing Dynamic Content to the Edge Server's Caching Proxy Component

You've seen how to configure dynamic cache on the application server and how to push static and dynamic content from there to the ESI processor on the HTTP server/plug-in node. Now, we'll complete the steps required to accomplish the third piece of the puzzle: pushing dynamic content to the Caching Proxy server (cp-host). For a reminder of what this architecture looks like, review Figure 15-1 again.

Step 1. To prepare the enterprise application to push content to the Caching Proxy server, open the cachespec.xml file you configured earlier for the snoop servlet, and add the following entry (as shown in Figure 15-26) to specify an external cache group. (In a clustered environment, perform this step on each cluster member.)

```
<property name="ExternalCache">CacheProxy</property>
```

```
<cache-entry>
    <class>servlet</class>
    <name>/snoop</name>
    <cache-id>
        <component id="*" type="parameter">
            <required>false</required>
        </component>
        <component id="" type="pathinfo">
            <required>false</required>
        </component>
        <component id="host" type="header">
            <required>false</required>
        </component>
        <property name="EdgeCacheable">true</property>
        <property name="ExternalCache">CacheProxy</property>
        <timeout>180</timeout>
    </cache-id>
</cache-entry>
```

Figure 15-26: Specifying the ExternalCache property

Save the file after making this change. The application server should pick up the change automatically. Next, you'll configure an external cache group named CacheProxy that points to the Caching Proxy server (cp-host).

Configure the External Cache Group and Member on the Application Server

The Caching Proxy's dynamic caching function enables you to cache responses from JSPs and servlets generated by the WebSphere application server. To avoid repeated requests to the application server when multiple clients request the same content, a Caching Proxy adapter module (com.ibm.websphere.edge.dynacache.WteAdapter) on the application server modifies the responses to cache them at the proxy server (entry point). The responses are also cached in the application server's dynamic cache. To configure the Caching Proxy as an external cache group, take the following steps.

Step 2. From the WebSphere admin console, expand **Servers**, navigate to **Application Servers|server1|Dynamic cache service|Container services|Dynamic Cache Service|External cache groups**, and click **New** to create a new external cache group named CacheProxy. (In a clustered environment, navigate to **Application Servers|*cluster-member*|Dynamic cache service|Container services|Dynamic Cache Service|External cache groups**.) Figure 15-27 shows the panel where you create the new group.

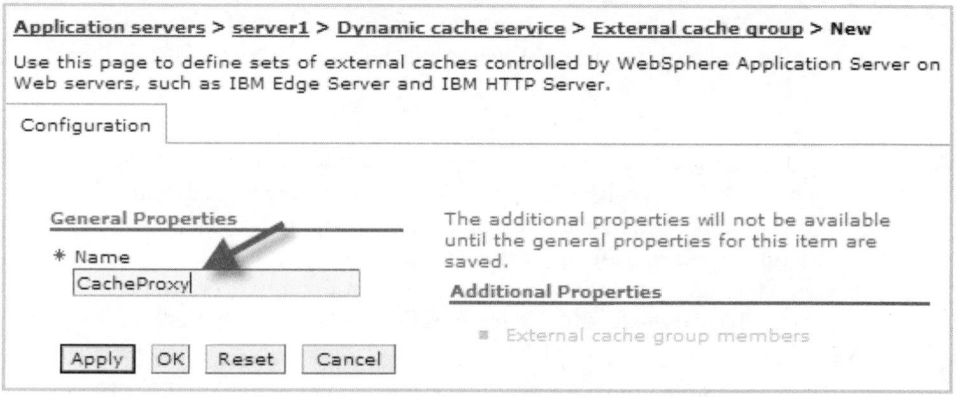

Figure 15-27: Creating an external cache group

The external cache group name (CacheProxy in this case) must match the **ExternalCache** property defined in the servlet or JSP cachespec.xml file (Step 1). You also need to use this group name when you configure the external cache manager directive in the Caching Proxy configuration file (ibmproxy.conf) on the Caching Proxy server (cp-host). You'll perform this step later.

Step 3. Click **Apply**, and then select **External cache group members** under the **Additional Properties** section. Provide the host name (or DNS entry) of the Caching Proxy server (cp-host in this example) and the adapter bean name (com.ibm.websphere.edge.dynacache.WteAdapter), as shown in Figure 15-28. (If the Caching Proxy isn't listening at port 80, provide the port number as well as the host name in the address field — for example, **cp-host:81**.)

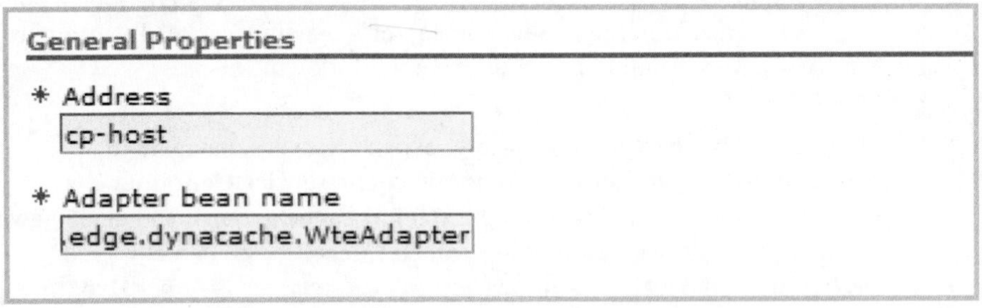

General Properties

* Address

cp-host

* Adapter bean name

.edge.dynacache.WteAdapter

Figure 15-28: Specifying the host address and adapter bean name

Click **OK**, and save the configuration. With this configuration, the application server can push cached content to the external caching device and control the cache (timeout) according to the configuration provided in file cachespec.xml.

Step 4. Next, on each application server node, create the file dynaedge-cfg.xml under the <WASV6-ROOT>\profiles\AppSrv01\properties directory to provide information about the external cache group. (If you're in a clustered environment, complete this step on each cluster member.) Use a text editor to create the information in the file, as shown in Figure 15-29. You can use the sample dynaedge-cfg.xml file in <WASV6-ROOT>\properties as a template.

The values in the file depend on your existing configuration. For the test environment described in this chapter, the values are as follows:

- for endpoint, "http://cp-host:80" (the host name of the Caching Proxy server and the port on which it is listening)

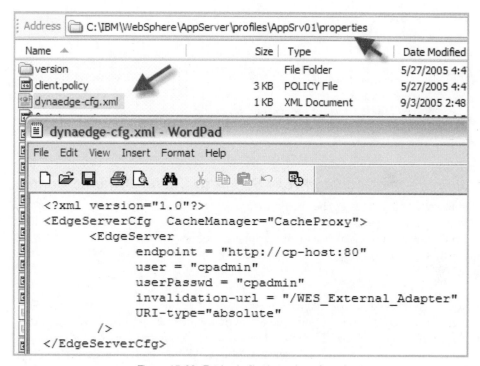

Figure 15-29: Entries in file dynaedge-cfg.xml

- for the Caching Proxy's administrative user ID and password, "cpadmin" and "cpadmin"

- for the invalidation URL, "/WES_External_Adapter" (you'll configure this JSP plug-in service in the ibmproxy.conf file on the Caching Proxy server)

- for the URI type, "absolute"

Step 5. Restart the application server (or cluster in a clustered environment).

Step 6. Review the file <WASV6-ROOT>/appserver/logs/edge/logs/dynaedge*time-stamp*.log on each application server to verify that your dynamic cache adapter was initialized properly. If any problems occurred, you should see errors in this log file. Figure 15-30 shows a sample file after a successful configuration.

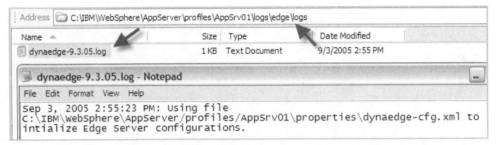

Figure 15-30: Log file contents after successful server restart

Configure the Caching Proxy Server to Cache Dynamic Content

Before performing this step, be sure you've completed Task 1 and verified a successful configuration. Also make sure you've installed the Caching Proxy and configured it with the HTTP server. For an overview of Caching Proxy installation and configuration, see the section "Install, Configure, and Verify the Caching Proxy Server" at the end of this chapter.

If you've configured a Load Balancer server to spray requests across multiple HTTP servers in your configuration, you need to configure the Caching Proxy with the Load Balancer instead of with HTTP Server. Use the cluster IP address or alias of the Load Balancer (noyb-cluster.noyb.com) instead of the HTTP Server IP address or alias (http-host) when following the instructions in this section. For more information about configuring the Load Balancer – Dispatcher component to spray requests across HTTP servers, see Chapter 13. Figure 15-31 depicts the architecture of a Caching Proxy server configured with Load Balancer servers in high-availability mode, as described in Chapters 13 and 14.

Step 7. Open the Caching Proxy configuration file, ibmproxy.conf (under the <CPROXY-ROOT>\edge\cp\etc\en_US directory, where <CPROXY-ROOT> is the directory where you installed the Caching Proxy). Search the file for "JSP Plug-in" and remove the comment to set the service directive to enable the dynamic caching plug-in (Figure 15-32). Make sure this command appears on a single line.

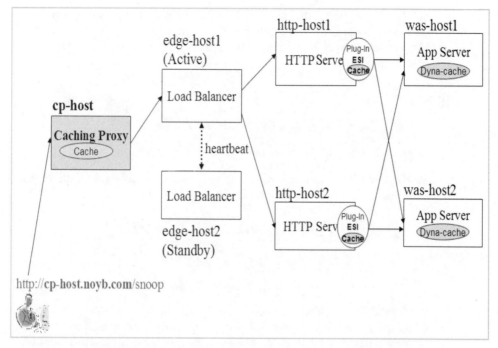

Figure 15-31: Caching Proxy configured with Load Balancer servers

```
# ===== JSP Plug-in =====
Service /WES_External_Adapter C:\IBM\edge\cp\lib\plugins\dynacache
\dyna_plugin.dll:exec_dynacmd
```

Figure 15-32: Setting the service directive

Step 8. Set the ExternalCacheManager directive, specifying the name you provided for the external cache group (CacheProxy) on the application server and a maximum expiration time for content if an invalidation request isn't received from the application server (Figure 15-33).

```
#     ExternalCacheManager directive:

      ExternalCacheManager CacheProxy 20 minutes
```

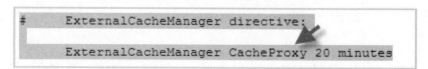

Figure 15-33: Setting the ExternalCacheManager directive

Step 9. Set the CacheQueries directive to always cache responses to queries if the URL pattern matches "http://http-host/*" (Figure 15-34). If you're using the Load Balancer, specify the cluster alias instead of http-host (i.e., http://*cluster-address*/*).

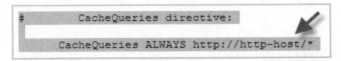

Figure 15-34: Setting the CacheQueries directive

Step 10. Set the CacheTimeMargin directive to specify not to cache files with expiration times less than three minutes (Figure 15-35).

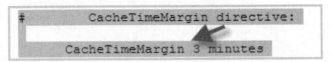

Figure 15-35: Setting the CacheTimeMargin directive

Step 11. Restart the Caching Proxy server. To do so, connect to the Caching Proxy's graphical admin console, and click the restart symbol. Using the host names defined in this chapter, the URL to invoke the console is **http://cp-host/pub/**. Figure 15-36 shows the Caching Proxy's console, from which you can perform various configuration and monitoring tasks related to the caching function.

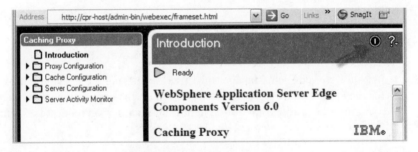

Figure 15-36: Caching Proxy console

Note: When you install the Caching Proxy server, the proxy caching directive will be set to ON (enable) by default. If this setting has been changed to OFF for some reason, you need to enable caching by editing file ibmproxy.conf, setting the caching directive to ON (Caching ON). You can also use the Caching Proxy's administrative console to set this directive. To do so, navigate to **Cache**

Configuration|Cache Settings, select the Enable proxy caching check box, and click Submit. Restart the Caching Proxy server after modifying the directive.

Verify External Cache – Caching Proxy Configuration

To verify your configuration, make sure you've started the Caching Proxy, HTTP server(s), Load Balancer (if you're using one), and application server(s). Then perform the following steps.

Step 12. Open a browser on a machine in the network, and issue **http://cp-host/snoop** to invoke the snoop servlet, sending the request through the Caching Proxy. Figure 15-37 shows the snoop servlet results for this request.

Figure 15-37: Snoop request served through Caching Proxy

Step 13. Open a browser on cp-host, and bring up the Caching Proxy console: **http://cp-host/pub/**. Expand **Server Activity Monitor**, and click **Proxy Access Statistics**. Click the **Refresh** button, and review the statistics to see that the first snoop request wasn't served from the Caching Proxy. (The first request will always be a miss and cache the output of the snoop servlet.)

Step 14. Refresh the browser page to reinvoke snoop (http://cp-host/snoop).

Step 15. Return to the Caching Proxy console, and click **Refresh** to verify that the subsequent request of snoop was served from the Caching Proxy. An entry in blue confirms that the Caching Proxy configuration is working. In Figure 15-38, the second line in the proxy statistics window represents this cache hit.

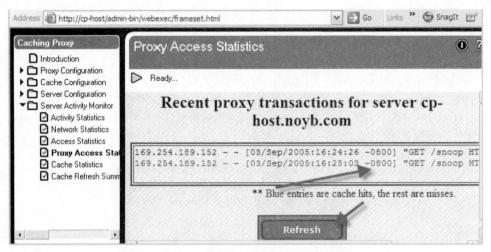

Figure 15-38: Proxy statistics for second snoop request

Note: If necessary, you can use Tivoli Performance Viewer during this exercise to tune the parameters related to dynamic caching.

Overview of Cluster-Aware Dynacache Object Caching (Cache Replication)

In a clustered environment, you can gain fault tolerance for cached content by enabling WebSphere's internal replication service. This is the same replication service you used in Chapter 11 to enable memory-to-memory replication of HTTP sessions for failover purposes.

If you're using external cache replication, there's no reason to employ the internal replication service feature unless your application configuration requires it. WebSphere Portal Server clusters, for example, require the cache replication feature to be enabled. Remember that all cached data on any cluster member will be replicated on the other cluster member(s) if you enable this feature, which could mean considerable memory use on each cluster member. There's little justification for this potentially high memory use on each JVM if the next request is being served from the external cache.

If you want to enable cache replication, take the following steps. (These steps assume you configured the Replication Domain and Replication Entries during cluster configuration. If that's not the case, you must configure these entries before enabling the cache replication feature.)

1. Expand **Servers**, and navigate to **Application servers|*cluster-member*| Container Services|Dynamic Cache Service** to display the settings shown in Figure 15-39.

2. Select the option to "Enable cache replication."

3. In the drop-down list, choose the replication domain for the replicator you created in Chapter 11.

4. For the replication type, select **Both push and pull**. This selection indicates that you want to send out identifiers of new entries and notify the other cluster members of updates to those entries.

5. Set the push frequency to **1** second (or a time appropriate for your configuration).

6. Click **OK**, and save the configuration.

7. Repeat these steps for each member of the cluster. Note that all cluster members must use the same replication type and push frequency settings.

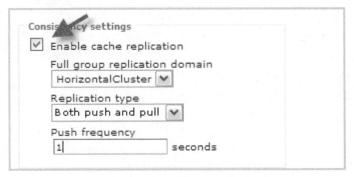

Figure 15-39: Enabling cache replication

Install, Configure, and Verify the Caching Proxy Server

In this section, we describe how to install the Caching Proxy server. This discussion assumes you've already downloaded and installed the WebSphere Edge Server and extracted the files to a temporary directory, as described in Chapter 13. Take the following steps to install, configure, and verify the Caching Proxy server.

Step 1.   Start the Launchpad (or use setup.exe on a Windows system) to initiate the Caching Proxy installation.

Step 2. In the Component Selection panel (Figure 15-40), select the options to install the Caching Proxy and its documentation. If necessary, change the installation directory (this example uses C:\IBM\edge\cp). Hereafter, we refer to this installation directory as <CPROXY-ROOT>.

Step 3. Click **Finish** to complete the install process. Be sure to restart the computer once installation is complete.

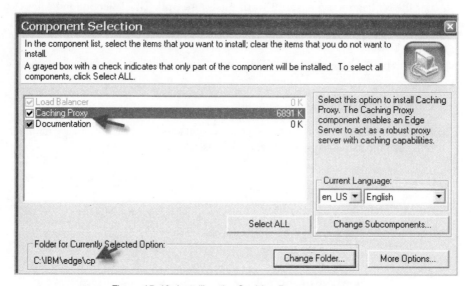

Figure 15-40: Installing the Caching Proxy component

Step 4. The procedure to start and stop the Caching Proxy server depends on your operating system. On Windows systems, the Caching Proxy is started automatically as a Windows service, as Figure 15-41 shows. On Linux, you use **/usr/sbin/ibmproxy** to start the process and use **kill proxy-process-id** to stop it. For more information about starting and stopping the Caching Proxy, review the Edge Server V6 documentation at *http://www-306.ibm.com/software/webservers/appserv/doc/v60/ec/infocenter/index.html*.

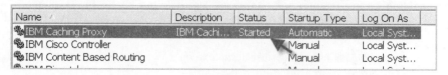

Figure 15-41: Caching Proxy Windows service

Step 5. Open a command prompt, and navigate to the directory <CPROXY-ROOT>\server_root\protect. Use the htadm command as shown in Figure 15-42 to add an administrator user.

```
C:\IBM\edge\cp\server_root\protect>htadm -adduser webadmin.passwd
Username:
cpadmin
Password:********
Verify:********
Real name:
```

Figure 15-42: Adding an administrator user

Step 6. Open file ibmproxy.conf under the <CPROXY-ROOT>\etc\en_US directory, and enter the mapping rule shown in Figure 15-43 to pass requests to the admin pages if the URL pattern matches "/pub/*". Be sure to enter the rule as the first line in the Mapping rules section.

```
#          URLs starting with /admin-bin/ will be understood as
#          script calls in the directory C:\IBM\edge\cp\Admin\
#

pass       /pub/*  C:\IBM\edge\cp\server_root\pub\en_US\*

Exec  /Docs/admin-bin/*  C:\IBM\edge\cp\server_root\Admin\*
Exec  /cgi-bin/*         C:\IBM\edge\cp\server_root\CGI-Bin\*
```

Figure 15-43: Mapping rule for admin pages

Step 7. Enter a mapping rule to pass all requests to the HTTP server (or dispatcher if you configured one). Be sure to enter this rule in the NEW MAPPING RULES section as shown in Figure 15-44.

```
#
# URL translation rules; If your documents are under
#
# NOTE: The installation defaults should be added below
# *** START NEW MAPPING RULES SECTION ***

proxy       /*  http://http-host/*

# if you configured Load Balancer then use cluster address/alias
# instead of http-host as shown below
# proxy      /*    http://noyb-cluster/*    169.254.213.100:80
# *** END NEW MAPPING RULES SECTION ***
```

Figure 15-44: Mapping rule for HTTP requests

Step 8.   Restart (stop and start) the Caching Proxy server.

Step 9.   Connect to the Caching Proxy admin console from the browser using the URL **http://cp-host/pub/**. Enter a user ID and password (cpadmin/cpadmin) to be authenticated (Figure 15-45).

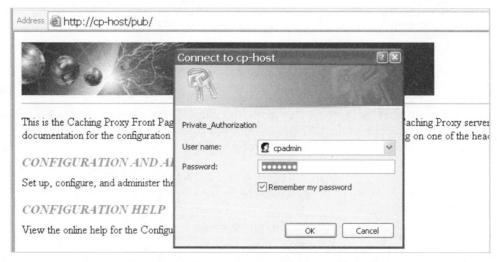

Figure 15-45: Connecting to the Caching Proxy server

Step 10.   Test the Caching Proxy configuration to verify that the requests are being sent to the HTTP server (or dispatcher) according to your configuration. To do so, open a browser, and enter **http://cp-host** to display the HTTP Server welcome page (Figure 15-46).

Figure 15-46: HTTP Server welcome page on Caching Proxy server

Step 11.   Enter **http://cp-host/snoop** to invoke the snoop servlet on the application server (Figure 15-47).

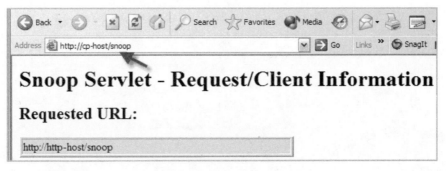

Figure 15-47: Invoking the snoop servlet

If you have any problems during the startup or runtime of the Caching Proxy server, consult the log files under the <CPROXY-ROOT>\server_root\logs directory, shown in Figure 15-48.

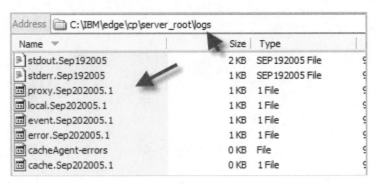

Figure 15-48: Caching Proxy log files

Starting the Caching Proxy from the Console

On Windows systems, you can start the Caching Proxy and review various logs from the console instead of from the **Services** panel by issuing the ibmproxy command from the command line. You can also enable and disable trace and restart the Caching Proxy server from the console using the options shown in Figure 15-49.

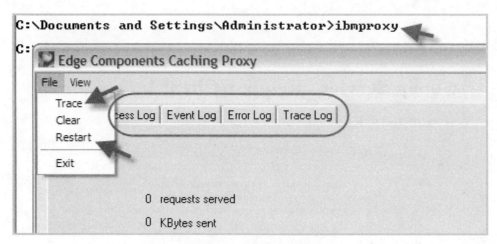

Figure 15-49: *Managing the Caching Proxy from the console*

16

Enabling WebSphere Application Server Security

WebSphere Application Server V6 supports J2EE security. In this chapter, we describe the steps needed to enable WebSphere security. Authentication and authorization are two aspects of security of particular interest in this chapter. *Authentication* is the act of proving identity. *Authorization* is the act of determining permission. To perform authentication and authorization, the processes in a WebSphere cell need what is referred to as a *registry*.

In the context of security, a registry is a collection of user and group definitions. Each user definition must include a unique user identifier (user ID) and some proof of identity. Depending on the registry implementation, the proof of identity can be a secret password or a public key digital certificate. The group definition includes a group identifier (group ID) and a list of users who are members of the group.

WebSphere supports three kinds of registries:

- *custom* — a user-provided class that implements the registry API

- *operating system* — the user and group registry used by the host operating system

- *LDAP* — a registry that supports the Lightweight Directory Access Protocol (LDAP)

This chapter covers the steps needed to set up WebSphere security using each of these registry types. As you'll see, much of the configuration process is the same regardless of which registry you use.

In addition, the chapter describes the steps to take to replace the "dummy" key and trust files that IBM ships with WebSphere Application Server. These dummy files are strictly for demonstration and easy out-of-the-box installation. Because the files are shipped with every copy of the product, the private portion of the key is obviously compromised. It's important to replace these files as part of the process of enabling WebSphere security.

Configuring Security Using the Sample Custom Registry

WebSphere comes with a sample custom registry implemented by a class named FileRegistrySample that uses a text file to maintain a collection of user and group definitions. The sample registry makes configuring WebSphere security quite convenient, but this registry is suitable only for development environments. Don't use the sample custom registry for production (it stores the passwords in the clear). This registry is also inappropriate for test environments because such environments should use the same type of registry as production.

Developing a custom registry suitable for production use is not an easy task and is beyond the scope of this text. The following example demonstrates the security configuration process using the sample custom registry.

Create the Custom Registry Files

Your first task is to create the registry files (users file and groups file) needed by the sample custom registry. You can put these files wherever you like in the host machine's file system. For this example, we'll place them in C:\FileRegistry. A property of the FileRegistrySample custom registry class specifies the location and name of the files. To create the two files, take the following steps.

Step 1. Create a directory named FileRegistry at the top level of the C drive.

Step 2. Create the users file. To do so, create a file named users.registry (or any name you prefer) in the FileRegistry directory, and edit the file to add users as described here.

Each line in the users file required by the sample custom registry must take the form

```
<userID>:<password>:<uid>:<groupIDs>:<displayName>
```

where

- <userID> is the user name

- <uid> is a unique identifier for the user name (the WebSphere processes use this value, comparable to the UID in a Unix user registry, to create a credential)

- <groupIDs> is a comma-separated list of group identifiers

Here's a sample users file with all passwords set to "password":

```
# <userID>:<password>:<uid>:<groupIDs>:<displayName>
wasadmin:password:101:501:"WAS Admin"
george:password:201:401,403:George
martha:password:202:401,403:Martha
moe:password:203:402:Moe
larry:password:204:402:Larry
curly:password:205:402:Curly
shemp:password:206:402:Shemp
admin1:password:207:403,501:"Admin One"
sibuser:password:208:403:"SI Bus User"
```

Step 3.   Next, create the groups file. To do so, create a file named groups.registry in the FileRegistry directory. Edit this file to add groups as described here. Each line in the sample groups file registry takes the form

```
<groupID>:<gid>:<userMembers>:<displayName>
```

Here, <userMembers> is a comma-separated list of user IDs. Here's a sample groups file:

```
# <groupID>:<gid>:<members>:<displayName>
hippos:401:george,martha:"Famous Hippos"
stooges:402:moe,larry,curly,shemp:"Famous Stooges"
sibUsers:403:sibuser,admin1,george,martha:"SI Bus Users"
SysAdmins:501:wasadmin,admin1:"WebSphere Administrators"
```

In reality, the groups you define will be relevant to the applications being developed in your development environment.

Step 4.   If you have more than one machine in your cell, you need to copy the users file and groups file to each machine, placing the files in the same location (C:\FileRegistry) on the other systems. (The overhead of keeping registry files synchronized on multiple machines is one reason why the sample custom registry isn't intended for use in a production cell, in addition to the fact that it's not a secure form of registry.) The operating system ID used by the WebSphere processes (Deployment Manager, node agents, and application servers) must have read access to the directory where the registry files are stored (e.g., C:\FileRegistry) and read access to the actual registry files (e.g., users.registry and groups.registry).

Configure WebSphere Security

Next, you'll perform the tasks to configure WebSphere security:

- configure the user registry
- configure the Lightweight Third Party Authentication (LTPA) mechanism
- enable security

The LTPA mechanism uses an encoded byte string referred to as a *token* that is created when a user or process authenticates (i.e., "logs in"). The LTPA token holds an identity and a configurable expiration time. The token is passed as a cookie back and forth between browser requests to provide the browser user's identity to the application server. When standalone Java clients authenticate, they get an LTPA token as well, and it is passed along with remote procedure calls to provide an identity to the remote WebSphere application server receiving the call. If more than one server is involved in fulfilling a request, the LTPA token is passed along with calls to other servers so that all servers in the request chain have evidence of an authenticated identity before executing a given request. After the expiration time, the LTPA token is no longer valid, and a user or process must re-authenticate to receive a new token.

The following discussion assumes you have a user named wasadmin that the WebSphere processes can use to authenticate. (We use the placeholder *<password>* instead of whatever password wasadmin actually has in your users file.) To configure WebSphere security, take the following steps.

Step 5.   Start the Deployment Manager (or your standalone application server), and open the admin console in a browser: **http://dmgr-host:9060/admin**. For a standalone server, specify was-host instead of dmgr-host in this URL.

Step 6.   In the left navigation pane of the console, expand **Security** and select **Global Security**.

Note: You may find it useful to shrink the context-sensitive help panel that appears in the upper-right corner of the admin console. This panel tends to get in the way of items you're trying to work with in this area of the console.

Step 7.   In the **User registries** section on the right side of the main panel (shown in Figure 16-1), select **Custom** to specify a custom user registry.

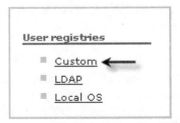

Figure 16-1: Custom user registry option

Under **General Properties** (Figure 16-2 shows this section), specify the options as follows:

a. For the **Server user ID**, enter **wasadmin**.

b. For the **Server user password**, enter *<password>*.

c. For the **Custom registry class name**, use the default value, **com.ibm.websphere.security.FileRegistrySample**.

d. Select the option to "Ignore case for authorization" (to disregard case in group names).

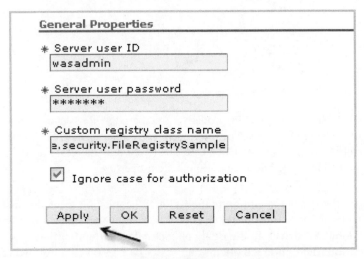

Figure 16-2: Custom user registry configuration parameters

After specifying the options, click **Apply** (otherwise, you'll lose your changes when you go to the custom properties in the next step). A message at the top of the main console panel informs you that configuration changes have been made. You needn't save these changes yet because you're going to make additional changes.

Step 8.   On the right side of the panel, under **Additional Properties**, select **Custom properties**. Click **New**, and add a new property as shown in Figure 16-3. In the **Name** field, enter **usersFile**. (You must use exactly this name to match the name used in the FileRegistrySample class.) In the **Value** field, enter **c:/FileRegistry/users.registry**. (You can use a forward slash, or /, in path names regardless of the underlying operating system. The JVM will use the proper syntax for the host file system.) For **Description**, enter **User registry** (or whatever text you prefer). Then click **OK**.

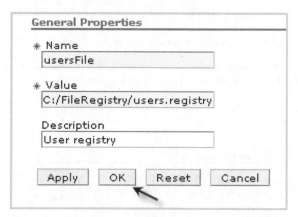

Figure 16-3: Specifying the users registry file

Step 9.   Click **New** again to add a property named groupsFile as shown in Figure 16-4. In the **Value** field, enter **c:/FileRegistry/groups.registry**. For the **Description**, enter **Groups registry**. Click **OK**, and save your changes. Figure 16-5 shows the newly created users and groups file properties.

Step 10.   Next, you need to configure the LTPA authentication mechanism. To do so, return to the admin console's Global Security panel (navigate to **Security| Global Security**). In the right column under **Authentication**, expand **Authentication mechanisms** and select **LTPA**. Take the following steps under **General Properties** (shown in Figure 16-6).

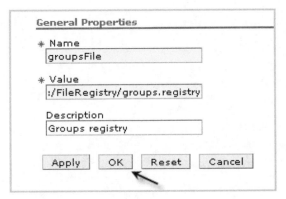

Figure 16-4: Specifying the groups registry file

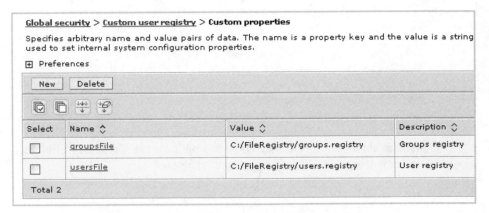

Figure 16-5: Custom properties list

a. Specify and confirm a password. (The LTPA password is used to encrypt and decrypt the LTPA keys for the cell.)

b. Accept the default **Timeout** value, or specify the cache timeout in seconds if you want a different value for your environment.

c. A key file is unnecessary for your purposes, so you can leave the last field blank. (You use LTPA keys when application servers in multiple WebSphere cells need to work together securely. The keys are used to encrypt the LTPA token that's passed among the servers.)

d. Click **Apply**.

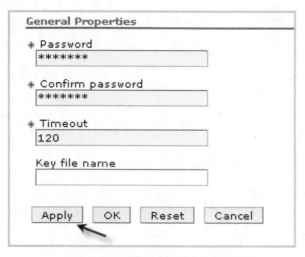

Figure 16-6: LTPA general properties

Step 11. On the right, under **Additional Properties,** you can optionally use the **Single signon (SSO)** item (shown in Figure 16-7) to set the single sign-on domain for LTPA. The SSO domain is the domain assigned to the LTPA cookie that WebSphere generates and returns to the browser. When you don't specify a domain name, the cookie is assigned the domain name of the host used in the URL of the request. For development purposes, you can leave the SSO domain blank. We'll talk more about this option when we cover configuring security using a local operating system registry.

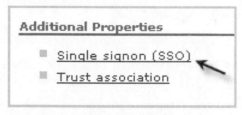

Figure 16-7: Single signon (SSO) property

Step 12. Save your configuration changes.

Step 13. Now, you're ready to enable WebSphere security. To do so, return again to the Global Security panel (**Security|Global Security**), and specify the General Properties as shown in Figure 16-8.

    a. Select to **Enable global security**.

    b. Clear the **Enforce Java 2 security** check box unless you plan to use Java 2 security in your development (this usually isn't the case).

    c. Leave the next two options, **Enforce fine-grained JCA security** and **Use domain-qualified user IDs**, unchecked.

    d. For development purposes, you can leave the **Cache timeout** value at the default of 600 seconds. The timeout value determines how often WebSphere refreshes items in the security caches. The setting of this value is very situation-specific and should be determined during the performance testing phase of development. For guidelines on setting the cache timeout value, consult the WebSphere V6 Information Center, *http://publib.boulder.ibm.com/infocenter/ws60help/index.jsp*.

    e. In the **Active protocol** list, select **CSI**. CSI, which stands for the Object Management Group's (OMG's) Common Secure Interoperability Version 2 (CSIv2) protocol, is the authentication protocol used for Remote Method Invocation/Internet Inter-ORB Protocol (RMI/IIOP) calls among application server Object Request Brokers (ORBs). (If you need backward compatibility with WebSphere 4.*x* servers, set the **Active protocol** value to **CSI and SAS**.)

    f. For the **Active authentication mechanism**, select **Lightweight Third Party Authentication (LTPA)**.

    g. For **Active user registry**, select **Custom user registry**.

When you're finished with this panel, click **Apply**.

Step 14.   If something isn't configured properly, you'll receive an error message at the top of the viewing pane after applying your changes. Common issues are incorrect paths to the registry files and an incorrect user ID or password for the server ID. Until you correct all problems, security won't be enabled.

If you've configured everything correctly, you'll receive a collection of warning messages similar to those shown in Figure 16-9. The main thing to realize is that you need to make sure all nodes in the development cell are synchronized and then stop and start all processes in the cell (Deployment Manager, all node agents, and all application servers).

After reviewing the messages, save your configuration changes.

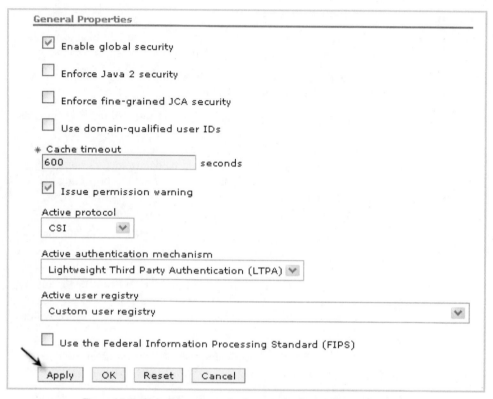

Figure 16-8: Global security general properties for custom registry type

Step 15. Log out of the admin console.

Step 16. Stop and start the Deployment Manager (or the standalone application server). If you're configuring security for a development cell that includes more than one machine, you need to copy the user and group registry files to the same directory (C:\FileRegistry) in the file system of each machine in the cell. (You may already have copied these files to the other machines in your cell in Step 4 above.) You also need to stop and start all node agents and application servers in the cell.

Step 17. Open an admin console in your browser. You can still use the nonsecure URL, http://dmgr-host:9060/admin. You'll be redirected to a secure URL, https://dmgr-host:9043/ibm/console/logon.jsp.

⊟ Messages

⚠ Changes have been made to your local configuration. Click <u>Save</u> to apply changes to the master configuration.

ℹ The server may need to be restarted for these changes to take effect.

⚠ The domain name for single signon is not defined. The Web browser defaults the domain name to the host name that runs the Web application. Single signon is restricted to the application server host name and does not work with other application server host names in the domain.

⚠ The security configuration is enabled or modified in a Network Deployment environment. The following steps need to be followed so that all the processes in this environment have the same security run-time settings: 1) Verify that all nodes are synchronized with these security configuration changes before stopping these processes. 2) If any node agents are currently stopped, issue a manual **syncNode** command before starting that node agent. 3) Stop all of the processes in the entire cell, including the deployment manager, node agents, and Application Servers. 4) Restart all of the processes in the cell; restart the deployment manager and node agents first, then Application Servers.

⚠ If Java 2 security is not enabled, the Java virtual machine (JVM) system resources are not protected. For example, applications can read and write to files on file systems, listen to sockets, exit the Application Server process, and so on. However, by enabling Java 2 security, applications might fail to run if the required permissions are not granted to the applications.

ℹ If any of the fields are changed, save the configuration and then stop and restart the server.

Figure 16-9: Security configuration warning messages

Your browser will warn you about receiving a Public Key Infrastructure (PKI) certificate certified by an unknown certificate authority. To proceed, you must accept the certificate. (To avoid this warning in the future, you can install the certificate in your browser. For details about this process, see Chapter 18.)

If you're using the Mozilla Firefox browser, you'll receive a separate warning about a domain name mismatch on the certificate. Click **OK** to proceed. (If you're using Microsoft Internet Explorer, the warnings about the unknown certificate authority and the domain name mismatch appear in one pop-up.)

Step 18. A login panel (Figure 16-10) is displayed next, prompting you to specify a user name and password. The first time you log in, you'll need to use the user name and password you specified for the server user ID when you configured global security. For the user ID, enter **wasadmin**. For the password, enter *<password>*. Then click **Log in** (or press Enter). You should now be logged in to the admin console.

479

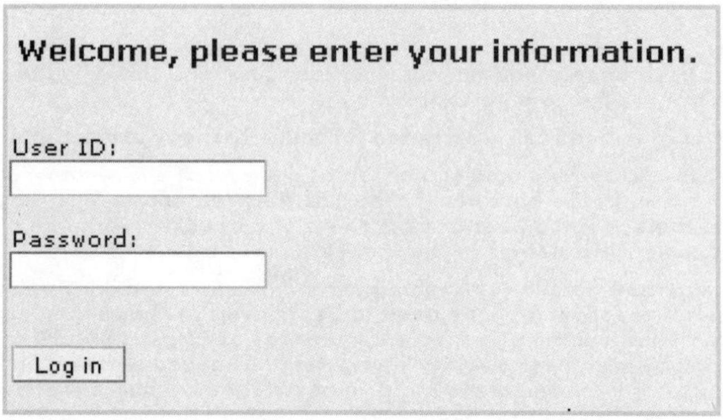

Welcome, please enter your information.

User ID:

Password:

Log in

Figure 16-10: WebSphere login panel requesting a user ID and password

Step 19. Even in development, it's unwise to let administrators use the same user ID for admin console login that the WebSphere processes use for authentication. (Instead, each administrator should use his or her own user name so you can track who makes changes to the configuration.) To address this issue, you can define a console administrators group.

To create the group, expand **System Administration**, select **Console Settings|Console Groups**, and click **Add** to add a new group. Specify the **General Properties** options (shown in Figure 16-11) as follows:

a. For the group name, enter **SysAdmins**, the name of the administrators group used in the sample groups.registry file. (You can use whatever name you like as long as you include it in the groups registry file and give it some members.)

b. In the **Role(s)** list, select **Administrator**. (We cover WebSphere roles in more depth later in this chapter.)

Click **OK** after entering these options, and save your configuration changes. Figure 16-12 shows the newly created SysAdmins console administrators group.

Step 20. Log out of the admin console.

Step 21. Bounce (i.e., stop and start) the Deployment Manager to have the configuration change take effect. You must perform this step when first adding a new

Figure 16-11: SysAdmins group general properties

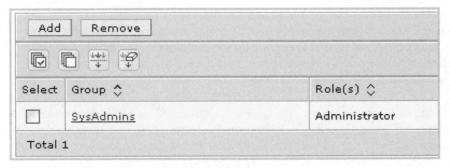

Figure 16-12: SysAdmins console administrators group

group or user to Console Groups or Console Users. Changing group membership in the groups registry (e.g., adding or removing members to or from the SysAdmins group) doesn't require a bounce of the Deployment Manager. Note that the security cache timeout affects how quickly changes in the groups registry take effect. If you want changes to be immediate, you need to bounce the Deployment Manager immediately after changing the groups registry.

Step 22. Log back in to the admin console using a member of the SysAdmins group. In this example, user admin1 is a member of this group, so you can enter **admin1**

481

for the user ID and *<password>* for the password on the login panel. (User admin1 is one of the users other than wasadmin assigned to the SysAdmins group used in the sample groups.registry file.) At this point, you've successfully configured WebSphere security using the sample custom registry.

Configuring Security Using the Local Operating System Registry

WebSphere supports the use of the local operating system registry for user and group information. For Unix operating systems, the WebSphere processes (Deployment Manager, node agents, and application servers) need to run as root to decrypt the passwords and use the APIs required to access user and group information. For Windows operating systems, the processes need to run as an administrator with "Act as part of operating system" rights to use the APIs required to authenticate users or access user and group information in the Windows registry.

For security reasons, most Unix system administrators permit as few processes as possible to run as root, and WebSphere is not typically run as root. Thus, it's unusual to use the local operating system registry when running WebSphere in Unix environments.

The operating system user which the WebSphere process runs needn't be the same user you specify in the WebSphere server user ID when configuring WebSphere security. For example, it would be unusual to use root as the server user ID in a Unix environment, but root is the user that the WebSphere processes need to run as if you use the local operating system registry for the WebSphere user registry.

Likewise, on Windows, the user ID specified as either the user account attribute of the Windows services defined for the WebSphere processes or the user ID of the user that starts the WebSphere processes from the command line can be one thing, and the WebSphere *server user ID* used by the WebSphere processes to authenticate and obtain WebSphere credentials can be another.

On Windows, the server user ID name can't be the same as the host name of any machine in the cell. If a machine is named george, for example, the server user ID specified for the WebSphere processes to use for WebSphere authentication can't be george. If a Windows machine is part of a Windows domain, the domain user registry is checked, and then the local user registry is checked.

Configure Users and Groups

For purposes of describing the steps involved in configuring security using the local operating system registry, we'll assume you've defined at least two users, wasadmin and admin1, and one group named WASAdmins. In a realistic setting, you'd define groups relevant to the applications running in your environment, mapping the groups to roles defined by your application security constraints. The users would be all the users defined in the Windows domain registry as well as in the local registries of the machines on which WebSphere is running.

Configure WebSphere Security

If you're configuring WebSphere security for a cell, the Deployment Manager must be running. If you're configuring security for a standalone application server, that server needs to be running. After starting the appropriate system, take the following steps to configure WebSphere security using the local operating system registry.

Step 1.   Open a browser, and enter the URL for the admin console: **http://dmgr-host:9060/admin.** (For a standalone server, specify was-host instead of dmgr-host in the URL.)

Step 2.   Expand **Security**, and select **Global Security**.

Step 3.   In the **User registries** section of the main panel (shown in Figure 16-13), select **Local OS**. Then, under **General Properties** (Figure 16-14), enter

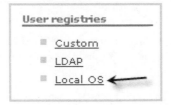

Figure 16-13: Local operating system user registry option

Figure 16-14: Local operating system registry general properties

wasadmin for the server user ID and *<password>* for the password. Click **OK**, and save your changes.

Step 4.   Next, configure the LTPA authentication mechanism:

a. Return to the admin console's Global Security panel (**Security|Global Security**).

b. On the right, under **Authentication**, expand **Authentication mechanisms** and select **LTPA**.

c. Specify and confirm a password.

d. The timeout value for the LTPA token controls how long the token is valid in units of minutes. The default of 120 minutes is appropriate for most uses, so you should leave this option as is unless you have a specific, well-understood need to change it. Securely communicating servers will need to reauthenticate after two hours to obtain a new LTPA token. If you do change the timeout, be sure the value you specify is greater than the security cache timeout specified on the Global Security panel. (You don't want invalid LTPA tokens hanging around in the cache.)

e. If you're configuring a cell that will have servers interacting with servers in other cells, specify a key file.

f. Click **Apply**.

g. If desired, use the **Single Sign-on (SSO)** item under **Additional Properties** to set the SSO domain. (For more information about this option, see the following paragraphs.)

h. Click **OK**, and save your configuration changes.

For development purposes, you can leave the SSO domain blank. If you're setting up a production configuration (or a test environment that needs to mimic a production environment), you'll likely want to configure the SSO domain. The online help provides a good description of this process.

Figure 16-15 shows the options you use to enable single sign-on.

In the **Domain name** field, the string to the right of the first period specifies the domain name. (Unless you specify a fully qualified host name, a leading period is appropriate in the value you provide here.)

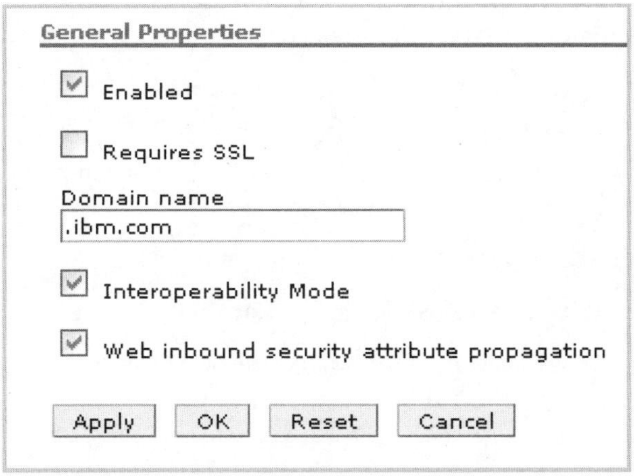

Figure 16-15: Single signon general properties

You can specify more than one domain by using a semicolon (;), comma (,), pipe (|), or space as a separation character. WebSphere will set the domain for the LTPA cookie to the first domain in the list that matches something in the host name of the request URL. (There's no attempt to make the "best match.") Another option is to specify the value **UseDomainFromURL**, which causes the WebSphere server to set the LTPA cookie to the domain of the host name used in the URL of the request. (If you leave the SSO domain empty, the default behavior is to use the domain from the URL. Likewise, if nothing in the SSO domain list matches the host name in the request URL, WebSphere uses the domain from the URL.)

Step 5.   To enable WebSphere security, return to the Global Security panel (**Security| Global Security**), and specify the options as shown in Figure 16-16. You'll notice that with the exception of the user registry type, you specify these options just as you did for the custom registry configuration.

a. Select **Enable global security**.

b. Clear the **Enforce Java 2 security** option unless you plan to use Java 2 security. (It's uncommon to select to enforce Java 2 security because of the additional processing overhead this option imposes at runtime. It would make sense to enforce Java 2 security if you were running an application whose author or source you didn't trust. Most sites, however, run only trusted applications.)

c. Leave the **Enforce fine-grained JCA security** and **Use domain-qualified user IDs** options unchecked.

d. Leave the **Cache timeout** value at the default of 600 seconds unless you have performance results that indicate you should do otherwise.

e. For Active protocol, select CSI. (For backward compatibility with WebSphere 4.x servers, select CSI and SAS.)

f. Set **Active authentication mechanism** to LTPA.

g. For **Active user registry**, choose **Local OS**.

When you're finished with this panel, click **Apply**.

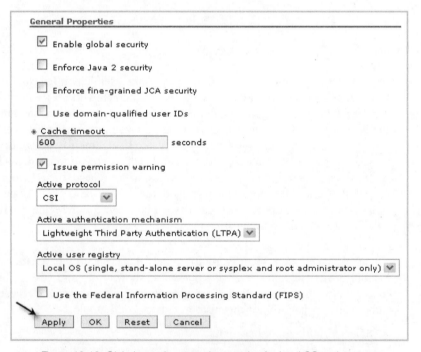

Figure 16-16: Global security general properties for local OS registry type

Step 6. If you've configured something incorrectly, you'll see an error message at the top of the viewing pane. For security configurations using a Local OS registry, a common issue is an incorrect user ID or password for the server ID. Until you correct all problems, security won't be enabled.

If you've configured everything properly, you'll receive warnings about the need to make sure all nodes in the cell are synchronized and to stop and start all processes in the cell. Review the messages, and save your configuration changes.

Step 7.   Log out of the admin console.

Step 8.   Stop and start the Deployment Manager (or the standalone application server). You also need to stop and start all node agents and application servers in the cell.

Additional Tasks

At this point, WebSphere security is enabled, but there are some other things you need to do to finish the configuration. One task is to create a console group with Administrator access to the WebSphere console. We describe the steps for doing that next. The other tasks are to replace the default digital certificate store files that come with WebSphere and to configure the browsers of your WebSphere administrators to trust the self-signed certificate you create for use by the WebSphere processes. We explain the steps for these tasks at the end of the chapter.

Step 9.   Open an admin console in your browser. You can still use the nonsecure URL, http://dmgr-:9060/admin. You'll be redirected to a secure URL, https://dmgr-host:9043/ibm/console/logon.jsp. As in the custom registry scenario, your browser will warn you about an unknown certificate authority and a domain name mismatch on the certificate. Click **OK** to proceed.

Step 10.   The first time you log in, you'll need to use the user name and password you specified for the server user ID when you configured global security. In the login panel, enter **wasadmin** for the user ID and *<password>* for the password. Then click **Log in** (or press Enter). You should now be logged in to the admin console.

Step 11.   To define a console administrators group, you use the same method as for the custom registry. Expand **System Administration**, select **Console Settings| Console Groups**, and click **Add** to add a new group. Under **General Properties**, enter the group name **WASAdmins**. (This is the name of a group created in the Windows registry. You can use whatever name you like as long as you define it in the Windows registry and give it at least one member.) In the **Role(s)** list, select **Administrator**.

Click **OK**, and save your changes. Figure 16-17 shows the newly created WASAdmins console administrators group.

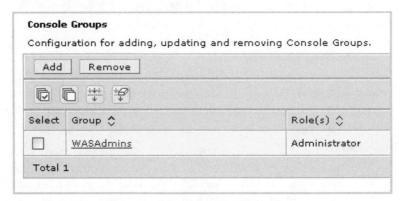

Figure 16-17: WASAdmins console group

Step 12.   Log out of the admin console.

Step 13.   Stop and start the Deployment Manager to have your configuration change to take effect.

Step 14.   Log back in to the admin console using a user that's a member of the WASAdmins group. In this example, user admin1 is a member of the WASAdmins group, so you can enter **admin1** for the user ID and *<pass-word>* for the password on the login panel. (In your environment, the members of WASAdmins would be the people trusted to administer the cell.)

At this point, you should replace the default key and trust files that come with WebSphere and configure your administrators' browsers to trust the self-signed certificate you create for use by the WebSphere processes. We describe the steps for these tasks later. (See this chapter's "Replacing the Default Digital Certificate Store Files" section and the "Importing a Public Certificate into a Browser" section of Chapter 18.)

Enabling WebSphere Security Using an LDAP Registry

In this section, you'll enable WebSphere security using a Lightweight Directory Access Protocol registry. LDAP is a well-established directory protocol with many provider options. LDAP registries can handle the large scale and high performance needs of

Internet Web applications. For production environments, an LDAP registry is the recommended registry to use.

This example uses an instance of the IBM Tivoli Directory Server (ITDS) as the LDAP server. The configuration of security to use an LDAP server from other vendors is similar. We assume you've installed and configured an instance of ITDS. For step-by-step instructions on this process, see Chapter 17.

In this description, the WebSphere server identity in the LDAP registry is uid=wasadmin, cn=roles,dc=ibm,dc=com. (Here, dc=ibm,dc=com is the root of the LDAP directory tree used for this example. In your specific case, you'd set up an identity in LDAP that's appropriate to your site and organization and that fits into your LDAP directory structure.) We assume the LDAP registry has an entry of object class inetOrgPerson with this distinguished name (DN). The server identity is what the WebSphere processes use to authenticate themselves to obtain a valid WebSphere login context. (As with a custom or local OS registry, this WebSphere server identity is independent of, and unrelated to, the operating system "process identity" associated with the WebSphere processes.)

The sample configuration doesn't use Secure Sockets Layer (SSL) communications between the LDAP server and the WebSphere processes. Because enabling WebSphere security is somewhat complicated, it's a good idea to first set up the configuration with non-SSL communications to make sure WebSphere security is working properly. Once you have WebSphere security working, enabling SSL communications between the LDAP server and the WebSphere processes is relatively straightforward. Any problems you encounter at that point are likely related to something wrong with the SSL configuration. (For more information about enabling SSL between WebSphere and ITDS, see Chapter 18.)

The steps for configuring WebSphere security using an LDAP registry are similar to configuring WebSphere security using a local OS registry. Obviously, the registry configuration details are different. Before performing the following steps, make sure the Deployment Manager and the IBM Tivoli Directory Server instance you plan to use are running.

Step 1.   Start an admin console: **http://dmgr-host:9060/admin**. (For a standalone server, specify was-host instead of dmgr-host in the URL.)

Step 2.   Expand **Security**, and select **Global Security**.

Step 3.   In the **User registries** section of the main panel (Figure 16-18), select **LDAP**.

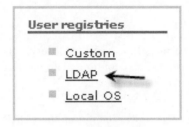

Figure 16-18: LDAP user registry option

Step 4.   Fill in the following attributes on the next panel (Figure 16-19) to define the LDAP user registry.

   a. For **Server user ID**, enter **wasadmin**. This is the user ID that the WebSphere processes use to authenticate themselves when they start. The LDAP directory must contain an entry with a uid attribute value that's the same as the string entered here. In the simple directory tree assumed for this example, one member of the tree is uid=wasadmin,cn=roles,dc=ibm,dc=com. (You can enter a fully qualified distinguished name in this field, but the convention is to use the value of the uid attribute.)

   b. For the **Server user password**, enter *<password>* (i.e., the password you used for the wasadmin entry in your LDAP directory tree).

   c. For **Host**, enter the fully qualified name of your LDAP host.

   d. For **Port**, enter **389**, the default non-SSL port for LDAP servers. If you used a different port when configuring your LDAP server, enter that value here instead. (When you set up SSL communications between the WebSphere processes and the directory server, you'll specify the SSL port of the directory server, which by default is 636.)

   e. The **Base distinguished name (DN)** entry specifies the root of the portion of the LDAP directory that the WebSphere processes will search for users and groups. In this example, we've used **dc=ibm,dc=com** as the root of the directory tree.

   f. The **Bind distinguished name (DN)** entry specifies the full distinguished name of the principal used by WebSphere processes to bind (i.e., open a connection) to the directory server to search the directory tree (starting at the base DN) for users and groups. The bind DN needs "search" and "compare" access rights to the entries in the portion of the directory tree rooted at the base DN. If you leave this field blank, the LDAP directory must grant anonymous connections search and compare access to the directory tree rooted at the base DN. The bind distinguished name needn't be the DN for the same identity as the WebSphere server user ID, but it commonly is the same.

g. Leave the **Search timeout** field at the default value of 120 unless your testing shows that you need to change this setting.

h. Leave the **Reuse connection** check box selected (unless you have a load balancer in front of a cluster of directory servers and the load balancer doesn't support affinity).

i. Leave the **Ignore case for authorization** check box selected. (For ITDS, this option must be checked. For more details about this field, see the WebSphere InfoCenter.)

j. For now, leave the **SSL enabled** option unchecked. Chapter 18 includes a section that describes the steps to take to enable SSL communications between the directory server and the WebSphere processes.

k. The **SSL configuration** entry references the SSL configuration repertoire that in turn points to where the WebSphere processes will find their key and trust files to use for opening SSL connections. Because for now SSL communications aren't enabled, you don't care about this setting. Leave it as it is. You'll learn more about SSL configuration repertoires later.

l. Click **Apply**. (You need to edit some items under **Additional Properties** next, but you must click **Apply** on this panel before doing so, or the values you've entered won't be persisted to the configuration work area.)

Step 5. Next, under **Additional Properties**, click "Advanced Lightweight Directory Access Protocol (LDAP) user registry settings." (You can see this option in the upper-right corner of Figure 16-19.) Make the following changes to the advanced settings, as shown in Figure 16-20.

a. The simple directory tree assumed for this example uses the objectclass inetOrgPerson, not ePerson. You therefore need to change the **User filter** value to use inetOrgPerson. Note that the search is on the UID attribute of the given object class.

b. Leave the **Group filter** value as is, but note the object classes used in the search filter and the fact that common name (CN) is the matching attribute.

c. You can leave the remaining attributes exposed on this panel at their defaults. Make a mental note that this panel is available for changing the more sophisticated aspects of the directory server interface. The InfoCenter provides a reasonably good description of each of these attributes.

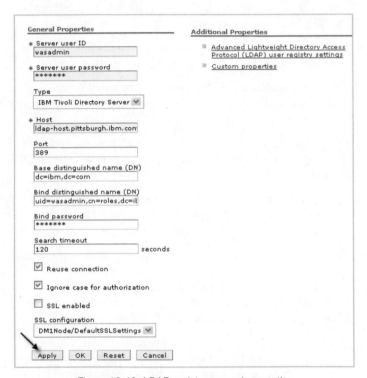

Figure 16-19: LDAP registry general properties

d. Click **OK**.

When you return to the main LDAP configuration panel, you'll see that the directory's Type value has been changed from IBM Tivoli Directory Server to Custom. This change occurred because you modified the user filter. Leave the directory type as Custom.

Step 6. Save your configuration. (You're not finished configuring, but now is a good time to save what you've set up so far.)

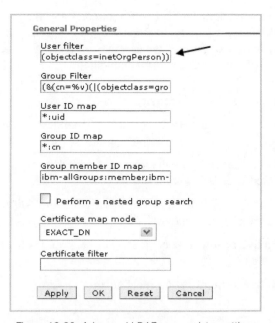

Figure 16-20: Advanced LDAP user registry settings

Step 7.   Next, configure the LTPA authentication mechanism.

a. Return to the admin console's Global Security panel (**Security|Global Security**).

b. On the right, under **Authentication**, expand **Authentication mechanisms** and select **LTPA**.

c. Specify and confirm a password. (The LTPA password is used to encrypt and decrypt the LTPA keys for the cell.)

d. If you're configuring a cell that will have servers interacting with servers in other cells, specify a key file.

e. Click **Apply**.

f. If desired, click **Single Sign-on (SSO)** under **Additional Properties** to set the SSO domain. (For more information about this option, see the local OS registry discussion.)

g. Click **OK**, and save your configuration.

Step 8. Now, to enable WebSphere security, return to the Global Security panel (**Security|Global Security**), and specify the options as shown in Figure 16-21. Again, with the exception of the user registry type, you specify these options the same as for the earlier registry configurations.

a. Select **Enable global security**.

b. Clear the **Enforce Java 2 security** option unless you plan to use Java 2 security.

c. Leave the **Enforce fine-grained JCA security** and **Use domain-qualified user IDs** options unchecked.

d. Leave the **Cache timeout** value at the default of **600** seconds unless your performance results indicate you should do otherwise.

e. For **Active protocol**, select **CSI**. (For backward compatibility with WebSphere 4.*x* servers, select **CSI and SAS**.)

f. Set **Active authentication mechanism** to LTPA.

Figure 16-21: Global security general properties for LDAP registry type

g. For **Active user registry**, choose **Lightweight Directory Access Protocol (LDAP) user registry**.

When you're finished with this panel, click **Apply**.

Step 9. If something isn't configured properly, you'll receive an error message at the top of the viewing pane. For security configurations using an LDAP registry, common issues are often caused by typos. Check for the following problems:

- incorrect identifier provided for the WebSphere server identity
- incorrect password for the server identity
- incorrect user filter (make sure the objects used to represent users in the LDAP directory are of the object class specified in the filter)
- incorrect host name or port number for the LDAP server
- incorrect base distinguished name
- incorrect bind distinguished name or password
- improper access privilege for the bind distinguished name
- network issues between the WebSphere processes and the LDAP server

Until you correct all problems, security won't be enabled.

If you've configured everything correctly, you'll see warnings about the need to make sure all nodes in the cell are synchronized and to stop and start all processes in the cell. Review the messages, and save your configuration changes.

Step 10. Log out of the admin console.

Step 11. Stop and start the Deployment Manager (or standalone application server) and all node agents and application servers in the cell. Make sure all WebSphere processes restart properly by checking the SystemOut.log file for each process. If all nodes in the cell didn't synchronize properly with the Deployment Manager before its shutdown, you need to run the syncNode utility for the nodes that aren't starting properly. You can tell you have a synchronization issue on a given node if the node agent can't contact the Deployment Manager because it isn't authenticated:

```
NodeSync       E   ADMS0005E: The system is unable to generate syn-
chronization request: javax.management.JMRuntimeException:
ADMN0022E: Access is denied for the getRepositoryEpoch operation on
ConfigRepository MBean because of insufficient or empty credentials.
```

If you receive this error, it's possible that either the Deployment Manager or the node agent was shut down very quickly after you enabled security, providing insufficient time for the node agent to obtain the latest configuration with security enabled. Another possibility is that the node that's having a problem wasn't running when you enabled security.

You run the syncNode command from a DOS command shell in the <PROFILE-ROOT>\bin directory on the host of the node you need to synchronize. The command's first argument is the host name of the Deployment Manager host. The second argument is the SOAP port used by the Deployment Manager, which defaults to 8879. Once security is enabled, you also need to provide a user name and password to syncNode.

```
syncNode dmgr-host 8879 -user wasadmin -password <password>
```

Additional Tasks

At this point, you've enabled WebSphere security, but, as with the local OS registry configuration, there are some other things you need to do to finish the configuration. You should create a console group with Administrator access to the WebSphere console. And you need to replace WebSphere's default digital certificate store files and configure your administrators' browsers to trust the self-signed certificate for use by the WebSphere processes. We describe the steps for the first task next and give those for the other tasks in the next section.

For this description, we assume there's a group (of object class groupOfNames or groupOfUniqueNames) defined in the LDAP registry with a common name (cn) of WASAdmins with at least one member.

Step 12. Open an admin console in your browser. You can still use the nonsecure URL, http://dmgr-host:9060/admin. You'll be redirected to a secure URL, https://dmgr-host:9043/ibm/console/logon.jsp. Your browser will warn you about an unknown certificate authority and a domain name mismatch on the certificate. Click **OK** to proceed.

Step 13. The first time you log in, you'll need to use the user name and password you specified for the server user ID when you configured global security. In the login panel, enter **wasadmin** for the user ID and *<password>* for the password. Then click **Log in** (or press Enter). You should now be logged into the admin console.

Step 14. To define a console administrators group, expand **System Administration**, select **Console Settings|Console Groups**, and click **Add** to add a new group. Under **General Properties**, enter the group name **WASAdmins**. (This is the common name of a group created in the LDAP registry. You can use whatever name you want as long as you define it in the LDAP registry and give it at least one member.) In the **Role(s)** list, select **Administrator**.

Click **OK**, and save your changes. Figure 16-22 shows the newly created WASAdmins console administrators group.

Figure 16-22: WASAdmins console group

Step 15. Log out of the admin console.

Step 16. Stop and start the Deployment Manager to have your configuration changes take effect.

Step 17. Log back in to the admin console using a user that's a member of the WASAdmins group. In this example, user george is a member of WASAdmins. On the login panel, enter **george** for the user ID and *<password>* for the password. (In your environment, the members of WASAdmins would be the people trusted to administer the cell.)

At this point, you should replace the default key and trust files that come with WebSphere and configure your administrators' browsers to trust the self-signed certificate. The next section describes the steps involved in these tasks.

Replacing the Default Digital Certificate Store Files

For authentication — for example, when creating an SSL connection — WebSphere processes use a digital certificate stored in a *key store file*. This file typically is reserved for the "personal" certificate and private key of the server or client processes. Access to the key store file must be carefully secured. The self-signed certificates of trusted servers (and clients) and the signer certificates from certificate authorities are kept in the *trust store file*. If no trust store file exists, it's assumed that certificates of trusted principals and certificate authorities are in the key store file.

IBM ships WebSphere with a DummyServerKeyFile and a DummyServerTrustFile that you should replace when you enable WebSphere security. This section describes the steps to take to replace these two files. In addition, WebSphere comes with a DummyClientKeyFile and DummyClientTrustFile, which you also should replace.

Although not a requirement, it's customary to use the same key and trust files for all the WebSphere server processes in a cell. This practice minimizes the overhead of managing the digital certificates associated with a cell. Once you create new key and trust files for the Deployment Manager node, you'll copy them to the other nodes (machines) that are members of the cell. (If you make changes to the key and trust files, you'll need to recopy the files to all nodes in the cell.)

The digital certificates are associated with WebSphere artifacts known as *SSL configuration repertoires*. You can view the SSL configuration repertoires in the admin console by expanding **Security** and selecting **SSL**. Figure 16-23 shows a sample repertoire list. As the figure shows, a DefaultSSLSettings repertoire is created for each node in the cell.

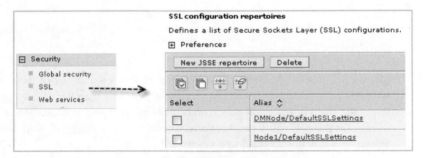

Figure 16-23: SSL configuration repertoires

Step 1.   Open the DefaultSSLSettings for your Deployment Manager node by clicking the appropriate line in the repertoire list.

Step 2. Several attributes are associated with an SSL repertoire, but the ones of immediate interest are the key file and the trust file. Figure 16-24 shows these attributes.

Figure 16-24: Key file and trust file attributes

The root directory of the default location for these files is defined by the WebSphere variable ${USER_INSTALL_ROOT}, which in the notation used in this book is <DMGR-PROFILE-ROOT>. ${USER_INSTALL_ROOT} isn't where the product is installed; it's the root-level directory where the WebSphere profile is located.

A number of transports defined for application servers, node agents, and the Deployment Manager reference the DefaultSSLSettings SSL configuration repertoire. If you decided to replace this repertoire, you'd need to edit all the secure transports to reference the replacement for DefaultSSLSettings. The InfoCenter provides the complete list of where DefaultSSLSettings is referenced. (We recommend you continue to use the DefaultSSLSettings repertoire. The important thing to do is replace the dummy key and trust files it references.)

Replace the DummyServerKeyFile and DummyServerTrustFile

In the next steps, you'll create a new key file and a new trust file to replace the DummyServerKeyFile.jks and DummyServerTrustFile.jks files. You'll use the IBM Key Management (iKeyman) utility to create the new files. While following the instructions given here, use <DMGR-PROFILE-ROOT> if you're in a Network Deployment environment and <PROFILE-ROOT> if you're performing the step in a standalone server environment.

Step 3. To start the iKeyman utility, open a DOS command window, change to the <WASV6ROOT>\bin directory, and enter **ikeyman.bat**. (If you want to open the dummy key or trust file, use the password shipped with WebSphere for access to these files, **WebAS**.)

Step 4.   Take the following steps to create a new key file.

a. Click the "Create a new key database file" icon in the utility's toolbar, or select **Key Database File|New** from the menu bar. Figure 16-25 shows the panel that's displayed.

b. For **Key database type**, select **JKS** to specify the Java Key Store (JKS) format.

c. For **File Name**, enter **WebSphereServerKeyFile.jks** (or whatever name you prefer).

d. For **Location**, specify the <DMGR-PROFILE-ROOT>\ssl directory (e.g., C:\WAS6\profiles\DM1\ssl) or whatever directory you prefer. (In this example, we use a new subdirectory, /ssl, to hold the certificate files to avoid confusion with the dummy files in directory <DMGR-PROFILE-ROOT>\etc.)

e. Click **OK**.

f. On the next panel (Figure 16-26), specify a password to be used to gain access to the key file. Later, when you define the new attributes for DefaultSSLSettings, this password will be lightly encoded and stored in the security.xml configuration file for the cell.

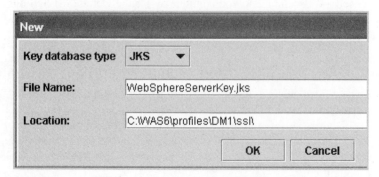

Figure 16-25: Creating a new server key file

The new key file is created now. By default, the iKeyman utility populates the file with a standard collection of signer certificates from commercial certificate authorities, Figure 16-27 shows.

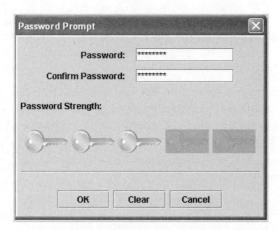

Figure 16-26: Specifying a key file password

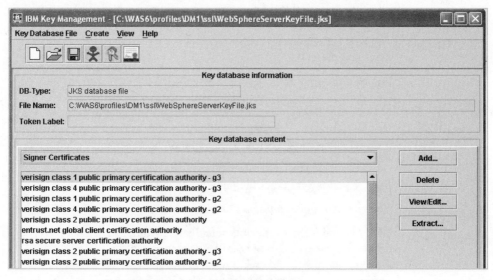

Figure 16-27: Signer certificates in newly created key file

Step 5. Delete all the signer certificates in the key file. (As we mentioned, it's customary to hold only the server certificate in the key file. The signer certificates are held in the trust file.) To delete the certificates:

a. Select the first signer certificate.
b. Scroll to the bottom of the list, and shift-select the last signer certificate.
c. Click the **Delete** button on the right side of the panel.
d. Click **Yes** in response to the delete confirmation pop-up.

Step 6. Next, create a new self-signed certificate for use by the WebSphere server processes:

a. From the pull-down menu at the top of the key database content panel, select the **Personal Certificates** portion of the key database (shown in Figure 16-28).

b. Click the **New Self-Signed** button in the panel's lower-right corner.

c. A dialog (Figure 16-29) pops up to collect certificate attribute values. You'll fill in these fields with values appropriate to your environment.

  i. For **Key Label**, enter **WebSphere Server Certificate** (or whatever label you prefer).

  ii. For **Common Name**, use the fully qualified host name of the Deployment Manager (because this is the digital certificate for the Deployment Manager node). (Note: This certificate will be passed to browsers used to access the admin console; to avoid a warning in the browser about the certificate, the common name should match the host name of the Deployment Manager host.)

  iii. For **Organization**, enter the name of your organization.

  iv. You may fill in the optional attributes or not.

  v. Note that the **Validity Period** defaults to 1 year. You can set this option to whatever period you like. It's important to make a note of the expiration date and create reminders to update the certificate before it expires. When you've enabled WebSphere security, the digital certificates used by the servers must be valid for the servers to run.

  vi. Click **OK** to create the certificate. Figure 16-30 shows the new certificate.

Step 7. Next, you need to extract the self-signed certificate so it can be imported into the server and client trust files. (Because you're using a self-signed certificate, you need to include it in the trust file used by any process that expects to set up an SSL connection with the server providing the key. In steps coming up soon, you'll add this certificate to the WebSphere server trust file. In a later section, you'll add the server certificate into the client trust file used by various WebSphere client processes.)

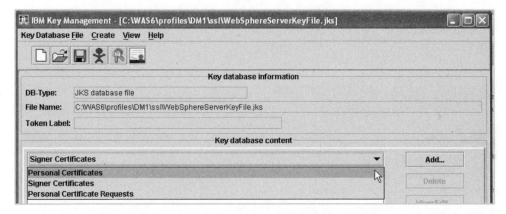

Figure 16-28: Personal Certificates option

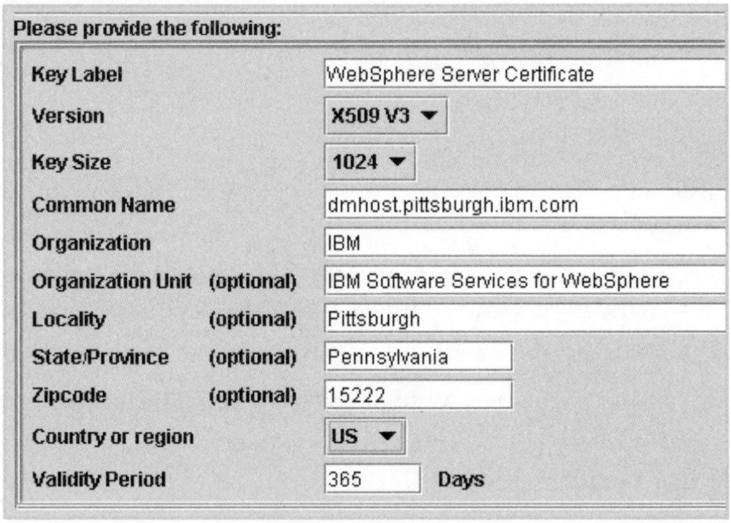

Figure 16-29: Certificate attributes

Figure 16-30: Newly created WebSphere server certificate

To extract the certificate, click the **Extract** button in the lower-right corner
of the database content panel. On the resulting panel (Figure 16-31), provide
a file name (e.g., WebSphereServerCertificate.arm) and a location
(e.g., <DMGR-PROFILE-ROOT>\ssl).

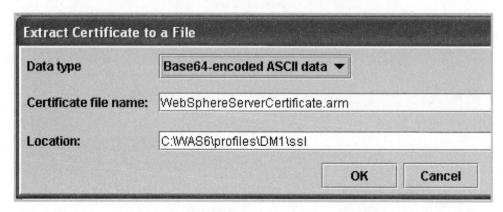

Figure 16-31: Extracting the self-signed certificate

Step 8.   Now, create a new trust file. To do so, you'll repeat the steps you performed
to create the key file, except you can leave the default signer certificates in
the trust store.

   a. Click the "Create a new key database file" icon in the toolbar, or select
   Key Database File|New from the menu bar.

   b. For **Key database type**, select **JKS**.

   c. For **File Name**, enter **WebSphereServerTrustFile.jks** (or whatever name
   you prefer).

   d. For **Location**, specify <DMGR-PROFILE-ROOT>\ssl (or whatever
   directory you prefer).

 e. Click **OK**.

 f. Enter a password to be used to gain administrative access to the trust file.

 The trust file is created and populated with the default signer certificates.

Step 9. Add the WebSphere server certificate to the trust file. (When you've enabled WebSphere security, WebSphere servers communicate with each other over SSL connections. To set up those connections, the servers need to trust each other's certificates.)

 a. With the signer certificates selected in the key database content panel, click the **Add** button.

 b. In the resulting panel (Figure 16-32), browse to the WebSphereServerCertificate.arm file in <DMGR-PROFILE-ROOT>\ssl that you created in the earlier step.

 c. Click **OK**, and specify a certificate label as shown in Figure 16-33.

 d. Click **OK**, and the certificate appears in the signer certificates list.

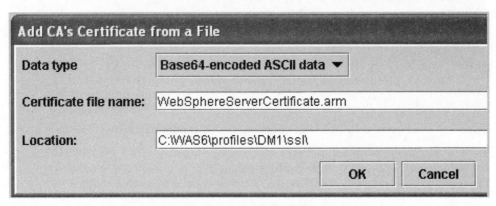

Figure 16-32: Adding the certificate

The next time you open the trust file, the certificate label will be converted to all lower case. The ordering of signer certificates isn't alphabetical, as you can see in Figure 16-34, so you may need to search for the certificate in the list. After you create a self-signed WebSphere client certificate in later steps, you'll add it to the WebSphere server trust file.

Figure 16-33: Certificate label prompt

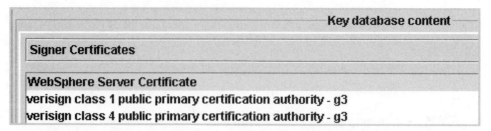

Figure 16-34: WebSphere certificate in signer certificates list

Step 10. Modify the Deployment Manager DefaultSSLSettings repertoire key file and trust file attributes to use the new files you've created.

a. Log in to an admin console, and navigate to **Security|SSL**.

b. Open the DefaultSSLSettings repertoire for the Deployment Manager node.

c. Modify the key file name and password as shown in Figure 16-35. Change the file name to provide the path to the key file you just created, and change the password to the password you created for this file. The password will be lightly encoded and stored in the security.xml configuration file for the cell.

d. Modify the trust file name and password as shown in Figure 16-36. Change the file name to provide the path to the new trust file, and change the password to the password you created for this file.

Step 11. Copy the new key and trust files to the file systems of each node in the WebSphere cell. (You may need to recopy these files to all nodes in the cell if you make changes to them, such as adding certificates to the trust file that you want all the servers to use.)

Figure 16-35: Modifying the key file name and password

Figure 16-36: Modifying the trust file name and password

Step 12. Change the DefaultSSLSettings SSL repertoire for each node in the cell to use the new key and trust files, making the same changes you made in Steps 10c and 10d for the Deployment Manager DefaultSSLSettings repertoire.

Replace the DummyClientKeyFile and DummyClientTrustFile

Once you replace the key and trust files used by the WebSphere server processes, it's important to replace the key and trust files used by client processes (e.g., command-line utilities such as startServer and stopServer) so they can communicate using SSL when WebSphere security is enabled. In this section, we describe how to replace the key and trust files used by the clients and change the soap.client.props file to use the new key and trust files. The steps for this task are the same as those for creating the new server key and trust files. To establish trust between WebSphere server and client processes that use their respective trust files, you'll import the self-signed server certificate into the client trust file and import the self-signed client certificate into the server trust file.

Step 13. Start the iKeyman utility (open a DOS window, change to <DMGR-PROFILE-ROOT>\bin, and enter **ikeyman.bat**).

Step 14. Create a new client key file, specifying the options as shown in Figure 16-37.

    a. For **Key database type**, select **JKS**.
    b. For **File Name**, enter **WebSphereClientKeyFile.jks**.
    c. For **Location**, specify <DMGR-PROFILE-ROOT>\ssl.
    d. Provide and confirm an access password.

Figure 16-37: Creating a new client key file

Step 15. Remove all the signer certificates from the client key file. (The client trust file will hold the signer certificates.)

Step 16. Create a new self-signed personal certificate as shown in Figure 16-38:

    a. For **Key Label**, enter **WebSphere Client Certificate**.

    b. For **Common Name**, enter something unique. (Actually, the name here isn't all that important. When this certificate is used for connections to WebSphere server processes, the common name isn't checked against the host name of the client using the certificate.)

    c. For **Organization**, enter your organization's name.

    d. For self-signed certificates, **Organization Unit** and the remaining attributes are optional.

e. The **Validity Period** defaults to 365 days. Whatever period you provide, make sure you set up a reminder system to replace the certificate near its expiration date. Just as the WebSphere servers will fail when their certificates expire, so too will the clients fail if their certificates expire.

f. Click **OK** to create the certificate. Figure 16-39 shows the new personal certificate.

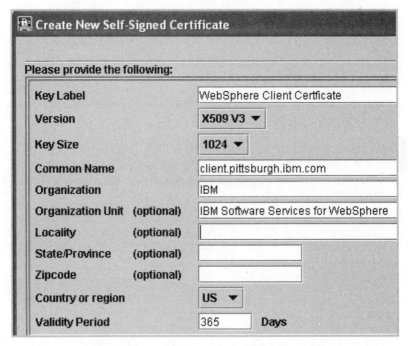

Figure 16-38: Specifying client certificate attributes

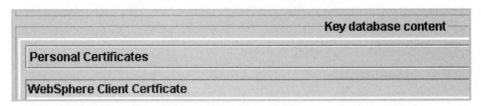

Figure 16-39: Newly created WebSphere client certificate

Step 17. Now, extract the self-signed certificate so it can be imported into the WebSphere server trust file. (Because you're using a self-signed client certificate, you need to include it in the WebSphere server trust file so the WebSphere servers can trust the clients using the key you've created.) In an upcoming step, you'll import the certificate into the WebSphere server trust file.

    a. Click the **Extract** button in the lower-right corner of the key database content panel.

    b. Provide a file name (e.g., WebSphereClientCertificate.arm).

    c. Provide a location (e.g., <DMGR-PROFILE-ROOT>\ssl).

Step 18. Create a new trust file. To do so, you'll repeat the steps you performed to create the key file, except you can leave the default signer certificates in the trust store.

    a. Click the "Create a new key database file" icon in the toolbar, or select **Key Database File|New** from the menu bar.

    b. For **Key database type**, select **JKS**.

    c. For **File Name**, enter **WebSphereClientTrustFile.jks** (or whatever name you prefer).

    d. For **Location**, specify <DMGR-PROFILE-ROOT>\ssl (or whatever directory you prefer).

    e. Click **OK**, and enter a password to be used to gain administrative access to the trust file.

At this point, the trust file is created and populated with the default signer certificates.

Step 19. Add the WebSphere server certificate to the trust file. (When you've enabled WebSphere security, WebSphere client processes communicate with the WebSphere server processes over SSL connections. The clients need to trust the WebSphere server certificates in order to set up those connections. It's recommended that you simplify the administration of these certificates by using the same key file for all WebSphere server processes in a cell. With this approach, you need to manage only one certificate for all WebSphere servers in the cell.)

    a. With the signer certificates selected in the key database content panel, click **Add**.

b. Browse to the WebSphereServerCertificate.arm file in <DMGR-PROFILE-ROOT>\ssl that you created in the earlier step.

c. Click **OK**, and specify a certificate label (e.g., WebSphere Server Certificate).

d. Click **OK**, and the certificate appears in the signer certificates list.

The next time you open the client trust file, the server certificate label will appear in all lowercase letters. Its location among the other signer certificates might not be obvious because they're not presented in alphabetical order.

Step 20. Copy the client key and trust files to the other nodes in the cell. (To simplify administration of these artifacts, it's best to use the same client key and trust files throughout the cell.)

Step 21. Next, add the WebSphere client certificate to the WebSphere server trust file. This step is necessary so that WebSphere servers will trust the self-signed client certificate when the client processes attempt SSL connections. Take the following steps:

a. Open the WebSphere server trust file using iKeyman. (In this example, the "master copy" of the WebSphere server trust file is in <DMGR-PROFILE-ROOT>\ssl and is named WebSphereServerTrustFile.jks. Here, <DMGR-PROFILE-ROOT> is the Deployment Manager profile root. Once you've modified the Deployment Manager trust file, you'll copy it to the other nodes in the cell. More specifically, you'll copy this file to <PROFILE-ROOT>\ssl for each node in the cell, assuming you set up an ssl directory in your node profiles as described for these examples. Because each node tends to be on a separate machine, you'll probably need to use FTP or some other remote file-copy utility to move the trust file to the machine for each node.)

b. Select the signer certificates in the key database content panel, and click **Add**.

c. Browse to the client certificate (WebSphereClientCertificate.arm) in <DMGR-PROFILE-ROOT>\ssl.

d. Click **OK**, and provide a certificate label (e.g., WebSphere Client Certificate).

e. Click **OK**.

The WebSphere client certificate should now appear among the signer certificates trusted by the WebSphere servers, as shown in Figure 16-40. As you can see, once you open and close the WebSphere server trust store, the certificate labels are converted to all lower case and the ordering is not alphabetical.

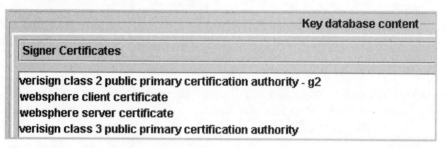

Figure 16-40: WebSphere client certificate added to trusted signer certificates

Step 22. Copy the updated WebSphere server trust file to the other nodes in your cell.

Step 23. One each node in the cell, you need to update the various client properties files that reference the WebSphere key and trust files to use the new key and trust files you've created. The following properties files in directory <DMGR-PROFILE-ROOT>\properties reference the key and trust files:

```
soap.client.props
sib.client.ssl.properties
sas.client.props
sas.stdclient.properties
sas.tools.properties
```

Unless you use standalone Java clients, many of these files aren't of interest to you. At a minimum, you need to change the soap.client.props file so that utilities such as startServer, stopServer, syncNode, and wsadmin will work properly when WebSphere Security is enabled. The following paragraphs demonstrate this change.

On each node in the cell, open soap.client.props with a text editor (e.g., WordPad). Change the following properties to reflect where the client key and trust files are located and the passwords needed to access those files.

```
com.ibm.ssl.keyStore
com.ibm.ssl.keyStorePassword
com.ibm.ssl.trustStore
com.ibm.ssl.trustStorePassword
```

Step 24. Use the utility PropFilePasswordEncoder to re-encode the keyStorePassword and trustStorePassword properties in the soap.client.props file. To do so, first make a copy of the soap.client.props file (e.g., copy.soap.client.props). (PropFilePasswordEncoder strips the file you give it of all comments and rearranges the properties in an arbitrary way.) Then open a DOS window, and run the utility on the copy of soap.client.props:

```
cd C:\WAS6\profiles\DM1\bin
PropFilePasswordEncoder.bat ..\properties\copy.soap.client.props
com.ibm.ssl.keyStorePassword
PropFilePasswordEncoder.bat ..\properties\copy.soap.client.props
com.ibm.ssl.trustStorePassword
```

Run the command for each password property in the properties file. Although the InfoCenter documentation gives the impression that you can provide a list of password properties to be encoded in the given file, in fact you can provide only one property at a time. (Of course, if both passwords are the same, you can run the command once and use that result.)

Next, cut and paste the XOR password that's created into your original soap.client.props file. (Include the "{xor}" in the text you copy into the original soap.client.props.)

For a cell with lots of nodes, it would make sense to put the key and trust files in exactly the same place in the file system on all nodes. That would let all nodes use the same copy of the client properties file (in this case, soap.client.props) because the values of the keyStore and trustStore properties could be the same on all nodes. The process would then be to change the values of the four properties above in one copy of the client properties file, run the password encoder utility, and then copy the file to the <PROFILE-ROOT>\properties directory on each node.

Step 25. The other commonly used file in the list above is sas.client.props, so you might need to modify that one as well.

Admin Roles

WebSphere supports coarse-grained security control and filtering functionality to protect administrative actions with the following four roles:

- Administrator
- Configurator

- Operator
- Monitor

Although this chapter's instructions mapped the users and groups in the registry to the WebSphere Administrator role, you may want to assign different levels of roles to different users or groups for better control of your environment. Figure 16-41 shows the relationship and hierarchy of the four roles supported by WebSphere.

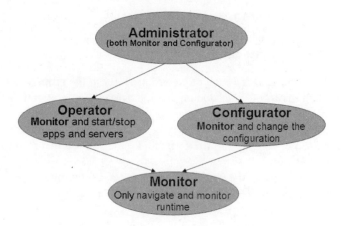

Figure 16-41: WebSphere admin roles

Figure 16-42 shows the relationship between users and groups in the registry and the WebSphere admin roles. For more information about this topic, consult the InfoCenter.

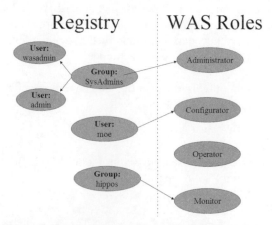

Figure 16-42: Relationship between user registry and admin roles

17

IBM Tivoli Directory Server Installation and Configuration

This chapter describes how to install and configure IBM Tivoli Directory Server (ITDS), a directory server compliant with the Lightweight Directory Access Protocol (LDAP). An LDAP directory server is one option for providing a registry that the WebSphere Deployment Manager, node agents, and application servers can use during the authentication and authorization processes.

When a user logs in, or when a WebSphere or user process needs to authenticate, the WebSphere application server sends a lookup request to the LDAP directory server, which in turn performs a lookup in its directory (database) to verify the user ID and password. WebSphere processes also send requests to the directory server to look up group memberships for a given user ID as part of the authorization process, to determine whether the user is permitted to use a given application. LDAP is a widely accepted standard protocol for directory servers, and many organizations run LDAP servers. ITDS is the IBM product you can use if you need an LDAP directory server.

After installing ITDS, you need to take some simple initialization steps to get started building a directory tree. Then you can use the ITDS administrative console to create a sample directory. As an alternative, you can use an LDAP Interchange Format (LDIF) file to load the directory contents. We step you through each of these aspects of ITDS in the following sections. We also explain the steps required to enable Secure Sockets Layer (SSL) connections to ITDS (e.g., for use by WebSphere processes).

For more information about ITDS, visit the product's home page, *http://www-306.ibm. com/software/tivoli/products/directory-server*. You can download the latest version of ITDS from there. Documentation for the product is available at the IBM Tivoli Directory

Server Information Center, *http://publib.boulder.ibm.com/infocenter/tivihelp/v2r1/index.jsp?toc=/com.ibm.IBMDS.doc/toc.xml*. For more information about LDAP, see the IBM Redbook *Understanding LDAP: Design and Implementation*, available online at *http://www.redbooks.ibm.com/abstracts/sg244986.html*.

Install ITDS V6 for Windows

The following steps demonstrate how to install ITDS on a Windows operating system. The installation process for Unix operating systems is similar. The example uses Version 6 of IBM Tivoli Directory Server. We assume you have the DB2 8.2 database with Fix Pack 1 installed on the machine on which you plan to install ITDS.

Step 1. Create a Windows user that will be the DB2 database instance owner, and make this user a member of the Windows Administrators group. Choose a user name no more than eight characters long. The DB2 instance you create will have the same name as the instance owner. For this example, we'll use the instance owner name LDAPDB2.

Step 2. Create a second Windows user that will be the directory instance owner.
(optional) Again, the name must not exceed eight characters, and, like the DB2 database instance owner, the directory instance owner must be a member of the Administrators group. Most installations use the DB2 instance owner for the directory instance owner. That's what we'll do for this example, using DB2 instance owner LDAPDB2 as our directory instance owner.

Step 3. If other WebSphere processes are installed on the machine on which you
(optional) plan to install ITDS and you want to be completely sure of no port conflicts, stop all WebSphere processes. An ITDS installation includes a WebSphere Express installation that's used to run the ITDS Web Administration Tool application. ITDS V6 considerably reduces the likelihood of port conflicts because the default ports used by the ITDS WebSphere Express application server are 12100, 12101 (Web container), 12102 (bootstrap), and 12103 (SOAP connector address).

Step 4. Unzip the download archive. Be sure to extract the archive to a directory path that has no space characters in its name.

Step 5. The top-level directory for the ITDS installation image is itdsV60. To start the installation process, go to the itds subdirectory under directory itdsV60, and double-click **setup.exe**.

Step 6. After the usual preliminary screens, a panel (shown in Figure 17-1) prompts you to specify the installation directory. We advise installing ITDS in a directory that has no space characters in its name. (ITDS predecessors used to fail during configuration if the installation directory path name contained either dashes or dots, but ITDS V6 has corrected this problem.) Hereafter, we refer to the ITDS installation root directory as <ITDS-ROOT>. For this example, we'll use C:\ITDS6 as the install directory. After specifying the directory on this panel, click **Next**.

Figure 17-1: Specifying the ITDS installation directory

Step 7. Next, on the panel shown in Figure 17-2, select the product components you want to install. (In this case, DB2 V8 and an appropriate version of the Global Security Kit are already installed.) Click **Next** after selecting the features to install.

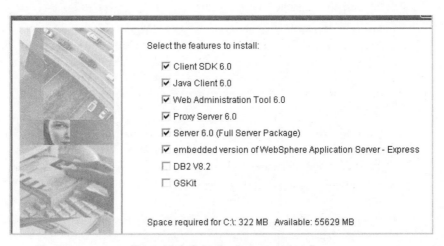

Figure 17-2: Selecting features to install

Step 8. When the ITDS installation wizard finishes, it displays a panel declaring that installation is complete. Click **Finish** on this panel.

Create a Directory Server Instance

Step 9. A second window, displaying the IBM Tivoli Directory Server Instance Administration Tool (Figure 17-3), is displayed next. Click the **Create** button on the right side of this panel to create a new directory server instance.

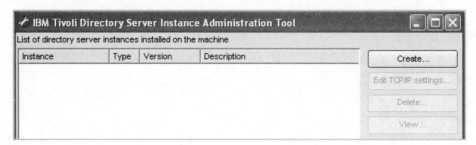

Figure 17-3: ITDS Instance Administration Tool

Step 10. On the next panel (Figure 17-4), specify the details for the new instance as follows:

a. For **User name**, enter **LDAPDB2**. (This field actually specifies the directory instance name. In our sample installation, the DB2 instance name and the directory instance name are the same.)

b. For **Install location**, select **C**. In Windows installations, the install location is a disk drive letter. The wizard will create the instance on that drive in directory idsslapd-*instance_name*, where *instance_name* is the name of the directory instance — in this case, LDAPDB2. Hereafter, we refer to the directory where the directory server instance is created as <ITDS-INSTANCE>.

c. For **Encryption seed string**, provide a minimum of 12 characters to be used to create an encryption key for encrypting and decrypting stored passwords and secret keys. You should record whatever value you provide and store it securely. (You may need it later for LDIF exports or to regenerate the key stash file.)

d. For **Instance description**, enter **IBM Tivoli LDAP Directory** (or whatever description you care to provide).

e. Click **Next**.

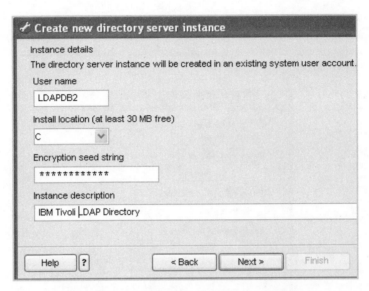

Figure 17-4: Creating a new directory server instance

Step 11. Next (Figure 17-5), specify the DB2 instance name. In our case, the name is LDAPDB2, the same name used for the directory instance and also for the Windows user you created earlier as a member of the Administrators group.

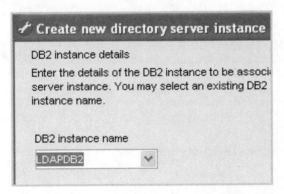

Figure 17-5: Specifying the DB2 instance

Step 12. On the next panel, you can choose which network interface to use if the server machine has more than one network interface card. In this example, the server machine has only one network interface, so simply click **Next** here.

Step 13. Next (Figure 17-6), choose the TCP/IP ports to use for the directory server and its administrative daemon. We advise sticking with the defaults, especially for the directory server, because these values are standard for an LDAP directory. Click **Next**.

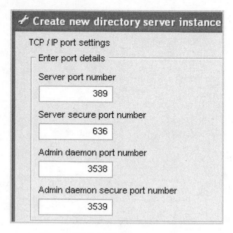

Figure 17-6: TCP/IP port settings

Step 14. The next panel (Figure 17-7) gives you the option to configure the administrator distinguished name (DN) and directory database now or postpone these tasks until later. To proceed with this configuration now, click **Next**.

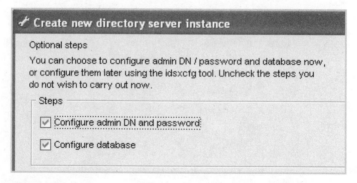

Figure 17-7: Options to configure the admin DN and directory database

Step 15. Specify the administrator DN and password (Figure 17-8). It's recommended that you use the default admin DN of **cn=root**. Click **Next**.

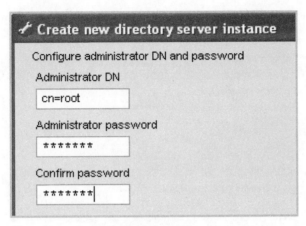

Figure 17-8: Specifying the admin DN and password

Step 16. Next (Figure 17-9), specify the database user name and password and the name of the database. For this example, enter the following values, and then click **Next**.

a. For **Database user name**, enter **LDAPDB2**.

b. For **Password**, enter <password>.

c. For **Database name**, enter **LDAPDIR**. (This value can actually be whatever you like as long as it meets the restrictions on database names in DB2. Use a name no longer than 12 characters, start it with an alpha character, and use only alphanumeric letters in the name.)

Figure 17-9: Configuring the database

Step 17. On the next panel (Figure 17-10), choose the disk drive to use to create the database, select the character set option, and click **Next**.

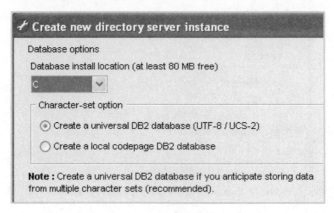

Figure 17-10: Database options

Step 18. The instance wizard now provides a summary of the configuration and gives you a chance to review your settings. You can go back and change things at this point if necessary. If you're satisfied with the settings, click **Finish**.

Step 19. You'll see a log window showing the commands being issued and their progress. When all tasks are completed, a little pop-up appears indicating so. Click **Close** on the task progress window.

Step 20. You should now see directory instance LDAPDB2 listed in the Instance Administration Tool, as shown in Figure 17-11.

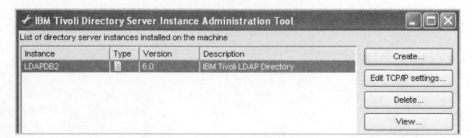

Figure 17-11: New directory instance in the Instance Administration Tool

You can close the administration tool now. Should you need to use it again, simply click the Windows **Start** button and navigate to **All Programs|IBM Tivoli Directory Server 6.0|Instance Administration Tool**.

Configure the Directory

Step 21. ITDS includes another graphical tool, IBM Tivoli Directory Server Configuration Tool, that lets you change the directory admin DN and password, configure directory suffixes, and perform other administrative tasks. You start this tool from the command line using the idsxcfg.cmd command as shown in Figure 17-12.

```
C:\>idsxcfg
(-) SHOW_TOOLBAR
(-) TEXT_BOTTOM
(+) NO_TEXT
(-) TASKPAD
```

Figure 17-12: ITDS Configuration Tool startup

You'll use the configuration tool to define a suffix to be the root of a sample directory tree. (The command-line tool to configure a suffix is idscfgsuf.cmd in the <ITDS-ROOT>\sbin directory.) In a suffix, the abbreviation for domain class is dc. You can define whatever suffix you like as long as you use it consistently (e.g., dc=yourco,dc=com or dc=yourorg,dc=org). Or you can use different attributes, such as organization (o) and country (c), to define the root of your tree (e.g., o=IBM,c=US).

For this example, we'll create the suffix dc=ibm,dc=com. Take the following steps to define this suffix:

a. Start the ITDS Configuration Tool by running **idsxcfg.cmd** from the command line. Figure 17-13 shows the configuration tool's main panel.

b. In the tool's left navigation pane, select **Manage suffixes**.

c. In the **Suffix DN** field that's displayed (shown in Figure 17-14), enter **dc=ibm,dc=com**.

d. Click **Add**. The new suffix will appear in the **Current suffix DNs** list, as shown in Figure 17-15.

e. Click **OK** to save the suffix in the configuration.

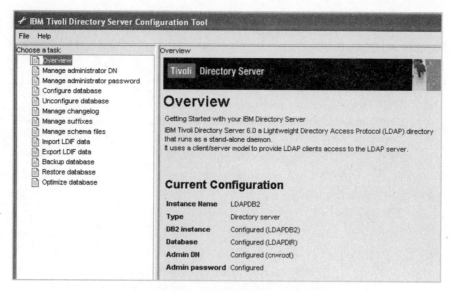

Figure 17-13: ITDS Configuration Tool main panel

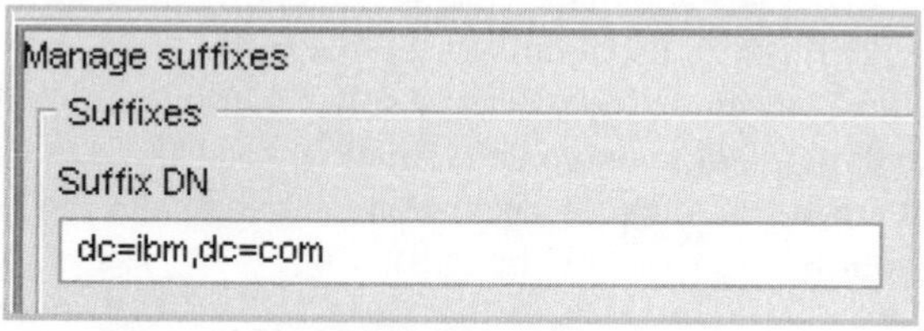

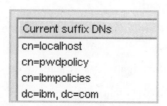

Figure 17-14: Defining a new suffix

Current suffix DNs
cn=localhost
cn=pwdpolicy
cn=ibmpolicies
dc=ibm, dc=com

Figure 17-15: New suffix in suffix DNs list

To ensure that the suffix has been properly defined in the configuration, check file ibmslapd.conf file in directory <ITDS-INSTANCE>\etc (in this case, in C:\idsslapd-LDAPDB2\etc). Search for "ibm-slapdSuffix" lines in the configuration file. You should find one that specifies your suffix.

Step 22. Next, verify that ITDS and the Directory Admin Daemon are installed as Windows services. To do so, click **Start**, and navigate to **Control Panel|Administrative Tools|Services**. You should see the two services shown in Figure 17-16 listed in the Windows **Services** panel.

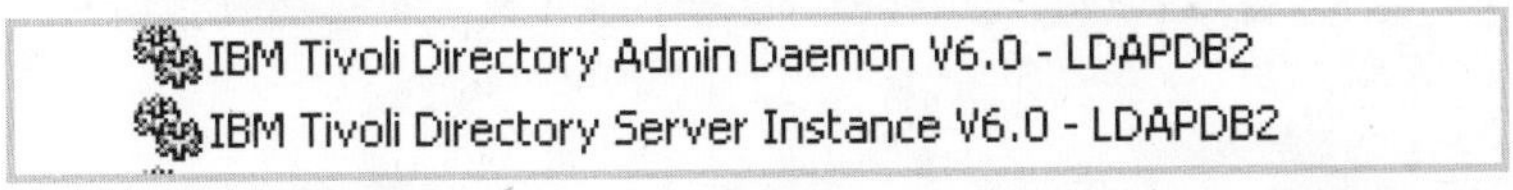

IBM Tivoli Directory Admin Daemon V6.0 - LDAPDB2
IBM Tivoli Directory Server Instance V6.0 - LDAPDB2

Figure 17-16: ITDS and Directory Admin Daemon Windows services

The Directory Admin Daemon needs to be running for you to be able to start and stop the directory server from ITDS's Web Administration Tool (which we'll talk about more in a moment). If the directory server isn't running, the admin daemon must be running to administer the server.

Administering the Directory

Step 23. After finishing the basic directory configuration, you use ITDS's Directory Server Web Administration Tool to administer the directory itself. (Numerous command-line tools that are also available for directory administration are beyond the scope of this text.) The administration tool is a J2EE Web application that runs on an instance of WebSphere Express. To access it, you must start the WebSphere Express server and then use a browser. As we noted earlier, the instance of WebSphere Express that's started uses ports 12100–12103.

To start the Web Administration Tool:

a. Open a command window, and change to directory <ITDS-ROOT>\appsrv\bin.

b. Issue the command **startServer.bat server1**. You can check the SystemOut.log file in directory <ITDS-ROOT>\appsrv\logs\server1 to make sure the application server started properly (i.e., with no exceptions).

c. Open a browser, and enter the URL **http://ldap-host:12100/IDSWebApp/ IDSjsp/Login.jsp**. (The WebSphere Express server is running on ldap-host in this example.) The administration tool's login panel, shown in Figure 17-17, is displayed.

d. To log in to the tool, enter the installed user name **superadmin** and the password **secret**, and then click **Login**.

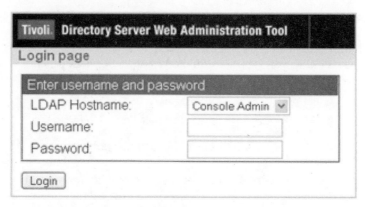

Figure 17-17: ITDS Web Administration Tool login panel

Step 24. After logging in to the Web Administration Tool as superadmin, you'll see the main panel shown in Figure 17-18.

Figure 17-18: ITDS Web Administration Tool main panel

Your first step here should be to change the console administrator user name and password to something known only to ITDS administrators. To change the user name, go the admin tool's left navigation pane, click the **Console administration** folder icon to "open" it, and select **Change console administrator login**. On the resulting panel (Figure 17-19), provide a new user name (e.g., itdsadmin) and the current password, and click **OK**.

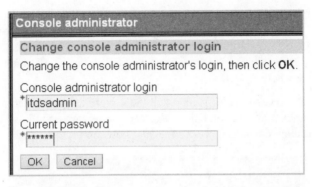

Figure 17-19: Specifying a new console administrator user name

Step 25. Next, to change the administrator password, select **Console Administration|Change console administrator password** in the navigation pane, and on the resulting panel (Figure 17-20) provide the current password, and then enter and confirm a new password. Click **OK**.

Figure 17-20: Changing the console administrator password

Step 26. Now, add the ITDS server you created to the list of servers managed by the Web Administration Tool:

a. Under **Console administration** in the admin tool's navigation pane, select **Manage console servers**.

b. Click **Add**.

c. On the resulting panel (Figure 17-21), supply the host name of the machine on which you installed the directory server (ldap-host in this case), and provide the port numbers used by the server and admin daemon. (If you used the default ports to define the ITDS server, you can accept the default values here.) Click **OK**.

d. You'll receive a notification that the server has been added to the Web Administration Tool. Click **OK**. You should now see the server listed in the **Manage console servers** panel, as shown in Figure 17-22.

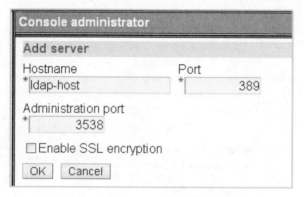

Figure 17-21: Adding the ITDS server

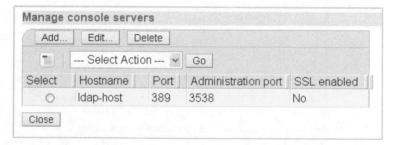

Figure 17-22: Manage console servers panel

Step 27. Click **Logout** in the navigation pane to log out of the administration tool.

Create a Small Directory Tree

At this point, you have the basic ITDS server set up and ready for creating a directory tree with the Web Administration Tool. The small tree you'll create in this section is intended simply for demonstration purposes. Figure 17-23 depicts this directory tree. The first thing you'll create is a root node to match the suffix you defined in the preceding section when initially configuring the ITDS server instance.

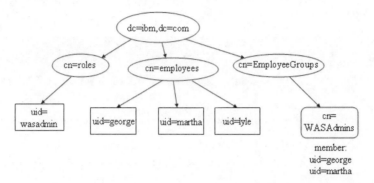

Figure 17-23: Sample directory tree

Step 1. Verify that the ITDS server is running. To do so, you can go to the Windows **Services** panel (**Start|Control Panel|Administrative Tools|Services**) and check the status of the IBM Tivoli Directory Server instance. You should also see an ibmslapd.exe entry in the Windows Task Manager's process list. If the ITDS server process isn't running, the Directory Admin Daemon (ibmdiradm.exe) needs to be running. You can use the admin daemon to start and stop the directory server from the Web Administration Tool.

Step 2. Log in to the ITDS server instance. To do so, use a browser as before, entering the URL **http://ldap-host:12100/IDSWebApp/IDSjsp/Login.jsp**. On the Web Administration Tool's login page (Figure 17-24), select the ITDS server (ldap-host in this case) in the **LDAP Hostname** list, provide the administrator distinguished name (e.g., cn=root) and password, and click **Login**.

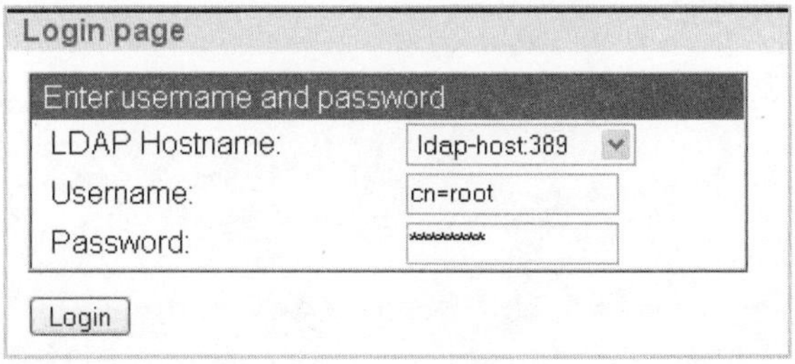

Figure 17-24: Logging in to the ITDS server instance

Figure 17-25 shows the Web Administration Tool after you've logged in and started the LDAP server from the console. As long as the Directory Admin Daemon is running, you can start and stop the directory server from the console.

Figure 17-25: Managing the directory server from the Web Administration Tool

Step 3.   To create the root node entry in the directory tree, open the **Directory management** folder in the navigation pane, and select **Manage entries** as shown in Figure 17-26.

Figure 17-26: Selecting to manage entries

Step 4.   In the **Manage entries** panel, shown in Figure 17-27, click the **Add** button.

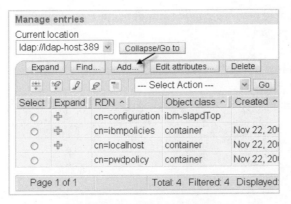

Figure 17-27: Manage entries panel

Step 5. In the **Add an entry** panel that appears, scroll down the **Structural object classes** list (shown in Figure 17-28), and select **domain**. Then scroll down the window until you see the **Next** button, and click it.

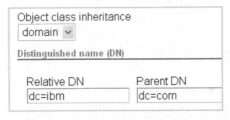

Figure 17-28: Structural object classes list

Step 6. Click **Next** to skip the **Select auxiliary object classes** panel.

Step 7. On the **Enter the attributes** panel, fill in the distinguished name fields as shown in Figure 17-29. For **Relative DN**, enter **dc=ibm**. For **Parent DN**, enter **dc=com**. Scroll down to the **Finish** button, and click it.

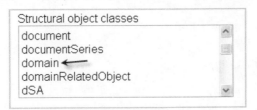

Figure 17-29: Specifying the domain attributes

531

Step 8. You should now see the **dc=ibm,dc=com** entry in the **Manage entries** panel, as shown in Figure 17-30.

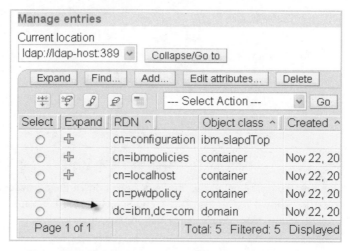

Figure 17-30: Entry for dc=ibm,dc=com in Manage entries panel

Creating Container Branches

The next set of steps creates a series of "containers" that are all at the same level in the directory tree under dc=ibm,dc=com. The container branches are named "roles," "employees," and "EmployeeGroups." (These branches of the directory tree are something we invented for this example. This approach isn't meant to represent a "best practice" way of organizing a directory.)

The roles branch of the directory tree is intended as a place to put users that aren't real people but rather generic users, such as wasadmin. These containers aren't groups in the sense of the groups used by WebSphere processes to determine a user's group membership. You'll add group (i.e., groupOfNames) objects later for this purpose, after creating some user (inetOrgPerson) objects.

Step 9. Add a container entry with the name cn=roles under the dc=ibm,dc=com root. To do so:

  a. Select the **dc=ibm,dc=com** entry in the **Manage entries** panel by clicking the radio button that appears in the **Select** column next to this entry and then clicking the **Add** button in the command bar (as shown in Figure 17-31).

Manage entries

Current location

| ldap://ldap-host:389 ☑ | Collapse/Go to |

| Expand | Find... | Add... | Edit attributes... | Delete |

| 🔧 | 🔧 | ♪ | ♪ | ☐ | --- Select Action --- ☑ | Go |

Select	Expand	RDN ^	Object class ^	Created ^
○	✚	cn=configuration	ibm-slapdTop	
○	✚	cn=ibmpolicies	container	Nov 22, 20
○	✚	cn=localhost	container	Nov 22, 20
○		cn=pwdpolicy	container	Nov 22, 20
◉	✚	dc=ibm,dc=com	domain	Nov 22, 20

| Page 1 of 1 | Total: 5 Filtered: 5 Displayed |

Figure 17-31: Adding an entry under dc=ibm,dc=com

b. Scroll down the **Select object class** panel's **Structural object classes** list, and select **container** to add an object of this type to the directory.

c. Scroll to the bottom of the panel, and click **Next**.

d. On the **Select auxiliary object classes** panel, click **Next** again.

e. Now, specify the container's distinguished name by entering **cn=roles** in the **Relative DN** field shown in Figure 17-32.

f. Scroll to the bottom of the window, and click **Finish**.

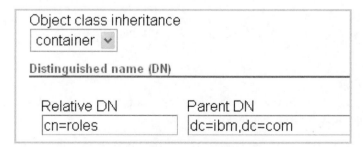

Object class inheritance

| container ☑ |

Distinguished name (DN)

Relative DN

| cn=roles |

Parent DN

| dc=ibm,dc=com |

Figure 17-32: Creating the cn=roles container entry

Step 10. Next, add a second container entry named cn=employees under dc=ibm,dc=com. To do so, make sure **dc=ibm,dc=com** is the selected node, and then add an object of type **container** with a relative DN of **cn= employees** (Figure 17-33).

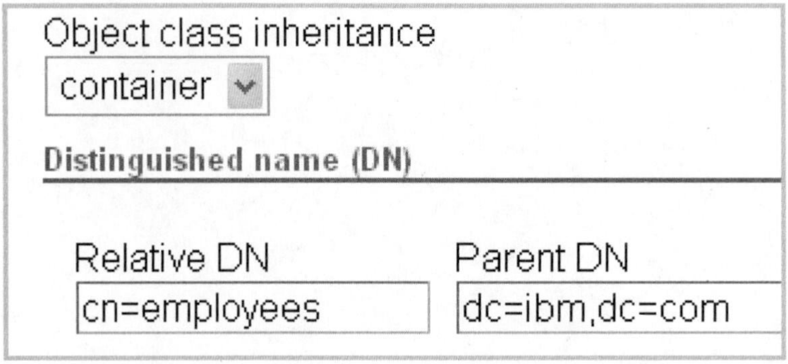

Figure 17-33: Creating the cn=employees container entry

Step 11. Add a third container entry under dc=ibm,dc=com named cn=EmployeeGroups. To do so, make sure **dc=ibm,dc=com** is the selected node, and add an object of type **container** with a relative DN of **cn=EmployeeGroups** (Figure 17-34).

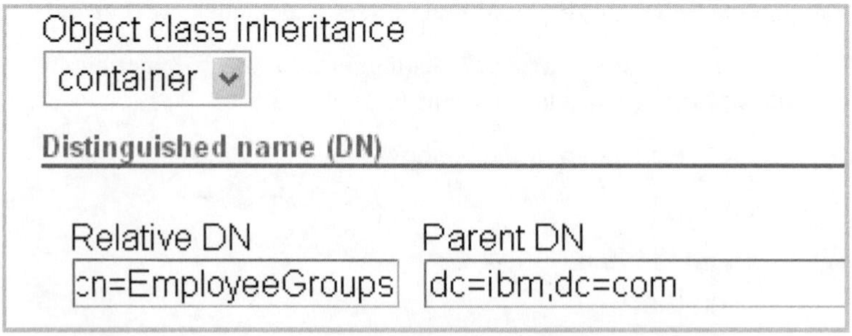

Figure 17-34: Creating the cn=EmployeeGroups container entry

Now, in the **Manage entries** panel, you should see three entries under dc=ibm,dc=com, as shown in Figure 17-35.

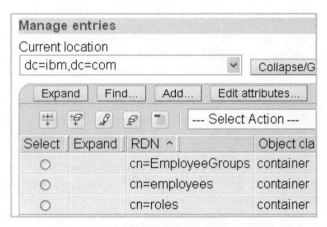

Figure 17-35: Newly created container entries

Figure 17-36 illustrates how the **Manage entries** panel lets you navigate the directory tree. You use the **Expand** button to expand selected nodes that appear with a plus sign icon to their left. You click the **Collapse/Go to** button to navigate the DN specified in the **Current location** attribute of a given view.

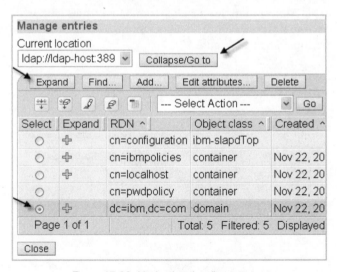

Figure 17-36: Navigating the directory tree

Creating User Entries

In the next steps, you'll create "user" entries (object class inetOrgPerson) in the directory tree. (A user may also be referred to as a *principal*.) For inetOrgPerson, the relative distinguished name (RDN) attribute is often the common name (cn), but it's recommended that you use the uid attribute instead. If you decide to use cn as the RDN, be sure to fill in the uid attribute of each user. The uid attribute is what the WebSphere processes use (by default) when looking up login names for authentication. If the uid attribute isn't filled in, users must provide a full DN when trying to authenticate when WebSphere security is enabled. With the uid attribute filled in, users need to type only the value of the uid attribute to be authenticated to WebSphere. This is true for applications as well as for the WebSphere admin console. (You can configure WebSphere security to use an attribute other than uid as the lookup key for login names. For more information about doing so, see the section titled "Configuring Lightweight Directory Access Protocol search filters" in the WebSphere V6 Information Center.)

Step 12. Create a wasadmin user in the roles container. This user will be the user assigned to the application server processes to bind to the directory to perform searches and password lookups and to authenticate when starting up. Take the following steps to create user wasadmin:

a. In the **Manage entries** panel, select the **cn=roles** item in the **dc=ibm,dc=com** view of the directory tree, and click the **Add** button in the command bar (Figure 17-37).

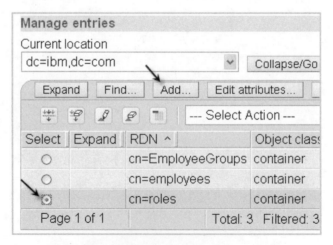

Figure 17-37: Adding a user to the roles container

b. In the **Structural object classes** list, select **inetOrgPerson**, as shown in Figure 17-38. Then click **Next** at the bottom of the main viewing pane.

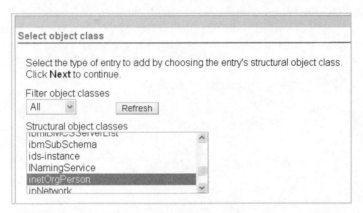

Figure 17-38: Selecting the inetOrgPerson object class for wasadmin

c. On the **Select auxiliary object classes** panel, click **Next** again.

d. On the **Enter the attributes** panel (Figure 17-39), enter **uid=wasadmin** in the **Relative DN** field.

Figure 17-39: Specifying the wasadmin user entry attributes

e. For **cn** (common name), enter **WebSphere Administrator** (or whatever name you like).

f. For **sn** (surname), enter **Administrator** (or whatever you like).

g. Click the **Optional attributes** link to the left of the **cn** and **sn** fields.

h. In the resulting property sheet, fill in the **userPassword** (Figure 17-40). The attributes on this panel are in alphabetical order, and you'll find the userPassword attribute near the bottom of the list. (You might notice that the **uid** field is blank here even though you've specified it for the RDN. The uid value will be filled in once you click the **Finish** button.)

i. At the bottom of the panel, click **Finish**.

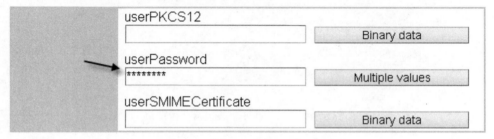

Figure 17-40: Specifying the user password

Step 13. Add some employee entries. (You'll use some of the employees as members of the WebSphere administrators group.) To do so:

a. In the **Manage entries** panel, select the **cn=employees** item in the **dc=ibm,dc=com** view of the directory tree, and click **Add** (Figure 17-41).

b. For the structural object class, select **inetOrgPerson**. Then click **Next**.

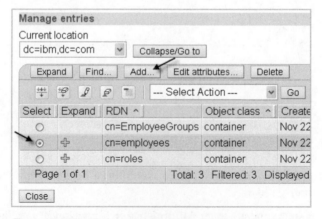

Figure 17-41: Adding an entry to cn=employees,dc=ibm,dc=com

c. Enter the values for this user as shown in Figure 17-42. For the relative DN, enter **uid=george**. For the common name, enter **George Hippo**. For the surname, enter **Hippo**.

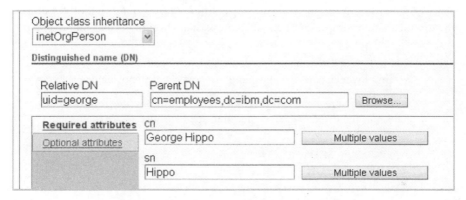

Figure 17-42: Adding employee George Hippo

d. Click Optional attributes, and set the **userPassword**.

e. Click **Finish**.

f. Repeat hese steps to create the employees Martha Hippo (**uid=martha**) and Lyle Crocodile (**uid=lyle**). Figure 17-43 shows the updated **Manage entries** panel listing the new employees.

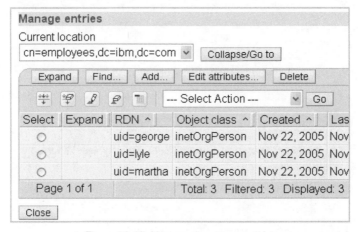

Figure 17-43: New employee user entries

Creating a User Group

In the next steps, you'll create a group (groupOfNames) in the EmployeeGroups container. The group name will be WASAdmins, and you'll add George and Martha as members of the group. WebSphere security is configured by default to look for objects of type groupOfNames or groupOfUniqueNames when checking group membership.

Step 14.   Add the groupOfNames object cn=WASAdmins to the cn=EmployeeGroups,dc=ibm,dc=com portion of the directory tree. To do so:

a. Select the **cn=EmployeeGroups** container in the **dc=ibm,dc=com** location in the directory tree, and click **Add** (Figure 17-44).

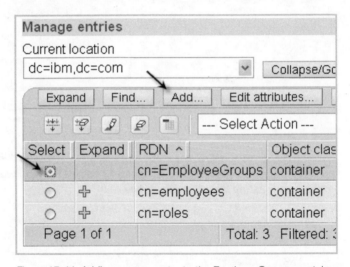

Figure 17-44: Adding a group entry to the EmployeeGroups container

b. For the structural object class, select **groupOfNames**. Then click **Next**.

c. Skip the **Select auxiliary object classes** panel (click **Next**).

d. On the panel shown in Figure 17-45, specify **cn=WASAdmins** for the relative DN.

Figure 17-45: Specifying the relative DN and group members for WASAdmins group

e. You can optionally fill in the **cn** field with the **WASAdmins** value as well. Because you've already specified cn=WASAdmins as the relative DN, WASAdmins will automatically be added to the cn attribute value when you finish adding the entry. The cn attribute is a multivalued attribute, so more than one common name is acceptable. To provide additional common names, you click the **Multiple values** button beside the **cn** field. If you add additional common names, you must specify WASAdmins explicitly. Note that when providing the attribute values, you don't include the attribute name abbreviation (e.g., cn) with the value you provide.

f. You must add at least one group member at the time you create the group. In this example, you'll add the distinguished name values for George and Martha. Click the **Multiple values** button beside the **member** field to add more than one member.

g. On the ensuing panel (Figure 17-46), add employee George by entering **uid=george,cn=employees,dc=ibm,dc=com** in the **member** field and clicking the **Add** button. To add employee Martha, enter **uid=martha, cn=employees,dc=ibm,dc=com**, and click **Add** again. (The group member values must be distinguished names of entries in the directory.)

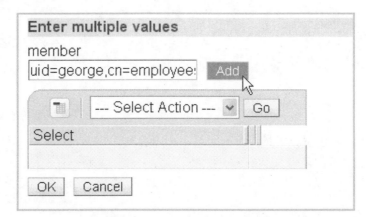

Figure 17-46: Adding multiple members to the WASAdmins group

h. Finish adding the values to the member attribute by clicking **OK** as shown in Figure 17-47. Doing so returns you to the **Enter the attributes** panel, where you'll see the new WASAdmins group (Figure 17-48).

i. Scroll to the bottom of the panel, and click **Finish**.

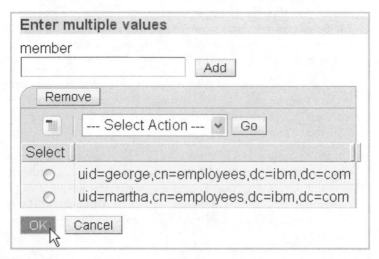

Figure 17-47: Completing the addition of multiple group members for the WASAdmins group

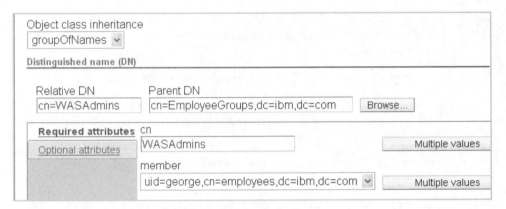

Figure 17-48: The completed WASAdmins group

At this point, you've created a simple directory tree that's sufficient to get started using an LDAP directory as the user registry for enabling WebSphere security.

Working with LDAP Interchange Format Files

Creating a directory tree using the Web Administration Tool is acceptable for small directories or for incremental additions to an existing directory. IBM Tivoli Directory Server also provides a mechanism for performing bulk loads of a directory from a text file in LDAP Interchange Format. This section demonstrates the details of working with LDIF files. First, you'll export an LDIF file for the directory you just built. Then you'll delete the directory tree you built and import the LDIF file to re-create the directory.

At the time this text was published, Version 6 of the ITDS Configuration Tool had a defect that didn't allow it to export or import LDIF files. The db2ldif and ldif2db (export and import) utilities exhibited the same problem when run in a DOS shell, yielding the following error message:

```
GLPRDB001E Error code -1 from function: "SQLAllocEnv"
```

To avoid this error, you'll use the db2ldif and ldif2db utilities (in <ITDS-ROOT>\sbin) in a Cygwin shell. To obtain usage information for either utility, use the –? option.

Step 1.   Create a directory where you want to dump the LDIF file. In this example, we'll use the destination <ITDS-ROOT>\ldif.

Step 2.   In the <ITDS-ROOT>\sbin directory, run the db2ldif command to export the directory tree to an LDIF file (we performed this step with a Cygwin shell on Windows XP):

```
$ ./db2ldif.cmd -o ../ldif/sample.ldif -s dc=ibm,dc=com
```

The output file (**–o**) specified by this command is sample.ldif. The LDIF is starting from subtree (**–s**) with root: dc=ibm,dc=com. The command's output should be

```
GLPD2L011I 9 entries have been successfully exported from the
directory.
```

Step 3.   Delete the directory tree from the directory. (You're doing this to see in the next step that you can import the LDIF file back into the directory server and re-create the directory subtree.) To delete the directory, select the **dc=ibm,dc=com** root node in the Web Administration Tool (as shown in Figure 17-49's **Manage entries** panel), click the command bar's **Delete** button, and confirm that you want to delete the subtree.

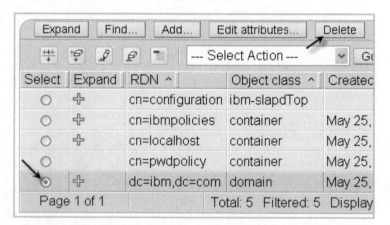

Figure 17-49: Deleting the directory tree

In some cases, the display pane isn't refreshed properly after the delete, and you'll continue to see **dc=ibm,dc=com** displayed. If this happens, bring up something else in the display pane, and then return to the **Manage entries** panel; the screen will then properly reflect the directory content.

Step 4.   Examine the LDIF file. You can see that it contains some encrypted information, as you might expect. You can also see that each entry has a "control" attribute. This attribute is specific to the directory server. You can use the **–j** option on the db2ldif command to omit this attribute from the entities dumped in the LDIF file.

Step 5.   Stop the directory server+6. (You can import an LDIF file only when the directory server is stopped.) You can stop the server from the Web Administration Tool by opening the **Server administration** item in the navigation pane and selecting **Start/stop/restart server**. On the resulting panel (Figure 17-50), click **Stop**, and wait until the server status changes from running to stopped. (It might take from 30 seconds to a minute to shut down the server.)

Figure 17-50: Stopping the directory server

Step 6.   To import the LDIF file, run the following ldif2db command in the <ITDS-ROOT>\sbin directory.

```
$ ./ldif2db.cmd -i ../ldif/sample.ldif

GLPCOM022I The database plugin is successfully loaded from
   c:/ITDS6/lib/libback-config.dll.

GLPRDB002W ldif2db: 9 entries have been successfully added out of 9
   attempted.
```

The ldif2db utility works reasonably well for a small number of items in the LDIF file. For large directories (more than 100,000 entries), it takes a long time to process the LDIF file. For large-scale loading of the directory from an LDIF file, you'll find the bulkload utility a better choice. For more information about this utility, see the ITDS InfoCenter.

Creating SSL Artifacts for IBM Tivoli Directory Server

In this section, we describe how to set up a key file and create a self-signed certificate for ITDS. These artifacts are necessary to support Secure Sockets Layer connections to the directory server. SSL provides encrypted communications between ITDS and its clients, such as WebSphere processes. It's important to encrypt the communications between ITDS and its clients to protect user name and password information passed on the network.

You administer ITDS key files using the IBM Key Management (iKeyman) utility. (You used this utility in Chapter 16 to create the replacement key and trust files for WebSphere.) The iKeyman utility either was installed when you installed ITDS or was already present on your machine.

ITDS comes with a default key file (ldapkey.kdb) located in directory <ITDS-ROOT>\etc. The password for the default file is ssl_password. (ITDS uses a password stash file, ldapkey.sth, also located in this directory. The stash file must have the same root name as the key file.)

Step 1.   For better organization of the SSL artifacts, we recommend creating a directory in <ITDS-ROOT> named ssl (e.g., C:\ITDS6\ssl) to hold only SSL-related files. The etc directory has a lot of other files in it that only get in the way when you're working with SSL configuration. Move the ldapkey.kdb and ldapkey.sth from the etc directory to the ssl directory.

Step 2.   The iKeyman utility needs a JVM to run. Make sure JAVA_HOME is specified properly in your environment. (In a DOS command window, you can echo %JAVA_HOME% to do so, or you can check the environment variables in the advanced system properties. To do the latter, right-click **My Computer**, select **Properties**, go to the **Advanced** tab, and click the **Environment Variables** button.)

Step 3.   Set up an iKeyman shortcut in the program start menu. If iKeyman was installed with ITDS, you may already have an iKeyman shortcut here for IBM Tivoli Directory Server 6.0. If not, look for the GSKit v7 executable in C:\Program Files\IBM\gsk7\bin. You can create a shortcut for gsk7ikm.exe and move it to C:\Documents and Settings\All Users\Start Menu\Programs\IBM Tivoli Directory Server 6.0. It turns out to be convenient to modify the iKeyman shortcut so that its "Start in" property is <ITDS-ROOT>\ssl (or wherever you've located your ITDS key file).

Step 4. Open the ldapkey.kdb key file by taking the following steps.

 a. Click the open folder icon in the toolbar, or select **Key Database File|Open**.

 b. In the resulting pop-up dialog (Figure 17-51), select **CMS** (Cryptographic Message Syntax) for the **Key database type**.

 c. For **File name**, browse to select **ldapkey.kdb**.

 d. For Location, enter <ITDS-ROOT>\ssl (or wherever you have your key file).

 e. Click **OK**.

 f. In the password dialog that appears, enter **ssl_password**, the default key file access password. (The next thing you'll do is change this password.)

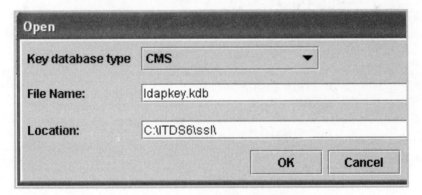

Figure 17-51: Opening the ITDS key file

The key file comes with a collection of certificate authority signer certificates. The ITDS server will trust any client certificate signed by one of these certificate authorities.

Step 5. Now, change the key file password:

 a. Select **Key Database File|Change Password** to display the **Change Password** panel (Figure 17-52).

 b. Enter and confirm a new password.

 c. If your organization has a password expiration policy, you can specify an expiration time on this panel; otherwise, leave that option unchecked. (Be sure to set up a reminder system to change the password shortly before expiration. If the key-file access password expires, ITDS won't support SSL properly, and clients such as WebSphere processes that are config-ured to use SSL with ITDS won't be able to access the directory server. If you have WebSphere security enabled and you're using ITDS for the user registry, a WebSphere process that can't authenticate with ITDS won't start.)

d. Select the **Stash the password to a file?** option. (The ITDS server needs to obtain the password at runtime.)

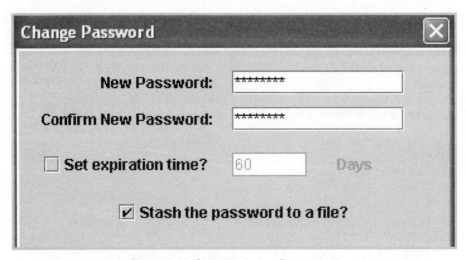

Figure 17-52: Changing the key file password

Step 6. Create a self-signed certificate for the ITDS server. Later, you'll export this certificate so that the WebSphere processes can import it into their trust file. To create the certificate:

a. Select the **Personal Certificates** section of the key database content from the pull-down menu (Figure 17-53). There should be no certificate defined here. (If there was, you'd delete it because it would be something that's compromised, having been shipped with every copy of ITDS.)

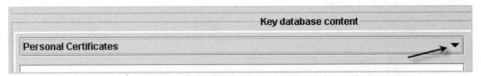

Figure 17-53: Personal Certificates section

b. In the toolbar, click the certificate icon (you can see this icon in Figure 17-54) to create a new self-signed certificate.

Figure 17-54: Creating a new certificate

c. Enter the attributes of the certificate as shown in Figure 17-55:

   i. For **Key Label**, enter **ITDS Self-signed Certificate** (or whatever text you like). You'll use this label when you configure ITDS to use SSL, to indicate which key ITDS should use for encryption.

   ii. For **Common Name**, enter your LDAP host name.

   iii. For **Organization**, enter the name your organization.

   iv. For **Validity period**, use 365 days. As with other certificates you're managing for your environment, it's critical to set up a reminder system so that you create a new certificate and circulate the public portion of it to clients (e.g., WebSphere processes) that need to trust the ITDS server shortly before this certificate expires.

   v. The remaining attributes are optional.

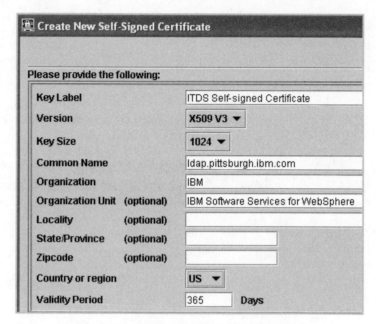

Figure 17-55: Defining the certificate attributes

d. Click **OK**. You should see the new certificate in the **Personal Certificates** list, as shown in Figure 17-56.

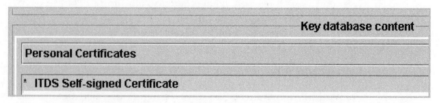

Figure 17-56: Newly created certificate in Personal Certificates list

Step 7. Extract the public certificate for the ITDS self-signed certificate. To do so:

a. Select the ITDS self-signed certificate, and click the **Extract** button in the lower-right corner of the iKeyman tool.

b. On the resulting panel (Figure 17-57), provide a file name (e.g., ITDSCertificate.arm).

c. For **Location**, specify <ITDS-ROOT>\ssl.

d. Click **OK**.

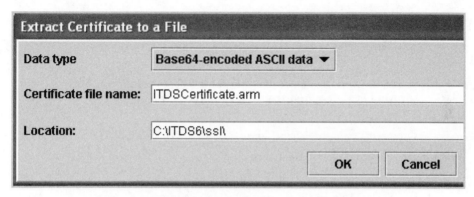

Figure 17-57: Extracting the public certificate

You should now have a public certificate file in <ITDS-ROOT>\ssl, as shown in Figure 17-58. You'll copy this public certificate file to the WebSphere server machine(s) where you configure the trust file for the WebSphere processes that need to trust the ITDS server. Chapter 18 describes the remaining details for setting up SSL connectivity between ITDS and WebSphere processes.

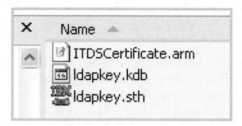

Figure 17-58: Public certificate file in <ITDS-ROOT>\ssl

Step 8. At this point, you can exit iKeyman.

Configure IBM Tivoli Directory Server to Allow SSL Connections

Now, you'll use the key file you set up in the preceding section to configure ITDS to support SSL communications.

Step 1. Make sure the IBM Directory Administration Daemon is running. (Check its status in the Windows **Services** panel, or look for the ibmdiradm.exe process in the Task Manager process list.)

Step 2. Start the ITDS admin application server if it's not already running. (To do so, issue the **startServer.bat server1** command in a DOS command window from the <ITDS-ROOT>\appsrv\bin directory.)

Step 3. Start a browser, and enter the URL for the ITDS admin console: **http://ldap-host:12100/IDSWebApp/IDSjsp/Login.jsp**.

Step 4. On the ITDS login panel (Figure 17-59), log in to your ITDS server instance.

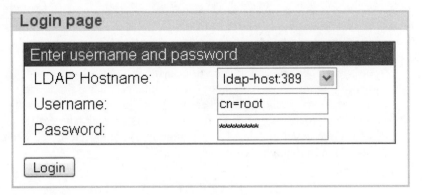

Figure 17-59: ITDS login panel

Step 5. If the ITDS server instance isn't running, start it. (You can't configure the security properties of the server unless it's running.) To do so, in the left navigation pane, open **Server administration**, and select **Start/stop/restart server**. Then, in the main viewing pane, click **Start**. The directory admin server will do the work of starting the directory server instance. The LDAP database instance will also be started.

Step 6. Configure the server instance for SSL communications:

    a. Under **Server administration**, select **Manage security properties**. The panel shown in Figure 17-60 will be displayed.

    b. Under **Enable secure connections**, select **SSL**. (This choice sets up the server to use both SSL and non-SSL connections.)

    c. For **Authentication method**, leave the default selection of **Server authentication**. (The **Server and client authentication** method is more secure, but it can require considerably more overhead to maintain the client certificates, depending on how many clients are involved. With an LDAP server, you usually have a lot of clients.)

d. Click **OK** (you may need to scroll down to see this button).

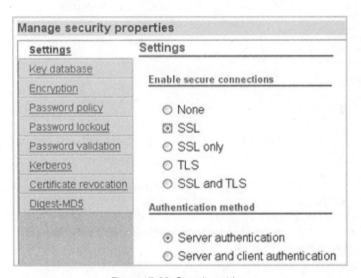

Figure 17-60: Security settings

Step 7.   Configure the key database file:

a. Select the **Key database** tab. Figure 17-61 shows this panel.

b. Provide a full path to the key file (e.g., C:\ITDS6\ssl\ldapkey.kdb).

c. We use a stash file in this example, so you don't need to provide an access password for the key file. (The password stash file must be in the same directory as the key file and must have the same root name.)

d. Enter the key label (e.g., ITDS Self-signed Certificate). (This label must match the key label you provided when you created the key for this server instance.)

e. Click **OK** (you may need to scroll down to see this button).

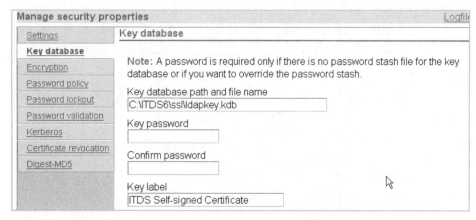

Figure 17-61: Key database tab

Step 8. If you want to use a port other than the default for LDAP SSL connections (port 636), you can set the SSL port under **Server administration|Manage server properties**. Figure 17-62 shows the panel where you make this change. (You're advised to use the default port 636 because that's the standard SSL port for LDAP servers, but in some situations you may need to use a different port.) Don't forget to click **OK** if you change the port.

Manage server properties

	General
*⃰**General**	
Performance	
Search settings	Hostname LDAP-HOST
Event notification	Version 6.0
Transactions	Note: The port number under "Manage console servers"
Suffixes	the server port numbers are modified. You must be logge
Referrals	administrator to manage console servers.
Attribute cache	Unsecure port
	*⃰[389]
	Secure port
	*⃰[636]
	Language tag support
	☐ Enable language tag support

Figure 17-62: Specifying the SSL port

Step 9. Stop and start the ITDS instance so that the SSL port will begin listening. You can run the command **netstat –an** in a DOS command window to verify that the SSL port is listening. (If you've configured the ITDS server instance as described in this chapter, port 389 should be listening as well.)

If the ITDS instance doesn't start, check the ibmslapd.log file for the ITDS instance. This file is in the logs directory of the ITDS instance root directory (e.g., in idsslapd-LDAPDB2). If the instance is started successfully, you should see the following lines in ibmslapd.log.

```
GLPSRV015I Configuration read securePort 636.

GLPCOM003I Non-SSL port initialized to 389.

GLPCOM004I SSL port initialized to 636.
```

The ITDS server instance is now prepared to accept SSL connections.

Basic Troubleshooting of ITDS

This section provides some hints and tips for troubleshooting ITDS problems, particularly with installation and configuration.

The log files associated with installation are in directory <ITDS-ROOT>\var: files ldap-inst.log, idsadm.log, and idsadmdb2cmds.log. The log files associated with an instance of ITDS are in directory <ITDS-INSTANCE>\logs (e.g., C:\idsslapd-LDAPDB2\logs). File ibmslapd.log addresses the instance itself. File db2cli.log captures DB2 client interface activity.

If you're using the default LDAP (non-SSL) port, you should see something listening on port 389 when the directory server is running. On Windows, the command **netstat –a** will show the port as "ldap" because port 389 is defined in the etc\services file. You can use **netstat –an** to avoid port number translation to the names in etc\services.

Make sure the LDAP DB2 instance gets created. You can use the **db2ilist** command in a DOS window to obtain a list of instances. One of the instances should be the one created for the directory server (LDAPDB2 in this example). You can perform further checks on the DB2 instance from a db2cmd window. Make sure the DB2INSTANCE environment variable is set to the name of the instance you created for the directory server (e.g., LDAPDB2):

```
C:\>echo %DB2INSTANCE%

LDAPDB2
```

Then, start a db2cmd window and list the nodes that are defined:

```
C:\>db2 list node directory

  Node Directory

  Number of entries in the directory = 1

Node 1 entry:

  Node name                           = IDSINODE

  Comment                             =

  Directory entry type                = LOCAL

  Protocol                            = LOCAL

  Instance name                       = LDAPDB2


C:\>db2 list db directory

  System Database Directory

  Number of entries in the directory = 1

Database 1 entry:

  Database alias                      = LDAPDIR

  Database name                       = LDAPDIR

  Database drive                      = C:\LDAPDB2

  Database release level              = a.00

  Comment                             =

  Directory entry type                = Indirect

  Catalog database partition number   = 0

  Alternate server hostname           =

  Alternate server port number        =
```

Notice that the type of instance is LOCAL, which means the database instance isn't available for remote access. (For security reasons, the directory server is intended to use a local instance.)

You can use the ITDS Configuration Tool (idsxcfg) to re-create the DB2 instance and database. If the instance isn't properly created (e.g., you don't see it listed in the output of the db2ilist command), or if you don't see the database created as shown in the list of databases for the instance, you might need to clean up the file system before trying to create the DB2 instance again. On Windows, for example, if the target drive is C and the instance name is LDAPDB2, you might see the directory C:\LDAPDB2 with a NODE000 directory in it. Assuming the LDAPDB2 instance seems to not be there completely, it's a good idea to remove the C:\LDAPDB2 directory tree before trying to configure the LDAP database again.

In earlier versions of ITDS, there were cases when the configuration tool would fail to properly create the directory instance but the command-line tool would succeed. If you're having trouble with the configuration tool, try using the idsicrt and/or idscfgdb utility.

On startup, the ITDS instance starts its own DB2 instance, so the DB2 instance needn't be running when you start the directory server. In earlier versions of ITDS, it was a good idea to let the ITDS instance start the associated DB2 instance. Version 6 seems to work well when it starts up the DB2 instance at the time the directory server is started.

If the directory server instance won't start and you aren't seeing any helpful diagnostic messages in the usual log files, try starting the instance in a DOS command window to see what sort of diagnostic messages it emits when it fails to start. The executable is in <ITDS-ROOT>\sbin\32; the file name is ibmslapd.exe.

If you're having trouble getting WebSphere to authenticate when you're using an LDAP registry, make sure ITDS is running. You should see an ibmslapd.exe process in Task Manager.

Make sure ITDS wasn't started in "configuration mode." Look on the **Start/stop/restart server** panel of the Web Administration Tool, and verify that the **Start/restart in configuration only mode** check box isn't selected. (When the directory server is running in configuration mode, the server status icon in the title bar of the administration tool's main display panel will be a yellow ball containing two vertical bars. This graphic appears as the center icon in Figure 17-63.)

Figure 17-63: Icon indicating directory server is running in configuration mode

Also, if you check the top level of the **Manage entries** panel and all you see is **cn=configuration** (as in Figure 17-64), you've started ITDS in configuration mode. This occurrence will lead to all sorts of problems when WebSphere processes try to authenticate. The directory database will appear to have been removed.

Select	Expand	RDN ^		Object class ^	Created
◯	✢	cn=configuration		ibm-slapdTop	
Page 1 of 1			Total: 1	Filtered: 1	Displayed: 1

Figure 17-64: Entry indicating ITDS is running in configuration mode

If ITDS will start only in configuration mode, some error is occurring during startup of the ITDS process (ibmslapd). You may find some clues to the problem in file ibmslapd.log in <ITDS-INSTANCE>\logs. (If you see no clues in the log, try starting ibmslapd.exe from a DOS command line to see whether it emits a trace that indicates the problem.)

Don't forget to check the db2cli.log for errors if you're having trouble getting the ITDS process to start.   If you see SQL1013N errors in the log — "The database alias name or database name <ldapdbname> could not be found" (where <ldapdbname> is the name of the database you configured when you created the directory server instance) — you might need to make sure the DB2INSTANCE environment variable is set properly for the startup environment of ibmslapd. If you're starting ITDS as a Windows service, you'll need to assign it a user name (that is a member of the Administrators group). Then properly set the DB2INSTANCE environment variable value for that user name to the name of the DB2 instance you created for the directory server to use (e.g., LDAPDB2).

With DB2 8.2, you may need to make sure the user ID you're using to run ITDS is a member of the DB2ADMNS group. DB2 8.2 defaults to being more rigorous about security checks than earlier versions.

ITDS V6 comes with a trace facility, the details of which are beyond the scope of this text. The ldtrc utility controls this facility.

A useful utility for diagnosing problems is ldapsearch (in <ITDS-ROOT>\bin). You can experiment with search filters that WebSphere or application programs might be using and make sure the results are as you expect, independently of WebSphere or an application that's using the directory.

18

Secure Sockets Layer Configuration and Verification

Secure Sockets Layer (SSL) is a protocol for providing encrypted data communications between two processes. Encryption is important for users of Internet sites that require secure communications, such as sites that accept credit-card payments or involve personal identity, health, or financial information.

SSL encryption relies on a combination of public key, or asymmetric, cryptography and symmetric cryptography. A public key is packaged in something referred to as a *certificate* that is either self-signed or, more typically, signed by a *certificate authority* that is trusted by the client (e.g., a Web browser). A standard known as X.509 governs the format and content of certificates.

To establish an SSL connection, a client and a server exchange a series of messages. In nearly all cases, only the server needs to present a certificate to authenticate to the client. But you can also configure a server to require clients to provide a certificate to authenticate to the server. (The administrative overhead of maintaining a large number of client certificates, along with loss and theft considerations, is among the factors that tend to deter use of X.509 certificates for client authentication.)

In this chapter, we describe how to set up SSL communications links between various processes in a typical WebSphere enterprise configuration:

- SSL between a browser and IBM HTTP Server (IHS)
- SSL between IHS and WebSphere Application Server
- SSL between WebSphere processes and IBM Tivoli Directory Server (ITDS)

Figure 18-1 provides a simplified view of the steps involved in an SSL handshake. The illustration assumes only server authentication takes place.

1. The client sends an initial request to the server that includes information about which SSL version and encryption algorithms it can support.

2. The server responds with a message that indicates which encryption algorithms it will use. The server sends an SSL session ID that identifies the connection. It also sends its signed X.509 certificate.

3. The client then sends a message to the server containing a preliminary (random-number) secret encrypted using the server's public key (which the client extracts from the server's certificate). The client and server use this preliminary secret to create a session key to use for the symmetric encryption of subsequent communications.

4. The client and server exchange messages that include the session key and the agreed-upon algorithm for symmetric encryption.

5. To provide a high degree of confidence that the exchanged messages were received without tampering, the client and server exchange messages containing digital signatures of all the exchanged messages.

6. The client and server switch to encrypted communications using the session key for symmetric encryption.

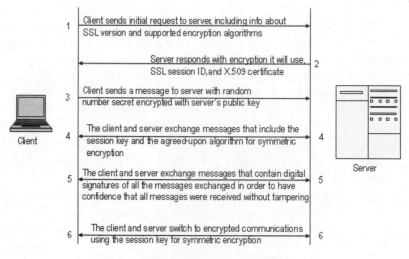

Figure 18-1: Simplified view of SSL handshake

The bulk of the performance cost for SSL lies in the computational and communications overhead of setting up an SSL connection. Once the connection is established, the performance impact of the symmetric encryption is relatively low and well worth the added security.

Some sites use "SSL accelerators" to alleviate the performance impact of SSL. You'd be wise to carefully test whether an SSL accelerator actually provides much of a boost in your situation. These accelerators help with only the symmetric encryption part of the communications and don't address the overhead of setting up the SSL connection. Depending on use patterns in your environment, an SSL accelerator may not improve performance much. In addition, consider the fact that SSL connections are usually terminated at an HTTP server that may not be very busy anyway, in which case you can let the HTTP server's CPU do the SSL encryption work.

Configuring SSL for IBM HTTP Server

You can use the IBM Key Management (iKeyman) utility that comes with IBM HTTP Server to create certificates for the Web server to use when setting up an SSL communications link with its browser clients. When installing IHS prior to Version 6, you had to do a "custom" install and include the Base Extensions for IHS to support SSL. With IHS V6, the "typical" install includes a Security package that contains the components needed to support SSL connections. (If the Security component of IHS has been installed, you should see an ikeyman directory in the directory tree where you installed IHS, and the modules directory should contain a mod_ibm_ssl.so file.)

Before WebSphere V6, the iKeyman utility used for IHS key file management was a different program than the iKeyman utility used for key file management for the WebSphere application server. With Version 6 of WebSphere and IHS, you can use the same iKeyman utility to manage key files for both servers. Keep in mind, however, that IHS uses a Cryptographic Message Syntax (CMS) type of key file and WebSphere uses a Java Key Store (JKS) key file.

Configuring IHS to support SSL communications with browser clients involves the following tasks:

1. Create the public key infrastructure (PKI) artifacts needed by IHS.

   - Create a key file for storing keys and certificates.

   - Create either a self-signed certificate or a certificate signed by a certificate authority.

2. Configure a virtual host on IHS to use secure HTTP (HTTPS).

   ■ Create a virtual host with the usual HTTPS port number (443).

   ■ Specify other attributes (e.g., document root) for the virtual host.

3. Enable SSL on IHS.

4. Test the connection using a browser.

In the following sections, we provide and illustrate the detailed steps involved in this configuration for a Windows installation.

Table 18-1 explains the symbolic file system references used in the following discussion. The path examples are typical install locations for a sample Windows installation. Exactly where you install the software on your machine will depend on whether it's a Windows or a Unix system and on the conventions you adopt regarding directory names. It's best to avoid using directory names that contain space characters, even on Windows machines. Spaces in directory names tend to introduce annoying problems when you want to write scripts to automate administration.

Table 18-1: Symbolic file system references

Symbolic reference	Description
<IHSV6-ROOT>	The root directory where IBM HTTP Server is installed. (In the example, IHS is installed in C:\IHS6.)
www.sandbox.com	The host name used in the step-by-step explanations.
<IHSV6-ROOT>\ssl	For this chapter's example, this is where the IHS public key infrastructure (PKI) artifacts (key file, trust file, and stash file) are stored.
<WASV6-ROOT>	The installation root directory for WebSphere V6 (e.g., C:\WAS6).
<PROFILE-ROOT>	The root directory of a given WebSphere profile. The default location for profiles is the <WASV6-ROOT>\profiles directory. For example, C:\WAS6\profiles\DM1 could be a profile root directory for a Deployment Manager profile.
<PLUGIN-ROOT>	The root directory for the WebSphere HTTP server plug-in installation.

Create the PKI Artifacts Needed by IHS

In this example, you'll store the key file and other public key infrastructure artifacts in a directory named "ssl" in the directory where you installed IBM HTTP Server. (In reality, you can store these items wherever you like.)

Step 1.   Create a key database file for IHS. To do so, start the IHS key management utility (iKeyman) by clicking the Windows **Start** button and navigating to **Programs|IBM HTTP Server|Start Key Management Utility**. (You can also start IHS's iKeyman utility from a command prompt, as you'll see later in the chapter.) Select **Key Database File|New** (or click the toolbar's "new key database file" icon) to display the panel shown in Figure 18-2.

a. Choose a key database type of **CMS**.

b. Provide a file name for the key file (e.g., ihsKeyfile.kdb).

c. Provide a path to the directory where the key file is to be stored (e.g., C:\IHS6\ssl).

d. Click **OK**.

Figure 18-2: Creating a new key database file

When prompted by the panel shown in Figure 18-3, enter a password and confirm it. (This is the password that you or another administrator will need to provide to access the key file you're creating.)

The default password expiration period is 60 days. You'll need to conform to your organization's policies on password expiration times. At many organizations, the expiration period is 90 days. This password is yet another thing for administrators to be diligent about updating.

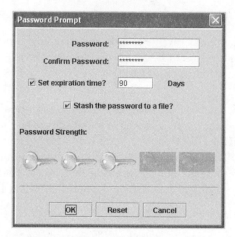

Figure 18-3: Key file password options

Select the password panel's option to stash the password to a file. IHS will need the password, too, when it accesses the key file at startup. One of the directives you'll configure for IHS is the path to the stash file.

Click **OK**. The utility will store the password in a file with the same path and root name as the key file and the extension **sth**, as the message shown in Figure 18-4 indicates.

Figure 18-4: iKeyman notification of password location

You now have a key store for IHS. The default collection of signer certificates appears under **Signer Certificates** in the key database content (Figure 18-5).

Step 2. Your next task is to create a self-signed certificate for IHS. From the iKeyman menu, select **Create|New self-signed certificate** (or click the toolbar's "create a new self-signed certificate" icon). Take the following steps on the resulting panel, shown in Figure 18-6:

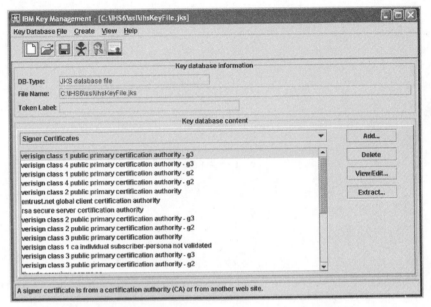

Figure 18-5: Default signer certificates in IHS key store

a. For **Key Label**, enter **myIHSCertificate**. (This will be the value of the SSLServerCert directive in the HTTP Server configuration file, httpd.conf.)

b. For **Common Name**, enter the host name of the HTTP server that will use the certificate. (For this example, we'll use the name www.sandbox.com.) It's important to make the common name of the certificate the same as the host name of the server using the certificate. Otherwise, browsers will issue an alert that the host name of the certificate doesn't match the host name of the server using it.

c. Fill in the certificate's other attributes as you see fit. Note that the validity period of the certificate defaults to one year. One administrative task associated with PKI certificates is maintaining a calendar of expirations and being diligent about renewing certificates before they expire.

d. Click **OK**. The certificate will be stored in the Personal Certificates part of the key store.

Step 3 Optionally extract the public certificate so clients can use it. This step is
(optional). optional because browsers typically provide the option to store a certificate

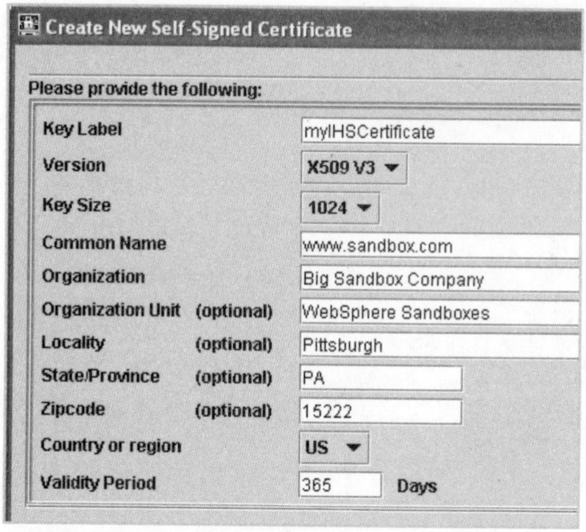

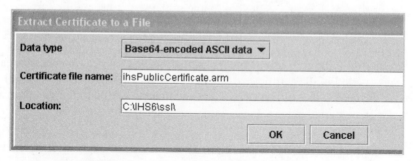

Figure 18-6: Creating a self-signed certificate

the first time it arrives. (If you distribute the certificate to browser clients, the browser users won't see an alert about a certificate signed by an unknown authority when the certificate arrives at the browser for the first time.)

To extract the certificate, click the **Extract** button on iKeyman's main panel. On the resulting panel (Figure 18-7), provide a certificate file name (e.g., ihsPublicCertificate.arm) and a location for the file (e.g., C:\IHS6\ssl\). Then click **OK**.

Figure 18-7: Extracting the self-signed certificate

Step 4.   Exit iKeyman. The next time you start the utility, no key database file will be open. To see the file, you'll need to select **Key Database File|Open** or click the toolbar's "open a key database file" icon and browse to the key file you just created (or provide the full path). Then supply the password associated with the file to open it.

Configure a Virtual Host on IHS to Use HTTPS

For purposes of setting up a test, you're going to create a virtual host in IHS associated with the default SSL port, 443. As you learned in Chapter 5, the file httpd.conf in the <IHSV6-ROOT>\conf directory specifies the configuration of Apache HTTP servers. (For comprehensive explanations of the directives used to configure an Apache HTTP server, see *Apache: The Definitive Guide* by Ben Laurie and Peter Laurie; O'Reilly, 2002.) The HTTP server process reads this file when it starts. If you make changes to the file, you must restart IHS for the changes to take effect. You can use any text editor to modify the httpd.conf file.

The following description includes the lines that are added to the httpd.conf file that specifies the configuration for the HTTP server. The httpd.conf.sample file in <IHSV6-ROOT>\conf contains documentation on the various directives associated with configuring SSL for an Apache Web server. You'll find this file a useful reminder when configuring SSL.

Step 1.   Make a backup of the original httpd.conf file. Because you'll be changing the file, it's a good idea to make a backup in case something goes wrong.

Step 2.   In the load module section of httpd.conf, add the following line:

```
LoadModule ibm_ssl_module modules/mod_ibm_ssl.so
```

Step 3.   To add a virtual host stanza to httpd.conf that has SSL enabled, find the section of the file where a virtual host is defined but commented out (search for "VirtualHost example"), and add the following lines:

```
Listen 443
<VirtualHost www.sandbox.com:443>
  DocumentRoot "htdocs/en_US"
  SSLEnable
  Keyfile "ssl/ihsKeyFile.kdb"
  SSLServerCert myIHSCertificate
  SSLStashFile "ssl/ihsKeyFile.sth"
  SSLV2Timeout 100
  SSLV3Timeout 1000
</VirtualHost>
```

The file paths here are relative to the IHS root directory (i.e., the directory where you installed IHS). If you decided to put the document root or the PKI artifacts in a directory outside <IHSV6-ROOT>, you'd use full paths.

Notice that the value of SSLServerCert is the certificate label you specified when creating the self-signed certificate.

Step 4.   Stop and start the IHS server to cause the changes to httpd.conf to take effect. Check the error.log file in directory <IHSV6-ROOT>\logs to make sure IHS starts correctly.

Step 5.   Next, you need to modify the hosts file on the Windows machine where you're going to run the browser to add www.sandbox.com to the hosts table. Once you add the entry to the hosts file, you can use "www.sandbox.com" in a URL entered at the browser, and the browser will be able to properly resolve the IP address where the IHS server is running.

Add a line to the hosts file that looks like this:

```
# IP address of IHS machine
12.34.56.789    www.sandbox.com
```

If the machine on which you're running the IHS server is the same as the machine on which you're running the browser, you can just add www.sandbox.com to the localhost line in the hosts file:

```
127.0.0.1    localhost www.sandbox.com
```

(On Windows, the hosts file is in either C:\WINDOWS\system32\drivers\etc or C:\WINNT\system32\drivers\etc, depending on the version of Windows you're using.)

Test the SSL Connection to IBM HTTP Server

Testing that you've set up the SSL configuration properly is as simple as using a browser to access the IBM HTTP Server welcome page using HTTPS. By default, browsers issue an alert when they receive a certificate they consider invalid. The browsers check whether the issuer (signer) of the certificate is known, whether the certificate has expired, and whether the name on the certificate matches the name of the server providing the page. It's up to the user to understand what the security alert means and take appropriate action.

It's interesting to consider the default response to this alert. As Figure 18-8 shows, the default action for Mozilla Firefox is to accept the certificate temporarily for the existing session, which means you'll connect to the site. For Microsoft Internet Explorer, the default action is not to "proceed" (Figure 18-9), which means don't connect to the site.

Consider the percentage of people who understand the implications of these security alerts. How many users would actually examine the certificate and be able to make a proper decision about connecting to the site? You can see that it would be a reasonable practice to always reject connecting to any site that uses an untrusted certificate. If you were to adopt such a policy, you'd need to take the steps described here to import the IHS public certificate into your browser.

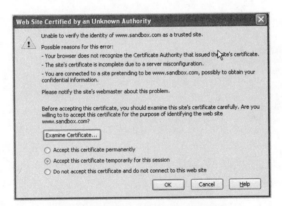

Figure 18-8: Firefox certificate alert

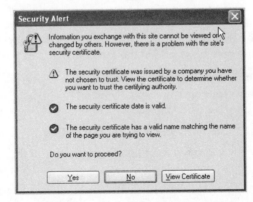

Figure 18-9: Internet Explorer certificate alert

Step 1.   Start a browser session, and try the URL: **https://www.sandbox.com/**. Note that the protocol is HTTPS, not HTTP. You should see a security alert.

Step 2.   Examine the certificate to make sure it's what you expect. Figure 18-10 shows the certificate for our example.

Step 3.   If you don't receive an alert when you access an HTTPS URL, check the following things:

- Use the command **netstat –an** to make sure something is listening on port 443. If nothing is listening, it's likely IHS didn't start properly.

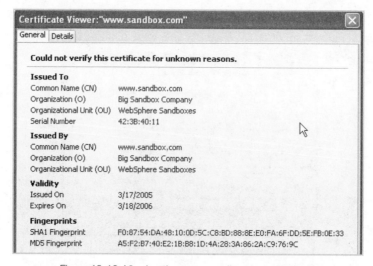

Figure 18-10: Viewing the www.sandbox.com certificate

- Check the IHS error log in <IHSV6-ROOT>\logs. Something configured incorrectly may have caused the server not to start properly.

- Make sure file paths for the KeyFile and SSLStashFile directives are correct for your configuration.

Importing a Public Certificate into a Browser

Browsers typically provide an option to import the certificate at the time they issue an alert. For Firefox, one option on the alert box is to "permanently" accept the certificate. For Internet Explorer, you can choose to "install" the certificate from the certificate viewer (Figure 18-11).

Browsers also include a certificate management utility that lets you import a certificate explicitly before visiting a site. Doing an explicit import of a self-signed certificate may make more sense from a security perspective because you can control the import process more carefully — for example, you can have a trained administrator do the import. If you exported the IHS public certificate file (ihsPublicCertificate.arm) as described above, you can import that certificate into your browser. You simply need to copy the IHS public certificate to the machine where you're configuring your browser or to a shared file system that the machine can access. The steps to do so differ slightly for Firefox and Internet Explorer. In the following description, the certificate file is in C:\Certificates.

Figure 18-11: Internet Explorer option to install the certificate

For Firefox, take the following steps to import the public certificate:

1. Under **Tools|Options** in the Firefox browser, click the **Advanced** icon, and scroll down to the portion of the viewer labeled **Manage Certificates.**

2. Click the **Manage Certificates** button.

3. On the **Certificate Manager** panel, select the **Web Sites** tab.

4. Click **Import**.

5. In the **Look in** drop-down list at the top of the next panel, browse to where you put the IHS public certificate (C:\Certificates in this example).

6. In the **Files of type** drop-down list at the bottom of the panel, select **All Files**.

7. Select the ihsPublicCertificate.arm file.

8. Click **Open**.

9. At this point, the **Purposes** entry for the certificate will be <Unknown>, as Figure 18-12 shows.

10. Select the certificate, and click **Edit**.

11. On the resulting panel (Figure 18-13), select the option to "Trust the authenticity of this certificate."

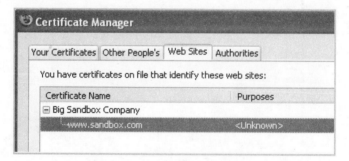

Figure 18-12: IHS public certificate in Firefox Certificate Manager

Figure 18-13: Selecting to trust the certificate

12. To conclude the import, click **OK** on each of the resulting panels.

13. Now exit Firefox, and retry the URL **https://www.sandbox.com/**. The browser should accept it without a security alert.

For Internet Explorer, take the following steps to import the public certificate:

1. Under **Tools Internet Options**, select the **Content** tab, and click the **Certificates** button.

2. Scroll to the right through the tabs on the **Certificates** panel to the **Trusted Root Certification Authorities** tab (Figure 18-14). You need to place the certificate in this store to indicate to the browser that the "root signer," www.sandbox.com, is trusted. If the certificate were signed by a recognized CA rather than self-signed, you'd put it in the **Trusted Publishers** store.

Figure 18-14: Trusted Root Certification Authorities tab

3. Leave the **Intended purpose** field at the top of the panel set to **<All>**.

4. Click the **Import** button to start the Certificate Import wizard.

5. Click **Next** to get past the initial screen, and then click **Browse**.

6. In the **Files of type** list, select **All Files** (to see .arm file types).

7. Navigate to where you stored the public certificate file (e.g., C:\Certificates).

8. Select the IHS certificate (ihsPublicCertificate.arm), and click **Open**.

9. Click **Next**, and you'll see the panel shown in Figure 18-15, where you can select the store into which you want to import the certificate. (The **Certificate store** field should say **Trusted Root Certification Authorities**

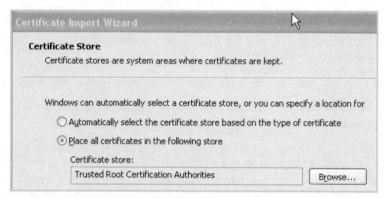

Figure 18-15: Selecting the certificate store

because you selected that tab when you started the import wizard. The **Browse** button on this panel lets you select the certificate store.)

10. Click **Next**.

11. On the next panel, click **Finish**.

12. You'll receive an alert similar to the one shown in Figure 18-16, questioning whether you want to add the certificate to the root store. Click **Yes**.

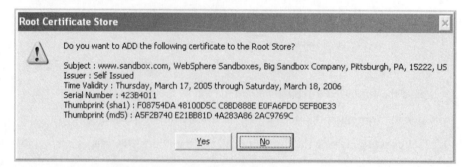

Figure 18-16: Adding the certificate to the root store

13. When you see the success pop-up notification, click **OK**.

14. You should now see the IHS certificate in the Trusted Root Certification Authorities store, as shown in Figure 18-17.

15. Close the **Certificates** panel, and click **OK** on the **Internet Options** panel to close it.

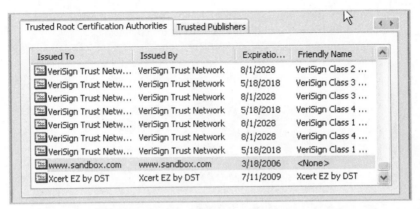

Figure 18-17: IHS certificate in Trusted Root Certification Authorities store

16. You should now be able to issue **https://www.sandbox.com/** and have the IHS welcome page appear without the browser displaying a security alert.

Creating a Certificate Signed by a Certificate Authority

In this section, we explain how to create a certificate that has been signed by a certificate authority. This is what you do for public-facing production servers that need to provide SSL connections. In this example, you'll obtain a 14-day trial signed certificate from VeriSign, Inc. In this description, the server is IBM HTTP Server. The process is essentially the same for any WebSphere server.

Note that there are several places in this set of instructions where you must cut and paste an ASCII representation of a digital certificate into a text file or a Web form. The beginning and ending of the certificate are marked by

```
---BEGIN CERTIFICATE---
---END CERTIFICATE---
```

When selecting the certificate text, you can select everything, including the "begin certificate" and "end certificate" text. Use a text editor that won't introduce any hidden formatting characters into the content (e.g., Notepad or WordPad on Windows).

Step 1.   Start the IHS iKeyman utility. To do so, open a DOS command window, change to directory <IHSV6-ROOT>\bin, and enter **ikeyman**.

Step 2.   Open the ihsKeyFile.kdb key file you created earlier in this chapter, specifying the file as shown in Figure 18-18.

     a. For **Key database** type, select **CMS**.

     b. For **File Name**, specify **ihsKeyFile.kdb**.

     c. For **Location**, use <IHSV6-ROOT>\ssl (e.g., C:\IHS6\ssl).

     d. Click **OK**.

     e. When prompted, provide the administrative password to access the file.

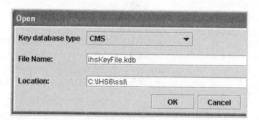

Figure 18-18: Opening the key file

Step 3.   From the pull-down menu in the key database content pane, select the **Personal Certificate Requests** list of database objects (Figure 18-19), which at this point is empty.

Figure 18-19: Selecting the Personal Certificates Requests list

Step 4.   Once you select the Personal Certificate Requests for the database content pane, you should see a different set of action buttons on the right side of the key database content pane. Click **New** here to create a new *certificate signing request (CSR)*.

When submitting a certificate signing request to VeriSign, you must fill out all the fields of the CSR (including the ones marked as optional). Specify the certificate attributes as shown in Figure 18-20:

     a. For **Key Label**, enter **IHS Server Certificate** (or whatever text you like). (In a later step, you'll specify the SSLServerCert directive value in file httpd.conf as the value of this label.)

     b. For **Common Name**, enter the fully qualified virtual host name for the site (e.g., www.sandbox.com). Browsers compare this name with the host name of the server presenting the certificate and issue an alert if the names don't match.

c. For **Organization**, name your organization.

d. For **Organization Unit**, enter your organization unit.

e. For **Locality**, supply your city or town.

f. For **State/Province**, enter the fully spelled-out name of your state or province.

g. For **Zipcode**, enter your ZIP code.

h. For **Country or region**, select the appropriate code from the pull-down list. The default value for this field is **US** (United States).

i. At the bottom of the panel, indicate where the certificate request file should be stored. For this example, we've specified <IHSV6ROOT>\ssl\IHSCertificateRequest.arm.

j. Click **OK**.

Figure 18-20: Creating a new certificate signing request

You should see a confirmation pop-up indicating that the CSR was created (Figure 18-21). When you visit the VeriSign site to request a signed certificate, you'll cut and paste the content of the certificate request file (IHSCertificateRequest.arm) into VeriSign's online request form.

Figure 18-21: Notification of successful certificate request creation

Step 5.   Open a browser, and enter **http://www.verisign.com/** to go to the VeriSign site. Click the **Free SSL Trial** link near the top of the page to request a 14-day trial signed certificate. Figure 18-22 shows this link.

Figure 18-22: Requesting a trial certificate from VeriSign

Step 6.   Enter your technical contact information in VeriSign's Web form.

Step 7.   Fill out the CSR information, taking note of the following points:

- If you don't see IBM HTTP Server in the list of server platforms, select **Server not listed**. (Even though IHS is based on Apache, its SSL support differs from Apache's, so don't specify Apache as the server platform.)

- To supply the CSR from the server, use a text editor to open the .arm file you created earlier (IHSCertificateRequest.arm), cut the content from the file, and paste it into the online form. (Use Notepad, WordPad, or another text editor that won't introduce formatting characters into the content.)

- In the "usage" list in the form's lower-right corner, choose **Web Server**. Then click **Continue**.

- If you don't fill out all the information in the CSR, the VeriSign Web form will report an error, noting that required information is missing. (It may not be clear that the required information is missing from the CSR, but that's likely what the problem is.)

Step 8. Confirm the CSR information, enter a challenge phrase and question, and finish out the ordering steps. The trial certificate and a Web site link with instructions for installing the certificate will show up in your e-mail shortly.

Step 9. Before you can install the trial certificate, you need to install a VeriSign Test CA Root certificate, cutting and pasting it from the VeriSign Web site specified in the e-mail message to a text file to be imported into the IHS server signer certificates. (In this example, you'll store the certificate file in <IHSV6-ROOT>\ssl, the directory created to hold the PKI artifacts for the IHS server.) For IHS (and other WebSphere processes that use iKeyman to manage their certificates), you need to copy VeriSign's Test CA Root certificate to install into the server key file. The VeriSign site may also have a Test Intermediate certificate, but you don't need that.

To copy the test certificate:

a. Create a text file to contain the Test CA Root certificate (e.g., VerisignTestCARootCert.txt).

b. Use Notepad, WordPad, or another text editor to paste the Test CA Root certificate from the VeriSign site into the text file.

c. Change the file's extension to .arm (e.g., VerisignTestCARootCert.arm).

Step 10. Now, install the VeriSign Test CA Root certificate into the signer certificates in the key file for the IHS server. (You need to install the Test CA Root certificate before iKeyman will let you install the trial server certificate signed by the Test CA.)

a. In the iKeyman tool with the ihsKeyFile.kdb file opened, select the Signer Certificates, and click **Add** on the right side of the key database content pane.

b. Browse to the location of the VerisignTestCARootCert.arm file (Figure 18-23), and click **OK**.

c. Enter a label for the certificate (e.g., Verisign Test CA Root Certificate), and click **OK**.

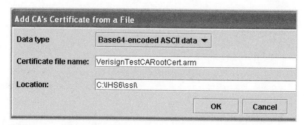

Figure 18-23: Selecting the VerisignTestCARootCert.arm file

The test certificate should now appear in the collection of signer certificates for the IHS server (Figure 18-24). This will allow the signed certificate for the IHS server to be accepted.

Figure 18-24: VeriSign test certificate in signer certificates list

Step 11. You're now ready to create a certificate file from the CA signed certificate you received in the VeriSign e-mail. Scroll to the bottom of the e-mail to find the certificate.

    a. Create a text file to hold the certificate content (e.g., IHSVerisignSigned14DayTrialCert.txt).

    b. Paste the certificate content into the file. (You can copy all the text from "Begin Certificate" to "End Certificate.")

    c. Change the file extension to .arm: IHSVerisignSigned14DayTrialCert.arm.

Step 12. Receive the VeriSign signed certificate:

    a. In the iKeyman tool with the ihsKeyFile.kdb opened, select the Personal Certificates, and click **Receive** on the right side of the key database content pane.

    b. Browse to the IHSVerisignSigned14DayTrialCert.arm file (Figure 18-25).

    c. Click **OK**.

    d. If you already have a key in the key file, a pop-up (Figure 18-26) will appear, prompting you to set the key associated with this signed certificate to be the default key for the database. Click **Yes**. If the key file is empty at the time you received the signed key, you won't see this pop-up.

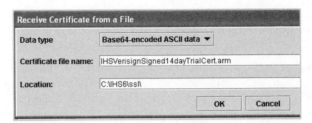

Figure 18-25: Specifying the file to receive the certificate

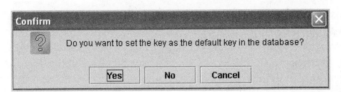

Figure 18-26: Default database key prompt

At this point, the signed certificate is now the key for the IHS server. You might also note that if you go look at the list of Personal Certificate Requests, the one associated with the certificate you just installed is gone. Once you've "received" a certificate, the CSR has no use and it is deleted.

Step 13. Make sure the certificate label specified in the HTTP Server configuration file (httpd.conf) is the same as the label in the IHS key file (ihsKeyFile.kdb). In this example, the label used for the trial signed certificate is "IHS Server Certificate" (this differs from the label used in the self-signed certificate). The SSLServerCert directive in httpd.conf specifies the label to use for a given SSL virtual host definition. The www.sandbox.com virtual host definition needs to look like the following:

```
<VirtualHost www.sandbox.com:443>
  DocumentRoot "htdocs/en_US"
  SSLEnable
  Keyfile "ssl/ihsKeyFile.kdb"
  SSLServerCert IHS Server Certificate
  SSLStashFile "ssl/ihsKeyFile.sth"
  SSLV2Timeout 100
  SSLV3Timeout 1000
</VirtualHost>
```

Notice that the value of the SSLServerCert directive is the certificate label used in the certificate signing request, and — no surprise — it is the label of the signed certificate as it appears in the Personal Certificates of the ihsKeyFile in iKeyman. Also notice that you don't put quotation marks ("") around the SSLServerCert attribute value even though it contains space characters.

If you don't get the SSLServerCert value right, the Firefox browser will issue an alert indicating "no data." Internet Explorer will issue a "server not found" error. You'll see an SSL handshake failure in the IHS error.log file:

```
SSL Handshake Failed, Specified label could not be found in the key
file.
```

Step 14. Install the Test CA Root certificate into your browser. (If you're getting a real signed certificate for your site, this step is unnecessary because browsers already have the VeriSign CA root certificates. However, for the trial certificate signed by the trial CA root, you need the Test CA Root certificate installed in any browser you're using for the test for your site's trial certificate to be trusted.)

In Firefox, you import certificates by selecting **Tools|Options** and then clicking **Advanced** in the left options column. Scroll down to **Manage Certificates**, and click the **Manage Certificates** button.

a. Choose the **Authorities** tab, and click **Import**.

b. In the **Files of type** list, select **All Files**.

c. Browse to where you created the Test CA Root certificate (e.g., <IHSV6-ROOT>\ssl), select the certificate file (e.g., VerisignTestCARootCert.arm), and click **Open**.

d. On the panel shown in Figure 18-27, select the option to indicate that you want to trust this CA to identify Web sites. You can view the CA certificate to make sure it's the Test CA Root from VeriSign. Click **OK** to accept it.

You can examine the installed Test Root CA certificate in Firefox under **Tools|Options|Advanced**. Scroll to **Manage Certificates**, click the **Manage Certificates** button, and select the **Authorities** tab in the Certificate Manager that pops up. Scroll down to the VeriSign certificates, and you'll see the Test CA Root certificate (Figure 18-28).

The installation of CA certificates using Internet Explorer is similar to the process for Firefox. You navigate to **Tools|Internet Options|Content|Certificates|Trusted Root Certification Authorities** and click **Import**. A wizard starts up. Browse to the Test CA Root certificate file

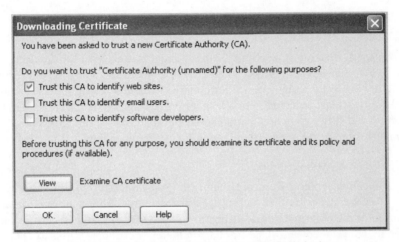

Figure 18-27: Option to trust the CA to identify Web sites

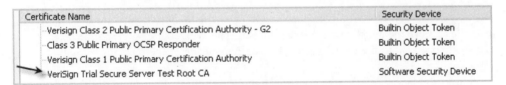

Figure 18-28: Test CA Root certificate in Firefox certificates list

(e.g., VerisignTestCARootCert.arm), and import it into "Trusted Root Certification Authorities."

Step 15. Now, test your configuration with an HTTPS URL. For example, **https://www.sandbox.com/** should return the IHS welcome page if you have a virtual host set up as described in this example. Assuming you've configured everything correctly, the browser shouldn't issue any alerts about certificates. Keep in mind that the host name of the certificate must match the host name in the URL. The browser needs to have the Test CA Root certificate installed properly. And the SSLServerCert value in httpd.conf must be correct.

Step 16. Make a backup copy of your IHS key file artifacts (i.e., ihsKeyFile.*), and store them in a secure place for recovery situations.

Configuring SSL Between the HTTP Server Plug-in and the Application Server

A common step in securing a WebSphere environment is to encrypt the connections between the WebSphere HTTP server plug-in and the WebSphere application server. The decision to do this is driven by a desire for a more "hardened" environment that adds a level of security against potential network snooping. Using SSL connections between HTPP servers and WebSphere application servers also adds a great degree of assurance that only the desired machines are involved in the communications.

The plug-in needs a key file in which to store its private key and the digital certificate from the application server's Web container. (The plug-in doesn't use the same key file as the HTTP server itself. Neither does it use a separate trust file for storing trusted certificates.) For the plug-in digital certificate, you can use a selfsigned certificate; you don't need to get a signed certificate from a commercial certificate authority. The plug-in certificate is added to the trust file of the Web container.

The application server's Web container needs a key file to store its private key and a trust file to store the certificate from the plug-in. The Web container self-signed certificate is added to the signer certificates in the key file of the plug-in.

A typical production environment will have multiple HTTP servers and multiple application servers. If you wanted to, you could create certificates for each HTTP server plug-in and each application server and exchange them, but that isn't necessary and would add tremendously to the administrative overhead of maintaining the cell. For most purposes, it's enough to use one key file for the HTTP server plug-in and copy it around to the other machines on which the HTTP servers reside. You can also use one Web container database and copy it to the machines on which the other application servers are running. (One reason it's feasible to use the same key database for multiple servers running on different hosts is that the plug-in and the Web container don't compare the host name in the certificates with the source of the request.)

Create the SSL Artifacts Needed by the Plug-in

This section describes the steps to take to set up the plug-in to use SSL. When you install the plug-in, a key file is created, along with its supporting artifacts, in the <PLUGIN-ROOT>\etc directory. The password for access to this key file is "WebAS". The first thing you'll do is delete the key in this key file and change the access password. Another option is to delete the key file artifacts (which are shown in Figure 18-29) and completely re-create them.

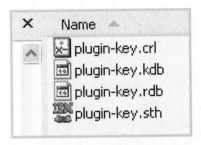

Figure 18-29: Key file artifacts

The configuration file that the plug-in reads when it starts up (plugin-cfg.xml) includes in it the path to the key file and the password stash file. The following lines show this portion of the file.

```
<Transport Hostname="was-host1.ibm.com" Port="9443"
Protocol="https">
<Property name="keyring" value="C:\IHS6\wasplugin/etc/plugin-
key.kdb"/> <Property name="stashfile"
value="C:\IHS6\wasplugin/etc/plugin-key.sth"/>
</Transport>
```

It turns out to be convenient to use the same name for the key file and leave it in the same directory. If you give the key file a different name or put it in a different directory, you must modify the generated plugin-cfg.xml file to use the different file name or directory.

Step 1. Start the iKeyman utility that comes with the HTTP server. There's an ikeyman.bat file in <PLUGIN-ROOT>\bin, but that may not properly start the iKeyman utility. Be sure to use the iKeyman that's installed with IBM HTTP Server. To do so, change to directory <IHSV6-ROOT>\bin, open a DOS window, and enter **ikeyman** on the command line.

Step 2. Open the plug-in key file (plugin-key.kdb) in <PLUGIN-ROOT>\etc. (In these instructions, we assume <PLUGIN-ROOT> is C:\IHS6\wasplugin — that is, we assume you installed the WebSphere plug-in in the <IHSV6-ROOT> directory.)

a. For **Key database type**, select **CMS**.
b. Browse to file plugin-key.kdb.
c. For **Location**, use <PLUGIN-ROOT>\etc (e.g., C:\IHS6\wasplugin\etc).

Step 3.   Next, delete the key that's present in Personal Certificates from the plug-in installation. To do so, select **WebSphere Plugin Key** in the Personal Certificates list, click **Delete**, and confirm.

Step 4.   Now, change the access password for the key file:

    a. From the menu bar, select **Key Database File|Change Password** to display the **Change Password** panel (Figure 18-30).

    b. Enter and confirm a new file access password.

    c. Set the expiration time according to your organization's password expiration policy. (You can clear the expiration time check box so that the password doesn't expire.)

    d. Select the option to stash the password to a file.

    e. Click **OK**.

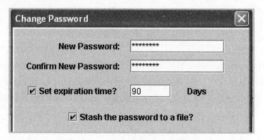

Figure 18-30: Change Password panel

Step 5.   Delete all the signer certificates from the plug-in installation. (You want the plug-in to trust only WebSphere application servers, so the only signer certificate it will have is the self-signed one for the application servers.)

    a. Select **Signer Certificates** from the key database content pull-down menu.

    b. Select the first certificate, and then shift-select the last certificate.

    c. Click **Delete**.

    d. The Signer Certificates section should now be empty, as in Figure 18-31.

Step 6.   Create a self-signed certificate for the plug-in. To do so, select **Personal Certificates** from the key database content pull-down menu, and click **New Self-Signed**. Specify the options as shown in Figure 18-32:

Figure 18-31: Signer Certificates section after deleting the signer certificates

a. For **Key Label**, enter **WebSphere HTTP Server Plugin Key**.

b. For **Common Name**, specify some generic name. (This value doesn't need to be a real host name. Plug-ins on more than one HTTP server will use the key, and the Web container doesn't compare the host name in the certificate with the host name of the connection source.)

c. For **Organization**, specify your organization.

d. The remaining organizational attributes are optional.

e. For **Validity Period**, use 365 days or whatever term makes sense to you. Be sure to set up a reminder system to replace the key and copy a new certificate to all the Web container trust files before the certificate becomes invalid. The plug-in and Web container will fail to communicate if the keys and certificates they're using are invalid.

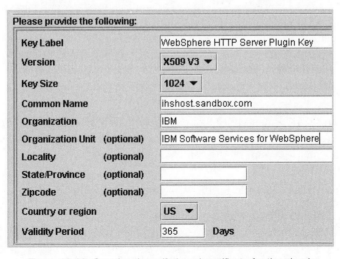

Figure 18-32: Creating the self-signed certificate for the plug-in

Step 7.   Extract the certificate from the plug-in key:

    a. Select **WebSphere HTTP Server Plugin Key**.

    b. Click **Extract**.

    c. Provide a file name: **WebSphereIHSPluginCertificate**.

    d. Export the certificate to <PLUGIN-ROOT>\etc with the rest of the plug-in SSL artifacts.

Step 8.   Copy the plug-in certificate file to the machine where you'll create the Web container trust file. (For this example, we'll assume you copy the file to the application server machine's <WASV6-ROOT>\ssl directory.) In the next section, you'll add this certificate to the signer certificates of the Web container trust file.

Step 9.   Exit iKeyman.

Create the SSL Artifacts Needed by the Application Server

This section explains the steps to take to set up the application server Web container to use SSL.

Step 1.   Create a directory where you can keep the key and trust file to be used by the Web container. In this example, the SSL artifacts directory is <WASV6-ROOT>\ssl. For <WASV6-ROOT>, you can use the WebSphere variable ${WAS_INSTALL_ROOT}. (<PROFILE-ROOT>\ssl would also work because you can use WebSphere variable ${USER_INSTALL_ROOT} for each node.) You need to define only one SSL repertoire artifact because the path to the key and trust file will be the same on all nodes if you use the appropriate WebSphere variable as the root for the path to the key and trust files.

Step 2.   Start the iKeyman utility that comes with WebSphere Application Server. To do so, change to directory <PROFILE-ROOT>\bin, open a DOS window, and enter **ikeyman** on the command line.

Step 3.   Create a new key file for the Web container (Figure 18-33):

    a. For **Key database type**, select **JKS**.

    b. For **File Name**, enter **WebContainerKeyFile.jks**.

    c. For **Location**, use <WASV6-ROOT>\ssl.

d. Click **OK**.

e. In the next pop-up dialog, specify and confirm a password for key file access.

Figure 18-33: Creating the key file for the Web container

Step 4.   Because WebSphere servers support the notion of a separate trust file, you should remove all signer certificates from the key file. To delete the certificates:

a. Select the first signer certificate in the list.
b. Scroll to the bottom of the list, and shift-select the last signer certificate.
c. Click **Delete**.

Step 5.   Next, create a new self-signed certificate for the Web container. To do so, select **Personal Certificates** in the pull-down for the key database content, and click **New Self-Signed**. Specify the options as follows.

a. For **Key Label**, enter **Web Container Key** (or whatever text you like).

b. For **Common Name**, specify a generic name. (The value doesn't need to be a real host name. Servers on more than one host are going to use it, and the plug-in doesn't compare the common name in the certificate with the source host name of the connection.)

c. For **Organization**, specify your organization.

d. The remaining organizational attributes are optional.

e. For **Validity Period**, use 365 days or whatever term makes sense to you. Be sure to set up a reminder system to replace the key and copy a new certificate to all the plug-in key stores before it becomes invalid. The plug-in and Web container will fail to communicate if the keys and certificates they're using are invalid.

Step 6.   Extract a certificate from the Web container key:

a. Select **Web Container Key**.

b. Click **Extract**.

c. For **Certificate file name**, enter **WebContainerCertificate.arm**.

d. For **Location**, use <WASV6-ROOT>\ssl.

e. Copy this certificate to the HTTP server machine on which you created the key file for the plug-in.

Step 7.   Create a trust file to be used by the Web container:

a. For **Key database type**, select **JKS**.

b. For **File Name**, enter **WebContainerTrustFile.jks**.

c. For **Location**, use <WASV6-ROOT>\ssl.

d. Click **OK**.

e. In the next pop-up dialog, provide and confirm a password for access to the trust file.

Step 8.   Delete all the signer certificates. (For this particular trust file, you want the Web container to trust only the plug-ins in the HTTP servers.)

Step 9.   Import the plug-in certificate:

a. With the Signer Certificates selected in the key database content pane, click **Add**.

b. Browse to where you copied the IHS plug-in certificate that you created in the previous section (Figure 18-34). (In this example, we copied the

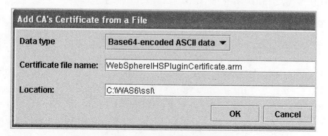

Figure 18-34: Importing the plug-in certificate

plug-in certificate to the application server machine's <WASV6-ROOT>\ssl directory.)

c. Click **OK**.

d. In the next panel, enter a label for the certificate (e.g., WebSphere IHS Plugin Certificate).

e. Click **OK**. The certificate will appear as the only entry in the Signer Certificates list (Figure 18-35).

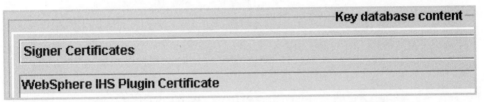

Figure 18-35: Plug-in certificate in application server's Signer Certificates list

Step 10. The Web container key and trust files are complete. Copy these two files to the other nodes (machines) in the cell that have application servers intended to communicate with the HTTP servers that will route requests to the application servers. Copy each file to the same directory on all installations (<WASV6-ROOT>\ssl) or profiles (<PROFILE-ROOT>\ssl) so you can define one SSL repertoire artifact to reference this key-and-trust-file pair on any node in the cell.

Step 11. Next, add the Web container certificate to the key file of the plug-in. (If you haven't done so already, copy the WebContainerCertificate.arm file to the IHS machine where you created the plug-in key file.) Take the following steps to perform this task.

a. If it's not already running, start iKeyman on the IHS server where you created the plug-in key file.

b. Open the plug-in key file. For **Key database type**, select **CMS**. For **File Name**, specify **plugin-key.kdb**. For **Location**, use <PLUGIN-ROOT>\etc (e.g., C:\IHS6\wasplugin\etc). Click **OK**.

c. Provide the key file access password.

d. Select the Signer Certificates view of the key database content, and click **Add**.

e. Browse to where you put the WebContainerCertificate.arm file (Figure 18-36). (In this example, the certificate file was copied to <PLUGIN-ROOT>\etc.)

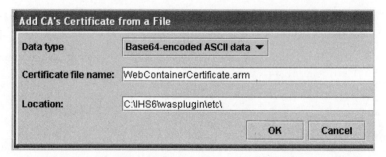

Figure 18-36: Adding the Web container certificate

f. Click **OK**, and provide a label (e.g., "Web Container Certificate") for the certificate in the next pop-up dialog.

g. Click **OK** to have the certificate added to the signer certificates (Figure 18-37).

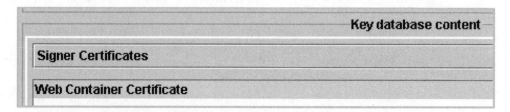

Figure 18-37: Web container certificate in IHS Signer Certificates list

Step 12. The plug-in key file is complete. You can now copy the plug-in key file artifacts to the <PLUGIN-ROOT>\etc directory on the other IHS machines you intend for use by application servers in the cell. Copy **plugin-key.*** (four files) to the other IHS machines.

Configuring SSL Between the Plugin and the Web Container

This section describes the steps to configure an SSL port for the Web container of the application server. You'll create an SSL configuration repertoire to define the attributes and artifact locations needed to create an SSL connection. (You learned about SSL configuration repertoires in Chapter 16.)

Step 1. Open an admin console on your Deployment Manager or standalone application server. In the left navigation pane, expand **Security**, and select **SSL** to manage the SSL configuration repertoire artifacts (Figure 18-38).

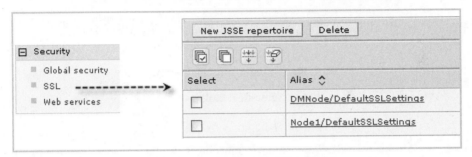

Figure 18-38: Managing the SSL artifacts

Step 2. To create an SSL configuration repertoire, click **New JSSE repertoire**. Specify the configuration attributes as follows:

a. For **Alias**, enter **PluginWebContainerSSLConnection** (or whatever you'd like to call this configuration).

b. You can leave most of the SSL configuration attributes at their default values. The only attributes you'll fill in are the key and trust file names and passwords.

- For the key file name, use ${WAS_INSTALL_ROOT} /ssl/Web ContainerKeyFile.jks.

- For the key file password, enter the password you specified when you created the Web container key file (*<password>*).

- For the trust file name, use ${WAS_INSTALL_ROOT} /ssl/ Web ContainerTrustFile.jks.

- For the trust file password, enter <password> (the Web container trust file password).

c. Click **OK**.

d. Save your configuration. Figure 18-39 shows the listing for the new SSL configuration repertoire.

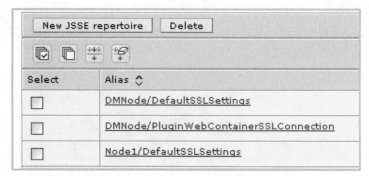

Figure 18-39: New SSL configuration repertoire

Step 3. Modify the SSL Web container transport to use the SSL configuration repertoire you just created:

a. Access the server Web container by expanding **Servers** and navigating to **Application Servers|*your-server*|Web Container Settings|Web container transport chains** (Figure 18-40).

b. Click the WCInboundDefaultSecure transport to open it.

c. Select the SSL inbound channel (Figure 18-41).

d. In the **SSL repertoire** list (Figure 18-42), choose the PluginWebContainerSSLConnection SSL repertoire.

e. Click **OK**.

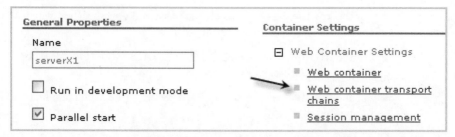

Figure 18-40: Selecting the server Web container

Step 4. Repeat the preceding steps for each server in the cluster or cell for which you want to enable SSL connections between the plug-in and application servers.

Step 5. Save your configuration changes.

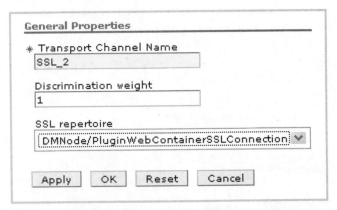

♦ SSL Inbound Channel (SSL 2)

  SSL repertoire DMNode/DefaultSSLSettings

Figure 18-41: Selecting the SSL inbound channel

General Properties

* Transport Channel Name

SSL_2

Discrimination weight

1

SSL repertoire

DMNode/PluginWebContainerSSLConnection ▼

| Apply | OK | Reset | Cancel |

Figure 18-42: Selecting the SSL repertoire

Step 6. Check the virtual host you're using (e.g., default_host) to make sure it has an alias for port 443 (e.g., *:443, www.sandbox.com:443). Unless you have an alias defined with the 443 port, HTTPS requests won't be routed from the plug-in to the application servers. (We assume you're using the standard HTTPS port, 443, on your HTTP server.) You'll find the virtual host artifacts under **Environment|Virtual Hosts**. Select the desired virtual host (e.g., default_host), and check its **Host Aliases**. Figure 18-43 shows host aliases display for the default_host virtual host. (For more information about host aliases, see Chapter 10.)

Select	Host Name ◇	Port ◇
☐	*	9080
☐	*	80
☐	*	9443
☐	*	443

Figure 18-43: Host aliases for the default_host virtual host

If you need to add an alias, you must generate a new plugin-cfg.xml file and copy it to the HTTP server machines where the plug-in expects to find it. You also need to stop and restart your application servers to load the new virtual host definition. (Note: In a production environment, it's a good practice to be explicit with the host name in the virtual host aliases rather than use the wildcard character for the host name as shown in this example. For testing purposes, it's handy to include the Web container ports — 9080 and 9443, for example — in the virtual host alias. In production, however, it's best not to include the port numbers of the application server Web container, as a deterrent to being able to access the Web container directly from a browser.)

You should see the 443 port listed for your virtual host in the plugin-cfg.xml file (see the second-to-last line in the following portion of the file):

```
<VirtualHostGroup Name="default_host">
    <VirtualHost Name="*:9080"/>
    <VirtualHost Name="*:80"/>
    <VirtualHost Name="*:9443"/>
    <VirtualHost Name="*:443"/>
</VirtualHostGroup>
```

Test the Connection

We assume you've set up your HTTP server to support SSL connections from a browser to IBM HTTP Server. (See the section at the beginning of this chapter for instructions about how to do that.) If a request arrives at the HTTP server on HTTPS and the plug-in determines that the request is intended for one of the application servers in its routing table (based on URL), then if an SSL option has been configured between the plug-in and the Web container for the given application server, an SSL connection will be used.

One way to test the SSL connection between the plug-in and the container is to turn on trace for the plug-in as we describe here and verify that when you make a request to an application running on an application server, the plug-in uses an SSL connection to reach the application server. (You need to have some application running on the application server configured with the Web module mapped to your HTTP server.) Make sure you use HTTPS to get to the Web server and some URL for an application that you've installed properly on the application server. You should see significant activity associated with the SSL connection between the plug-in and the Web container when you make a request on HTTPS using an application URL.

Troubleshooting the Connection

If you have problems that you think are related to the plug-in, you can turn on plug-in trace by changing the LogLevel attribute of the Log tag in file plugin-cfg.xml. Setting the level to "Trace" provides a verbose trace of plug-in activity in the given http_plugin.log.

```
<Log LogLevel="Trace"
Name="C:/IHS6/wasplugin\logs\IHS1\http_plugin.log"/>
```

If you have problems that you think are related to the Web container side of the connection, you can turn on trace associated with the HTTP Channel, the SSL Channel, and (if necessary) the HTTP Transport. Figures 18-44 and 18-45 show WebSphere traces associated with the HTTP Channel and the SSL Channel, respectively.

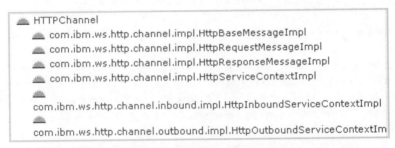

Figure 18-44: WebSphere trace associated with the HTTP Channel

Figure 18-45: WebSphere trace associated with the SSL Channel

To set trace levels in WebSphere V6, select the **Change Log Detail Levels** item in the **Troubleshooting** section of the admin console's application server page (Figure 18-46 shows this item). You can choose to trace either **Components** or **Groups**. HTTPChannel and SSLChannel are groups. Figure 18-47 shows the WebSphere trace specification after enabling "all" trace for the HTTP Channel and SSL Channel groups.

Figure 18-46: Option to change log detail levels

Figure 18-47: WebSphere trace specification with "all" trace enabled for the HTTP Channel and SSL Channel groups

By default, the trace log shows up in the same directory as file SystemOut.log for the server you're tracing. You can control the destination of the trace and other attributes of the log file by clicking the **Logging and Tracing** link on the application server page of the admin console and then selecting **Diagnostic Trace** (as shown in Figure 18-48).

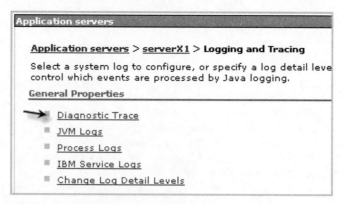

Figure 18-48: Logging and tracing properties

Configuring SSL Between WebSphere and IBM Tivoli Directory Server

If you have WebSphere security enabled and you're using an LDAP directory server (e.g., IBM Tivoli Directory Server) for the user registry, it's a good idea to use SSL for the communications between the WebSphere processes and the directory server. Using SSL protects the user name and password information that passes over the network between WebSphere and the LDAP server.

This section describes the steps to take to configure the use of SSL on the connections between the WebSphere processes and IBM Tivoli Directory Server. (The steps are similar regardless of the LDAP directory server you're using.) We assume you have already enabled WebSphere security, are using ITDS for the LDAP registry, and have configured ITDS to accept SSL connections (as described in Chapter 17).

As you might expect, the WebSphere processes need a key and trust file. In this case, you'll use the DefaultSSLSettings SSL configuration repertoire to reference the key and trust file to use. When WebSphere is installed, the DefaultSSLSettings repertoire references a "dummy" key and trust file included in the installation. One of the tasks associated with enabling WebSphere security is replacing the dummy key and trust file. In the following description, the application server key file is WebSphere Server Key File.jks, and the trust file is WebSphereServerTrustFile.jks. (For details about the steps to take to replace the dummy key and trust files, see Chapter 16.)

Add the ITDS Public Key Certificate to the WebSphere Trust File

Chapter 17 describes the process of creating a self-signed public key certificate for the directory server. For the WebSphere processes to trust the directory server, the trust file referenced by the WebSphere DefaultSSLSettings SSL configuration repertoire must have the directory server public certificate in its list of signer certificates. (Either that or the directory server needs to use a certificate signed by a certificate authority that has a signer certificate in the trust file referenced by the SSL configuration.)

Step 1.   You need a copy of the public certificate file for the ITDS server instance that the WebSphere processes are going to use. (In this example, this-certificate file is named ITDSCertificate.arm, as you can see in Figure 18-49, and has been copied to the <PROFILE-ROOT>\ssl directory for the Deployment Manager. This is the same place where you're keeping the key and trust file for the Deployment Manager.)

Step 2.   Start the iKeyman key management tool by opening a DOS command window, changing to directory <WASV6ROOT>\bin, and entering **ikeyman**.

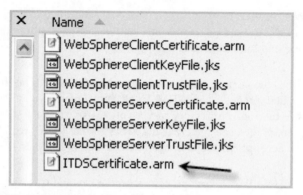

Figure 18-49: Public certificate file for the ITDS server instance

Step 3. Open the WebSphereServerTrustFile in the ssl directory in the Deployment Manager profile root.

    a. For **Key database type**, select **JKS**.
    b. For **File Name**, specify **WebSphereServerTrustFile.jks**.
    c. For **Location**, use <PROFILE-ROOT>\ssl.
    d. Click **OK**.
    e. Provide the key file access password in the subsequent pop-up dialog.

Step 4. Add the ITDS certificate to the trust file. (For the WebSphere processes to trust the ITDS server, you need to add its self-signed certificate to the WebSphere trust file.) When you open the WebSphere trust file, the Signer Certificates part of the key database content should be selected by default.

    a. In the right column of the viewing pane, click **Add** to display the panel where you add the certificate (Figure 18-50).

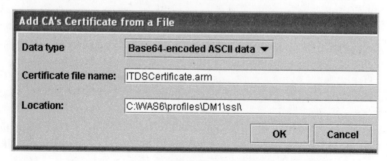

Figure 18-50: Adding the ITDS certificate to the trust file

b. Provide the certificate file name (e.g., ITDSCertificate.arm).
c. Provide the location: <PROFILE-ROOT>\ssl.
d. Click **OK**.
e. In the next pop-up dialog (Figure 18-51), provide a certificate label.

Figure 18-51: Specifying the certificate label

When you first add a certificate to a trust file, the case of the letters in the label is maintained (as Figure 18-52 shows), but the next time you open the trust file, the label will be in all lower case (Figure 18-53).

Figure 18-52: Initial display of added certificate

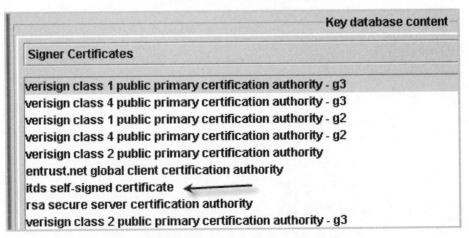

Figure 18-53: Subsequent display of added certificate

Step 5.   Exit iKeyman.

Step 6.   Copy file WebSphereServerTrustFile.jks to the <PROFILE-ROOT>\ssl directories of all nodes in the cell.

Configure WebSphere to Use SSL with Its LDAP Registry Communications

Unless you're very experienced with configuring WebSphere security, it's a good idea to first get WebSphere security working correctly without SSL enabled between the LDAP server and the WebSphere processes. Once you have everything working with non-SSL communications, you can take the steps described here to enable SSL communications. If any problems occur, you know they're likely to be related only to the configuration of SSL. (For instructions on setting up WebSphere security, see Chapter 16.)

Once you make the conversion from non-SSL to SSL communications, you must stop and restart all WebSphere processes in the cell to have the changes take effect for each process. The restart is necessary to get them all using Lightweight Third-Party Authentication (LTPA) tokens from the same "security realm." When you change the port number used to connect to the LDAP server, you're changing the security realm identifier, which is made up of the host name and port number of the LDAP server. The security realm is part of what makes up the LTPA token that's passed among WebSphere processes when they make requests (e.g., synchronization requests) among each other. If a WebSphere process doesn't trust the security realm of a requesting process, it ignores the request and throws an exception. Until you restart all the processes in the cell, they won't trust each other and won't work together.

For this example, we assume you have WebSphere security enabled using the IBM Tivoli Directory Server and have configured ITDS to accept SSL connections.

Step 1.   Open a WebSphere admin console in your browser, and log in.

Step 2.   Expand **Security**, and select **Global Security**. In the right column of the viewing pane under **User registries**, select **LDAP**.

     a. Change the LDAP port to **636**, the standard SSL port for LDAP servers.

     b. Select the **SSL enabled** check box.

     c. The selected **SSL configuration** should be **DefaultSSLSettings**.

d. Click **OK**, and save your configuration changes. Either check the **Synchronize changes with Nodes** check box when you save your changes, or allow time for all nodes in the cell to synchronize before you take the next step of restarting all the WebSphere processes in the cell.

Step 3. To force the change to using the SSL connection between the WebSphere processes and the LDAP server, you need to stop and start all the processes in the cell. Start with the Deployment Manager, and then restart the node agents and application servers on each node in the cell.

Until you restart all the processes, you'll see errors in the Deployment Manager's SystemOut.log file regarding LTPA tokens with realms that don't match the current realm (due to the change in the LDAP host port number from 389 to 636). There will also be errors in the node agent SystemOut.log regarding insufficient credentials to perform a synchronization.

If you don't let the nodes all properly synchronize before restarting the Deployment Manager, you'll need to use the syncNode command-line utility from the <PROFILE-ROOT>\bin directory of any unsynchronized node to manually force a synchronization. (Issue **syncNode –?** to obtain usage information.)

The SystemOut.log file of the WebSphere processes will indicate that they are using the SSL port of the LDAP server:

```
SASRas    A    JSAS0001I: Security configuration initialized.
SASRas    A    JSAS0002I: Authentication protocol: CSIV2
SASRas    A    JSAS0003I: Authentication mechanism: LTPA
SASRas    A    JSAS0004I: Principal name: ldap-
host.ibm.com:636/wasadmin
```

19

Installing Product Updates

Installing product updates is a common administrative task. In this chapter, we describe the process for WebSphere Application Server so you can be confident you're installing updates properly.

To ensure that your organization is aware of the availability of updates, it's important to assign someone in the administration group the task of regularly checking the WebSphere Support Web site, *http://www-306.ibm.com/software/webservers/appserv/was/support*. Also key is having a well-defined process for accepting product updates in the various environments used by the organization. The specifics of the update-acceptance process will differ depending on the type of product update.

IBM's product update terminology has changed from earlier releases of WebSphere. Table 19-1 defines some commonly used terms.

Table 19-1: Product update terminology

Update type	Definition
Release	This is the term used by WebSphere Development and Support for a "major" version of WebSphere. The first two digits of the product version number identify the release (e.g., 6.0, 6.1).
Refresh pack	This is a new term used to identify an update to the product version that typically contains only defect fixes but may also include feature additions and changes. The third digit of the version number identifies a refresh pack (e.g., 6.0.**1**, 6.0.**2**).
Fix pack	This is the term now used to describe a product update that in fact includes only defect fixes. (The previous term for this type of update was *cumulative fix*.) The version number's fourth digit identifies a fix pack (e.g., 6.0.1.**1**, 6.0.1.**2**).
Fix or interim fix	These two terms indicate a temporary or emergency product update focused on a specific defect. (This type of update used to be referred to as an *emergency fix* or *efix*.) A fix isn't identified by digits in the product version number. You'll find fixes listed in the output of the version Info utility.

Depending on the type of update, the acceptance process starts in development and moves through different test environments to staging and finally to production. Acceptance of *releases* should start with the development team environments because releases contains major product enhancements and changes. Acceptance of *refresh packs* and *fix packs* tends to start in the test team environments. If a test team discovers some incompatibility between an application and a refresh or fix pack, the development team should get involved. Once the product update has been run through all the testing stages, the operations team can be confident that the applications will run properly on the updated version of WebSphere Application Server.

You should install the product updates referred to as *fixes* (or *interim fixes* or *efixes*) only if your development or test team has determined that a fix is needed in order for applications running in a given environment to operate properly. IBM intends fixes as emergency corrections to defective product behavior. If the applications you're developing, testing, or running aren't experiencing the defect addressed by a fix, don't install the fix.

The introduction of an *update installer* tool has made installing WebSphere Application Server updates a well-defined process. In the past, there were times when you needed to make sure you had the proper version of the update installer to ensure that a given update would be installed correctly. Because the update itself didn't come with the necessary update installer, users had problems determining which installer to use. Now, IBM packages an update installer program with each update (except for fixes). (As you'll see later in the chapter, the update installer requires a JDK to run.)

In this chapter, we describe how to use the graphical version of the update installer. You can also run the update installer in "silent" mode using a response file. For details about this procedure, see the readme_updateinstaller documentation that comes with the update installer in the "docs" directory.

As WebSphere Application Server has matured, the ability to determine what's running in a given installation has also changed and improved. An important tool to be familiar with in this regard is *versionInfo*. This utility can examine a WebSphere installation and report on every update that has been installed.

Because the Deployment Manager (DM) must always run at the highest version of any installation in a cell, the DM installation is always the first WebSphere component to be updated. Although the release notes for updates claim that you can mix refresh packs and fix packs among installations in a cell as long as the DM is running the most recent version, in practice this statement hasn't always been true. As a practical matter, it's a good idea to run all the installations in a cell at exactly the same version.

As you learned in the early chapters of this book, Version 6 of WebSphere Application Server introduces the notion of profiles. Multiple profiles share the same installation. When you update an installation, you update all the profiles based on that installation. If multiple profiles share the same installation in a given environment (e.g., development, test, production), it's important to make sure all parties involved are agreed to moving forward with the update.

One word of warning: Don't run concurrent updates on the same machine. The update installer isn't built to have multiple instances running at the same time.

WebSphere Application Server Updates in a Nutshell

Performing a WebSphere product update is a straightforward process, and much of the procedure is the same regardless of which component you're updating. The following summary gives an overview of the tasks involved.

1. Use the versionInfo utility to determine the version of WebSphere installed on your machine.

2. Find out what updates are available by visiting the WebSphere Support home page.

3. Retrieve an update from the support site.

4. Stop all WebSphere processes that use the installation.

5. Back up your configuration(s) using the backupConfig command.

6. Extract the update ZIP archive file to <wasv6-root>.

7. Run the update.exe program.

8. Restart the Deployment Manager and any node agents for profiles associated with the installation.

9. Check the SystemOut.log files of the restarted processes to make sure the processes started cleanly.

10. Repeat these steps for the other nodes in the cell.

In the remainder of this chapter, we present the detailed steps involved in updating the following WebSphere components:

- WebSphere Application Server
- IBM HTTP Server (IHS)

- the HTTP server plug-in
- the Load Balancer Edge Component

Table 19-2 explains the symbolic file system references used in these descriptions.

Table 19-2: Symbolic file system references

Symbolic reference	Description
<WASV6-ROOT>	The file system location for the root directory of the WebSphere Application Server product installation.
<DM-PROFILE>	The file system location for the root directory of the Deployment Manager profile. It's often the case that the DM profile directory is in <WASV6-ROOT>\profiles, but that location is merely the default convention.
<NODE-PROFILE>	The file system location for the root directory of a node profile. Again, the convention is for this directory to be in <WASV6-ROOT>\profiles.
<IHS-ROOT>	The file system location for the root directory of the IBM HTTP Server installation.
<PLUGIN-ROOT>	The file system location for the root directory of the HTTP server plug-in installation. In this chapter, the WebSphere HTTP server plug-in is installed in <IHS-ROOT>\wasplugin, but you can install it where you prefer.
<EDGE-ROOT>	The file system location for the root directory of the Edge Component installation. The Load Balancer is the Edge Component of interest in this chapter.

Detailed Guide to Updating WebSphere Application Server

Use the following procedure to update the WebSphere Application Server product.

Step 1. Determine the version of your current installation. The Deployment Manager, node agents, and application servers leave a version signature similar to the following in their respective SystemOut.log file each time they start.

```
WebSphere Platform 6.0 [ND 6.0.0.1 o0445.08]
```

You can also use the versionInfo utility to obtain a product version report. To do so, open a DOS window, navigate to <WASV6-ROOT>\bin or <DM-PROFILE>\bin, and run **versionInfo.bat** (on Unix, run **versionInfo.sh**). Listing 19-1 shows sample output from this program for a WebSphere 6.0 install.

Listing 19-1

Sample versionInfo.bat output for a WebSphere 6.0 installation

```
WVER0010I: Copyright (c) IBM Corporation 2002; All rights reserved.
WVER0011I: WebSphere Application Server Release 6.0
WVER0012I: VersionInfo Reporter Version 1.15, Dated 9/20/03


----------------------------------------------------------------
IBM WebSphere Application Server Product Installation Status Report
----------------------------------------------------------------


Report at date and time 2005-03-30T15:41:03-05:00

Installation
----------------------------------------------------------------
Product Directory    C:\WAS6
Version Directory    C:\WAS6\properties\version
DTD Directory        C:\WAS6\properties\version\dtd
Log Directory        C:\WAS6\logs\update
Backup Directory     C:\WAS6\properties\version\backup
TMP Directory        C:\DOCUME~1\pvs\LOCALS~1\Temp

Installation Platform
----------------------------------------------------------------
Name           IBM WebSphere Application Server
Version        6.0

Technology List
----------------------------------------------------------------
ND             installed

Installed Product
----------------------------------------------------------------
Name           IBM WebSphere Application Server - ND
Version        6.0.0.1
ID             ND
Build Level    o0445.08
Build Date     11/10/04


----------------------------------------------------------------
End Installation Status Report
----------------------------------------------------------------
```

Step 2. The WebSphere Support site's home page lists the most current updates for the various supported versions of WebSphere Application Server. To see the update list, go to *http://www-306.ibm.com/software/webservers/appserv/was/support,* and look for the **Download** heading. Figure 19-1 shows a sample update list. From here, you can view the available updates by version, see a list of recommended updates, or view all downloads. The Support home page also offers a search function (shown in Figure 19-2) that you can use to find the updates you need.

For each update, the support site provides a description, prerequisites information, a readme file, and other installation and support particulars.

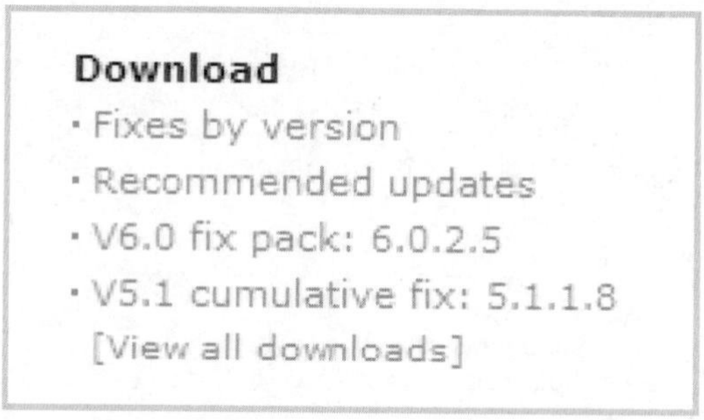

Figure 19-1: List of WebSphere Application Server updates

Figure 19-2: WebSphere support site's search function

Depending on where you are in the site, you may find the updates organized by WebSphere version, platform (e.g., AIX, Linux, Windows), product component (e.g., HTTP Server, plug-ins, Load Balancer), or processor. Figure 19-3 shows a sample download table.

Download package					What is DD?	
Download	**RELEASE DATE**	**LANGUAGE**	**SIZE(Bytes)**	**Download Options**		
Windows Express/Base/ND	3/31/2005	US English	307897358	FTP	DD
Windows Application Client	3/31/2005	US English	96481056	FTP	DD
Windows IBM HTTP Server	3/31/2005	US English	15281558	FTP	DD
Windows Plug-ins	3/31/2005	US English	63046074	FTP	DD
Windows Edge Load Balancer V6.0.1	3/31/2005	US English	100209676	FTP	DD
Windows Edge Caching Proxy V6.0.1	3/31/2005	US English	79358337	FTP	DD

Figure 19-3: Obtaining the WebSphere Application Server update

Like most support destinations, the WebSphere Support site is always changing. The tables you see when you visit the site may differ somewhat from this one. They might be organized by platform or processor, for example, instead of by product component. But the procedures we describe in this chapter give you the general steps to follow to install WebSphere updates.

To begin the download process, click the appropriate link in the download table to obtain the desired update. Each update is delivered as a ZIP archive file. In the following steps, we'll install the Express/Base/ND for Windows update.

Step 3. Review the readme document for your update. To do so, either click the **Readme** link on the update page or view the document in the update archive once you've downloaded and unzipped the update.

Step 4. Stop all Java processes that may be using the installation: application servers, node agents, Deployment Managers, Java Message Service servers (if you're using the V5 Embedded Messaging option), and Java clients. Use the Windows Task Manager (on Unix systems, issue **ps –ef | grep java**) to make sure the JVMs are actually stopped.

Step 5. Use the backupConfig utility to make a backup of your configurations. (For usage information, issue **backupConfig.bat –?**. For more information about the backupConfig utility, see Chapter 22.) From directory <DM-PRO-FILE>\bin, run **backupConfig.bat** to create a copy of the Deployment Manager configuration in <DM-PROFILE>\backups:

```
$ ./backupConfig.bat ../backups/DMbackup-2005330.zip
ADMU0116I: Tool information is being logged in file
           C:\WAS6\profiles\DM1\logs\backupConfig.log
ADMU0128I: Starting tool with the DM1 profile
ADMU5001I: Backing up config directory C:\WAS6/profiles/DM1\config
           to file
           C:\WAS6\profiles\DM1\backups\DMbackup-2005330.zip
ADMU0505I: Servers found in configuration:
ADMU0506I: Server name: dmgr
ADMU2010I: Stopping all server processes for node DMNode
ADMU0512I: Server dmgr cannot be reached. It appears to be stopped.
...........................................................
...........................................................
ADMU5002I: 176 files successfully backed up
```

Then, from <node-profile>\bin, run **backupConfig.bat** again to make a backup copy of the Node1 configuration in <DM-PROFILE>\backups:

```
$ ./backupConfig.bat ../backups/Node1backup-20050330.zip
ADMU0116I: Tool information is being logged in file
           C:\WAS6\profiles\Node1\logs\backupConfig.log
ADMU0128I: Starting tool with the Node1 profile
ADMU5001I: Backing up config directory C:\WAS6/profiles/Node1\config
           to file
           C:\WAS6\profiles\Node1\backups\Node1backup-20050330.zip
ADMU0505I: Servers found in configuration:
ADMU0506I: Server name: nodeagent
ADMU0506I: Server name: serverX1
ADMU0506I: Server name: serverX2
ADMU2010I: Stopping all server processes for node Node1
ADMU0512I: Server nodeagent cannot be reached. It appears to be
           stopped.
ADMU0512I: Server serverX1 cannot be reached. It appears to be
           stopped.
ADMU0512I: Server serverX2 cannot be reached. It appears to be
           stopped.
...........................................................
...........................................................
ADMU5002I: 235 files successfully backed up
```

Step 6. On the Deployment Manager node, extract the contents of the ZIP archive. (Note that PKUnzip might not properly extract the archive. We advise using some other utility, such as WinZip, to do the extraction.) You must extract WebSphere V6 updates to the <WASV6ROOT>\updateinstaller directory. The archive is rooted in updateinstaller, so you can extract the files directly to <WASV6ROOT> (e.g., C:\WAS6).

Step 7. If you've installed any interim fixes, you need to uninstall them before proceeding with a refresh or fix pack installation. (This extra administrative overhead is one reason to avoid interim fixes unless absolutely necessary.)

Step 8. From the updateinstaller directory, run the **update** program. When you execute this program with no arguments, the update installer utility starts in graphical user interface mode. The utility's opening panel presents some information about the update installer. (On this and succeeding panels of the update installer, click **Next** to proceed.)

The install wizard next prompts you (as shown in Figure 19-4) for the installation directory for WebSphere. (The provided default directory is likely to be correct.)

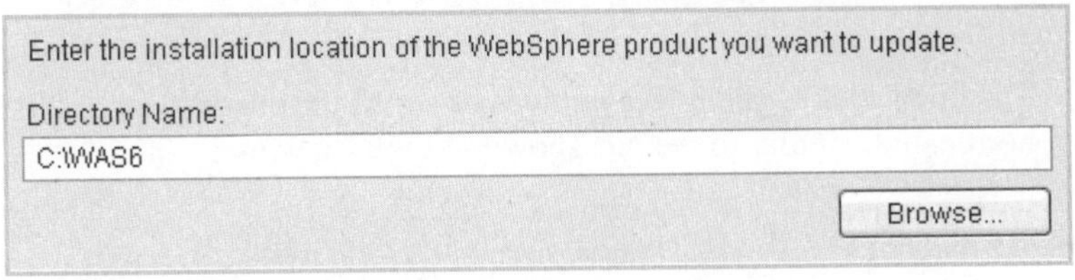

Enter the installation location of the WebSphere product you want to update.

Directory Name:

C:\WAS6

Browse...

Figure 19-4: Specifying the WebSphere update installation location

The next panel asks whether this is a maintenance package install or uninstall. Install is the default response.

The next panel (Figure 19-5) prompts for the path name to the maintenance package. (Again, the default is likely to be correct.)

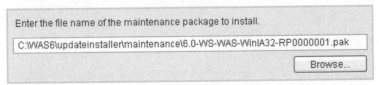

Enter the file name of the maintenance package to install.

C:\WAS6\updateinstaller\maintenance\6.0-WS-WAS-WinIA32-RP0000001.pak

Browse...

Figure 19-5: Specifying the WebSphere update name and path

Depending on the JDK version initially used by the update installer, the next panel may indicate that the "installed JDK" is going to be updated. (If the JDK that was used to start the update installer is at a sufficient revision level, you won't see this panel.) The message text is somewhat confusing. The installed JDK itself isn't updated; it is copied to a new location and then updated. The update installer is then restarted, and the actual update begins, as signaled by a panel similar to the one shown in Figure 19-6.

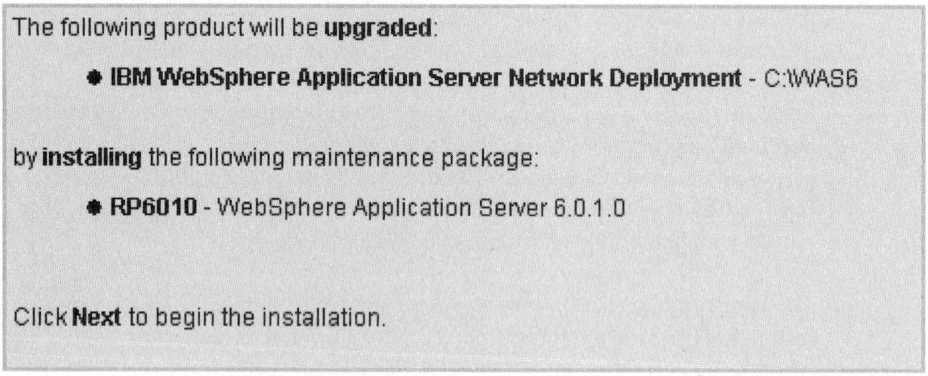

The following product will be **upgraded**:

   ◆ **IBM WebSphere Application Server Network Deployment** - C:\WAS6

by **installing** the following maintenance package:

   ◆ **RP6010** - WebSphere Application Server 6.0.1.0

Click **Next** to begin the installation.

Figure 19-6: WebSphere update notification panel

The update takes about five minutes or so. At the conclusion, you'll see a notification similar to the one shown in Figure 19-7.

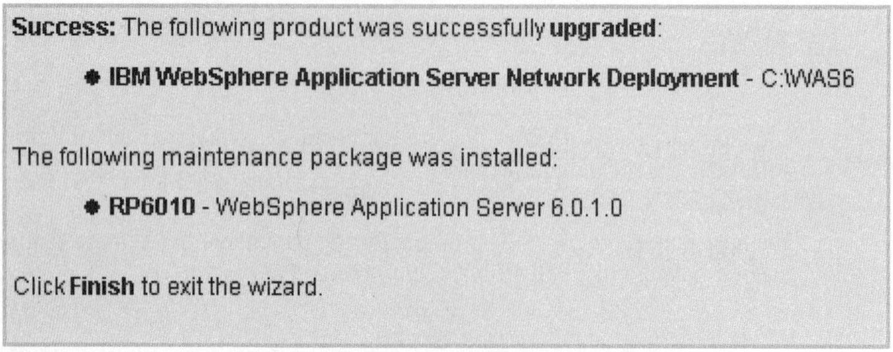

Success: The following product was successfully **upgraded**:

   ◆ **IBM WebSphere Application Server Network Deployment** - C:\WAS6

The following maintenance package was installed:

   ◆ **RP6010** - WebSphere Application Server 6.0.1.0

Click **Finish** to exit the wizard.

Figure 19-7: Notification of successful WebSphere update

Step 9.   Restart the Deployment Manager and the node agents or standalone application servers of any other profiles sharing the installation.

Step 10.   Check the SystemOut.log file(s) to make sure all processes started correctly and left an appropriate version signature in the log:

```
WebSphere Platform 6.0 [ND 6.0.1.0 o0510.18]
```

Step 11.   Restart the application servers of any nodes associated with the updated installation.

Step 12.   Repeat the preceding steps for the other nodes in the cell.

Detailed Guide to Updating IBM HTTP Server

This section explains the steps to install updates to IBM HTTP Server. The machine running a production HTTP server is usually stripped of any software that someone could use to compromise the operation of the site. For these security reasons, a JDK isn't usually installed on a production HTTP server. However, the update installer needs a JDK to run, so the first task in updating a production HTTP server machine is to install a JDK and modify the PATH environment variable to include the path to the Java bin directory. For nonproduction HTTP server machines, it's not necessary to remove the JDK, so you don't need to install a JDK before installing the IHS update.

Step 1.   Determine the version of your current IHS installation. The easiest thing to check is the version.signature file in <IHS-ROOT>. As of IHS 6.0.1, the server also leaves a version signature in file error.log in <IHSROOT>\logs when it starts. IHS does not have a versionInfo utility.

Step 2.   Go to the WebSphere Support site, and locate and download the latest update for IHS. For this example, we assume the server is IBM HTTP Server on Windows.

Step 3.   Extract the IHS update ZIP file archive to directory <IHS-ROOT>. The archive is rooted at updateinstaller, so you'll have an <IHS-ROOT>\update-installer directory with the update in it.

Step 4.   Stop the HTTP server. (On Windows systems, you can stop and start the server from the Windows **Services** panel.)

Step 5.   Run the **update** program in <IHS-ROOT>\updateinstaller.

The first panel introduces the update installer. The second (Figure 19-8) prompts for the install location of the product you're updating. In this case, you're updating IBM HTTP Server installed in <IHS-ROOT> (e.g., C:\IHS6).

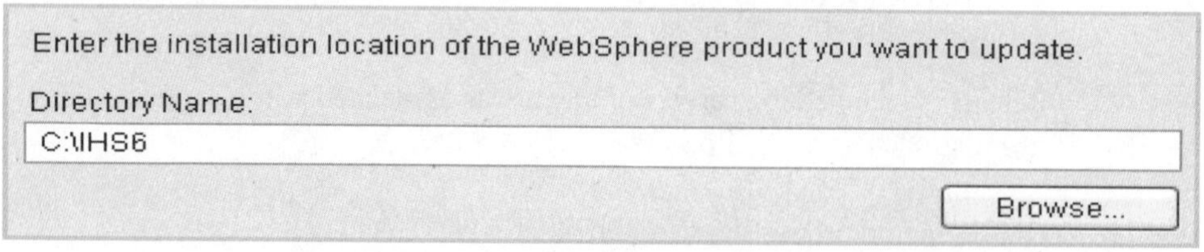

Enter the installation location of the WebSphere product you want to update.

Directory Name:

C:\IHS6

Browse...

Figure 19-8: Specifying the IHS update installation location

The next panel asks whether you want to install or uninstall a maintenance package. The default is to install, which is what you want to do.

Next (Figure 19-9), you're prompted for the location of the maintenance package file. The provided path is likely to be correct.

Enter the file name of the maintenance package to install.

C:\IHS6\updateinstaller\maintenance\6.0-WS-IHS-WinIA32-RP0000001.pak

Browse...

Figure 19-9: Specifying the IHS update name and path

The next panel (Figure 19-10) indicates that the update is about to start. The IHS update goes quickly. At the conclusion, you'll see a notification similar to the one shown in Figure 19-11.

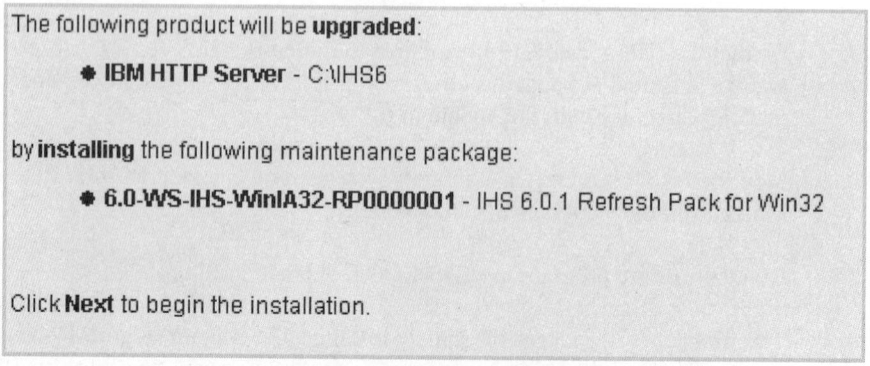

The following product will be **upgraded**:

    ✦ **IBM HTTP Server** - C:\IHS6

by **installing** the following maintenance package:

    ✦ **6.0-WS-IHS-WinIA32-RP0000001** - IHS 6.0.1 Refresh Pack for Win32

Click **Next** to begin the installation.

Figure 19-10: IBM HTTP Server update notification panel

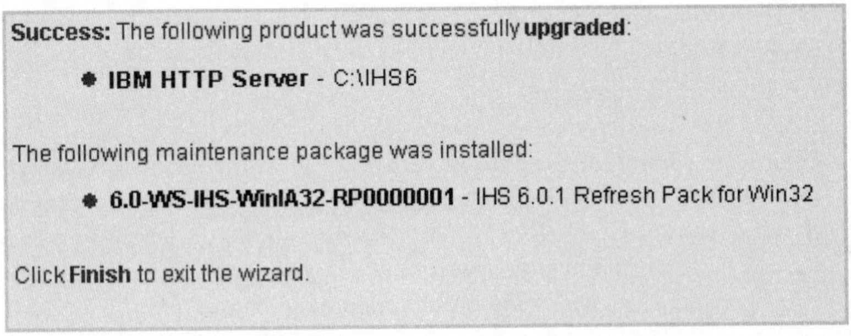

> **Success:** The following product was successfully **upgraded**:
>
> * **IBM HTTP Server** - C:\IHS6
>
> The following maintenance package was installed:
>
> * **6.0-WS-IHS-WinIA32-RP0000001** - IHS 6.0.1 Refresh Pack for Win32
>
> Click **Finish** to exit the wizard.

Figure 19-11: Notification of successful IBM HTTP Server update

Step 6.   Check the <IHS-ROOT>\version.signature file to see that it contains the proper version number.

Step 7.   Restart IBM HTTP Server, and check file error.log in <IHSROOT>\logs to verify that the server started correctly. Also make sure the file shows the expected version number:

```
IBM_HTTP_Server/6.0.1 Apache/2.0.47 (Win32) configured — resuming
normal operations
Server built: Mar  2 2005 11:29:24
```

Step 8.   If IHS is running on a production machine, remove the JDK you installed to enable the update installer to run.

Detailed Guide to Updating the HTTP Server Plug-in

This section describes how to install updates to the HTTP server plug-in. In this example, the target HTTP server is IBM HTTP Server. The steps to install updates to the plug-in of other HTTP servers are the same.

For security reasons described briefly in the preceding section, the machine running a production HTTP server doesn't usually have a JDK installed on it. The update installer needs a JDK to run, so the first step in updating the HTTP server plug-in on a production HTTP server machine is to install a JDK and change the PATH environment variable to include the path to the Java bin directory. For nonproduction HTTP server machines, this step is unnecessary.

When you installed the HTTP server plug-in, a JVM was installed in the same directory as the plug-in. Various utilities, including versionInfo and iKeyman (the IBM Secure Sockets Layer configuration utility), use this JVM. The update installer uses it, too. In a production environment, it's a good practice to delete this JVM because it isn't needed by the plug-in at runtime and would be available for malicious activity if the HTTP server machine were compromised.

Step 1.   Check the version of the plug-in you're using. If the installation doesn't have a JVM (as it shouldn't in production), you can look at file http_plugin.log file in directory <PLUGIN-ROOT>\logs\<*servername*>, where <*servername*> is the HTTP server name you specified when you installed the plug-in (e.g., IHS1). This file provides the build version and date as part of the startup trace:

```
PLUGIN: Plugins loaded.
PLUGIN: ----------System Information---------
PLUGIN: Bld version: 6.0.0
PLUGIN: Bld date: Oct 31 2004, 11:15:26
```

In nonproduction environments, you can use the versionInfo utility to obtain plug-in version information.

Step 2.   Download the HTTP server plug-in update from the WebSphere Support site.

Step 3.   Extract the update to <PLUGIN-ROOT>. The plug-in archive is rooted in updateinstaller, so you can extract it directly to where the plug-in is installed (e.g., C:\IHS6\wasplugin).

Step 4.   Stop the HTTP server. In this case, the server is IBM HTTP Server on Windows, and you can start and stop it from the Windows **Services** panel.

Step 5.   Run the **update** program in <PLUGIN-ROOT>\updateinstaller.

The first panel provides information about the update installer. The second panel (Figure 19-12) prompts for the install location of the product you're updating. In this case, it's the IHS plug-in installed in <PLUGIN-ROOT>.

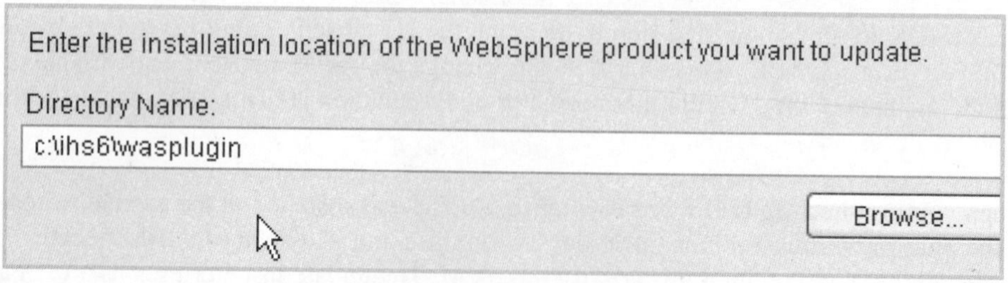

Figure 19-12: Specifying the plug-in update installation location

The next panel asks whether you want to install or uninstall a maintenance package. The default is to install, which is what you want to do. Next (Figure 19-13), you're prompted for the location of the maintenance package file. The provided path is likely to be correct.

Figure 19-13: Specifying the plug-in update name and path

Depending on the version of the JDK initially used by the update installer, you may see a panel indicating that the "installed JDK" needs to be updated. The JDK is copied to a new directory (which defaults to where you extracted the update archive) and updated. This process takes about a minute. The update installer is then restarted, picking up at the point where it prompts for the maintenance package to install.

The next panel (Figure 19-14) indicates that the update is about to start. The plug-in update proceeds quickly. At the conclusion, you'll see the notification shown in Figure 19-15.

Figure 19-14: Plug-in update notification panel

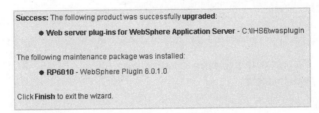

Figure 19-15: Notification of successful plug-in update

Step 6.   Restart HTTP Server, and check the http_plugin.log file in <PLUGIN-ROOT>\logs\<*servername*> to verify that the plug-in started correctly. Make sure the file shows the expected version number.

```
PLUGIN: Plugins loaded.
- PLUGIN: ----------System Information---------
- PLUGIN: Bld version: 6.0.1
- PLUGIN: Bld date: Mar  7 2005, 19:43:29
```

Step 7.   If this is a production machine, remove the JDK you installed to run the update installer. Also check the <PLUGIN-ROOT>\updateinstaller directory for Java if the update installer updated the JDK. Remove this JDK as well.

Detailed Guide to Updating the Load Balancer

This section provides step-by-step instructions for installing updates to the Load Balancer Edge Component of the WebSphere V6 Network Deployment package. The Load Balancer doesn't use the same update installer as the other components, so its update process differs considerably.

The Load Balancer has been known in the past as "Network Dispatcher" or "IBM Dispatcher," and the Dispatcher name is still present in the product as a particular component of the product suite. You'll notice several references to it in the following installation instructions.

> **Note:**   The Version 6.0.1 Load Balancer update installer has had some problems that as of this writing had not been corrected. The installer doesn't retain the software license for using the Load Balancer, nor does it retain the configuration files associated with the existing install. In the following steps, we instruct you to make backup copies of the directories holding these artifacts so you can manually restore them after running the update installer.
>
> Note that the Load Balancer V6.0.1 update installer does correctly uninstall the existing Load Balancer version. You'll be instructed to uninstall the Load Balancer using Add/Remove Programs in Windows. Reboot your machine, and then install the new version of the Load Balancer.

Step 1.   If you need to determine the current Load Balancer version installed:

a. Use a text editor to open the server.log file in <EDGE-ROOT>\servers\ logs\dispatcher.

b. Search back from the end of the log file for the point where the Load Balancer (Dispatcher) emitted a trace at its most recent startup that indicates its version:

```
KNDServer Version: 06.00.00.00 - 10/28/2004-14:25:49-GMT-8:00
```

Step 2.   Download the Load Balancer update from the WebSphere Support site.

Step 3.   Extract the update to the file system of the Load Balancer host machine (e.g., C:\LBUpdates\extracted).

Step 4.   Stop the Load Balancer. Because the Load Balancer is installed as a Windows service, you can start and stop it from the Windows **Services** panel. In the panel, you'll see the Load Balancer service listed as "IBM Dispatcher," as shown in Figure 19-16. (In the Task Manager process list, the Load Balancer process is named dsservice.exe.)

IBM Content Based Routing	Manual	LocalSystem
IBM Dispatcher	Automatic	LocalSystem
IBM Metric Server	Manual	LocalSystem
IBM Site Selector	Manual	LocalSystem

Figure 19-16: Load Balancer (a.k.a. IBM Dispatcher) in Windows Services panel

Step 5.   Make a backup copy of the directories <EDGE-ROOT>\servers\conf and <EDGEROOT>\servers\configurations. Figure 19-17 shows these two directories. The conf directory holds the license for the Load Balancer. The update wizard doesn't back up and restore this license. The configuration directory holds the runtime configuration for the Edge Components you've installed, such as Load Balancer, Site Selector, Content Based Routing, and any other components. The install wizard for Load Balancer V6.0.1 doesn't

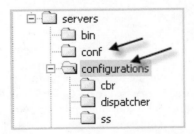

Figure 19-17: Load Balancer configuration directories

back up and restore the configuration files. (This is a defect that may be corrected in later releases of the update installation wizard.)

Step 6. Now, you need to uninstall the current version of the Load Balancer. (You must perform this step because the Load Balancer update installer has problems uninstalling the existing version followed by an immediate installation of the new version.) To uninstall the Load Balancer and the other Edge Components, click **Start** and navigate to **Control Panel|Add/Remove Programs**. Figure 19-18 shows the components to remove.

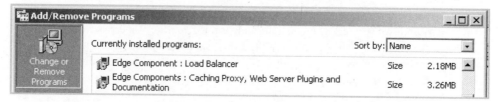

Figure 19-18: Load Balancer and Edge Components in Add/Remove Programs

First select the Load Balancer, and click the **Change/Remove** button to remove it. When the Load Balancer has been uninstalled, a dialog will appear regarding rebooting the machine. Decline the reboot at this time because you need to remove the second Edge Components item. Then you'll reboot.

Select the other Edge Components item (the documentation), and click **Change/Remove**. For this item, a dialog will appear; select the **Remove** option (shown in Figure 19-19).

Figure 19-19: Removing the other Edge Components

When prompted, reboot the machine. After the system reboots, delete the <EDGE-ROOT> directory tree (e.g., C:\LB6*x*). (There will likely be some remnants of the original install that you don't want to mix with the update installation.) At this point, you're ready to install the new version of the Load Balancer.

Step 7. In the top-level directory of the extracted update (e.g., C:\LBUpdates\extracted), run **setup.exe** to launch the Load Balancer for Windows Setup wizard. Click **Next** on the opening panel.

The next panel prompts for the location where you want to install the new version of the Load Balancer. The default location is C:\Program Files\IBM\edge\lb, but you can click **Browse** and select a desired <EDGE-ROOT> directory (e.g., C:\LB6*x*).

The next panel prompts for the type of installation you want: **All** or **Your choice**. It's unlikely you're using every Load Balancer component. The **Your choice** option lets you use the list shown in Figure 19-20 to update only the components you're using.

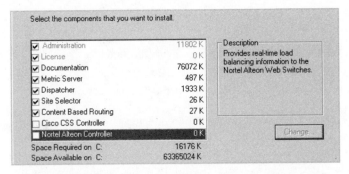

Figure 19-20: Selecting the Load Balancer components to install

The next panel declares that files will be copied, giving you a chance to make sure you've selected the proper components to be installed (Figure 19-21). Click **Next** to proceed.

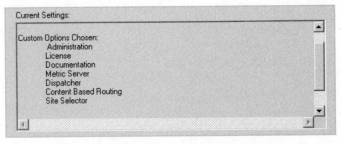

Figure 19-21: Notification of components to be installed

The wizard copies the files to the target directory. When it finishes, it prompts you to reboot the machine (Figure 19-22). At this time, choose not to restart so you can copy the license and configuration files into the proper directories in the new installation.

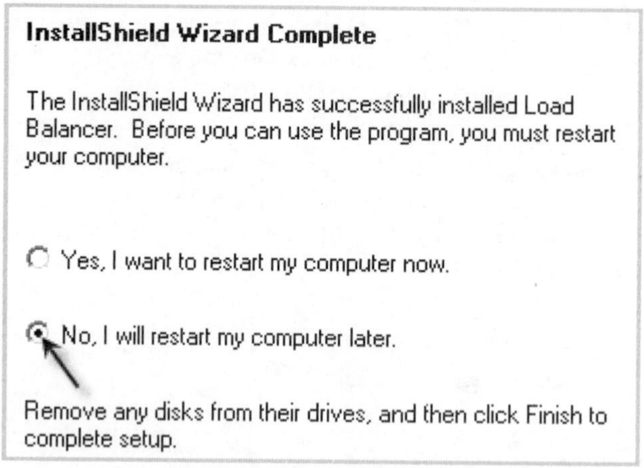

InstallShield Wizard Complete

The InstallShield Wizard has successfully installed Load Balancer. Before you can use the program, you must restart your computer.

○ Yes, I want to restart my computer now.

⊙ No, I will restart my computer later.

Remove any disks from their drives, and then click Finish to complete setup.

Figure 19-22: Load Balancer successful installation notification

Step 8. Copy the license and configuration directories from their backup location to the new <EDGE-ROOT>\servers directory. (You can click **Yes to all** when prompted about overwriting existing folders and files with the same name.) The <EDGE-ROOT>\servers\conf directory should now have the license files lb60Full.LIC and nodelock in it, and the <EDGE-ROOT>\servers\configurations\dispatcher directory should have the proper default.cfg directory in it.

Step 9. Restart the machine. The new version of the Load Balancer should start (assuming you have the IBM Dispatcher service set to automatic). Check the dispatcher log file to make sure the version signature is as you expect it:

```
KNDServer Version: 06.00.01.00 - 03/08/2005-09:33:26-GMT-8:00
```

Also check the log file to see that the Load Balancer started cleanly (make sure the license-check messages are proper):

```
EDT LIC: performing license check
EDT LIC: Starting license monitor!
EDT LIC: Permanent license installed!
```

You should also see the trace of the dscontrol commands for your configuration (abbreviated in the following sample).

```
Loaded kernel successfully.
AppendLoad command: dscontrol cluster add ...
        AppendLoad command: dscontrol cluster set ...
        AppendLoad command: dscontrol executor configure ...
        AppendLoad command: dscontrol port add ...
        AppendLoad command: dscontrol server add ...
        etc
        AppendLoad command: dscontrol manager start manager.log ...
        The manager has been started.
        AppendLoad command: dscontrol advisor start ...
```

For further verification, you can start the Load Balancer admin console and check out your cluster definitions and the status of the cluster members (use **Start|Programs|IBM WebSphere|Edge Components|Load Balancer|Load Balancer** to start the console). If you didn't properly save and restore your license files, the console won't properly display your configuration. If you didn't properly save and restore your configuration files, you won't see your configuration from the original installation. Figure 19-23 shows a sample HTTP Server cluster viewed in the Load Balancer admin console.

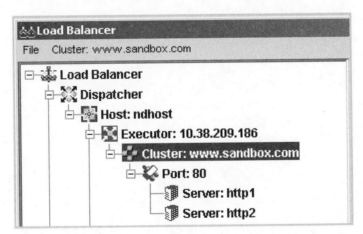

Figure 19-23: Load Balancer console view of HTTP server cluster members

20

Registering and Running WebSphere Processes as Windows Services

When you install WebSphere components on Windows operating systems, you have the option to register the following Java processes as services in the Windows registry.

- application server process (server1)

- deployment manager process (dmgr)

- node agent process — when you federate the node under a profile to the deployment manager cell (node agent)

By registering these processes as services, you gain the flexibility to

- start WebSphere services during system startup

- automatically restart failed processes (using a built-in feature of Windows)

- manage (e.g., start, stop, check the status of) WebSphere processes from the Windows **Services** panel instead of issuing commands from the command line

As requirements change in the corporate environment, you may want to add a WebSphere service to the registry (if you didn't register it during installation), remove a service from the registry, change a service's name, or modify the arguments for a service after installation. WebSphere's WASService.exe command-line utility lets you perform all these tasks with ease.

You use the WASService command to configure WebSphere processes in the Windows registry. By default, the utility is located in directory <WASV6-ROOT>\bin (where <WASV6-ROOT> is the directory in which you installed the WebSphere product binaries). Once you've registered a WebSphere process as a Windows service, the

WebSphere-specific command-line utilities for managing the process (e.g., startServer.bat, startManager.bat, startNode.bat) in turn call the WASService command to process those requests.

To obtain help for WASService command syntax, open a command prompt, navigate to <WASV6-ROOT>\bin, and issue **wasservice.exe**. Figure 20-1 shows the usage help that's displayed when you execute this command.

```
C:\IBM\WebSphere\AppServer\bin>wasservice.exe    ←
Usage: WASService.exe (with no arguments starts the service)
                    || -add <service name>
                       -serverName <Server>
                       -profilePath <Server's Profile Directory>
                            [-wasHome <Websphere Install Directory>]
                            [-configRoot <Config Repository Directory>]
                            [-startArgs <additional start arguments>]
                            [-stopArgs <additional stop arguments>]
                            [-userid <execution id> -password <password>]
                            [-logFile <service log file>]
                            [-logRoot <server's log directory>]
                            [-encodeParams]
                            [-restart <true | false>]
                            [-startType <automatic | manual | disabled>]
                    || -remove <service name>
                    || -start <service name> [optional startServer.bat p
                    || -stop <service name> [optional stopServer.bat par
                    || -status <service name>
                    || -encodeParams <service name>
```

Figure 20-1: WASService command syntax information

Register WebSphere Processes as Windows Services

As we've noted, you have the option to register the WebSphere processes as Windows services at the time of installation. You encountered this option in the sample installations you worked through in the early chapters of this book. Figure 20-2 shows the installation wizard panel that provides this option during a WebSphere Base/Express package installation. Note, as the panel indicates, that the user account that runs the service must possess rights to act as part of the operating system and log on as a service.

In the following paragraphs, we show you how to register the WebSphere processes manually, after installation, by using the WASService command.

Register the Deployment Manager Process

To register the deployment manager process, open a command prompt on dmgr-host, change to directory <WASV6-ROOT>\bin, and issue the following WASService command (on a single line).

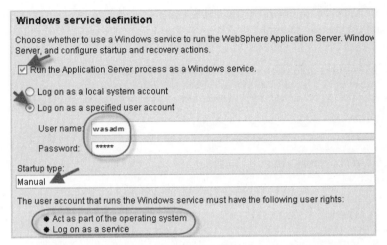

Figure 20-2: Installation wizard's Windows service definition panel

```
WASService -add <SERVICE-NAME> -serverName <SERVER-NAME> -profilePath
<DMGR-PROFILE-ROOT> -wasHome <WASV6-ROOT> -restart [true|false] -startType
startup-type
```

The command argument values are as follows:

- <SERVICE-NAME> is the display name of the WebSphere process as it will appear in the **Services** panel. For this value, provide a meaningful name appropriate for your environment. In this example, we'll use the default name that's provided during the creation of the profile when you choose, during installation, to run as a service: *hostname*CellManager01 for the deployment manager process.

- <SERVER-NAME> is the name of the deployment manager. When you create a deployment manager profile, a server named dmgr is created by default.

- <DMGR-PROFILE-ROOT> is the path to the deployment manager profile. In a Network Deployment environment, the profile's default path is <WASV6-ROOT>\profiles\Dmgr01.

- <WASV6-ROOT> is the installation directory for the application server product binaries (C:\IBM\WebSphere\AppServer in this case).

- The restart parameter tells Windows whether to restart (**–restart true**) or not to restart (**–restart false**) the service if the process fails.

- The startType argument indicates the startup type of the service as defined in the **Services** panel: automatic, manual, or disabled.

Figure 20-3 shows the command given above being executed to register the deployment manager process for our example.

```
C:\IBM\WebSphere\AppServer\bin>WASService -add dmgr-hostCellManager01
-serverName dmgr -profilePath c:\IBM\WebSphere\AppServer\profiles\Dmgr
01 -wasHome c:\IBM\WebSphere\AppServer -restart true -startType automa
tic
Adding Service: dmgr-hostCellManager01
        Config Root: c:\IBM\WebSphere\AppServer\profiles\Dmgr01\config

        Server Name: dmgr
        Profile Path: c:\IBM\WebSphere\AppServer\profiles\Dmgr01
        Was Home: c:\IBM\WebSphere\AppServer\
        Start Args:
        Restart: 1
IBM WebSphere Application Server V6 - dmgr-hostCellManager01 service s
uccessfully added.
```

Figure 20-3: Registering the deployment manager process

After executing the WASService command, click the Windows **Start** button, navigate to **Control Panel|Administrative Tools|Services** to display the **Services** panel, and look for the deployment manager process. You should see that the service has been added with the service name dmgr-hostCellManager01, as shown in Figure 20-4.

Figure 20-4: Newly registered deployment manager process in Windows Services panel

Register the Application Server Process

To register the application server process, open a command prompt on was-host, change to directory <WASV6-ROOT>\bin, and issue the following command:

```
WASService -add <SERVICE-NAME> -serverName <SERVER-NAME> -profilePath
<PROFILE-ROOT> -wasHome <WASV6-ROOT> -restart [true|false] -startType
startup-type
```

Specify the command argument values as follows:

- <SERVICE-NAME> is the name of the WebSphere process as it will appear in the **Services** panel. Provide a meaningful name appropriate for your environment. For this example, we'll use the default name assigned during the creation of the profile when you choose to run as a service: *hostname*Node01 for the application server process.

- <SERVER-NAME> is the name of the application server. When you create an application server profile, an application server named server1 is created by default. You can create additional application servers (e.g., server2, server3) if needed. In this case, we're registering the default application server (server1).

- <PROFILE-ROOT> is the path to the application server profile. By default, this path is <WASV6-ROOT>\profiles\AppSrv01 in a Network Deployment environment. (In a Base/Express installation, the default path will specify "default" instead of "AppSrv01".)

Figure 20-5 shows the command given above being executed to register the application server process.

```
C:\IBM\WebSphere\AppServer\bin>wasservice -add was-hostNode01 -serverName server1
 -profilePath c:\IBM\WebSphere\AppServer\profiles\AppSrv01 -wasHome c:\IBM\WebSph
ere\AppServer -restart true
Adding Service: was-hostNode01
        Config Root: c:\IBM\WebSphere\AppServer\profiles\AppSrv01\config
        Server Name: server1
        Profile Path: c:\IBM\WebSphere\AppServer\profiles\AppSrv01
        Was Home: c:\IBM\WebSphere\AppServer\
        Start Args:
        Restart: 1
IBM WebSphere Application Server V6 - was-hostNode01 service successfully added.
```

Figure 20-5: Registering the application server process

After executing the WASService command, open the **Services** panel, and look for the application server process. You should see that the service has been added with the service name was-hostNode01, as shown in Figure 20-6.

When you create a cluster, you need to register a service for each cluster member. For example, when you create a vertical cluster, you create a separate service for the second cluster member (server2) under the same application server profile (<PROFILE-ROOT>). Use the following command to register the second cluster member. Note the values specified for the –add and –servername parameters.

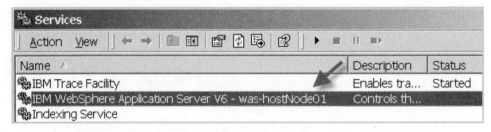

Figure 20-6: Newly registered application server process in Windows Services panel

```
WASService -add was-hostNode01-server2 -serverName server2 -profilePath
c:\IBM\WebSphere\AppServer\profiles\AppSrv01 -wasHome
c:\IBM\WebSphere\AppServer -restart true -startType automatic
```

Register the Node Agent Process

To register the node agent process, open a command prompt on was-host, change to
<WASV6-ROOT>\bin, and issue the following command:

```
WASService -add <SERVICE-NAME> -serverName <SERVER-NAME> -profilePath
<PROFILE-ROOT> -wasHome <WASV6-ROOT> -restart [true|false] -startType
startup-type
```

Specify the command argument values as follows:

- <SERVICE-NAME> is the name of the WebSphere process as it will appear on
  the **Services** panel. Provide a meaningful name appropriate for your environment. For this example, we'll use the default name assigned during the creation
  of the profile when you choose to run as a service: *hostname*Node01 for the
  application server process.

- <SERVER-NAME> is the name of the application server. When you create an
  application server profile, an application server named server1 is created by
  default. You can create additional application servers (e.g., server2, server3) if
  needed. In this case, we're registering the default application server (server1).

- <PROFILE-ROOT> is the path to the application server profile (remember,
  there will be no node agent profile). By default, the path for this profile will be
  <WASV6-ROOT>\profiles\AppSrv01 in a Network Deployment environment.

Figure 20-7 shows the command given above being executed to register the node agent
process.

```
C:\IBM\WebSphere\AppServer\bin>wasservice -add was-hostNode01 -serverName server1
 -profilePath c:\IBM\WebSphere\AppServer\profiles\AppSrv01 -wasHome c:\IBM\WebSph
ere\AppServer -restart true
Adding Service: was-hostNode01
        Config Root: c:\IBM\WebSphere\AppServer\profiles\AppSrv01\config
        Server Name: server1
        Profile Path: c:\IBM\WebSphere\AppServer\profiles\AppSrv01
        Was Home: c:\IBM\WebSphere\AppServer\
        Start Args:
        Restart: 1
IBM WebSphere Application Server V6 - was-hostNode01 service successfully added.
```

Figure 20-7: Registering the node agent process

After executing the WASService command, open the **Services** panel, and look for the node agent process. You should see that the service has been added with the service name was-hostNode01_nodeagent, as shown in Figure 20-8.

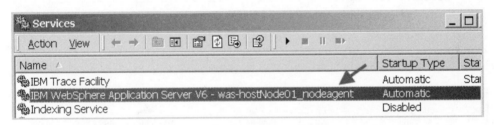

Figure 20-8: Newly registered node agent process in Windows Services panel

Securing Argument Values in the Registry by Encoding

When you enable global security, you must supply user credentials to perform certain administrative tasks. For instance, to stop a WebSphere process, you must supply a user name and password. When you register a WebSphere process as a service, you need to provide user name and password information for a user that has permission to stop, for example, an application server or a Deployment Manager. When using the WASService command, you supply these values as arguments to the startArgs and stopArgs parameters.

To protect this information in the registry, you may want to encode these parameter values. To do so, either add –**encodeParams** *service-name* to the end of the WASService command when adding the service or execute the command with just the –encodeParams parameter to encode the values for an existing service.

Figure 20-9 shows the WASService command being executed with the –encodeParams argument (and stopArgs) at the time the application server process (server1) is added as a service.

```
C:\IBM\WebSphere\AppServer\bin>WASService -add was-hostNode01
-serverName server1 -profilePath c:\IBM\WebSphere\AppServer\pr
ofiles\AppSrv01 -stopArgs "-username admin -password admin123"
 -encodeParams was-hostNode01
Adding Service: was-hostNode01
        Config Root: c:\IBM\WebSphere\AppServer\profiles\AppSr
v01\config
        Server Name: server1
        Profile Path: c:\IBM\WebSphere\AppServer\profiles\AppS
rv01
        Was Home: C:\IBM\WebSphere\AppServer\
        Start Args:
        Restart: 1
```

Figure 20-9: Encoding the user name and password for a new service

Figure 20-10 shows the WASService command being executed with the –encodeParams argument to encode the argument values in an existing service.

```
C:\IBM\WebSphere\AppServer\bin>WASService -encodeParams was-hostNode01_nodeagent

Encoded parameters for service IBMWAS6Service - was-hostNode01_nodeagent
```

Figure 20-10: Encoding the user name and password for an existing service

Managing WebSphere Processes

Once you've registered a WebSphere process as a Windows service, you can manage the process — start it, stop it, and check its status, for example — from the Windows **Services** panel. The panel's toolbar buttons and menu options let you perform these tasks with the click of a mouse button, as you can see in Figure 20-11.

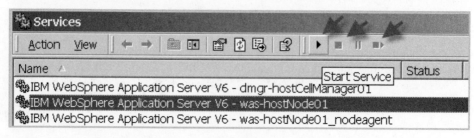

Figure 20-11: Managing WebSphere services from the Windows Services panel

As an alternative, you can use the WASService command from a command prompt to perform these management activities. Issue the following commands to manage a WebSphere process using the WASService command.

- To start the service, use **WASService –start** *service-name*.
- To stop the service, use **WASService –stop** *service-name*.
- To check the status of the service, use **WASService –status** *service-name*.

You'll find that it's generally helpful and convenient to create desktop shortcuts for these commands.

Removing WebSphere Processes from the Windows Services Panel

If you use the WASService command to register a WebSphere service manually, it is your responsibility to remove the service from the Windows registry when it's no longer valid. If you uninstall WebSphere, for example, you must remove such services yourself. WebSphere's uninstall utility doesn't remove services created by the WASService command, although it can remove those that the installation wizard creates during WebSphere installation.

Removing a WebSphere process from the **Services** panel is straightforward. You simply locate the process you plan to remove in the **Services** panel's list of services (Figure 20-12), and issue the following WASService command:

```
WASService -remove service-name
```

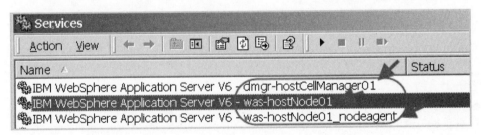

Figure 20-12: WebSphere processes in Windows Services panel

Let's take a closer look at the specific steps required to remove the WebSphere deployment manager, application server, and node agent processes. For these examples, we'll assume you registered the processes as Windows services when creating the profiles and federating the node (for the node agent process), as described in the earlier chapters of this book.

Remove the Deployment Manager Process

To remove the deployment manager process, open the **Services** panel and look for the deployment manager process on dmgr-host. The default service name for this process during its creation is *hostname*CellManager01. In Figure 20-12, the deployment manager service is named dmgr-hostCellManager01. To remove this process, open a command prompt, change to <WASV6-ROOT>\bin, and issue the following command, as shown in Figure 20-13.

```
WASService -remove dmgr-hostCellManager01
```

```
C:\IBM\WebSphere\AppServer\bin>WASService -remove dmgr-hostCellManager01
Remove Service: dmgr-hostCellManager01
Successfully removed service
```

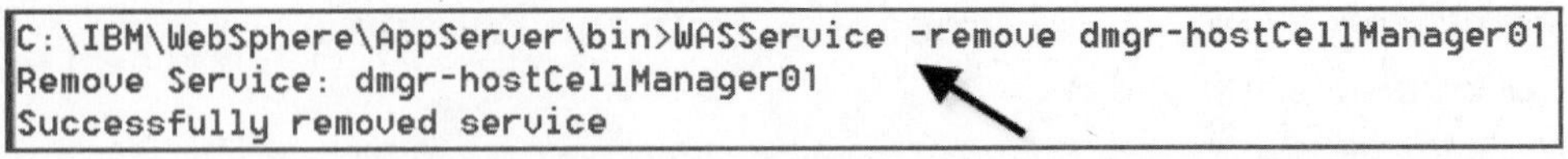

Figure 20-13: Removing the deployment manager process

Refresh the contents of the **Services** panel, and you'll see that the deployment manager process has been removed.

Remove the Application Server Process

To remove the application server process, open the **Services** panel and look for the application server process on was-host. The default service name for this process during its creation is *hostname*Node01 (was-hostNode01 in Figure 20-12). Open a command prompt, change to directory <WASV6-ROOT>\bin, and issue the following command to remove the application server process.

```
WASService -remove was-hostNode01
```

Refresh the **Services** panel to observe that the application server process has been removed.

Remove the Node Agent Process

To remove the node agent process, open the **Services** panel and look for the node agent process on was-host. The default service name for the node agent process during its creation is *hostname*Node01_nodeagent (was-hostNode01_nodeagent in Figure 20-12).

Open a command prompt, change to directory <WASV6-ROOT>\bin, and issue the following command to remove the node agent process.

```
WASService -remove was-hostNode01_nodeagent
```

Refresh the **Services** panel to observe that the application server process has been removed.

21

Service Integration Bus Web Services Enablement

WebSphere Application Server comes with a Web services enablement component for the Service Integration Bus (SIBus). This component, referred to as *SIBWS* in the WebSphere Information Center documentation, enables the use of Web services in a WebSphere installation. As you learned in Chapter 12, an SIBus is an element defined as part of a WebSphere cell with bus members that can be standalone application servers or, more typically, clusters of application servers. For each bus member, a messaging engine (ME) supports destinations defined for that bus member.

In addition to enabling the highly available messaging functionality you learned about in Chapter 12, the SIBus can be used to support Web services destinations in a WebSphere environment. Web services are self-contained, modular applications that can be described, published, located, and invoked over a network. Through SIBWS, you can

- take an internally hosted service at a bus destination and make it available as a Web service through the SIBus (*inbound service*)

- take an externally available Web service and make it available as an internal Web service at the bus destination (*outbound service*)

In this chapter, you'll learn the basics of installing SIBWS components and configuring them to invoke a stock quote Web service (a WebSphere sample application) as an inbound service through the SIBus infrastructure.

The diagram in Figure 21-1 depicts the message flow from a Web services client to the destination to invoke a Web service available as an inbound service at an SIBus destination. Here's an overview of the process:

1. The Web services client sends a request to an *endpoint listener* application (HTTPSOAPChannel1 in this example). An endpoint listener is the address at which Simple Object Access Protocol (SOAP) requests are received from clients.

2. The endpoint listener passes the request to an "InboundPort". (Each endpoint listener is associated with an inbound port.)

3. The inbound port invokes the Web Services Security (WS-Security) protocol and/or JAX-RPC handlers (if they're associated with the port). (JAX-RPC, which stands for *Java API for XML-based Remote Procedure Call*, is also known as *JSR 101*.)

4. The inbound port then sends the message to an inbound service for processing.

5. The response is returned using the same path in the reverse direction.

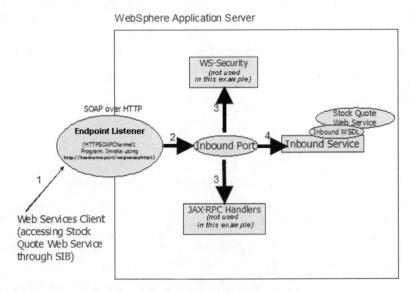

Figure 21-1: Sample inbound Web service architecture

After reflecting on the message flow and examining the architecture diagram, you'll quickly understand how powerful it is to be able to configure and invoke a Web service through an SIBus rather than invoking it directly. The unique advantages of invoking a Web service through an SIBus include the ability to accomplish the following:

- authenticate Web services clients using endpoint listener authentication

- apply security externally to a Web service using WS-Security after receiving the client request and before running the Web service (you can apply operation-level security using role-based authorization)

- invoke JAX-RPC handlers to do some preprocessing before invoking the Web service (e.g., capturing the message received from the client and modifying it before invoking the Web service, changing the message destination depending on a condition)

- define Qualities of Service (QoS), such as message persistence and out-of-band priority messages

- automatic protocol transformation — You might use one messaging protocol (e.g., SOAP over HTTP) to invoke Web services, while your partners employ another (e.g., SOAP over JMS). Using an SIBus component called the Web Services Gateway, you can trap the request from the client and transform it to another messaging protocol.

Web Services Without SIBWS

Before we look at how to install, configure, and test SIBWS and invoke a Web service through an SIBus component, it's useful to see how you invoke a Web service without SIBWS, using only the basic WebSphere Application Server Web service supporting infrastructure. (This support works almost the same way Web service invocation worked in WebSphere Application Server 5.1.) In this example, you'll install and test a Web service application that IBM provides with the WebSphere Application Server V6 download.

Step 1. If you're on a Windows platform, start the Samples Gallery by clicking the **Start** button and navigating to **IBM WebSphere|Application Server V6|profiles|Default|Samples Gallery**. Otherwise, open a browser, and enter the URL **http://was-host:9080/WSSamples**.

Step 2. The navigation pane of the Samples Gallery lists the installed and installable samples. Check to see whether **Web Services Samples** appears under the **Installable Samples** item (as in Figure 21-2). If it does, you need to install the samples to proceed with this example.

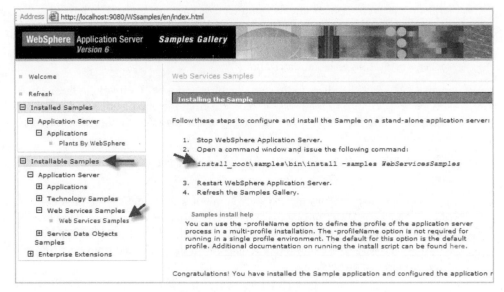

Figure 21-2: Web Services Samples option in Samples Gallery

To install the samples on a standalone application server:

a. Click the **Web Services Samples** link, and read the installation instructions that appear in the panel's main pane.

b. Stop WebSphere Application Server.

c. Open a command window, change to the <WASV6-ROOT>\samples\bin-directory, and issue the following command to install the Web Service Samples:

```
install -samples WebServicesSamples
```

d. Restart WebSphere.

e. Refresh the Samples Gallery to make sure **Web Services Samples** now appears under **Installed Samples** (as in Figure 21-3).

f. Connect to the WebSphere administrative console (**http://was-host:9060/ibm/console**), and verify that the Web Services Samples application is running.

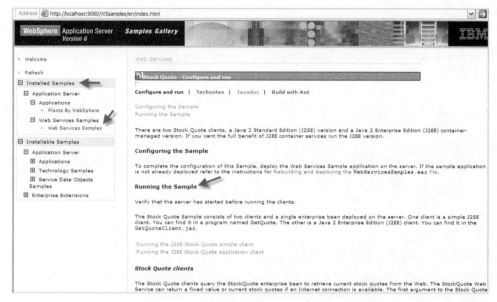

Figure 21-3: Web Services Samples installed

Step 3.   Verify that the Stock Quote functionality is working by completing the following test. To do so, first make sure the application server is started. Then open a command prompt, navigate to the <PROFILE-ROOT>\bin directory, and run **setupCmdLine.bat (.sh** on Unix). Next, navigate to the <WASV6-ROOT>\bin directory, and run **setupCmdLine.bat (.sh).**

Now, issue the following command, all on one line —

```
"%JAVA_HOME%\bin\java" %WAS_LOGGING%
-Djava.ext.dirs="%JAVA_HOME%\jre\lib\ext;%WAS_EXT_DIRS%" -classpath "%
    WAS_CLASSPATH%;%WAS_HOME
    %\samples\lib\WebServicesSamples\simpleClients.jar"
    samples.stock.GetQuote <URL> <symbol>
```

where

- <URL> is the service endpoint address http://<was-host>:<port>/ StockQuote/services/xmltoday-delayed-quotes, with <was-host> being the WebSphere application server system and <port> being the HTTP transport number (default is 9080)

- <symbol> is either a stock symbol, such as DELL or IBM (if you have an Internet connection) or XXX (if you're testing the function offline)

A successful run of the Stock Quote client on a Windows system displays the output shown in Figure 21-4.

```
C:\WebSphere6\AppServer\bin>
C:\WebSphere6\AppServer\bin>"%JAVA_HOME%\bin\java" %WAS_LOGGING% -Djava.ext.dirs
="%JAVA_HOME%\jre\lib\ext;%WAS_EXT_DIRS%" -classpath "%WAS_CLASSPATH%;%WAS_HOME%
\samples\lib\WebServicesSamples\simpleClients.jar" samples.stock.GetQuote http:/
/localhost:9080/StockQuote/services/xmltoday-delayed-quotes IBM
IBM: 95.5

C:\WebSphere6\AppServer\bin>"%JAVA_HOME%\bin\java" %WAS_LOGGING% -Djava.ext.dirs
="%JAVA_HOME%\jre\lib\ext;%WAS_EXT_DIRS%" -classpath "%WAS_CLASSPATH%;%WAS_HOME%
\samples\lib\WebServicesSamples\simpleClients.jar" samples.stock.GetQuote http:/
/localhost:9080/StockQuote/services/xmltoday-delayed-quotes DELL
DELL: 40.82
```

Figure 21-4: Sample Stock Quote commands and output

Stock Quote Implementation Details

The Stock Quote Web service function is implemented using the JAX-RPC/JSR 109 specification. This example uses a stateless session bean. As the illustration in Figure 21-5 depicts, when a client sends a request to a Web container, the HTTP router servlet (webServicesServlet) forwards the request to the StockQuote stateless session bean.

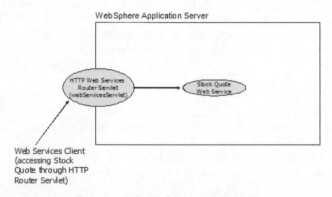

Figure 21-5: Stock Quote implementation

To see the complete implementation details of the Stock Quote Web service, you can examine its source under <WASV6-ROOT>\samples\src\WebServicesSamples\stockEJB and its installation details under <WASV6-ROOT>\profiles\default\installedApps *hostname*Node01Cell\WebServices Samples.ear.

SIBWS Installation

When you install WebSphere Application Server (or a WebSphere upgrade or fix pack), the installation program doesn't install (or upgrade) the Web services enablement portion of the Service Integration Bus (as of fix pack 6.0.1). The installation program simply copies the SIBWS files into directories within your application server directory structure; you must then install them into your application server as a separate task.

When you install WebSphere, the files required to run the SIBWS are copied into your file system under directory <WASV6-ROOT>. Table 21-1 lists the files needed to run the Stock Quote Web service. For a complete list of files required to run the SIBWS, review the documentation at the WebSphere InfoCenter.

Table 21-1: Files required by the Stock Quote Web service

File(s)	Purpose	Location
installSdoRepository.jacl	The script used to create and install the Service Data Objects (SDO) repository	/bin
SDO repository resources	The resource files used to configure SDO to work with various databases	/util/SdoRepository
sib.ra.rar	The resource adapter application (this application isn't SIBWS-specific but is shared by several components of the service integration technologies)	/lib
sibws.ear	The SIBWS application	/installableApps
sibwsInstall.jacl	The script used to install the SIBWS and the resource adapter	/util
soaphttpchannel1.ear	The SOAP-over-HTTP endpoint listener-1 application	/installableApps

To set up the SIBWS installation, you'll complete the following tasks:

1. Create an SIBus.
2. Add the application server as a member of the bus.
3. Create a Service Data Objects (SDO) repository.
4. Install the resource adapter.
5. Install the SIBWS application.
6. Install the endpoint listener application.
7. Configure an endpoint listener.
8. Create a new inbound service configuration.

9. Update the Web service client to use the SIBus.

10. Test the SIBWS.

Installation Steps

Take the following steps to install the SIBWS components in preparation for setting up your Web services environment.

Step 1.   In the WebSphere admin console, expand **Service integration**, select **Buses**, and click **New** to create a new SIBus. On the resulting panel (Figure 21-6), give the bus a name (e.g., MyBus) and a description. Then click **OK**.

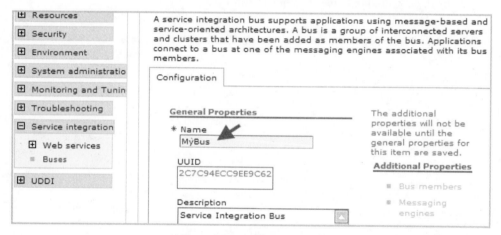

Figure 21-6: Adding an SIBus

Step 2.   Navigate to *bus-name*|**Bus members**|**Add**, and add the server (or cluster) as a member of the bus. Specify the options as follows (as shown in Figure 21-7) for a standalone server environment:

a. Choose the **Server** option, and, in the **Server** drop-down list, select the server you want to add as a bus member.

b. Select the **Default** data store check box option to use Cloudscape to persist the messages. (In a production environment, it's best to use a production-quality database and specify the data source you created instead of using the default data source.)

c. Click **Next**.

d. Click **Finish**, and save your changes to the master configuration.

(In a clustered environment, you'd choose the **Cluster** option, select the cluster name in the **Cluster** drop-down list, and specify the data source you want to use to persist messages.)

The server is added to the bus now, and a default messaging engine is created for the server. If you want to use the SIBus only for Java Message Service (JMS) applications (i.e., as a messaging bus only), you can skip the following steps. You're ready to deploy and configure JMS applications at this point.

Figure 21-7: Adding a server as a bus member

Step 3.   SIBus Web services enablement uses a Service Data Objects (SDO) repository to store and serve Web Service Definition Language (WSDL) definitions. SDO is an open standard for enabling applications to handle data from different data sources in a uniform way. Your next step is to create and install an SDO repository using the installSdoRepository.jacl script. To do so, open a command prompt, navigate to the <WASV6-ROOT>\bin directory, and enter the following wsadmin command.

```
wsadmin -f <WASV6-ROOT>\bin\installSdoRepository.jacl -createDb
```

The optional –createDb flag tells the command to create a default (i.e., Cloudscape) database. If you omit this flag, the command installs the SDO repository application without creating the database.

Note: You can install the SDO repository on many database configurations. For instructions, see the following link in the WebSphere V6 InfoCenter: *http://publib.boulder.ibm.com/infocenter/wasinfo/v6r0/topic/com.ibm. websphere.pmc.doc/tasks/tjw_install_sdo.html.*

Step 4. Next, install the resource adapter using the sibwsInstall.jacl script with the INSTALL_RA parameter. The SIBWS uses this adapter to invoke Web services at outbound ports. To install the adapter, open a command prompt, navigate to the <WASV6-ROOT>/bin directory, and enter the following command:

```
wsadmin -f sibwsInstall.jacl INSTALL_RA installRoot
install_root_using_forward_slashes -nodeName node_name
```

For example:

```
wsadmin -f ..\util\sibwsInstall.jacl INSTALL_RA -installRoot
"c:/IBM/WebSphere/AppServer" -nodeName was-hostNode01
```

In this sample command, the install root is C:/IBM/WebSphere/AppServer, and the node_name is was-hostNode01. The use of forward slashes (/) in file path names is compulsory for the wsadmin command, even on Windows systems.

Step 5. Install the SIBWS application using the sibwsInstall.jacl script with the INSTALL parameter. The SIBWS application enables Web services configuration and access through an SIBus. (Before installing the SIBWS or endpoint listener application, be sure you've installed the resource adapter.)

```
wsadmin -f sibwsInstall.jacl INSTALL -installRoot
install_root_using_forward_slashes -serverName server_name -nodeName
node_name
```

For example:

```
wsadmin -f ..\util\sibwsInstall.jacl INSTALL -installRoot
"c:/IBM/WebSphere/AppServer" -serverName server1 -nodeName
was-hostNode01
```

Again, the use of forward slashes is required. In this example, the install root is C:/IBM/WebSphere/AppServer, the node_name is was-hostNode01, and the server name is server1.

Step 6. Next, install the Endpoint Listener (HTTP) application. An endpoint listener is the address at which messages for an inbound service are received. The endpoint listeners supplied with WebSphere support SOAP-over-HTTP and SOAP-over-JMS bindings. In this example, we're using only SOAP-over-HTTP binding. Execute the following command:

```
wsadmin -f sibwsInstall.jacl INSTALL_HTTP -installRoot
install_root_using_forward_slashes -serverName server_name -nodeName
node_name
```

For example:

```
wsadmin -f ..\util\sibwsInstall.jacl INSTALL_HTTP -installRoot
"c:/IBM/WebSphere/AppServer" -serverName server1 -nodeName was-
hostNode01
```

Again, the use of forward slashes is required. In this example, the install root is C:/IBM/WebSphere/AppServer, the node_name is was-hostNode01, and the server name is server1.

Restart the application server to have your changes take effect.

Create a New Endpoint Listener Configuration

Step 7. Take the following steps to create a new endpoint listener configuration:

a. Start the WebSphere admin console.

b. Expand **Servers**, and navigate to **Application servers|***server***|Endpoint listeners** to display the endpoint listener collection panel.

c. Click **New**.

d. On the endpoint listener settings panel (Figure 21-8), specify the general properties as follows:

- The endpoint listener **Name** must match the name of the Listener application. It should be **SOAPHTTPChannel1**.

- The **URL root** field specifies the context root of the endpoint enterprise application. Enter **http://*was-host:port*/wsgwsoaphttp1**, where *was-host* and *port* are the host name and port number for your application server. On our system, for example, we used the following URL: **http://was-host:9080/wsgwsoaphttp1**.

- For **WSDL serving HTTP URL root**, enter
  http://*was-host:port*/wsgwsoaphttp1. (Even if the documentation says
  this entry is optional, you won't be able to proceed unless you enter a
  value here. Use the same URL here as the URL root.)

e. Click **Apply**.

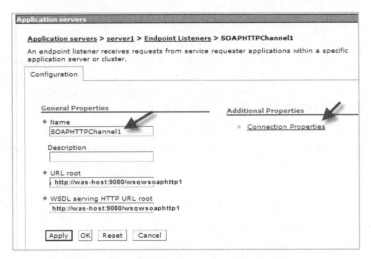

Figure 21-8: Configuring the endpoint listener

f. Under **Additional Properties**, click **Connection properties**.

g. Click **New**. The SIBus connection properties settings panel (Figure 21-9)
   is displayed.

h. In the **Bus name** list, choose an available service integration bus — for
   example, MyBus (assuming you created an SIBus named MyBus as
   suggested in an earlier step).

i. Click **OK**, and save the configuration.

If the processing is completed successfully, the list of service integration
buses connected to this endpoint listener will be updated to include the new
bus. (Otherwise, you'll see an error message.) You're now ready to select
this endpoint listener for use with the sample Web service.

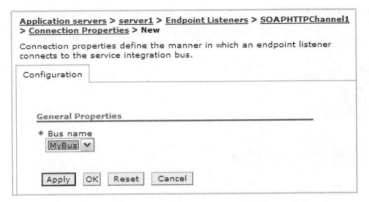

Figure 21-9: Defining the SIBus connection properties

Create a New Inbound Service Configuration

Step 8. Your next task is to configure the Stock Quote Web service as an inbound service to make this internal service available at an SIBus destination. The Stock Quote WSDL file (StockQuoteFetcher.wsdl) defines the service. This WSDL is made available at a URL. An inbound service WSDL is usually a subset of the WSDL of a Web service in a real production system. For this example, we'll use the same WSDL file.

a. Connect to the admin console.

b. Expand **Service Integration**, and navigate to **Buses|*bus-name*|Inbound Services** (e.g., **Buses|MyBus|Inbound Services**).

c. Click **New** to launch the Inbound Service wizard to create the new inbound service configuration.

d. On the resulting panel (Figure 21-10), select the service destination by choosing the StockQuoteService destination name in the drop-down list.

e. Set the **Template WSDL location type** to **URL**.

f. For the **Template WSDL location**, use <WASV6-ROOT> \samples\src\WebServicesSamples\stockEJB\ META-INF\wsdl\StockQuoteFetcher.wsdl.

g. Click **Next**.

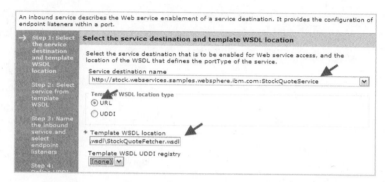

Figure 21-10: Specifying the service destination and WSDL location

h. Next, select the desired service (StockQuote) from the template WSDL, as shown in Figure 21-11.

i. Click **Next**.

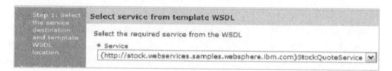

Figure 21-11: Specifying the service from the template WSDL

j. On the next panel (Figure 21-12), specify the name of the inbound service (e.g., MyBusInboundService), and select the endpoint listener (SOAPHTTPChannel1).

k. Click **Finish**, and save the configuration.

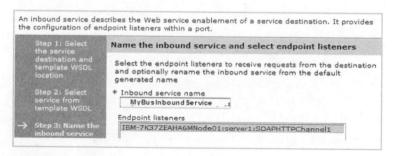

Figure 21-12: Naming the inbound service and selecting endpoint listeners

Update the Web Service Client to Use the SIBus

Step 9.   Next, you need to download the new WSDL files (as a ZIP archive) and generate and test the Web service client so that Web service requests are made via the SIBus rather than directly through the Web service router servlet. To update the client:

a. Connect to the administrative console.

b. Expand **Service Integration**, and navigate to **Buses|*bus-name*|Inbound Services|** *inbound-service-name* (e.g., **Buses|MyBus|Inbound Services|MyBusInboundService**).

c. On the right side of the resulting panel (Figure 21-13), under **Additional Properties**, click **Publish WSDL files to ZIP file**.

d. Select the *inbound-service-name*.zip file (e.g., MyBusInboundService.zip), and save it to your favorite location.

Figure 21-13: Publishing the WSDL files to a ZIP file

Test the SIBWS by Invoking the Web Service Through the SIBus Infrastructure

Step 10.   To test your SIBWS setup, complete the following steps.

a. Start the Rational Application Developer (use **Start|IBM Rational|IBM Rational Application Developer V6|Rational Application Developer**).

b. Create a simple project (**File|Project|Simple|Project**), and specify a name. For this example, we'll use the name MyBus.

c. Right-click **MyBus Project**, and select **import**.

d. Select **Zip file**, and enter the WSDL zip file location you generated earlier.

e. Right-click **MyBusInboundServiceService.wsdl**, and choose **Web Services|Test with Web Service Explorer**. Figure 21-14 shows this menu path.

f. In the explorer's Navigator pane (shown in Figure 21-15), click **getQuote**. Then, in the panel's main pane, enter either a stock symbol (if you have a Internet connection) or **XXX** (to test the function offline).

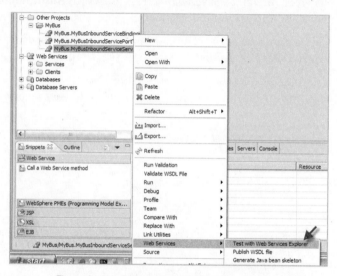

Figure 21-14: Starting the Web Services Explorer

Note: Unfortunately, the Application Server Toolkit doesn't provide the functionality of testing Web services using the Web Services Explorer. If you don't have Rational Application Developer, generate the Web services client using the WSDL2JAVA command. For information about how to use this tool to generate a Web services client from a WSDL file, consult the following WebSphere InfoCenter link:

http://publib.boulder.ibm.com/infocenter/wasinfo/v6r0/index.jsp?topic= /com.ibm.websphere.base.doc/info/aes/ae/rwbs_wsdl2java.html

---

Summary

The service integration functionality within WebSphere Application Server provides a highly flexible messaging system that supports a service-oriented architecture with a wide spectrum of quality-of-service options, supported protocols, and messaging patterns. It supports both message-oriented and service-oriented applications. This messaging system is based on the concept of a service integration bus that provides service-oriented capabilities:

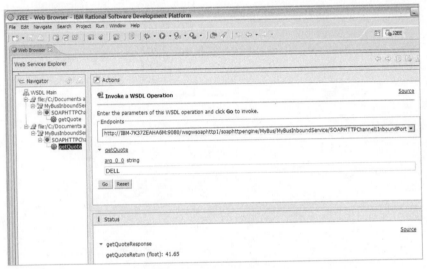

Figure 21-15: Invoking the Web service through the Web Services Explorer

- a service-oriented infrastructure to support application description, deployment, and invocation

- reliable message transport capability

- both tightly and loosely coupled communications options

- intermediary logic (mediations) to adapt message flow at the message engine layer

- implementation of relevant Web services standards

You can configure service integration in a variety of different ways — for example, to tailor the functionality to meet specific messaging requirements without the need for specialized messaging products. Within WebSphere Application Server, the SIBus provides

- the default JMS 1.1–compliant messaging provider, fully integrated with the application server, supporting multiserver configurations, and interoperable with WebSphere MQ

- an infrastructure for Web services integration of applications by leveraging the service-oriented architecture based on Web services standardization

- support for the Web Services Gateway, which provides a single point of control, access, and validation of Web service requests and allows control of which Web services are available to different groups of Web service users

22

Managing the WebSphere V6 Environment

WebSphere Application Server V6 comes with a healthy set of diagnostic and monitoring aids to help you manage even the most sophisticated WebSphere environment. From basic logging and tracing to backup/restore and performance monitoring, you'll find a variety of features in V6 to assist you. In this chapter, we introduce you to the key tools at your disposal for managing a WebSphere installation:

- WebSphere tracing
- collector tool
- First Failure Data Capture
- Log Analyzer
- thread dumping
- heap dump analysis
- configuration archive backup and restore
- Tivoli Performance Viewer
- Dump Name Space

WebSphere V6 Tracing

Tracing lets you obtain detailed information about the execution of WebSphere Application Server components, including application servers, clients, and other processes in the environment. Trace files show the time and sequence of methods called by WebSphere base classes; you can use these files to pinpoint a failure. IBM technical support personnel often request trace collection when troubleshooting a problem. If you're not familiar with the internal structure of WebSphere Application Server, the trace output might not be meaningful to you.

The steps to enable WebSphere tracing are straightforward:

1. Configure an output destination to which the trace data will be sent.

2. Enable trace for the appropriate WebSphere application server or application components.

3. Run the application or operation to generate the trace data.

4. Analyze the trace data, or forward it to the proper organization for analysis.

You can configure the application server to start in a trace-enabled state by setting the appropriate configuration properties. You can enable trace for an application client or standalone process only at process startup.

Tracing and Logging

WebSphere V6 uses a new logging infrastructure that extends Java logging. This enhancement results in some changes to the configuration of the WebSphere Application Server logging infrastructure:

- Loggers defined in Java logging are equivalent to, and configured in the same way as, trace components introduced in previous versions of WebSphere. We refer to both as *components*.

- You can use both Java logging levels and WebSphere Application Server trace levels. The following is a complete list of valid levels, in ascending order of severity:

  - all
  - finest or debug
  - finer or entryExit
  - fine or event
  - detail
  - config
  - info
  - audit
  - warning
  - severe or error
  - fatal
  - off

- Setting the logging and tracing level for a component to **all** enables all the logging for that component. Setting the logging and tracing level for a component to **off** disables all the logging for that component.

- You can configure a component to only one level. However, configuring a component to a certain level enables it to perform logging on the configured level and on any higher severity level.

- Several levels have equivalent names: **finest** is equivalent to **debug**; **finer** is equivalent to **entryExit**; **fine** is equivalent to **event**; and **severe** is equivalent to **error**.

Java logging doesn't distinguish between tracing and message logging, but earlier versions of WebSphere made a clear distinction between these kinds of messages. In WebSphere V6, the differences between tracing and message logging are as follows:

- Tracing messages are messages with lower severity. (For example, tracing messages are logged on levels **fine**, **finer**, **finest**, **even**, **entryExit**, and **debug**.)

- Tracing messages are generally not localized.

- When tracing is enabled, a much higher volume of messages is produced.

- Tracing messages provide information for problem determination.

Trace and Logging Strings

In WebSphere Application Server 5.1.1 and earlier, the trace service for all WebSphere Application Server components was disabled by default. To request a change to the current state of the trace service, you passed a *trace string* to the service. The trace string encoded the information detailing which level of trace to enable or disable and for which components.

In WebSphere V6, the trace string becomes a logging string; you use it to configure both tracing and message logging. The tracing for all components is disabled by default. To change the current state of the tracing and message logging, you must construct a logging string and pass it to the server. The logging string specifies which level of trace or logging to enable or disable for specific components.

You can type in trace strings (or logging strings) or construct them using WebSphere's administrative console. Trace and logging strings must conform to a specific grammar. For Version 5.1.1 and earlier, the specification of the grammar is

```
TRACESTRING=COMPONENT_TRACE_STRING[:COMPONENT_TRACE_STRING]*
    COMPONENT_TRACE_STRING=COMPONENT_NAME=LEVEL=STATE[,LEVEL=STATE]*
```

where

```
LEVEL = all|entryExit|debug|event
STATE = enabled|disabled
COMPONENT_NAME = COMPONENT|GROUP
```

Version 6 supports this earlier syntax; however, IBM has added a new grammar to better represent the underlying infrastructure:

```
LOGGINGSTRING=COMPONENT_LOGGING_STRING[:COMPONENT_LOGGING_STRING]*
    COMPONENT_TRACE_STRING=COMPONENT_NAME=LEVEL
```

where

```
LEVEL = all|(finest|debug)|(finer|entryExit)|(fine|event)|detail|
    config|info|audit|warning|(severe|error)|fatal|off
COMPONENT_NAME = COMPONENT|GROUP
```

The COMPONENT_NAME element in the string specification is the name of a component or group registered with the trace service logging infrastructure. WebSphere components typically register using a fully qualified Java class name (e.g., com.ibm.servlet. engine.ServletEngine). You can also use the asterisk (*) wildcard character to terminate a component name and indicate multiple classes or packages. For example, use the component name **com.ibm.servlet.** * to specify all components whose names begin with com.ibm.servlet. When you use * by itself in place of the component name, the level the string specifies will be applied to all components.

A few notes:

- In Version 5.1.1 and earlier, you could set the level to **all=disabled** to disable tracing. In V6, this syntax results in **LEVEL=info**; tracing is disabled, but logging is enabled.

- The logging string is processed from left to right. During processing, part of the string might be changed or removed if another part of the string overrides the levels the earlier part has configured.

- In V6, **info** is the default level. If the specified component is not present (i.e., if *=*xxx* is not found), *=**info** is always implied. Any component that is not matched by the trace string will have its level set to **info**.

- If the logging string doesn't start with a component logging string that specifies a level for all components (using the * in place of a component name), one will be added, setting the default level for all components.

- In V6, you need not specify **STATE=enabled|disabled**. If used, this parameter has the following effect: **enabled** sets the logging for the specified component to the specified level, and **disabled** sets the logging for the specified component to one level above the specified level.

Table 12-1 lists the effects of disabling on logging level. Table 22-2 shows some legal trace string examples using the V5 and V6 syntaxes.

Table 22-1: Effects of disabling on logging level

Logging string	Resulting logging level	Notes
com.ibm.ejs.ras=debug=disabled	com.ibm.ejs.ras=finer	debug (Version 5) = finest (Version 6)
com.ibm.ejs.ras=all=disabled	com.ibm.ejs.ras=info	Specifying **all=disabled** disables tracing; logging is still enabled.
com.ibm.ejs.ras=fatal=disabled	com.ibm.ejs.ras=of	
com.ibm.ejs.ras=off=disabled	com.ibm.ejs.ras=off	Off is the highest severity.

Table 22-2: Legal trace string examples

Version 5 syntax	Version 6 syntax
com.ibm.ejs.ras.ManagerAdmin= debug=enabled	com.ibm.ejs.ras.ManagerAdmin= finest
com.ibm.ejs.ras.ManagerAdmin= all=enabled,event= disabled	com.ibm.ejs.ras.ManagerAdmin= detail
com.ibm.ejs.ras.*=all=enabled	com.ibm.ejs.ras.*=all
com.ibm.ejs.ras.*=all= enabled:com.ibm.ws.ras=debug= enabled,entryexit=enabled	com.ibm.ejs.ras.*=all:com.ibm.ws. ras=finer

Enabling Trace at Server Startup

The Diagnostic Trace configuration settings for a server process determine the initial trace state for a server process. The configuration settings are read at server startup and used to configure the trace service. You can also change many trace service properties or settings while the server process is running.

The **Application Servers** page of the admin console lists the application servers in the cell and the nodes holding the application servers. If you're using the WebSphere Network Deployment package, this panel also shows the status of the application servers, indicating whether each server is running, stopped, or encountering problems. Here's a summary of the information you'll find on this panel:

- **Name**—The logical name of the server. (For WebSphere Application Server for z/OS, this value is sometimes called the *long name*.)

- **Node**—The name of the node for the application server.

- **Version**—The version for the application server.

- **Status**—The state (e.g., started, stopped) of the application server (Network Deployment environments only). If the status is listed as Unavailable, the node agent isn't running on that node, and you must restart the node agent before you can start the server.

When you select an application server on the **Application Servers** page, a panel is displayed that lets you choose which log or trace task to configure for that application server. To view this panel, expand **Troubleshooting** in the admin console's navigation tree, and select **Logs and Trace**. You use the **Log and Trace** settings page to view and configure the logging and trace settings for the server. Choose a server from the list, and then select the service with which you want to work.

To enable the trace service at application server startup, take the following steps:

1. Start the WebSphere admin console.

2. In the console navigation tree, expand **Troubleshooting**, and select **Logs and Trace**.

3. On the resulting panel, select your server (e.g., server1), and then click **Diagnostic Trace** to configure the trace service.

4. Go to the **Configuration** tab of the resulting page. Figure 22-1 shows the properties you can set here.

Figure 22-1: Logs and Trace Configuration tab

5. To enable trace, select the **Enable Log** check box. (Clear this option to disable trace.)

6. Choose whether to direct trace output to an in-memory circular buffer or to a file.

   - If you select the in-memory circular buffer for the trace output (i.e., the **Memory Buffer** option), set the size of the buffer (in thousands of entries). This value indicates the maximum number of entries the buffer will retain at any given time.

   - If you select a file for trace output (the **File** option), set the maximum size (in megabytes) to which the file should be allowed to grow, and indicate the number of history files to keep. When the file reaches the specified size, the existing file will be closed and renamed, and a new file with the original name will be opened. The new file name will be based on the original name, with the addition of a timestamp qualifier.

7. Select the desired format for the generated trace.

8. Save the changed configuration.

9. Now, enter a trace string to set the trace specification to the desired state:

   a. In the console navigation tree, expand **Troubleshooting**, and select **Logs and Trace** again.

   b. Select your server.

   c. Click **Change Log Level Details** to display the page shown in Figure 22-2. You use this page to select which components and groups to trace.

Figure 22-2: Change Log Detail Levels page

d. If **All Components** has been enabled on this page, you might want to turn it off and then enable specific components.

e. To enable trace for a component or group, click the component or group name. (If the selected server isn't running, you won't be able to see individual components in graphic mode.) Then enter a trace string in the trace string box to set the log detail level.

f. Click **Apply** and then **OK**.

10. Allow enough time for the nodes to synchronize, and then start the server.

Enabling Trace on a Running Server

You can change the trace service state that determines which components are being actively traced for a running server by using the following procedure.

1. Start the WebSphere admin console.

2. Expand **Troubleshooting**, and click **Logs and Trace**.

3. Select a server, and then click **Diagnostic Trace**.

4. Go to the **Runtime** tab. Figure 22-3 shows the properties you can set on this tab.

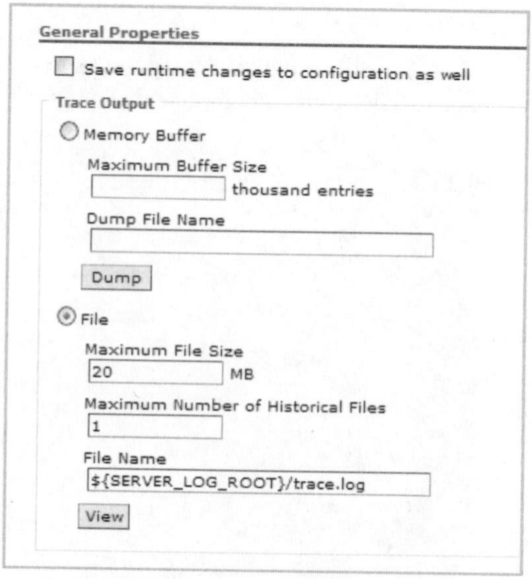

Figure 22-3: Log and Trace Runtime tab

5. Select the check box option to Save runtime changes to configuration as well if you want to write your changes back to the server configuration.

6. Configure the trace output if a change from the existing settings is desired.

7. Click **Apply**.

Enabling Trace on Client and Standalone Applications

When standalone client applications (e.g., Java applications that access WebSphere-hosted Enterprise JavaBeans) have problems interacting with WebSphere Application Server, it may be useful to enable tracing for those applications. Enabling trace for client programs causes the WebSphere classes used by those applications (e.g., naming-service client classes) to generate trace information. A common troubleshooting technique is to enable tracing on both the application server and the client applications and then match records according to timestamp to try to understand where a problem is occurring.

To enable trace for the WebSphere classes in a client application, you add the –DtraceSettingsFile=*filename* system property to the startup script or command of the client application. The location of the output and the classes and detail included in the trace follow the same rules as for adding trace to WebSphere application servers. For example, to trace the standalone client application program named com.ibm.sample.MyClientProgram, you'd enter the following command:

```
java -DtraceSettingsFile=MyTraceSettings.properties
com.ibm.sample.MyClientProgram
```

The file identified by *filename* must be a properties file placed in the classpath of the application client or standalone process. You can find a sample file in the <WASV6-ROOT>\properties\TraceSettings.properties directory.

You can't use the –DtraceSettingsFile=TraceSettings.properties property to enable tracing of the Object Request Broker (ORB) component for thin clients. To direct ORB tracing output for thin clients, set the com.ibm.CORBA.Debug.Output = debugOutputFilename parameter in the command line.

You can use the traceFileName property to configure the MyTraceSettings.properties file to send trace output to a file. Specify one of two options:

- the fully qualified name of an output file (e.g., traceFileName=C:\\ MyTraceFile.log) — You must specify this property to generate visible output.

- stdout — When you use this option, output is written to System.out.

You can also specify a trace string for writing messages with the traceString property. Specify a startup trace specification similar to that available on the server. For your convenience, you can enter multiple individual trace strings into the trace settings file, one trace string per line.

Here are the results of using each optional property setting:

- Specify a valid setting for the traceFileName property without a trace string to write messages to the specified file or System.out only.

- Specify a trace string without a traceFileName property value to generate no output.

- Specify both a valid traceFileName property and a trace string to write both message and trace entries to the location specified in the traceFileName property.

Managing the Application Server Trace Service

You can manage the trace service for a server process while the server is stopped and while it is running. You can specify which components to trace, where to send trace output, what the characteristics of the trace output device are, and which format to generate trace output in. Use the following procedure to manage the application server trace service.

1. Start the WebSphere admin console.

2. Expand **Troubleshooting**, and click **Logs and Trace**.

3. Select your server and then **Diagnostic Trace**.

4. If the server is running, go to the **Runtime** tab.

5. For a running server, select the check box option to write your changes back to the server configuration. If you don't choose this option, the changes you make will apply only for the life of the server process that's currently running.

6. Perform the desired operation:

   - To dump the in-memory circular buffer, enter the file name, and click **Dump**.

   - To change the trace destination from a file to the in-memory circular buffer or to a different file, or to change from the in-memory circular buffer to a file, select the appropriate radio buttons, and then click **Apply**.

- To change the format in which trace output is generated, choose the appropriate value from the drop-down list.

7. Click **Apply**.

Interpreting Trace Output

As you've learned, on an application server, you can direct trace output to either a file or an in-memory circular buffer. If you send trace output to the in-memory circular buffer, you need to dump the output to a file before you can view it. On an application client or standalone process, you can direct trace output to either a file or the process console window. In all cases, trace output is generated as plain text in basic, advanced, or log analyzer format, according to your specification.

The basic and advanced formats for trace output are similar to the basic and advanced formats available for the JVM message logs. These formats use many of the same fields and formatting techniques. The fields you'll encounter in the basic and advanced trace output formats include the following:

- TimeStamp — A timestamp formatted using the locale of the process in which it is formatted. It includes a fully qualified date (*yymmdd*), a 24-hour time with millisecond precision, and the time zone.

- ThreadId — An eight-character hexadecimal value generated from the hash code of the thread that issued the trace event.

- ThreadName — The name of the Java thread that issued the message or trace event.

- ShortName — The abbreviated name of the logging component that issued the trace event. This is typically the class name for WebSphere Application Server internal components, but it may be some other identifier for user applications.

- LongName — The full name of the logging component that issued the trace event. This is typically the fully qualified class name for WebSphere Application Server internal components, but it may be some other identifier for user applications.

- EventType — A one-character field that indicates the type of trace event. Trace types are in lower case. Possible values include

Value	Description
>	a trace entry of type **method entry**
<	a trace entry of type **method exit**

Value	Description
1	a trace entry of type **fine** or **event**
2	a trace entry of type **finer**
3	a trace entry of type **finest, debug,** or **dump**
Z	a placeholder to indicate that the trace type wasn't recognized

- ClassName — The class that issued the message or trace event.

- MethodName — The method that issued the message or trace event.

- Organization — The organization that owns the application that issued the message or trace event.

- Product — The product that issued the message or trace event.

- Component — The component within the product that issued the message or trace event.

Basic Format

Trace events displayed in basic format take the following form:

```
<timestamp><threadId><shortName><eventType>[className][methodName]
<textMessage>
     [parameter 1]
     [parameter 2]
```

Advanced Format

Trace events displayed in advanced format take the following form:

```
<timestamp><threadId><eventType><UOW><source=longName>[className]
   [methodName] <Organization><Product><Component>[thread=threadName]
      <textMessage>[parameter 1=parameterValue][parameter 2=parameterValue]
```

Log Analyzer Format

Specifying the log analyzer format lets you open trace output using the Log Analyzer tool. This option is useful if you're trying to correlate traces from two different server processes because it lets you use the Log Analyzer's merge capability. You'll learn more about the Log Analyzer later in this chapter.

Diagnostic Trace Service Settings

This section provides a detailed explanation of the options available on the **Configuration** and **Runtime** tabs of the Diagnostic Trace Service settings page. (You view this page by expanding **Troubleshooting** in the WebSphere admin console and navigating to **Logs and Trace|*server*|Diagnostic Trace**).

On the Configuration tab:
Enable Log

This check box option enables the log service. If you select this option, the Trace Output and Trace Output Format configuration properties you specify are passed to the application server trace service at server startup.

Trace Output

The Trace Output properties specify where trace output should be written. The output can be written directly to an output file or stored in memory and written to a file on demand (using the **Dump** button found on the **Runtime** tab).

- **Memory Buffer** — Specifies that the trace output should be written to an in-memory circular buffer. If you choose this option, you must specify the following parameter:

    - **Maximum Buffer Size** — The number of entries, in thousands, that can be cached in the buffer. When this number is exceeded, older entries are over-written by new entries.

- **File** — Specifies to write the trace output to a self-managing log file. The self-managing log file writes messages to the file until the specified maximum file size is reached. When the file reaches the specified size, logging is temporarily suspended, and the log file is closed and renamed. The new name is based on the original name of the file plus a timestamp qualifier that indicates when the renaming occurred. Once the renaming is complete, a new, empty log file with the original name is reopened, and logging resumes. No messages are lost as a result of the rollover, although a single message may be split across the two files. If you choose the **File** option, you must specify the following parameters:

    - **Maximum File Size** — The maximum size, in megabytes, to which the output file is allowed to grow. This attribute is valid only if you select the **File** output option. When the file reaches this size, it is rolled over as described above.

    - **Maximum Number of Historical Files** — The maximum number of rolled-over files to keep.

    - **File Name** — The name of the file to which the trace output is written.

Trace Output Format

You use this drop-down list to specify the format of the trace output. You can choose one of three levels for trace output:

- **Basic (Compatible)** — Preserves only basic trace information. Choose this option to minimize the amount of space taken up by the trace output.

- **Advanced** — Preserves more-specific trace information. Choose this option to see detailed trace information for use in troubleshooting and problem determination.

- **Log Analyzer** — Preserves trace information in a format compatible with the Log Analyzer tool. Choose this option if you want to use the trace output as input to the Log Analyzer.

On the Runtime tab:

With the exception of the **Enable Log** check box, the **Runtime** tab of the Diagnostic Trace Service settings page contains the same parameters as the **Configuration** tab, and you can enable tracing on either tab. The difference is that changes you make on the **Configuration** tab are applied only when the server is restarted. Changes made on the **Runtime** tab take effect immediately.

Two additional options are unique to the **Runtime** tab:

Save changes to configuration

This check box option saves changes made on the **Runtime** tab to the trace configuration as well. Select this option to copy runtime trace changes to the trace configuration settings. Doing so will cause the changes to persist even if the application is restarted.

Dump File Name

This field specifies the name of the file to which the memory buffer will be written when it is dumped (using the **Runtime** tab's **Dump** button).

Collector Tool

The collector tool gathers information about your WebSphere installation and packages it in a Java archive (JAR) file that you can send to IBM Customer Support to assist in determining and analyzing a problem. Information in the JAR file includes logs, property files, configuration files, operating system and Java data, and a notation of the presence and level of each software prerequisite. When you execute the collector tool, the collector program traverses the system to gather relevant files and command results to produce the JAR file of information needed to determine and solve a problem.

There are two phases to using the collector tool. In the first phase, you run the tool on your WebSphere Application Server product to produce the JAR file. The IBM Support team performs the second phase, which is analyzing the JAR file produced by the collector program. The collector program runs to completion as it creates the JAR file despite any errors it might find (e.g., missing files or commands), collecting as much data in the JAR file as possible.

You can optionally run the collector tool in summary mode to collect summary data only. The collector summary option produces a lightweight collection of version and other information in a text file and on the console. The lightweight information is useful for getting started in communicating your problem to IBM Support.

Running the Collector Tool

Take the following steps to run the collector tool in full (i.e., non-summary) mode.

Step 1. Log on to the system as an Administrator (on Windows systems) or root (on Unix systems).

Step 2. Verify that Java 1.2.2 or later is available in the path. The collector program requires Java code to run. It also collects data about the IBM Developer Kit, Java Technology Edition in which it runs. If you have multiple Developer Kits on the system, make sure the one used by WebSphere Application Server is the one in the path for the collector program. If the Developer Kit being used by WebSphere isn't available, you can put another Developer Kit in the path for the collector program to have the collector gather all data except information about the Developer Kit.

Step 3. Verify that the path being used by the collector program contains all necessary information, and make sure you're not running the program from within the WebSphere installation root directory. (You can't run the collector tool in a directory under the WebSphere installation directory.) If your system is a Windows platform, include regedit in the path. If the system is a Unix (or Linux) platform, make sure the path contains system directories /bin, /sbin, /usr/bin, and /usr/sbin.

Step 4. Create a working directory from which you can start the collector program, and make this directory the current directory. The collector program writes its output JAR file to the current directory. The program also creates and deletes several temporary files in the current directory. Creating a work directory to run the collector program avoids naming collisions and simplifies cleanup.

Step 5. Run the collector program by entering the command **collector** from the command line. Specifying the command with no parameters gathers one copy of the node data and data from each server in the node and stores the data in a single JAR output file. To gather data from a specific server in the node, use

```
collector.bat -servername servername
```

where *servername* is the name of the problem server. (On Unix systems, use **collector.sh** instead of **collector.bat**.)

You can also enter a fully qualified path to the collector command. For example, use this command in a default installation on a Windows platform:

```
C:\WebSphere\AppServer\bin\collector.bat
```

> **Note:** To use the nonqualified version of the collector command, be sure to set the path correctly. For Windows platforms, <WASV6-ROOT>\bin must be in the path for the system to locate the collector.bat command. For Unix platforms, <WASV6-ROOT>/bin must be in the path to locate the collector.sh command. The WebSphere installation root directory is determined at installation. The setupCmdLine.bat file on Windows platforms and the setupCmdLine.sh file on Unix systems identify this directory.

The collector program creates a log file, Collector.log, and the output JAR file in the current directory. The name of the JAR file is based on the host name and package of the WebSphere Application Server product, in the format *hostname-cellname-nodename-profile*. The Collector.log file is one of the files collected in the *hostname-cellname-nodename-profile* file. Send the *hostname-cellname-nodename-profile* file to IBM Support for analysis.

Analyzing Collector Tool Output

The collector tool was developed so that IBM Support could ask customers to run the tool and collect (into a single JAR file) all pertinent information about the installation at the time a customer logged a problem. IBM Support could then analyze the collector tool output sent to it. You can use this section to understand the JAR file content in case you decide to perform your own analysis.

You can view the files contained in the JAR archive file without extracting them, but it's easier to extract all files and view the contents of each file individually. To extract the files, use one of the following two commands:

```
jar -xvf WASenv.jar v
unzip WASenv.jar
```

where WASenv.jar represents the name of the JAR file created by the collector tool. For easy access to the gathered files and simplified cleanup, unzip the JAR file to an empty directory.

The JAR file contains the following items:

- the collector tool log file, Collector.log
- copies of stored WebSphere Application Server files and their full paths
- operating system information in a directory named OS
- Java information in a directory named Java
- WebSphere Application Server information in a directory named WAS
- collector shell script (or batch file) execution information in a directory named debug
- MQ information in a directory named MQ (if you installed WebSphere MQ or the embedded messaging feature)
- a JAR file manifest

Tips and Suggestions

When examining the collector tool output, check the Collector.log file for errors. Some errors might be normal or expected. For example, when the collector tries to gather files or directories that don't exist for your specific installation, it logs an error about the missing files. A nonzero return code means that a command the collector tool tried to run doesn't exist. This result might be expected in some cases, but if this type of error occurs repeatedly, you might actually have a problem.

On Unix systems, a file named commands in the OS directory contains the location of all commands used. If you're missing command output, check this file to see whether the collector tool found the command.

The collector runs some shell scripts on Unix systems. The script output is saved in files in the OS directory, while the corresponding debug information is saved in the debug directory. If the output of a shell script is missing, check the corresponding file in the debug directory.

When you issue the collector command in an environment with multiple installation instances, the tool that runs depends on what is in the PATH statement. For example, if you install both the base WebSphere Application Server and the Deployment Manager product on the same machine, the bin directory that appears first in the PATH variable is the one that furnishes the collector tool. To work around this problem, use a fully qualified file path when calling the collector tool, as in the following example for a Windows platform:

```
C:\WebSphere\AppServer\bin\collector.bat
```

On Windows systems, the OS directory includes a file named installed.out. This file contains a list of programs found in the Add/Remove Programs list. You can find the same information in the file Desktop\My Computer\Control Panel\Add/Remove Programs\Install/Uninstall.

Collector Summary

Starting with Version 5.0.2, WebSphere Application Server includes an enhancement to the collector tool that helps you communicate with WebSphere technical staff at IBM Support. The *collector summary option* produces a lightweight text file and console version of some of the information in the JAR file produced by the collector tool.

You can use the collector summary option to retrieve basic configuration and prerequisite software level information when starting a conversation with IBM Support. The option produces version information for the WebSphere Application Server product and the operating system and additional information, storing the results in the Collector_Summary.txt file and writing it to the console. You can use this information to answer initial questions from IBM Support, or you can send the Collector_Summary.txt file directly to IBM. If IBM Support needs more information to solve your problem, run the collector command to create the JAR file.

To use the collector summary option, you run the collector command with the –Summary option. Start from a temporary directory outside the WebSphere installation root directory, and issue the appropriate command for your operating system:

On Windows platforms:

```
<WASV6-ROOT>\bin\collector.bat -Summary
```

On Unix platforms:

```
<WASV6-ROOT>/bin/collector.sh -Summary
```

Collector Tool Examples

Listings 22-1 through 22-5 shows several examples of the collector tool in action. Listing 22-1 shows what happens if you try run the tool from the WebSphere installation directory. Listing 22-2 illustrates running the collector tool in full mode. (For space considerations, we've omitted a large portion of the display output that's generated when you run the tool in full mode.)

Listing 22-3 displays the JAR file created by the collector tool. Listing 22-4 shows how to run the collector tool in summary mode, and Listing 22-5 displays the text file created by the tool when run in this mode.

Listing 22-1

Attempt to run the collector from the WebSphere installation directory

```
C:\Program Files\IBM\WebSphere\AppServer\bin>collector
2005/06/26 09:51:34 URL is: jar:file:/C:/Program Files/IBM/WebSphere/AppServer/
        lib/collector.jar!/com/ibm/websphere/rastools/collector/

Collector.class
2005/06/26 09:51:34 Collector version: 6.0.0.0
2005/06/26 09:51:34 Log File name: C:\Program Files\IBM\WebSphere\AppServer\
        bin\Collector.log
2005/06/26 09:51:34 Case sensitive: false
2005/06/26 09:51:34 Inventory file: C:/Program Files/IBM/WebSphere/AppServer/
        lib/collector.jar
2005/06/26 09:51:34 Please run the Collector tool in a temporary working
        directory.
2005/06/26 09:51:34 The Collector tool can not be run in the WebSphere install
        directory or a WebSphere install subdirectory: C:\Program Files\
        IBM\WebSphere\AppServer
```

Listing 22-2

Running the collector tool in full mode

```
C:\temp>C:\Progra~1\IBM\WebSphere\AppServer\bin\collector.bat
2005/06/26 09:52:43 URL is: jar:file:/C:/Program Files/IBM/WebSphere/AppServer/
      lib/collector.jar!/com/ibm/websphere/rastools/collector/

Collector.class
2005/06/26 09:52:43 Collector version: 6.0.0.0
2005/06/26 09:52:43 Log File name: C:\temp\Collector.log
2005/06/26 09:52:43 Case sensitive: false
2005/06/26 09:52:43 Inventory file: C:/Program Files/IBM/WebSphere/AppServer/
      lib/collector.jar
2005/06/26 09:52:47 Compression:   9
2005/06/26 09:52:47 User:   null

The Collector program should be run as user id Administrator or a
user id that has Administrator authority because some of the commands
to be executed require Administrator authority.  However, if you
proceed without Administrator authority, much of what Collector does
will work just fine.

2005/06/26 09:52:48 EXECUTE: echo
2005/06/26 09:52:48 Execute return code: 0
2005/06/26 09:52:48 EXECUTE: echo
2005/06/26 09:52:48 Execute return code: 0

<CONTENT OMITTED TO SAVE SPACE>

2005/06/26 09:57:12 Including file: C:\Program Files\IBM\WebSphere\AppServer/
      profiles/default/logs/server1/trace.log
2005/06/26 09:57:12 Error - File does not exist: C:\Program Files\IBM\
      WebSphere\AppServer/profiles/default/logs/server1/trace.log
2005/06/26 09:57:12 Including file: C:\Program Files\IBM\WebSphere\AppServer/
      profiles/default/logs/activity.log
2005/06/26 09:57:12 Number possible errors:        36
2005/06/26 09:57:12 Log File name:  C:\temp\Collector.log
2005/06/26 09:57:12 Output Jar name:  C:\temp\IBM-79D6XZF0P9F-IBM-
      79D6XZF0P9FNode01Cell-IBM-79D6XZF0P9FNode01-default-WASenv.jar
2005/06/26 09:57:12 Including file: C:\temp\Collector.log
2005/06/26 09:57:12 Return code:  0, Elapsed Time: 00:04:25.101

C:\temp>
```

Listing 22-3

JAR file created by the collector tool

```
C:\temp>dir *.jar
  Volume in drive C has no label.
```

```
Volume Serial Number is 5CC0-9DEE

Directory of C:\temp

06/26/2005  09:57 AM          4,653,970 IBM-79D6XZF0P9F-IBM-
        79D6XZF0P9FNode01Cell-IBM-79D6XZF0P9FNode01-default-WASenv.jar
              1 File(s)      4,653,970 bytes
              0 Dir(s)  39,338,934,272 bytes free

C:\temp>
```

Listing 22-4

Running the collector tool in summary mode

```
C:\temp>C:\Progra~1\IBM\WebSphere\AppServer\bin\collector.bat -Summary
2005/06/26 10:10:40 URL is: jar:file:/C:/Program Files/IBM/WebSphere/AppServer/
        lib/collector.jar!/com/ibm/websphere/rastools/collector/

Collector.class
2005/06/26 10:10:40 Collector version: 6.0.0.0

The Collector program should be run as user id Administrator or a
user id that has Administrator authority because some of the commands
to be executed require Administrator authority.  However, if you
proceed without Administrator authority, much of what Collector does
will work just fine.


Hostname: IBM-79D6XZF0P9F   Nodename: IBM-79D6XZF0P9FNode01
-------------------------------------------------------------------------------
IBM WebSphere Application Server Product Installation Status Report
-------------------------------------------------------------------------------

Report at date and time 2005-06-26 10:10:49-0700

Installation
-------------------------------------------------------------------------------
Product Directory        C:\Program Files\IBM\WebSphere\AppServer
Version Directory        C:\Program Files\IBM\WebSphere\AppServer\
        properties\version
DTD Directory            C:\Program Files\IBM\WebSphere\AppServer\
        properties\version\dtd
Log Directory            C:\Program Files\IBM\WebSphere\AppServer\logs
Backup Directory         C:\Program Files\IBM\WebSphere\AppServer\properties\
        version\update\backup
TMP Directory            C:\DOCUME~1\ADMINI~1\LOCALS~1\Temp

Installation Platform
-------------------------------------------------------------------------------
Name                     IBM WebSphere Application Server
```

```
Version                 6.0

Product List
------------------------------------------------------------------------
BASE                    installed

Installed Product
------------------------------------------------------------------------
Name                    IBM WebSphere Application Server
Version                 6.0.1.0
ID                      BASE
Build Level             o0510.18
Build Date              3/11/05


------------------------------------------------------------------------
End Installation Status Report
------------------------------------------------------------------------

Java Full Version:
J2RE 1.4.2 IBM Windows 32 build cn142sr1a-20050209 (JIT enabled: jitc)

Operating System: Windows XP, 5.1
```

Listing 22-5

Text file created by the collector tool in summary mode

```
C:\temp>dir Collector*
 Volume in drive C has no label.
 Volume Serial Number is 5CC0-9DEE

 Directory of C:\temp

06/26/2005  10:10 AM                     0 Collector.log
06/26/2005  10:10 AM                 1,820 Collector_Summary.txt
               2 File(s)          1,820 bytes
               0 Dir(s)   39,338,749,952 bytes free

C:\temp>
```

First Failure Data Capture

The First Failure Data Capture tool is another troubleshooting feature available in WebSphere V6. This tool preserves the information generated from a processing failure and returns control to the affected engines. The tool saves the captured data in a log file for use in analyzing the problem.

The First Failure Data Capture tool is intended primarily for use by IBM Service. It runs as part of WebSphere Application Server, and you can't start or stop it. It's recommended that you not try to configure the First Failure Data Capture tool. If you experience conditions requiring you to contact IBM Service, your IBM Service representative will assist you in reading and analyzing the First Failure Data Capture log. The tool does not affect the performance of WebSphere Application Server.

Log Analyzer and showlog

WebSphere's Log Analyzer takes one or more service or activity logs, merges all the data, and displays the entries. Based on its symptom database, the tool then analyzes and interprets the event or error conditions in the log entries to help you diagnose problems. The Log Analyzer has a special feature that enables it to download the latest symptom database from the IBM Web site.

WebSphere Application Server creates the service or activity log file from the activity of the various components. The log file, activity.log, is a binary file in the logs directory of the profile (e.g., C:\Program Files\IBM\WebSphere\AppServer\profiles\default\logs).

You can't use a text editor to view the service or activity log, but you can view it using the Log Analyzer. To do so, change to directory <WASV6-ROOT>\bin, and run the **waslogbr** script file. On Windows systems, this file is named waslogbr.bat; on Unix systems, it is waslogbr.sh.

Once the Log Analyzer starts, use **File|Open** to open the activity.log file containing the events you want to view. The file will be in the logs directory for the profile you're interested in. For example, you'll find the default profile's activity.log file in the <WASV6-ROOT>\profiles\default\logs directory. Figure 22-4 shows the Log Analyzer main window after a log file is opened.

To analyze the log file records, right-click an entry in the tree on the left (the **Logs** pane), select **UnitOfWorkView** from the resulting context menu, and then select **Analyze**. A green check mark will appear next to any record that matches a record in the Log Analyzer's symptom database. When you select a check-marked record, you'll see an explanation of the problem in the **Analysis** pane (in the lower-right corner of the Log Analyzer window).

By default, the **Logs** pane displays log entries by unit of work (UOW). It lists each UOW instance and its associated entries from the logs you've opened. You may find the

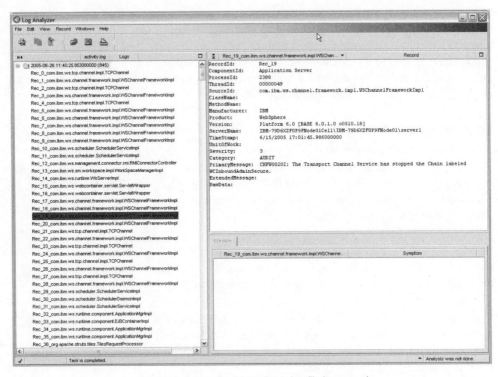

Figure 22-4: Log Analyzer after a log file is opened

UOW grouping useful when you're trying to find related entries in the service or activity log or when diagnosing problems across multiple machines. The file name of the first log you open appears in the pane's title bar. You'll see a root folder in the pane; under it, each UOW has a folder icon that you can expand to show all the entries for that UOW. Log entries without any UOW identification are grouped into a single folder in this tree view.

The UOW folders are sorted to show the UOW with the latest timestamp at the top of the list. The entries within each UOW are listed in the reverse sequence — that is, the first (earliest) entry for that UOW appears at the top of the list. If you've merged several logs in the Log Analyzer, all the log entries are merged in timestamp sequence within each UOW folder, as if they all came from the same log.

Each log entry is assigned an entry number, Rec_*nnnn*, when you open a log in the Log Analyzer. If more than one file is opened (i.e., in the case of merged files), the Rec_*nnnn* identification won't be unique because the number is relative to the entry sequence in the original log file, not to the merged data the Log Analyzer is displaying.

By default, each entry in the **Logs** pane is color-coded to help you quickly identify entries that have high-severity errors. The following color values are the defaults for the entries displayed in the pane.

- A nonselected log entry with a background color of

    - pink indicates a severity 1 error
    - yellow indicates a severity 2 error
    - white indicates a severity 3 error

- A selected log entry with a background color of

    - red indicates a severity 1 error
    - green indicates a severity 2 error
    - blue indicates a severity 3 error

This color coding is configurable; you can change it on the Log Analyzer Preferences dialog (**File|Preferences|Logs|Severity**). For details about how to do this, as well as an explanation of the different error severity levels, see the help for the Severity page in the Log Analyzer Preferences notebook. You can also use different groupings to display entries in the **Logs** pane. To set the grouping filters, use the **Logs** page of the Log Analyzer Preferences notebook.

Once you've invoked the Analyze action, the following icons provide more information about analyzed log entries in the **Logs** pane:

- A check icon indicates that the entry has some analysis information in one or more pages in the **Analysis** pane.

- A cascading plus sign (+) indicates that the entry has some analysis information and that it has a reraised or remapped exception. You may want to look at the log entry prior to this one when diagnosing problems.

- A question mark (?) indicates that the entry has a severity 1 or 2 error but that no additional analysis information is available for it.

- An "x" icon indicates that the entry has a severity 3 error and has no analysis information.

When you select an entry in the **Logs** pane, you see the entry in the **Record** pane (upper-right corner of the Log Analyzer window). The entry identification appears in the pane's title bar, and the Rec_*nnnn* number appears as the **RecordId** in the first line of the pane. Right-click in the **Record** pane to see actions you can perform on the selected entry. A drop-down arrow at the top of the pane lets you look at the last 10 records you've viewed. (The Log Analyzer doesn't display associated analysis data for these cached records. To see analysis information for cached data, you must reselect the entry in the **Logs** pane.) To change the cache for the historical data (10 by default), use the Log Analyzer Preferences notebook's **General** page.

To print the **Record** pane's contents, select **Record|Print** with the **Record** pane in focus. You can enable or disable line-wrap mode for the pane using the **Record** page of the Log Analyzer Preferences notebook.

When you've invoked the Analyze action and additional information is available, the information will appear in the **Analysis** pane. If this pane's **Symptom** tab is grayed out, there is no information in that page.

Updating the Symptoms Database

As we stated, the Log Analyzer works in conjunction with IBM's symptom database to help analyze the root cause of errors. From time to time, IBM updates this database, so periodically you'll want to download the current version. To obtain the latest updates to the symptom database, open the Log Analyzer interface, and select either **File|Update Database|WebSphere Application Server Symptom Database** (for WebSphere Base or Express installations) or **File|Update Database|WebSphere Application Server Network Deployment Symptom Database** (for WebSphere Network Deployment).

showlog

The Log Analyzer tool can't view remote files. If you're running WebSphere on an operating system that doesn't support a graphical interface, you can transfer the activity log file in binary mode to the system on which you're running the WebSphere admin console, and use the Log Analyzer there. In cases where transferring the file is impractical or inconvenient, you can use an alternate viewing tool, showlog, to view the service or activity log file. The showlog tool dumps a WebSphere binary log file to either stdout or a text file.

To use showlog, first change to the bin directory of<WASV6-ROOT>. Execute the command with no parameters to display usage instructions. On Windows systems, run **showlog.bat**; on Unix systems, run **showlog.sh**. Listing 22-6 shows the usage information displayed for the command.

Listing 22-6

Usage information for the showlog command

```
C:\Program Files\IBM\WebSphere\AppServer\bin>showlog
This program dumps a Websphere binary log file to standard out or a file.
Usage: showlog [-format CBE-XML-1.0.1] binaryFilename [outputFilename]
where:
        -format specifies the output format.  Currently only CBE-XML-1.0.1
    format is supported (this complies with the Common Base Event specification
    version 1.0.1).  If no format is given, showlog outputs in a tabular format.

        binaryFilename should be a binary log filename in the WASHOME/logs
    directory or a fully-qualified binary log filename.  showlog will not look
    in the current directory.

        outputFilename is optional.  If no filename is given, showlog dumps
    binaryFilename to standard out.  Otherwise, outputFilename will be created
    in the current directory unless it is a fully-qualified filename.
```

To direct the service or activity log contents to stdout, use the command **showlog activity.log**. Listing 22-7 shows a portion of the output that results for this command. To dump the service or activity log to a text file for viewing with a text editor, use **showlog activity.log** *textFileName*.

Listing 22-7

Directing the service or activity log to stdout

```
C:\Program Files\IBM\WebSphere\AppServer\bin>showlog activity.log
$LANG = en_US
$CODESET = Cp1252
----------------------------------------------------------------
ComponentId:    Application Server
ProcessId:      2388
ThreadId:       0000000a
ThreadName:     P=763023:O=0:CT
SourceId:       com.ibm.ws.tcp.channel.impl.TCPChannel
ClassName:
MethodName:
Manufacturer:   IBM
Product:        WebSphere
Version:        Platform 6.0 [BASE 6.0.1.0 o0510.18]
ServerName:     IBM-79D6XZFOP9FNode01Cell\IBM-79D6XZFOP9FNode01\server1
TimeStamp:      2005-06-15 11:40:42.737000000
UnitOfWork:
Severity:       3
Category:       AUDIT
PrimaryMessage: TCPC0001I: TCP Channel TCP_2 is listening on host *  (IPv4)
```

```
    port 9080.
ExtendedMessage:
-------------------------------------------------------------
ComponentId:        Application Server
ProcessId:          2388
ThreadId:           0000000a
ThreadName:         P=763023:0=0:CT
SourceId:           com.ibm.ws.channel.framework.impl.WSChannelFrameworkImpl
ClassName:
MethodName:
Manufacturer:       IBM
Product:            WebSphere
Version:            Platform 6.0 [BASE 6.0.1.0 o0510.18]
ServerName:         IBM-79D6XZF0P9FNode01Cell\IBM-79D6XZF0P9FNode01\server1
TimeStamp:          2005-06-15 11:40:42.797000000
UnitOfWork:
Severity:           3
Category:           AUDIT
PrimaryMessage:     CHFW0019I: The Transport Channel Service has started chain
    WCInboundDefault.
ExtendedMessage:
-------------------------------------------------------------
ComponentId:        Application Server
ProcessId:          2388
ThreadId:           0000000a
ThreadName:         P=763023:0=0:CT
SourceId:           com.ibm.ws.tcp.channel.impl.TCPChannel
ClassName:
MethodName:
Manufacturer:       IBM
Product:            WebSphere
Version:            Platform 6.0 [BASE 6.0.1.0 o0510.18]
ServerName:         IBM-79D6XZF0P9FNode01Cell\IBM-79D6XZF0P9FNode01\server1
TimeStamp:          2005-06-15 11:40:42.857000000
UnitOfWork:
Severity:           3
Category:           AUDIT
PrimaryMessage:     TCPC0001I: TCP Channel TCP_3 is listening on host *   (IPv4)
port 9043.
ExtendedMessage:

<REMAINDER OF CONTENT OMITTED TO SAVE SPACE>
```

Thread Dumping

Dumping threads from your application server can help you diagnose problems such as blocked threads. To dump threads, issue the **wsadmin** command, as shown in Listing 22-8. Each time you run this command, a new Java Core file is generated in the profile directory with the file name javacore.<*timestamp*>.txt — for example, C:\Program Files\IBM\WebSphere\AppServer\profiles\default\javacore.20050525.102138.836.txt.

> **Unix note:** The popular way to take thread dumps on Unix platforms is by issu-
> ing a **KIll -3 <pid>** commmand.

Listing 22-8

Dumping threads using the wsadmin command

```
C:\Program Files\IBM\WebSphere\AppServer\bin>wsadmin
WASX7209I: Connected to process "server1" on node IBM-79D6XZF0P9FNode01 using
        SOAP connector;  The type of process is: UnManagedProcess
WASX7029I: For help, enter: "$Help help"
wsadmin>set jvm [$AdminControl completeObjectName type=JVM,process=server1,*]
WebSphere:name=JVM,process=server1,platform=dynamicproxy,node=IBM-
79D6XZF0P9FNode01,j2eeType=JVM,J2EEServer=server1,version=6.0.0.1,type=JVM,mbea
        nIdentifier=JVM,cell=IBM-79D6XZF0P9FNode01Cell
wsadmin>$AdminControl invoke $jvm dumpThreads

wsadmin>
```

Heap Dump Analysis

Heap dumps occur in conjunction with dumping an application server's threads. Heap
dumps are important because they give you a snapshot of all the objects in your heap
space. This information is useful when you're trying to diagnose various memory-related
exceptions (e.g., "out of memory" exceptions).

To set up your environment to enable heap dumps, you need to define several environment variables. To set the environment entries from the admin console, expand **Servers**,
and navigate to **Application Servers|***server***|Java and Process Management|Process
Definition|Environment Entries|New**. Then add the name and value pairs shown in
Table 22-3. Last, don't forget to save your changes to the master configuration.

Table 22-3: Heap dump environment variables and values

Name	Value
IBM_HEAPDUMP	True
IBM_HEAP_DUMP	True
IBM_HEAPDUMPDIR	*your_directory*
IBM_HEAPDUMP_OUTOFMEMORY	True
IBM_JAVADUMP_OUTOFMEMORY	True

Figure 22-5 shows the heap dump variables in the WebSphere admin console.

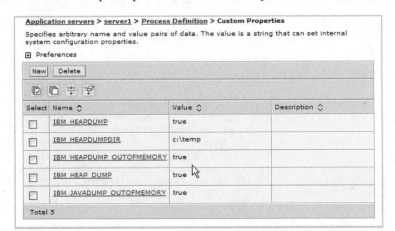

Figure 22-5: Heap dump variables in WebSphere admin console

Each time you make a thread dump, a new heap dump file is generated. You'll find the file in the directory specified by variable IBM_HEAPDUMPDIR. The file will be named using the format heapdump.*<timestamp>*.phd — for example, C:\temp\heap-dump.20050525.104348.1852.phd.

Once you've dumped your heap, you'll need to analyze its contents. Multiple tools are available for this task. One tool you should definitely consider using is the Memory Dump Diagnostic for Java tool. For information about this tool, visit *http://www-128.ibm.com/developerworks/websphere/downloads/memory_dump.html.*

BackupConfig Archive

In addition to the stable of troubleshooting and diagnostic tools we've discussed, WebSphere Application Server V6 provides some operational tools that make system tasks such as backup, recovery, and performance monitoring easier. One of these tools, the backupConfig utility, gives you the ability to back up your WebSphere configuration files from the command line.

To obtain usage on the utility, issue **backupConfig -?**. The backupConfig command takes the form

```
backupConfig [backup_file] [-nostop] [-quiet] [-logfile <filename>]
    [-replacelog] [-trace] [-username <uid>] [-password <password>]
    [-profileName <profile>] [-help]
```

where

- backup_file specifies the name of the file to which the backup is written. If you don't specify a file name, the system generates a unique name.

- –nostop specifies that no servers will be stopped. (By default, they will be.)

- –quiet suppresses the progress information that the command prints in normal mode.

- –logfile <filename> specifies the location of the log file to which information is written.

- –replacelog replaces the log file instead of appending to the current log.

- –trace generates trace information into the log file for debugging purposes.

- –username <uid> (or –user <uid>) specifies the user name (uid) for authentication if you've enabled security in the server.

- –password <password> specifies the password for authentication if you've enabled security in the server.

- –profileName <profile> defines the profile of the application server process in a multiprofile installation. (This option isn't required in a single-profile environment.) The default value for this option is the default profile.

- –help (or –?) prints a usage statement.

Listing 22-9 demonstrates using the backupConfig command to back up the default profile configuration.

Listing 22-9

Backing up the default profile configuration

```
C:\Program Files\IBM\WebSphere\AppServer\bin>backupConfig
ADMU0116I: Tool information is being logged in file C:\Program Files\IBM\
        WebSphere\AppServer\profiles\default\logs\backupConfig.log
ADMU0128I: Starting tool with the default profile
ADMU5001I: Backing up config directory C:\Program Files\IBM\WebSphere\
        AppServer/profiles/default\config to file
            C:\Program Files\IBM\WebSphere\AppServer\bin\
            WebSphereConfig_2005-07-04.zip
ADMU0505I: Servers found in configuration:
ADMU0506I: Server name: server1
ADMU2010I: Stopping all server processes for node IBM-79D6XZF0P9FNode01
ADMU7702I: Because server1 is registered to run as a Windows Service, the
            request to stop this server will be completed by stopping the
```

```
                  associated Windows Service.
..............................................................................
ADMU5002I: 331 files successfully backed up
```

Restore Config Archive

To restore your configuration files, WebSphere V6 provides the command-line restoreConfig utility. To obtain usage on the utility, issue **restoreConfig −?**. The restoreConfig command takes the following form:

```
restoreConfig backup_file [-location restore_location] [-quiet]
    [-nowait] [-logfile <filename>] [-replacelog] [-trace] [-username
    <uid>] [-password <password>] [-profileName <profile>] [-help]
```

The following three parameters are unique to the restoreConfig command; the others function the same as for the backupConfig command.

- backup_file specifies the file to be restored. If you don't specify a file, the restoreConfig command won't run.

- −location <restore-location> specifies the directory to which the backup file is restored (the location defaults to the <WASV6-ROOT>\config directory).

- −nowait tells the command not to stop the servers before restoring the configuration.

Listing 22-10 demonstrates using the restoreConfig command to restore the default profile configuration.

Listing 22-10

Restoring the default profile configuration

```
c:\Program Files\IBM\WebSphere\AppServer\bin>restoreConfig
      WebSphereConfig_2005-07-04.zip

ADMU0116I: Tool information is being logged in file C:\Program Files\
      IBM\WebSphere\AppServer\profiles\default\logs\restoreConfig.log

ADMU0128I: Starting tool with the default profile
ADMU0505I: Servers found in configuration:
ADMU0506I: Server name: server1
ADMU2010I: Stopping all server processes for node IBM-79D6XZF0P9FNode01
ADMU7702I: Because server1 is registered to run as a Windows Service, the
      request to stop this server will be completed by stopping the
      associated Windows Service.
ADMU5502I: The directory C:\Program Files\IBM\WebSphere\AppServer\profiles\
      default\config already exists; renaming to C:\Program Files\IBM\
```

```
        WebSphere\AppServer\profiles\default\config.old
ADMU5504I: Restore location successfully renamed
ADMU5505I: Restoring file WebSphereConfig_2005-07-04.zip to location C:\Program
        Files\IBM\WebSphere\AppServer\profiles\default\config
..................................................................
ADMU5506I: 331 files successfully restored
ADMU6001I: Begin App Preparation -
ADMU6009I: Processing complete.
```

Performance Monitoring Using Tivoli Performance Viewer

WebSphere Application Server can collect performance metrics using the Performance Monitoring Infrastructure (PMI). PMI is the core monitoring infrastructure for WebSphere Application Server and WebSphere family products, such as Commerce, Portal, and so on. The performance data provided by WebSphere PMI helps to monitor and tune the performance of the application server.

Enabling your application server to collect PMI data will affect your system's performance, so be sure to consider this impact when choosing the amount and level of PMI data to collect. Note that collecting PMI data on Enterprise JavaBeans (EJBs) can be very costly.

To display and log PMI data, you can use the Tivoli Performance Viewer (TPV). Before you can use TPV, you first need to enable PMI data for your application server using the admin console. Take the following steps to do so:

1. In the WebSphere admin console, expand **Servers**, and click **Application Servers**.

2. Select an application server (e.g., server1).

3. Under **Performance**, click **Performance Monitoring Infrastructure (PMI)**.

4. Make sure you select the **Enable Performance Monitoring Infrastructure (PMI)** option.

5. Next, choose a statistic set to monitor: **None, Basic, Extended, All**, or **Custom**.

6. Click **Apply**, and save your configuration.

To view the performance data:

1. In the admin console, select **Monitoring and Tuning**, and click **Performance Viewer**.

2. Select either **Current Activity** or **View Logs**. To look at live data, choose **Current Activity**. (TPV can also save collected data in log files.)

3. Select your server, and click the **Start Monitoring** button to start the data collection. Notice that the collection status changes to Active.

4. Click on a server to view its data. The Tivoli Performance Viewer will be displayed. The viewer's left pane provides four areas to investigate: **Adviser, Settings, Summary Reports**, and **Performance Modules**.

   ■ Select **Adviser** to display a graphic that can help you decide which WebSphere runtime parameters to tune for better performance.

   ■ Select **Settings** to configure TPV. You can specify the rate at which data is collected, how data is viewed (under **User settings**), and how output will be logged (under **Log settings**).

   ■ Select **Summary** to select preconfigured TPV reports on commonly viewed statistics.

   ■ Select **Performance Modules** to specify any combination of metrics to be viewed together graphically. Figure 22-6 shows TPV's performance module view.

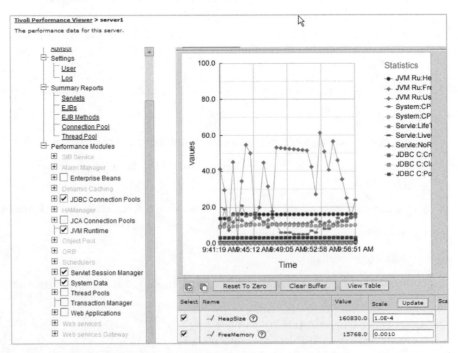

Figure 22-6: Performance modules being viewed in Tivoli Performance Viewer

Obtaining WebSphere Version Information

WebSphere's versionInfo command provides an easy way to obtain version information for your WebSphere installation. Listing 22-11 shows the command being executed for a sample installation.

Listing 22-11

Using the versionInfo command to obtain WebSphere version information

```
C:\Program Files\IBM\WebSphere\AppServer\bin>versionInfo
WVER0010I: Copyright (c) IBM Corporation 2002, 2005; All rights reserved.
WVER0011I: WebSphere Application Server Release 6.0
WVER0012I: VersionInfo reporter version 1.15.1.7, dated 2/17/05


--------------------------------------------------------------------------

IBM WebSphere Application Server Product Installation Status Report
--------------------------------------------------------------------------


Report at date and time 2005-07-04 14:04:40-0700

Installation
--------------------------------------------------------------------------

Product Directory        C:\Program Files\IBM\WebSphere\AppServer
Version Directory        C:\Program Files\IBM\WebSphere\AppServer\
                         properties\version
DTD Directory            C:\Program Files\IBM\WebSphere\AppServer\
                         properties\version\dtd
Log Directory            C:\Program Files\IBM\WebSphere\AppServer\logs
Backup Directory         C:\Program Files\IBM\WebSphere\AppServer\
                         properties\version\update\backup
TMP Directory            C:\DOCUME~1\ADMINI~1\LOCALS~1\Temp

Installation Platform
--------------------------------------------------------------------------

Name                     IBM WebSphere Application Server
Version                  6.0

Product List
--------------------------------------------------------------------------

BASE                     installed

Installed Product
--------------------------------------------------------------------------
```

```
Name               IBM WebSphere Application Server
Version            6.0.1.0
ID                 BASE
Build Level        o0510.18
Build Date         3/11/05


-----------------------------------------------------------------------

End Installation Status Report
-----------------------------------------------------------------------
```

Verbose Garbage Collection and Class Loader

By enabling both verbose garbage collection (GC) and class loading, you can learn much about the operation of WebSphere Application Server. To enable these features, you need to change some parameters on the application server:

1. In the WebSphere admin console, expand **Servers**, and click **Application Servers**.

2. Select your server (e.g., server1).

3. Under **Server Infrastructure**, click **Java and Process Management**.

4. Click **Process Definition**.

5. Under **Additional Properties**, click **Java Virtual Machines**.

6. Select the **Verbose class loading** option and the **Verbose garbage collection** option.

7. Click **Apply**, and save your configuration.

8. Restart the application server.

After restarting the server, you'll see the extra output in the following file (for the default profile): C:\Program Files\IBM\WebSphere\AppServer\profiles\default\ logs\server1\native_stderr.log.

Verbose GC

Garbage collection is a fact of life for every JVM. As objects are no longer referenced, a background GC thread walks the heap memory and removes these objects. In addition, the GC thread shuffles objects around to make the heap memory contiguous again. If the GC thread runs too often or too long, you start to have problems, with the GC thread consuming large amounts of CPU time and effectively freezing your Java or J2EE application. If you experience such problems, your application may be creating and destroying too many objects (a leading performance-degradation issue).

The overall objective in JVM performance tuning is to minimize the overhead of garbage collection. A good rule of thumb is to ensure GC overhead doesn't exceed 15 percent. To see whether the GC thread is too intrusive, you must enable verbose GC.

To verify that verbose garbage collection is enabled, check to see that file native_stderr.log contains the following line:

```
[ JVMST080: verbosegc is enabled ]
```

You'll notice that this file is filled with garbage-collection events. Listing 22-12 shows an example of one event.

Listing 22-12

Sample verbose garbage collection results

```
<AF[31]: Allocation Failure. need 528 bytes, 5562 ms since last AF>
<AF[31]: managing allocation failure, action=1 (0/159820576) (3474752/3755744)>
  <GC(31): GC cycle started Tue May 24 15:15:56 2005
  <GC(31): freed 60471768 bytes, 39% free (63946520/163576320), in 277 ms>
  <GC(31): mark: 253 ms, sweep: 24 ms, compact: 0 ms>
  <GC(31): refs: soft 0 (age >= 32), weak 0, final 92, phantom 0>
<AF[31]: completed in 278 ms>
```

Garbage Collector

Garbage Collector is a useful utility available to analyze the garbage-collection events collected by verbose GC. Figure 22-7 shows the Garbage Collector in action.

You can download the Garbage Collector tool from *http://w3.alphaworks.ibm.com/ techs/overview.jsp?tech=gcdiag*. The utility is distributed as a ZIP file.

Garbage Collector requires two additional files, jfreeChart-0.9.21.jar and jcommon-0.9.6.jar, that are part of Version 0.9.21 of the open-source software tool JFreeChart. JFreeChart isn't distributed with Garbage Collector, but you can download it from SourceForge at *http://sourceforge.net/projects/jfreechart*. The SourceForge link should let you download both current and previous releases of JFreeChart. Locate Version 0.9.21, download the file jfreechart-0.9.21.zip, and extract from it files jfreeChart-0.9.21.jar and jcommon-0.9.6.jar. (Another way to download JFreeChart is through the JFreeChart project home page, *http://www.jfree.org/jfreechart/index.html*.)

To run Garbage Collector:

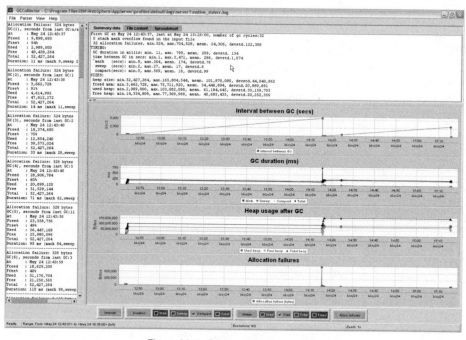

Figure 22-7: Garbage Collector utility

1. Extract the contents of the ZIP file GCCollector.zip into a directory of your choice.

2. Place files jfreeChart-0.9.21.jar and jcommon-0.9.6.jar in the lib directory that was created when you unzipped GCCollector.zip.

3. Execute **GCCollector.bat**, which you'll find in the directory where you unzipped GCCollector.zip.

The GCCollector.bat program is written in Java, so it will run only if you have a Java runtime environment installed (JDK 1.2.2 or later). Make sure your PATH environment variable points to the location of java.exe on your system (or edit GCCollector.bat to include the full path of the java command).

The GCCollector.bat file has only one command line, which specifies the parameter –Xmx300m to set the maximum Java heap size to 300 MB. This size should be enough to work with more than 10,000 garbage collection cycles, but if you experience any "out of memory" exceptions, go ahead and modify the Xmx parameter.

Verbose Class Loader

Once you've enabled verbose class loading (as described above), you'll see an entry for every class that's loaded. You'll also see where each class was loaded from — information that's helpful if you suspect a class is being loaded from a JAR you didn't expect. Listing 22-13 shows some sample output from the verbose class loader.

Listing 22-13

Sample verbose class loading output

```
[Opened C:\Program Files\IBM\WebSphere\AppServer\java\jre\lib\core.jar in 0 ms]
[Opened C:\Program Files\IBM\WebSphere\AppServer\java\jre\lib\graphics.jar
       in 0 ms]
[Opened C:\Program Files\IBM\WebSphere\AppServer\java\jre\lib\security.jar
       in 0 ms]
[Opened C:\Program Files\IBM\WebSphere\AppServer\java\jre\lib\server.jar
       in 10 ms]
[Opened C:\Program Files\IBM\WebSphere\AppServer\java\jre\lib\xml.jar in 0 ms]
[Opened C:\Program Files\IBM\WebSphere\AppServer\java\jre\lib\charsets.jar
       in 0 ms]
[Opened C:\Program Files\IBM\WebSphere\AppServer\java\jre\lib\ibmcertpathprovider.
       jar in 0 ms]
[Opened C:\Program Files\IBM\WebSphere\AppServer\java\jre\lib\
       ibmjaasactivelm.jar in 0 ms]
[Opened C:\Program Files\IBM\WebSphere\AppServer\java\jre\lib\ibmjaaslm.jar
       in 0 ms]
[Opened C:\Program Files\IBM\WebSphere\AppServer\java\jre\lib\ibmjcefw.jar
       in 0 ms]
[Opened C:\Program Files\IBM\WebSphere\AppServer\java\jre\lib\
       ibmjgssprovider.jar in 0 ms]
[Opened C:\Program Files\IBM\WebSphere\AppServer\java\jre\lib\ibmjssefips.jar
       in 0 ms]
[Opened C:\Program Files\IBM\WebSphere\AppServer\java\jre\lib\
       ibmjsseprovider.jar in 0 ms]
[Opened C:\Program Files\IBM\WebSphere\AppServer\java\jre\lib\ibmorb.jar
       in 0 ms]
[Opened C:\Program Files\IBM\WebSphere\AppServer\java\jre\lib\ibmorbapi.
       jar in 0 ms]
[Opened C:\Program Files\IBM\WebSphere\AppServer\java\jre\lib\ibmpkcs.jar
       in 0 ms]
[Loaded java.lang.NoClassDefFoundError from C:\Program Files\IBM\WebSphere\
       AppServer\java\jre\lib\core.jar]
[Loaded java.lang.Class from C:\Program Files\IBM\WebSphere\AppServer\
       java\jre\lib\core.jar]
```

Dump Name Space

J2EE environments and applications depend on a service called the Java Naming and Directory Interface (JNDI) service. The JNDI service provides a central repository for the addresses of all the J2EE resources — EJBs, Java Message Service (JMS) resources, and Java Database Connectivity (JDBC) resources, and so on. If you start receiving a "name not found" exception, it's usually a clue that some issue exists with how or whether the resource is registered in the JNDI name space.

IBM ships WebSphere with a utility you can use to dump your JNDI name space. To invoke the dumpnamespace utility (.bat on Windows and .sh on Unix), go to the <WASV6-ROOT>\bin directory, and run **dumpnamespace** as shown in Listing 22-14.

Listing 22-14

Running the dumpnamespace utility

```
C:\IBM\WAS\AppServer\bin>dumpnamespace

Getting the initial context
Getting the starting context


===============================================================================
Name Space Dump
    Provider URL: corbaloc:iiop:localhost:2809
    Context factory: com.ibm.websphere.naming.WsnInitialContextFactory
    Requested root context: cell
    Starting context: (top)=OWEN-T40Node01Cell
    Formatting rules: jndi
    Time of dump: Wed Feb 08 15:53:02 PST 2006
===============================================================================


===============================================================================
Beginning of Name Space Dump
===============================================================================

    1 (top)
    2 (top)/cells                                       javax.naming.Context
    3 (top)/legacyRoot                                  javax.naming.Context
    3    Linked to context: OWEN-T40Node01Cell/persistent
    4 (top)/domain                                      javax.naming.Context
    4    Linked to context: OWEN-T40Node01Cell
    5 (top)/clusters                                    javax.naming.Context
    6 (top)/cell                                        javax.naming.Context
    6    Linked to context: OWEN-T40Node01Cell
    7 (top)/cellname                                    java.lang.String
    8 (top)/nodes                                       javax.naming.Context
```

```
 9 (top)/nodes/OWEN-T40Node01                          javax.naming.Context
10 (top)/nodes/OWEN-T40Node01/node                     javax.naming.Context
10    Linked to context: OWEN-T40Node01Cell/nodes/OWEN-T40Node01
11 (top)/nodes/OWEN-T40Node01/servers                  javax.naming.Context
12 (top)/nodes/OWEN-T40Node01/servers/server1          javax.naming.Context
13 (top)/nodes/OWEN-T40Node01/servers/server1/servername
13                                                      java.lang.String
14 (top)/nodes/OWEN-T40Node01/servers/server1/thisNode
14                                                      javax.naming.Context
14    Linked to context: OWEN-T40Node01Cell/nodes/OWEN-T40Node01
15 (top)/nodes/OWEN-T40Node01/servers/server1/services
15                                                      javax.naming.Context
16 (top)/nodes/OWEN-T40Node01/servers/server1/services/cache
16                                                      javax.naming.Context
17 (top)/nodes/OWEN-T40Node01/servers/server1/services/cache/distributedmap
17                                                      com.ibm.websphere.cache.
                                                        DistributedObjectCache
18 (top)/nodes/OWEN-T40Node01/servers/server1/services/cache/basecache
18                                                      com.ibm.websphere.cache.
                                                        DistributedObjectCache
19 (top)/nodes/OWEN-T40Node01/servers/server1/plantsby
19                                                      javax.naming.Context
20 (top)/nodes/OWEN-T40Node01/servers/server1/plantsby/MailerHome
20                                                      com.ibm.websphere.
                                                        samples.plantsbyweb
                                                        sphereejb.MailerHome
21 (top)/nodes/OWEN-T40Node01/servers/server1/plantsby/CatalogHome
21                                                      com.ibm.websphere.
                                                        samples.plantsbyweb
                                                        sphereejb.CatalogHome
22 (top)/nodes/OWEN-T40Node01/servers/server1/plantsby/LoginHome
22                                                      com.ibm.websphere.
                                                        samples.plantsbyweb
                                                        sphereejb.LoginHome
23 (top)/nodes/OWEN-T40Node01/servers/server1/plantsby/SuppliersHome
23                                                      com.ibm.websphere.
                                                        samples.plantsbyweb
                                                        sphereejb.SuppliersHome
24 (top)/nodes/OWEN-T40Node01/servers/server1/plantsby/BackOrderStockHome
24                                                      com.ibm.websphere.
                                                        samples.plantsbyweb
                                                        sphereejb.BackOrder
                                                        tockHome
25 (top)/nodes/OWEN-T40Node01/servers/server1/plantsby/BackOrderHome
25                                                      com.ibm.websphere.
                                                        samples.plantsbyweb
                                                        sphereejb.BackOrderHome
26 (top)/nodes/OWEN-T40Node01/servers/server1/plantsby/ResetDBHome
26                                                      com.ibm.websphere.
                                                        samples.plantsbyweb
                                                        sphereejb.ResetDBHome
```

S

```
27 (top)/nodes/OWEN-T40Node01/servers/server1/plantsby/ReportGeneratorHome
27                                                      com.ibm.websphere.
                                                        samples.plantsbyweb
                                                        sphereejb.ReportGenera
                                                        torHome
28 (top)/nodes/OWEN-T40Node01/servers/server1/plantsby/SupplierHome
28                                                         com.ibm.websphere.
    samples.plantsbywebsphereejb.SupplierHome
29 (top)/nodes/OWEN-T40Node01/servers/server1/plantsby/ShoppingCartHome
29                                                      com.ibm.websphere.
                                                        samples.plantsbyweb
                                                        sphereejb.Shopping
                                                        CartHome
30 (top)/nodes/OWEN-T40Node01/servers/server1/wm      javax.naming.Context
31 (top)/nodes/OWEN-T40Node01/servers/server1/wm/default
31                                                      com.ibm.websphere.
    asynchbeans.WorkManager
32 (top)/nodes/OWEN-T40Node01/servers/server1/cell     javax.naming.Context
32    Linked to context: OWEN-T40Node01Cell
33 (top)/nodes/OWEN-T40Node01/servers/server1/jdbc     javax.naming.Context
34 (top)/nodes/OWEN-T40Node01/servers/server1/jdbc/PlantsByWebSphereDataSource
34                                                      javax.resource.cci.
                                                        ConnectionFactory
35 (top)/nodes/OWEN-T40Node01/servers/server1/jdbc/DefaultEJBTimerDataSource
35                                                      javax.resource.cci.
                                                        ConnectionFactory
36 (top)/nodes/OWEN-T40Node01/servers/server1/tm       javax.naming.Context
37 (top)/nodes/OWEN-T40Node01/servers/server1/tm/default
37                                                      com.ibm.ws.asynchbeans.
                                                        timer.TimerManagerImpl
38 (top)/nodes/OWEN-T40Node01/servers/server1/com      javax.naming.Context
39 (top)/nodes/OWEN-T40Node01/servers/server1/com/ibm  javax.naming.Context
40 (top)/nodes/OWEN-T40Node01/servers/server1/com/ibm/websphere
40                                                      javax.naming.Context
41 (top)/nodes/OWEN-T40Node01/servers/server1/com/ibm/websphere/scheduler
41                                                      javax.naming.Context
42 (top)/nodes/OWEN-T40Node01/servers/server1/com/ibm/websphere/
                    scheduler/calendar
42                                                      javax.naming.Context
43 (top)/nodes/OWEN-T40Node01/servers/server1/com/ibm/websphere/scheduler/
                    calendar/DefaultUserCalendarHome
43                                                      com.ibm.websphere.
                                                        scheduler.UserCalen
                                                        darHome
44 (top)/nodes/OWEN-T40Node01/servers/server1/com/ibm/websphere/ejbquery
44                                                      javax.naming.Context
45 (top)/nodes/OWEN-T40Node01/servers/server1/com/ibm/websphere/
                    ejbquery/Query
45                                                      com.ibm.websphere.
                                                        ejbquery.QueryHome
46 (top)/nodes/OWEN-T40Node01/servers/server1/ejb      javax.naming.Context
```

```
47 (top)/nodes/OWEN-T40Node01/servers/server1/ejb/ivtEJBObject
47                                                    com.ibm.websphere.
                                                      ivt.ivtEJB.ivtEJBHome
48 (top)/nodes/OWEN-T40Node01/servers/server1/ejb/mgmt
48                                                    javax.naming.Context
49 (top)/nodes/OWEN-T40Node01/servers/server1/ejb/mgmt/MEJB
49                                                    javax.management.
                                                      j2ee.ManagementHome
50 (top)/nodes/OWEN-T40Node01/servers/server1/mail    javax.naming.Context
51 (top)/nodes/OWEN-T40Node01/servers/server1/mail/PlantsByWebSphere
51                                                    javax.mail.Session
52 (top)/nodes/OWEN-T40Node01/servers/server1/DefaultDatasource
52                                                    javax.resource.cci.
                                                      ConnectionFactory
53 (top)/nodes/OWEN-T40Node01/servers/server1/eis     javax.naming.Context
54 (top)/nodes/OWEN-T40Node01/servers/server1/eis/DefaultDatasource_CMP
54                                                    javax.resource.cci.
                                                      ConnectionFactory
55 (top)/nodes/OWEN-T40Node01/servers/server1/eis/jdbc
55                                                    javax.naming.Context
56 (top)/nodes/OWEN-T40Node01/servers/server1/eis/jdbc/
                  PlantsByWebSphereDataSource_CMP
56                                                    javax.resource.cci.
                                                      ConnectionFactory
57 (top)/nodes/OWEN-T40Node01/servers/server1/jta     javax.naming.Context
58 (top)/nodes/OWEN-T40Node01/servers/server1/jta/usertransaction
58                                                    java.lang.Object
59 (top)/nodes/OWEN-T40Node01/cell                    javax.naming.Context
59     Linked to context: OWEN-T40Node01Cell
60 (top)/nodes/OWEN-T40Node01/domain                  javax.naming.Context
60     Linked to context: OWEN-T40Node01Cell
61 (top)/nodes/OWEN-T40Node01/nodename                java.lang.String
62 (top)/nodes/OWEN-T40Node01/persistent              javax.naming.Context
63 (top)/persistent javax.naming.Context
64 (top)/persistent/cell javax.naming.Context
64     Linked to context: OWEN-T40Node01Cell
```

```
================================================================================
End of Name Space Dump
================================================================================
```

23

J2EE Packaging, Enhanced EARs, and the Application Server Toolkit

As you learned about in Chapter 1, WebSphere Application Server V6 supports the full Java 2 Platform, Enterprise Edition (J2EE) 1.4 programming model. The J2EE specification consists of several functional subspecifications. However, it isn't always obvious how you should put together the different elements to form a complete J2EE application. In this chapter, we take a closer look at J2EE packaging and explain the role IBM Enhanced EAR files and the WebSphere Application Server Toolkit (AST) play in creating a J2EE application.

J2EE Packaging at a Glance

The J2EE specification provides guidelines for the structuring and creation of J2EE applications, and one of the major ones relates to *packaging*. Individual specifications provide guidelines for the packaging of individual components, such as Enterprise JavaBeans (EJBs), Java Server Pages (JSPs), and servlets. The J2EE specification then dictates how these heterogeneous components are themselves to be packaged together.

This section provides an analysis of the J2EE packaging mechanism, focusing on the relationships these components have within an *Enterprise Application Archive (EAR)* file and the process involved in building EAR files. Some of the questions we'll ask are

- What are the rules for using J2EE packaging as opposed to component packaging?

- What can you place into a J2EE package?

- Is J2EE packaging necessary, and are there behavioral changes that occur as a result of using J2EE packaging?

As we answer these questions, you'll learn

- how J2EE class loading schemes work
- how to create EAR files
- how to deal with dependency and utility classes

J2EE Packaging Overview

A J2EE application is composed of

- one or more J2EE components
- a J2EE application deployment descriptor

When one or more heterogeneous J2EE components need to use one another, you must create a *J2EE application*. When building a J2EE application, you must take into account many considerations, including

- the types of J2EE components you can package into a J2EE application

- the roles people play when creating J2EE packages

- the current limitations of J2EE packaging

- the class loading approaches different vendors use to meet the needs of J2EE component interactions

What Can Be Packaged?

The J2EE specification differentiates between resources that run within a container and resources that can be packaged into a J2EE EAR file:

> "An EAR file is used to package one or more J2EE modules into a single module so that they can have aligned classloading and deployment into a server."

J2EE clarifies the difference between runtime containers and deployment modules. *Runtime containers* are request-level interceptors that provide infrastructure services around components of the system. A *deployment module* is a packaging structure for components that will ultimately execute in a runtime container. Recall how J2EE containers are structured:

- *EJB container* — The EJB container provides containment and request-level interception for business logic. The EJB container lets EJBs access Java Message Service (JMS), Java Authentication and Authorization Service (JAAS), the Java Transaction API (JTA), JavaMail (which uses JavaBeans Activation

Framework, or JAF), the Java API for XML Processing (JAXP), Java Database Connectivity (JDBC), and the Connector architecture.

- *Web container* — The Web container provides interception for requests sent over HTTP, File Transfer Protocol (FTP), Simple Mail Transfer Protocol (SMTP), and other protocols. Most Web containers support only HTTP (and HTTPS) but could support a broader range of protocols. The Web application container lets JSPs and servlets have access to the same resources the EJB container provides.

- *Application client container* — An application client container provides request-level interception for standalone Java applications. These applications run remotely, in a different JVM from that in which the Web container and the EJB container operate.

  A program running in an application client container is similar to a Java program with a main() method. However, instead of a JVM controlling the application, a wrapper controls the program. This wrapper is the application client container. Application client containers are a new concept in the J2EE specification, your application server provider should provide them.

  An application client container can optimize access to a Web container and an EJB container by providing direct authentication, performing load balancing, allowing failover routines, providing access to server-side environment variables, and properly propagating transaction contexts. Programs that run within an application client container have access to JAAS, JAXP, JDBC, and JMS resources on a remote application server.

- *Applet container* — An applet container is a special type of container that provides request-level interception for Java programs running in a browser. An important point to remember is that an applet container doesn't provide access to any additional resources, such as JDBC or JMS.

  Applets running within an applet container are expected to request resources directly from an application server (as opposed to making the request to the container and letting the container ask the application server). The EJB specification doesn't regulate how an applet should communicate with an EJB container, but the J2EE specification does. J2EE requires applets that want to directly use an EJB to use the HTTP(S) protocol and tunnel Remote Method Invocation (RMI) invocations. Many application server vendors support a form of HTTP tunneling to support this functionality.

The components you can package into a J2EE EAR file don't directly correlate to the components that contain containers. There are no basic requirements for what an EAR file must minimally include. An EAR file consists of any number of the following components:

- *EJB application JAR files* — An EJB application JAR file contains one or more EJBs.

- *Web application WAR files* — A WAR file contains a single Web application. Because an EAR file can contain multiple Web applications, each Web application in an EAR file must have a unique deployment context. The deployment mechanism for EAR files allows just such a specification of different contexts.

- *Application client JAR files* — The application client JAR file contains a single, standalone Java application that's intended to run within an application client container. The application client JAR file contains a specialized deployment descriptor and is composed similarly to an EJB JAR file. The JAR file also contains the classes required to run the standalone client as well as any client libraries needed to access JAAS, JAXP, JDBC, JMS, or an EJB client.

- *Resource adapter RAR files* — The resource adapter RAR file contains Java classes and native libraries required to implement a Java Connector Architecture (JCA) resource adapter to an enterprise information system. Resource adapters don't execute within a container; rather, they're designed to execute as a bridge between an application server and an external enterprise information system.

Each of these components is developed and packaged individually apart from the EAR file and its own deployment descriptor. A J2EE EAR file combines one or more of these components into a unified package with a custom deployment descriptor.

Packaging Roles

During the building, deployment, and use of an EJB, Web application, or other component, different people will play different roles. The J2EE specification defines broad *platform roles* that developers play during the creation of an enterprise application. Even though there are many roles individuals assume during the development and deployment process, these roles are nothing more than logical constructs that let you better plan and execute an application. It's likely (and expected) that a single individual or organization will perform multiple roles.

The common roles involved in building, deploying, and using an EAR file include the following:

- *J2EE product provider* — The J2EE product provider supplies an implementation of the J2EE platform, including all appropriate J2EE APIs and other features defined in the specification. The J2EE product provider is typically an application server, Web server, or database system vendor who provides an appropriate implementation by mapping the specifications and components to network protocols.

- *Application component provider* — The application component provider provides a J2EE component — for example, an EJB application or a Web application. Many roles within the J2EE specification can also be characterized as application component providers, including document developers, JSP authors, enterprise bean developers, and resource adapter developers.

- *Application assembler* — The application assembler is responsible for combining one or more J2EE components into an EAR file to create a J2EE application. This person is also responsible for creating the J2EE application deployment descriptor and identifying any external resources (e.g., class libraries, security roles, naming environments) on which the application may depend. The application assembler will commonly use tools provided by the J2EE product provider and the tool provider (described next).

- *Tool provider* — A tool provider furnishes utilities to automate the creation, packaging, and deployment of a J2EE application. A tool provider can provide tools that automate the generation of deployment descriptors for an EAR file, the creation of an EAR file, and the deployment of an EAR file into an application server. Utilities supplied by a tool provider can be either platform-independent (i.e., work with all EAR files irrespective of the environment) or platform-dependent (working with the native capabilities of a particular environment).

- *Deployer* — The deployer is responsible for deploying Web applications and EJB applications into the server environment, producing container-ready Web applications, EJB applications, applets, and application clients that have been customized for the target environment of the application server.

  The deployer isn't responsible for deploying a resource adapter archive or an application client archive but may be responsible for additional configuration of these components. These components, although packaged as part of a J2EE EAR file, aren't considered when the enterprise application is deployed. They're part of the J2EE application but don't group through the runtime "activation" process that Web application and EJB containers go through during deployment.

Resource adapter archives are simply libraries that are dropped into a valid JCA implementation. Although packaged as part of a J2EE EAR file, they don't operate within the context of a J2EE container. Therefore, because resource adapter archives don't have a J2EE container, they don't need to have a J2EE deployer involved with their activation.

Application client programs do operate within the context of a J2EE container, but they aren't deployed into an application server. Application client programs run standalone, and the deployer isn't responsible for configuring the container environment for these programs.

- *System administrator* — The system administrator is responsible for configuring the networking and operational environment within which application servers and J2EE applications execute. The system administrator is also responsible for the monitoring and maintenance of J2EE applications.

In this chapter, when we discuss the creation of EAR files and the resolution of conflicts, we'll be acting in the roles of application assembler and deployer.

The Limitations of Packaging

EAR files meet the basic requirements for packaging an application because most Web-based J2EE applications consist solely of Web and EJB applications. However, EAR files lack the capability to package complicated J2EE applications. For example, you can't declare the following components in an EAR file, but they are often used in J2EE applications:

- JDBC DataSource objects

- JMS ConnectionFactory and Destination objects

- Java Management Extensions (JMX) MBeans

- some JMS consumers that run within an application server, such as a MessageConsumer, which runs as part of a ServerSession

- classes triggered when an application is deployed or undeployed (these classes are vendor-provided proprietary extensions not defined in the J2EE specification; however, all vendors generally supply them)

At present, these components must be manually configured and deployed via an administration interface provided by the implementation vendor and are the system administrator's responsibility. The use of these items will increase over time, and it will be important for EAR files to support the packaging of these components to enable application portability. Starting with WebSphere V6, you can include these components in an EAR. This form of EAR file is called an *Enhanced EAR*.

Understanding Class Loading Schemes

At runtime, when a class is referenced, it needs to be loaded by the Java Virtual Machine. The JVM uses a standard class loading structure to load classes into memory. A class loader is a Java class that's responsible for loading Java classes from a source. Java classes can be loaded from disk or some other media; they can reside anywhere. Class loaders are hierarchical in the sense that they can be chained together in a parent-child relationship. Classes loaded by a child class loader have visibility (i.e., can use) classes loaded by any of the parent class loaders. Classes loaded by a parent class loader don't have visibility to classes loaded by any of the parent's children's class loaders. Class loaders and EAR files are important because application server vendors can deploy application modules using common or different class loaders.

If, within an application, a Web application needs to access an EJB, the Web application will need to be able to load those classes it requires. Because of this implied dependency between different modules, application server vendors must consider different approaches for structuring EAR class loaders to resolve these dependencies.

A standalone application is deployed in its own class loader. This means that if you deploy a Web application archive and an EJB application archive separately, the respective classes for each application will be loaded in different class loaders that are siblings of one another. The classes in the Web application class loader won't be visible to the classes loaded by other class loaders. This circumstance creates a problem for Web applications that want to use EJBs that have been deployed separately.

Before the advent of EAR files, many developers would deploy an EJB and then repackage the same EJB JAR file as part of the WEB-INF\lib directory of the Web application. The same class files would exist in two different places so that the overall application could work correctly — a situation to be avoided. EAR applications were introduced to solve this problem. EAR files aren't just a convenient packaging format; they also provide a special class loading scheme that lets applications within the EAR file access the classes of other applications.

The J2EE 1.3 specification makes no specific requirements as to how an EAR class loader should work, giving application server vendors the flexibility to determine how to load classes. Before implementing an EAR class loader, a vendor must decide the following questions:

- Will all classes in all applications in the EAR file be loaded by a single class loader, or will separate files be loaded by different class loaders?

- Should there be any parent-child class loader relationships between different applications in the EAR file? For example, if two EJB applications depend on log4j.jar, should appropriate visibility be maintained by loading log4j.jar in a parent class loader and loading the EJB applications in a child class loader so that the JAR file is visible to both applications?

- If a hierarchy of class loaders is created, to what depth will the hierarchy be allowed to extend?

- EJBs have inherent relationships with one another but Web applications don't. So, will EJB applications be loaded differently from Web applications so that Web application integrity can be maintained?

Class Loading Starting with EJB 2.0

The EJB 2.0 Public Final Draft 2 specification introduced the concept of local interfaces and placed an interesting twist on the EAR class loading problem. Local interfaces let colocated clients and EJBs be accessed using pass-by-reference semantics instead of pass-by-value semantics.

Having visibility to the public interfaces and stub implementation classes of an EJB is not sufficient for a client of an EJB to perform pass-by-reference invocations. The client needs to have a direct reference to the implementation classes of the EJB's container. With local interfaces, clients of EJBs need access to much more than before. This restriction means that the class loading scheme used before EJB 2.0 won't work. To solve this problem, the class loaders of any applications that act as clients to an EJB must be loaded as children of the EJB class loader.

In this model, Web application class loaders are children of the EJB class loader. This arrangement enables all Web applications to have visibility to the files they need to allow them to behave as clients of the EJBs. Each Web application is still loaded in a custom class loader to achieve isolation, though. The overall structure of this implementation is simpler to understand because it doesn't require the EJB class loader to export any files to the EAR class loader.

An Ambiguity in the J2EE Specification

Certain implementations have exposed an ambiguity in the J2EE specification. The ambiguity arises because the J2EE specification is unclear about how dependency libraries of a Web application should be loaded. It's very clear that a utility library specified by WEB-INF\lib should remain isolated and be loaded by the class loader of the Web application only. However, the specification doesn't state whether a utility library specified as a dependency library of the Web application should be loaded by the Web application's class loader or exported to the EAR class loader. This distinction can have a behavioral impact. If it's known that a dependency utility library will be loaded only once for all Web applications, the Web applications can take advantage of knowing that a singleton class will create one object that all the Web applications can share. But if each Web application's class loader isolated the utility library, a singleton class (which is a class intended to create only a single instance in the virtual machine) will create one object in each Web application.

At present, WebSphere loads any utility library specified as a dependency library of a Web application at the EAR class loader level. This approach makes sense because you can always achieve Web application isolation by placing utility libraries in WEB-INF\lib. This solution provides the best of both worlds: a dependency library loaded at the EAR class loader level or a dependency library loaded at the Web application class loader level.

Configuring J2EE Packages

Now that you have a basic grasp of how the J2EE architecture is implemented — specifically, of the different roles and the behavior of class loaders — you're ready to configure and deploy enterprise applications. To do so, you need to understand the process of EAR file creation and the contents of the deployment descriptors that describe the EAR file contents.

The Enterprise Application Development Process

The overall process used to build an enterprise application is as follows:

1. Developers build individual components. These components can be EJBs, JSP pages, servlets, and resource adapters.

2. Some number of components is packaged into a JAR file along with a deployment descriptor to a J2EE module. A J2EE module is a collection of one or more J2EE components of the same component type, so an EJB module can contain more than one EJB, a Web application module can consist of multiple JSP pages and servlets, and a resource adapter archive can consist of multiple resource adapters.

3. One or more J2EE modules are combined into an EAR file along with an enterprise application deployment descriptor to create a J2EE application. The simplest J2EE application is composed of a single J2EE module. Multiple J2EE modules make up more complicated J2EE applications. A complex J2EE application consists of multiple J2EE modules and dependency libraries that are used by the classes contained within the modules. A J2EE application may also contain help files and other documents to aid the deployer.

4. The J2EE application is deployed into a J2EE product. You install the application on the J2EE platform and then integrate it with any infrastructure that exists on an application server. As part of the J2EE application deployment process, each J2EE module is individually deployed according to the guidelines specified for deployment of that respective type. Each component must be deployed into the correct container that matches the type of the component.

For example, if you have a my.ear file with a my.jar and a my.war contained within it, when you deploy the application, the application server's deployment tool will copy the my.ear file into the application server. Next, the application server's deployment mechanism will extract the my.jar and my.war modules and deploy them separately following the class loading guidelines of that platform. If each module is deployed successfully, the J2EE application is considered to have been deployed successfully.

The Structure of a J2EE Package

The structure of a J2EE enterprise application package is straightforward; it is composed of one or more J2EE modules and a deployment descriptor named application.xml in a directory named META-INF\. The files are packaged using the JAR file format and stored in a file with an .ear extension. You can optionally include dependency libraries within the EAR file. The general structure of an EAR file is

```
EJB .jar files
Web application .war files
Resource adapter .rar files
Application client .jar files
Dependency library .jar files
META-INF\
              application.xml
```

Issues with Dependency Packages

Given the standard definition of J2EE, where are dependency libraries supposed to be placed so that they can be redeployed with an application at run time? There are two creative, yet ultimately undesirable, solutions.

In the first approach, you can place dependency libraries that are packaged as JAR files in the WEB-INF\lib directory of a Web application. In general, you should use WEB-INF\lib primarily for the storage of servlet classes, but servlets and JSP pages will look for classes in this directory when loading new ones. If only your servlets and JSP pages need the utility libraries you're using, this solution will be sufficient. However, if EJBs, JMS consumers, or startup and shutdown classes also need the same libraries, this option won't work because the WEB-INF\lib directory isn't visible to these items.

In the second approach, you place a complete copy of all the utility libraries in each EJB JAR file as well as in the WEB-INF\lib directory. When you deploy an EJB, an EJB class loader will look only within its own JAR file for any utility classes that are referenced. It won't look in the JAR files of other EJB applications that have been deployed or in WEB-INF\lib. If all your EJB applications require the use of the same library, placing a copy of that library's classes in each JAR file will meet your needs. The utility classes will be redeployable along with the EJB.

Although the second scenario achieves redeployability of dependency libraries, it is incredibly inefficient. The purpose of having multiple JAR files for packaging is to promote application modularity, and placing the same class in multiple JAR files destroys this benefit. In addition, having multiple copies of the same classes unnecessarily bloats your applications. Last, the build process requires an extra step because you need to rebuild every JAR file if you want to change even a single library.

With the release of Java Development Kit (JDK) 1.3, Sun Microsystems redefined the "extension mechanism," which is the functionality necessary to support optional packages. The extension mechanism is designed to support two things:

- JAR files can declare their dependency on other JAR files, enabling an application to consist of multiple modules.

- Class loaders are modified to search optional packages and application paths for classes.

In addition, the J2EE 1.3 specification mandates that application servers support the extension mechanism as defined for JAR files. This requires any deployment tool that references a JAR file to be capable of loading any optional libraries defined through the extension mechanism. It also implies that if an application server or deployment tool supports runtime undeployment and redeployment of EJB applications that use libraries via the extension mechanism, that tool or application server must also support undeployment and redeployment of any dependent libraries.

Support for the extension mechanism doesn't exist for EAR or resource adapter applications as defined in the J2EE specification because these applications aren't directly loaded by an instance of ClassLoader. Web applications have the freedom to use the extension mechanism or the WEB-INF\lib directory when specifying a dependency library. As we discussed earlier, the way a dependency library is loaded can vary depending on whether you specify the library using the extension mechanism or WEB-INF\lib.

Enterprise applications need to repackage any libraries required by the Web application or EJB application as part of the EAR file. After this repackaging, the extension mechanism provides a standard way for Web application WAR files and EJB application JAR files to specify which dependency libraries in the enterprise application EAR file they need.

How does the extension mechanism work with EJB applications? A JAR file can reference a dependent JAR file by adding a Class-Path attribute to the manifest file contained in every JAR file. The jar utility automatically creates a manifest file to place in a JAR file and names it manifest.mf by default. You can edit this file to include a Class-Path attribute entry in addition to the other entries that already exist in the file.

The Class-Path manifest attribute lists the relative URLs to search for utility libraries. The relative URL is always from the component that contains the Class-Path entry (not the root of the EAR file). You can specify multiple URLs in a single Class-Path entry, and a single manifest file can contain multiple Class-Path entries. The general format for a Class-Path entry is

```
Class-Path: list-of-jar-files-separated-by-spaces
```

Inside a Sample EAR File

WebSphere Application Server provides an example of a packaged J2EE application named WebSphere Bank, delivered as a sample in the WebSphere SamplesGallery. Like every J2EE application, the WebSphere Bank sample is packaged in an EAR. Go ahead and open it with a utility such as WinZip. You'll see that the EAR contains these J2EE modules:

Web modules:
BankCMRQLWeb.war, DepositJCAWeb.war, BankGallery.war

EJB modules:
BankCMRQLEJB.jar

Connector modules:
BankRA.rar

Dependent JAR modules:
BankAdapterInterface.jar, WsaEJBDeployUtility.jar

Application client JAR modules:
TransferJMSClient.jar, GetAccounts.jar, FindAccounts.jar

Remember that each module contains deployment descriptor files you can locate and view. Another thing to note is that EARs configured for WebSphere can have IBM proprietary deployment descriptor files. These files are always named ibm-application-bnd.xmi and ibm-application-ext.xmi. These files, when present, contain proprietary parameters for the WebSphere Application Server platform.

If you're viewing the contents of WebSphereBank.ear, you'll notice many files packaged in a directory called Database. These files contain the Cloudscape files to support the WebSphere Bank sample. This approach is a common practice when packaging an EAR. The technique lets any files be packaged with the EAR and be available relative to where the EAR is deployed.

Configure an Enhanced EAR

One oversight, some might say, of J2EE packaging is that there is no standard way to package all the parameters for all the J2EE resources a J2EE application might require. If there were, these parameters could be used to automatically create the resources when you deploy the application. Instead, you must script this step (or perform it manually), and the process differs for each J2EE environment (e.g., WebSphere, WebLogic).

IBM has tried to address this issue with the advent of Enhanced EARs. Using the WebSphere Application Server Toolkit, you can enhance your EAR with files that will be used to create the resources for the EAR when you deploy it.

Within the AST, you use the WebSphere Enhanced EAR editor to edit server configurations for WebSphere Application Server V6. The server configuration data you specify in this editor is embedded within the application itself. By preserving the existing server configuration, this technique improves the administration process of publishing to WebSphere when you install a new application to an existing local or remote WebSphere server.

As of Version 6, server-specific configurations for WebSphere Application Server are set in the WebSphere administrative console. You can use the Enhanced EAR editor to set the configuration settings specific to an enterprise application. The Enhanced EAR editor is available on the deployment page of the AST's Application Deployment Descriptor editor. Use this editor to configure the following elements that are specific to an enterprise application:

- data sources
- resource adapters and connection factories
- substitution variables
- authentications
- shared libraries
- virtual hosts
- class loader policies

When you enhance an EAR with the above configurations, several XML files are added to your EAR directory. Table 23-1 lists these files.

Table 23-1: XML files added to the EAR directory

File name	EAR directory
deployment.xml	\<AST_workspace>\\<EAR_PROJECT>\META-INF\ibmconfig\cells\defaultCell\applications\defaultApp\deployments\defaultApp
resources.xml	\<AST_workspace>\\<EAR_PROJECT>\META-INF\ibmconfig\cells\defaultCell\applications\defaultApp\deployments\defaultApp
variables.xml	\<AST_workspace>\\<EAR_PROJECT>\META-INF\ibmconfig\cells\defaultCell\applications\defaultApp\deployments\defaultApp
libraries.xml	\<AST_workspace>\\<EAR_PROJECT>\META-INF\ibmconfig\cells\defaultCell\nodes\defaultNode\servers\defaultServer
security.xml	\<AST_workspace>\\<EAR_PROJECT>\\META-INF\ibmconfig\cells\defaultCell
virtualhosts.xml	\<AST_workspace>\\<EAR_PROJECT>\\META-INF\ibmconfig\cells\defaultCell

To illustrate how to locate the WebSphere Enhanced EAR editor, let's test a sample data source:

1. In the Application Server Toolkit, switch to the J2EE perspective.

2. In the Project Explorer view, expand the **Enterprise Applications** folder.

3. Under the enterprise application project folder for which you want to test the data source, double-click **Deployment Descriptor** to open the Application Deployment Descriptor editor. (We're doing this to get to the Enhanced EAR editor.)

4. At the bottom of the editor window, select the **Deployment** tab to open the WebSphere Enhanced EAR editor.

Note: Before adding or removing J2EE modules using the Application Deployment Descriptor editor's **Module** page, you must first click the **Deployment** tab to activate the functions in the **Deployment** page. Then add or remove your modules from the **Module** page. You must complete this task for each Application Deployment Descriptor editor session that you want to have add or remove modules from the **Module** page.

If the WebSphere Enhanced EAR editor is opened and you make changes to its dependent files either on the file system or using another editor, the changes aren't reloaded on the **Deployment** page. To refresh the changes on this page, you must close and reopen the Enhanced EAR editor.

Let's step through the process of configuring an Enhanced EAR with the configuration information for a new data source for the WebSphere Bank sample application. To begin, you must start the AST (you can do so from the Windows **Start** menu). Then import the EAR you want to enhance:

1. Select **File|Import**.

Figure 23-1: WebSphereBank imported into an AST workspace

2. Select **EAR File**, and click **Next**.

3. Browse to the WebSphere Bank EAR file (<WASV6-ROOT>\samples\lib\WebSphereBank\WebSphereBank.ear), and click **Finish**.

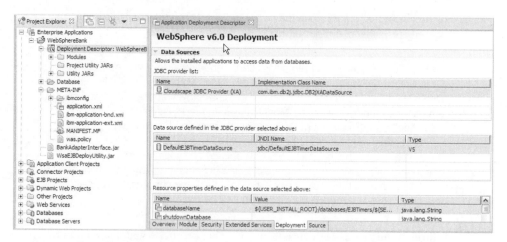

Figure 23-2: WebSphereBank EAR's deployment descriptor opened in editor

After you import the EAR, your Project Explorer should look as shown in Figure 23-1.

Now, double-click the WebSphere Bank EAR's deployment descriptor to open up the Application Deployment Descriptor editor. Then go to the **Deployment** tab. This is where you'll access the Enhanced EAR editor. Figure 23-2 shows the WebSphereBank EAR's deployment descriptor opened in the editor.

As a test, go ahead and add a new data source:

1. To the right of the panel labeled "Data source defined in the JDBC provider selected above," click the **Add** button (note that this button doesn't appear in the figure).

2. Select **Cloudscape JDBC Provider (XA)**, and then click **Finish**, accepting all defaults.

After adding enhanced parameters (as you just did), new enhanced EAR files will appear in your Project Explorer; look for deployment.xml, resources.xml, variables.xml, and security.xml. Depending on what you added (or didn't add), some files may not be created. Figure 23-3 shows sample results for our example.

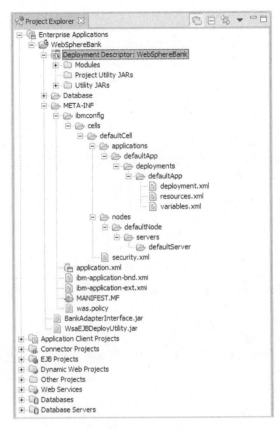

Figure 23-3: Enhanced EAR's added files

Once you've finished with the AST, you can export your EAR and deploy it as normal. During the deployment, the enhanced EAR files will be detected, and the resources will be created.

24

Manually Install WebSphere Bank

I n Chapter 4, you saw how to use a WebSphere –samples script from the command line to install the WebSphere SamplesGallery application, one element of which is the WebSphere Bank sample you learned about in Chapter 24. What you didn't see are all the resources that were created for you at that time. In this chapter, we review the resources created for the WebSphere Bank application and explain how you can create them yourself using the WebSphere administrative console.

Installing resources manually is a common requirement to successfully deploy any J2EE application because the J2EE specification doesn't define how to package this information in the Enterprise Archive (EAR) file. As you learned in Chapter 23, IBM has solved this issue in a proprietary way with Enhanced EARs. In that chapter, you used the WebSphere Application Server Toolkit (AST) to create an enhanced WebSphere Bank EAR. In most cases, however, the J2EE developer/packager will tell you which resources the application requires, and, as the system administrator, you'll need to create these resources using either WebSphere's admin console or the wsadmin command-line tool.

As it turns out, WebSphere Bank needs the following resources to run:

- a J2C resource adapter called *WebSphere Relational Resource Adapter* that, luckily, is created automatically when you install WebSphere

- a J2C authentication alias named *IBM-79D6XZF0P9FNode01Cell/samples* (note that the first part of this name contains the name of the node/cell where the alias is created and so will vary from node to node)

- a JDBC provider named *Samples Cloudscape JDBC Provider (XA)*

- a data source named *BANKDS*

- a connection factory named *BANKDS_CF* (which, as you'll see, is also created automatically)

- a service integration bus (SIBus) named *IBM-79D6XZF0P9FNode01SamplesBus* (again, the first part of the name is the node name where the bus is created and so will vary from node to node)

- an SIBus member for the SIBus named *IBM-79D6XZF0P9FNode01SamplesBus*

- an SIB Java Message Service (JMS) connection factory named *BankJMSConnFactory*

- an SIB JMS queue named *BankJMSQueue*

- an SIB queue named *BankJSQueue*

- an SIB JMS activation specification named *BankActivationSpec*

Last, but not least, you'll need to enable the SIB service for the application server (server1). Let's walk through the steps to set up each required resource.

Verify the Existence of the J2C Resource Adapter

First, take the following steps to make sure the required J2C resource adapter, WebSphere Relational Resource Adapter, has been created.

1. In the WebSphere admin console's navigation tree, expand **Resources**, and click **Resource Adapters**.

2. Verify that WebSphere Relational Resource Adapter appears in the list of installed resource adapters.

Create the J2C Authentication Alias

Next, create the required J2C authentication alias, IBM-79D6XZF0P9FNode01Cell/ samples:

1. In the console, navigate to **Security|Global Security** to display the **Global Security** panel.

2. Under the **Authentication** heading, select **JAAS configuration|J2C authentication data** to display the **J2C Authentication Data Entries** panel.

3. Click **New**.

4. On the resulting configuration panel (shown in Figure 24-1), enter the required values: a unique alias name (IBM-79D6XZF0P9FNode01Cell/samples), a valid user ID (samples), a valid password (samples), and a short description (JAAS Alias for WebSphere Samples).

5. Click **Apply** or **OK**.

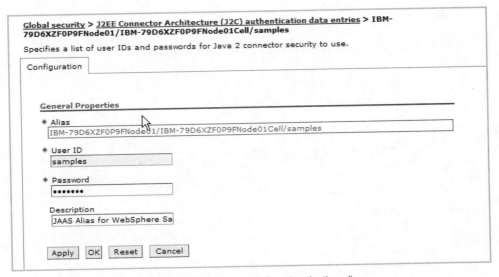

Figure 24-1: Creating a J2C authentication alias

Create the JDBC Provider

Next, create the JDBC provider resource, Samples Cloudscape JDBC Provider (XA):

1. Navigate to **Resources|JDBC Providers**.
2. On the resulting panel, make sure the scope is set to Server.
3. Click **New**.
4. Enter the values as shown in Figure 24-2 to create the JDBC provider.

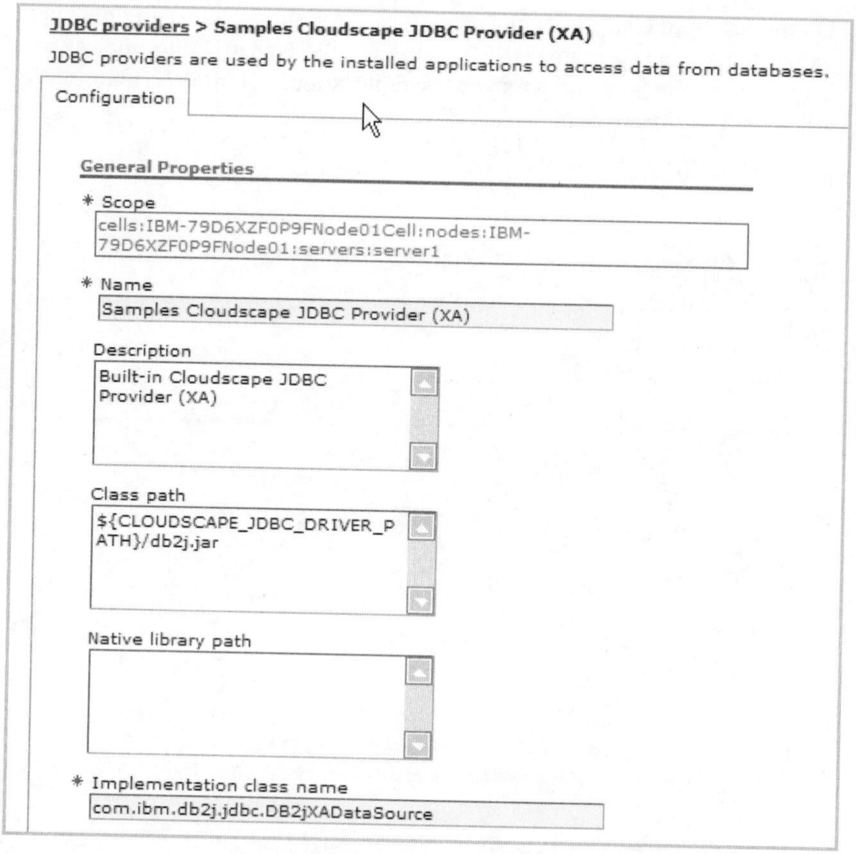

JDBC providers > Samples Cloudscape JDBC Provider (XA)

JDBC providers are used by the installed applications to access data from databases.

Configuration

General Properties

* Scope
cells:IBM-79D6XZF0P9FNode01Cell:nodes:IBM-79D6XZF0P9FNode01:servers:server1

* Name
Samples Cloudscape JDBC Provider (XA)

Description
Built-in Cloudscape JDBC Provider (XA)

Class path
${CLOUDSCAPE_JDBC_DRIVER_PATH}/db2j.jar

Native library path

* Implementation class name
com.ibm.db2j.jdbc.DB2jXADataSource

Figure 24-2: Creating a JDBC provider

Create the Data Source

Next, create the BANKDS data source:

1. Again, navigate to **Resources|JDBC Providers**.

2. Select theJDBC provider you just created, **Samples Cloudscape JDBC Provider (XA)**.

3. Click **Data Sources**.

4. Click **New**.

5. Enter the data shown in Figure 24-3 to create the data source.

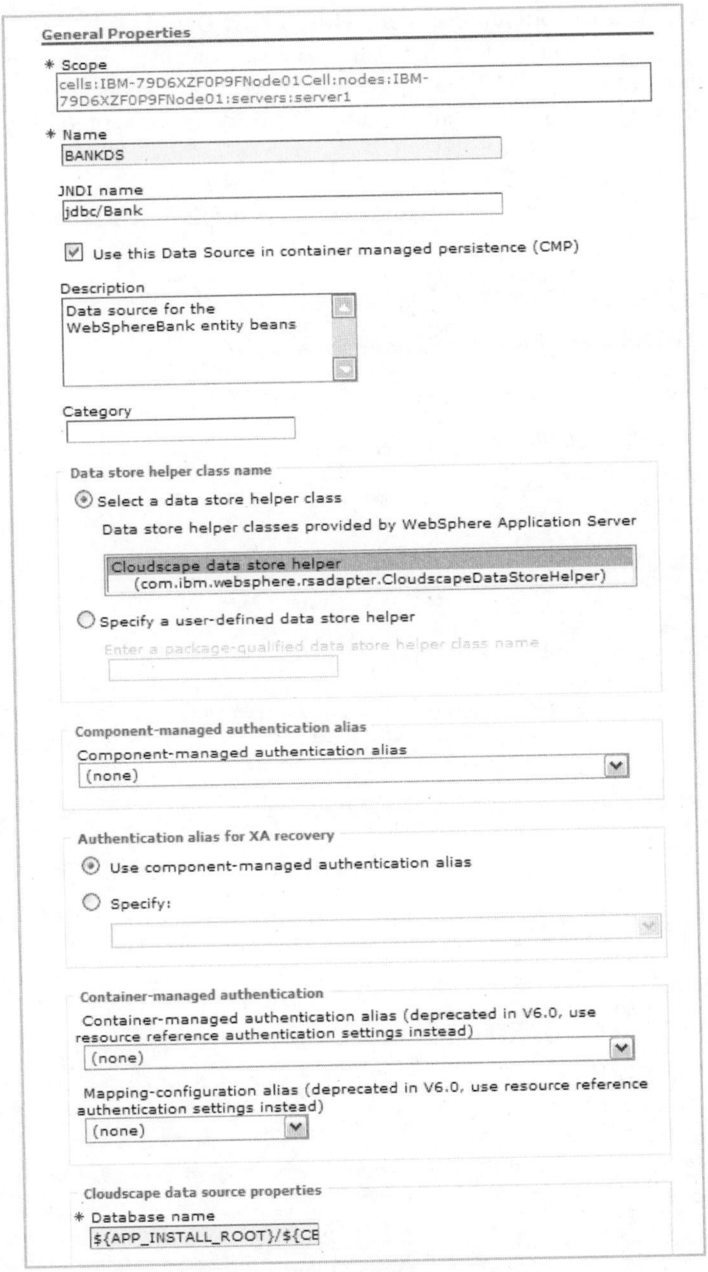

Figure 24-3: Creating a data source

Verify That the Connection Factory Has Been Created

When you select the option to "Use this Data Source in container managed persistence (CMP)" when creating the BANKDS data source, the required connection factory, BANKDS_CF, is created for you automatically. To verify the creation of this connection factory:

1. Navigate to **Resources|Resource Adapters** to display the **Resource Adapters** panel.

2. Make sure the scope is set to Server.

3. Click **WebSphere Relational Resource Adapter**.

4. Click **CMP connection factories**.

5. Verify that BANKDS_CF is created. Figure 24-4 shows the connection factory's general properties.

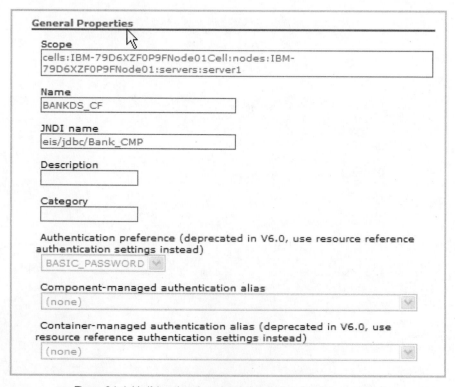

Figure 24-4: Verifying that the connection factory has been created

Create the SIBus

Next, create the service integration bus, IBM-79D6XZF0P9FNode01SamplesBus:

1. Navigate to **Service Integration|Buses**.
2. Click **New**.
3. Enter the values shown in Figure 24-5 to create the required SIBus.
4. Click **Apply** or **OK**.

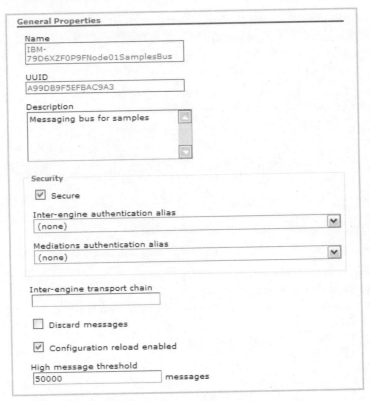

Figure 24-5: Creating an SIBus

Create an SIBus Member for the SIBus

To create the SIBus member:

1. Again navigate to **Service Integration|Buses**.

2. Click **IBM-79D6XZF0P9FNode01SamplesBus**.

3. Under **Additional Properties**, click **Bus members**.

4. Click **Add**.

5. Select **Server** or **Cluster**, accept the default values, and click **Next**.

6. Confirm the addition of a new bus member as shown in Figure 24-6, and then click **Finish**.

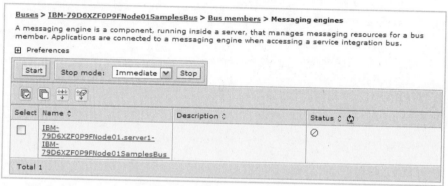

Figure 24-6: Adding an SIBus member

Create the SIB JMS Connection Factory

Take these steps to create the JMS connection factory named BankJMSConnFactory:

1. Navigate to **Resources|JMS Providers**.
2. Click **Default messaging**.
3. Under **Connection Factories**, click **JMS connection factory**.
4. Click **New**.
5. Enter the parameters as shown in Figure 24-7.
6. Click **OK**.

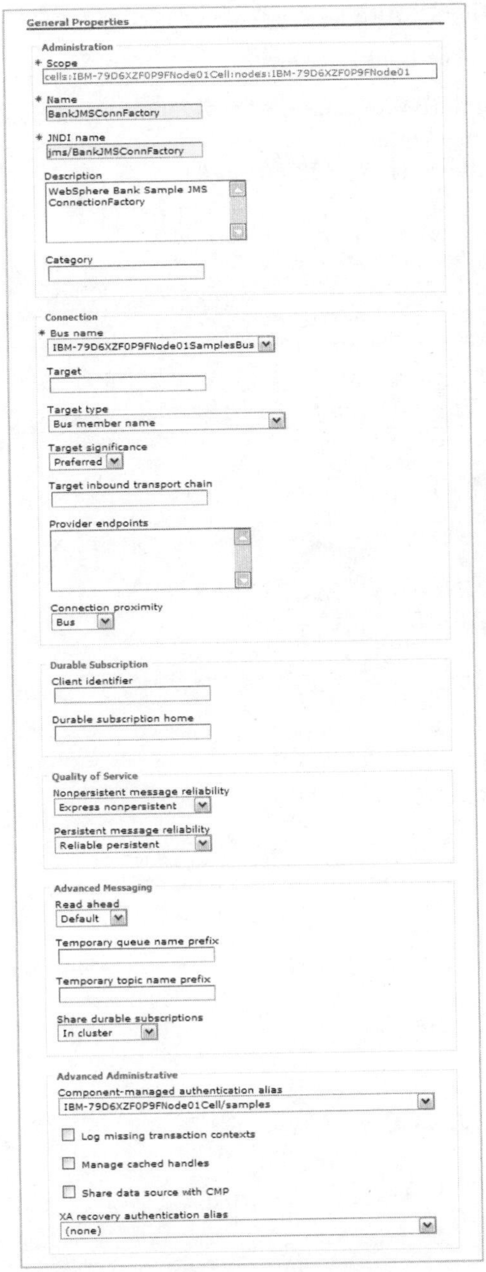

General Properties

Administration

* Scope
`cells:IBM-79D6XZF0P9FNode01Cell:nodes:IBM-79D6XZF0P9FNode01`

* Name
`BankJMSConnFactory`

* JNDI name
`jms/BankJMSConnFactory`

Description
`WebSphere Bank Sample JMS ConnectionFactory`

Category

Connection

* Bus name
`IBM-79D6XZF0P9FNode01SamplesBus`

Target

Target type
`Bus member name`

Target significance
`Preferred`

Target inbound transport chain

Provider endpoints

Connection proximity
`Bus`

Durable Subscription

Client identifier

Durable subscription home

Quality of Service

Nonpersistent message reliability
`Express nonpersistent`

Persistent message reliability
`Reliable persistent`

Advanced Messaging

Read ahead
`Default`

Temporary queue name prefix

Temporary topic name prefix

Share durable subscriptions
`In cluster`

Advanced Administrative

Component-managed authentication alias
`IBM-79D6XZF0P9FNode01Cell/samples`

☐ Log missing transaction contexts

☐ Manage cached handles

☐ Share data source with CMP

XA recovery authentication alias
`(none)`

Figure 24-7: Creating a JMS connection factory

Create the SIB JMS Queue

Next, create the JMS queue BankJMSQueue:

1. Navigate again to **Resources|JMS Providers**.
2. Click **Default messaging**.
3. Under **Destinations**, click **JMS Queue**.
4. Click **New**.
5. Enter the parameters as shown in Figure 24-8.
6. Click **OK**.

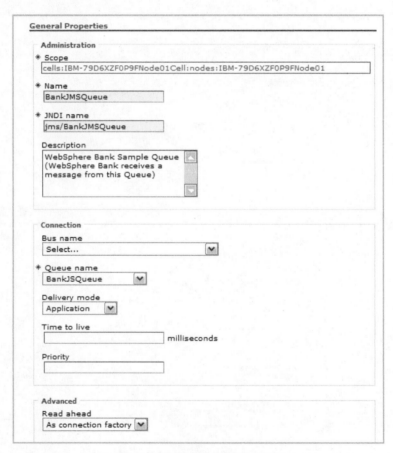

Figure 24-8: Creating a JMS queue

Create the SIB Queue

Create the BankJSQueue SIB queue:

1. Navigate to **Service Integration|Buses**.

2. Select **IBM-79D6XZF0P9FNode01SamplesBus**.

3. Under **Additional Properties**, click **Destinations**.

4. Click **New**.

5. On the **Create new destination** panel, select **Queue** and click **Next**.

6. For the identifier, enter **BankJSQueue**. Leave the description field blank, and click **Next**.

7. On the **Assign the queue to a bus member** panel, accept server1 as the bus member, and click **Next**.

8. On the **Confirm queue creation** panel, click **Finish**.

9. Verify that the BankJSQueue looks as shown in Figure 24-9.

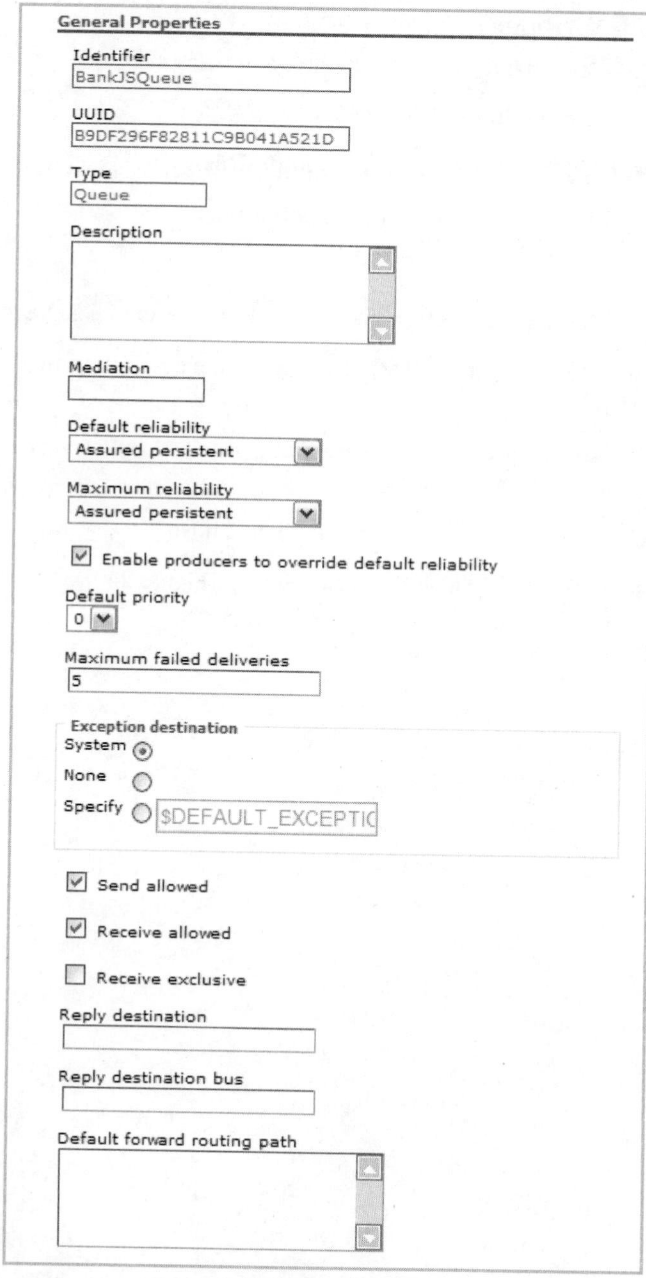

General Properties

Identifier

BankJSQueue

UUID

B9DF296F82811C9B041A521D

Type

Queue

Description

Mediation

Default reliability

Assured persistent

Maximum reliability

Assured persistent

☑ Enable producers to override default reliability

Default priority

0

Maximum failed deliveries

5

Exception destination
System ◉

None ○

Specify ○ $DEFAULT_EXCEPTIC

☑ Send allowed

☑ Receive allowed

☐ Receive exclusive

Reply destination

Reply destination bus

Default forward routing path

Figure 24-9: Creating an SIB queue

Create the SIB JMS Activation Specification

To create the SIB JMS activation specification BankActivationSpec:

1. Navigate to **Resources|JMS Providers**.
2. Click **Default messaging**.
3. Under **Activation specifications**, click **JMS Activation specification**.
4. Click **New**.
5. Enter the parameters shown in Figure 24-10.

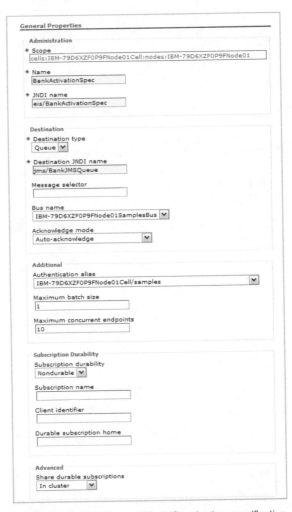

Figure 24-10: Creating an SIB JMS activation specification

Verify That the SIB Service for the Application Server Is Enabled

Your final task is to verify that the SIB service for the application server, server1, is enabled. To do so:

1. Navigate to **Servers|Application Servers**.
2. Select **server1**.
3. Click **SIB service**.
4. Verify that the service is enabled. If it's not, enable it.

25

WebSphere Rapid Deployment (WRD)

WebSphere Rapid Deployment (WRD), a feature new to WebSphere Application Server in Version 6, is designed to simplify the development and deployment of WebSphere applications. WRD is a collection of Eclipse plug-ins that can be integrated within development tools or run in a "headless" mode, without headers, from a user file system. WRD is currently integrated in Application Server Toolkit, Rational Application Developer, and Rational Web Developer. Initially, WRD's features are supported only in headless mode.

During development, you use annotation-based programming with WRD. The developer adds into the application source code metadata tags used to generate artifacts that the code requires, thus reducing the number of artifacts the developer needs to create. The application is then packaged into an Enhanced EAR file that contains the J2EE EAR file along with deployment information, application resources, and properties (e.g., environment variables, JAAS authentication entries, shared libraries, class loader settings, and JDBC resources). During installation, WRD uses this information to create the necessary resources. Moving an application from one server to another also moves the resources. WRD automates the installation of applications and modules onto a running application server by monitoring the workspace for changes and then driving the deployment process.

Invoking WRD

You can use the rapid deployment launch tool (wrd.bat or wrd.sh) to specify that you want WRD to start listening for application artifacts that are dropped into a monitored project. The wrd command runs in a nongraphical mode using a command-line interface:

- On Windows, enter **wrd.bat [<*optional parameters*>]**.
- On Unix, enter **wrd.sh [<*optional parameters*>]**.

The command supports the following optional parameters:

- **–monitor** — Enables console feedback from the rapid deployment tool.

- **–project <*"project_name"*>** — Specifies the name of the rapid deployment project you want to target to run in batch mode. You use this parameter only in conjunction with the –batch parameter.

- **–batch** — Enables batch mode on a specified target project. Batch mode runs a full build on a rapid deployment workspace and then shuts down the process.

- **–usage** — Displays the optional parameters for the command.

Deploying Applications with WRD

You can configure WRD to automatically install (or uninstall) J2EE applications (EAR files) that are deposited in its workspace or to construct and deploy a J2EE-compliant application from artifacts or modules you create or drop into a freeform project. In this section, we review the steps for both of these alternatives.

Automatically Install an EAR

To set up WRD to automatically install J2EE applications packaged as EARs, the first thing you should do is open a command prompt window. Then, create a source directory into which you'll drop the EAR to be deployed and define an environment variable called WORKSPACE to point to that directory. For this example, we'll use the following values for the source directory and environment variable:

```
C:\Program Files\IBM\WebSphere\AppServer\bin>md c:\WRD
C:\Program Files\IBM\WebSphere\AppServer\bin>set WORKSPACE=c:\WRD
```

Next, you need to configure the workspace you just created. You use the rapid deployment configuration command, wrd-config, to do so. For this example, we'll use the AutoAppInstall style of deployment. Listing 25-1 shows the command and its execution. Accept the default parameter configuration settings by pressing the Enter key.

Listing 25-1

Configuring the WRD workspace for AutoAppInstall mode

```
C:\Program Files\IBM\WebSphere\AppServer\bin>wrd-config -project "AutoInstall"
-style "autoappinstall"
Launching WebSphere Rapid Deployment configuration.  Please wait...
```

```
Starting Workbench...

Starting up the workbench.

------------------------------------------------------------
Parameter Configuration Settings
------------------------------------------------------------
Press ENTER to accept defaults
The * symbol denotes required input

 Enter the server name* ( server1 ) :
 Enter the server JMX host name* ( localhost ) :
 Enter the server JMX port number* ( 8880 ) :
 Enter your server username ( ) :
 Enter your server password ( ) :

WebSphere Rapid Deployment configuration completed.
Shutting down the workbench.
```

Next, start the WRD utility. We'll start the tool in monitor mode to have all messages sent to the console window. Listing 25-2 shows the command execution.

Listing 25-2

Starting WRD in monitor mode

```
C:\Program Files\IBM\WebSphere\AppServer\bin>wrd -monitor
Launching WebSphere Rapid Deployment.  Please wait...
Starting Workbench...

Starting up the workbench.
WebSphere Rapid Deployment ready for e-business...

Type 'q', 'quit', or 'exit' to shut down WebSphere Rapid Deployment processes.
```

Now, we'll use the WebSphere Bank application (which you worked with in previous chapters) to illustrate how the rapid deployment tool works. Copy the WebSphereBank.ear file to the C:\WRD\AutoInstall directory. As soon as you do that, the WRD utility will detect the EAR and begin to install it. Listing 25-3 shows the installation's progress. You can verify that the WebSphere Bank application has indeed been installed by viewing it in the admin console. (Select **Applications|Enterprise Applications** in the navigation tree to do so.)

Listing 25-3

Command-line notifications for WebSphere Bank installation

```
[04:19:16 PM]    !INSTALL_EAR_FILE WebSphereBank.ear!
[04:19:16 PM]    Publishing WebSphereBank to server_510658053
```

```
[04:19:19 PM]    Updating Application. WebSphereBank
[04:19:55 PM]    Installation Completed Successfully:
[04:19:55 PM]    Starting Application:  WebSphereBank
[04:19:55 PM]    Application Started Successfully:  WebSphereBank
```

Automatically Remove an EAR

If you delete the EAR, WRD will remove the application. Figure 25-1 illustrates the deletion of the EAR file for the WebSphere Bank application.

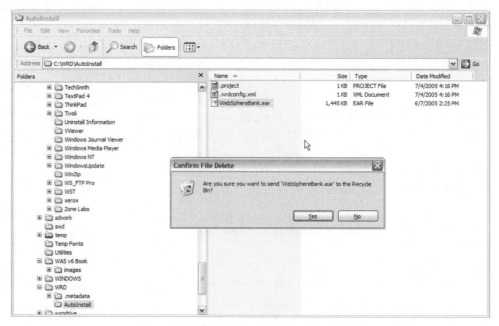

Figure 25-1: Deleting the WebSphereBank EAR

To see WRD removing the application, check the command prompt (Listing 25-4).

Listing 25-4

Command-line notifications for WebSphere Bank removal

```
[04:41:23 PM]    !DELETE_EAR_WRAPPER WebSphereBank.ear!
[04:41:23 PM]    Uninstalling WebSphereBank:server_510658053
[04:41:50 PM]    Application Uninstalled:  WebSphereBank
```

Automatically Deploy a Freeform Application

The WRD tool's freeform configuration lets you create or drop your J2EE artifacts or modules into a freeform project. J2EE artifacts include source code, annotated source code or class files of servlets, Java Server Page (JSP) files, static Web content files, enterprise beans, and so on. WRD takes the artifacts you drop into the freeform project directory, automatically places them into the appropriate J2EE project structure, generates any additional required artifacts (e.g., deployment descriptors) to create a fully compliant J2EE application, and then deploys the application.

To deploy an application using this method, you first need to configure the freeform project. Listing 25-5 shows the wrd-config command being executed to set the required configuration parameters.

Listing 25-5

Configuring a WRD freeform project

```
C:\Program Files\IBM\WebSphere\AppServer\bin>wrd-config -project "Hello" -
style "freeform"
Launching WebSphere Rapid Deployment configuration.  Please wait...
Starting Workbench...

Starting up the workbench.

----------------------------------------------------------
Parameter Configuration Settings
----------------------------------------------------------
Press ENTER to accept defaults
The * symbol denotes required input

  Enter the server name* ( server1 ) :
  Enter the server JMX host name* ( localhost ) :
  Enter the server JMX port number* ( 8880 ) :
  Enter a path for containing the exported EAR ( ) :
  Enter your server username ( ) :
  Enter your server password ( ) :

WebSphere Rapid Deployment configuration completed.
Shutting down the workbench.
```

Next, start WRD as before, by issuing the **wrd −monitor** command.

At this point, let's assume that a Java source file called HelloWorld.java exists in the directory C:\temp\HW\com\orc\helloworld. Listing 25-6 shows the HelloWorld.java source file.

Listing 25-6

HelloWorld.java source file

```java
package com.orc.helloworld;

import java.io.IOException;
import java.io.PrintWriter;

import javax.servlet.ServletException;
import javax.servlet.http.HttpServlet;
import javax.servlet.http.HttpServletRequest;
import javax.servlet.http.HttpServletResponse;

/**
 * @version      1.0
 * @author       O. Cline
 */
public class HelloWorld extends HttpServlet {

    /**
     * @see javax.servlet.GenericServlet#void ()
     */
    public void destroy() {

            super.destroy();
    }

    /**
     * @see javax.servlet.http.HttpServlet#void (javax.servlet.http.HttpServ-
letRequest, javax.servlet.http.HttpServletResponse)
     */
    public void doDelete(HttpServletRequest req, HttpServletResponse resp)
            throws ServletException, IOException {

    }

    /**
     * @see javax.servlet.http.HttpServlet#void (javax.servlet.http.
HttpServletRequest, javax.servlet.http.HttpServletResponse)
     */
    public void doGet(HttpServletRequest req, HttpServletResponse resp)
            throws ServletException, IOException {

            resp.setContentType("text/html");
            PrintWriter out = resp.getWriter();

            out.print("Hello World");

            out.close();
    }
```

```
        /**
         * @see javax.servlet.http.HttpServlet#void (javax.servlet.http.
HttpServletRequest, javax.servlet.http.HttpServletResponse)
         */
        public void doPost(HttpServletRequest req, HttpServletResponse resp)
                throws ServletException, IOException {
                doGet(req, resp);

        }

        /**
         * @see javax.servlet.http.HttpServlet#void (javax.servlet.http.
HttpServletRequest, javax.servlet.http.HttpServletResponse)
         */
        public void doPut(HttpServletRequest req, HttpServletResponse resp)
                throws ServletException, IOException {

        }

        /**
         * @see javax.servlet.GenericServlet#java.lang.String ()
         */
        public String getServletInfo() {

                return super.getServletInfo();

        }

        /**
         * @see javax.servlet.GenericServlet#void ()
         */
        public void init() throws ServletException {

                super.init();

        }

        /**
         * @see java.lang.Object#java.lang.String ()
         */
        public String toString() {

                return super.toString();

        }

}
```

Copy this file and its package directories to the WRD freeform project directory. Figure 25-2 shows the WRD directory after you've completed this step.

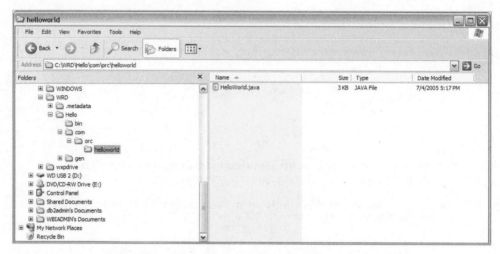

Figure 25-2: Freeform project directory after source code copied

Once you've copied the source code to the freeform project, WRD will detect its presence and then build and deploy a J2EE application. Listing 25-7 shows the command-line notifications you'll see as WRD takes the steps required to create and deploy the HelloWorld application.

Listing 25-7

WRD notification of successful application creation and deployment

```
[05:13:17 PM]    [/Hello/com/orc/helloworld/HelloWorld.java] Added
[05:13:23 PM]    [/Hello/bin/com/orc/helloworld/HelloWorld.class] copied to
                 project [HelloWeb]
[05:13:23 PM]    [/Hello/com/orc/helloworld/HelloWorld.java] Added
[05:13:24 PM]    Servlet added to web.xml: HelloWorld
[05:13:24 PM]    Servlet mapping added.  URL is: [HelloWeb/HelloWorld]
[05:13:24 PM]    Publishing IBMUTC to server_510658053
[05:13:24 PM]    Publish requested for this change.
[05:13:26 PM]    Updating Application. IBMUTC
[05:13:38 PM]    Installation Completed Successfully:
[05:13:38 PM]    Starting Application:   IBMUTC
[05:13:38 PM]    Application Started Successfully:  IBMUTC
[05:13:38 PM]    J2EE deployment started.
[05:13:39 PM]    J2EE deployment completed.
[05:13:39 PM]    Publishing HelloApp to server_510658053
[05:13:39 PM]    Installing New Application:  HelloApp
[05:13:42 PM]    Installation Completed Successfully:
[05:13:42 PM]    Starting Application:  HelloApp
[05:13:43 PM]    Application Started Successfully:  HelloApp
```

Now, you can test your application. Figure 25-3 shows a successful test of HelloWorld.

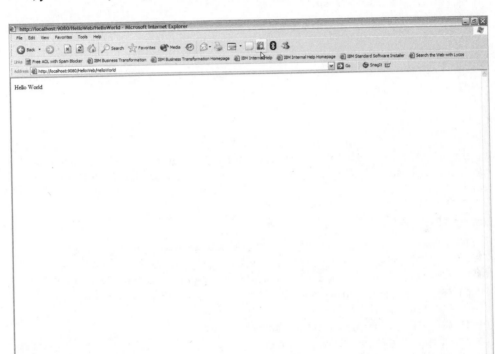

Figure 25-3: Verifying that the HelloWorld application is deployed

Next, let's see how WRD reacts when you modify the source file. Edit the HelloWorld.java file directly inside the freeform project by changing the string output by the application from "Hello World" to "Hello World AGAIN". Listing 25-8 shows the modified section of source code.

Listing 25-8

Modifying the HelloWorld output string

```
        .
        .
        .
public void doGet(HttpServletRequest req, HttpServletResponse resp)
      throws ServletException, IOException {
```

```
    resp.setContentType("text/html");
    PrintWriter out = resp.getWriter();

    out.print("Hello World AGAIN");

    out.close();

}

        .
        .
        .
```

As soon as you save the HelloWorld.java file, WRD will detect that you've done so and update the application. Listing 25-9 shows the command-line confirmation you'll receive.

Listing 25-9

Command-line notifications for updated HelloWorld application

```
[05:17:47 PM]    [/Hello/com/orc/helloworld/HelloWorld.java] Modified
[05:17:48 PM]    [/Hello/bin/com/orc/helloworld/HelloWorld.class] copied to
                 project [HelloWeb]
[05:17:48 PM]    Publish requested for this change.
[05:17:48 PM]    J2EE deployment started.
[05:17:48 PM]    J2EE deployment completed.
[05:17:48 PM]    [/Hello/com/orc/helloworld/HelloWorld.java] Modified
[05:17:48 PM]    Publishing HelloApp to server_510658053
```

As a last step, verify that your change was deployed successfully. Figure 25-4 shows the output you can expect.

Figure 25-4: Verifying that the change to HelloWorld was successful

26

WebSphere V6 System Management Using the J2EE Management API

As you've seen in earlier chapters of this book, you can administer WebSphere Application Server and your applications using tools that come with the product — specifically, the administrative console, the wsadmin scripting tool, and the administrative command-line tools. WebSphere Application Server also supports access to the administrative functions through a set of Java classes and methods. In this chapter, we examine the task of WebSphere V6 system management using the J2EE Management API.

The J2EE Management Specification was developed through the Java Community Process as JSR-077 to provide a standard model for managing J2EE server platforms, including WebSphere Application Server. The specification directs that application servers provide a Management Enterprise JavaBean (MEJB) to surface the Java Management Extensions (JMX) interface. Using JSR-077 (or MEJB) will (or should) make your system-management code usable by any J2EE application server.

Dumping the Java Naming and Directory Interface (JNDI) namespace for a running WebSphere application server (by executing the <WASV6_ROOT>\bin\dumpnamespace script as you learned in Chapter 22) provides a good way to verify that WebSphere's MEJB session bean is active and available to you. Listing 26-1 shows a snippet of the dumpnamespace output demonstrating that the MEJB session bean is running.

Listing 26-1

Partial dumpnamespace output verifying that MEJB session bean is active

```
65 (top)/nodes/IBM-79D6XZF0P9FNode01/servers/server1/ejb/mgmt
65                                                      javax.naming.Context
```

```
66 (top)/nodes/IBM-79D6XZF0P9FNode01/servers/server1/ejb/mgmt/MEJB
66                                      javax.management.j2ee.ManagementHome
```

To test this functionality, let's look at a servlet that accesses the MEJB to let you start and stop enterprise applications on your application server. To create the servlet, use Rational Application Developer (RAD) to create a Dynamic Web Project called SystemManagement and a servlet called TSM. Listing 26-2 shows the TSM.java source code. Deploy the EAR containing the TSM servlet to a WebSphere application server. Then execute the servlet by issuing the URL **http://localhost:9080/SystemManagement/TSM** in your browser. Figure 26-1 shows the results you should see.

Listing 26-2

TSM.java source code

```java
import java.io.IOException;
import java.io.PrintWriter;
import java.rmi.RemoteException;
import java.util.Arrays;
import java.util.Calendar;
import java.util.Enumeration;
import java.util.GregorianCalendar;
import java.util.Iterator;
import java.util.Set;

import javax.ejb.CreateException;
import javax.management.AttributeNotFoundException;
import javax.management.InstanceNotFoundException;
import javax.management.MBeanException;
import javax.management.MalformedObjectNameException;
import javax.management.ObjectName;
import javax.management.ReflectionException;
import javax.management.j2ee.Management;
import javax.management.j2ee.ManagementHome;
import javax.management.j2ee.statistics.BoundedRangeStatistic;
import javax.management.j2ee.statistics.JVMStats;
import javax.naming.Context;
import javax.naming.InitialContext;
import javax.rmi.PortableRemoteObject;
import javax.servlet.ServletException;
import javax.servlet.http.HttpServlet;
import javax.servlet.http.HttpServletRequest;
import javax.servlet.http.HttpServletResponse;

/*
 * @version 1.0 @author
 */
public class TSM extends HttpServlet {
```

```
        /**
         * @see javax.servlet.http.HttpServlet#void
         *      (javax.servlet.http.HttpServletRequest,
         *      javax.servlet.http.HttpServletResponse)
         */

        private ManagementHome home;

        public void init() throws ServletException {
                super.init();
                try {
//                      Properties props = new Properties();
//                      props.setProperty(Context.PROVIDER_URL, "iiop://myhost:2809");
//                      Context ic = new InitialContext(props);
//                      Object obj = ic.lookup("ejb/mgmt/MEJB");
                        Context initial = new InitialContext();
                        java.lang.Object objref = initial
// This works too but you do need a local reference defined in your WAR
                        project deployment descriptor
//                                      .lookup("java:comp/env/ejb/mgmt/MEJB");
// Do a global JNDI lookup but remember this is not best practice
                                        .lookup("ejb/mgmt/MEJB");
                        home = (ManagementHome) PortableRemoteObject.narrow(objref,
                                        ManagementHome.class);
                } catch (Exception ex) {
                }
        }

        public void doGet(HttpServletRequest req, HttpServletResponse resp)
                        throws ServletException, IOException {
                System.out.println("doGet - Management Bean Test");
                resp.setContentType("text/HTML");
                PrintWriter out = resp.getWriter();
                out
                                .println("<HTML><HEAD><TITLE>Test System
                                                Management</TITLE></HEAD><BODY>");
                out.println("<FORM ACTION=\"/SystemManagement/TSM\" METHOD=POST>");
                try {
                        out.println("<P>Creating an instance of the ManagementBean.</P>");

                        /* Find all J2EEApplication managed objects on this system */
                        Management mejb = home.create();
                        ObjectName searchpattern = new ObjectName(
                                        "*:j2eeType=J2EEApplication,*");
                        Set managed_object_set = mejb.queryNames(searchpattern, null);
                        out.println("<P>found " + managed_object_set.size()
                                        + " objects matching
                                                \"j2eeType=J2EEApplication\". </P>");
                        out.println("<TABLE border=\"1\">");
                        out
                                        .println("<TH>Enterprise Application
```

```
Name<TD><input type=submit value=\"Start\" name=\"Button\"><TD><input type=sub-
mit value=\"Stop\" name=\"Button\"> <TH> State");

                /* Get the status (started / stopped) for each: */
                Iterator managed_objects = managed_object_set.iterator();
                while (managed_objects.hasNext()) {
                        ObjectName objectname = (ObjectName)
managed_objects.next();
                        /*
                         * display the state attribute (from JSR77.5.1.1.1)
                                                                if it is
                         * StateManageable
                         */
                        if (((Boolean) mejb.getAttribute(objectname,
                                                "stateManageable"))
                                .equals(Boolean.TRUE)) {
                                out.println("<TR><TD>" +
objectname.getKeyProperty("name"));
                                out
                                         .println("<TD colspan=\"2\"
align=\"center\"><input type=checkbox value=\"\" name=\""
+ objectname.getCanonicalName() + "\" > ");
                                Object state = mejb.getAttribute(objectname,
                                                "state");
                                switch (state.hashCode()) {
                                case 0:
                                        out.println("<td> STARTING");
                                        break;
                                case 1:
                                        out.println("<td> RUNNING");
                                        break;
                                case 2:
                                        out.println("<td> STOPPING");
                                        break;
                                case 3:
                                        out.println("<td> <font color=FF0000
                                                        STOPPED </font>");
                                        break;
                                case 4:
                                        out.println("<td> <font color=FF0000
                                                        FAILED </font>");
                                        break;
                                }
                        }
                }
                Calendar cal = new GregorianCalendar();
                out.println("</TABLE><BR><P>Status refreshed at "
                        + cal.get(Calendar.HOUR) + ":" +
                                                cal.get(Calendar.MINUTE)
                        + ":" + cal.get(Calendar.SECOND) + " (server
                                                        time) </P>");
```

```
        } catch (Exception ex) {
                out.println("<P>Caught an unexpected exception!</P>");
                ex.printStackTrace(out);
        }
        out.println("</BODY></HTML>");
        out.close();
    }


    /**
     * @see javax.servlet.http.HttpServlet#void
     *      (javax.servlet.http.HttpServletRequest,
     *      javax.servlet.http.HttpServletResponse)
     */
    public void doPost(HttpServletRequest req, HttpServletResponse resp)
                throws ServletException, IOException {
        resp.setContentType("text/HTML");
        PrintWriter out = resp.getWriter();
        out
                    .println("<HTML><HEAD><TITLE>Test System
Management</TITLE><meta http-equiv=\"refresh\" content=\"8;
url=/TD/TDSMServlet\"></HEAD><BODY>");
        out.println("<FORM ACTION=\"/SystemManagement/TSM\" METHOD=GET>");
        out
                    .println("\""
                                    + req.getParameter("Button")
                                    + "\" was clicked with the following
applications selected: <BR>");
        String action = "";
        if (req.getParameter("Button").equals("Start")) {
                action = "start";
        } else {
                action = "stop";
        }
        try {
                Management mejb = home.create();
                for (Enumeration e = req.getParameterNames();
                                            e.hasMoreElements();) {
                    Object nextApp = e.nextElement();
                    if (nextApp.equals("Button")) {
                    } else {
                        try {
                                ObjectName appName = new
                                        ObjectName(nextApp.toString());
                                out.println("<P><B>" +
                                        appName.getKeyProperty("name")
                                        + "</B></P>");
                                mejb.invoke(appName, action, null,
                                                            null);
                        } catch (Exception ex) {
                                out.println("<P>Caught an unexpected
                                                    exception!</P>");
```

```
                                    ex.printStackTrace(out);
                    }
                }
            }
    } catch (Exception ex) {
            out.println("<P>Caught an unexpected exception!</P>");
            ex.printStackTrace(out);
    }
    out.println("<input type=submit value=\"OK\" name=\"OK\" > ");
    out.println("</BODY></HTML>");
    }

}
```

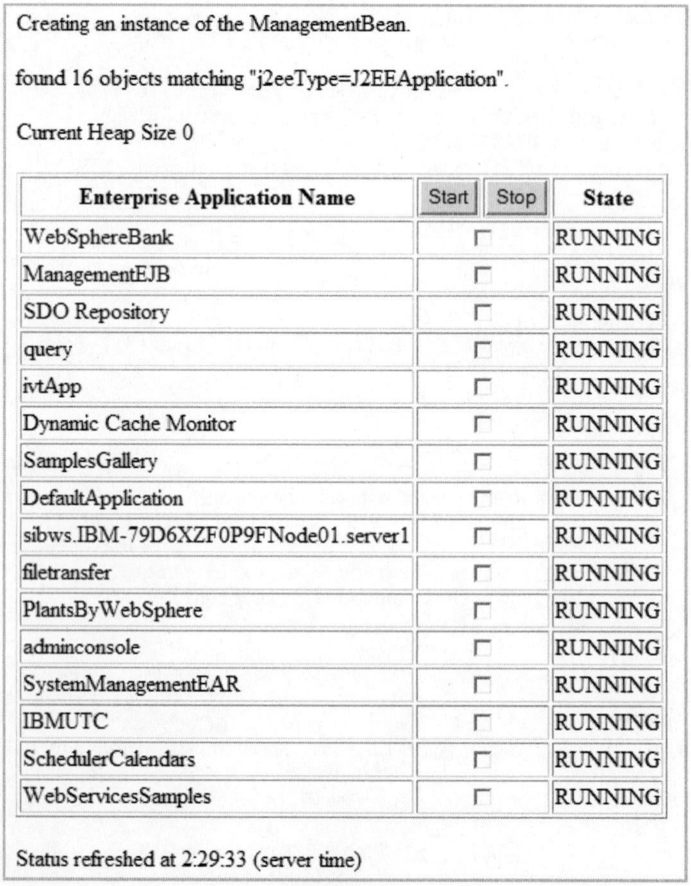

Creating an instance of the ManagementBean.

found 16 objects matching "j2eeType=J2EEApplication".

Current Heap Size 0

Enterprise Application Name	Start	Stop	State
WebSphereBank	☐		RUNNING
ManagementEJB	☐		RUNNING
SDO Repository	☐		RUNNING
query	☐		RUNNING
ivtApp	☐		RUNNING
Dynamic Cache Monitor	☐		RUNNING
SamplesGallery	☐		RUNNING
DefaultApplication	☐		RUNNING
sibws.IBM-79D6XZF0P9FNode01.server1	☐		RUNNING
filetransfer	☐		RUNNING
PlantsByWebSphere	☐		RUNNING
adminconsole	☐		RUNNING
SystemManagementEAR	☐		RUNNING
IBMUTC	☐		RUNNING
SchedulerCalendars	☐		RUNNING
WebServicesSamples	☐		RUNNING

Status refreshed at 2:29:33 (server time)

Figure 26-1: TSM servlet in action

Creating a Custom Java Administrative Client

WebSphere Application Server administrative APIs give you control over the operational aspects of your distributed system and the ability to update your configuration. In this section, we describe how to develop a Java program to access the WebSphere administrative system using these APIs. This task requires a basic familiarity with JMX API programming. For more information about this and the other topics covered in this section, consult the administrative API documentation, the JMX API documentation, and the MBean API documentation. You can find this documentation in the <WASV6-ROOT>\web directory.

When you develop and run administrative clients that use the various JMX connectors and have security enabled, follow these guidelines:

- Create and use a single administrative client before you create and use another administrative client.

- Create and use an administrative client on the same thread.

- Use one of the following ways to specify a user ID and password to create a new administrative client:
  › Specify a default user ID and password in the property file. You define these values in the soap.client.props file, which you'll find in the properties directory of the WebSphere profile being used. Look for the com.ibm.SOAP.loginUserid and com.ibm.SOAP.loginPassword properties.
  › Specify a user ID and password other than the default in your administrative client by defining these properties in your Property object: AdminClient.USERNAME and AdminClient.PASSWORD.

By following these rules, you guarantee the behavior among different JMX connector implementations. Any programming model that strays from these principles is unsupported.

You'll take the following steps to create the sample administrative client program:

1. Create an AdminClient instance.
2. Find an MBean.
3. Use the MBean.
4. Register for events.
5. Handle the events.

Step 1. Create an AdminClient Instance

An administrative client program needs to invoke methods on the AdminService object that is running in the Deployment Manager (or the application server in a Base installation). The AdminClient class provides a proxy to the remote AdminService object through one of the supported JMX connectors. The Java code in Listing 26-3 shows how to create an AdminClient instance. (Note that this example is for a WebSphere Network Deployment environment because it looks up a node agent MBean, which wouldn't be present in a WebSphere Base installation.)

Listing 26-3

Creating an AdminClient instance

```
// Port 8879 is the default SOAP port for the Deployment Manager. This value
// may differ in your environment.
Properties connectProps = new Properties();
connectProps.setProperty(
AdminClient.CONNECTOR_TYPE, AdminClient.CONNECTOR_TYPE_SOAP);

connectProps.setProperty(AdminClient.CONNECTOR_HOST, "localhost");
connectProps.setProperty(AdminClient.CONNECTOR_PORT, "8879");
AdminClient adminClient = null;
try
{
        adminClient = AdminClientFactory.createAdminClient(connectProps);
}
catch (ConnectorException e)
{
        System.out.println("Exception creating admin client: " + e);
}
```

Step 2. Find an MBean

Once you obtain an AdminClient instance, you can use it to access managed resources in the administration servers and application servers. Each managed resource registers an MBean with the AdminService through which you can access that resource. MBeans are registered with the MBeanServer instance running in a WebSphere Application Server process. The AdminService is like a wrapper to the MBeanServer and provides much of the same functionality in addition to WebSphere-specific distributed support and enhanced security.

The MBean is represented by an ObjectName instance that identifies the MBean. An ObjectName consists of a domain name followed by an unordered set of one or more key properties. For WebSphere Application Server, the domain name is "WebSphere" and the key properties defined for administration include the following (not all are listed in this table):

Property	Description
Type	The type of MBean (e.g., Server, TraceService, Java Virtual Machine)
Name	The name identifier for the individual instance of the MBean
Cell	The name of the cell the MBean is running
Node	The name of the node the MBean is running
Process	The name of the process the MBean is running

You can locate an MBean by querying for it using ObjectNames that match desired key properties. For example, the code in Listing 26-4 shows how to find the MBean for the NodeAgent of node MyNode.

Listing 26-4

Finding an MBean

```
String nodeName = "MyNode";
String query = "WebSphere:type=NodeAgent,node=" + nodeName + ",*";
ObjectName queryName = new ObjectName(query);
ObjectName nodeAgent = null;
Set s = adminClient.queryNames(queryName, null);
if (!s.isEmpty())
    nodeAgent = (ObjectName)s.iterator().next();
else
    System.out.println("Node agent MBean was not found");
```

Step 3. Use the MBean

What a particular MBean lets you do depends on that MBean's management interface. It may declare attributes you can obtain or set. It may declare operations you can invoke. It may declare notifications for which you can register listeners. For the MBeans provided by WebSphere, you can find information about the interfaces they support in the MBean API documentation. The example in Listing 26-5 invokes one of the operations available on the NodeAgent MBean we located above. This sample code starts the MyServer application server.

Listing 26-5

Using the MBean

```
String opName = "launchProcess";
String signature[] = { "java.lang.String" };
String params[] = { "MyServer" };
try
{
    adminClient.invoke(nodeAgent, opName, params, signature);
}
catch (Exception e)
{
    System.out.println("Exception invoking launchProcess: " + e);
}
```

Step 4. Register for Events

In addition to supporting the managing of resources, the JMX API supports application monitoring for specific administrative events. Certain events produce notifications, for example, when a server starts. Administrative applications can register as listeners for these notifications. WebSphere Application Server provides a full implementation of the JMX notification model and includes additional function so you can receive notifications in a distributed environment. For a complete list of the notifications emitted from WebSphere Application Server MBeans, see the com.ibm.websphere. management.NotificationConstants class in the MBean API documentation.

Here's an example of how an object can register itself for event notifications emitted from an MBean using the node agent ObjectName:

```
adminClient.addNotificationListener(nodeAgent, this, null, null);
```

In this example, the null value will result in receiving all the node agent MBean event notifications. You can also use the null value with the handback object.

Step 5. Handle the Events

Objects receive JMX event notifications via the handleNotification method, which is defined by the NotificationListener interface and which any event receiver must implement. Listing 26-6 shows an implementation of handleNotification that reports the notifications it receives.

Listing 26-6

Handling events

```
public void handleNotification(Notification n, Object handback)
{
        System.out.println("*****************************************************");
        System.out.println("* Notification received at " + new
                        Date().toString());
        System.out.println("* type      = " + ntfyObj.getType());
        System.out.println("* message   = " + ntfyObj.getMessage());
        System.out.println("* source    = " + ntfyObj.getSource());
        System.out.println(
        "* seqNum    = " + Long.toString(ntfyObj.getSequenceNumber()));
        System.out.println("* timeStamp = " + new Date(ntfyObj.getTimeStamp()));
        System.out.println("* userData  = " + ntfyObj.getUserData());
        System.out.println("*****************************************************");
}
```

Listing 26-7 shows the complete administrative client program. Copy the contents to a file named AdminClientExample.java, and place the file in directory <WASV6_ROOT>\bin. (You can download this code from the MC Press Online Web site, at *http://www.mcpressonline.com/mc/Forums/Reviews/5077.*)

This example does two things. If you run it in a WebSphere Network Deployment environment and specify the correct node name and application server name, the program starts the named application server. If you run it in a WebSphere Base environment, the program dynamically obtains the process identifier (PID) of server1 and displays it. (You can find documentation for the MBeans and their attributes and methods in directory <WASV6_ROOT>\web\mbeanDocs.)

Listing 26-7

Sample Java administrative client program

```
import java.util.Date;
import java.util.Properties;
import java.util.Set;

import javax.management.InstanceNotFoundException;
import javax.management.MalformedObjectNameException;
import javax.management.Notification;
import javax.management.NotificationListener;
import javax.management.ObjectName;

import com.ibm.websphere.management.AdminClient;
```

```
import com.ibm.websphere.management.AdminClientFactory;
import com.ibm.websphere.management.exception.ConnectorException;

public class AdminClientExample implements NotificationListener
{

    private AdminClient adminClient;
    private ObjectName nodeAgent;
    private ObjectName server;
    private long ntfyCount = 0;

    public static void main(String[] args)
    {
        AdminClientExample ace = new AdminClientExample();

        // Create an AdminClient
        ace.createAdminClient();

            /*
             * Test Case #1: In a WAS ND environ, connect to a node agent
                                            and start an app server
             */
//      ace.getNodeAgentMBean("localhost"); // Use your host name instead of
                                                                localhost
//      ace.invokeLaunchProcess("server1");
//      ace.registerNodeAgentNotificationListener();    // For node agent

            /*
             * Test Case #2: In a WAS Base environ, connect to server1 and
                                            output its PID
             */
        ace.getAppServerMBean("server1");
        ace.getAppServerPid("server1");
        ace.registerAppServerNotificationListener();    // For server1

        // Run until interrupted
        ace.countNotifications();
    }

    private void createAdminClient()
    {
        // Set up a Properties object for the JMX connector attributes
        Properties connectProps = new Properties();
        connectProps.setProperty(
        AdminClient.CONNECTOR_TYPE, AdminClient.CONNECTOR_TYPE_SOAP);
        connectProps.setProperty(AdminClient.CONNECTOR_HOST, "localhost");
            // If you're trying to go to a WAS Base installation, 8880 is
                                                probably the port to use.
            // If you're trying to target a node in a cell (via a node
                                                agent), port 8879 is
            // probably the right one.
```

```
        connectProps.setProperty(AdminClient.CONNECTOR_PORT, "8880");

        // Get an AdminClient based on the connector properties
        try
        {
            adminClient = AdminClientFactory.createAdminClient(connectProps);
        }
        catch (ConnectorException e)
        {
            System.out.println("Exception creating admin client: " + e);
            System.exit(-1);
        }

        System.out.println("Connected and Admin Client created ");
    }


private void getNodeAgentMBean(String nodeName)
{
    // Query for the ObjectName of the NodeAgent MBean on the given node
    try
    {
        String query = "WebSphere:type=NodeAgent,node=" + nodeName + ",*";
        ObjectName queryName = new ObjectName(query);
        Set s = adminClient.queryNames(queryName, null);
        if (!s.isEmpty())
            nodeAgent = (ObjectName)s.iterator().next();
        else
        {
            System.out.println("Node agent MBean was not found");
            System.exit(-1);
        }
    }
    catch (MalformedObjectNameException e)
    {
        System.out.println(e);
        System.exit(-1);
    }
    catch (ConnectorException e)
    {
        System.out.println(e);
        System.exit(-1);
    }

    System.out.println("Found NodeAgent MBean for node " + nodeName);
}

private void getAppServerMBean(String appServerName)
{
    // Query for the ObjectName of the NodeAgent MBean on the given node
    try
```

```
    {
        String query = "WebSphere:type=Server,*";
        ObjectName queryName = new ObjectName(query);
        Set s = adminClient.queryNames(queryName, null);
        if (!s.isEmpty())
            server = (ObjectName)s.iterator().next();
        else
        {
            System.out.println("App Server MBean was not found");
            System.exit(-1);
        }
    }
    catch (MalformedObjectNameException e)
    {
        System.out.println(e);
        System.exit(-1);
    }
    catch (ConnectorException e)
    {
        System.out.println(e);
        System.exit(-1);
    }

    System.out.println("Found App Server MBean for server " +
                                            appServerName);
}

private void invokeLaunchProcess(String serverName)
{
    // Use the launchProcess operation on the NodeAgent MBean to start
    // the given server
    String opName = "launchProcess";
    String signature[] = { "java.lang.String" };
    String params[] = { serverName };
    boolean launched = false;
    try
    {
        Boolean b = (Boolean)adminClient.invoke(nodeAgent, opName,
                                            params, signature);

        launched = b.booleanValue();
        if (launched)
            System.out.println(serverName + " was launched");
        else
            System.out.println(serverName + " was not launched");
    }
    catch (Exception e)
    {
        System.out.println("Exception invoking launchProcess: " + e);
    }
```

```
    }

    private void getAppServerPid(String serverName)
    {
        String opName = "getPid";
        String signature[] = { "" };
        String params[] = { "" };

        try
        {
            // PID is an attribute on the Server MBean. You could also use a
                                                             getAttribute
// function to get the mbean attribute.
            String thePid = (String)adminClient.invoke(server, opName, null,
                                                               null);

            System.out.println(" PID for server1 is  " + thePid);

        }
        catch (Exception e)
        {
            System.out.println("Exception invoking getPid: " + e);
        }
    }

    private void registerNodeAgentNotificationListener()
    {
        // Register this object as a listener for notifications from the
        // MBean. Don't use a filter, and don't use a handback object.
        try
        {
            adminClient.addNotificationListener(nodeAgent, this, null, null);
            System.out.println("Registered for event notifications");
        }
        catch (InstanceNotFoundException e)
        {
            System.out.println(e);
        }
        catch (ConnectorException e)
        {
            System.out.println(e);
        }
    }

    private void registerAppServerNotificationListener()
    {
        // Register this object as a listener for notifications from the
        // MBean. Don't use a filter and don't use a handback object.
        try
        {
            adminClient.addNotificationListener(server, this, null, null);
            System.out.println("Registered for event notifications");
```

```
        }
        catch (InstanceNotFoundException e)
        {
            System.out.println(e);
        }
        catch (ConnectorException e)
        {
            System.out.println(e);
        }
    }

    public void handleNotification(Notification ntfyObj, Object handback)
    {
        // Each notification that the MBean generates will result in
        // this method being called
        ntfyCount++;

  System.out.println("*****************************************************");
        System.out.println("* Notification received at " + new
                                                 Date().toString());
        System.out.println("* type     = " + ntfyObj.getType());
        System.out.println("* message  = " + ntfyObj.getMessage());
        System.out.println("* source   = " + ntfyObj.getSource());
        System.out.println(
        "* seqNum   = " + Long.toString(ntfyObj.getSequenceNumber()));
        System.out.println("* timeStamp = " + new
                                        Date(ntfyObj.getTimeStamp()));
        System.out.println("* userData = " + ntfyObj.getUserData());

  System.out.println("*****************************************************");

    }

    private void countNotifications()
    {
        // Run until killed
        try
        {
            while (true)
            {
                Thread.currentThread().sleep(60000);
                System.out.println(ntfyCount + " notification have been
                                                    received");
            }
        }
        catch (InterruptedException e)
        {
        }
    }
}
```

To compile the code, go to <WASV6_ROOT>\bin, and run **setupCmdline.bat**. Then execute this compilation instruction (all on one line):

```
"%JAVA_HOME%\bin\javac" -classpath "%WAS_CLASSPATH%" -extdirs
"%WAS_EXT_DIRS%" AdminClientExample.java
```

To run the code, create a file called ace.bat containing the lines shown in Listing 26-8 (be sure to edit the directory paths to match your installation). (You can download this code from the MC Press Online Web site, at *http://www.mcpressonline.com/ mc/Forums/Reviews/5077.*) When you execute the batch file, you'll see results similar to those shown in Listing 26-9.

Listing 26-8

Contents of file ace.bat

```
@echo on

rem -Dwas.install.root=C:/progra~1/ibm/websphere/AppServer -
Xbootclasspath/p:C:\progra~1\ibm\websphere\AppServer\java\jre\lib\ext\ibmorb.ja
r -Djava.security.auth.login.config=C:\progra~1\ibm\websphere\AppServer\proper-
ties\wsjaas_client.conf -
Djava.ext.dirs=C:\progra~1\ibm\websphere\AppServer\java\jre\lib\ext;C:\progra~1
\ibm\websphere\AppServer\java\jre\lib;C:\progra~1\ibm\websphere\AppServer\class
es;C:\progra~1\ibm\websphere\AppServer\lib;C:\progra~1\ibm\websphere\AppServer\
lib\ext;C:\progra~1\ibm\websphere\AppServer\properties -
Djava.naming.provider.url=corbaloc:iiop:IBM-79D6XZF0P9F:2809 -Djava.naming.fac-
tory.initial=com.ibm.websphere.naming.WsnInitialContextFactory
-Dserver.root=C:\progra~1\ibm\websphere\AppServer -
Dcom.ibm.CORBA.ConfigURL=file:C:\progra~1\ibm\websphere\AppServer\properties\sa
s.client.props -Dcom.ibm.CORBA.BootstrapHost=IBM-79D6XZF0P9F
"%JAVA_HOME%\bin\java" "%CLIENTSAS%" "-Dwas.install.root=C:/progra~1/ibm/web-
sphere/AppServer" "-
Xbootclasspath/p:C:\progra~1\ibm\websphere\AppServer\java\jre\lib\ext\ibmorb.ja
r" "-Djava.security.auth.login.config=C:\progra~1\ibm\websphere\AppServer\prop-
erties\wsjaas_client.conf" "-
Djava.ext.dirs=C:\progra~1\ibm\websphere\AppServer\java\jre\lib\ext;C:\progra~1
\ibm\websphere\AppServer\java\jre\lib;C:\progra~1\ibm\websphere\AppServer\class
es;C:\progra~1\ibm\websphere\AppServer\lib;C:\progra~1\ibm\websphere\AppServer\
lib\ext;C:\progra~1\ibm\websphere\AppServer\properties" -
Djava.naming.provider.url=corbaloc:iiop:IBM-79D6XZF0P9F:2809 -Djava.naming.fac-
tory.initial=com.ibm.websphere.naming.WsnInitialContextFactory
"-Dserver.root=C:\progra~1\ibm\websphere\AppServer" "-
Dcom.ibm.CORBA.ConfigURL=file:C:\progra~1\ibm\websphere\AppServer\profiles\defa
ult\properties\sas.client.props" -Dcom.ibm.CORBA.BootstrapHost=IBM-79D6XZF0P9F
"-Dwas.repository.root=%CONFIG_ROOT%" -Dcom.ibm.CORBA.BootstrapHost=%COMPUTER-
NAME% -classpath
"%WAS_CLASSPATH%;c:\progra~1\ibm\websphere\appserver\classes;c:\progra~1\ibm\we
bsphere\appserver\lib\admin.jar;c:\progra~1\ibm\websphere\appserver\lib\wasjmx.
```

```
jar;c:\progra~1\ibm\websphere\appserver\lib\management.jar;c:\progra~1\ibm\web-
sphere\appserver\lib\wsexception.jar;c:\progra~1\ibm\websphere\appserver\lib\sa
s.jar;c:\progra~1\ibm\websphere\appserver\lib\utils.jar;c:\progra~1\ibm\web-
sphere\appserver\lib\wssec.jar;c:\progra~1\ibm\websphere\appserver\lib\emf.jar;
c:\progra~1\ibm\websphere\appserver\lib\ras.jar;c:\progra~1\ibm\websphere\appse
rver\lib\ffdc.jar;c:\progra~1\ibm\websphere\appserver\lib\soap.jar" c:\pro-
gra~1\ibm\websphere\appserver\bin\AdminClientExample.class %*
```

Listing 26-9

Running the administrative client program

```
C:\PROGRA~1\IBM\WebSphere\AppServer\bin>ace

C:\PROGRA~1\IBM\WebSphere\AppServer\bin>rem -
Dwas.install.root=C:/progra~1/ibm/websphere/AppServer -Xbootclasspath/p:C:\pro-
gra~1\ibm\websphere\AppServer\java\jre\lib\ext\ibmorb.jar
-Djava.security.auth.login.config=C:\progra~1\ibm\websphere\AppServer\proper-
ties\wsjaas_client.conf -
Djava.ext.dirs=C:\progra~1\ibm\websphere\AppServer\java\jre\lib\ext;C:\progra~1
\ibm\websphere\AppServer\java\jre\lib;C:\progra~1\ibm\websphere\AppServer\class
es;C:\progra~1\ibm\websphere\AppServer\lib;C:\progra~1\ibm\websphere\AppServer\
lib\ext;C:\progra~1\ibm\websphere\AppServer\properties -
Djava.naming.provider.url=corbaloc:iiop:IBM-79D6XZF0P9F:2809 -Djava.naming.fac-
tory.initial=com.ibm.websphere.naming.WsnInitialContextFactory
-Dserver.root=C:\progra~1\ibm\websphere\AppServer -
Dcom.ibm.CORBA.ConfigURL=file:C:\progra~1\ibm\websphere\AppServer\properties\sa
s.client.props -Dcom.ibm.CORBA.BootstrapHost=IBM-79D6XZF0P9F

C:\PROGRA~1\IBM\WebSphere\AppServer\bin>"C:\Program
Files\IBM\WebSphere\AppServer\java\bin\java" "-
Dcom.ibm.CORBA.ConfigURL=file:C:\Program Files\IBM\WebSphere\AppServer/pro-
files/default/properties/sas.client.props"
"-Dwas.install.root=C:/progra~1/ibm/websphere/AppServer" "-
Xbootclasspath/p:C:\progra~1\ibm\websphere\AppServer\java\jre\lib\ext\ibmorb.ja
r" "-Djava.security.auth.login.config=C:\progra~1\ibm\websphere\AppServer\prop-
erties\wsjaas_client.conf" "-
Djava.ext.dirs=C:\progra~1\ibm\websphere\AppServer\java\jre\lib\ext;C:\progra~1
\ibm\websphere\AppServer\java\jre\lib;C:\progra~1\ibm\websphere\AppServer\class
es;C:\progra~1\ibm\websphere\AppServer\lib;C:\progra~1\ibm\websphere\AppServer\
lib\ext;C:\progra~1\ibm\websphere\AppServer\properties" -
Djava.naming.provider.url=corbaloc:iiop:IBM-79D6XZF0P9F:2809 -Djava.naming.fac-
tory.initial=com.ibm.websphere.naming.WsnInitialContextFactory
"-Dserver.root=C:\progra~1\ibm\websphere\AppServer" "-
Dcom.ibm.CORBA.ConfigURL=file:C:\progra~1\ibm\websphere\AppServer\profiles\defa
ult\properties\sas.client.props" -Dcom.ibm.CORBA.BootstrapHost=IBM-79D6XZF0P9F
"-Dwas.repository.root=C:\Program
Files\IBM\WebSphere\AppServer/profiles/default\config" -
Dcom.ibm.CORBA.BootstrapHost=IBM-79D6XZF0P9F -classpath "C:\Program
Files\IBM\WebSphere\AppServer/profiles/default\properties;C:\Program
```

```
Files\IBM\WebSphere\AppServer\properties;C:\Program
Files\IBM\WebSphere\AppServer\lib\bootstrap.jar;C:\Program
Files\IBM\WebSphere\AppServer\lib\j2ee.jar;C:\ProgramFiles\IBM\WebSphere\AppSer
ver\lib\lmproxy.jar;C:\Program
Files\IBM\WebSphere\AppServer\lib\urlprotocols.jar;c:\progra~1\ibm\websphere\ap
pserver\classes;c:\progra~1\ibm\websphere\appserver\lib\admin.jar;c:\progra~1\i
bm\websphere\appserver\lib\wasjmx.jar;c:\progra~1\ibm\websphere\appserver\lib\m
anagement.jar;c:\progra~1\ibm\websphere\appserver\lib\wsexception.jar;c:\pro-
gra~1\ibm\websphere\appserver\lib\sas.jar;c:\progra~1\ibm\websphere\appserver\l
ib\utils.jar;c:\progra~1\ibm\websphere\appserver\lib\wssec.jar;c:\progra~1\ibm\
websphere\appserver\lib\emf.jar;c:\progra~1\ibm\websphere\appserver\lib\ras.jar
;c:\progra~1\ibm\websphere\appserver\lib\ffdc.jar;c:\progra~1\ibm\websphere\app
server\lib\soap.jar"
c:\progra~1\ibm\websphere\appserver\bin\AdminClientExample.class
Oct 3, 2005 2:43:31 PM com.ibm.websphere.management.AdminClientFactory
WARNING: ADMC0046W
Connected and Admin Client created
Found App Server MBean for server server1
 PID for server1 is  4912
Oct 3, 2005 2:43:32 PM com.ibm.ws.util.ImplFactory
WARNING: WSVR0072W
Registered for event notifications
0 notification have been received
0 notification have been received
0 notification have been received
0 notification have been received
0 notification have been received
0 notification have been received
Terminate batch job (Y/N)? y

C:\PROGRA~1\IBM\WebSphere\AppServer\bin>
```

Extending WebSphere Administration with Custom MBeans

You can extend the WebSphere Application Server administration system by supplying and registering new JMX MBeans in one of the WebSphere processes. JMX MBeans represent the management interface for a particular piece of logic. All managed resources within the standard WebSphere infrastructure are represented as JMX MBeans. There are a variety of ways in which you can create your own MBeans and register them with the JMX MBeanServer running in a WebSphere process. For more information, consult the MBean API documentation and the JMX 1.0 specification (which you can find online at *http://java.sun.com/products/JavaManagement*).

Create Custom JMX MBeans

When creating MBeans to extend the WebSphere administrative system, you have some alternatives from which to choose. You can use any existing JMX MBean from another application. You can register any MBean you tested in a JMX MBean server outside the WebSphere Application Server environment in a WebSphere process, including Standard MBeans, Dynamic MBeans, Open MBeans, and Model MBeans. In addition, you can use special distributed extensions provided by WebSphere to create a WebSphere ExtensionMBean provider. This option provides better integration with the distributed functions of the WebSphere administrative system.

An ExtensionMBean provider implies that you supply an XML file that contains an MBean Descriptor based on the Document Type Definition (DTD) shipped with WebSphere. The descriptor tells the WebSphere system all the attributes, operations, and notifications your MBean supports. With this information, the WebSphere system can route remote requests to your MBean and register remote listeners to receive your MBean event notifications.

All internal WebSphere MBeans follow the Model MBean pattern. Pure Java classes supply the real logic for management functions. The WebSphere MBeanFactory class reads the description of these functions from the XML MBean Descriptor and creates an instance of a ModelMBean that matches the descriptor. This ModelMBean instance is bound to your Java classes and registered with the MBeanServer running in the same process as your classes. Your Java code now becomes callable from any WebSphere administrative client through the ModelMBean created and registered to represent it.

Register the New MBeans

There are various ways to register your MBean, either with the WebSphere Application Server administrative service or with the MBeanServer in a WebSphere Application Server process. The following paragraphs describe the available registration options in order of preference.

Option 1: Go through the MBeanFactory class. For the greatest possible integration with the WebSphere Application Server system, use the MBeanFactory class to manage your MBean's life cycle through the activateMBean and deactivateMBean methods of the MBeanFactory class. Use these methods by supplying a subclass of the RuntimeCollaborator abstract superclass and an XML MBean descriptor file. With this approach, you supply a pure Java class that implements the management interface defined in the MBean descriptor. The MBeanFactory class creates the actual ModelMBean and registers it with the WebSphere administrative system on your behalf. This option is recommended for registering Model MBeans.

Option 2: Use the JMXManageable and CustomService interface. You can make the process of integrating with WebSphere administration even easier by implementing a CustomService interface that also implements the JMXManageable interface. Using this approach, you can avoid supplying the RuntimeCollaborator. When your CustomService interface is initialized, the WebSphere MBeanFactory class reads your XML MBean descriptor file and creates, binds, and registers an MBean to your CustomService interface automatically. After the shutdown method of your CustomService is called, the WebSphere system automatically deactivates your MBean.

Option 3: Go through the AdminService interface. You can call the registerMBean() method on the AdminService interface, and the invocation is delegated to the underlying MBeanServer for the process after appropriate security checks. You can obtain a reference to the AdminService using the getAdminService() method of the AdminServiceFactory class. This option is recommended for registering Standard, Dynamic, and Open MBeans. Implement the UserCollaborator class to use the MBeans and to provide a consistent level of support for them across distributed and z/OS platforms.

Option 4: Get MBeanServer instances directly. You can get a direct reference to the JMX MBeanServer instance running in any WebSphere process by calling the getMBeanServer() method of the MBeanFactory class. You get a reference to the MBeanFactory class by calling the getMBeanFactory() method of the AdminService interface. Registering the MBean directly with the MBeanServer instance can result in that MBean not participating fully in the distributed features of the WebSphere administrative system.

Regardless of the approach you use to create and register your MBean, you must set up proper Java 2 security permissions for your new MBean code. (You can optionally define an explicit MBean security policy. If you don't do so, WebSphere uses the default security policy.) The WebSphere AdminService and MBeanServer are tightly protected using Java 2 security permissions, and if you don't explicitly grant your code base permissions, security exceptions are thrown when you try to invoke methods of these classes. If you're supplying your MBean as part of your application, you can set the permissions in the was.policy file that you furnish as part of your application metadata. If you're using a CustomService interface or other code that's not delivered as an application, you can edit the library.policy file in the node configuration or even the server.policy file in the properties directory for a specific installation.

The sample code in Listings 26-10 through 26-12 shows how to create and register a standard MBean with the WebSphere administrative service. The listings show the

SnoopMBean.java, SnoopMBeanImpl.java, and SnoopMBean.xml source code, respectively.

Listing 26-10

SnoopMBean.java

```
/**
 * Use the SnoopMBean MBean, which has a standard MBean interface.
 */
public interface SnoopMBean {
    public String getIdentification();
    public void snoopy(String parm1);
}
```

Listing 26-11

SnoopMBeanImpl.java

```
/**
 * SnoopMBeanImpl - SnoopMBean implementation
 */
public class SnoopMBeanImpl implements SnoopMBean {
    public String getIdentification() {
        System.out.println(">>> getIdentification() called...");
        return "snoopy!";
    }

    public void snoopy(String parm1) {
        System.out.println(">>> snoopy(" + parm1 + ") called...");
    }
}
```

Listing 26-12

SnoopMBean.xml

```
<?xml version="1.0" encoding="UTF-8"?>
<!DOCTYPE MBean SYSTEM "MbeanDescriptor.dtd">
<MBean type="SnoopMBean"
 version="5.0"
 platform="dynamicproxy"
 description="Sample SnoopMBean to be initialized inside an EJB.">


 <attribute name="identification" getMethod="getIdentification"
type="java.lang.String" proxyInvokeType="unicall"/>

 <operation name="snoopy" role="operation"  type="void"
```

```
targetObjectType="objectReference"
    impact="ACTION" proxyInvokeType="multicall">
  <signature>
    <parameter name="parm1" description="test parameter"
type="java.lang.String"/>
  </signature>
 </operation>
</MBean>

//The method MBeanFactory.activateMBean() requires four parameters:
//String type: The type value that you put in this MBean's descriptor. For this
//example, the string type is SnoopMBean.
//RuntimeCollaborator co: The UserMBeanCollaborator user MBean collaborator
//instance that you create.
//String id: Unique name that you pick.
//String descriptor: The MBean descriptor file name.


import com.ibm.websphere.management.UserMBeanCollaborator;
//Import other classes here.
    .
    .
    .
static private ObjectName snoopyON = null;
static private Object lockObj = "this is a lock";
    .
    .
    .
/**
 * ejbCreate method: Register your MBean.
 */
public void ejbCreate() throws javax.ejb.CreateException {
    synchronized (lockObj) {
        System.out.println(">>> SnoopMBean activating for --|" + this + "|--");
        if (snoopyON != null) {
            return;
        }
        try {
            System.out.println(">>> SnoopMBean activating...");
            MBeanFactory mbfactory = AdminServiceFactory.getMBeanFactory();
            RuntimeCollaborator snoop = new UserMBeanCollaborator(new
                                                 SnoopMBeanImpl());

            snoopyON = mbfactory.activateMBean("SnoopMBean", snoop,
                                      "snoopMBeanId", "SnoopMBean.xml");

            System.out.println(">>> SnoopMBean activation COMPLETED! --|" +
                                                 snoopyON + "|--");

        } catch (Exception e) {
            System.out.println(">>> SnoopMBean activation FAILED:");
            e.printStackTrace();
        }
    }
}
```

```
}
        .
        .
        .
/**
 * ejbRemove method: Unregister your MBean.
 */
public void ejbRemove() {
    synchronized (lockObj) {
        System.out.println(">>> SnoopMBean Deactivating for --|" + this + "|--");
        if (snoopyON == null) {
            return;
        }
        try {
            System.out.println(">>> SnoopMBean Deactivating ==|" + snoopyON +
                                        "|== for --|" + this + "|--");
            MBeanFactory mbfactory = AdminServiceFactory.getMBeanFactory();
            mbfactory.deactivateMBean(snoopyON);
            System.out.println(">>> SnoopMBean Deactivation COMPLETED!");
        } catch (Exception e) {
            System.out.println(">>> SnoopMBean Deactivation FAILED:");
            e.printStackTrace();
        }
    }
}
```

Appendix

Web Resources

WebSphere Application Server

WebSphere Application Server V6 Information Center:
http://publib.boulder.ibm.com/infocenter/ws60help/index.jsp

WebSphere V6 trial version download:
http://www-106.ibm.com/developerworks/websphere/downloads
http://www14.software.ibm.com/webapp/download/home.jsp

WebSphere V6 system requirements:
http://www-306.ibm.com/software/webservers/appserv/doc/latest/prereq.html
http://www-306.ibm.com/software/webservers/appserv/was/requirements

WebSphere V6 product details:
http://www-306.ibm.com/software/webservers/appserv/was

WebSphere product updates and support:
http://www-306.ibm.com/software/webservers/appserv/was/support

WebSphere V6 migration guide:
http://www.redbooks.ibm.com/redbooks/pdfs/sg246369.pdf

IBM WebSphere developerWorks:
http://www-130.ibm.com/developerworks/websphere

Introduction to WebSphere:
http://www-128.ibm.com/developerworks/websphere/newto

WebSphere V6 training and certification:
http://www-106.ibm.com/developerworks/websphere/education

Configuring the Service Data Objects (SDO) repository:
http://publib.boulder.ibm.com/infocenter/wasinfo/v6r0/topic/com.ibm.websphere.pmc.doc/tasks/tjw_install_sdo.html

WSDL2Java command:
http://publib.boulder.ibm.com/infocenter/wasinfo/v6r0/index.jsp?topic=/com.ibm.websphere.base.doc/info/aes/ae/rwbs_wsdl2java.html

HTTP Server

IBM HTTP Server V6 Information Center:
http://publib.boulder.ibm.com/infocenter/ws60help/index.jsp

Edge Components

IBM Edge Components for WebSphere Information Center:
http://www-306.ibm.com/software/webservers/appserv/doc/v602/ec/infocenter/index.html

Tivoli Directory Server

IBM Tivoli Directory Server home page:
http://www-306.ibm.com/software/tivoli/products/directory-server

IBM Tivoli Directory Server Information Center:
http://publib.boulder.ibm.com/infocenter/tiv2help/index.jsp?toc=/com.ibm.IBMDS.doc/toc.xml

IBM Tivoli Directory Server documentation (under the D document category):
http://publib.boulder.ibm.com/tividd/td/tdprodlist.html

IBM Redbook *Understanding LDAP: Design and Implementation*:
http://www.redbooks.ibm.com/abstracts/sg244986.html

Java and J2EE

Java 2 Platform, Enterprise Edition (J2EE) specification:
http://java.sun.com/j2ee

Java Management Extensions (JMX) documentation:
http://java.sun.com/products/JavaManagement

Other References

DB2 UDB Server Edition V8.2 Information Center:
http://publib.boulder.ibm.com/infocenter/db2help/index.jsp

Garbage Collector tool download:
http://www.alphaworks.ibm.com/tech/gcdiag

SourceForge's JFreeChart download:
http://sourceforge.net/projects/jfreechart

JFreeChart project home page:
http://www.jfree.org/jfreechart/index.html

Index

E